CHRISTIAN SPIRITUALITY
High Middle Ages and Reformation

World Spirituality

An Encyclopedic History of the Religious Quest

Board of Editors and Advisors

EWERT COUSINS, *General Editor*

Volume 17 of
World Spirituality:
An Encyclopedic History
of the Religious Quest

CHRISTIAN SPIRITUALITY

HIGH MIDDLE AGES AND REFORMATION

Edited by

Jill Raitt

in collaboration with
Bernard McGinn and John Meyendorff

CROSSROAD • NEW YORK

1997

The Crossroad Publishing Company
370 Lexington Avenue, New York, NY 10017

World Spirituality, Volume 17
Diane Apostolos-Cappadona, Art Editor

Printed in the United States of America

Library of Congress Cataloging-in-Publication Data

Christian spirituality
(World spirituality ; v. 17)
Includes bibliographies and indexes.
1. Spiritual life—History of doctrines—Middle Ages,
600–1500. 2. Spiritual life—History of doctrines—16th
century. I. Raitt, Jill. II. McGinn, Bernard, 1937–
III. Meyendorff, John, 1926–   . IV. Series.
BV4490.C48   1987   248′.09′02   86-29212
ISBN 0-8245-0765-7
ISBN 0-8245-0967-6 (pbk)

Contents

Part Two: Themes

Preface to the Series

T HE PRESENT VOLUME is part of a series entitled World Spirituality: An Encyclopedic History of the Religious Quest, which seeks to present the spiritual wisdom of the human race in its historical unfolding. Although each of the volumes can be read on its own terms, taken together they provide a comprehensive picture of the spiritual strivings of the human community as a whole—from prehistoric times, through the great religions, to the meeting of traditions at the present.

Drawing upon the highest level of scholarship around the world, the series gathers together and presents in a single collection the richness of the spiritual heritage of the human race. It is designed to reflect the autonomy of each tradition in its historical development, but at the same time to present the entire story of the human spiritual quest. The first five volumes deal with the spiritualities of archaic peoples in Asia, Europe, Africa, Oceania, and North and South America. Most of these have ceased to exist as living traditions, although some perdure among tribal peoples throughout the world. However, the archaic level of spirituality survives within the later traditions as a foundational stratum, preserved in ritual and myth. Individual volumes or combinations of volumes are devoted to the major traditions: Hindu, Buddhist, Taoist, Confucian, Jewish, Christian, and Islamic. Included within the series are the Jain, Sikh, and Zoroastrian traditions. In order to complete the story, the series includes traditions that have not survived but have exercised important influence on living traditions—such as Egyptian, Sumerian, classical Greek and Roman. A volume is devoted to modern esoteric movements and another to modern secular movements.

Having presented the history of the various traditions, the series devotes two volumes to the meeting of spiritualities. The first surveys the meeting of spiritualities from the past to the present, exploring common themes that

A longer version of this preface may be found in Christian Spirituality: Origins to the Twelfth Century, *the first published volume in the series.*

can provide the basis for a positive encounter, for example, symbols, rituals, techniques. The second deals with the meeting of spiritualities in the present and future. Finally, the series closes with a dictionary of world spirituality.

Each volume is edited by a specialist or a team of specialists who have gathered a number of contributors to write articles in their fields of specialization. As in this volume, the articles are not brief entries but substantial studies of an area of spirituality within a given tradition. An effort has been made to choose editors and contributors who have a cultural and religious grounding within the tradition studied and at the same time possess the scholarly objectivity to present the material to a larger forum of readers. For several years some five hundred scholars around the world have been working on the project.

In the planning of the project, no attempt was made to arrive at a common definition of spirituality that would be accepted by all in precisely the same way. The term "spirituality," or an equivalent, is not found in a number of the traditions. Yet from the outset, there was a consensus among the editors about what was in general intended by the term. It was left to each tradition to clarify its own understanding of this meaning and to the editors to express this in the introduction to their volumes. As a working hypothesis, the following description was used to launch the project:

> The series focuses on that inner dimension of the person called by certain traditions "the spirit." This spiritual core is the deepest center of the person. It is here that the person is open to the transcendent dimension; it is here that the person experiences ultimate reality. The series explores the discovery of this core, the dynamics of its development, and its journey to the ultimate goal. It deals with prayer, spiritual direction, the various maps of the spiritual journey, and the methods of advancement in the spiritual ascent.

By presenting the ancient spiritual wisdom in an academic perspective, the series can fulfill a number of needs. It can provide readers with a spiritual inventory of the richness of their own traditions, informing them at the same time of the richness of other traditions. It can give structure and order, meaning and direction to the vast amount of information with which we are often overwhelmed in the computer age. By drawing the material into the focus of world spirituality, it can provide a perspective for understanding one's place in the larger process. For it may well be that the meeting of spiritual paths—the assimilation not only of one's own spiritual heritage but of that of the human community as a whole—is the distinctive spiritual journey of our time.

EWERT COUSINS

Introduction

For all who are led by the Spirit of God
are children of God.
Romans 8:14

THE SECOND VOLUME in the Christian spirituality trilogy covers a time of movements, restlessness, and change, prompted by the need to adapt to the breakdown in the feudal system and the requirements of a rising bourgeoisie.[1] The papacy attempted to deal with these changes by increasing its bureaucracy and its centralized power. Popes faced opposition internally from conciliarists. Political theorists such as Marsiglius of Padua and William of Ockham aided both conciliarist cardinals and increasingly powerful heads of state to oppose the spiritual hegemony and territorial aspirations of popes and curia. At the grass-roots level, people sought ways to compensate for an increasingly ineffectual clergy and an incomprehensible liturgy. Some movements, like that of Peter Waldo, failed and went underground to reemerge in the sixteenth century; some movements resulted in heresy like the Albigensians; others formed new religious orders like the Dominicans and Franciscans, which received papal approval. Meanwhile crusades and pilgrimages drained off some of the energies of western Europe but, in turn, brought back new appetites for Eastern goods and ideas and further stimulated trade and curiosity.

In Eastern Christianity, the patriarchs had all they could do to maintain their churches against Islamic incursions from the south and rapacious crusaders from the west. In fact, Eastern Christendom lost ground continually until its greatest gem, Constantinople, fell in 1453. In the face of such continual menace, Eastern Christendom maintained its medieval ways into and beyond the period covered by this volume. Its strengths were its use of vernacular in its liturgy, its married clergy, and the wholeness of the cosmos it presented to its people in architecture, icons, language, and liturgy. There were, however, not dissimilar battles concerning poverty and religious life which were waged within or against a political background.

In the West, however, the failed reforms within the Roman Catholic Church resulted in one reform that in less than two decades resulted in the permanent break of the "protesters," the Protestants, from the Roman Catholic Church. The Reformation of the sixteenth century begun by Martin Luther went further than Luther foresaw and resulted in three basic forms of European Protestantism: Lutheran, Reformed, and Anabaptist. Jolted by these developments, the Roman Catholic Church finally mounted an effective reform-minded council, the Council of Trent. But the Tridentine reform is the root of the spirituality of later centuries and so is reserved for the third volume of the Christian series.

This volume therefore holds between its covers three quite different traditions. The Roman Catholic and Eastern Orthodox churches broke apart in the eleventh century; the Protestant Reformation split Western Christendom in the sixteenth century. In all three traditions, the word "spirituality" has been differently interpreted, reflecting different ways of affirming the Christian calling to be the heirs, the followers, of Christ and participants in the life of the Spirit. For Roman Catholics, the adoption by God of those reborn in Christian baptism is no legal fiction but results in a real change in the baptized. On the basis of that change, that adoptive inclusion in Christ, Christians can respond to grace and cooperate in their sanctification. In continuity with both monastic and lay practices set forth in the first volume of Christian spirituality, men and women sought union with God through the next centuries. Essentially adaptive to the new needs of changing societies, Western Christendom developed yet another way, a "middle way." In the burgeoning towns and around the new universities of the High Middle Ages, the orders of friars combined the active and the contemplative life. Their founders sought to share the strength and joy they found in prayer through teaching and preaching. Women affiliated with these new orders were not allowed to share the wandering life of the friars nor to teach or preach. They found, however, ways of making the spirit of their founders their own and taught and preached in spite of their cloistered lives. Indeed, their influence was often widely felt, as in the case of Catherine of Siena.

Orthodox Christians also emphasized the gift of divine life which God shares with those deified by baptism. Those who devoted themselves to God through prayer and asceticism hoped for the gift of *theōsis* or divinization so that they could be true *icons*, true images of God in the world. Laity found a coherent spirituality presented to them in the liturgy and iconography of their richly symbolic churches. There, through praying and singing in their own language and through hearing the Scriptures and sermons, Byzantine Christians received spiritual sustenance.

Not all Christians sought sanctity in either Eastern or Western Christianity. The exploitation of religion for money, power, and prestige was no less common in the Middle Ages than it is today. In fact, so many abuses had entered the government of the Roman Catholic Church by the thirteenth century that Pope Innocent III called a reforming council, Lateran IV, in 1215. When its reforms proved ineffectual, reforming cardinals, together with equally reform-minded laypeople and clergy, tried to place the government of the church in the hands of regularly called councils. The "conciliarist" movement almost succeeded in the fourteenth century but came to grief in the latter half of the fifteenth century. The reform of the Western Christian church was precipitated in the early sixteenth century by a remarkable Augustinian named Martin Luther. Efforts on the part of Emperor Charles V, the German lords, and theologians to keep the church whole failed when, in 1530, Philip Melanchthon presented the Augsburg Confession to the emperor and it was rejected.

Luther's understanding of what it meant to be a Christian was quite different from the dominant models in both Eastern and Western Christendom. For Luther, the fallen, sinful state of humankind renders it incapable of doing anything at all, even with grace, to cooperate with God. Rather, when sinners recognize their sinfulness and cry to God for mercy, they are offered salvation in Jesus Christ. When sinners believe that Jesus Christ has died and risen *for them*, then they are justified by that faith. The righteousness of Christ himself is imputed to them and their sins are covered. They remain sinners in themselves, but they are righteous in Christ. Their gratitude for so great a gift should then prompt them to live as good Christians, spending themselves in the service of their neighbor.

The chapters in this volume deal with spiritualities based on one or another of these three fundamental visions of how salvation and sanctification are offered by God to Christians. But before presenting a preview of the contents of this volume, readers may properly ask why the dates 1150 to 1600 were chosen and, given that choice, why there are no sixteenth-century Roman Catholics represented. Any division or periodization of the past depends on somewhat arbitrary decisions on the part of historians. In this instance, the editors were required to divide Christian history into material for three volumes. The first volume ended as the High Middle Ages began with their crusades, commerce, towns, universities, great cathedrals, pilgrimages, and all the hustle and bustle of a world successfully emerging from the havoc of repeated invasions. The old monasteries remained, as did their classic spirituality. But a new sort was beginning, and so the twelfth century seems a good transition point.

This volume also sides with those who prefer to see lines of continuity between the Middle Ages and the Reformation. Even though the break was—and remains—grievous, the Protestant Reformation nevertheless began as a reform movement within the "Old Church" and became a decisive rupture only when all means of reconciliation had failed and differences were hardened into political realities by the Peace of Augsburg in 1555. This volume might have taken 1555 as its final date were it not for the necessity of following Protestantism into its most radical forms, forms that were not clear until the end of the sixteenth century.

On the other hand, Roman Catholic spirituality, prompted by the Reformation, took on new forms that continued in the seventeenth century. Volume three of the Christian series will therefore deal with Ignatius of Loyola and the Jesuits, the Council of Trent and its reforms, Teresa of Avila, John of the Cross, and Francis de Sales, all of whom lived in the sixteenth century.

As was volume 16, this volume is divided into two sections; however, unlike in volume 16, the division is not so equal. Rather, Part 1, "Schools and Movements," is much longer than Part 2, "Themes." This arrangement is due more to the variety that must be included in Part 1 than to a lack of themes that might be discussed at length in Part 2.

Part 1, "Schools and Movements," presents the variety of new orders and reform movements in the period from 1150 to 1500 and then turns to the spirituality of the Protestant Reformation. Readers may find peculiar the splitting of the sixteenth century which attaches the Reformation to the spirituality of the Middle Ages while reserving the Roman Catholic Ignatian, Tridentine, and Carmelite reforms for the third Christian volume in this series. Any periodization or division will be questioned. The lives of people are not lived in this age or that. They are lived in a continuum of events, which historians then divide for purposes of conceptualization and because, as in this case, a break must be made somewhere.

The continuities the series editors wished to emphasize were those of reform and spiritual kinship. It is too easy to see the Protestant Reformation as radically discontinuous and to ignore the common roots that Protestants and Roman Catholics share. The choice here was at least partly dictated by ecumenical concerns. Just as problematic is the wrenching of sixteenth-century Roman Catholic spirituality from its temporal context and its relation to sixteenth-century Protestantism. The editors' decision here was to see the Roman Catholic reforms of the sixteenth century as the roots of the spiritual developments of the modern period. The editors hope that such an arrangement may be more conducive to fruitful reflection than to the endless debate on the "beginnings of modernity."

The theme of reform is sounded in the first chapter by church historian George Tavard. Monasteries of monks and nuns continued to be places of prayer and of ferment, but new orders arose and new voices were heard in the thirteenth century, influenced at its beginning by Lateran Council IV. Following this transitional chapter between volumes 16 and 17 in this series is Part 1, "Schools and Movements." The major new mendicant orders appear in chapter 2, "The Mendicants." In spite of similarities among the orders of friars, their spiritualities developed different emphases and schools, which affected their relationships with cities, universities, kings, and the Holy Roman Emperor and their missions in Europe and even into the Muslim world. Simon Tugwell's essay demonstrates the degree of spiritual flexibility that resulted from Dominic's concern for preaching and teaching. Wayne Hellmann presents Dominic's contemporary, Francis of Assisi, as a reformer whose person and life were a strong ingredient in Franciscan spirituality. He then invites the reader to see how Franciscans interpreted and then divided over their interpretations of Francis's requirement that all the brothers should strive "to follow the humility and poverty of Our Lord Jesus Christ."

Two mendicant orders began through the inspiration of individual saints, Dominic and Francis. Two were the result of modifications of existing groups, the Augustinians and the Carmelites. Of the latter two, the origins of the Carmelites are least known. Hence, the essay by Keith Egan begins: "The anonymity of Carmelite origins. . . ." It was from such anonymity, however, that the Carmelite Order took form in the Holy Land and migrated at various times in the thirteenth century to Europe. By 1247, the Carmelite constitutions had been approved by Innocent IV. The combination of the contemplative and active lives that marked the mendicant orders remained a tension, since some Carmelites preferred the hermetic life. More than the other three orders, then, contemplation remained a strong force in Carmelite spirituality and would bear fruit in the sixteenth century in the reform led by the two greatest Carmelite mystics, Teresa of Avila and John of the Cross.

A smoother transition from hermits to mendicants marked the approval of the Order of the Hermits of St. Augustine in 1256. This order arose from the combining of Italian communities of hermits who lived according to the *Rule of St. Augustine.* Following a clear emphasis in the works of Augustine, the Hermits of St. Augustine stressed the exercise of the divine gift of charity, love for God and neighbor. Adolar Zumkeller's essay stresses the fraternal love practiced in the community, which flowed out into their preaching and teaching. The emphasis on grace and God's action in the

Christian is an emphasis that would become the basis of the reforming theology of an Augustinian of the sixteenth century, Martin Luther.

With chapter 3, "Major Currents in Late Medieval Devotion," Richard Kieckhefer begins a series of essays devoted to the spiritualities of the fourteenth and fifteenth centuries. Kieckhefer works deftly to present the complex picture of popular devotions, represented by various and not easily accessible bodies of literature. He locates popular devotion in the liturgy, that is, the Mass and the Divine Office, and also in the feast-day celebrations of aspects of Christian life and worship, for example, Corpus Christi or the commemoration of popular saints. Kieckhefer's sources are not only written texts but also iconography, architecture, and drama. Some of the major themes introduced by Kieckhefer are treated at greater length in Part 2, "Themes," for example, the passion of Christ, Marian devotion, and the Eucharist.

The academic side of medieval life is represented by William Courtenay's essay, "Spirituality and Late Scholasticism." Courtenay looks "beneath the surface of more familiar aspects of university life" to find its spirituality. He looks at the role of biblical studies, the lives of scholars, and the communal life of masters and students as these gathered in "colleges" run by religious orders, dioceses, or geographical regions.

Excluded from the wandering life of the friars and from the universities as well, women in the Middle Ages nevertheless developed modes of religious life that were as influential and significant as those of their less restricted brothers. In her essay, "Religious Women in the Later Middle Ages," Caroline Bynum finds that "for the first time in Christian history, we can identify a women's movement (the beguines) and can speak of specifically female influences on the development of piety." She looks at the rapid growth in numbers of women who lived lives dedicated to Christian prayer and service, from which came increasing numbers of women saints. Women also found more freedom in groups that were labeled heretical, a circumstance not unlike conditions in early Christianity. Within orthodox forms of Christian life, most often in convents, women became spiritual leaders whose lives were published by their confessors and adherents. Bynum keeps her eye on the ways in which women found their way in a religious world dominated by men, and she deftly sorts out the particularities of female spirituality within the context of a church directed by males.

The influence of women mystics is part of the history of late medieval mysticism in Europe, on the Continent and in England. The continental history is admirably laid out by Alois Haas, and a particularly influential development, the *devotio moderna,* is treated by Otto Gründler. Bernard McGinn presents a survey of English mysticism.

In his essay, "Schools of Late Medieval Mysticism," Haas begins with the earlier *Frauenmystik*, the mysticism of women, which influenced the great male and female mystics of the fourteenth and fifteenth centuries. He presents the Cistercian Beatrice of Nazareth and the beguine Hadewijch, followed by Mechthild of Magdeburg, who lived first as a beguine and then as a Cistercian. This section finishes with Marguerite Porete, whose themes of annihilation and freedom were not unlike those of Meister Eckhart. Haas then turns to Dominican mysticism and the controversial Meister Eckhart and his followers, Tauler, Suso, and the nuns who were directed by, but also inspired, their male counterparts. Sections on the Friends of God and the *Theologia deutsch* (later translated by a young Martin Luther) precede Haas's treatment of Franciscan mysticism, the eclectic but unified spirituality of Ruysbroeck, and Carthusian mysticism. Haas then crosses the Alps to encompass the three Catherines—of Siena, of Bologna, and of Genoa. He concludes his essay by presenting two great theologians who were also mystics: Jean Gerson and Nicholas of Cusa.

Basing his reform on a Christ-centered piety, Geert Groote of Deventer in the Netherlands inspired the founding of the Brothers of the Common Life and the Sisters of the Common Life in the late fourteenth century. Otto Gründler presents the development of this "modern devotion" from its origins, through its best-known book, *The Imitation of Christ*. The spirit of the *devotio moderna*, he affirms, was indebted to the monastic tradition and "was modern not because it broke with any *devotio antiqua*, but because it advocated the *current* practice of the latter both inside and outside the cloister."

The fourteenth-century wealth of mystics was not confined to the Continent. The distinctiveness of English mysticism might better be attributed to the distinctiveness of English mystics. Richard Rolle and Margery Kempe were idiosyncratic. Walter Hilton was in the Augustinian tradition, while his contemporary, the anonymous author of the *Cloud of Unknowing*, relied upon Pseudo-Dionysius. Julian of Norwich "is the great original among English mystics," writes McGinn, and indeed, her "showings" and her theology are both remarkably original and theologically profound, especially with regard to the fall, redemption, and the motherhood of Christ as God.

At the beginning of the fourteenth century, other problems were differently addressed in the Orthodox East. In Thessalonica, the hesychast Gregory Palamas devoted himself to prayer and the liturgy. When the hesychast method of contemplation became a matter of dispute in the fourteenth century, Palamas began to write in defense of contemplation. As a result, not only was the Christian church enriched by the lucid explication of Orthodox spirituality, it was also benefited by explanations that demonstrated the nature of a theological spirituality and a spiritual theology based on Scripture and the Greek fathers of the church. George Mantzaridis makes clear the theological base of Palamas's treatises and the Greek answer to the problem of how finite creatures can know, and even participate in, the radiance of an infinite God.

Bridging the period from the late Middle Ages into the sixteenth century is the monastic controversy in Russia. Sergei Hackel discusses the problem of the "possessors and the nonpossessors," which curiously mirrors the European debates over Franciscan poverty. The Russian problem, however, centers on the teaching of the monastic elder Nil Maikov, who wished the monasteries to return to the poverty of the desert fathers. Because the ownership of land was not only a religious but also a political question, the debate involved also Ivan III, grand prince of Moscow, who was interested (as was his near contemporary Henry VIII) in enriching the state by the dispossession of the monasteries. The background to this debate lies in the Mongol invasions of the thirteenth century and the spiritual writings of fourteenth-century monks who rebuilt the devastated monasteries. Through this complex world Hackel guides the reader to the results of the council in 1503 that left property in the hands of the monasteries and thereby established the Russian church as a political, because landed, power in the Muscovite state.

Two essays on the spirituality of Renaissance humanism tie together the late Middle Ages and the sixteenth-century Reformation in Europe. Many of the humanists were concerned with reform in church, state, and society as well as in letters. William Bouwsma brings his mastery of Renaissance thought to focus on the spirituality of the major figures—Petrarch, Salutati, and Valla. James Tracy examines the humanist use of the Scriptures as spiritual nourishment in Erasmus and Lefèvre d'Étaples with special attention to Erasmus's *Paraphrase* of the Gospel of Luke.

The stage is now set for the Reformation. Marc Lienhard looks at Luther and Lutheranism to delineate the theological source of that piety which, however altered in other Protestant traditions, is nevertheless the key to them all: justification by faith alone. Out of this principle flowed not only Luther's opposition to many Roman Catholic doctrines and practices but also the preaching that has inspired Protestants to trust God and serve their neighbors.

While Luther was elaborating his biblically inspired theology, Huldrych Zwingli was also preaching reform and the doctrine of justification by faith in Zurich. After establishing the reformation there, Zwingli was killed in 1531, but his place was filled by Heinrich Bullinger, who guided Zurich until his own death in 1575. By then Zurich's school and Bullinger's theology were known across Europe and especially in England, where Bullinger's *Decades* were required reading in Puritan seminaries. The Christ-centered spirituality of these Zurich reformers is admirably laid out in Fritz Büsser's essay. Fifteen years after Zwingli's death, a young Frenchman stopped in Geneva on his way, so he thought, to Strasbourg. But John Calvin stayed to become the great reformer in Geneva. William Bouwsma finds the roots of Calvin's spirituality in a single-minded dedication to God nourished by Scripture and founded on faith in Christ and the work of the Spirit. Of particular interest are the humanist influences that Bouwsma finds in Calvin's complex mind.

Hounded by Roman Catholics, Lutherans, and Swiss Reformed alike, those groups, gathered under the capacious label "radical reformation," knew the meaning of persecution. It is little wonder that the passion of Christ meant so much to them and was a major subject for their meditation. Timothy George's sources for his essay are the materials the people themselves wrote and used: prayers, stories about martyrs, letters, catechisms. The radical reformation had few leaders as well known as Luther, Zwingli, or Calvin. Nor did they found academies or teach in universities. These folk lived simply and fervently tried to build "a new congregation according to Christian order."

The center of the spirituality of all the groups represented in Part 1 is Christ. In the twelfth and thirteenth centuries, attention to the humanity of Christ was increasingly directed to the sufferings of Christ. Crucifixes portrayed the agony rather than the triumph of Christ on the cross. Worshipers were more and more drawn to contemplate the love Christ expressed through his passion. Ewert Cousins studies this devotion to Christ crucified in Francis of Assisi and Bonaventure. His essay compassionately examines the growth of a spirituality centered on the humanity and passion of Christ.

Under the cross stood Mary, the mother of Jesus. Marian devotion grew rapidly in the Middle Ages and was expressed in hymns like the Salve Regina and the Stabat Mater, in practices like the Rosary and the Angelus and iconographically, in many forms. Mary was celebrated as virgin, as mother, as protectress and intercessor. The Christ lay in her lap as an infant or as her crucified son. Mary stood valiantly or swooned beneath the cross, or she stood triumphant upon the head of a dragon, crowned with stars. Through all of these images, Elizabeth Johnson traces the uses and abuses of Marian devotion in the Western church.

Central to the liturgy of the Christian churches in the East and the West is the Eucharist. The rich liturgy of the Byzantine churches is examined by

Robert Taft, and James McCue does not hesitate to point out the liturgical abuses as well as the benefits associated with the Eucharist in the Western church.

The grievous split between East and West, efforts at reunion, and the theological differences that continue to separate Eastern and Western Christians are carefully described by John Meyendorff. This essay provides an overview from the Eastern perspective of medieval events to the fall of Constantinople in 1453.

The last essay reviews the divergences and convergences of the medieval and Reformation spiritualities under the title "Saints and Sinners." It is a chapter that looks back at volume 17 and ahead to volume 18 in this series. The focal point of Jill Raitt's essay is the way the different theologies conceive of justification and sanctification and hence how they draw their followers into a closer following of Christ under the inspiration of the Holy Spirit, the origin and the finisher of all Christian spirituality.

JILL RAITT

Note

1. See the introduction to volume 16, *Christian Spirituality: Origins to the Twelfth Century* (pp. xv–xvii), for an explanation of editorial choices governing all three Christian volumes (16, 17, and 18) in this series.

General Bibliography
and Abbreviations

Sources

Classics of Western Spirituality. Edited by Richard J. Payne and John Farina. New York: Paulist Press. 1978–. 50+ vols.

[*PG*] Migne, J. P., ed. *Patrologiae cursus completus. Series graeca.* Paris: J. P. Migne, 1857–66. 161 vols.

[*PL*] Migne, J. P., ed. *Patrologiae cursus completus. Series latina.* Paris: J. P. Migne, 1844–64. 221 vols. and 4 index vols.

[WA] Weimarer Ausgabe, D. Martin Luthers Werke. Kritische Gesamtausgabe. Weimar: H. Böhlau, 1883ff.

Studies

Bouyer, Louis, Jean Leclercq, and François Vandenbroucke. *A History of Christian Spirituality.* 3 vols. New York: Seabury, 1982. Vol. 1, *The Spirituality of the New Testament and the Fathers.* Vol. 2, *The Spirituality of the Middle Ages.* Vol. 3, *Orthodox Spirituality and Protestant and Anglican Spirituality.* The original French edition of this series also included Louis Cognet, *La spiritualité moderne* as part 2 of vol. 3 (Paris: Aubier, 1966).

Cross, F. L., and E. A. Livingstone. *The Oxford Dictionary of the Christian Church.* 2nd ed. Oxford: Oxford University Press, 1974.

[*Dict. Sp.*] *Dictionnaire de spiritualité ascétique et mystique doctrine et histoire.* Edited by Marcel Viller, assisted by F. Cavallera, J. de Guibert. Paris: Beauchesne, 1937–. This is the most useful single work for the history of Christian spirituality. As of 1983 it had reached volume 12 (fascicles LXXVI– LXXVII) and the letter *P.* The richly detailed and lengthy articles, as well as the generally excellent bibliographies, make this an indispensable work.

Dizionario degli Istituti di Perfezione. Rome: Edizioni Paoline, 1974–. This work, devoted to the history of religious groups and orders, has thus far reached seven volumes, up to the letter *R.*

The Westminster Dictionary of Christian Spirituality. Edited by Gordon S. Wakefield. Philadelphia: Westminster, 1983.

1

Apostolic Life and Church Reform

GEORGE H. TAVARD

T HE EXPRESSION "Renaissance of the twelfth century" is commonly accepted.[1] It designates that aspect of the twelfth century that was creative of new movements and dimensions in Latin theology and spirituality. Many of the most important authors in fact died around 1150. Rupert of Deutz, Hugh of St. Victor, William of St. Thierry, Bernard, Peter the Venerable: all died between 1141 (Hugh) and 1156 (Peter). Yet the rest of the century was not without influential personalities. Several events that happened after 1150 were in fact determinative for the future. Among these, the Carmelite Order was founded in Palestine around 1154 by St. Berthold (d. 1195), and it received its original rule in 1209 from Albert of Vercelli, the Latin patriarch of Jerusalem.

It was in other ways a remarkable period. Peter Lombard, the father of scholastic theology, finished his *Book of Sentences* around 1150 and died in 1164. Medieval canon law was codified in Gratianus's decree in 1150–1151. Both Dominic and Francis of Assisi were born in this period; Dominic was preaching in southern France in 1206, and Francis initiated his movement in 1208. In 1163, building started for the cathedral of Paris, Notre-Dame, which inaugurated, after the abbey church of St. Denys, the spread of Gothic architecture.[2] In a different direction, the Fourth Crusade, which ended in a disastrous way with the crusaders' attack on Constantinople on 13 April 1204, had started with the usual enthusiasm.

Undoubtedly, the period that goes from 1150 to 1215 is, in spirituality as in theology, a time of transition. One may see a sign of this in that two rather distinct trends can easily be discerned in the spiritual writings of the period. An abundant spiritual literature came to light in the second half of the twelfth century. Most of it continued the main trends of the previous centuries. It is often called "monastic" for the obvious reason that it was written in monasteries, primarily to meet the needs of monks and nuns

1

engaged in the contemplative way. Some of it, however, looked forward to something new, leaning as it did toward a new eschatological, more or less prophetic, vision of the Christian life. This prophetic movement itself had two forms: the first, literary and theological, found in theological writings and biblical commentaries; and the second, popular, largely untheological, concerned with orthopraxis more than with the formulation of theory. These three aspects of the period determine the first three sections of the present chapter. A fourth section will be added, as some of the concerns of these movements converged at Lateran Council IV, in 1215, a council called in large measure to deal with some of the most disconcerting aspects of the time under survey.

The Literature of Contemplation

Many monastic authors continue the spiritual traditions of the great orders. Guigue II the Carthusian (d. 1188) at the Grande Chartreuse in the Alps, describes in his *Letter on the Contemplative Life* the four degrees of the spiritual ladder: reading, meditation, prayer, contemplation; and his twelve *Meditations* provide guidance for spiritual growth through these degrees. In a similar spirit, the Cistercian Aelred of Rievaulx (1110–1167), in England, composed *Rule for Recluses (De Institutione Inclusarum)*: these were women (and also a few men) who lived a life of prayer and solitude at the service of a particular church building and its congregation, thus realizing the ideal of uniting together action and contemplation.

Others, like the Premonstratensian Philip of Harvengt (d. 1183), in the low countries, commented on the Song of Songs, taking it as a paradigm of the soul eagerly expecting the return of Christ, or who, like the English Cistercian and archbishop of Canterbury, Baldwin of Ford (d. 1190), explained the spiritual dimension of the New Testament passages on the Eucharist. Adam the Scot (d. ca. 1210), who joined the Carthusians after being a Premonstratensian abbot, authored several treatises concerning contemplation. Such an abundant flourishing of spiritual writing seems to express the temperament of western Europe before the dawn of the thirteenth century, if we realize that the literature of mysticism is also at home in the Judaism of the period: this is the time of the great Maimonides (1135–1204) of Cordoba, Spain. It is equally at home among the Muslims of southern Spain: Abu-Madyan (d. 1193) of Sevilla is considered one of the founders of the *sadili* school, which was to flourish in North Africa.

Among all the spiritual authors, however, pride of place belongs to the great Richard of St. Victor (d. 1173), a Scotsman who became prior of St. Victor, near Paris, where he succeeded his spiritual teacher, Hugh of St.

Victor. Richard's best-known mystical writing is probably his treatise *The Four Degrees of Passionate Love*. But the most fundamental ones are the two volumes called *Benjamin*, named on the assumption that Benjamin, the youngest son of Jacob, was a model of the contemplative life, an idea that came from the Latin Vulgate rendering of Ps 67:28 ("There, young Benjamin, in ecstasy of mind . . ."). In *Benjamin minor*, Richard prepares the soul for contemplation through a self-knowledge that is both psychological and spiritual. This self-knowledge should, at the limit, coincide with God-knowledge. In the longer *Benjamin major*, the soul is led to the grace and the experience of contemplation. There are, for Richard, six degrees of contemplation, the first four being natural or psychological. The last two are mystical: it "is above the human and exceeds human thinking or human capacity." In other words, it is effected entirely by divine grace, as the soul is made to rise above itself.

Seers and Prophets

More creative and original in her approach and methods for the life of prayer is Hildegard of Bingen (1109–1179) in Germany. Raised as a child by a recluse, Jutta of Spanheim, essentially unlettered and deprived of formal education but rich in popular wisdom, Hildegard gained so much fame through her writings, her extensive correspondence with bishops, abbots, princes, and ordinary people, that she has been nicknamed "the Sybil of the Rhine." She lived as a nun in several monasteries until she was elected abbess in 1136 at Disibodenberg, from where, a few years later, she moved the community to Bingen on the Rhine. Her visions gave her the reputation of a seer and brought her fame in her lifetime. Through several secretaries, both nuns and priests, she wrote extensively in the area of folk medicine, and, after obtaining in 1141 some profound insights into the spiritual meaning of Scripture, on the life of piety. She also composed a number of prose poems, mostly liturgical, and a psychological-moral drama, *Ordo virtutum* (*Order of the Virtues*).

The *Scivias* (that is, *Sci vias lucis, Know the Ways of Light*) is her most important theological work. Finished before 1151, it is a spiritual compendium remarkably illustrated with colored pictures. These images, undoubtedly inspired by her visions and modeled, it would seem, on manuscript illuminations that were fashionable, were drawn by various artists under her supervision. Hildegard had learned from her folk medicine the therapeutic virtualities of pictures and images. She transposed this basic idea into theology and the teaching of piety. Both the subjects and the colors have symbolic intent. The traditional content and purpose of her spiritual writings place her squarely in the line of the great orthodox mystics of her century. Her spirituality is very trinitarian, even though she frequently uses unusual images to convey her perception of the Three Persons' life and action. The pictures and meditations of her later composition, *De Operatione Dei* (*On the Work of God*), of 1170, show the universe as a sort of cosmic egg, containing a human person and itself resting within the womb of God. The pictures, more artistic than in the *Scivias*, were added after Hildegard's death but in keeping with the descriptions given in her text. Hildegard conceives God as essential love. Her unusual style of teaching makes it appropriate to see her as a pioneer of new ways. Hildegard, who must have been aware of this, considered herself a prophet, freely appropriating images from Old Testament prophecy and from the Apocalypse. And she was so considered by those around her.

As an author in the field of theology and piety, Hildegard may be compared with her predecessor, Hroswitha of Gandersheim (ca. 1000), and with her successors, Gertrude of Helfta (1256–1302), the two Mechthilds (of Magdeburg, 1210–1295, and of Hackeborn, 1241–1299), and the many women mystics of the fourteenth and fifteenth centuries. She is more deeply religious than Hroswitha, more creative than Gertrude, but perhaps not so profound a mystic as Gertrude.

Hildegard had a direct influence on another notable woman mystic of her time, Elizabeth of Schönau (1129–1164), a Benedictine nun in the twin abbeys of Schönau. Her brother Eckbert of Schönau (1132–1184) became a monk at the same abbeys and eventually the abbot. He directed her spiritually and he later wrote her life. Elizabeth's *Book of the Ways of God* is largely inspired by the *Scivias*. Her visions, which followed an illness she suffered in 1157, lean to the fantastic. They were written down with the help of her brother. Eckbert was himself a notable spiritual writer, the author, among other volumes, of *Stimulus amoris,* which has often been wrongly attributed to Bernard and to Anselm.

Some of Hildegard's interests relate her indirectly to the prophetism of Joachim of Fiore (ca. 1135–1202).[3] There is no direct influence. Yet, like Hildegard, Joachim stressed the place of the Trinity in theology and spirituality; like her too he oriented the spiritual life toward eschatology. But he gave a different twist to these two concerns.

Joachim, a Calabrian, entered the Cistercian order after making a pilgrimage to the Holy Land. He left it in 1196, with the approval of Pope Celestine III, to establish a new monastic order, the Order of St. John, which he started in Fiore, Calabria. By the time Joachim died, the order had grown to sixty houses, thirty-eight of which were concentrated in southern Italy. Bernard remained the spiritual model of these monks, but Joachim

brought a new spirit, unknown to the Cistercian tradition, to the foundation. As his writings show, he was primarily a biblical commentator, very
orthodox in his formal beliefs. But he brought to the task of commenting
on Scripture a new spirit and a new principle. The new spirit was that the
real purpose of biblical interpretation is prophecy. The past is there only
for the future. In studying it we may know the future. This future is what
Joachim tried to describe. The new principle was that the key to the biblical
meanings, or what would be called today the "canon within the canon," is
the book of the Apocalypse. Interest in the Apocalypse was not unusual in
the Middle Ages. What made Joachim unique was that he read in the
Apocalypse the promise of a new age to come, the age of the Spirit, which
would succeed and supersede the age of the Son (corresponding to the New
Testament), as this had already succeeded and superseded the age of the
Father (corresponding to the Old Testament). From this he drew remarkable consequences for the understanding of history and for the nature of the
church itself. And this, precisely, makes Joachim relevant to a history of
spirituality, because these conclusions themselves entailed a new accent in
Christian piety and because they presupposed a new conception of the relationships between the Holy Trinity and the created world.

One of Joachim's main concerns was to explore the parallelisms between
the two Testaments. Thus, the seven periods which he, after Augustine,
identified in the unfolding of the Old Testament, were to have their parallel
in the history of the New, that is, in the unfolding of the church. But,
unlike Augustine, Joachim sought the meaning of the sevenfold pattern in
a broader one, which he constructed on the heavenly model of the Three
Persons. His insights so impressed Pope Lucius III in 1184 that the pope
commissioned him to compose two major works, his *Concord* (of the Old
and the New Testaments) and his *Exposition on the Apocalypse*. In regard to
history, Joachim used his threefold pattern to reinterpret the theological
outline of history that had been inherited from Augustine: six ages of the
world (or seven, depending on whether the seventh age, corresponding to
the sabbath of creation, is seen to run parallel to the sixth or to come after
it). For Joachim, the world is coming to the end of the sixth age. After the
time of the laity (the Old Testament and God the Father) and that of the
clergy (the New Testament and the Word incarnate), there will soon come
the age of monks (the state of perfection and the Holy Spirit). A new
religious order was to be expected. Joachim even prophesied—mistakenly,
of course—that Pope Urban III would have no successor! At any rate,
Joachim set the tone for a spirituality of expectation, nourished by the
Apocalypse, waiting for, and perhaps imagining, visions of the times to
come. In these times, the institutional church, structured on the clergy,

would cease and be replaced by a purely spiritual church on a monastic model, centered on the perceived presence and action of the Holy Spirit.

Whether Joachim was himself a mystic, the recipient of special graces of spiritual insight, would seem to be questionable. He was certainly gifted in pedagogy. Indeed, the abundant illustrations of his works bring him close to Hildegard's concerns for a holistic approach to the spiritual life. Joachim's pictures are inspired by Gothic architectural drawing as well as by manuscript illuminations. They belong to what may be called a holy geometry: there are intertwining circles, eagles shaped like trees, triangles, circles, squares, and straight lines, the whole being covered with names and words from the Scriptures. Joachim likes foliage well enough, but he also draws wild animals, real or mythical, like dragons, serpents, and seven-headed beasts. His pictures do not really feed the soul. They are mnemonic devices for the mind rather than mandalas destined to open up hitherto undiscerned perspectives. They undoubtedly contributed to the astonishing success of his books and ideas. But they also point to the reason for Joachim's ultimate posthumous failure: besides whatever personal piety he presumably had, Joachim's contributions distorted Christian piety and theology. His pictures, like his visions of history, are matters for the head, not for the heart. They may fill and clutter the mind, but they do not nurture it. A new meaning of Scripture may indeed emerge in subsequent experience, meditation, and insight, but it cannot be invented through intellectual cleverness. Joachim was clever.

The Church of the Poor

Hildegard's interest in folkways also relates her to a growing concern for spiritual simplicity and poverty which comes to light in several sectors of Western Christendom. Small groups searching for a simple Christianity were not rare, especially in the countryside, throughout the twelfth century. The first movement of this kind dates back to the early years of the century, in northern Italy, where it was organized in monastic fashion, following the *Rule of St. Benedict*, by Giovanni d'Oldrado (d. 1159). The group was known as the Humiliati. Many lay people of northern Italy, inspired by the same ideal, lived a simple life as artisans in the towns of Lombardy, devoted to almsgiving and meditation.

The best-known such movement, however, is that of Peter Waldo.[4] As far as can be known in the absence of uncontested documentation, Waldo was a rich merchant of the city of Lyon, who, under the impact of a spiritual experience, chose poverty and simplicity as a way of life. This was in part inspired by the legend of St. Alexis.[5] As it took place in the 1170s, it may

1. Interior of Durham Cathedral.

2. Interior of Chartres Cathedral.

have been related to the great famine of 1176. Waldo soon had a number of followers, who may have given Waldo the name Peter. Their ideal was that of a wandering life, sustained by alms, preaching, and setting the example of Christian love. They wanted to imitate the seventy-two disciples sent by Jesus two by two to announce the kingdom of God. They lived without any specific rule, and they preached in public, inviting people to simplicity and poverty. Waldo and some of his companions traveled to Rome at the time of Lateran Council III (1179), probably to secure the pope's protection and the permission to preach. Known as "the Poor of Lyon," they were well received by Pope Alexander III, who generally approved their way of life but did not authorize them to preach, except where the clergy would ask for them, for they were without theological education. In 1180 a regional council of Lyon imposed on Waldo a profession of faith which is strongly trinitarian and which he accepted without difficulty, but permission to preach was still refused. It is not certain that Waldo himself continued to preach, yet many of his followers did; occasionally the Waldensian preacher was a woman, although this did remain exceptional.

The movement, however, was condemned by Pope Lucius III at the regional council of Verona in 1184, along with that of the Humiliati (bull *Ad Abolendam*, 4 November 1184). The same council took action against the Cathars, who were numerous in northern Italy and southern France.[6] The Poor of Lyon were soon expelled from the diocese of Lyon by the bishop, John of Canterbury. But this expulsion helped their growth: they more or less amalgamated with some of the Humiliati of Lombardy, and they are found later in much of eastern and southern France, in the low countries, in southern Germany and Austria, and in much of northern and central Italy. They gained a reputation for heresy, perhaps because they rejected the ordinance forbidding lay preaching or because they were confused with the Cathars, whose doctrines, however, they strongly opposed. Yet at the origin they showed every sign of orthodoxy. The opposition of the hierarchy had been occasioned only by their zeal for preaching in spite of being relatively unlettered and, most of them, unordained. In many ways, the Poor of Lyon anticipated the Franciscan movement, but their problems with the bishops over lay preaching marginalized them to the point where they eventually veered into heterodoxy.

Lateran Councils III and IV

Lateran III, a reforming council, was called chiefly to end the situation created after Pope Hadrian IV died in 1159: two different popes had been elected by rival factions of cardinals. At the death of Callistus III (1164–1168), the third of the minority line, the Third Lateran Council, called by Alexander III (1159–1181), met in 1179 to settle the quarrel with the emperor, which was largely responsible for the schism. It deserves to be mentioned here only because, although it strongly condemned the Cathar movement, it said nothing against Waldo and his disciples: the distinction between the two groups was still made. The Cathars were heretics; the Poor of Lyon were orthodox.

Simplicity, poverty, purity: the Poor of Lyon sought the first two. The third was the watchword of the Cathars. This may be seen as a spiritual movement that was unorthodox from the start and was inspired to a large extent by an old dualistic tradition going back to the Persian Mani, which had had a resurgence in eastern Europe and had started its westward march around the time of the First Crusade.[7] In spite of several local condemnations, this movement flourished in southern France and in various parts of central and northern Italy. There were also, especially in Italy, more revolutionary groups: the Amaurians (followers of Amalric of Bene, d. ca. 1206), who taught a kind of pantheism; the Arnoldists (disciples of Arnold of Brescia, executed in 1155), who believed that the church of Rome had lost all validity; the Speronists (founded by Ugo Speroni, a lawyer in Brescia), who taught a strict doctrine of predestination and who anticipated the Quakers in their belief that the true church is purely interior to the conscience.

Deeply concerned about the radicalization of such movements and their largely unchecked proliferation, Pope Innocent III (1198–1216) called another "general council of the West,"[8] Lateran Council IV, in 1215, to meet this growing challenge to orthodoxy. Yet the pope's intent was broader: he wanted to remove one of the causes of such movements by reforming the church; he also wanted to persuade, or oblige, the bishops and the Christian princes to form a common front against all heterodoxies. Accordingly, the council formulated the Catholic faith and adopted measures against the trinitarian conceptions of the late Joachim, against the "heretics," the anti-Latin Greeks, and the Jews. It tried to stem the proliferation of conventicles by forbidding the formation of new religious orders. It attempted to reform pastoral care, chiefly by recommending that priests be well instructed in liturgical matters and that those in charge of churches be noted for their moral life and their knowledge of letters. It also tried to bring monks and clerics under stricter control by taking measures against those involved in concubinage or who practiced dueling. In this context, the heretics in question included the Waldensians, along with the other movements of a more heterodox bent.

Precisely when the Poor of Lyon were being pushed out because of their disobedience to authority, the church of the poor showed its resilience: both Dominic and Francis were at the gate.

* * * * * * * *

During the thirteenth century, the seat of theological authority moved from monasteries to universities, just as the seat of economic power passed from agricultural domains to the concentrated commerce and fairs of the cities, and the seat of political power began to shift from the provincial aristocracy to the court of the king in a central capital. As a transition between the period of monastic theology and that of scholastic theology, the years from 1150-1215 serve two functions. They bring the previous time to an end, and they inaugurate a new Christian culture. As far as spirituality was concerned, the previous time was dominated by the monasteries and the meditative writings of monks; there was, by the nature of things, a close connection between spirituality and theology, even to the point of identity. By developing theology as a special discipline, the specialty of the universities, the period of scholastic theology began a separation of theology and spirituality which reached its high point at the end of the Middle Ages and was taken for granted at the dawn of the modern age.

Like the past to which it succeeds, the transition period still saw monks doing spiritual theology or theological spirituality in their cloisters: in the context, the two expressions are tantamount to the same thing. Yet, like the future it heralded, the transition already brought to the surface trends in which some sort of psychology was set in the very warp and woof of spiritual meditation. In the popular movements of the church of the poor it even pushed the distinction between theology and spiritual experience, orthodoxy and orthopraxis, to the point of mutual ignorance.

It is, of course, not a useful exercise, eight centuries later, to apportion blame for the errors and mistakes of the past. Yet one cannot help feeling a nostalgic regret that those who held positions of leadership were then unable to read the signs of the times—until it was too late and drastic measures became unavoidable, on the pattern of those of Lateran Council IV.

Notes

1. This is the title of a classic, H. Haskins, *The Renaissance of the Twelfth Century* (Cambridge, MA: Harvard University Press, 1927).

2. Studies of medieval and Gothic art are many; for an overview, see Andrew Martindale, *Gothic Art* (London: Thames & Hudson, 1967); Ann Mitchell, *Cathedrals of Europe* (London: Hamlyn, 1968); *Larousse Encyclopedia of Byzantine and Medieval Art*, ed. René Hyughe (New York: Prometheus, 1968).

3. Henri de Lubac has studied Joachim's principles of biblical exegesis in *Exégèse*

mediévale: Les quatre sens de l'écriture, vol. 3 (Paris: Aubier, 1961) chap. 6. Joachim's influence has been widespread; de Lubac has traced it in both religious and secular movements until our own time (*La Postérité spirituelle de Joachim de Flore* (2 vols.; Paris: Lethielleux, 1978, 1981).

4. His name is also given as Valdès, not to be confused with Juan Valdès, a Spanish spiritual author of the early sixteenth century, who was connected with the movement of the "Catholic Evangelicals." The date of Peter Waldo's death is not known, but he seems to have lived a long life, well into the thirteenth century, supported by the veneration of his followers.

5. A Greek legend, mentioned for the first time in the ninth century, told the story of a wealthy citizen, the son of a Roman senator, who in the fifth century would have left his wife on their wedding day and lived thereafter as a poor hermit. The legend became popular in the West. In some forms of it, this saint, called Alexis, returned to his home after seventeen years as a beggar and lived there as a servant for another seventeen years, unrecognized until he died. He was believed to be buried in Edessa (Syria). The feast of St. Alexis is celebrated in the Roman calendar on 17 July.

6. The Cathars (the name means "the Pure") appeared in France in the eleventh century (condemned at the Council of Orleans in 1022). The sources also call them Albigensians (from the city of Albi, in France) and Patarines (apparently from a confusion: the Patarini, followers of Ariald, a cleric in Milan around 1056, had maintained that the clergy must be pure by refraining from concubinage). The Cathars taught a dualistic doctrine, in which matter and the flesh were identified with evil. They may have been related to the Bogomils (in Bulgaria, eighth century), who taught a similar doctrine. By the beginning of the thirteenth century, the Cathars were so numerous in southern France that a crusade was called against them.

7. Mani, a priest in Iran in the third century, had taught a heterodox doctrine that was a mixture of Christianity and Zoroastrianism (the religion of the Iranian prophet of the sixth century B.C., Zoroaster, also called Zarathustra). Mani distinguished between a substance of the good and a substance of evil and attributed them to different creators. Manicheanism had been a major heresy in the patristic times of the church. (St. Augustine had been a Manichee for eleven years.) Both the Bogomils and the Cathars held to a kind of dualism on the Manichean model, although the historical links of their movements with that of Mani have remained obscure.

8. The expression is from Pope Paul VI; see G. Tavard, "What Elements Determine the Ecumenicity of a Council?" *Concilium* 9 (1983) 45–49.

Bibliography

Fox, Matthew. *Illuminations of Hildegard of Bingen.* Santa Fe, NM: Bear, 1985.

Kirchberger, Clare, ed. *Richard of Saint Victor: Selected Writings on Contemplation.* New York: Harper, n.d.

Lambert, M. D. *Medieval Heresy: Popular Movements from Bogomil to Hus.* New York: Holmes & Meier, 1977.

Leclercq, Jean. *The Love of Learning and the Desire for God: A Study in Monastic Culture.* New York: Fordham University Press, 1961.

Reeves, Marjorie. *Joachim of Fiore and the Prophetic Future.* London: SPCK, 1976.

——, and Beatrice Hirsch-Reich. *The "Figurae" of Joachim of Fiore.* Oxford: Clarendon Press, 1972.

Southern, R. W. *The Making of the Middle Ages.* Manchester: University Press, 1921.

Part One
SCHOOLS AND MOVEMENTS

2

The Mendicants

I. *The Spirituality of the Dominicans*

Simon Tugwell

The Order of Preachers

THE DOMINICAN ORDER was officially founded in 1216 by Dominic Guzman (ca. 1170–1221) "to be and to be called 'order of preachers.'" The official name of the order is, in fact, The Order of Preachers. In the words of an important declaration added to the constitutions in 1220, "Our order is known to have been founded from the beginning for the sake of preaching and the salvation of souls, and our efforts ought above all to be directed primarily and enthusiastically towards being able to be useful to the souls of our neighbors." In one form or another this declaration has remained in the Dominican constitutions to this day.

A revival of preaching was a recognized need in the church in the early thirteenth century. The bishops, who were the official ministers of the word of God, were all too frequently "dumb dogs who will not bark," as Innocent III complained. Recognizing that often they were in fact prevented from preaching by their other responsibilities, the Fourth Lateran Council in 1215 called for the appointment in each diocese of auxiliary preachers to help them. It has been suggested that this decree was influenced by the experiment initiated earlier in the same year in the diocese of Toulouse, where Bishop Fulk had appointed Dominic and his first associates to be official preachers.

Dominic himself, however, was already beginning to think in larger terms. He envisaged his friars going out in pairs, like the preachers sent out by Christ, into all the world. In 1216 his order was approved by Honorius III as an Order of Preachers not confined to any one diocese and not

dependent on any bishop for its mandate to preach. The Dominicans thereafter were not simply people who were available to be called upon to preach;
they were, by right and by definition, preachers.

So urgent did Dominic consider this task to be that even though at first
he had only a few friars—and they were, on the whole, young and not very
well educated—he sent them out confidently to preach, supporting them
with his prayers and bidding them have confidence in God. Moreover,
instead of consolidating his first foundation in Toulouse, he disbanded his
friars, sending them out to preach and to make new foundations.

Poor Preachers

Judged by the prevailing monastic norms, Dominic's action was rather
foolhardy. For decades the Dominicans, like the Franciscans, had to defend
themselves against the charge that their way of life was "exceedingly dangerous." It was considered highly improper for religious, particularly young
religious, to go gadding about the world instead of staying within the
disciplined environment of the monastery. The Dominicans retorted that
Christ was not a black monk or a white monk, but a poor preacher, and
they were content to follow his example. If they were "gyrovagues," well and
good; so was St. Paul. And if their life was, humanly speaking, exposed to
enormous risks, they relied on God and on the Mother of God to protect
them.

The fifth master of the order, Humbert of Romans (ca. 1200–1277), one
of the most authoritative exponents of Dominican life, was quite categorical
that, for anyone who has a "grace of preaching," preaching must take priority over all other spiritual practices, even prayer and the celebration of the
sacraments. It would be wrong for such a person to abstain from preaching
because of a preference for a quiet life at home in the convent. Even when
the preacher is at home, resting between his preaching expeditions, he
should be preparing to resume his task.

In a letter written in about 1270 to encourage his novices to persevere, the
English Dominican provincial, Robert Kilwardby, expresses his order's
boast:

> You should notice the usefulness of our state of life, my beloved novices. In
> this, unless I am mistaken, our state of life ought, on any true calculation,
> to be preferred to all others. For all our chapters and discussions and debates
> and all the order's study aim at nothing else than to prepare people and make
> them fit for the salvation of souls, and, when they are prepared and equipped
> in their way of life and in knowledge, to direct them to the task of converting
> sinners. So I reckon that no other order works as hard in its concern for this

as ours does, or achieves so much by its work. Therefore those who have such a vocation ought rightly to rejoice since it is well known that at the last judgment the reward is to be meted out in accordance with what people merit by their useful labour.[1]

Kilwardby was no doubt well aware that the traditional doctrine linked merit with the infused grace of charity, but charity is expressed precisely in the concern to be useful to others. Preaching is itself an act springing from charity. Dominic had longed to pour himself out totally for the salvation of others, reckoning that only so would he really be a member of the Body of Christ, and some of his followers felt guilty about taking their evening meal if they had not preached to at least one person during the day. In its own way, a life totally dedicated to preaching was considered to be as heroic as martyrdom or virginity.

Educated Preachers

In the thirteenth century a fairly sharp distinction was made between doctrinal preaching, which was reserved to the clergy, and exhortation. The Dominicans were essentially committed to the former, and this meant that they needed to be intellectually prepared for the task. The Lateran Council recognized this too as a major need in the church and called for the setting up of diocesan schools of theology. Dominic, once again, had anticipated the council. Almost as soon as his first community was formed in Toulouse in early 1215, he went with his brethren to the classes being given there by an English theologian, Alexander Stavensby. Dominic even went so far as to obtain a bull from the pope summoning masters of theology from Paris to teach in Toulouse, though he never actually used this bull. Instead, in 1217, he sent some of his friars to Paris to study in the university there. In Bologna, where the friars first settled in 1218, there was no faculty of theology, but the Dominicans studied together every day, under the guidance of one of their number.

Study was from the outset an essential element in Dominican life. Every house was to have a resident lecturer in theology, and many Dominican houses became centers of theological study. In 1221 the bishop of Metz supported the founding of a house in his diocese because he wanted his clergy to benefit from the friars' theological teaching.

Dominic's first recruits were characterized more by zeal than by intellectual prowess, but the order soon began to attract much more educated recruits. Dominic's successor, Jordan of Saxony (d. 1237), regarded universities as prime recruiting ground and was so successful in attracting students to the order that he was known as "the harlot of the schools." There seems to have been some tension between those who were more interested in piety than study and those who thought study all-important for the order's work, but there is no doubt on which side the order's officials came down. Jordan, in an encyclical written in 1233, warns that people's very lives are endangered by the friar's lack of fidelity to study. Humbert of Romans talks dismissively of one friar who became "silly through excess of devotion."

From the middle of the thirteenth century, the order established a very comprehensive program of education with elaborate academic structures, even if it did not always have enough qualified teachers in them. The order contributed some of the greatest theologians of the period, such as Albert the Great (ca. 1200–1280) and Thomas Aquinas (ca. 1225–1274).

As the order became more involved in the universities, it inevitably became involved in a more intellectual apostolate. One of the needs of the time was for a serious attempt to cope theologically with the new, Aristotelian learning which posed a serious threat to orthodoxy. Albert and Thomas in particular helped to disentangle the genuine teaching of Aristotle and to show how it could be made to serve orthodox theology. Later on there was a similar problem with the new humanism of the Italian Renaissance, and once again Dominicans were prominently involved. Even those who were overtly opposed to many facets of humanism, like John Dominici (ca. 1355–1419) and Savonarola (1452–1498), were influenced by it and influential on it.

Albert and Thomas espoused a radically intellectualist account of the Christian life. It is through the intellect that one is to be united with God, and the contemplative ascent to God is an intellectual process, though it must be motivated by charity and have an affective component. Over against the prevailing unintellectual, if not anti-intellectual, notion of the contemplative life, Thomas uses the phrase to mean a life in which speculative interests predominate. In this sense he acknowledges realistically that contemplatives love God less than people engaged in the active life, though they are more loved by God, in that their lives approximate more closely the life of heaven.

Apostolic Preachers

Although the intellectual element in preaching was important, there was also at the outset a great emphasis on imitation of the apostolic way of life. The Order of Preachers grew out of the preaching campaign against the heretics in the south of France, in which Dominic, with his bishop, Diego, became involved in 1206. Diego realized that the heretics, whether Albigensian or Waldensian, were winning converts largely because they appeared much more obviously evangelical in their way of life than did the Catholic preachers and clergy. He therefore suggested that the Catholic missionaries ought also to "imitate in everything the form of the apostles."[2] He and Dominic therefore initiated a style of itinerant, mendicant preaching, which had previously been regarded with considerable suspicion in the church.

From this experience Dominic retained a devotion to poverty that was almost as extreme as that of Francis. His first community in Toulouse did have a certain income, but the friars were not to take money or provisions with them when they traveled. In 1220 he persuaded the order to go even further and renounce all properties, except the actual buildings in which the friars lived. The whole order was thereafter to be funded exclusively by begging.

Dominic himself wanted the brethren to display real poverty in the simplicity of their buildings and clothing, but it is not clear that the brethren saw eye to eye with him on this. It was also taken for granted that there would be no individual ownership of goods within the community, but the essential feature of Dominican poverty was the abandonment of guaranteed revenues. The Dominicans, unlike all other religious including the Franciscans, never attempted to earn their living by undertaking paid labor or to provide for themselves by any form of manual work. The Dominicans, were, from the beginning, mendicant.

Over the years, however, the practice of poverty changed. First of all, it was found that relying on daily begging took up too much time, so in 1240 the General Chapter ruled that supplies for up to one year could be kept in the house. Later on, it became harder and harder to finance the order by begging, and from early in the fourteenth century it became common for some houses to acquire benefactions that would give them a more secure income and even to acquire properties on which money could be raised. This practice was defended by the order's canonists and theologians as a realistic adaptation; the order's superiors, it was argued, had the right to give whatever dispensations were needed, including the dispensation from mendicancy. Finally, at the request of the General Chapter, in 1475 the pope permitted the order as a whole to be possessionate. The reason given was that mendicancy was found to be an intolerable hindrance to the order's work.

From the outset poverty had been adopted for apostolic reasons; however, many extra, more ideological, motives may have been involved as well. Already by the middle of the thirteenth century writers like Thomas Aquinas and Kilwardby were explaining Dominican poverty almost entirely in functional terms, so it is not surprising that the order eventually concluded that mendicancy would have to be sacrificed to study and preaching.

The regime of mendicancy itself caused a modification in the traditional principle of community of goods. In the nature of the case, some benefactions were made to individual friars, and it became normal for those who were able to provide their own clothing, for instance, thanks to their personal contacts, to do so. This led to wild disparity between the provision made for different brethren, and by the end of the thirteenth century we find references to the "poor" brethren, meaning those without personal benefactors.

In addition to this, it was soon recognized that academics, at least, needed to have their own books, and this was soon extended to recognizing the usefulness of their having some funds of their own with which to procure books. By the middle of the fourteenth century, there was evidently a high level of de facto private ownership in the order, even though technically all goods belonged to the community. It was pointed out by Thomas that things that belong to everybody get looked after by nobody, and this argument was later used by Raphael of Pornassio (d. 1467) to defend contemporary relaxed practice.

Obedient Preachers

The order began to come into existence as an institution in 1215, when two burghers of Toulouse "gave themselves" to Dominic. Until then, though he had had various people associated with him in his preaching, none of them had bound themselves to him by any profession of obedience. When the order was recognized by the pope, the promise of obedience to Dominic remained its structural linchpin, and to this day the Dominican formula of profession contains only the vow of obedience. The Dominicans never adopted a formal profession rite like those of the monks and canons, so that the personal self-oblation of the new friar to the master of the order remained highlighted.

Unlike the members of the traditional orders, the Dominicans were not regarded as submitting themselves primarily to the regime of a religious house; they were putting themselves at the disposal of the master of preaching. The rules of the order were certainly important, and Dominic expected and exacted a high level of fidelity to them; but they were not regarded as the essential element in Dominican life, nor were they regarded as a discipline needed to contain the frailty and depravity of human instincts. In the nature of the case, preachers who were to spend much of their time out of their convents had to be responsible for themselves. The Dominicans therefore stressed personal responsibility and, above all, generosity rather than the precautions that had been traditional.

3. *The Nativity with Six Dominicans,* Italian, ca. 1275.

Dominic himself had begun his religious life as a reformed canon at Osma, and since, as a result of the Lateran Council, his new order had to adopt one of the existing *Rules,* it is not surprising that he and his companions chose the *Rule of St. Augustine,* the canons' rule. They also took over some of the more austere customs of the reformed canons, drawing on the constitutions of the Premonstratensians. To some extent, then, they regarded themselves as akin to the reformed canons. But they did not take over the detailed timetable that was characteristic of reformed legislation, and they made unprecedented provision for dispensations from conventual observance in order to facilitate the study and preaching of the brethren.

This meant that inevitably there was much less sense of discipline in a Dominican house than would have been expected in a traditional religious community. Humbert of Romans, in spite of his taste for uniformity, acknowledged that there cannot be all that much uniformity in Dominican observance. Preachers and, even more, teachers have to be given considerable freedom if they are to do their job properly. It was to be expected that some people would abuse this freedom. It is significant that Humbert, rather than trying to tighten up the discipline, tried to ensure that novices developed good habits from the outset, avoiding the company of the more frivolous brethren and learning how to make good use of their time.

Evidently the common life suffered considerably from the accumulating dispensations which the brethren enjoyed. An indication of how far things had gone is provided by an early fourteenth-century customary from one of the German priories, which rules that the brethren must eat together in the refectory on the days for receiving communion—that is, about fifteen times a year! Later reforming chapters in the middle of the century rule that at least half the community must eat in the refectory every day. An attempt is also made to restrict the number of people dispensed from the common liturgy in choir.

It had generally been assumed that religious rules in some way had the authority of divine law and so were binding in conscience. The Dominicans added a sentence to their constitutions in 1236 explicitly denying this, and Dominic himself is credited with saying that if he thought the brethren were taking the constitutions as being binding in conscience he would personally destroy every copy of them. The principle that Dominican law is only human law, having no supernatural sanctions attached to it, is greatly insisted on by thirteenth-century Dominicans. It is meant to relieve people of undue nervousness and to leave room for truly generous motivation. But the principle was stressed so much that by the end of the fourteenth century, evidently some people were saying that Dominican law did not oblige the brethren at all and that it was only a kind of recommendation. What was meant to liberate people into generosity was turned into a justification for self-will.

However, the principle of personal obedience to the superior was retained as the essential element in Dominican obedience. This was never meant to involve a constant running to the superior for instructions, much less a surrender of the individual's freedom of judgment; the typical Dominican obedience consisted in doing the job one had been given to the best of one's ability, applying one's mind and will to it, even if one thought that the superior was actually wrong. Being given a job meant being given the responsibility for doing it, and priors were not meant to interfere unnecessarily with the way people did their jobs. Gradually more emphasis came to be put on the superior's role as watchdog over the brethren's religious observance, but this was often ineffective as, seemingly, the superiors were generally no more observant than their subjects.

Active Preachers

The ingredients that made up Dominican life were many, and the resulting mixture was not entirely stable. There were, as we have seen, tensions between poverty and study and between the demands of the job and the demands of conventual life. Nor was there an obvious model that could hold the whole mixture together. Whereas the monks and reformed canons could, without undue difficulty, base themselves on the model of the early church in Jerusalem as depicted in the Acts of the Apostles, the chosen Dominican model, Christ the wandering poor preacher, did not suggest any way of holding together itinerant preaching and conventual life. The Franciscans, initially, abandoned conventual life in favor of the model of the apostolic life given in Matthew 10, but from the beginning the Dominicans were conventual. Nor did the Dominicans make any serious attempt to take Dominic himself as enshrining the full reality of the Dominican vocation. The early biographers present him as being inimitable, but, what is more serious, Dominic had not encouraged the brethren to view him as a model. He had made the brethren take full responsibility with him for forming the structures and rules of the order, and they had on occasion ventured to disagree with his ideas. The order was always intended to be adaptable to new situations, so there could be no fixed model for all times any more than there could be fixed statutes for all times.

In addition to this, there was, of course, no concept of "Dominican spirituality," calling for a systematic exploration of how the various ingredients were related to one another. In their edifying writings, Dominicans were generally unoriginal, even when the writings were intended for the use of their brethren. Humbert's *Letter on Religious Life* is largely derived from Cistercian writings or from the canons regular; the treatise written for novices by the Toulouse novice master at the end of the thirteenth century is similarly derivative. In the same way, in the seventeenth century, we find Dominicans adopting the current norms of piety, such as "mental prayer" and spiritual exercises (we even find them doing the *Exercises* of St. Ignatius), with no discussion of how such pious practices are or are not related to Dominican spirituality. Dominican sources, therefore, give us only piece-meal and incidental indications of how the rather heady mixture inherited from the founding fathers of the order can and should work.

If preaching and intellectual life are to be undertaken seriously, it is clear that they must be allowed to follow their own rhythm, regardless of the convent timetable. This was conceded almost from the outset, with the principle of dispensations for the sake of the work. But they will also become all-absorbing, leaving little time and less energy for the cultivation of moral and spiritual perfection, which was generally regarded as the goal of religious life, or for the responsibilities of the common life. This too was conceded by Humbert. Preachers must not be expected to play a full part in the conventual observances, nor must they be expected to carry the burdens of community functions. Teachers must be positively cosseted and should not be expected to come to choir even if at the time of choir they are only relaxing. . . .

It had generally been assumed that it was impossible to undertake a serious active life and, at the same time, be an exemplary religious. Humbert fully accepted this. He warned that it is a trivial reason for holding back from preaching that one is afraid of "the sins which will unavoidably occur." Similarly, early in the fourteenth century, Jordan of Pisa (ca. 1260–1311) tells people not to be surprised that the Dominicans are not perfect: cities, with all their temptations, are no proper place for religious, but "we are here for your good."[3] The wear and tear inseparable from a busy apostolic or ac-demic life make it almost impossible to sustain the austerities usually expected of religious, and they make it extremely probable that tempers will sometimes fray. In Humbert's view, this was simply a risk that had to be taken. The goodness inherent in this apostolic service of others is more than enough to wash away any taint of sin that the preacher may contract.

From the time of Jordan of Saxony on, we find prominent Dominicans complaining that they are hardly ever able to pray, so they ask the nuns to pray for them. They do not infer that they ought to abandon their work.

The "collapse" of regular life of which mid-fourteenth-century chapters keep complaining was not simply due to the loss of religious fervor. Even if the level of private life was unacceptable, even if the original austerity had largely disappeared, this was at least in part derived from the legitimate option made in the thirteenth century in favor of the work of the order. But the problem was considerably exacerbated by the decimation of the order during the period of the Black Death. Drastically reduced numbers made it even harder to sustain conventual life, and a lamentably undiscriminating recruiting policy was adopted to replenish the order. By the end of the fourteenth century, a fair number of people found the situation insufferable.

Reformed Preachers

The various attempts to reform the order's regular life in the fourteenth century seem to have had little effect, so in the 1380s there was talk of establishing at least one convent in which there could be a return to strict and complete observance. In 1389 the first reformed community was established in Colmar, and a year later a program was announced for the establishment of one such convent in each province under the jurisdiction of the provincials, but with considerable independence. Later on, the reformed convents were withdrawn from the jurisdiction of the provincials and taken under the immediate jurisdiction of the master of the order, who governed them through specially appointed vicars. Later still, reformed convents began to be formed into reformed congregations, which sometimes came close to complete independence even of the master of the order. The various reforms in the order, however well-intentioned and even necessary they may have been, illustrate the precariousness of the original Dominican mixture.

One of the first dreams of the reformers was for a quiet house out in the country where the brethren would not be seriously distracted from their contemplative and regular life. Nothing came of this first plan, but later on it reappeared, especially in Spain. This kind of reform certainly tended to make the Dominicans better religious, but only at the expense of their apostolate and sometimes of their study. Even short of these extremes, the emphasis on conventual discipline militated against the wholehearted dedication to preaching and study by restricting the traditional dispensations and relative independence that had previously been enjoyed by the most active brethren. Observance came to be an end in its own right, simply juxtaposed to the apostolate, so that Dominican life came to be seen as a "mixed life" rather than a single apostolic life.

The reformers varied in their attitude to poverty. Some, like John Dominici and Savonarola, rejected any suggestion that the order could abandon its mendicancy; others were simply concerned with eliminating or severely restricting the amount of money and goods effectively controlled by individuals. But it is not clear that mendicancy was really a viable option any longer. Savonarola proposed financing his reformed congregation by recruiting lay brothers who would make money by painting miniatures, which was just as contrary to the original Dominican practice as was any other proposed solution. And, as was pointed out by Raphael of Pornassio, individual funding was in fact the main surviving element of genuine mendicancy in the order. He was probably right that a combination of a certain amount of property and a certain reliance on benefactions, whether made to individuals or communities, was as close as it was possible to get to the original Dominican practice. A rigorous insistence that no individual should have control of any resources whatsoever was more typical of the reformed canons than of the early Dominicans.

There were also problems about obedience. As we have seen, the principle that Dominican law does not bind in conscience was being abused. But the contrary principle, asserted most famously by John Dominici, that Dominican law does bind in conscience, was flagrantly contrary to the intention of Dominic.

The reformers themselves were quick to resort to the equally un-Dominican practice of seeking outside help to bolster their positions, relying to a considerable extent on papal decrees and even on lay support to guarantee them against their own superiors. When the community of Padua consulted two prominent lawyers about the reform, the lawyers had no hesitation in pronouncing it contrary to Dominican law. The reform, no doubt, did something to counteract the excesses that had become widespread in the order, but, in the long run, it was not able to suppress what seems to be a basic Dominican instinct for a rather casual approach to religious life and a generous but benign view of humanity which expects people to rise to heights of self-denial and heroism only when external circumstances require it of them.

Dominican observance must, it seems, tend to be either intermittent because of the order's work or impressive at the expense of the order's work.

The Spiritual Life

Thomas Aquinas

Although with regard to their ascetic and spiritual doctrine the Dominicans were, on the whole, unoriginal, they did make a few distinctive and important contributions to the understanding of spiritual life. Thomas Aquinas is, of course, an abiding witness that the intellectual life, undertaken with full seriousness, can itself be a genuine form of piety, provided it is motivated by charity, and especially if it is also motivated by a desire to communicate the truth to other people. In subsequent centuries, when intellectuals fell into increasing disfavor in devout circles, the Dominicans at least did something to redress the balance.

On particular points of doctrine, we should notice Thomas's insistence that Christian perfection means the perfection of charity and that this is possible, strictly speaking, only in heaven. Here on earth there is a minimum that is required for salvation; beyond this there is a kind of image of perfection enshrined in the evangelical counsels. But the religious state can be called a "state of perfection" only in the sense that it is a state (because it is established by public vow) in which a person is committed to three renunciations which are, in themselves, *means* to the perfection of charity. Thomas thus rules out, for instance, the doctrine of Thomas of York, O.F.M., that perfection *consists* in material poverty. On this basis he can challenge the almost universally accepted principle that a life of greater austerity must necessarily be more perfect; rather, means have to be taken in an appropriate quantity like medicine, not always in the largest possible quantity. Thomas also rules out the possibility of there being different kinds of perfection in the church, such that religious (or mystics) could be regarded as having or as aiming at a perfection different from the objective of perfect charity common to all Christians.

Thomas's doctrine of prayer is also worth noting. He offers a magisterial exposition of the significance of prayer in its traditional (and popular) sense of petition. By formulating our purposes precisely as petition, we are sacrificing our planning intellect to God—no mean sacrifice, as he points out. We are acknowledging that all good comes from God and that all plans must be subject to him. We are learning to have recourse to him at all times, and we are, under the prompting of the Holy Spirit, becoming fellow workers with him in the execution of his purposes. This sane and cogent doctrine shows why we do not need to lose our nerve about the most straightforward petitionary prayer and why we do not need to take refuge in seemingly more "spiritual" notions of prayer. Thomas also explains very sensibly why it is often useful to pray out loud. In accordance with the old monastic tradition, he says that, though we can go on praying for an extended period of time if we want to (other things being equal), we should not force ourselves to go on once we start getting bored. Frequent, brief prayer is what we need to cultivate (*Summa Theologiae* II–II q. 83; cf. I q. 23 a.8).

Thomas shows little interest in preternatural phenomena, except prophecy (which was on the agenda for all theologians at this time). But it is worth noting his insistence that genuinely supernatural operations never contradict the working of our natural powers, except in the extreme case of rapture (and he reckons that there are only two known instances of rapture: Moses and St. Paul). Any preternatural phenomenon that does contradict the workings of our natural powers is to be ascribed to the devil, not to the Holy Spirit (*Super Ev. Matt.* 849; Marietti ed.). The true criterion of supernaturalness is charity, not the presence of something phenomenologically peculiar. This same principle is found later in Henry Suso (ca. 1295–1366), for all his interest in preternatural experiences (*Horologium Sapientiae* 2.5; ed. P. Kunzle, p. 581), and is a major factor in the Dominican reluctance to accept the mystical doctrines that became common in the sixteenth and seventeenth centuries.

Meister Eckhart

Meister Eckhart (ca. 1260–1328) is undoubtedly one of the great names of Dominican spirituality, but the interpretation of his doctrine is much debated, at least in part because of genuine obscurities in his thought. Too much of his time was spent with admiring but uncritical and uncomprehending audiences for him to be forced to declare more exactly what he meant.

It is characteristic of his thought that he largely deduced his spirituality from metaphysical considerations; he was not very interested in pious practices or devotional experiences. A crucial virtue for him is *Abgeschiedenheit,* usually translated "detachment," but better rendered "separateness." It is primarily a philosophical term meaning "abstraction"; just as the philosopher abstracts from particulars, so in our lives we must wean ourselves from "this and that." God is equally present in everything and God's will is done in all that is done; if we seek God in some particular way, we shall find the way and let go of God. Even "God" must not be understood as a particular. He can be identified as "God" only by reference to creatures which are not God. "God," *as a relative term,* is insufficient for our bliss. Nor must we want to be anything in particular, any more than we should want to possess or know anything in particular. We should aim to be as we were before we were created, when we, as it were, preexisted in God with no distinctions of any kind. God is "No-thing," and we must become no-thing to be one with him.

Rather than try to ascend to God, then, we must acknowledge that he is indifferently in everything and learn from the whole experience of life what it means to be one with him. Thus, in one sermon, Eckhart upturns the usual allegorical interpretation of Mary and Martha to suggest that Martha is, in fact, the mature Christian because she has learned from life, with all its hurly-burly.

The essential thing is that we should live from the very ground of God who is our ground. We must give birth to the divine Son in union with the Father, and this means giving birth to him by acting from the ground, as spontaneously as God acts. Life has no reason for living; it simply lives. All true virtue is qualified by the same spontaneity and lack of purposiveness.

Eckhart certainly did not intend his doctrine to be antinomian. Living spontaneously, for him, meant living within whatever one's circumstances happen to be; if one is a religious, it would mean living within the terms of one's religious life. But it is not surprising that echoes of his doctrine should be found in antinomian circles and that some of his more ill-considered statements should have been condemned. His supposed disciples, Suso and John Tauler (d. 1361), offer a considerably reduced version of his teaching, with more moralism and devotionalism and with little of his speculative agility.

John of the Cross

In sixteenth-century Spain, it seems to have been largely the Dominicans who resisted the burgeoning new spirituality with its intense interest in interiority and fervor. In particular, the Dominican John of the Cross (who entered the order in 1524) rejects the appropriation of "spirit" words to describe conditions of inner fervor and unction and insists that any Christian who performs the tasks assigned to him with willingness and dedication is "spiritual." Charity is expressed in all the works of the Christian life, and some people may have no special gift for private prayer or for fervent devotion.[4]

The Dominican theologians retain the traditional intellectual sense of "contemplation" against the new sense of "spending a long time in a state of elevation, thinking nothing" (as recommended especially by Osuna).[5] They also retain the traditional sense of "prayer" as meaning petition, with no radical distinction between mental prayer and vocal prayer. They reject the idea that there are "grades" of prayer, recognizing only two such grades: there is the prayer of the person in a state of grace, and there is the prayer of the person not in a state of grace. This doctrine passed from Bartolomé Carranza (d. 1576) to the official Roman Catechism, which was largely the work of Dominicans.

Over against the increasingly prevalent interiorism, Dominicans stressed that what matters is what one does, not what one feels like while doing it. It is going to Mass that expresses devotion, whether or not one feels inspired by it. Saying prayers, with a serious intention of addressing God, is real prayer, even if one's mind wanders and even if one feels no devotion. In ways like this, the Dominicans tried to safeguard both the practicality and the integrity of the Christian life against the tendency toward a restrictive notion of what can count as spiritual.

Notes

1. Simon Tugwell, *Early Dominicans*, 150.
2. Ibid., 87.
3. Jordan of Pisa, *Prediche*, ed. D. M. Manni (Florence, 1739) 9; see also Tugwell, *Way of the Preacher*, 50–51.
4. John of the Cross, *Dialogo sobre la Necesidad de la Oracion Vocal*, ed. V. Beltran de Heredia, in *M. Cano, D. Soto, J. de la Cruz: Tratados Espirituales* (Madrid: B.A.C., 1962).
5. Francisco de Vitoria, *Commentarios a la Secunda secundae de Santo Tomas*, q. 182 a. 4, ed. V. Beltran de Heredia (Salamanca: Biblioteca de teólogos españoles, 1952) 312. Cf. Francisco de Osuna, *Third Spiritual Alphabet*, tr. 21, chap. 5.

Bibliography

The standard life of Dominic is Vicaire, and the major history of the order in English is Hinnebusch, of which only the first two volumes were published before the author's death. An introduction to early Dominican spirituality with a substantial selection of thirteenth-century texts is Tugwell (*Early Dominicans*). A selection of texts from Albert the Great and Thomas Aquinas is in preparation for Classics of Western Spirituality (New York: Paulist Press). For a good introduction to Meister Eckhart, with a selection of texts, see Colledge and McGinn, and a complete and reliable translation of the German works of Eckhart is being published in Walshe, of which two volumes have appeared. A translation of the Dominican John of the Cross is in preparation for Dominican Sources (Chicago: Dominican Publications). This series is publishing texts from all periods; thus far two volumes have appeared. For a brief introduction to the earliest phase of the Dominican reform, see the introduction to Raymund of Capua, *Life of Catherine of Siena*, trans. C. Kearns. On the Dominicans in sixteenth-century Spain, see Peers, esp. vol. 3, and Tugwell ("A Dominican Theology," 128–44).

Colledge, Edmund, and Bernard McGinn. *Meister Eckhart*. Classics of Western Spirituality. New York: Paulist Press, 1981.

Hinnebusch, William A. *The History of the Dominican Order*. 2 vols. Staten Island, NY: Alba House, 1965, 1973.

Jordan of Saxony. *On the Beginnings of the Order of Preachers*. Dominican Sources. Chicago: Dominican Publications, 1982.

Lacordaire, H. D. *Essay on the Reestablishment in France of the Order of Preachers*. Dominican Sources. Chicago: Dominican Publications, 1983.

Peers, Allison. *Studies of the Spanish Mystics*. London: Sheldon Press, 1960.

Raymund of Capua. *Life of Catherine of Siena*. Translated by Conleth Kearns. Dublin: Dominican Publications, 1980.

Tugwell, Simon. "A Dominican Theology of Prayer." *Dominican Ashram* 1 (1982) 128–44.
——. *Early Dominicans: Selected Writings.* Classics of Western Spirituality. New York: Paulist Press, 1982.
——. *The Way of the Preacher.* Springfield, IL: Templegate, 1979.
Vicaire, M. H. *St. Dominic and His Times.* Translated by Kathleen Pond. London: Darton, Longman & Todd, 1964.
Walshe, M. O'C. *Meister Eckhart.* 2 vols. London: Watkins, 1979, 1981.

II. *The Spirituality of the Franciscans*

J. A. WAYNE HELLMANN

THE WRITINGS OF ST. FRANCIS OF ASSISI are a primary source for Franciscan spirituality.[1] From his own writings emerges a Francis who was shaped by events, movements, and a spirituality of an age flowing out of the Gregorian reform. His response to his age and his perspective on various issues reveal not only his spiritual insight but also the development of his own personal spiritual experience.

Although Francis is foundational for Franciscan spirituality, he is not enough. The memory of Francis's spiritual experience was reflected on, interpreted, and applied in the development of the broadly based band of men and women who, across the centuries, have followed him in the First, Second, and Third Orders, namely, the friars, the Poor Clare nuns, and the laity. In manifold ways the spiritual experience and vision of Francis of Assisi have been expanded and enriched. Specifically chosen to illustrate the diversity and communality of the Franciscan spiritual experience are St. Clare of Assisi, Brother Thomas of Celano, Blessed Angela of Foligno, St. Bonaventure, the Spirituals, and subsequent First-Order reforms that began within the community, the Conventuals, and ended as separated and juridically distinct orders, the Observants and the Capuchins.

Francis of Assisi

Influences on Francis of Assisi

Francis of Assisi was born in 1181/1182 in central Italy. As a boy Francis learned his Latin and other elements of the basic education of his time at

his parish church of St. George in Assisi, where he also became aware of
other ecclesial developments. The landscape of monastic reform that began
in Cluny in 910 and was renewed at Citeaux in 1098 and, of course, the
teachings of St. Romuald (d. 1027) and St. Peter Damian (d. 1072) were all
formative of the attempts at renewal of the church. Thus, one can see traces
of the *Rule of St. Benedict* and axioms of early Christian monasticism within
the text of the rules Francis later wrote.

The Third Crusade was called in 1198, when Francis was a boy of fifteen
years. He was drawn into a love for the land upon which Jesus walked. The
humanity of Christ, already fostered by Romuald and preached by Bernard
of Clairvaux (d. 1153), easily became the pivotal point of his consciousness
in living the Christian life. The *fuga mundi,* or flight from the world, was
no longer focused on the flight into the stability of monastic life but into
the unsettling practice of both pilgrimages and crusades. Francis embraced
the instability of life on the road as "pilgrims and strangers" in chapter 6
of the *Later Rule:* "The brothers shall not acquire anything as their own,
neither a horse nor a place nor anything else. Instead, as pilgrims and
strangers in this world who serve the Lord in poverty and humility, let them
go begging for alms with full trust."

It is from within the hierarchical church that Francis embraced the lay
evangelical and penitential movements of his age.[2] In the spirit of these lay
movements, he encouraged his brothers in the *Earlier Rule:* "Let us, therefore, hold onto the words, the life, and the teaching of the Holy Gospel of
Him who humbled Himself" (chap. 22). In doing so, however, "all the
brothers must be Catholics and live and speak in a Catholic manner"
(*Earlier Rule,* chap. 19). The Catholic emphasis of Francis's gospel life is
particularly apparent in the last several chapters of his *Earlier Rule,* which
indicate the influence of the directives of the Fourth Lateran Council of
1215 upon Francis's manner of life.[3]

Francis was formed by and responded to the many conflicting spiritual,
political, and ecclesiastical currents prominent at the close of the twelfth
century and the beginning of the great thirteenth century. His own writings
show acute awareness of these movements as well as an appreciation of both
the scriptural and liturgical texts. He readily incorporated, synthesized, and
reconciled much of what was considered by many as impossibly fragmented.
The secret of his spirituality which achieved this synthesis is clearly written
in chapter 22 of the *Earlier Rule:* "Let us pay attention, all my brothers, to
what the Lord says: *Love your enemies* and *do good to those who hate you* for
our Lord Jesus Christ, whose footprints we must follow, called his betrayer
'friend' and gave himself willingly to those who crucified him." In generous

response to every situation, Francis is and remains the *forma minorum* for Franciscan life and spirituality.

The Spiritual Experience of St. Francis

From the earliest years of his conversion in 1205 and 1206 up to the last months of his life in 1226, Francis of Assisi left a legacy of twenty-eight writings, in addition to dictated letters or blessings found in various biographical sources. Among these writings are the *Earlier Rule*, the *Later Rule*, and the *Testament*. These, along with his *Canticle of Brother Sun*, are the best known, but they are impoverished without an awareness of his letters, admonitions, and prayers. All of them together provide a portrait revealing the experience, vision, and wisdom of Francis as he incarnates the gospel of Jesus Christ.

In the very first lines of his *Testament*, written shortly before his death, Francis reflects on his life's journey:

> The Lord granted me, Brother Francis, to begin to do penance in this way: While I was in sin, it seemed very bitter to me to see lepers. And the Lord himself led me among them and I had mercy upon them. And when I left them that which seemed bitter to me was changed into sweetness of soul and body; and afterward I lingered a little and left the world.

The foundation of his conversion was his experience of the Lord leading him among the lepers. It was an experience of mercy that moved his heart to a new and deep compassion. For the first time his heart was opened to his outcast brothers and sisters, and in his embrace of them he was embraced. He realized that it was the Lord who led him, and thus to be among the lepers was his response to God's holy and true command. In the ninth chapter of the *Earlier Rule*, Francis encouraged his own brothers toward the same experience: "And they must rejoice when they live among people who are considered to be of little worth and who are looked down upon, among the poor and the powerless, the sick and the lepers, and the beggars by the wayside." In the same chapter he gave the reason for this joy; it is because all the brothers should strive "to follow the humility and poverty of Our Lord Jesus Christ."

As he was led to the lepers, Francis was led to Christ. But the heroic action of overcoming his own disgust and prejudice was not something Francis claimed for himself. It was rather the work of God within him that prompted and moved him; he was inspired with the gift of the Spirit. Even more fundamental than his experience of mercy and the new sweetness with lepers was his sense and knowledge of the presence of the Lord leading him to them. He bent his own will to the will of his Father, the Father of his Lord Jesus Christ. In this he emptied himself of self-will and of the ways of the world in order to receive the inspiration and the gifts of the Lord through the liberating Spirit. It is understandable why he wrote in chapter 10 of the *Later Rule* that his brothers "must desire above all things: to have the Spirit of the Lord and his holy manner of working."

The Spirit, which Francis desired, identified him with the mortified and despised flesh of the humble Christ, and the Spirit gave Francis the power to be vulnerable and free from any desire for self-glory, dominion, or control over others. The Spirit mortified Francis's own flesh and made him at home with the despised. With the Spirit dwelling within, Francis's eyes were focused on "the Good Shepherd who suffered the passion of the cross to save his sheep" (*Admonition 4*). The poverty, patience, humility, wisdom, and divine love Francis experienced were a knowledge and an experience of the passion of the cross given to him by the Spirit of the Lord.

Brotherhood and the brothers themselves are gifts of the Spirit. "The Lord gave me brothers" (*Testament*). Their unity, communion, and love for each other are gifts and as such determine their relations to each other. According to chapter 5 of the *Earlier Rule*, "Nor should any brother do evil or say something evil to another; on the contrary, through the charity of the Spirit, they should voluntarily serve and obey one another." Experience of the brotherhood is living the life of Christ, who took the last place. "And the one should wash the feet of the others" (*Earlier Rule*, chap. 6). This is their loving obedience to each other.

This disposition of Francis before God and before his brothers illustrates his spiritual charism and plan of life. It is his *minoritas* before both creator and creature. Therein is the key to his great sense of interior and personal poverty intimately linked to an appreciation of honest humility. "Blessed is the servant who esteems himself no better when he is praised and exalted by people than when he is considered worthless, simple, and despicable; for what a man is before God, that he is and nothing more" (*Admonition 19*). Francis had the same disposition before all: saint, sinner, unbeliever, or persecutor. Those friars who went among the fierce Saracens and enemies of Christianity Francis directed "not to engage in arguments or disputes, but to be subject to every human creature for God's sake" (*Earlier Rule*, chap. 16).

Francis identified his whole life and the life of his brothers as "the life of the Gospel of Jesus Christ." In his *Testament*, he writes that the Spirit of the Lord which led him to the lepers also revealed to him that he should "live according to the form of the Holy Gospel." His respect and love for the Scriptures, in which he found "Spirit and life," were shown not only in his way of life but also in his reverence for the written words themselves.

"Likewise, wherever the written words of the Lord may be found in unbecoming places, they are to be collected and kept in a place that is becoming" (*A Letter to Clergy*). For Francis, the words of Scripture were the voice of the Son of God, and he understood that his life was to hold fast to the holy words.

The Christ of the Gospel, who humbly handed himself over to his executioners and who spoke the word of love to his enemies, was also present to Francis's eyes of faith in the Eucharist, in the sacrament of his body and blood. In the first *Admonition* Francis speaks of belief in this sacrament "according to the Spirit." The same faith required of those who walked with and touched the human flesh of Jesus while he was yet on earth is required now of those who approach the Eucharist. The mystery of the humility of God is the same, and only in the embrace of humility can one enter into the Eucharistic relationship. Humility allows the Spirit of the Lord dwelling within to receive "the most holy body and blood of the Lord." Only with the eyes of the Spirit can one see him; and only with the power of the Spirit can one receive him, who humbles himself under the appearances of bread and wine in order to be always present to us. According to the first *Admonition*, it is by the Spirit that one can hear his voice in the Gospel, and it is by that same Spirit that one can see him in the Eucharist:

> See, daily he humbles himself as when he came from the royal throne into the womb of the Virgin; daily he comes to us in a humble form; daily he comes down from the bosom of the Father upon the altar in the hands of the priest. And as he appeared to the holy apostles in true flesh, so now he reveals himself to us in the sacred bread. And as they saw only his flesh by means of bodily sight, yet believed him to be God as they contemplated him with the eyes of faith, so, as we see bread and wine with our bodily eyes, we too are to see and firmly believe them to be his most holy body and blood living and true.

It was the Lord Jesus Christ of the Gospel and of the Eucharist who bound Francis to the word and to church. He could not live apart from the ministers of the Roman church: "And let all of us firmly realize that no one can be saved except through the holy words and blood of our Lord Jesus Christ which the clergy pronounce, proclaim and minister. And they alone must administer them, and not others" (*Second Version of the Letter to the Faithful*). Thus Francis's writings often promote respect for liturgical objects and norms. A deep ecclesial sense is seen in his love for the Divine Office. In the *Earlier Rule*, the *Later Rule*, and the *Letter to the Entire Order*, he stressed the liturgical hours. Francis's own composition, *Office of the Passion*, reveals his roots in the Judeo-Christian tradition of prayer with the psalms. The inclusion and interspersion of texts from liturgical hymns demonstrate his own familiarity with scriptural and liturgical prayer.

The Spirit of the Lord which led Francis to the lepers, opened his heart to the word of God, and gave him faith in churches is the same Spirit which led him to Mount La Verna, where while secluded in prayer in September of 1224, two years before his death, he received the stigmata marking his body with the five wounds of Christ crucified. This is attested by all thirteenth-century sources, and it is described as occurring at the appearance of a six-winged seraph. Bonaventure, in his *Major Life of St. Francis,* writes that in the stigmata Francis was "totally transformed into the likeness of Christ crucified, not by the martyrdom of the flesh, but by the fire of his love consuming his soul" (13.12).

Shortly after this experience of God on Mount La Verna, Francis composed his great *Canticle of Brother Sun.*[4] This poetic hymn, although written when he was nearly blind and suffering acute abdominal pain, is praise of the Most High by a man fully at peace and in harmony with all the elements of creation and the whole cosmos. All the elements are brothers and sisters and they mirror the communion of the praise of the church with the Virgin Mary and all the angels and saints. In his final song, Francis is swept away in praise of the Most High and he is in harmony with the hidden nature of all the cosmic elements, which are, according to Francis, in the depths of their own innermost being a choir of voices praising God. His final submission and definitive act of loving obedience is echoed in this canticle. When he greets Sister Death, he sings: "Praised be you, my Lord, through our Sister Bodily Death, from whom no living man can escape. Woe to those who die in mortal sin. Blessed are those whom death will find in your most holy will, for the second death shall do them no harm." The final testimony of his life and spirituality is given in the simple invitation uttered as death visited him on the eve of 3 October 1226 in his beloved "little portion" or *portiuncula,* the church of St. Mary of the Angels: "Praise and bless my Lord and give Him thanks and serve Him with great humility."

St. Clare of Assisi

St. Clare of Assisi, Clara di Offreduccio, born in 1193/1194, was some twelve years younger than Francis of Assisi and she lived until August 1253, nearly twenty-seven years after the death of her spiritual teacher and guide. Clare knew Francis longer in life than most of his followers and treasured his memory in death for many years. It was on Palm Sunday, 19 March 1212, that Clare was clothed in the habit of poverty by Francis at St. Mary of the Angels and was taken shortly thereafter to the church of San Damiano, where she would spend the rest of her years. Clare would have heard of Francis much earlier, probably in 1206, when he first entered upon his own life of conversion and penance. In her *Rule*, approved in 1253 after many years of struggle, Clare claimed to be "the little plant of the most blessed Father Francis" (chap. 1). Her long years of fidelity to the memory and vision of Francis speak of a deep spiritual relationship with him.

Sources for Clare's spirituality are few but very rich. Her *Rule* and *Testament*, five letters, four of which are written to Blessed Agnes of Prague and one to Ermetrude of Bruges, and a blessing for the same Agnes are all that have come down to us. At the beginning of her religious life, Clare received a form of life from Francis. However, after the conciliar decree of the Fourth Lateran prohibited new rules, Clare received from Cardinal Hugolino, the future Gregory IX, a form of the *Rule of St. Benedict.* Later, in 1247, Innocent IV wrote a second rule, a modification of Hugolino's rule. Through long years, Clare resisted the traditional monastic rule not because of its prescriptions to the cloister but because she wished to write her own rule, which would incorporate a strict and absolute poverty—the "privilege of poverty," as she called it. Finally, on 9 August 1253, two days before her death, her lifetime wish was granted, when Innocent IV approved her own rule.

The chief legacy Clare received from Francis was poverty, experience of mutual love, and shared contemplation of "the Lord who was poor as he lay in the crib, poor as he lived in the world, who remained naked on the cross" (*Testament*). Her letters, written in the later years of her life, reflect the long years of distilled spiritual wisdom learned in the silence of San Damiano. Her love for poverty was not for preaching or penance but for the sake of contemplation, which enabled her to see, know, and touch Christ. Poverty is the key to spousal union with the poor Christ. In her *Second Letter to Agnes,* Clare wrote:

> But as a poor virgin, embrace the poor Christ. Look upon him who became contemptible for you, and follow him, making yourself contemptible in the world for him. Your spouse, though more beautiful than the children of men, despised, struck, scourged untold times throughout his whole body, and then died amid the sufferings of the Cross. O most noble Queen, gaze upon him, consider him, contemplate him, as you desire to imitate him.

The themes of poverty and contemplation fused into a light that illumined the charism of Francis. Clare mirrored to Francis the depth of his own heart. Without Clare the depth and vision of Francis's own life and charism would have remained blurred. "In Clare," wrote Alexander IV in the bull of her canonization, "a clear mirror is given."

Thomas of Celano

Less than two years after his death, Francis was proclaimed a saint by his friend Cardinal Hugolino, the newly elected Gregory IX, in a celebration in Assisi. It was on this occasion in July 1228 that Pope Gregory IX not only laid the cornerstone of what was to become the magnificent basilica of San Francesco; he also commissioned an official life of the saint. This *First Life* by Brother Thomas of Celano became the foundation for the subsequent literary tradition that developed concerning the saint. This work is called the *First Life* because during the General Chapter of 1246 Thomas was commissioned to write a *Second Life*. His trilogy on Francis was completed in 1253 with his *Treatise on Miracles*, which gathered all the known miracles attributed to the popular saint.

Brother Thomas of Celano presents the spirituality of Francis as a renewal in the spirit of the Gospel, which in turn renews the church. Humility and charity are the two principal virtues that flow from the Gospel words of Our Lord Jesus Christ. In Gospel meditation, "the humility of the incarnation and the charity of the passion occupied his memory particularly, to the extent that he wanted to think of hardly anything else" (*First Life*=I *Cel.* 84). It is not surprising that part 1 of Celano's *First Life* finishes with the story where Francis recalled the memory of the child born in Bethelem. In Greccio, the Child Jesus, who had been forgotten, "was brought to life again through his servant Francis" (I *Cel.* 86).

The second part of the *First Life* unfolds the charity of the passion. In this section, treating the last years of Francis's life, all the Gospel words Francis hears speak of the suffering and passion of Jesus. Upon hearing the passion of Jesus, Francis is overwhelmed by charity, represented by the seraph, which appears at the moment of the stigmata. "This is a great mystery and shows forth the majesty of the prerogative of love" (I *Cel.* 90). In hearing, preaching, living, and teaching the Gospel message of the humility and poverty of the Word made flesh, Brother Thomas shows a Francis who discovers the great love of Christ crucified. He is transformed into a "crucified servant of the crucified Lord" (I *Cel.* 95). Both the humility of Greccio and the charity of La Verna are signs that Francis was faithful to his vocation to fill "the whole earth with the Gospel of Christ" (I *Cel.* 97).

Blessed Angela of Foligno

Blessed Angela of Foligno (1248–1309) illustrates the development of Franciscan spirituality as it influenced the penitential movement of the late thirteenth century. In 1291 as a penitent widow, Angela was received into

4. Sassetta (Stefano di Giovanni), *St. Francis before the Crucifix*, ca. 1437–1444.

the Third Order. This Franciscan style of Christian life was developing successfully among women, who include not only Angela but also St. Elisabeth of Hungary (d. 1231), St. Rose of Viterbo (d. 1252), St. Margaret of Cortona (d. 1297), St. Clare of Montefalco (d. 1308), and St. Dauphine of Puimichel (d. 1360). Elisabeth followed in the tradition of Gospel service to the poor, but among the others there was a shift toward the mystical with a focus on the inner life.

Among these Third-Order women, the search for mystical union followed the path of intense meditations on the passion of Christ, which was the favorite theme of Francis's meditation. Through mystical experience, these women, who were not allowed to preach the word, became spiritual masters for their confessors and directors and thereby became teachers of the spiritual life even in their own age. Angela followed the practice of other women mystics of her age, in which spiritual direction and confession were regular. It is because of her Franciscan confessor, Brother Arnaldo, that Angela's journey of intense spiritual experience has been preserved. In numerous encounters between 1290 and 1296, she poured out her soul to him and dictated to him the stages and struggles of her conversion, despair, and ecstasy. In the *Memorial* of Arnaldo, her spiritual itinerary, which is divided into thirty steps, unfolds.

The *Memorial* begins Angela's conversion with her prayer to St. Francis to find her a confessor. Upon finding Arnaldo, she made "a full confession to him." From confession and the embrace of a life of penance, she began to look at the cross and to perceive how Christ had died for her. She began to see her sins against the crucified and his love for her. This prompted her one day to strip herself of all her clothing before the cross and promise him "perpetual chastity in all her members and accusing each part, one after the other, of past sins."

With the cross as the inspiration of her prayer and visions she discovered new abilities to see, taste, feel, and smell. She received the ability to return the love to Christ crucified which he had given to her. Therein she experienced the cross from within as she entered into the experience of Christ, who made himself "poor of friends, poor of relatives, poor of himself to the point of helplessness."

In the sixth and seventh supplementary steps of the *Memorial,* Angela moved from the absolute poverty and helplessness of Christ on the cross into a "most horrible darkness" and suffering:

> I am incapable of finding any other comparison than that of a man hanged by the neck who, with his hands tied behind him and his eyes blindfolded, remains dangling from the gallows and yet lives, with no help, no support, no remedy. (no. 97)

Her anguished cry for death as she beseeched "him to send me to hell without delay" was her descent into the abyss of darkness, where she struggled with the last enemy of all—pride. Yet from this she comes forth into rapture, the seventh and final supplementary step, in which she experienced "a state of joy so great that it is unspeakable. In it I knew everything I wanted to know, possessed all I wanted to possess. I saw the All Good. In this state the soul delights in the All Good."

In Angela's description of her own experiences, particularly in the sixth and seventh supplementary steps, she participated in the complete self-emptying of Christ crucified, whom she had embraced and followed. In a radical new experience of God, she touched the uncreated All-Good, dark to the human mind, which is limited by created categories. In her spiritual journey, there is something akin to that which Bonaventure articulates at the conclusion of *The Journey of the Soul into God:* "With Christ Crucified let us pass out of this world to the Father so that when the Father is shown to us we may say with Philip: It is enough for us" (7.6).

St. Bonaventure

St. Bonaventure, born in Bagnoregio around 1217, entered the order in Paris in 1243. In this great center of learning he wrote his commentaries on the Scriptures and on the *Sentences.* He became regent master of the Franciscan School in 1257, the same year he was elected minister general of his order, only thirty-one years after the death of Francis. It was a turbulent time in the order's history, and he served his brothers as minister general up to the last years of his life. In May 1273, he was elevated to the cardinalate and was consecrated bishop of Albano. During his work as bishop and cardinal at the Council of Lyons, death came to him on 15 July 1274.

As minister general he wrote works important for Franciscan spirituality. Among them are his *Disputed Questions on Gospel Perfection, Defense of the Mendicants,* and his last work, *The Collations on the Six Days.* In the *Disputed Questions,* Bonaventure defends poverty as the basis of Gospel perfection, which is closely associated with humility. The *Defense of the Mendicants* follows the same general theme, but in the *Collations* Bonaventure presents a Franciscan eschatology incorporating some of the elements of the thought of Joachim of Fiore. Here Francis is seen as the fulfillment of the eschatological age, and his Gospel perfection places him already in the seraphic order as the fulfillment of history, while his followers, distinct from Francis in perfection, remain in the cherubic order. The Franciscan Order is providentially geared to the last days, and it points the church toward the final era, into which Francis, fully transformed into the crucified Christ in the stigmata on Mount La Verna, has already entered.

Although Bonaventure made a distinction between Francis and the Franciscan Order, most of his works as minister general make explicit references to the relationship of Francis and the friars. Bonaventure himself had a deep sense of relationship to Francis, even though he had never met him. Bonaventure's greatest speculative and mystical work, *The Journey of the Soul into God*, was written in 1259 shortly after his election as minister general. In the eremitical silence of Mount La Verna, Bonaventure explicitly remembered Francis, as he masterfully articulated a plan of the Franciscan mystical journey. In the prologue of his great masterpiece, Bonaventure wrote:

> While I was there reflecting on various ways by which the soul ascends into God, there came to mind, among other things, the miracle which had occurred to blessed Francis in this very place: the vision of a winged Seraph in the form of the Crucified. While reflecting on this, I saw at once that this vision represented our father's rapture in contemplation and the road by which this rapture is reached.

Contemplation is both the goal and the journey. The transforming rapture of contemplation which Francis experienced on Mount La Verna and the journey toward that rapture are experienced through contemplation of the indwelling presence of the Triune God in creation, in the depths of self, and in the graced experience of virtue, the gifts of the Spirit. This is the summit and the fulfillment of Francis's vocation. All those who share in the vocation of Francis are called to the contemplative journey. Bonaventure believed that contemplation is for all men and women, and so he had a message for all: "Open your eyes, alert the ears of your spirit, open your lips and apply your heart so that in all creatures you may see, hear, praise, love and worship, glorify and honor your God lest the whole world rise against you."

The contemplative journey up the mountain begins with a love for Christ crucified:

> There is no other path but through the burning love of the Crucified, a love which so transformed Paul into Christ when he was carried up to the third heaven that he could say: "With Christ I am nailed to the cross. I live, now not I, but Christ lives in me."

The completion of the journey in contemplative rapture is intimacy with Christ crucified, this intimacy itself being the fulfillment of Francis's journey. It is not merely the Franciscan spiritual journey, but rather it is the fulfillment of the Christian journey and the human vocation, because it is according to the image of the Word made flesh that all are created: "With Christ crucified let us pass out of this world to the Father so that when the

Father is shown to us, we may say with Philip: It is enough for us." The following of Christ is fulfilled in contemplation; it is entrance into the passover of Christ to his Father.

Another of Bonaventure's writings that is significant for Franciscan spirituality is the *Legenda Maior*, or *The Major Life of St. Francis*. It was written at the request of the General Chapter of 1260, and within three years this theological interpretation and presentation of Francis's life was complete. In 1266 Bonaventure's theological biography became the official life, and it was distributed throughout the entire order. Every friary was to have a copy, and other biographies or legends were to be destroyed. Thus, this text became one of the most widely distributed pieces of later medieval literature. Its influence upon the spiritual formation of the friars and upon Franciscan literature, art, and popular devotion is enormous.

Bonaventure unfolds a spirituality as he thematically presents the life of Francis using both the structure and insights of the Dionysian spiritual tradition of purgation, illumination, and perfection. Within this structure, the central spiritual experience of Francis is compassion: Both his conversion and the completion of his journey in contemplation are experiences of compassion. Compassion is Francis's life and love. His spirituality is thus realized in relationship to the humanity of his brother the leper and the humanity of his brother Jesus on the cross. Compassion is that which admitted Francis into the seraphic order at the summit of Mount La Verna: "By the Seraphic ardour of his desires, he was being born aloft into God; and by his sweet compassion he was being transformed into him who chose to be crucified because of the excess of his love" (*Major Life* 13.3). In compassion, Francis reached the deepest level of likeness to God, and this he realized by sharing in the human poverty and humility of Christ.

For Bonaventure, the stigmata of Francis is central to understanding the mystery of the Lord revealed in the poor man of Assisi. Marked with the sign of the cross in his flesh, Francis becomes himself a revelation of the mystery of God's infinite love. Although in the *Major Life* the link between Francis's experience with the leper and his experience on Mount La Verna is compassion, Bonaventure, in his sermons on Francis, emphasized the foundation of compassion, namely, humility: "Christ's cross is the sign of the most perfect humility." As identified with the cross of Christ on La Verna, Francis reveals the humility of Christ. In the stigmata, Francis is the true "friar minor." This spirituality, however, is not simply for Franciscans. Bonaventure believed that the humble embrace of the humbled Christ on the cross is central to salvation for all. In his sermon on the feast of St. Francis in 1255, Bonaventure underlined the universal significance of Franciscan spirituality: "Although it is not for everyone to take the habit and

profess the Rule of the Friars Minor, it is necessary for everyone who wants
to be saved to be a friar minor in the sense of being meek and humble."

The Spirituals

A study of the development of Franciscan spirituality cannot overlook the
movement within the order that was notably visible between 1274, the year
of the death of Bonaventure, and 1322, the year John XXII issued his *Ad
conditorem canonum*, which rejected papal title to Franciscan property. This
bull was the radical rejection of the previous attempts of papal authority to
mediate the disputes within the order on the question of interpreting the
Rule in matters related to poverty. As early as 1229 Gregory IX issued *Quo
Elongati*, which declared Francis's *Testament* not binding in its injunction to
observe the *Rule* simply, *sine glossa*. Already at this time there were friars
unhappy with papal intervention. It appeared to some friars that the aspect
of poverty "to possess neither a house, nor a place nor anything else" was
undergoing substantial mitigation at the hands of both the order's leaders
and the papal curia. The minority dissatisfied with these developments were
basically located in the hermitages of central Italy and in Provence in
southern France.

In 1254 the initial breach began with the condemnation of Gerard of
Borgo San Donnino's *Introduction to the Eternal Gospel*, which took
Joachim of Fiore's works as authoritative for the new age. Despite the condemnation, the thought of Joachim of Fiore was readily received by those
seeking stricter observance of the *Rule*. Where else could the triumph of
Christ on earth be seen than in the new event of the stigmata of Francis
and in the new order of poverty inaugurated by him? Combining the
thought of Bonaventure, for whom the miracle of the stigmata was central
to any understanding of Francis, and the thought of Joachim concerning the
dawning of a new age of perfection in the Spirit, a new eschatological
spirituality found a theological base in the radical newness of the stigmata
of Francis.

Those most commonly considered teachers and leaders of the rigorist
friars who became known as the Spirituals are Peter John Olivi of Provence
(d. 1298) and his student while he taught in Florence, Ubertino da Casale
of Tuscany (d. ca. 1329–1341). Jacopone da Todi (d. 1306) verged toward the
mystical in his *The Lauds* of poverty, and Angelo Clareno (1245–1337),
representing the tradition of the Marches of Ancona, knew the tribulations
of public and political controversy with both Boniface VIII and John XXII
after he had earlier enjoyed the protection of the short-reigned Celestine V,
who resigned the papacy. Although the Spirituals lasted no longer than their

leaders, the influence of their teaching contributed to the patrimony of the Franciscan Order and became particularly significant in the Observant movement of the subsequent century and influential in later Franciscan sources such as the *Mirror of Perfection* and the *Fioretti*.

It is the work of Peter John Olivi, particularly his *Postilla in Apocalypsim*, that inspired the vision and writing of Ubertino da Casale. In 1287 when the minister general, Matthew of Acquasparta, appointed Olivi lector at Santa Croce in Florence, Ubertino readily absorbed the Joachimist leanings and indomitable Franciscan ideal of poverty from his teacher. In 1299, the year after the death of Peter John Olivi, when his books were condemned by a chapter of the order, Ubertino took up the Spiritual cause. This eventually sent him into exile, when he was ordered by his superiors to retire to the hermitage on Mount La Verna. There in 1305 he finished his classical work, *Arbor Vitae Crucifixae Jesu*.

In this work, *The Tree of the Crucified Life of Jesus*, the schema of Bonaventure's *Tree of Life* and extensive sections of Olivi's *Postilla* are visible as he presents a quasi-autobiographical account of the life of Jesus extending back to his uncreated Being with the Father. In this text, the crucified Christ is central as both point of departure and point of arrival. Meditation leads into the interior suffering of Christ as one would enter through the wound in his side into the very heart of Christ. In the prologue, Ubertino remarks that the journey is "to contemplate the immense sorrow of his most sacred heart." The concluding book celebrates the triumph of Christ crucified: "The fifth and last book is about the numerous offspring from the Gentile Church joined to Jesus by a new martyrdom, extending up until the everlasting wedding banquet of a human nature universally beatified."

The one joined to Jesus by a new martyrdom is Francis, and thus Francis's seraphic love for Christ restores human nature and inaugurates the third age. Francis signed by the stigmata is the angel of the sixth seal (Apoc 3:7–13). This new world of the Spirit's seraphic love is characterized by sublime poverty, manifestations of humility, ecstasies of contemplation, and the intimate communion of all the saints. The Spirituals sought to advance the final perfection of the church by clinging to the transforming power of evangelical poverty as realized by Francis in his "seraphic" rule. Theirs was an eschatological spirituality based on the Spirit's movement in a radical revolution of poverty. The seraphic rule was looked upon as God's gift for the renewal of the world. The Spirituals, in turn, in their perfect observance of the rule, were the prototypes of what all true Christians would be. Thus, they were not separatists within the order or church but rather the "saving remnant."

From the identification of absolute poverty as the summit of evangelical perfection there emerged the question of the poverty of Christ, which also must be absolute. This position was condemned by John XXII as heretical. In the ensuing conflict with John XXII, Angelo Clareno entered directly into the debate with his small band of followers, who had once enjoyed the protection of Celestine V as his Poor Hermits. Although condemned by John XXII, they clung to their privilege from Celestine and became known as the Fraticelli. During the peak of this conflict and the turning point in the demise of the Spirituals, Angelo finished in 1325 his famous *History of Seven Tribulations,* which describes the trials of the *Rule*'s faithful observers at the hands of the order, beginning with the generalate of Brother Elias. Angelo composed this work while banished and separated from the order as a monk in the Sacro Speco of Subiaco, where the short-lived struggle of the Spirituals died with him.

Conventual and Observant Spirituality

At the dawn of the fifteenth century, the reform movement in the order that came to be known as the Observance demonstrated regard for a stricter interpretation of the rule while accenting the ministry of popular itinerant preaching. In the following century this led to a separation in the order between those following the observance and those following the tradition of the conventuals.

The term "conventual" comes from those larger urban convents of at least thirteen friars attached to churches for pastoral ministry or to centers of study. Brother Thomas Eccleston's chronicle, *The Coming of the Friars Minor to England,* gives witness to a spirituality developing already among the friars of the 1230s and 1240s which accented the development of larger friaries, chapters, study, liturgy, and sacramental life more than strict interpretations of poverty.

The Observants desired the simpler life and cultivated the tradition that arose in the rural or more eremitical friaries. Their fortune was enhanced with the arrival of four friars who became exceptional spiritual leaders: St. Bernardine of Siena in 1402, John of Capistrano in 1415, Albert Sarteano in 1415, and James of the Marches in 1416. Central to their thought and preaching was Francis, the *alter Christus,* another Christ. The *Arbor Vitae Crucifixae Jesu* of Ubertino da Casale as well as *The Book of Conformity of the Life of St. Francis to the Life of the Lord Jesus* written around 1390 by Bartholomew of Pisa were two works that influenced the spirituality of these men, especially Bernardine of Siena (1380–1444).

Bernardine is best known for his devotion to and preaching of the holy name of Jesus. This devotion was not original with him; it was already popular in the writings of the English mystic Richard Rolle (d. 1349), but it is essentially consistent with the love Francis bore toward the humanity of Christ as witnessed in the preaching of Bonaventure in his sermon *The Five Feasts of the Child Jesus:* "Oh, how fruitful and blessed is the name endowed with so great a power and efficacy!"

In sermon 49, entitled *The Glorious Name of Our Lord Jesus Christ,* Bernardine shows how the name of Jesus was foretold in the Old Testament, announced by the angel, revealed in the circumcision, and finally proclaimed after the resurrection. The name of Jesus spans the whole history of salvation, and therefore in his name there is a spirituality of human history and of personal history. In Jesus' name everything that pertains to salvation and to the glory of the final age is revealed. Thus, the heart of every prayer and the center of every religious experience are purely and simply rooted in the speaking and in the savoring of that wonderful word of salvation, "Jesus." "O glorious name, O gracious name, O lovely and worthy name. Through you sins are wiped away, adversaries are overcome, the sick are delivered, those suffering trials are strengthened and consoled."

Capuchin Spirituality

In 1525, shortly after Pope Leo X's bull *Ite et Vos,* which finally and juridically separated the Observants and the Conventuals, the Observant friar Fra Matteo Bascio (d. 1552) of the Marches of Ancona set out for Rome seeking permission to live a more fervent eremitical Franciscan life. In 1528 Clement VII issued the bull *Religionis zelus,* in which he gave the small band initiated by Matteo Bascio but organized and led by Ludovico da Fossombrone (d. 1560) autonomy and juridical status. Within ten years their numbers increased to seven hundred, spread throughout twelve provinces. The fortunes of these Friars Minor of Eremitical Life, later called Capuchins, were helped early on with able leaders such as Francesco da Jesi (d. 1549), Giovanni da Fano (d. 1539), and Bernardino d'Asti (d. 1554).

The spirituality of these early years was built on desire for primitive evangelical simplicity expressed in solitary contemplative prayer and a life of strict poverty. As popular preachers close to the common folk, they became promoters of mental prayer among the faithful. Giovanni da Fano's *L'Arte de la unione* published in Brescia in 1536 is among the first of a long line of popular mystical works. As the Capuchins moved into France, this same tradition appeared in the writing of Benet Canfield (d. 1610) in his famous mystical treatise, *La regle de la perfection,* published in Paris in 1609. His preference for the affective way as the way toward intimate union with

God is clearly stated in his development of devotion to the passion of Christ, the Eucharist, and to Mary as the secure way to Christ.

St. Lawrence of Brindisi (1559–1619), sometimes called the greatest of Capuchins, was a towering figure in the Catholic Restoration after the Council of Trent. He braved new inroads for the Capuchins north of the Alps, as he entered Hussite, Calvinist, and Lutheran strongholds to foster the Catholic faith. In 1601 he even trod the battlefield in central Hungary to encourage the outnumbered Christian troops against the Turks. Christian victory was attributed to his presence. Yet in the midst of this activity he fostered an interior mystical life which energized him in his efforts to preach against heretics and to strengthen embattled Catholics. His mysticism is decisively Marian.

In the first of the fifteen volumes of Lawrence's collected works, there is found one of the richest treasures of Marian discourses composed by a single person. It is his *Mariale,* which consists of eighty-four discourses. His praise of the Virgin Mary is directed toward her consent to and participation in the mystery of the Word made flesh. In this praise Lawrence stands in the tradition of Francis of Assisi, who praised "this Word of the Father—so worthy, so holy and glorious—in the womb of the holy and glorious Virgin Mary, from which he received the flesh of humanity and our frailty" (*Second Version of the Letter to the Faithful*). Bonaventure built on this when he wrote that Francis "embraced the mother of the Lord Jesus with an indescribable love because she had made the Lord of Majesty our brother" (*Major Life* 9.3). Lawrence synthesized the best of nearly four hundred years of Franciscan Marian theology and piety. Her motherhood is at the center of his Marian thought, and this is because of her free consent and her choice to be receptive to the power of the Word of God: "How momentous was the Virgin's fiat! For when it was uttered the Word was made flesh" (*Sermo* 7).

* * * * *

Franciscan spirituality focuses on the passion of Christ and touches the heart of human, cosmic, and divine reality. Franciscan spirituality is not simply a gazing upon the cross but an entering into the experience of the poverty of the cross to know there the compassionate wisdom of God from within God. Franciscan wisdom is to know God in the poverty of the cross as Jesus, in his identification with the suffering and rejected, knows his Father. It is this wisdom which Bonaventure, in his second sermon on the nativity of the Lord, described as a union in which "immensity is tempered by smallness; strength by weakness; clarity by obscurity; immortality by mortality; divinity by humanity; and riches by poverty." Smallness, humanity, and poverty are the rich legacy of Francis of Assisi. His spirituality proclaims a radical denial of power in a power-hungry world. Franciscan love for Christ crucified bequeathes a compassionate tenderness toward all and a witness to what is possible in a world torn by war and alienation.

Notes

1. The definitive Latin text is best represented by *Opuscula Sancti Patris Francisci Assisiensis*, ed. K. Esser, O.F.M. (Grottaferrata: Collegium S. Bonaventurae, 1978).

2. For studies concerning influence of the lay penitential movements on Francis, see *Dossier de l'ordre de la penitence au XIIIe siècle*, ed. G. G. Meersseman (Fribourg: Editions universitaires, 1961); and Alphonse Pompei, O.F.M. Conv., "Il movimento penitenziale nei sec XII-XIII," in *Atti del Convegno di Studi Francescani* (Assisi: Edizione Franciscane, 1973).

3. Francis of Assisi was never ordained a priest. For consideration of the question of his diaconate, see Mariano D'Alatri, O.F.M. Cap., *San Francesco d'Assisi diacono nella Chiesa* (Rome: Istituto Storico dei Cappuccini, 1977).

4. For a fine study, see Eloi Leclercq, *The Canticle of Creatures: Symbols of Union*, trans. Matthew J. O'Connell (Chicago: Franciscan Herald Press, 1978).

Bibliography

Sources

Angela of Foligno. *Il Libro della beata Angela da Foligno*. Edizione critica. Ludger Thier, O.F.M., Abele Calufett, O.F.M. Grottaferrata: Editiones Collegii S. Bonaventurae ad Clara Aquas. 1985.

Bonaventure. *The Soul's Journey into God, The Tree of Life, The Life of St. Francis*. Translated by Ewert Cousins. New York: Paulist Press, 1978.

———. *Sermons on St. Francis of Assisi [The Disciple and the Master]*. Translated by Eric Doyle, O.F.M. Chicago: Franciscan Herald Press, 1983.

———. *The Works of Bonaventure*. Translated by Jose de Vinck. 5 vols. Paterson, NJ: St. Anthony Guild Press, 1960–1970.

Francis of Assisi. *St. Francis of Assisi: Writings and Early Biographies, English Omnibus of the Sources for the Life of St. Francis*. Edited by Marion A. Habig, O.F.M. Chicago: Franciscan Herald Press, 1973.

Francis of Assisi and Clare of Assisi. *Francis and Clare: The Complete Works*. Translated by Regis Armstrong and Ignatius Brady. New York: Paulist Press, 1982. This volume contains excellent introductions and bibliographical references.

Jacopone da Todi. *The Lauds*. Translated by Serge and Elizabeth Hughes. New York: Paulist Press, 1982.

Thomas of Celano. *The First Life of St. Francis* in *St. Francis of Assisi: Writings and Early Biographies, English Omnibus of the Sources for the Life of St. Francis*, 225–354. Edited by Marion A. Habig, O.F.M. Chicago: Franciscan Herald Press, 1973.

Ubertino da Casale. *Arbor Vitae Curcifixae Jesu*. Edited by Charles T. Davis. Monumenta politica et philosophica rariora 4. Turin: Bottega d'Erasmo, 1961.

Studies

De Robeck, Nesta. *St. Clare of Assisi.* Milwaukee, WI: Bruce, 1951.

Englebert, Omer. *St. Francis of Assisi: A Biography.* Translated by Eve Marie Cooper. 2nd Eng. ed. revised and augmented by Ignatius Brady, O.F.M. Chicago: Franciscan Herald Press, 1965. Contains a St. Francis of Assisi Research Bibliography by Raphael Brown.

Esser, Cajetan. *Origins of the Franciscan Order.* Translated by Aedan Daly and Irina Lynch. Chicago: Franciscan Herald Press, 1970.

Flood, David, O.F.M., and Thadee Matura, O.F.M. *The Birth of a Movement: A Study of the First Rule of St. Francis.* Chicago: Franciscan Herald Press, 1975.

Fortini, Arnaldo. *Francis of Assisi.* Translated by Helen Moak. New York: Crossroad, 1981.

Hayes, Zachery. *The Hidden Center: Spirituality and Speculative Christology in St. Bonaventure.* New York: Paulist Press, 1981.

Iriarte, Lazaro de Aspurz, O.F.M. Cap. *The Franciscan Calling.* Translated by Carole Marie Kelly. Chicago: Franciscan Herald Press, 1974.

———. *Franciscan History: The Three Orders of St. Francis of Assisi.* Translated by Patrica Ross. With an appendix, "The Historical Context of the Franciscan Movement," by Lawrence C. Landini, O.F.M. Chicago: Franciscan Herald Press, 1983.

LaChance, Paul, O.F.M. *The Spiritual Journey of the Blessed Angela of Foligno according to the Memorial of Frater A.* Rome: Athenaeum Antonianum, 1984.

Reeves, Marjorie. *The Influence of Prophecy in the Later Middle Ages.* Oxford: Clarendon Press, 1969.

III. *The Spirituality of the Carmelites*

Keith J. Egan

THE ANONYMITY OF CARMELITE BEGINNINGS profoundly affected medieval Carmelite consciousness. Bereft of a Benedict, a Dominic, or a Francis, medieval Carmelites lacked a known charismatic founder and early heroic figures. Not one of the original Carmelites is known by name; in fact, not until the late fourteenth century was B., prior of the earliest known community of Carmelites, expanded to read Brocard. Moreover, Simon Stock, the alleged dynamic prior general of the Carmelites in the mid-thirteenth century and the supposed visionary recipient of the brown scapular, emerged out of the same late-fourteenth-century legends. Modern research is still looking for any certain contemporary references to Simon, once a key figure in Carmelite tradition.[1] Plagued by the absence of heroes, the Carmelites felt compelled during the late Middle Ages to fabricate as their founder the prophet Elijah, upon whose mountain they came into existence and who had long served as a model for monks. Moreover, medieval Carmelites emphasized a connection with the Virgin Mary in ways that strained even the medieval taste for the extraordinary. The modern recognition of the legendary quality of many of these traditions allows for a concentration on events and documents that are, in fact, more central to an understanding of the spiritual life of medieval Carmelites than were peripheral issues, even though the latter were associated with key symbolic figures in Carmelite spirituality.

Origins

One can trace the origins of the Carmelites to the years immediately preceding the approval by Albert, patriarch of Jerusalem, of their formula of life, *vitae formulam* (1206–1214). This brief formula describes a way of life for predominantly lay penitents who lived in separated small cells located around a chapel, an arrangement reminiscent of earlier Palestinian laura. The spirituality of these first Carmelites was that of the medieval Latin eremitic tradition, a tradition that would soon be giving way to the rising mendicant movement. Like other hermits of the Middle Ages, the Carmelites lived a life of prayer (chiefly the psalms), silence, solitude in a communal setting, and penance with a special emphasis on an intense relationship to Jesus (*in obsequio Jesu Christi* of their formula of life).[2] Each of the brothers was to remain in his cell or near it, meditating day and night on the law of the Lord, watching in prayer. When possible, perhaps dependent upon the availability of a priest, there was a daily gathering for the Eucharist. The Carmelite formula of life made no provision for public ministry by the brothers. These first Carmelites were hermits, pure and simple, without fame in their own time. The Dutch Carmelite scholar Victor Roefs, in fact, has claimed that "the glory of the Carmelite order is its striking anonymity."[3] The eremitism of the formula of life had a communitarian context, which prepared the Carmelite hermits to embrace a mendicant style of life once they had emigrated to Europe.[4]

Located only five kilometers south of the medieval port of Haifa at the wadi 'Ain es-Siāh in a ravine facing the blue waters of the Mediterranean Sea, these Carmelite hermits did not have long to enjoy their solitude. All of them would be driven from the Holy Land by 1291, although some of them had emigrated to Europe about 1238.[5] The earlier migrations headed for

Cyprus, Sicily, England, and southern France. The first years in Europe, not even a decade long, presented insurmountable difficulties for the continuation of their eremitic style of life. A General Chapter held at Aylesford, England, sent two representatives, Reginald and Peter de Folsham, to the Holy See to seek revisions in their formula of life. The work of revision was entrusted to two former Dominicans, Cardinal Hugh of St. Cher and William of Reading, bishop of Tortosa.[6] The selection of these two former Dominicans and other unknown factors determined that the Carmelites would develop constitutions very similar to those of the Dominicans. On 1 October 1247, Innocent IV approved the revised formula of life, which, with his approval, became a formal rule (*regula*).

The revisions of the formula had permanent effects upon the spirituality of the Carmelites. No longer were they held to accepting only eremitic sites. They could now undertake new foundations, wherever they were given to them, as long as they were suitable for their observance. The revision also called for a common refectory and shortened the period of absolute silence to early evening until the following morning. The Carmelites were now allowed to eat food cooked with meat, so that they would not be a burden to their hosts. Those who could do so were required to recite in common the canonical hours.[7] The changes in the text of the formula may not appear monumental, but their implementation led to a new identity for the hermits from Mount Carmel. These changes quickly resulted in a rapid expansion of the order to the cities of Europe where the Dominicans and the Franciscans were settled, a more cenobitical form of life, and a clericalization of the brethren. The changes in the formula of life, in fact, set the Carmelites firmly on the road to a mendicant identity. The revisions of 1247 also established the tension that has existed ever since for the Carmelite friars, the paradox of the call to a contemplative solitude and at the same time a call to ministerial service out of the context of communal living. The once simple hermits had now to prepare themselves to preach, to teach, to administer the sacraments—in fact, to be ready to respond to the religious needs of their neighbors, as the Dominicans and Franciscans were doing. The friars were riding the popular wave of evangelization initiated by the Fourth Lateran Council. Unable to resist this successful trend, the Carmelites chose to identify with the mendicant way of life. Yet the Carmelites did not fully attain all the privileges of the mendicants until 1326, when John XXII extended to them the full provisions of Boniface VIII's *Super cathedram*.[8] Nevertheless, the Carmelites began to act very much like friars immediately upon the change of the eremitic formula into a full-fledged rule, a revision that opened up a new way of life for the Carmelites, who had come to Europe as hermits only a few years before and who were now pursuing the ideals of the friars.[9]

The assimilation of the Carmelites into the mendicant ranks did not go unchallenged externally or internally. The antimendicant feelings of the seculars and the apprehensiveness of the Dominicans and the Franciscans about the dilution of their ascendancy in the church culminated in the constitution *Religionum diversitatem* of the Second Council of Lyons. This document put the future status of the Carmelites and the Austin Friars into doubt until a later time.[10] The official ambivalence of the church toward the mendicancy of the Carmelites was reversed only in 1298, when Boniface VIII changed the wording of *Religionum diversitatem* so that the Carmelites and the Austin Friars no longer had to fear that their existence as a mendicant order was in jeopardy.[11]

Internally, the most significant resistance to the transformation of the Carmelites from hermits to friars was voiced by Nicholas the Frenchman (Gallicus), prior general from 1266 until 1271, when he resigned his office, probably in protest against the new identity of his brothers. In his circular letter entitled *The Fiery Arrow* (*Ignea sagitta*), Nicholas castigated those who had chosen life in the cities in place of their former solitude.[12] He condemned them for taking on the ministry of the mendicants, namely, teaching, preaching, and counseling. This jeremiad is, in fact, a belated death knell for the strictly eremitic life of the Carmelite order. Within Nicholas's lifetime, his brothers had already taken definitive steps that would identify them for the rest of the Middle Ages and beyond with Chaucer's "ordres foure."[13] Even Teresa of Jesus, whose reform looked back for inspiration to the hermits of Mount Carmel, developed a cenobitic model for the nuns and friars.[14] Moreover, Teresa never envisioned a termination of the public ministry of the friars. Once the revision of 1247 had occurred, there was no turning back from what would be the perennial and pivotal tensions of Carmelite spirituality: usually between contemplative solitude and ministerial community and sometimes, as for Teresa's nuns, solitude and community. Yet even Teresa felt the pull of public ministry not possible to her and her sisters in the sixteenth century.[15]

The contemplative orientation of the Carmelites is not only apparent in their original formula of life; it is explicitly mentioned in the earliest extant constitutions, those of 1281 and 1294, which remind the younger members of the order that their predecessors had contemplated heavenly things in the solitude of Mount Carmel.[16] The contemplative orientation of Carmelite spirituality during the Middle Ages did not have, however, the strong mystical elements that would be so pervasive in the writings of Teresa of Jesus and John of the Cross. Interest in the specifically mystical was only occasional during this era. However, the *Institution of the First Monks*

(1379–1391) and the recollection of the solitude of the first Carmelites laid the groundwork for the sixteenth-century mysticism of Teresa and John and the subsequent Carmelite Reform of Touraine.[17]

The first of the two key documents in medieval Carmelite spirituality, the formula of life, later approved as the *Rule,* has already been discussed in part. Although the text of the *Rule* as approved by Innocent IV remained unchanged, mitigating clauses were added, the most important of which was the mitigation of Eugene IV in 1432, granted in response to the petition of the Carmelites themselves. Now the Carmelite friars were permitted to eat meat on three days during the week except in Advent and Lent. In addition, the obligation to be in or near one's cell was mitigated.[18] During the rest of the fifteenth century there were further dietary concessions. Although these concessions indicate a general lack of spirit at the same time that they appear insignificant to a modern mentality, the conscientiousness with which the Carmelites sought these mitigations indicates "the great respect in which the letter of the Rule was held."[19] On the other hand, the mitigation of Eugene IV would become a key target of the Teresian reform. Teresa referred to the friars who did not participate in her reform as the "Mitigated Friars."[20] One should also note that Teresa saw her reform as a restoration of what she thought to be the *regla primera* or the *regla primitiva.*[21] In fact, Teresa knew only the text of the *Rule* approved by Innocent IV.[22] What is important is to realize that Teresa and her medieval Carmelite forebears had an abiding reverence for the text of the *Rule,* a reverence shared by centuries of women and men in Western monasticism for the various rules by which they lived.

Second only to the *Rule* in importance for Carmelite spirituality during the late Middle Ages was the *Institution of the First Monks,* which Otger Steggink has called the "chief book of spiritual reading in the Carmelite order" until the seventeenth century.[23] Modern Carmelites have neglected this text, which is the first part of a four-part work from the late fourteenth century and which was almost certainly composed by Philip Ribot, Catalonian Carmelite provincial. Ribot passed off his work as a collection of earlier writings that he merely edited.[24] The purported author of the *Institution* is John XLIV, supposedly patriarch of Jerusalem, who allegedly wrote this text in Greek in 412.[25] The *Institution* tells of the founding of the Carmelite order by the prophet Elijah and of a fanciful history of the order in the pre- and early Christian era. Unfortunately, the legendary character of this document has, by and large, eliminated its use by modern readers. As a consequence, the spiritual doctrine of the *Institution* concerning the personal experience of God in the Carmelite tradition has been unavailable to most inquirers into Carmelite spirituality. There is yet no critical edition

5. "Initial T introducing the introit of the Mass for the Dedication of the Church,"
Carmelite Missal, Add. ms. 29704 f.68 fragment no. 89.

of the *Institution* or of the other three parts of the document, which, for convenience, can be referred to as the Ribot Collection.

The *Institution of the First Monks* portrays Carmelite spirituality as a withdrawal from the usual preoccupations of life and an entering into solitude, as a purification of the heart and finally as the reception of the gift of union with God in love. The culmination of Carmelite life is experiential union with God, according to the *Institution*. This Carmelite journey one lives in the prophetic spirit of Elijah. These themes of the *Institution* are both a manifestation of a spiritual doctrine about the personal experience of God held up as an ideal for medieval Carmelites and are a prelude to post-Reformation mystical doctrine of both the Teresian reform and the Touraine Reform, which so creatively built on the spiritual doctrine of the *Institution*.[26] Not enough, however, is known about how effective its doctrine was for Carmelites of the later Middle Ages.

After 1247, like the other mendicant orders, the Carmelites developed close ties with the laity, both women and men, who shared on various levels the spiritual life of the Carmelite friars. Although an argument has been made for the existence of Carmelite sisterhoods in Italy as early as the thirteenth century,[27] the weight of historical evidence supports a much later date for the inauguration of the Carmelite sisters as an officially recognized group within the church. It was not, in fact, until 1452 that with the bull *Cum nulla* the papacy gave approval for the reception of women into the Carmelite order.[28] In large measure, the growth of the Carmelite sisterhood in the late Middle Ages was due to the patronage and reforming activities of Blessed John Soreth, prior general of the order from 1451 until 1471.[29] Further research is needed into the spirituality of the laity who associated themselves with the Carmelite order throughout the Middle Ages and into the lives of the women who constituted the Carmelite sisterhoods after 1452. These Carmelite sisters were both the predecessors of Teresa of Jesus and other women Carmelites who did not become part of the Teresian reform. No plausible theory has been advanced for the lack of an official Carmelite sisterhood before 1452, since monasteries of Dominican and Franciscan sisters had existed since the thirteenth century. In the post-Reformation church, Carmelite women would become prominent in ways that they were not during the Middle Ages. Perhaps an integrated articulation of Carmelite spirituality that appealed widely to women occurred only with Teresa of Jesus. Whatever the reasons, women do not hold the place in medieval Carmelite spirituality that they would eventually occupy after the advent of Teresa of Jesus.

Reforms

Reform was in the air and much discussed among the religious orders of the Western church throughout the late Middle Ages. On the whole, however, long-term and widespread reform eluded these religious during that era despite numerous valiant attempts at renewing religious life, especially through Observant reform movements. Decline in the observance of the common life and abuses of personal and corporate poverty were foremost in the minds of the reformers. Carmelites were, like other mendicant orders, well aware of their failures in these matters, and they made various attempts at reform. Some of these efforts—for example in Italy and in France—were important. The desire for reform was manifest in various ways among the Carmelites. By 1413 a significant movement of reform had begun among the Carmelites in northern Italy. This reform became known as the Congregation of Mantua, and in 1442 it was approved by Pope Eugene IV. The Congregation of Mantua set aside the mitigations of the *Rule* allowed by the same pope in 1432, fostered a sense of solitude reminiscent of the original Carmelite ideal of solitude, and, like other reforms of the time, sought a restoration of the observance of common life and of poverty.[30] The best-known member of the Mantuan Congregation was Blessed Baptist Spagnoli (1447–1516), known as the Mantuan.[31] Unfortunately, for reasons that could have been avoided, the Mantuan Congregation became a separatist movement, and, as a result, it failed to have a significant impact upon the Carmelite order as a whole.[32]

The most effective Carmelite reformer before the sixteenth century was Blessed John Soreth from Normandy, who was prior general of the Carmelite order from 1451 until 1471.[33] Soreth sought faithful observance of the *Rule* and the constitutions of the order. He even composed an influential commentary on the *Rule* which reveals much of his own personal experience as a Carmelite.[34] What is most significant, Soreth fostered among the friars as well as among the Carmelite sisters whom he brought into the order a spirit of recollection that hearkened back to the primitive Carmelite spirit of solitude.[35] Soreth's immediate successors in office, however, were not much interested in reform. Consequently, Soreth's strenuous and sustained efforts at reform soon lost the momentum that they had had under his able and zealous leadership. The fifteenth-century Observant reforms among the Carmelites may have fallen short of the goals the reformers desired. One ought to remember, however, that besides John Soreth and Baptist of Mantua, these reforms produced an imposing list of Carmelite blesseds: Angelus Mazzinghi (d. 1438), Frances d'Amboise (d. 1485), Aloysius Rabatà (d. 1490), Joan Scopelli (d. 1491), Bartholomew Fanti (d. 1495), Arcangela Girlani (d. 1495).[36]

The lives of these better-known fervent Carmelites and the lives of those not publicly celebrated for their sanctity are the most valuable outcome of the persistent attempts at reform throughout the fifteenth century and affirm the validity of Carmelite life during an era not recognized for many religious successes.

Soreth's ideals of reform eventually found a worthy successor in Nicholas Audet, who, in his long term as prior general (1524–1562), vigorously worked for the reform of the Carmelite order.[37] Audet had the energy of Teresa of Jesus but not her creativity. He, like Teresa, sought a return to the primitive life of the order, but Audet lacked Teresa's gift of intuiting what would galvanize her followers into living in a revolutionary way the solitude of the original hermits of Mount Carmel.[38]

Carmelite Spirituality

Much research remains to be done before there is anything like a basic understanding of medieval Carmelite spirituality. The literary activity of the Carmelites did not get under way in earnest until the second quarter of the fourteenth century.[39] For the rest of the Middle Ages and well beyond, Carmelite literature was excessively self-conscious and apologetic about its own identity. Often bent on defending the legend that the prophet Elijah had founded the order, this literature also was preoccupied with propagating the vision of Simon Stock as well as fictitious stories about the prehistory and the early years of the order. Much energy that could more profitably have been spent on other endeavors also went into controversies over these claims of the order. There is a distinct danger, however, in writing off as frivolous and meaningless the apologetic literature of the medieval Carmelites. Dates of foundations, demographic data, and constitutional regulations all reveal something of what it meant to be a Carmelite in the Middle Ages. Nonetheless, the literature that flowed from the passion of the heart has a potential for a revelation of the meaning of Carmelite spirituality that has not yet been mined. The legendary stories about Elijah, Mary, and Simon Stock as well as others need to be analyzed rather than jettisoned. Elijah and Mary are invaluable archetypal symbols of the Carmelite spiritual journey.[40] Elijah called the Carmelites to an awareness of their origins on Mount Carmel and to their contemplative mission in the church. Mary connected them intimately with Jesus. This intimacy with Jesus was a hallmark of the lives of medieval hermits and a distinctive characteristic of the Carmelite *Rule*.[41]

Medieval Carmelite spirituality is rooted in its *Rule*, often referred to as the *Rule of Saint Albert*, after the patriarch of Jerusalem who approved this *Rule*. This rootedness goes beyond the usual relationship of a mendicant order to its rule. The Dominicans and the Austin Friars looked much more to constitutions than to the *Rule of St. Augustine*, which they shared. The Franciscans sought inspiration more in Francis than in his *Rule(s)*. Medieval Carmelites, on the other hand, found their spirituality in the *Rule* as they received it from Albert and as it was revised into a mendicant text in 1247. The Carmelite *Rule* remains the central and most basic text of Carmelite spirituality. Important to an interpretation of Carmelite spirituality is an understanding of the original formula of life and the evolution of this formula into a mendicant rule in 1247. Thus, modern research shows that fraternity was already a crucial element in the formula of life before the new mendicant identity further emphasized community.[42] It ought to be noticed, therefore, that in the very origins of the Carmelite order there appears the basic paradox of Carmelite spirituality: solitude and community.

Next to the *Rule* the most basic document in medieval Carmelite spirituality is the *Institution of the First Monks* with its intimation of a subsequent mystical doctrine. However, the most obvious identity of the Carmelites during the Middle Ages was their thoroughgoing assimilation into the ranks of the mendicant orders. From the second half of the thirteenth century, no one during the Middle Ages could have taken the Carmelites for anything other than friars. This mendicant identity was not only canonical but reached into every level of Carmelite consciousness. Known also as the Whitefriars, the Carmelites were ubiquitous throughout Europe. They were, like the other mendicant orders, popular preachers, teachers, and spiritual guides. Their spirituality was simple and unpretentious. The very strong devotion to Mary, their special patroness after whom they were called the Brothers of the Blessed Virgin Mary of Mount Carmel, appealed to the medieval mentality.[43] Yet there was ever present in Carmelite life an inspiration for an intense life of solitude and prayer. Somewhere below the surface of Carmelite consciousness, there was always half-forgotten and half-remembered the heritage of the simple lay penitents who had sought solitude on Mount Carmel. This elusive memory, nonetheless, gave rise during the Middle Ages to various, albeit inconclusive, reforms. Eventually this remembering of the spirit of the original Carmelites inspired the magnificent Teresian reform and the later but much-neglected Reform of Touraine.

The contemplative orientation of Carmelite spirituality, first in the general monastic sense of a contemplative life-style and later in the evolution of contemplation as the personal and perceptual experience of God, emerged from the Middle Ages as the lasting and highly distinctive characteristic of this spirituality. After 1247, however, the contemplative character of Carmelite spirituality was in the manner of the friars, who saw contemplation as the basis of a ministerial mission in the church. This attitude was articulated by Thomas Aquinas: it is better to share the fruits of contemplation with others than simply to contemplate (*Summa Theologiae* II–II, 188.6). The paradox of a call to solitude and at the same time a call to ministerial community was, during the Middle Ages and thereafter, the critical source of the vitality of Carmelite spirituality.

Notes

1. *Santi del Carmelo,* ed. Ludovico Saggi (Rome: Institutum Carmelitanum, 1972) 320–23; Keith J. Egan, "An Essay toward a Historiography of the Origin of the Carmelite Province in England," *Carmelus* 19 (1972) 92–96.

2. For the Latin text and an English translation of the formula and the *Rule* of 1247, see *The Rule of Saint Albert,* ed. Bede Edwards (Aylesford and Kensington: The Friars and Carmelite Book Service, 1973) 77–93. For the Latin text of the *Rule,* see *Constitutiones Ordinis Fratrum B.V. Mariae de Monte Carmelo . . . praemissa Regula S. Alberti* (Rome: Curia Generalizia Ordinis Carmelitarum, 1971).

3. Victor Roefs, "The Earliest Evidence concerning the Carmelite Order," trans. Sean O'Leary, *The Sword* 19 (1956) 244.

4. *Carmelite Rule,* ed. Otger Steggink, Jo Tigcheler, Kees Waaijman (Almelo, Netherlands: Privately printed, 1979) 4–5. See also Otger Steggink, "Fraternità e possesso in commune: L'ispirazione presso i mendicanti," *Carmelus* 15 (1968) 5–35.

5. Egan, "An Essay," 67.

6. Ibid., 91.

7. Ibid., 91–92.

8. *Bullarium Carmelitanum* (Rome, 1715) 1:56–57.

9. There was a rush of English Carmelites to towns right after the revision: London (1247), Cambridge (1249 closer to town), York (1253), Oxford (1256), Bristol (1256), Norwich (1256). See Keith J. Egan, "Medieval Carmelite Houses, England and Wales," *Carmelus* 16 (1969) 188, 164, 224, 211, 158, 208, 143 (chronological list of dates of foundations in England).

10. John Dominic Mansi, *Sacrorum conciliorum nova et amplissima collectio,* 24:96–97. *Religionum diversitatem* was promulgated to the Carmelites 31 March 1275 (*Bullarium Carmelitanum,* 1:34–35).

11. *Bullarium Carmelitanum,* 1:48–49. On the definitive character of the approval of 1298, see S. Kuttner, "Conciliar Law in the Making: The Lyonese (1274) Constitutions of Gregory X," *Miscellanea Pio Paschini* (Rome: Facultas Theologica Pontificii Athenaei Lateranensis, 1949) 2:74 and n. 116.

12. For the text, see "Nicolai Prioris Generalis Ordinis Carmelitarum *Ignea sagitta*," ed. Adrian Staring, *Carmelus* 9 (1962) 237–307.

13. *The Works of Geoffrey Chaucer*, ed. F. N. Robertson (2nd ed.; Boston: Houghton Mifflin, 1961) General Prologue, line 210.

14. Teresa of Jesus, *The Way of Perfection* in *The Collected Works of St. Teresa of Avila*, trans. Kieran Kavanaugh and Otilio Rodriguez (Washington, DC: Institute of Carmelite Studies, 1980) 2:11, 4.

15. *The Way of Perfection*, 1:2; see also in the same volume *The Interior Castle*, 7, 4, 14.

16. "... sancti patres tam veteris quam novi testamenti ejusdem solitudinem pro contemplatione celestium tamquam veri amatores. . . ." ("Constitutiones capituli Londinenis anni 1281," ed. Ludovico Saggi, *Analecta Ordinis Carmelitarum* 15 [1950] 208; "Constitutiones capituli Burdigalensis anni 1294," ed. Ludovico Saggi, *Analecta Ordinis Carmelitarum* 18 [1953] 131).

17. For a list of editions of the *Institution*, see Otger Stegginck, *La reforma del Carmelo español: La visita canónica del general Rubeo y su encuentro con Santa Teresa (1566-1567)* (Rome: Institutum Carmelitanum, 1965) 357-58. On the reform, see Joachim F. Smet, *The Carmelites*, vol. 3, part 1, 36-62.

18. For the text, see Ludovico Saggi, "La mitigazione del 1432 della Regola Carmelitana, tempo e persone," *Carmelus* 5 (1958) 20-22.

19. *The Rule of Saint Albert*, 30.

20. Teresa of Jesus, *Book of Foundations*, in *The Complete Works of St. Teresa of Jesus*, trans. E. Allison Peers (London: Sheed & Ward, 1946) 3:150.

21. For references to Teresa's use of these designations, see Stegginck, *La reforma*, indexes.

22. Smet, *The Carmelites*, 2:33.

23. Stegginck, *La reforma*, 357; see n. 17 above.

24. Egan, "An Essay," 79-80.

25. Stegginck, *La reforma*, 357-59; Smet, *The Carmelites*, 1:63.

26. Bruno [of Jesus], *St. John of the Cross* (New York: Sheed & Ward, 1932) 25-70; Stegginck, *La reforma*, indexes: *Liber de institutione*, Ribot; Ludovico Saggi, "Santa Teresa 'Carmelitana,'" *Carmelus* 18 (1971) 42-63; Saggi, "Agiografia Carmelitana"; *Santi del Carmelo*, indexes, Riboti.

27. Claudio Catena, *Le Carmelitane: Storia e spiritualità* (Rome: Institutum Carmelitanum, 1969) 410-16.

28. Smet, *The Carmelites*, 1:104-5; *Santi del Carmelo*, 325.

29. *Santi del Carmelo*, 324-25.

30. Ludovico Saggi, *La Congregatione Mantovana dei Carmelitani* (Rome: Institutum Carmelitanum, 1954); Smet, *The Carmelites*, 1:87-90.

31. *Santi del Carmelo*, 326-28.

32. Smet, *The Carmelites*, 1:89-90.

33. *Santi del Carmelo*, 324-25.

34. John Soreth, *Expositio paraenetica in regulam Carmelitarum* (Paris, 1625); *Santi del Carmelo*, 324-25.

35. Smet, *The Carmelites*, 1:92-109.

36. *Santi del Carmelo*, 295-96, 211-12, 312, 319, 210, 249.

37. Adrianus Staring, *Der Karmelitengeneral Nikolaus Audet und die Katholische Reform des XVI. Jahrhunderts* (Rome: Institutum Carmelitanum, 1959).

38. Keith J. Egan, "Teresa of Jesus: Daughter of the Church, Woman of the Reformation," *Carmelite Studies* 3 (1984) 84-87.

39. Rudolf Hendriks, "La succession héréditaire (1280-1451)," in *Elie le Prophète* 2: 41-81, *Études Carmelitaines* 35 (1956).

40. Bruno de Jésus-Marie, Charles Baudouin, Carl-Gustav Jung, René Laforgue, "Puissance de l'Archétype," *Elie le Prophète* 2:11–33.

41. Rudolf Hendriks, "De primogenia ordinis Carmelitarum inspiratione in regula expressa," *Carmelus* 15 (1968) 46–53; English translation in *The Rule of Saint Albert*, 67–72.

42. *Carmelite Rule*, 4–5. See also Steggink, "Fraternità," 12–20.

43. Ludovico Saggi, "Santa Maria del Monte Carmelo," in *Santi del Carmelo*, 109–35.

Bibliography

Periodical resources include *Carmelus: Journal of the Institutum Carmelitanum* (Rome, 1954–), which includes an annual bibliography in the second number of each year; and *Ephemerides Carmeliticae* (Florence, 1947–), which became *Teresianum* in 1982.

Brandsma, Titus. *Carmelite Mysticism: Historical Sketches.* Chicago: Carmelite Press, 1936.

——. "Carmes (Spiritualité de L'Ordre des)," In *Dict. Sp.* 2, cols. 156–71.

Cicconetti, Carlo. *La Regola del Carmelo: Origine, natura, significato.* Rome: Institutum Carmelitanum, 1973.

Friedman, Elias. *The Latin Hermits of Mount Carmel: A Study in Carmelite Origins.* Rome: Teresianum, 1979.

Paul-Marie de la Croix. "Carmelite Spirituality." In *Some Schools of Catholic Spirituality*, 110–85. Edited by Jean Gautier. Translated by Kathryn Sullivan. New York: Desclée, 1959.

Secondin, Bruno. *La Regola del Carmelo: Per una nuova interpretazione.* Rome: Presenza del Carmelo, 1982.

Smet, Joachim. *The Carmelites.* 3 vols. Darien, IL: Carmelite Spiritual Center, 1975, 1976, 1982. See the German translation of vol. 1 by Ulrich Dobhan for extensive additional bibliography, *Die Karmeliten* (Freiburg: Herder, 1981).

Steggink, Otger, and Efrén de la Madre de Dios. "Carmelite Spirituality." In *New Catholic Encyclopedia*, 3:114–18. New York: McGraw-Hill, 1967.

IV. *The Spirituality of the Augustinians*

A D O L A R   Z U M K E L L E R

THE AUGUSTINIAN ORDER (*Ordo eremitarum sancti Augustini,* now the *Ordo fratrum sancti Augustini*) arose from a combination of a number of Italian communities of hermits of the twelfth and thirteenth centuries, whose union was based on the *Rule of St. Augustine* (*Regula sancti Augustini*). The development was accomplished in 1256 at a General Chapter in Rome by the so-called *Magna Unio* (great union) and was confirmed by the bull *Licet Ecclesiae* of Pope Alexander IV in the same year. Already at the time of this union, five provinces of the order had been founded in Italy and one each in Germany, England, France, and Spain. Its further expansion was quickly accomplished. In Germany at the end of the thirteenth century, there were almost eighty convents, which, along with the Franciscans and the Dominicans, took over the work of the care of souls in the burgeoning cities. An inescapable condition for this growth of the Augustinian Order was the good religious and theological formation of its members in its houses of study, the so-called *studia generalia*. Not a few Augustinians enrolled also at the universities of Paris, Oxford, and Cambridge or at one of the numerous new foundations of the fourteenth and fifteenth centuries. The study of theology was considered to be the foundation of the order (*fundamentum ordinis,* Constitutions of 1290, chapter 17).

Sources and Characteristics of the Spirituality

The spirituality of the Augustinians was stamped decisively from the very beginning by the spirit of Augustine and his *Rule*. Precisely because no dominant founding figure rocked the cradle of the order, Augustine, the father of the rule, was chosen as "the exemplar and rule of all our action." Indeed, an early legend traced the foundation of the order to Augustine himself.[1] The *Rule of St. Augustine,* deeply inspired by the Bible, is especially directed toward *caritas,* the love of God and of neighbor. The real goal of the monastic life as seen by Augustine is the actualization of a community of love founded in God according to the model of the first Christian community, which stressed love and common property, "one mind and one heart in God" (*Rule* 1.2; cf. Acts 4:32–35).[2] Such a community matures, according to Augustine, through common prayer, a common table, and a common life and, finally, through the nurturing of religious esteem for one another: "Honor God in each other, whose temples you have become" (*Rule* 1.8). By consideration and patience with one another, by prompt forgiveness after disputes, and by the daily selfless effort for the community, love should be proved in the daily routine of the monastery. Personal poverty and the common use of goods are understood as expressions of love. In the same way, the relation of superiors and their charges rests in love and mutual trust. The *Rule of St. Augustine* breathes in all this the spirit of mildness and discretion and shows a strong tendency toward spiritualization and interiorization of the monastic life. Augustine stresses emphatically that one should follow the rules in Christian freedom, "not as slaves under the law, but as free men firmly established in grace" (*Rule* 8.1). He also reminds us that the true fulfillment of the rule obliges us to give thanks to God because all goodness in human beings is ultimately only a gift of God (*Rule* 8.2). This basic thought of the *Rule of St. Augustine* had already been worked out by Jordan of Saxony around 1350 in his *Liber Vitasfratrum* (*The Life of the Brothers*) as the perduring spiritual basis for the monastic life of the Augustinians.

Other works of Augustine which decisively affected the monastic spirituality of the Augustinians are the following: the short work *On the Work of Monks* (*De opere monachorum*), with which Augustine gave a theological basis for a monastic and Christian work ethic in opposition to certain monks of his time who shunned work; *Sermons* 355 and 356, in which he defended the monastic life of his monastery of clerics (*monasterium clericorum*) as being poor and holding all goods in common; and *Letter* 48, in which he exhorts the monks of a contemplative monastery on the isle of Capraria not to prefer their leisure to the needs of the church and not to refuse the church their service when it has need of it. In fact, Augustine's close connection of apostolic activity and contemplative life (see *On the City of God* [*De civitate Dei*] 19.19) was characteristic of the order from the very beginning and contributed to the ideals of "evangelical poverty" and "apostolic brotherhood," propagated by the ecclesial reform movement of the High Middle Ages. In this regard, the Augustinians understand themselves as a community of "brothers" and also see in the office of superior only a service of love to the community: "Let your Superior not deem himself happy in using his authority, but in serving you with love" (*Rule* 7.3).

Next to the sacred scripture, the works of St. Augustine were for the Augustinians a major source of their spiritual teachings. Certainly it is a given that Augustinism has exercised a general influence on Christian spirituality. Yet, over and above that, certain common views are found among the spiritual teachers of the Augustinians, which justify speaking about an Augustinian spirituality of the order. Contributing to this spirituality is a theology that rather consistently taught the primacy of will over intellect. Further, just as Augustine had, Augustinians saw love as the special goal of theology and considered theology to be neither speculative nor practical but rather an affective knowledge. In addition, the following characteristics of the spiritual teaching of the order may be deduced, although they assuredly are not present in every author to the same degree of importance.[3]

1. According to the teaching of sacred scripture, Christian perfection consists basically in love (caritas). This point is greatly accentuated by the spiritual writers of the order in the same sense as Augustine. First, the love given by God and then directed back to God and neighbor grants to all other virtues life and growth. The goal, essence, and steps of the Christian life are clarified by the classical formulation of Augustine in On Nature and Grace (De natura et gratia 70.84): "The beginning of charity is the beginning of justice, the growth of charity is the growth of justice, great charity is great justice, perfect charity is perfect justice. . . . But it is not poured out in our hearts by the resources either of nature or of the will which lie in us: rather [it is poured out] 'by the Holy Spirit which has been given to us' (Romans 5:5)."[4]

2. Even when every trend of Christian spirituality teaches that the spiritual life is rooted on the one side in the grace of God and on the other side has human free cooperation as prerequisite, still there are characteristic differences in the way in which one or the other is brought about. Totally in the sense of Augustine, as is clear in the previous quotation, the Augustinians emphasize the activity of God. Thus Giles of Rome, the first great theologian of the order (d. 1316), writes in his Commentary on the Sentences (2.28.2.2; [Venice, 1581] p. 374)

> If, therefore, we wish to avoid acting badly, this is the sole available remedy, that we, having the grace of God, permit Him to move, drive, and lead us; . . . for as soon as we will to be moved merely by our own perceptions . . . we fail to do good acts. If, therefore, we want to persevere in the good, we are really more acted on than acting.

In addition, the Augustinian theologian Johannes Klenkok of Erfurt (d. 1374), drawing upon the post-Augustinian work Hypomnesticon (3.11.20),[5] speaks repeatedly about the fact that the human will is guided and set in motion by the grace of God to accomplish all good deeds, even as a riding horse is ruled and driven (regitur . . . agitur). Johannes Zachariae (d. 1428), one of the first Augustinian professors at the University of Erfurt, interprets the saying "compel people to come in" (*compelle intrare!* [Luke 14:23]) as follows: "This happens by a compulsion of what pleases, not by any violent compulsion; . . . God so inclines the mind that one freely chooses to seek the good and in the same way John says (6:44) 'No one comes to me unless my Father draw him,' that is: unless my Father has changed that person's will" (*Collecta super Lucam,* MS Soest 10, p. 373a).

3. The more basic reason why the necessity of the help of divine grace in the spiritual life was emphatically stressed by the Augustinians lies in their conviction that human beings are severely weakened in their powers to know and to will because of the fall. Already Giles of Rome speaks of a wounding of human nature, "but he [Adam] was wounded in his natural powers, but not so that he lost what was natural . . . , but . . . because those natural powers were useless for doing good, and were useful for sin" (*Commentary on the Sentences* 2.28.1.2).[6] What is to be understood by that in particular is explained by the Augustinian theologians through the concepts of "ignorance and difficulty" from Augustine's *On Free Choice* (*De libero arbitrio*) 3.18.52. Human understanding is so obscured that it takes falsehood for truth, and the power of the will is so weakened that doing good is very difficult. Giles writes, "On account of sensual repugnance and because we see a law in our members fighting against the law of the mind (cf. Romans 7:23), it is difficult to do good. For there is in us, however good we are and however much we are in a state of grace, a continual struggle with vices" (*Commentary on the Sentences* 2.28.1.2.1).[7] In a similar sense, Johannes Zachariae teaches, appealing to Augustine, that the constant rebellion of the flesh against the spirit is the reason why God is not yet loved *ex toto* by people on earth (*Expositio in Apocalypsim;* MS Trier 106/1086, folio 138vb–139ra).

4. Accordingly, the authors of the order often emphatically stress the lack of good works and warn against false self-righteousness which praises its works and trusts in its merits. The Italian theologian of the order, Albert of Padua (d. 1323 or 1328) writes in his *Liber predicationum super evangeliis dominicalibus:*

> No living persons, however great their merit may be, ought to trust in their own righteousness for four reasons: first . . . , because our righteousness is uncertain, for no one can know for certain whether one's works are really just. . . . Second . . . , because our works of justice are not unadulterated but always have some stain of sin attached. . . . Third, our own righteousness is not to be trusted because it is not firm, hence anyone can fall away from one's own righteousness. . . . Fourth . . . , because our works of justice are not yet

approved, but still have to be brought before the strict judgment of God. (Venice 1476, folio s 1v–2r)

These thoughts are taken over by a number of German Augustinian theologians and preachers.[8] In addition, the great Spanish preacher St. Thomas of Villanova (d. 1555) warned emphatically against self-praise and trust in one's own righteousness.

> Blessed are they to whom the Lord grants both to do good and not to presume about their works, but to glory in Christ Jesus. . . . In Him alone, therefore, our hope is to be fixed who gives life to our dead works by His grace and illumines them that they may be worthy of eternal life. . . . Our righteousness, therefore, is to be despised and the righteousness of God to be magnified. For however much is taken away from our own merit, so much is attributed to grace, and those who, distrusting themselves, lean on God, are secure in God, working diligently through charity and through humility forgetting those same good works, so that they may be remembered by God. (*Opera* 1; Manila 1881, 179)

5. Without denying the merit of good works before God, the Augustinians liked to refer to the teaching of Augustine, that "all our good merits (*merita*) are only gifts of God" (*Enchiridion* 107.28).[9] So wrote also the German Augustinian theologians Hermann von Schildesche (d. 1357), Johannes Zachariae, and Johannes von Dorsten (d. 1481).[10]

Important Spiritual Writers

The order fostered no small number of spiritual writers and through them exercised a significant influence on the religious and ecclesial life of the Middle Ages and the beginning of the modern era. Only the most important of these writers can be mentioned here.

Augustine of Ancona (d. 1328), as a final part to his widely circulated *Summa de ecclesiastica potestate,* added an essay on the spiritual life, and in his treatise *De amore Spiritus Sancti* discoursed also on the gifts of the Holy Spirit and the mystical gifts of grace. Michael of Massa (d. 1337) composed *Tractatus de passione Domini,* which was highly regarded in the Middle Ages. In addition to several other ascetical works, he produced a life of Christ in the form of meditations (MS Leipzig 800). It was recently proved to be "the most important and immediate source" of the influential work *Life of Christ* written by the Carthusian Ludolph of Saxony (d. 1378) and therefore influenced indirectly the whole of piety of the late Middle Ages and the beginning of the modern era up to the *Spiritual Exercises* of Ignatius of Loyola.[11] Of great influence on the piety of the late Middle Ages, especially in Germany, was Blessed Simon Fidati of Cascia (d. 1348), an exemplary leader in the spiritual life. His comprehensive and later repeatedly published main work *De gestis Domini Salvatoris* calls for conformity to Christ, who represents the perfect model for the moral and spiritual life of every man and woman. The raising up of people to God by means of Christian virtues is represented in nine ascetic-mystical steps. In addition to these important spiritual writers, the Italian Augustinians of the contemplative monastery of Lecceto near Siena deserve mention. Several members of this monastery belonged to the circle formed around Catherine of Siena (d. 1380): the English Augustinian theologian William Flete (d. 1388) spent the last thirty years of his life in Lecceto and was Catherine's spiritual director from 1367 to 1373 and wrote the essay *De remediis contra tentationes*. Felix Tancredi of Massa (d. 1386), who accompanied Catherine to Avignon in 1376, is the author of the poem *La fanciullezza di Gesù*. The long-time prior of the monastery, Philipp Agazzari (d. 1422), was known for his *Assempri*, a collection of pious legends of that time, also prized for their literary beauty. A series of popular ascetical works were left by Jerome of Siena (d. 1420), who appears to have been influenced by Simon of Cascia.

The German Augustinians already possessed several important spiritual writers in the first half of the fourteenth century who were strongly influenced by contemporary German mysticism. These members of the Saxon-Thuringian province of the order were Henry von Friemar the Elder (d. 1340), Hermann von Schildesche, and Jordan von Quedlinburg (d. 1370 or 1380). All three worked for a long time at the general *studium* of their order in Erfurt, that is, in the city where Eckhart was prior of the Dominican priory, around 1294–1300. Henry is numbered among the most distinguished spiritual writers of the late Middle Ages in Germany. Next to his very widespread *Tractatus de decem praeceptis,* his *Tractatus de occultatione vitiorum sub specie virtutum* enjoyed high esteem. In it he sought to show how vices are often disguised as virtues. His *Tractatus de quatuor instinctibus* is the first comprehensive treatment of the criteria for the discernment of the spirits; here he displays a typical Augustinian attitude when, with considerable reserve, he discusses both the so-called natural instincts and pagan philosophy. A valuable addition to the theology of mysticism are two other works by Henry, his treatises *De adventu Verbi in mentem* and *De adventu Domini.* According to Henry, the mystical union with God is accompanied and completed by a special kind of love of God which he terms a "consuming, wounding and binding love." But perhaps he opposes Eckhart when he asserts that this "mystical union" is not to be understood "according to the identity of a real existence" but rather "according to a certain likeness of conformity and transformation."[12] Hermann von Schildesche has left, among his other ascetical treatises, a comprehensive spiritual

6. Master of St. Augustine, *Augustine Made Bishop*, ca. 1490.

handbook for cloistered religious under the title *Claustrum animae*. In it, and also in his *Postilla super Cantica,* he uses the image of the "*claustrum spirituale*" and an allegorical interpretation of the Song of Songs to illustrate the life of grace and virtue of the Christian and also infused contemplation and the mystical experience of God. Jordan of Quedlinburg (or of Saxony), a strong religious personality, strongly influenced the piety of the late Middle Ages in Germany not only by his *Liber Vitasfratrum* but also by his *Meditationes de passione Christi,* which was early translated into German. Ascetical and mystical material is assimilated also in his widespread works on preaching. In several of these sermons he used Eckhart's commentary on John as a source. Repeatedly he set himself against the pantheistic mysticism of the Brethren of the Free Spirit.

Like the Augustinians in middle Germany, so also the monastery of Strasbourg was washed by the stream of German mysticism. Witness to that are the numerous mystical sermons of an anonymous Augustinian whose manuscripts were destroyed in 1870 in a fire at the Municipal Library of Strasbourg. In close association with the group of the so-called Friends of God gathered about the Strasbourg layman Rulman Merswin was Johannes von Schaftholzheim (d. after 1381), to whom we owe the Latin revision of Merswin's *Neunfelsenbuch.* Johannes von Rynstett (d. 1421) wrote with pleasing objectivity, clarity, and meaning a life of the Blessed Brother Heinrich, an otherwise unknown Friend of God from Strasbourg.[13]

That the north German Augustinians finally took part in the mystical movement is shown by a mystical sermon of Gyso of Cologne (d. after 1409), a professor at the university,[14] by the comprehensive ascetical-mystical work *De triplici adventu Verbi* by Matthäus von Zerbst (or of Saxony; d. after 1390), and by the *Invitatorium exulantis animae tendentis ad caelestem Jerusalem* by Johannes von Hoxter (d. after 1419).

Other respected spiritual writers among the German Augustinians originated from the monastic reform movement of the fifteenth century. These are Oswalt Reinlein of Nuremberg (d. after 1466) and Conrad von Zenn (d. after 1460);[15] the professors of Erfurt University Johannes von Dorsten (d. 1481) and Johannes von Paltz (d. 1511);[16] and the superiors of the German reform congregation of the Augustinians, Andreas Proles (d. 1503) and Johannes von Staupitz (d. 1524), who was the superior and spiritual director of a young Augustinian, Martin Luther.[17] The *Liber de monastica vita* by Zenn is counted among the most comprehensive books on monastic reform of the time. The most widespread works in print were the *Coelifodina* and the *Supplementum Coelifodinae* by Paltz, who wanted to promote principally the right form of Christian life among the people. Dorsten edited, among other things, a *Quaestio quodlibetalis de tertio statu mundi* (*On the Third State of the World*) in 1465, a theme that would be taken up by Paltz in 1486 at another *Quodlibet* at Erfurt. Both Augustinians ranged themselves against contemporary apocalyptic expectations. Indeed, the assumption that such expectations were lively in the Augustinian monastery of Erfurt at that time is ungrounded. Also untenable is the proposed thesis of M. Reeves, who argues that the spirituality of the order has shown a lasting tendency toward spiritualistic and apocalyptical or Joachimist ways of thought.[18]

John Waldeby (d. ca. 1372) was a distinguished spiritual writer of the Middle Ages in England who was influenced by English mysticism. Among the French authors of the order, Jacobus Legrand (d. 1414/15) achieved great significance through his widespread *Sophilogium*, an original attempt to express the truth and grace of Christ for Renaissance people in a contemporary language. He treats exhaustively of the virtues and vices, as well as the right way of life for the clergy.

Already at the beginning of the fourteenth century, the Spanish Augustinians produced a respected spiritual writer in Bernard Oliver (d. 1348), whose *Excitatorium mentis ad Deum* shows characteristic traits of Augustinian spirituality. Among the Spanish Augustinian authors of the sixteenth century, there was an actual school of spirituality whose doctrine was characterized by its Christocentricity and by its basis in the Bible and in the writings of the fathers, especially Augustine.[19] One of its main representatives was Thomas of Villanova, who by his exemplary personality and his preaching ability exercised a lasting influence on the spirituality of his time. His published *Conciones* form a basic part of the spiritual literature of Spain. One of the most frequently read mystical writers of that time was Blessed Alfonso of Orozco (d. 1591), whose numerous Spanish works were repeatedly printed and translated into other languages. A work that achieved an even larger circulation was *Trabalhos de Jesus,* observations of mystical interiority on the life of Jesus written in poetic language by the Portuguese Thomas of Andrade (or Thomas de Jesus), who died in 1582 in prison in Morocco. Considered to be a high point in religious literature, *De los nombres de Cristo* by the Spanish poet Luis of Leon (d. 1591) offers biblically deep expositions to teach the reader to know and love Christ in a more profound way.

The importance of the Augustinians for the spirituality of the Christian Middle Ages should be seen as equal to that of the other mendicant orders. Firmly built on Augustine's spiritual teaching, the Augustinians emphatically stressed the centrality of love (*caritas*), together with the necessity of helping grace for all good works, the lasting consequences of original sin, the insufficiency of good works and the gift-character of human merits. Through their spiritual writings, some Augustinians had an influence far beyond their order and their native countries. In the fourteenth century the Italians Michael of Massa and Simon of Cascia and the Germans Henry of Friemar and Jordan of Quedlinburg were especially influential; and in the sixteenth century the Spaniards Thomas of Villanova, Alfonso of Orozco, and Luis of Leon and the Portuguese Thomas de Jesus continued the Augustinian tradition stressing love and grace.

Notes

1. See Henricus de Frimaria, *Tractatus de origine et progressu ordinis fratrum eremitarum sancti Augustini* (1334), ed. Rudolph Arbesmann, *Augustiniana* 6 (1956) 37–145, esp. 90–110.

2. The best critical edition of the *Regula sancti Augustini* (=Praeceptum) is by Luc Verheijen in *La Règle de Saint Augustin* (Paris: Études augustiniennes, 1967) 1:417–37.

3. See David Gutiérrez, "Ermites," in *Dict. Sp.* 4, cols. 1004–6.

4. "Caritas ergo inchoata, inchoata iustitia est; caritas provecta, provecta iustitia est; caritas magna, magna iustitia est; caritas perfecta, perfecta iustitia est; . . . non tamen diffunditur in cordibus nostris vel naturae vel voluntatis opibus quae sunt in nobis, sed 'per Spiritum Sanctum qui datus est nobis.' . . ." *Sancti Aurelii Augustini: De natura et gratia* 70.84 (Corpus Scriptorum Ecclesiasticorum Latinorum 60); Vienna and Leipzig: F. Tempsky-G. Freytag, 1913) 298–99).

5. Adolar Zumkeller, *Erbsünde, Gnade, Rechtfertigung und Verdienst nach der Lehre der Erfurter Augustinertheologen des Spätmittelalters* (Würzburg: Augustinus-Verlag, 1984) 87, 90–94, 98.

6. "Fuit autem vulneratus in naturalibus, non quod naturalia perderet . . . , sed . . . quia ipsa naturalia fuerunt inhabilitata ad bene agendum et habilitata ad peccandum."

7. Other Erfurt Augustinians taught the same doctrine: Angelus Dobelinus (d. after 1420), Johannes von Dorsten (d. 1481) and Johannes von Paltz (d. 1511); see Zumkeller, *Erbsünde, Gnade*, 147, 333, 355, and 397–98.

8. See Adolar Zumkeller, "Das Ungenügen der menschlichen Werke bei den deutschen Predigern des Spätmittelalters," in *Zeitschrift für katholische Theologie* 81 (1959) 265–305; idem, *Erbsünde, Gnade*, 288–90, 379–85.

9. Similarly *Epistula* 194.5.19 and elsewhere.

10. See Zumkeller, *Erbsünde, Gnade*, 289, 378.

11. See Walter Baier, *Untersuchungen zu den Passionsbetrachtungen in der Vita Christi des Ludolf von Sachsen* (Analecta Cartusiana 44.1–3; Salzburg, 1977).

12. Henricus de Frimaria, *Tractatus ascetico-mystici I*, ed. Adolar Zumkeller (Würzburg: Augustinus-Verlag, 1975). See also Adolar Zumkeller, "Ein Zeitgenosse Eckeharts zu Fehlentwicklungen in der damaligen mystischen Bewegung," *Würzburger Diözesan-Geschichtsblätter* 37/38 (1975) 229–38.

13. See Adolar Zumkeller, *Manuskripte der Autoren des Augustiner Eremitenordens in mitteleuropäischen Bibliotheken* (Würzburg: Augustinus-Verlag, 1966) 577, 581–83, 656, 860.

14. See Adolar Zumkeller, "Neuendeckte Sermones des Augustinermagisters Gyso von Köln," in *Wahrheit und Verkündigung, M. Schmaus zum 70. Geburtstag* (Munich and Paderborn: Schöningh, 1967) 1121–40.
15. See Zumkeller, *Manuskripte,* nos. 223–26.
16. See Zumkeller, "Der Predigtband Cod. Berolinensis Lat. Fol. 851 des . . . Johannes von Dorsten," *Augustiniana* 27 (1977) 402–30; 28 (1978) 34–90; also idem, *Erbsünde, Gnade,* 307–431.
17. See David Steinmetz, *Luther and Staupitz: An Essay in the Intellectual Origins of the Protestant Reformation* (Durham, NC: Duke University Press, 1980).
18. See Zumkeller, "Joachim von Fiore und sein angeblicher Einfluss auf den Augustiner-Eremitenorden," *Augustinianum* 3 (1963) 382–88.
19. See David Gutiérrez, "Asceticos y misticos," 224–38.

Bibliography

Bavel, Tarsicius van. "The Evangelical Inspiration of the Rule of Saint Augustine." *Downside Review* 93 (1975) 83–99.
Bertalia, Olimpia. "Fray Luis de Leon, Mistico." *Revista Augustiniana de Espiritualidad* 2 (1961) 149–78, 381–409; 3 (1962) 308–40.
Brocardo, Pietro. "Jérôme de Sienne." In *Dict. Sp.* 8, cols. 939–42.
Chaurand, Jacques. "Jacques Legrand." In *Dict. Sp.* 8, cols. 46–48.
Ciolini, Gino. "Scrittori spirituali agostiniani dei secoli XIV e XV in Italia." In *Sanctus Augustinus,* 2:339–87.
Gutiérrez, David. "Asceticos y misticos agustinos de España, Portugal y Hispano-américa." In *Sanctus Augustinus,* 2:147–238.
———. "Ermites de Saint-Augustin." In *Dict. Sp.* 4, cols. 983–1018.
———. *History of the Order of St. Augustine.* 2 vols. thus far. Villanova: Augustinian Historical Institute, 1979–.
———. "Michel de Massa." In *Dict. Sp.* 10, cols. 1182–83.
Gutiérrez, Gilberto. "La vita espiritual en los escritos de Santo Tomas de Villanueva." *Revista Augustiniana de Espiritualidad* 1 (1960) 24–34; 2 (1961) 411–26; 4 (1963) 197–220.
Hackett, M. Benedict. "Guillaume Flete." In *Dict. Sp.* 6, cols. 1204–8.
———. "The spiritual life of the English Austin friars of the fourteenth century." In *Sanctus Augustinus,* 2:421–92.
Hamm, Berndt. *Frömmigkeitstheologie am Anfang des 16. Jahrhunderts. Studien zu Johannes von Paltz und seinem Umkreis.* Tübingen, 1982.
Sanctus Augustinus, vitae spiritualis Magister. 2 vols. Rome: Analecta Augustiniana, 1959.
Lang, F. "Alphonse de Orozco." In *Dict. Sp.* 1, cols. 392–95.
Martin, François-Xavier. "Jean Waldeby." In *Dict. Sp.* 8, cols. 788–90.
Romanis, Alphonse de. "Charité: 6. L'École Augustinienne." In *Dict. Sp.* 2, cols. 627–36.
Ros, Fidèle de. "La Contemplation au XVIe siècle: 3. Les Augustins." In *Dict. Sp.* 3, cols. 2018–20.
Toner, Nicholas. "Augustinian spiritual writers of the English province in the fifteenth and sixteenth centuries." In *Sanctus Augustinus,* 2:493–521.
Viller, M. "Agazzari, Philippe." In *Dict. Sp.* 1, col. 250.
Zumkeller, Adolar. "Henri de Freimar." In *Dict. Sp.* 7, cols. 191–97.
———. "Hermann de Schildesche." In *Dict. Sp.* 7, cols. 302–8.
———. "Jean de Huxaria." In *Dict. Sp.* 8, cols. 556–57.

——. "Jean de Rynstett." In *Dict. Sp.* 8, cols. 697–98.

——. "Jean de Schaftholzheim." In *Dict. Sp.* 8, cols. 722–23.

——. "Jourdain de Saxe." In *Dict. Sp.* 8, cols. 1423–30.

——. "Die Lehrer des geistlichen Lebens unter den deutschen Augustinern vom dreizehnten Jahrhundert bis sum Konzil von Trient." In *Sanctus Augustinus,* 2:239–337.

——. "Mattieu de Saxe." In *Dict. Sp.* 10, cols. 814–16.

——. "Oswald Reinlein." In *Dict. Sp.* 11, cols. 1054–55.

——. "Paltz (Jean Jeuser de)." In *Dict. Sp.* 12, cols. 145–48.

——. "Proles (André)." In *Dict. Sp.* 12, cols. 2406–9.

3

Major Currents in
Late Medieval Devotion

RICHARD KIECKHEFER

ERHAPS THE MOST SIGNIFICANT DEVELOPMENT in late medieval Christianity was the rise of devotionalism. In the last centuries of the Middle Ages, devotions of all kinds flourished in unprecedented profusion: pilgrimages, veneration of relics, Marian devotions, meditations on the passion of Christ, penitential exercises, and more. Development of the Rosary was essentially a late medieval phenomenon. The Stations of the Cross, which attained their modern form by the early sixteenth century, arose out of devotional practices of the late Middle Ages. Eucharistic devotions, often connected with the feast of Corpus Christi, likewise stem from this age. The image of the Sacred Heart, in literary and artistic manifestation, can be traced to the last centuries before the Reformation. Devotional literature proliferated even before the invention of printing, and all the more afterward: classics such as *The Imitation of Christ* and myriad other works less widely known and often unpublished. Devotional art too enjoyed a heyday; this was the era of lavishly ornamented books of hours commissioned for wealthy patrons, of small devotional ivory panels for private devotion, of inexpensive and generally crude woodcuts for popular consumption, and of intricate polyptychs to decorate both high altars and side altars in churches and chapels. Themes with major significance in European devotional art, such as the pietà, emerged during this period; others, like the man of sorrows, attained new-found popularity. This explosion of devotional forms unmistakably changed the tenor of Christian life.

The rise of devotional Christianity has been viewed both favorably and unfavorably. Johan Huizinga saw the multiplication of devotions as one element in the general diffuseness of late medieval culture; the "extreme

saturation of the religious atmosphere" involved the heaping up of benedic-
tions, amulets, cults of saints, feast days, and so forth, in ever greater
superfluity. Indeed, Huizinga cites contemporary authors such as Peter
d'Ailly as critics of the multiplication of festivals, images, fasts, hymns, and
other usages. On the other hand, Bernd Moeller points to the great demand
for such devotions as a sign of "churchliness" in pre-Reformation Germany.
Far from being alienated from the ecclesiastical establishment, Germans in
the waning Middle Ages hungered insatiably for its blessings.[1]

Because it is so diffuse, devotional religion eludes precise definition. One
can, however, locate it on a conceptual map between the liturgical and contemplative elements in religion. *Liturgical* exercises are in principle public
and official; they form the core of the church's common religious experience, and even in eras of diversity and experimentation their shared
character means that they remain essentially constant in their structure. The
Mass and the Divine Office form the backbone of the church's liturgical life.
Contemplative piety, on the other hand, is fundamentally private, unofficial,
and unstructured. It is what the individual does in those moments when she
or he stands alone before God. It is best cultivated in solitude, and the noted
contemplatives of the late Middle Ages, like their counterparts of earlier
centuries, were typically monks or recluses. When Dominicans or other
mendicants gravitated toward contemplative piety, the tension between
their contemplation and their active involvement could be severe.

The *devotional* type of piety stands as an intermediate phenomenon.
Smaller or larger groups can practice devotions, but individuals as well can
cultivate them. A parish or a confraternity might commemorate the feast
of some patron saint with special fervor, but the nearest relic of that saint
might rest in the private collection of some fortunate layperson. Devotions
pass, often without fanfare, from the realm of unofficial religion to that of
official exercise, for example, the Corpus Christi procession. (Indeed, one of
the most interesting aspects of devotionalism is often the way it develops
into, grows out of, or otherwise relates to official liturgical observance.)
Devotions need not be universal or even widespread, but often they do
spread widely, whether at the grassroots level (as with veneration of the
Fourteen Auxiliary Saints) or through official sanction (as with the feast of
Corpus Christi and its associated practices). With increasing popularity
they may acquire ever more rigid structure, but they may also give birth
to greater variation. They are hard to pin down. Unlike liturgy and contemplation, devotions are defined more by their objects than by their form:
a devotion is usually to a particular saint, or to the Virgin, or to the suffering Christ, or to the Eucharist, or to some other object. In any case, their
importance in late medieval Christendom is paramount. From the twelfth

century on, and with extraordinary momentum as the centuries proceeded, devotions proliferated and aroused both clerical and lay fascination.

Manifestations of Devotion

Devotions manifested themselves in three basic ways: in literary expression, in artistic depiction, and in performance. In other words, people read devotional texts or heard them read or sung; they saw devotional themes in art; and they gave themselves over to devotional exercises. Evidence for the literary and artistic expression is readily at hand: texts, paintings, statues, and other such works survive in abundance. These survivals have long held interest for scholars, whether as sources for general trends and historical contexts or for the inherent religious or artistic merit of individual works. Devotional performance is harder to study, since one can approach it only indirectly, through material vestiges (such as prayer beads) and written accounts. Before analyzing specific devotional trends, one must have some acquaintance with the sources for these various manifestations of piety.

Devotional Literature

Literary sources take numerous forms. First, there are meditative works (prayers, moral exhortations, reflections on the life of Christ, etc.) intended mainly for the private use of individuals. These were conceived as aids to meditation on one's state of soul or on the goodness of God. Fifteenth-century treatises on "the art of dying" fall into this category,[2] as do meditations on the passion of Christ, the personal letters of such figures as Catherine of Siena, and other specific genres. Second, there were works meant primarily for public performance or delivery. Around the fourteenth century, religious drama developed as a literary form outside of its earlier liturgical context; with laypeople as actors, plays linked together biblical scenes or portrayed saints' lives in outdoor playing areas.[3] Lyrics, sung by or for laypeople, represent another such genre. Franciscan or other popular preachers might draw street-corner crowds by singing pious lyrics.[4] In some parts of Europe there were confraternities formed to sing devout songs, such as Italian confraternities for singing of *laudi*.

Related to this second category was a third, that of sermons, which might be delivered either in church (in a liturgical setting) or outdoors. In many ways this is the most important of all categories, since the religious culture of the later Middle Ages was in large measure a preached culture. Although there were many laypeople who might read the ever-proliferating devotional literature of the age, there were far more who would gladly have it preached to them. On Sundays, major feast days, and sometimes every day during Lent, sermons might be delivered to large and avid congregations. The texts that we have are at times complete versions delivered as they were written, but more often they are notes or rough drafts paraphrased in oral delivery, or transcripts taken down by someone in the audience. Some sermons were in a popular style, and others were technical and scholastic. The Italian sermons of Bernardino of Siena, for example, abound with folksy anecdotes and colorful language and frequently break off to comment on people in the congregation who are dozing or chattering. In contrast, the same preacher's Latin sermons are tightly structured and intricately articulated disquisitions explaining, for example, how the Virgin resembles the morning star.[5] Usually a sermon was based on a scriptural text. Though the link between the text and the sermon might be allegorical and by modern standards rather tenuous, such conventions allowed for creative reflection on established authorities.

A fourth category of literary source is the compilation, usually intended as a quarry to be mined by the preacher. Collections of sermon exempla (or anecdotes) are the most obvious case in point. A treatise on virtues and vices such as that of William Peraldus; a string of theological consolations for people bearing various afflictions, like John of Dambach's *Consolation of Theology;* a collection of saints' lives, such as James of Voragine's classic *Golden Legend;* or a life of Christ like Ludolph of Saxony's—all such compilations provided rich materials for the preacher. They might have the loose structure of a florilegium or some semblance of a tightly organized summa. Works of this kind were enormously popular in the later Middle Ages. Although they could be used for private devotion by individuals, they testify mostly to the importance of sermons in this era and to the care taken in providing fresh materials for the edification and entertainment of the congregation.

As the laity became increasingly literate and cultured, devotional literature was increasingly available in the vernacular languages. There was some of this in the thirteenth century: sermons by the Franciscan preacher Berthold of Regensburg from the mid-thirteenth century are among the important early examples of German prose. By the fourteenth century vernacular writings were routine. Works intended for public performance most clearly called for use of the vernacular. Thus, a substantial portion of the literature in Middle English is religious: original lyrics, translations or adaptations of earlier Latin poems and prose texts, and mystery plays. In some cases even these publicly performed works incorporated fragments of Latin alongside the vernacular, thus showing the clerical element even in works composed for the laity. Macaronic Christmas carols of the era, such as "In dulci iubilo" with its mixture of German and Latin, furnish good examples. The texts least likely to be written in the vernacular were the compilations. Material from these would be translated or adapted anyway when it was incorporated in sermons, and there was no point in spoiling the international market by appealing to a specific vernacular public.

Devotional Art

Literary texts are essential for understanding the devotional trends of the late Middle Ages, and the art of the era is likewise a rich source of information.[6] This is particularly true of panel painting, in which the artist was free to incorporate a wide variety of primary and secondary motifs. The Flemish painting of the fifteenth century, for example, is well known for its elaborate symbolism: not only conventional details such as saints' attributes but also specific vestments worn by angels could hold symbolic value. The painter of an annunciation scene, for example, could draw upon several kinds of symbolic and expressive vocabulary: nuances of emotion might be conveyed in the Virgin's facial expression and posture; the painter might suggest linkage between the Old and New Testaments by showing Mary with a Bible open to a prophetic text; an anachronistic (or prophetic) portrait of Jesus might hang on the wall behind his mother-to-be; Trinitarian theology could be expressed by showing the Father hovering above the scene, while the Holy Spirit in the form of a dove winged its way from the Father to the Virgin along a beam of celestial light; and the artist might use flowers, candles, and other objects for their established symbolic value.

In the later Middle Ages, panel painting was increasingly used to represent narrative scenes as well as static portraits (or icons): scenes from the life of Christ, the legend of the Virgin, and legends of the saints were favorite narrative motifs. The accumulation of symbolic, iconic, and narrative elements reached its fullest development as individual panels were assembled in large or small diptychs, triptychs, and polyptychs. The *Ghent Altarpiece* by Hubert and Jan van Eyck is one of the best known examples. Unfortunately, many of the panels originally intended for polyptychs have now been dispersed, but the original contexts can often be reconstructed hypothetically or by comparison with extant panels in various museums.

Other forms of art were limited in various ways. Sculpture (in stone, ivory, wood, and alabaster) is important for the history of devotions because one can gauge the significance of motifs from the frequency of their occurrence; madonnas, for example, were ubiquitous. But the possibilities for development of motifs were restricted. The sculptor might represent the madonna as standing or enthroned, gracefully curved or rigidly erect, crowned or bare-headed, but the sculptor could not represent her in an entire setting (such as a rose garden) and could not readily relate the madonna to other figures (such as John the Baptist), as could the painter. These limitations were less severe in the case of relief carving, but opportunities for such work were relatively rare, except for the small ivory panels that were especially popular in the fourteenth century. Miniaturists, working on an illuminated manuscript, were bound by constraints of a different sort: they had limited space (often they had to produce thumbnail sketches, and their choice of subject matter was largely dictated by the text. Stained glass and woodcuts, although clearly different from each other in many respects, shared the limitation of requiring work in bold outline, whether for clear visibility or for ease of recognition. Thus, although none of these media can be neglected in the history of devotions, work done in them seldom attained the richness and sophistication of panel painting.

In the last centuries of the Middle Ages the range of motifs available to the artist widened. In the twelfth and thirteenth centuries, while other themes were certainly used, there was a decided preponderance of certain basic motifs: the madonna and child, the crucifixion, and a few other scenes abounded. By the fifteenth century, partly because of the greater emphasis on narrative, the range of options was greater; for example, Christ would more often be shown as the man of sorrows, and events such as the bodily assumption of Mary or her coronation as Queen of Heaven might be represented in media as diverse as panel painting and alabaster carving.

The role of art within medieval devotionalism cannot be understood without knowing about the institution of patronage. A literary composition too might be commissioned by a patron, but this was not often done, and even a letter addressed to a specific person might quickly reach a much broader audience. A painting or a book of hours, however, was typically done for a particular person or a specific place. The artist was commissioned by an individual or a group (often a confraternity or a guild) to produce a single work of art, which would in principle remain in the possession of the patron or would be donated to a church or chapel. Frequently the patron would be represented in the artwork itself, with hands folded in prayer; he or she would be portrayed smaller than the sacred figures who dominated the work—until about the fifteenth century, when patrons typically appeared as full-sized sharers in the sacred space, just as laypeople at this time came increasingly to claim a role in the religious life around them.

Devotional Practice

For medieval women and men, the literature and art we have discussed was no doubt valuable but secondary. It helped them in their devotional practice, but it did not form the substance of that practice. Devotions were not primarily what one read or saw, but what one did. Devout Christians manifested their devotion by saying their prayers, going on pilgrimage, fasting, participating in processions, joining in the activities of confraternities, wearing hairshirts, giving alms, attending sermons, and performing other pious acts. The deeds themselves were then over and done with. We know about them only indirectly: they are recounted in chronicles, in saints' lives, in fictional narratives, or in letters; they are represented in art (for example, in paintings that show Bernardino of Siena preaching in the piazza); material objects bear witness to them (such as the lead tokens a pilgrim would receive at a place of pilgrimage); and in their ideal form they are sketched in prescriptive manuals (treatises on how to pray, guidebooks for pilgrims, and the like).

Although some devotions could take place anywhere, the most important were commonly linked with special locations. Liturgical religion is marked primarily by a sense of special times, and contemplative religion by an effort to transcend both place and time, but devotional religion attends mainly to the veneration of sacred places or to the objects that make these places holy. Relics, images, and consecrated Hosts are the mainstay of devotional practice. Even meditational reading is typically an aid to the exercise of meditation, in which attention is fixed on an image, perhaps an ivory diptych or a privately owned panel painting. The image most often cited in saints' lives as the center for meditation is the crucifix. Sacred objects might be found within one's own home, at times in a special room (an oratory) or a particular corner. The crucifix or other object would define that special part of the otherwise profane space as especially appropriate for devotion. Outside the home there were shrines everywhere: roadside shrines, distant chapels in secluded spots, and so forth. The greatest concentration of devotional spaces, however, would usually be in a church—whether an established parish church, a monastic church, or the church of a mendicant order. In the later Middle Ages a church would often be subdivided into several more or less enclosed spaces; the sanctuary would be separated from the nave by a screen, and side chapels would serve various devotional purposes quite separate from the liturgy. Indulgences could be secured for those who visited certain churches, chapels, or shrines. At times these shrines would be erected in imitation of sites in the Holy Land, such as the sepulcher of Christ (the most important of the holy places in Jerusalem, according to fifteenth-century sources). For those who were truly devout, domestic oratories and local churches usually did not suffice: for such persons, the very act of traveling to a place of pilgrimage, whether a few miles outside of town or on the other side of the Alps or across the sea, was a process that helped to define one's destination as a special and sacred location.

Many of the sources for devotional practice are thus "archaeological": they are concrete objects or structures used for devotion. Remaining chapels and shrines constitute important evidence, though it is seldom possible to be sure what form they had or quite how they were furnished in the Middle Ages. Works of art, to the extent that they were linked with devotional practice, give insight into the performative element in devotion. One need only stand before a work such as Memling's brilliant *St. John Altarpiece* in Bruges to realize how captivating such a painting might be and how effectively it could serve as an entryway into meditation. Monstrances for display of the Host or of relics—ornate vessels, commonly of silver—give some sense of what devout Christians would exert themselves to behold.

Literary accounts of devotional practice, outside of saints' lives and prescriptive manuals, are not as common as archaeological sources, though there are examples: the anonymous thirteenth-century *Quest of the Holy Grail,* for instance, testifies eloquently to the rise of eucharistic devotion. When nonfictional accounts were composed, it was usually because some particular devotional center attracted an exceptional crowd for some occasion. The classic cases are the jubilees that brought throngs of pilgrims to Rome for the jubilee indulgence. When Boniface VIII proclaimed the first jubilee for 1300, the crowds were so great that many people were crushed, and Giovanni Villani reported that throughout the year there were as many as two hundred thousand persons in the city. During the 1450 jubilee, crowds were so dense that an overcrowded bridge was the scene of confusion: a mule's kicking led to general melee, and ultimately about two hundred persons lost their lives. (Medieval chroniclers not uncommonly seem to gauge the significance of an event by the number whose death it occasioned!) In the mid-fourteenth century, likewise, the penitential devotions of the flagellants aroused the interest of many a chronicler.[7]

Another vital element in devotional practice was preaching. We have already considered the sermon as text; in addition, one must consider the sermon as event. To comprehend how a sermon or a series of sermons could become a noteworthy event, one must recognize that sermons sometimes entered the public record and were duly observed by local chroniclers. Vincent Ferrer drew multitudes when he preached, and he provided a kind of edifying diversion for people whose lives were otherwise absorbed in routine labor. It is claimed that when John Brugman had preached for five hours his audience pleaded for more. Both Dominicans and Franciscans devoted themselves fervently to the homiletic mission, and going to hear them preach constituted an important part of later medieval devotional practice. Evidence for this occurs not only in chroniclers' reports but in some of the sermons themselves, in which the preachers make reference to those present. During one Lenten sermon, Bernardino of Siena called upon his hearers to send food and clothing to prisoners rotting in the town jail—also beds and mattresses, so they would have something to lie on after being tortured. The next time he preached, he noted that his exhortations had so far netted only two shirts, two pairs of drawers, and one ragged pair of stockings for the prisoners to share, and so he repeated his entreaty. In this and in many other ways the preacher entered into the devotional, social, and political life of the town. Bernardino was known as a promoter of devotion to the holy name of Jesus; in contemporary art he is shown holding a plaque with the monogram IHS (for the Greek form of "Jesus") in a medallion, surrounded by rays of light. Such a plaque would itself be a center for meditative devotion, and Bernardino's use of it in preaching was a way of fostering private devotion at a public assembly. The emblem was also Bernardino's own substitute for the devices or banners borne by warring political factions within the town.[8] If late medieval religious culture was largely a preached culture, this was partly because preaching impinged on all aspects of the audience's religious life—or at least the preachers *endeavored* to exert such pervasive influence.

Although devotional practice can be approached only indirectly, the sources clearly show that here too, as in devotional literature and art, there was an increase of fervor and of available options in the later centuries of the medieval period.

Main Devotional Themes

We turn now from the form to the content of late medieval devotion and to the specific themes that dominated the era's religious life. The range of devotional motifs in the late Middle Ages was wide, but the contours of late medieval piety can be discerned in four of the most important devotions: those to the passion of Christ, to Mary, to the saints, and to the Eucharist.

The Passion of Christ

Devotion to the passion was ubiquitous in late medieval piety.[9] This was a case in which devotional fervor far outran strict liturgical necessity. In liturgical commemoration the passion was seasonal: each Mass throughout the year might constitute a reenactment of the sacrifice of Calvary, but it was specifically during Holy Week, at the end of Lent, that the passion itself became the focus of attention. There were days in May and September commemorating the finding and exaltation of the cross, and the latter observance became extended to the three days preceding the original feast, yet these were relatively minor events. Votive Masses for the passion might be celebrated on Fridays throughout the year, but this weekly observance was the expression of a devotional urge rather than a liturgical norm. But while the passion held a vital but limited place in liturgy, it was all-pervasive in extraliturgical piety.

Bernard of Clairvaux and others in the twelfth century promoted a form of spirituality that was firmly grounded in meditation on Christ's humanity; to this the Franciscans and others in later centuries added much poignancy and intensity. Francis of Assisi himself composed an *Office of the Passion,* and his stigmatization became the single most important event in his life for later Franciscan tradition. Important Franciscan authors, Bonaventure among them, enriched the stock of literature on this theme. Although non-Franciscans shared this devotion, it was Franciscans in particular who popularized it.

Like most devotions, this one was bound to a concept of sacred space. The obvious place connected with the passion was Jerusalem, the site of the great, archetypal Christian pilgrimage. The journey was arduous and dangerous; from 1187 on, the city was under Muslim control. In the later Middle Ages the Franciscans served as guardians and polyglot guides to the holy places. From the late thirteenth century, the standard tour of Jerusalem focused on a series of "stations," or places important in the passion or in general Christian antiquity: the place where Simon of Cyrene was forced to take Christ's cross, the spot where Mary swooned on meeting her son, the house of Mary, even a house displayed as that of Dives (the rich man of the parable in Luke 16)! Other stations were added later, such as the house of Veronica. One fifteenth-century account lists over one hundred of them. The most important location, however, was the church of the Holy Sepulcher, whose precincts incorporated several shrines and chapels, including one at the spot where Christ was supposed to have been crucified. Felix Fabri, who made the pilgrimage in 1480 and left a detailed account, speaks with awe and excitement of the nighttime hours he spent at this site. He also testifies to the importance of indulgences: pilgrims to the holy places gained indulgences for praying at these spots or venerating them with kisses and prostrations. From the fourteenth century on, it was believed that these indulgences had been granted by Sylvester I at the request of Constantine and Helen.[10]

Some who had made this pilgrimage, and others who wished they could, set up replicas of these holy places back at home. In 1378 an Augustinian named John of Schaftolsheim established a model of the Mount of Olives, with a chapel of the Holy Sepulcher. When two knights returned from Jerusalem in the early fifteenth century they set up a model of the Sepulcher at Bruges. Later in the century a Poor Clare in Italy built models of various holy sites (the house of Mary, the room where the Last Supper took place, the garden of Gethsemane, the praetorium of Pilate, Calvary, etc.), which she used for her daily meditations. A pilgrim from Nuremberg named Martin Ketzel, on returning home, engaged a sculptor to carve a series of stations representing the "seven falls," or the points in his passion when Christ fell to the ground. Late fifteenth- and early sixteenth-century authors wrote reflections on these stations, to be used for meditation as a person proceeded from one image to another. Among the most important of these authors was a Belgian Carmelite, John Pascha, who in the early sixteenth century devised a list of fourteen stations identical to those used in modern devotion.[11]

These passion-centered devotions exemplify some of the ways literature, art, and performance could be linked. Artwork such as statues or relief plaques representing the stations served as centers for devotional practice. Literature such as John Pascha's guided the devout Christian in meditation on these stations, and written accounts by Felix Fabri and others give information about deeds actually performed.

The cross or crucifix was of central importance for both liturgy and devotion. Paintings by Cimabue, Giotto, and Fra Angelico depict Mass being celebrated on altars adorned only by crosses. As already mentioned, crucifixes were common foci of private devotion, and roadside shrines commonly featured a crucifix. Furthermore, the crucifixion was one of the most frequent subjects in art throughout the Middle Ages.

During the last medieval centuries there were four major developments in art of the passion. First, especially in the fifteenth century, there was increasing interest in the entire sequence of events, including those before the crucifixion (the agony in the garden, the arrest, the flagellation, the imprinting of Christ's image on Veronica's veil, etc.) and those after it (the deposition from the cross, the lamentation, and the burial). Second, even in representation of the crucifixion itself the depiction became more complex. A full cast of characters appeared: not only Christ himself, Mary, and John, but also Mary Magdalene (with her arms around the cross), the Virgin's companions (supporting her as she swoons), and a band of soldiers and officials. Toward the end of the Middle Ages artists commonly included the thieves, anonymous throngs, and even an entourage of postbiblical saints. Angels might be depicted worshiping Christ or gathering his blood in chalices, an obvious eucharistic symbol. Other symbolic or allegorical motifs included the skull of Adam at the foot of the cross, the pelican feeding its young with its own blood, the sun and moon, and other devices.

Third, there were particular moments from the postcrucifixion narrative that were increasingly isolated for iconic portrayal. The pietà, or Christ spread on his mother's lap, was common in German woodcarving during the fourteenth century; in the following century it appeared in various regions and in diverse media, painted as well as sculpted. The man of sorrows, in which the deceased Christ displays his wounds, became a motif almost as common as the crucifixion itself. Painted versions of the man of sorrows usually showed Christ standing upright in his sarcophagus, yet still suffering and even cadaverous, and not truly risen. Similar detachment from narrative context shows in the fourth development: in the fifteenth century especially there was a fondness for emblems of the passion, either isolated or in combinations—the flagella with which Christ was whipped, the crown of thorns, the veil of Veronica, the instruments of crucifixion, the wounds, etc. One of the most common of these "arms of Christ" was his wounded heart. For example, a fifteenth-century woodcut shows a large heart (with clearly visible aorta) superimposed on the cross; in the corners are medallions with pierced hands and feet, while a spear coming from the left side pierces the heart itself. In these early depictions the wound is more important than the heart itself—as is the case also in early literary references to the wound, in which the devout Christian mystically enters through pious meditation.

Literature on the passion, found in a wide variety of genres, was as diverse in content as in form. Two representative texts, one a series of meditations and the other a sermon, may convey some sense of this variety.

The meditations are those of an anonymous author from around 1300, though in the late Middle Ages they were ascribed to the Venerable Bede (*PL* 94, cols. 561–68). The preface addresses a specific reader who has requested a series of meditations on the passion corresponding to the seven canonical hours. The author says he will set forth the basic principles without going into much detail, "because the contemplative and spiritual soul draws much from a few things, while the crude and carnal soul understands little in many things." If the reader is serious about the business of meditation, however, he (or she) must abstain from indulgence in unnecessary food or drink, vain words, games, and merrymaking, for "carnal consolation and contemplation of the Lord's passion do not belong together." (The author uses "meditation" and "contemplation" interchangeably.) Thus morally prepared, readers must imagine that they are present at the very time of the passion and must feel grief as if the Lord were suffering before their very eyes.

The schema for these meditations was a common one, resembling that of the influential Pseudo-Bonaventuran meditations on the life of Christ: at compline, the reader is to meditate on the Last Supper, the agony in the garden, and the arrest of Christ; after sleeping, the reader should awake at matins still suffused with tears and sorrow from the earlier meditation and should ponder the beginning of Christ's trial; and so on, through the canonical hours, concluding with meditation on Christ's burial at vespers. At every stage the author suggests specific reflections. Christ's prayer in Gethsemane becomes a lesson in how to pray: as Christ prayed three times, for example, so we too should pray not once but often. There are descriptive details, as when Christ is arrested and his disciples are imagined casting themselves to the ground and crying out like orphans. In the course of the trial, the readers are to imagine themselves pleading with the authorities to stop tormenting Christ, and are to embrace the Lord and offer themselves as objects of the blows. When the Jews go off to sleep, Jesus will be left alone, weary and cold (because it is winter). The reader is to sit beside him and kiss his hands, feet, and chains, and proffer a shoulder as a resting-place for Christ's head.

Mary appears as a major figure in the drama, an "example of sorrow for all who love Christ." She is led forth by older women, as if she herself were dead, and when she meets her son she falls as if lifeless to the ground. From the cross, Christ entrusts not only John but his entire church to her. When he dies, she pours out an eloquent lament and then falls to the ground. (The repeated falls, which we have already seen emphasized in early stations of the cross, underscore not merely the pain and grief of Christ and his mother but the utter powerlessness of those who have renounced the means of power.)

Whereas Pseudo-Bede emphasizes the concrete detail of the passion narrative, Thomas Brinton in a sermon for Good Friday concerns himself more with allegorical and moral reflections.[12] The text for this late-fourteenth-century sermon is John 19:34, "There came out blood," but the focus is not the historical event of Christ's passion. Instead, Brinton proceeds immediately to moral exhortation. We dare not approach the Father for pardon when our own hands are stained with blood from sins against his Son. Alas, England abounds in thieves, murderers, and other criminals who go unrepentent and unpunished. As Hosea 4:1f. says, there are sins throughout the land, "and blood hath touched blood." Brinton tells the exemplum of a priest who dared to celebrate Mass after sleeping with a concubine. When he looked into the chalice he saw that the sacred elements had turned black as pitch. He considered pouring them onto the ground, but finally consumed them with great dread and found them exceedingly bitter. After Mass he hastened to his bishop to confess his sin. Brinton then tells other miracles involving the blood of Christ. Most of the sermon, though, deals with the seven times Christ shed his blood: at the circumcision, in Gethsemane, at the flagellation, at the crowning with thorns, and in the perforation of his hands, his feet, and his side. Each occasion receives allegorical or moral interpretation. Because hands signify works, for example, the piercing of Christ's hands represents the cleansing of the guilty soul by good works. The sermon abounds in Old Testament figures. Leviticus 16:14, which speaks of sevenfold propitiatory sprinkling with calf's blood, prefigures the seven times Christ shed his blood. 1 Maccabees 6:34 says that the blood of grapes and mulberries was shown to elephants to provoke them to fight; so too, the blood of Christ is displayed to arouse zeal in spiritual combat, particularly in defense of the church's liberties. Types of Christ are found throughout the Old Testament: he was figuratively killed in the person of Abel, denuded in Noah, bound to wood in Isaac, persecuted in Jacob, sold in Joseph, spat upon and blasphemed in Job, flagellated in Jeremiah, and entombed in Jonah. Whereas Pseudo-Bede used narrative detail to arouse pious compassion, Brinton used allegorical interpretation to inspire moral reform. What they have in common is their careful, point-by-point meditation on biblical texts. Brinton's sermon develops a more traditional technique of analysis, however, and Pseudo-Bede better represents the fascination and sympathy of later medieval authors for the suffering Christ.

One of the most significant developments in late medieval literature on the passion is the rise of the vernacular passion play, performed outdoors by a largely lay cast.[13] Earlier passion plays, in Latin, had grown out of liturgical drama performed within the church building. Around the fourteenth century these plays shed their essentially liturgical character—but not entirely, since among the various sources used in these plays were the liturgical texts used during Holy Week. The plays followed the Gospel accounts for much of their material, but drew from liturgical formulations as well and borrowed heavily from apocryphal Gospels, commentaries and treatises, and other sources. Through imaginative embellishment they developed a full range of characters, both major and minor. The York play represents Herod as gleeful when Jesus comes before him: "Oh, my heart hops for joy to see now this prophet appear!" In the French *Palatine Passion*, four soldiers emerge as great braggarts, boasting, for example, of the treatment they will mete out to anyone who tries to steal Christ's body. The same play has a smith whose hands are miraculously stricken when he is asked to forge nails for the crucifixion; his shrewish wife has to do the job. At the same time that panel paintings were showing new interest in an array of personages on Calvary and in narrative details of the entire passion story, the same tendencies manifested themselves in drama.

Often, however, the art and literature of the passion reveal not so much a sense of curiosity as a violence of emotion that startles modern viewers and readers. German crucifixes of the fourteenth century frequently portray Christ's body in grotesquely distorted fashion, with blood gushing profusely from his wounds. Something of the same effect comes from Julian of Norwich's vision of the crucifixion, in which Christ's body undergoes almost kaleidoscopic transformation through various shades of blue, brown, and black, as a piercing cold wind dries his flesh. Perhaps the most striking grotesquerie, however, is in accounts of the barbaric cruelties inflicted on Christ by his tormentors—accounts which find their artistic analogue in the paintings of Hieronymus Bosch and his followers. Devotion to the passion thus displayed a feverish intensity widespread in late medieval piety.[14]

Marian Devotion

Alongside devotion to the passion, and often linked with it, Marian themes were ubiquitous in late medieval Christianity.[15] Relics, shrines and pilgrimages, feast days, hymns, motets, legends, plays, paintings and statues, patronage of churches and monasteries, sermons, devotional treatises, visions, theology—in all these areas Mary was not merely present but vitally important. Marian devotion was so pervasive and diffuse that it is difficult to trace even the main lines of development. If one looks for increasing emphasis on Mary's humility one will find ample evidence. But if one seeks the theme of Mary's majesty, her exaltation to regal status, her unparalleled perfection, one will find abundant signs of this as well. Special motifs arose in Marian art—Mary in the company of Christ and St. Ann, Mary with grains of wheat on her gown, and so forth—but these by no means displaced earlier themes. If there is any principle that applies to Marian devotion in the later Middle Ages, it is that of accumulation. Virtually anything that could be said, sung, displayed, or thought in Mary's honor found its place in the mélange.

Marian devotion arose against a rich background of liturgical development. In the early Middle Ages there were four Marian feast days: the Purification, the Annunciation, the Assumption, and the Nativity of Mary. A feast in honor of the Visitation arose in the thirteenth century in some parts of Western Christendom, and efforts to make it universal included a bull by Boniface IX in 1389 and a prescription of the Council of Basel in 1441. In the fourteenth century a feast of Mary's Presentation in the Temple was gradually taken over from the Eastern church. The following century saw efforts to establish a feast of the Betrothal; John Gerson proposed this in honor of both Mary and Joseph. As early as the eleventh century it was common to celebrate a votive Mass honoring the Mother of God on Saturdays, either because she maintained faith in her son's divinity even before his resurrection or because Saturday was God's day of rest and Mary's womb was Christ's place of rest. All these feasts, distributed throughout the year, gave rise to liturgical texts, including hymns, antiphons, and motets. A "little office" for Mary, traceable to monastic observance of the eighth century, became an important part of private lay devotions in the later Middle Ages.

It may seem ironic that the major shrines of medieval Christendom did not include a Marian shrine: Canterbury, Santiago, and Rome were centers for veneration of saints, and Jerusalem was the destination for which enthusiasts of the passion yearned, but Marian shrines tended to be local and of lesser significance. There was no medieval Lourdes or Fatima. Yet this was the great strength of Marian devotion. Thomas Becket was associated closely with Canterbury, and other saints with the places where their bones lay buried or where they had figured prominently during their lifetimes, but Mary was the universal patroness. The Cistercians, not wishing to link themselves too closely with any one part of Christendom, had made Mary their special patroness, dedicated all their monasteries to her, and named many of them in her honor. The Franciscans had shared much of this sense of Mary as the universal patroness and helped to disseminate it. Marian shrines were thus found everywhere.

In keeping with the principle that a sacred place must have a focal object, relics and images lay readily at hand. Mary's bodily assumption into heaven was a precondition for the universality of her cult: because no one place on earth could claim her remains, she was equally present in all places. Nonetheless, there were shrines that displayed samples of her hair (usually blonde), vials of her milk, snippets of her veil, or even the girdle which (according to legend) she dropped from heaven into the doubting Thomas's lap as proof of her assumption. Skeptical voices were at times raised; one preacher protested that all the cows of Lombardy could not yield as much milk as was ascribed to the Virgin. But even if there had been no relics at all, there were images in every form imaginable.

Artistic representations of Mary fall into two general categories: iconic portrayals of the madonna and scenes from her life. The madonna was one of the most common motifs of medieval art, in both painting and sculpture. The painted madonna was usually seated on a throne, while in sculpture she might be either enthroned or standing. In the later Middle Ages, as her regal status was taken for granted, she routinely bore a crown. The most interesting evolution of the madonna is found in panel painting, where angels and saints accompany the Virgin, and where settings (interiors, gardens, etc.) become increasingly elaborate. Frequently the Virgin or her child is seen holding an object (often a book, a piece of fruit, a flower, even a bird), not

7. *Devotional Diptych*, Italian, late 14th century.

simply as a bit of genre realism but usually as a symbol of the redemption or the sin that required it.

Scenes from the life of Mary, especially common in the panel painting of the late Middle Ages, fall into four main groups: those connected with the "protevangelium," or the narrative of events in Mary's childhood (her conception and birth, presentation, and betrothal); those relating to Christ's infancy (the annunciation, visitation, nativity, and so on); those dealing with the passion of Christ (the crucifixion with Mary at the foot of the cross, the pietà and more elaborate lamentation scenes, and the burial); and those connected to what one might call the "postevangelium," the events occurring after those of the canonical Gospels (especially Mary's "dormition" or death, assumption, and coronation in heaven). There was no real interest in the years between Christ's infancy and his passion, partly because Mary did not play a major role in Christ's ministry and partly also because representations of Christ himself during these years are relatively uncommon. (Mary did appear in the occasional paintings of the wedding feast at Cana.)

The increasing dignity of Mary is seen in fifteenth-century depictions of her coronation, in which she is typically crowned not only by her son but by the entire Trinity. On the other hand, nativity scenes from the same era show her kneeling in adoration of her son, who is usually laid on the ground (following a vision of St. Bridget of Sweden). Her role as protectress is accented most forcefully in paintings and statues of the Madonna of Mercy, whose mantle expands to envelop her huddled devotees. Occasionally those thus protected include representatives of the various stations in society (pope, king, bishop, burgher, etc.); at times the most prominent figures are hooded members of the flagellant confraternities that commissioned the artwork.

The same variety of themes can be found in legends of the Virgin, which began to evolve in Christian antiquity (see *The Protevangelium of James*) and became enshrined in later compilations such as the *Golden Legend*. What the later Middle Ages had to add to the legends of her life were primarily miracle stories showing her providential care for those who venerated her. Stories of this kind had been told by Gregory I and Gregory of Tours, among others. Collections became especially popular in the High Middle Ages; often they focused on the miracles occurring in a particular place. Frequently they involved pardon of sin and entry into heaven for sinners, whose guilt was mitigated by their devotion to the Virgin—a theme that preachers could develop to good effect by using such stories as exempla in their sermons. Another important literary development was the poetic "Lamentation of Mary," in which Christ's mother pours out her grief on seeing her son removed from the cross and laid out for burial. Closely related was the poetic "Dispute between Mary and the Cross," in which Mary bemoaned the fate to which the cross had subjected her son, and the cross itself then argued the need for Christ's sacrifice. Ubertino of Casale composed a Latin version of such a poem in the early fourteenth century, and vernacular versions followed. In these as in other literary works, Mary appeared as a model of compassion and as "coredemptrix," participating in her son's redemptive work. Other poems, treatises, and sermons likewise honored the Virgin in these and other ways.

Prayers to the Mother of God were numerous. From the twelfth century on the most important and popular of these was the angelic salutation (of Luke 1:28), the Ave Maria, to which the exclamation of Elizabeth (from Luke 1:42) had already been added. Twelfth-century manuscripts tell of a nun who knelt daily before a picture of Mary and prayed the Ave Maria 150 times, until Mary herself appeared and suggested doing so only fifty times but slowly and with greater devotion. Such multiplication of prayers, counted on prayer beads, led in the later Middle Ages to the formation of the Rosary. The Dominicans especially cultivated this practice, and in the early fifteenth century they combined the recitation of prayers with a system of meditation on events from the life of Mary, and later in that century encouraged the formation of special confraternities for use of this exercise.

The importance of Marian devotion for late medieval music can be seen from the example of Jacob Obrecht: of the twenty-four motets by him that survive, fully one quarter are on Marian texts. The Old Hall Manuscript, a collection of English music from the late fourteenth and early fifteenth centuries, contains twenty-six motets, of which roughly two-thirds are Marian. One of the non-Marian motets from this collection, a piece for All Saints' Day, begins with the words "Christ has ascended into heaven and has prepared a place of immortality for his most chaste mother." While corresponding music for the passion was oddly uncommon, Marian piety made itself everywhere manifest.

The Cult of the Saints

Like devotion to the Virgin, the veneration of saints was firmly rooted in liturgical practice.[16] Indeed, the process of canonization that certified a deceased person as a saint was essentially a determination that this person was worthy of public veneration in the liturgy of the universal church. In the early centuries of Christianity this decision was made by the Christian community which had witnessed the saint's virtuous life and heroic martyrdom.

Throughout the early Middle Ages, bishops and synods held control of the process. Beginning around 1200, the pope asserted sole right to canonize saints—and since papal canonization was the most effective way to secure a widespread cult, those fostering the veneration of a prospective saint were happy to recognize this claim. What emerged was an elaborate quasi-judicial process, involving scrutiny of witnesses and composition of a canonization biography or vita. (In many cases a vita was written before the process began and could be a means for arousing the required interest in canonization.) Once canonized, new saints could be honored with the full range of liturgical and devotional accolades. They could be invoked in public prayers; churches could be dedicated to them; liturgy could be celebrated in their honor on their feast days; their relics could be enclosed in precious vessels and displayed for veneration; and they could be represented in art with the full nimbus or halo of a saint. Until they had been canonized, they could receive only private and local veneration as blessed, or *beati*, a term that in the later Middle Ages referred merely to prospective saints who had not yet been canonized by the pope.

Because there were far more than 365 recognized saints, selection had to be made of individuals who would be venerated in a particular place on each day of the year. Throughout the Middle Ages this process remained flexible; bishops could institute feast days in their own dioceses, and particular churches or monasteries had considerable liberty in drawing up and changing the "sanctoral" section of their own liturgical calendars. Not every day was celebrated as the feast of a saint. Some measure of standardization and much filling-in of gaps in the calendar occurred in the thirteenth and following centuries, when saints' feasts were increasingly used on documents as a form of dating—a system that required some uniformity. Still, there remained much flexibility in deciding which saints merited vigils, octaves, and special honors such as public processions or other rituals outside the church.[17]

The relics of the saint almost always formed the center of devotion. Often the entire body or skeleton was preserved in one shrine, but in theory even the smallest fragment was equivalent to the saint's *corpus* (like the consecrated Host, which was undiminished when divided). If the cult was already recognized when the saint died, the body might be enshrined at once in a sarcophagus within a church, where devotees could pay their veneration. Otherwise the body might be "translated" from its grave to an accessible place of honor. People seeking favors from the saint would bring offerings; if they had made vows to the saint and consequently received the requested favors, they would bring *ex voto* offerings to the shrine as compensation for the blessing rendered. Those wanting cures might spend the night beside the saint's tomb, a practice known as incubation. Shrines with the remains of particularly popular saints might attract pilgrims from far and wide, especially if these shrines could claim exclusive possession of these relics.

The ready availability of saints' relics made their artistic images less important than they no doubt would otherwise have been. Still, the saints were common subjects for art. Like Mary, they could be shown either in portraits or in narrative scenes taken from their legends. An elaborate system of attributes helped the viewer to identify the saint portrayed in an iconic portrait: Peter typically appeared with his keys, Catherine of Alexandria with the spiked wheel on which she was tortured, and so forth. There were also generic attributes, such as the palm borne by a martyr. Throughout the Middle Ages, the classical saints of the early church were preferred subjects for art, though a few "modern" saints such as Francis of Assisi did gain popularity. One study of seven hundred Italian panel paintings from the late eleventh through the early fourteenth century found that Christ was depicted in 35 percent of them, the Virgin in 55 percent, unidentified saints in 15 percent, and identified saints in 9 percent. Among the identified figures, Francis of Assisi was the most common; others frequently portrayed were mainly apostles and early martyrs, though Clare of Assisi and Dominic were also important. Studies for other places and times similarly show a preference for classical—and male—saints.[18]

Fondness for the saints can also be seen in the adoption of saints' names. This was a custom of long standing, but in the later centuries of the Middle Ages it became increasingly common. Thus, a study of Genoese rulers shows that in the twelfth century only about 12 percent of them had saints' names, whereas in the thirteenth century the figure reached 23 percent, and in the fourteenth it climbed to 67 percent. It is surely no coincidence that the custom of giving a name at baptism became widespread at the same time.[19] Apart from this baptismal patron, in some parts of Europe it was expected that everyone would choose a patron apostle, and adherence to this custom could even become a test of orthodoxy. One German evidently amused an inquisitor by telling him that his patron apostle was the archangel Michael.[20]

Patronage was not restricted to churches and individuals. Organizations too could adopt saints as their patrons, as was common among confraternities in some parts of Europe. Members of these confraternities would join in commemoration of their patron's feast day. Particularly important in this regard in northern Germany, for example, was St. Ann.

Veneration of saints was no less important in literature. James of Voragine's *Golden Legend* (compiled around 1270) was one of the more important collections of pious legend in medieval literature; its distillation of earlier hagiography, particularly the legends of early Christian saints, provided material for later authors and preachers for generations to come. While this standard compilation contained legends for 159 saints, later works were often more inclusive, even if at the expense of superficiality. Thus, Peter Calo's fourteenth-century *Legends of the Saints* covered 853 figures, again mostly classical ones. These saints were also celebrated on occasion in drama; in the fifteenth century especially, plays reenacted the legends of St. Barbara, St. Sebastian, and other classical figures.[21]

Lives of contemporary saints were seldom thus romanticized, but there were other interesting developments in the treatment of these figures. As canonization proceedings became more rigorous, vitae for prospective saints in the thirteenth and fourteenth centuries became more meticulous, more exhaustive, and more concerned with the saints' virtues than with the miracles they performed while alive. Lists of posthumous miracles, attesting both the popular cult of the saints and the divine approbation of that cult, were appended to the vitae. On the other hand, from the thirteenth century on there was often an emphasis on the saints' mystical experiences and on the inner life of the saints generally. Precedent for this can be seen in the saints' own accounts of their visions. This emphasis on inwardness was especially pronounced in autobiographies and in vitae written by the saints' spiritual fathers and confessors; the autobiography of Henry Suso and the vita of Catherine of Siena exemplify this tendency.[22]

The cult of saints holds special importance in the history of devotionalism because in the earlier Middle Ages, before the twelfth century, this veneration held *the* central place in Christian devotion. Extraliturgical observances, semipublic and semiprivate, were attached mainly to the cult of holy men and women. Before devotion to the passion attained great popularity, and before an upsurge in literacy and the rise of the mendicant orders evoked new interest in multiform devotions, the relics of saints were the primary devotional foci through most of Europe. Interest in saints did not wane in the late Middle Ages, but there were other devotional fascinations which aroused enthusiasm in the ever-richer accumulation of options.

The Eucharist

The evolution of devotions out of earlier liturgical practice can nowhere be more clearly seen than in the eucharistic devotions of the late Middle Ages.[23] When the Franciscan John of Winterthur said in the fourteenth century that the Eucharist was the sacrament in which his contemporaries' devotion most especially consisted, he did not mean that there was a new-found enthusiasm for liturgical observance. Rather, he was pointing to a rapidly increasing fascination for the consecrated Host itself, whether within the liturgy or outside of it.

The first clear sign of this devotion came in the early thirteenth century, when quite suddenly the institution of elevating the Host after the consecration at Mass became widespread. The earliest instance is in the diocese of Paris, around 1200. By the middle of the century the custom had spread widely throughout Western Christendom, and clearly it answered to a popular craving to see the miraculously transubstantiated Host. The doctrine of transubstantiation, clarified in the wake of eleventh-century controversy, had been formally promulgated by the Fourth Lateran Council in 1215. Eucharistic devotions may have been fostered by the clergy as a way of reinforcing this doctrinal formula, but popular appetite for the miraculous was surely a more vital factor. By the end of the thirteenth century many bishops were granting indulgences for veneration of the elevated Host. Bells would be rung to call distracted people to attention at the moment of elevation. It has been claimed that for many Christians attending Mass meant essentially seeing the elevated Host. Gottschalk Hollen in the fifteenth century commented of such people, "They come when they hear the bell, entering to see the elevation, and when it is over they leave, running and fleeing, as if they have seen the devil."

Soon it was not enough to see the Host merely at the time of elevation, and in some places it would be displayed outside the liturgy, in a monstrance, usually placed on the altar. This practice began in northern Europe in the fourteenth century. The monstrance itself was modeled after earlier cases for display of relics; it usually had the form of a tower or cross, sometimes a human or angelic figure, with a glass container for the Host. Encased in such a monstrance and left exposed on the altar, the Host was a primary center for devotions. Dorothy of Montau, who was keenly devoted to the Eucharist, could have seen it a hundred times a day and still not felt satisfied. In the fourteenth and fifteenth centuries the mere act of seeing the consecrated Host was sometimes thought to have a kind of magical effect: protection from sudden death was among the many benefits it bestowed. A countertrend was veneration of the Eucharist even in a closed tabernacle; the custom began in the fifteenth century and was fostered in some places by means of indulgences.

The greatest impetus to eucharistic devotion, both liturgical and extraliturgical, was the institution of a special eucharistic feast, that of Corpus Christi. The inspiration came from the Belgian visionary Juliana of Cornillon (1192–1258), who reported that the establishment of this feast was Christ's will. One might have thought that Holy Thursday was already a feast in honor of the Eucharist and that in fact every Mass was a celebration of this sacrament. Such objections were raised by contemporaries; Juliana encountered fierce opposition to her proposal from those who saw it as superfluous. In 1246 the feast was nonetheless instituted in the diocese of Liege, and in 1264 Urban IV (formerly of that diocese) proclaimed it for the church at large. Only in the early fourteenth century, however, was any effort made to enforce this decree, with strong support from the Dominicans.

The practice of carrying the Host as the central focus in a Corpus Christi procession emerged in northern Europe, where it became common around the mid-fourteenth century. Such processions were occasions for joyous and triumphant display. As the Host was carried from church to church, there was much singing and ringing of bells, and much show of ornaments, banners, and statues. Almost immediately there were disputes between clerics and among guilds and confraternities, contending with each other for places of honor in the procession. In some places the celebration took on a markedly secular character, with games and diversions of all sorts. Another departure from the original intention came when the procession moved out into the fields as a kind of blessing for protection against destructive weather.

The principle of multiplication exerted itself further: in addition to the Corpus Christi procession proper, there were other processions during the octave of the feast. When the processions were over, the monstrance with the consecrated Host came to be displayed on an altar. (This was the main source for extraliturgical veneration of the Host: once the custom of such display at Corpus Christi time was established, it became habitual throughout the year.) As a papal legate to Germany in the mid-fifteenth century, Nicholas of Cusa sought to curb these tendencies by limiting exposition of the Host to the feast of Corpus Christi and its octave. In his words, the Eucharist "was instituted as food, not as an item of display." But what he was opposing was a widespread and firmly established tradition. In effect, he was offering futile opposition to the growth of devotion out of liturgy—to the shift of focus from sacred time (the feasts of the liturgical calendar) to sacred space (the altar defined as exceptionally holy through the presence of the exposed Host).

It was for the feast of Corpus Christi that the best-known eucharistic hymns were composed. "Pange lingua" and "Verbum supernum prodiens" (also known as "Tantum ergo" and "O salutaris hostia"), attributed to Thomas Aquinas, were written at the time Urban IV established the feast. "Adoro te devote," also ascribed to Thomas though on dubious evidence, comes from the same general time but was not intended for the office of Corpus Christi. In many ways the subtlest of the three, it emphasizes the hiddenness of Christ's presence in the Eucharist and declares that while sight, touch, and taste are deceived by the appearance of bread, the sense of hearing gives access to the mysterious truth about the sacrament.

Devotion to the Eucharist received powerful support from reports of miracles connected with it. These were extraordinary miracles, which might be taken as confirmation that the Eucharist itself was miraculous, but which might also distract from the essential miracle of transubstantiation. One of the most famous of these events is said to have occurred at Bolsena in 1263, though the earliest report is from around 1340. A priest, tormented by doubts about transubstantiation, saw the Host at Mass transformed into visible flesh, from which drops of blood fell onto the corporal in the form of a bleeding face. Urban IV was notified and had the miraculous Host brought to Orvieto, where it was received in procession. Before long there were many other miraculous Hosts venerated in western Europe. One study lists 117 shrines in Germany (particularly pilgrimage churches in Bavaria) where eucharistic miracles were commemorated. The legends connected with these shrines typically begin with the story of a desecrated Host. Some miscreant (usually a Jew) steals the Host, mistreats it (by abuse such as piercing or beating), and is astounded when it displays miraculous properties (usually bleeding). The culprit tries to hide the Host, but it is discovered (typically by miraculous light shining on it or by animals that venerate it), whereupon a shrine is built on the spot. Legends of this sort arose as early as the late twelfth century, but the high point in their formation came around 1300.[24]

Although eucharistic devotion did not often manifest itself in art (apart from the applied art of metalwork required for monstrances), there were occasional paintings in the late Middle Ages depicting eucharistic miracles. A set of panels from Regensburg, done around 1476, shows a thief casting a stolen Host into a cellar; as he does so it is guarded by two hovering angels. The missing Host is then discovered and retrieved by a formal procession of clerics, accompanied by banners and by the same angelic escorts as they gather about the sacred object in the cellar.[25] More typical than this was the depiction of "St. Gregory's Mass," in which Christ appears as the man of sorrows while the saint celebrates Mass.

Lives of late medieval saints, especially women, frequently refer to eucharistic wonders: sometimes the saints look at the altar during Mass and perceive not a Host but Christ in the form of a small child; at other times the Host is miraculously brought to the saints by an angel. Women's particular devotion to the Eucharist has been interpreted as compensation for women's exclusion from holy orders. If women could not consecrate the Host, they could at least have an extraordinarily close relationship to it in their visions and through miraculous contact.[26] What is important here is that most of these mystics wanted not merely to see but to receive the Eucharist, as frequently as they could. Male mystics, such as John Tauler in his sermons for Corpus Christi and to a lesser extent Meister Eckhart, likewise encouraged reception of the Eucharist rather than extraliturgical display and veneration. On this matter there was thus a kind of alliance of contemplative and liturgical religion working against devotional tendencies.

It is impossible to gauge how effective Tauler, Nicholas of Cusa, and others of their sort were in persuading people to receive rather than merely venerate the sacrament. The Fourth Lateran Council required annual communion; such evidence as we have suggests that few people received much more than annually, if that often. To the end of the Middle Ages, the Eucharist was used perhaps more as a focus for devotion than as a sacrament.

General Trends in Devotionalism

This brief survey scarcely covers the forms of late medieval devotionalism exhaustively. Even from what has been said, however, certain general conclusions emerge.

First, the developments that occurred in late medieval piety were essentially cumulative. Little of significance was lost, and much was added, as time progressed. The Virgin was represented as Queen of Heaven but also as a humble servant of God. The sufferings of Christ were graphically portrayed, but at times he appeared also as the regal conqueror of death. Sermons and devotional treatises used narrative detail to evoke compassion, yet earlier modes of allegorical interpretation persisted. For this reason it is misleading to characterize the emerging devotionalism of the later Middle Ages as a shift from one tendency to another. Instead, what one finds are proliferating variations on traditional themes.

Second, the devotions that evolved were often imitative. The Rosary, meditations on the passion, and books of hours were so many lay imitations of the monastic hours. Stations of the Cross originated as substitutes for the pilgrimage to Jerusalem. Those who could do so, particularly Christians from the social or clerical elites, made the greater devotional commitment; new devotions were often quite literally poor people's (or middle classes') substitutes for other pious exercises.

Third, devotions of all kinds tended to center on some sort of sacred space, public or private. The focal point in the sacred space which defined it as distinctively holy was an object set apart for veneration: a relic, a consecrated Host, or a work of art. The Rosary might be said anywhere, but it is not coincidental that the legendary nun who said 150 Ave Marias daily did so before an image of the Virgin. Typical settings for devotion were churches and chapels, but statues and paintings could convert part of a home into a makeshift oratory.

Fourth, the intermediate position of devotions, between the public acts of liturgy and the private act of contemplation, provided not just for flexibility but also for a sense of linkage between church and home. Like Roman Catholic children who play at celebrating Mass, pious Christians of the late Middle Ages could show their "churchliness" by bringing home with them what they had seen in churches and chapels. The sword was, however, double-edged: while showing their affiliation with the church, they were also in some measure making themselves independent of it. Domestic devotions could breed either a sense of attachment to the church or a feeling of detachment from it. From this perspective it is not surprising that a land like Germany, teeming with "churchliness," could give birth to the Reformation.

Fifth, devotionalism often went hand in hand with particularism. A confraternity, with its special devotional exercises, was a kind of miniature church—an *ecclesiola in ecclesia*, as one scholar has put it.[27] Devotions could thus become symbolic reinforcement for social or political boundaries within society. A town devoted to a particular saint was cultivating *its* saint as a symbol of civic pride. Even in a Corpus Christi procession, different guilds and confraternities rivaled each other with their banners and other items of display. Devotions could serve to unite the church: Marian piety linked devotees from throughout Christendom, and pilgrims returning from the Roman jubilee might bring home a heightened devotion to the holy city and even to its bishop. Probably more often, however, the effect was divisive.

Sixth, devotions represent a mixture of clerical and lay initiative. It is generally impossible to tell where the true initiative lay. Was it laypeople who promoted a particular saint's cult and clergy who responded with enthusiasm? Was it the clerics who wrote and supervised production of a given play and the people who then joined as actors and spectators? Seldom can we give clear and full answers. Perhaps the best symbols of this mixed culture are the macaronic poems where the clerical Latin is interspersed with the lay vernacular, though works of this sort were presumably penned by clerics for lay consumption. One of the most common ways for the clergy to promote devotions was by indulgences: prayers, pilgrimages, veneration of the consecrated Host, and other devotional acts could be performed for their inherent value and also for the indulgences attached. The system of indulgences had originated as a way of encouraging crusaders to wage war, but by the time Boniface VII proclaimed the jubilee indulgence for 1300 the institution of the devotional indulgence was already well established.

Excursus: Penance and Penitence

Whether one can properly speak of "penitential devotion" is not a simple question. If devotions are defined in terms of their objects, it would seem that penitence is not devotional: one can speak in the same way of devotion to the Virgin or to a saint, but one cannot speak of devotion to penitence. Yet the very linkage between devotions and indulgence suggests a strong penitential element to late medieval devotionalism. There were many reasons for joining in pious exercises, but one of the strongest motives was to gain indulgences and thus obtain remission of the punishment for one's sins. In other ways as well devotions and penitence intersected. One of Mary's most important functions was to protect sinners and win mercy for them at the throne of judgment. On the other hand, devotion to the passion heightened the conviction of guilt for one's sins: it was the sins of humankind, including those of the devotee, that caused Christ to undergo his torments. While the penitential spirituality of the late Middle Ages may not be per se a kind of devotion, it is nonetheless an important ingredient in the devotionalism of the era.[28]

The foundations for late medieval penitential practice were laid in 1215 at the Fourth Lateran Council. The twenty-first canon of this council, *Omnis utriusque sexus,* has been referred to as "perhaps the most important legislative act in the history of the Church."[29] Requiring annual confession for all, it subjected the laity to clerical authority and gave the clergy greater opportunity than ever before to learn about and to guide the lives of the people. The relevant provisions of the canon are essentially six. First, every faithful Christian who has reached the age of discretion must confess his or her sins at least once a year and carry out the penance that the priest imposes. Second, anyone who fails to do this will be denied entrance into church (or, upon death, ecclesiastical burial). Third, this statute should be proclaimed often in churches so that no one can claim ignorance of it. Fourth, the confession must be to one's own priest, and only with his permission can one confess instead to another priest and receive absolution for one's sins. Fifth, the priest must be discreet and careful; like an experienced physician he must apply wine and oil (cf. Luke 10:34) to the penitent's spiritual wounds, and he must inquire about the circumstances of the sin and of the sinner, so as to give proper counsel and suggest fitting remedy for the habit of sin. Sixth, the priest must be careful not to betray the secrecy of the confession; if he needs to consult anyone for counsel he must do so without revealing the penitent's name, for if he reveals a sin told him in confession he will be deposed from priestly office and sentenced to perpetual punishment in monastic confinement. The most important of these provisions were the first, which laid out the duties of the faithful, and the fifth, which specified the basic responsibilities of the priests.

This legislation provoked a flood of literature on confession, written to teach both priests and laity how they should comply with its requirements. Some of it was technical writing by theologians or canon lawyers: seven questions (containing forty articles) in the supplement to Thomas Aquinas's *Summa Theologiae* deal with the sacrament of penance, and much of the detail in Thomas's discussion of virtue and vices is clearly inspired by the needs of the confessional. More relevant for present purposes, however, are works written for laypersons and preachers—writings which in their didactic tone resemble much of the era's devotional literature.

In the mid-fifteenth century a German priest named Johannes Wolff drew up an examination of conscience and had it published.[30] His pamphlet illustrates the kind of popular penitential literature that flourished in his day. He gives counsel for children who are just learning to confess their sins, and then provides aid for adults, who are assumed to be more advanced in the art of confession, if not in sinning. Children reflecting on whether they have violated the commandment "Thou shalt not kill" are advised to consider whether any of the following applies to them: "I threw snowballs and stones twice with my friends. Four times I scuffled with them, got into blows with them, knocked them about, hit them. For a long time I have borne anger, envy, enmity against them in my heart.... I have thrown things at people's chickens, ducks, and geese. I killed the emperor with a battle-axe." At this point the priest is to interrupt, "Be careful to tell the truth!" Under the heading "Thou shalt not steal" the fledgling penitents are to ponder yet more possibilities: "I have stolen pens, paper, wooden shoes, etc., from my companions seven times. I have taken pears, apples, nuts, cheese, rolls, from my mother three times.... I found a small coin and didn't return it.... I stole ten thousand guilders from the town council at Frankfurt." Again the confessor breaks in, "Take care, and don't lie!"

One of the most entertaining compendia of guidance on confession is the third book of Caesarius of Heisterbach's *Dialogue on Miracles*.[31] Caesarius gives stories illustrating the power of confession: at times those who have just confessed their sins have miraculous abilities, such as the power to defeat strong adversaries in single combat! More often, his tales show the correct and incorrect ways of confessing one's sins, the dangers of failing to carry out one's assigned penance, and so forth. One of Caesarius's exempla is about a woman in Cologne who went to confess her sins one Lent but had nothing to say but praise for her own good deeds. Asked why she did not instead tell her sins, she was flummoxed and claimed she had committed none. The priest then asked her what she did for a living, and she said she sold scrap iron. The confessor asked whether she ever put smaller pieces of iron into bundles along with larger ones, to deceive her customers, and when she acknowledged this misdeed he informed her that it was a mortal sin. Likewise, every time she lied, perjured herself, maligned her rivals, or was envious of those more successful in the trade than she—for these offenses she would burn in hell unless she atoned by vigorous penance.

From various sources we get some notion of how confession was carried out. Typically the penitent knelt before the priest in a public place (not a confessional), greeted the priest piously, and received the response, "The Lord be with you." Preliminary inquiry, if needed, gave the confessor some basic information on the penitent's marital status, profession, and place of residence. A brief catechetical session ensued, in which the priest might ascertain whether the penitent knew the Pater Noster, the Ave Maria, and the Apostles' Creed. Then the priest was to exhort the penitent to confess all his sins properly without being held back by shame. Following these preliminary stages, the penitent told all the sins he could remember, typically incorporating them into an adapted form of the Confiteor (or liturgical profession of sin). The confessor was not to be content with this recitation of sins, however, but was to probe further. Using any of various schemas (the Ten Commandments, the seven deadly sins, etc.), he was to ask in some detail whether the penitent had perhaps neglected to confess this or that offense—but not in such detail as to give fresh ideas for later sin! (A penitential manual ascribed to Richard Rolle instructs the priest to ask whether a male penitent has emitted his seed "in any other way except the natural way with his wife," but if the penitent wants examples of what the priest has in mind, the latter should immediately close his eyes and "proceed cautiously to something else.") Then the priest was to assign penance and give absolution. Upon leaving, the penitent was expected (though not required) to give the priest alms and request his prayers.[32]

The penance given in confession might itself be some form of devotional exercise: a few prayers at the least, or for some serious offense perhaps even a pilgrimage. The widespread tendency was toward lenience in selection of penance. Richard Rolle suggests that the confessor remind the penitent of the church's earlier severity in these matters, but then impose merely a Pater Noster or Ave Maria, or the endurance of ordinary labors and hardships as a form of penance, leaving the rest for the sinner to make up in purgatory. "And it is far better to give a light penance so that the sinner will perform it and thus go to purgatory, than to give a heavy and burdensome penance which the sinner fails to perform and so goes to hell." He then cites Christ himself as an example; Christ never assigned heavy penance, but even told the adulterous woman merely "Go and sin no more." In this as in other ways, the confessor was to comfort as well as discipline the confessing Christian.[33]

* * * * *

Virtually all the manifestations of devotion we have surveyed became intensely controversial in the sixteenth century. One of the abuses that aroused Martin Luther's wrath was an indulgence granted for a visiting display of relics. When he set out to purify the church, devotionalism was one of his targets—though of course there have always been Protestant forms of devotionalism. Having found them useless in his own life, he jettisoned them in the practice he laid down for others. He could accommodate the concept of sainthood, but not the veneration of saints he had learned in his own youth. He retained the institution of confession, but stripped it of its sacramental and disciplinary character. While maintaining the doctrine of Christ's real presence in the Eucharist, he repudiated the notion of transubstantiation—in part because of the magical conceptions it had spawned. Like earlier critics he saw devotionalism as focusing attention unduly on outward practice; unlike most of his predecessors he had a theology that accorded outward deeds no inherent value for sanctification or salvation. Works of discipline and charity remained important as manifestations of inner faith, but devotions reflected nothing but a Pelagian quest for salvation through works. Whatever their disagreement on other matters, the other Reformers shared these views with Luther.

Devotional fervor persisted in Roman Catholicism, however, and underwent further development in the Counter-Reformation and through the modern era. One of the most striking effects of the reforms following Vatican II was the severe reaction against this continuing devotionalism. But whether the interplay between devotional piety and puritanism is a linear or a cyclical process is a question beyond the bounds of historical inquiry.

Notes

1. J. Huizinga, *The Waning of the Middle Ages;* Bernd Moeller, "Piety in Germany around 1500," in *The Reformation in Medieval Perspective,* ed. Steven E. Ozment (Chicago: Quadrangle, 1971) 50–75.

2. Rainer Rudolf, *Ars moriendi: Von der Kunst des heilsamen Lebens und Sterbens* (Cologne: Böhlau, 1957).

3. Francis Edwards, *Ritual and Drama: The Mediaeval Theatre* (Guildford: Lutterworth, 1976).

4. David L. Jeffrey, *The Early English Lyric and Franciscan Spirituality.*

5. Saint Bernardino of Siena, *Sermons,* ed. Nazareno Orlandi; trans. Helen Josephine Robins (Siena: Tipografia sociale, 1920); Bernardinus Senensis, *Opera omnia* (Quaracchi: Collegium S. Bonaventurae, 1950–65).

6. Hans H. Hofstätter, *Art of the Late Middle Ages,* trans. Robert Erich Wolf (New York: Abrams, 1968); Emile Mâle, *Religious Art;* Gertrud Schiller, *Iconography of Christian Art.*

7. Henry Charles Lea, *A History of Auricular Confession and Indulgences in the Latin Church* (Philadelphia: Lea, 1896) vol. 3.

8. Orlandi's edition gives various sermons that stress the significance of the Holy Name (e.g., no. 18) and the evils of factions and their banners (e.g., no. 17).

9. Carl Richstaetter sets this theme in a broad context in *Christusfrömmigkeit in ihrer historischen Entfaltung: Ein quellenmässiger Beitrag zur Geschichte des Gebetes und des mystischen Innenlebens der Kirche* (Cologne: Bächem, 1949).

10. On this see especially Herbert Thurston, *The Stations of the Cross: An Account of their History and Devotional Purpose* (reprint, London: Burns & Oates, 1914) 1–61.

11. See especially Thurston, *Stations,* 46–95.

12. *The Sermons of Thomas Brinton, Bishop of Rochester (1373–1389),* ed. Sister Mary Aquinas Devlin (London: Royal Historical Society, 1954) 1:87–94.

13. Sister John Sullivan's *A Study of the Themes of the Sacred Passion in the Medieval Cycle Plays* (Washington, DC: Catholic University of America Press, 1943) is useful especially for the sources of material for the plays.

14. Richard Kieckhefer, *Unquiet Souls,* chap. 4.

15. See especially Stephan Beissel, *Geschichte der Verehrung Marias in Deutschland während des Mittelalters: Ein Beitrag zur Religionswissenschaft und Kunstgeschichte* (Freiburg i. Br.: Herder, 1909). Useful material can be found also in Marina Warner, *Alone of All Her Sex: The Myth and the Cult of the Virgin Mary* (New York: Knopf, 1976). For Marian theology, see especially Hilda C. Graef, *Mary: A History of Doctrine and Devotion* (New York: Sheed & Ward, 1963–65).

16. Eric Walram Kemp, *Canonization and Authority in the Western Church* (London: Oxford University Press, 1948); André Vauchez, *La sainteté en occident aux dernières siècles du moyen âge, d'après les procès de canonisation et les documents hagiographiques* (Bibliothèque des études françaises d'Athènes et de Rome 241; Rome: École Française de Rome, 1981); Donald Weinstein and Rudolph M. Bell, *Saints and Society: The Two Worlds of Western Christendom, 1000–1700* (Chicago: University of Chicago Press, 1982); an exceptionally useful bibliography can be found in *Saints and Their Cults: Studies in Religious Sociology, Folklore and History,* ed. Stephen Wilson (Cambridge: University Press, 1983).

17. See the dissertation (unfortunately not yet published) of M. G. Dickson, "Patterns of European Sanctity: The Saints in the Later Middle Ages (with Special Reference to Perugia)" (Edinburgh University, 1975) 1:133, 136–37.

18. Ibid., tables between pp. 85 and 86.

19. Ibid., 95, 99–100.

20. Dietrich Kurze, "Zur Ketzergeschichte der Mark Brandenburg und Pommerns, vornehmlich im 14. Jahrhundert: Luziferianer, Putzkeller und Waldenser," *Jahrbuch für die Geschichte Mittel- und Ostdeutschlands* 16/17 (1968) 85 and n. 189.

21. Dickson, "Patterns," 292–302.

22. This is a central theme of Kieckhefer, *Unquiet Souls.*

23. Peter Browe, *Die Verehrung der Eucharistie im Mittelalter* (Munich: Huebner, 1933); for the theology especially, see also Edouard Dumoutet, *Le désire de voir l'hostie et les origines de la dévotion au Saint-Sacrament* (Paris: Beauchesne, 1926).

24. Romuald Bauerreiss, *Pie Jesu: Das Schmerzensmann-Bild und sein Einfluss auf die mittelalterliche Frömmigkeit* (Munich: Widmann, 1931) 15–107.

25. In the Germanisches Nationalmuseum, Nuremberg.

26. Caroline Bynum, *Jesus as Mother: Studies in the Spirituality of the High Middle Ages* (Berkeley and Los Angeles: University of California Press, 1982) esp. 256–58.

27. Otto Clemen, *Die Volksfrömmigkeit des ausgehenden Mittelalters* (Dresden and Leipzig: Studien zur religiösen Volkskunde, 1937) 7.

28. Lea, *History of Auricular Confession;* more recently, Thomas N. Tentler, *Sin and Confession on the Eve of the Reformation* (Princeton, NJ: Princeton University Press, 1977); and Nicole Bériou, "Autour de Latran IV (1215): La naissance de la confession moderne et sa diffusion," in Group de la Bussiére, *Pratiques de la confession des Pères du désert à Vatican II: Quinze études d'histoire* (Paris: Cerf, 1983) 73–136.

29. Lea, *History,* 1:230.

30. Clemen, *Volksfrömmigkeit,* 38–41.

31. Caesarius of Heisterbach, *The Dialogue on Miracles,* trans. H. von E. Scott and C. C. Swinton Bland (London: Routledge, 1929).

32. Tentler, *Sin and Confession,* 82–95; John Philip Daly, *An Edition of the* Judica Me Deus *of Richard Rolle* (Salzburg: Institut für Anglistik und Amerikanistik, 1984) 54–55, 106.

33. Daly, *Edition,* 56–57., 106. The combination of discipline and consolation is a main theme in Tentler, *Sin and Confession.*

Bibliography

Boase, T. S. R. *Death in the Middle Ages: Mortality, Judgment and Remembrance.* New York: McGraw-Hill, 1972. Covers both literature and art.

Brooke, Rosalind B., and Christopher Brooke. *Popular Religion in the Middle Ages: Western Europe, 1000–1300.* London: Thames & Hudson. Good for early manifestations of devotionalism.

Coulton, George Gordon. *Five Centuries of Religion.* Cambridge: University Press, 1923–50. Dated and tendentious, but a useful mine of information.

Gougaud, Louis. *Devotional and Ascetic Practices in the Middle Ages.* Translated by L. Gougard and G. C. Bateman. London: Burns, Oates & Washbourne, 1927. Collection of essays; old but useful.

Huizinga, J. *The Waning of the Middle Ages: A Study of the Forms of Life, Thought and Art in France and the Netherlands in the XIVth and XVth Centuries.* Translated by F. Hopman. London: Arnold, 1924. A classic.

Jeffrey, David L. *The Early English Lyric and Franciscan Spirituality.* Lincoln: University of Nebraska Press, 1975. Indicates the pervasiveness of Franciscan influence.

Kieckhefer, Richard. *Unquiet Souls: Fourteenth-Century Saints and Their Religious Milieu.* Chicago: University of Chicago Press, 1984. Chapter on devotion to the passion is especially relevant.

Leff, Gordon. *The Dissolution of the Medieval Outlook: An Essay on the Intellectual and Spiritual Change in the Fourteenth Century.* New York: Harper, 1976. More an interpretive essay than an introduction.

Mâle, Emile. *Religious Art: From the Twelfth to the Eighteenth Century.* Rev. English ed. Princeton, NJ: Princeton University Press, 1982. The broadest of several works by this important author.

Manselli, Raoul. *La religion populaire au Moyen Age: Problèmes de méthod et d'histoire.* Montreal: Institut d'Etudes Médiévales Albert-le-Grand, 1975.

Oakley, Francis. *The Western Church in the Later Middle Ages.* Ithaca, NY: Cornell University Press, 1979. A particularly useful synthesis of religious and ecclesiastical life.

Rothkrug, Lionel. *Religious Practices and Collective Perceptions: Hidden Homologies in the Renaissance and Reformation=Historical Reflections* 7/1 (Spring 1980). Rich and provocative essay on German shrines and on much else as well.

Schiller, Gertrud. *Iconography of Christian Art.* Translated by Janet Seligman. London: Humphries, 1971–72. Exceptionally detailed synthesis.

Sumption, Jonathan. *Pilgrimage: An Image of Mediaeval Religion.* London: Faber & Faber, 1975.

Trinkaus, Charles, and H. Oberman, eds. *The Pursuit of Holiness in Late Medieval and Renaissance Religion: Papers from the University of Michigan Conference.* Studies in Medieval and Reformation Thought 10. Leiden: Brill, 1974. An important collection of articles.

Wilmart, André. *Auteurs spirituels et textes dévots du moyen âge latin: Etudes d'histoire littéraire.* Reprint. Paris: Etudes Augustiniennes, 1971. A classic series of essays on prayers and other devotional texts.

4

Spirituality and Late Scholasticism

WILLIAM J. COURTENAY

Few areas of late medieval life seem as removed from spirituality as the university classrooms of late scholasticism. The highly abstract, rational, logic-oriented theology of the late Middle Ages or the career-conscious goals of the average student of arts, theology, and canon law seem to contrast markedly with the deeply emotional religious commitment associated with monastic spirituality or the various forms of lay piety. When sixteenth-century reformers decried the debilitating effects of Aristotelian logic and canon law on Christian theology, they decried to a large extent the curriculum and focus of late medieval universities that prepared students in a form of scholasticism seemingly devoid of spirituality. Thus, in looking for piety among late scholastics, one must search beneath the surface of more familiar aspects of university life. This essay will therefore examine, however briefly, the place of biblical studies, biographies of individual scholars, and features of late scholasticism that link it closely with the spirituality of late medieval mysticism and with the *devotio moderna*.

Religious Life within the University

Most university scholars before the sixteenth century, even those whose academic aspirations lay no higher than the arts degree, expected to pursue church careers after the university. To be a student was to be a cleric and under ecclesiastical authority and law. Some students were already in religious orders, had come to the university through those agencies, and would continue in their service after the university. Others expected to receive an ecclesiastical living, either as a parish priest or as the recipient of a benefice while attached to the household of some prelate or governmental official. No matter how secular some of those later careers may have been, they functioned within an institution that was also the bearer of religious life and spirituality for the Christian world.

What was expected of the religious life of university scholars? Probably far more than was achieved. Churches within university districts held daily services. Their bells marked the beginning and end of instruction and disputations. They were the scene of examinations, promotions, and magisterial meetings. Students were expected to attend Mass on a regular basis. Theological students were engaged in the study of the Bible and moral theology as well as speculative theology centered on the *Sentences* of Peter Lombard.

In addition to the study of the Bible, theological students were required to preach at various points in their academic career. The periods as biblical bachelor and bachelor of the *Sentences* began and ended with sermons given by the candidate. His inception as *magister* also usually contained the obligation to preach a sermon. All of these sermons before the late fourteenth century, however, tended to be more academic than religious, inasmuch as they displayed the knowledge and wit of the candidate far more than the degree of his religious insight, depth, or commitment.

Religious houses of study and, to a lesser degree, secular colleges served to promote and ensure some form of communal religious life in the midst of a worldly setting. The mendicant orders established convents in university towns at the very beginning of their entrance into academic life. Later in the thirteenth century, monastic orders responded to the needs of young monks already attending universities by creating houses of study to protect their students from the dangers posed by life in the streets and halls of Bologna, Paris, or Oxford. Colleges were initially founded to provide room and board for poor students and a proper atmosphere for study, but they soon came to serve a secondary purpose of protecting moral virtue and providing something of a communal religious life, centered in the college chapel.

Among all these opportunities and safeguards for the spiritual life of university students and masters, the role of Scripture in the theological faculty is of utmost importance, for it was around the place and meaning of Scripture that the crises of university spirituality took place.

The Place of the Bible in Late Scholasticism

It is well known that from the entrance of the mendicant orders into universities beginning around 1230 until the last decades of the fourteenth century the religious orders dominated university biblical studies.[1] Secular theologians and Austin Canons, who had contributed so much in the twelfth century, did not in the thirteenth, as is sometimes suggested, concentrate their attention on scholastic theology, leaving scriptural teaching and exegesis to the mendicants. The most prominent theologians in the period from 1230 to 1280, with a few exceptions, were mendicants, who produced both speculative theology and biblical commentaries, while their secular colleagues produced comparatively little in either area.

In assessing the changing status of biblical studies in universities of northern Europe in the next two centuries, one must be careful to distinguish between what was provided by way of regular teaching, what was circulated in manuscript form, and what evidence of the latter has survived into our day. Every university maintaining a faculty of theology required its theological students, both secular and religious, to attend lectures on the Bible for several years before becoming a bachelor of theology. It was also an obligation of masters of theology to provide those lectures on the Bible—the major teaching responsibility of regent masters. There is no reason to doubt that most fulfilled that task in some form or other. Abundant scriptural citations and analogies used in the scholastic works of the late Middle Ages attest to extensive familiarity with the content of the Bible for almost any late medieval theologian.

Perhaps nothing illustrates better the relative disparity between the actual importance of the Bible and the amount of time devoted to it by theological bachelors than the cases of Paris and Oxford in the early fourteenth century. At Paris the first stage of the baccalaureate consisted of one or more years as biblical *cursor* (bachelor lecturer on the Bible). Only after the successful completion of this could one be admitted to lecture on the *Sentences*. At Oxford a newly formed bachelor read on the *Sentences* before reading on the Bible, the latter activity being reduced in the fourteenth century to a semester or a short series of lectures given during summer vacation. On the surface this suggests that biblical study played a far smaller role for students at Oxford and that the concentration of the theological curriculum was centered on speculative theology approached through the techniques of logic and physics. The difference in this matter between Paris and Oxford, however, may not have been that great. Roughly the same amount of time attending biblical lectures, the same availability of magisterial lectures on the Bible, the wide biblical knowledge displayed throughout most scholastic theological treatises, commentaries, *questiones*, and *summa*, and the impressive biblical commentaries produced by Oxford masters—albeit only the mendicants until the 1370s—suggest that the Bible remained as fundamental a part of the late medieval theological curriculum in England as on the Continent.

Having said that, it must also be noted that production and dissemination of biblical commentaries (not necessarily biblical teaching or learning) declined among university scholars in the fourteenth century, even among mendicants. From Godfrey of Fontaines to Nicole Oresme, inclusive, no biblical commentaries have survived from Parisian secular theologians. Similarly, the rich array of contemporary Oxford secular masters, including Walter Burley, Richard Fitzralph, and Thomas Bradwardine, left behind no specific works of biblical scholarship. What is more remarkable, leading university theologians in the religious orders of that period contributed very few biblical commentaries. This is not so surprising for those who never attained the doctorate (William of Ockham and probably John of Mirecourt) or for those whose regency and subsequent teaching were cut short by death (John Duns Scotus), but it is surprising that we have no commentaries or biblical works from Durand of St. Pourçain, Francis Mayronnis, Thomas of Strasbourg, Gregory of Rimini, or Hugolino of Orvieto at Paris, nor from William of Alnwick, John of Reading, John of Rodington, Walter Chatton, or Robert of Halifax at Oxford. Mystical writers from or beyond the fringe of universities, such as Rudolf of Biberach and Richard Rolle, contributed far more. The first three decades of the fourteenth century saw the last of any extensive biblical work among Parisian mendicants for some time: Alexander of Alexandria, Peter Aureoli, and Gerard Odonis among the Franciscans; Peter Palude, James of Lausanne, and Meister Eckhart among the Dominicans; Augustinus Triumphus and Michael of Massa among the Augustinians; and John Baconthorp among the Carmelites. The only mendicant biblical commentators of any note in the period between 1330 and 1370 were English, and of those the only one of first rank whose works were popular enough to survive in number was Robert Holcot.[2]

When university biblical commentaries began to reappear late in the third quarter of the fourteenth century, the impetus was as much from secular theologians as from religious, and more from Prague and Oxford than from Paris. (A further change is the number of bachelor lectures on biblical texts that were preserved.) The list begins with Henry Totting of Oyta's bachelor lectures at Prague in 1362–1367 on the Gospel of Mark, followed soon by the Austin Friar John Klenkok's magisterial lectures on Matthew and Acts, probably both given at Prague during the years 1365–1372. At the same time the Italian Carmelite Michael Aiguani lectured on Luke, Paul's letter to the Romans, and Psalms during his regencies at Paris (1362–1379) and Bologna (1380–1400). Paris, however, retained its new-found importance as a center for biblical study. Pierre d'Ailly, as theological bachelor, lectured there between 1374 and 1381 on the opening chapters of Genesis, on Psalms, and the Song of Songs. He wrote various treatises, questions, and sermons relating to Scripture. Moreover, beginning in 1381 Peter Gracilis, O.E.S.A., began his lengthy lectures on the Gospel of Luke, and Peter of Candia, a Franciscan and the future Alexander V, began his lectures on the Apocalypse. The predominant attraction of Old Testament books in the first half of the fourteenth century, especially the wisdom literature, gave way in the late fourteenth to a renewed interest in the New Testament.

The most crucial events in the development of biblical studies in the late fourteenth century were the treatises and commentaries of John Wyclif, especially those on the Gospels and Pauline epistles written during the period 1375–1384, and his translation of portions of the Bible into English. Despite the orthodoxy of his treatment of Scripture, the storm raised by his other opinions in combination with his thoroughgoing biblicism reawakened the fear that the Bible might become the vehicle for the dissemination of heresy, particularly if insufficient attention were given to it among orthodox theologians in the universities.

Wyclif's death in 1384 marked a turning point in a renewed commitment to biblical study in universities, especially among secular theologians. Henry Totting of Oyta at Prague (1381–1384) and Vienna (1384–1397) gave extensive lectures on the Gospel of John and on the Psalms. A Prague contemporary of Oyta, Matthew of Janov, who also taught at Paris and who wrote at Prague in 1389–1392 the six books of his *De regulis novi et veteris testamenti*, expressed a spiritual attachment to the Bible that went well beyond the historical and anagogical glosses of the thirteenth and early fourteenth centuries. Henry Heimbuch of Langenstein began his lengthy lectures on Genesis at Vienna in 1385. Vienna, in fact, became a center for biblical commentaries, rivaled only by Prague in the late fourteenth century and by Cracow in the fifteenth. But other universities contributed as well. The turn of the fourteenth century was to see the monumental exegetical works of Jean Gerson at Paris, Marsilius of Inghen at Heidelberg, Nicholas of Dinkelsbühl at Vienna, and James of Soest at Prague and Cologne. The challenge of the Hussite movement in the first half of the fifteenth century only made this commitment to orthodox exegesis all the more important.

The production of scriptural commentaries continued throughout the fifteenth century at almost the late fourteenth-century level. Vienna and Cracow were the two most active university centers, although Heidelberg contributed a significant number. The majority of commentators were secular theologians, most of them German. Among all, the New Testament was slightly favored over the Old, and the most frequently chosen books of earlier generations remained popular: the Psalms, the Gospel of Matthew, and the Apocalypse.

Against Vain Curiosity

Throughout the fourteenth century the Bible had remained a source for scholastic theology, and for many scriptural commentaries done by scholastics—for example, those of Holcot—the techniques and questions of the schools of that age were used to interpret or at least treat biblical texts. In addition, the massive commentaries of the late fourteenth and the early fifteenth century became windows on the world, filled with social, political, scientific, and theological views by and on that age. Those produced by university scholars, however, were seldom written with the devotional life of the author or reader in mind. This very dichotomy between the religious message of Scripture and the indifferent and sometimes contrary assumptions and language of the classroom bothered many in their post-university years, even among those who wrote no biblical commentaries.

Thomas Bradwardine, while chancellor of St. Paul's in London in the early 1340s, looked back on his study of philosophy at Oxford with just such an attitude.

> Idle and unlearned in the knowledge of God when I was pursuing philosophical studies, I was tempted away by an unorthodox error. I sometimes heard the theologians deal with the question [grace], and the position of Pelagius seemed to me nearest to truth. . . . At the schools of philosophy I rarely used to hear about grace, except in an ambiguous way. But the whole day I would hear that we are masters of our own free acts and that it is in our own power to do good or evil, to have virtues or sins, and many things like that. . . . And if sometimes I heard Paul magnify grace and belittle free will in the Epistle reading in church, as is the case in Romans 9: "So then it is not of him that willeth, nor of him that runneth, but of God that sheweth mercy," and many similar things, then that view of grace displeased me, ungrateful as I was.
>
> However, even before I became a theological student [ca. 1325] the text mentioned came to me as a beam of grace and in a mental representation of the truth I thought I saw from afar how the grace of God precedes all good works in time and in nature: that is, the gracious will of God, who in both these ways wills before hand that he who does deserving works should be saved, and who in the natural medium performs the man's merits in him earlier than he does himself, since in all movements He is the first Mover.[3]

Even more to the point is the contemporary and oft-cited observation of Richard Fitzralph, written around 1340 at the papal court in Avignon:

> Nor were You, the Solid Truth, absent from me those six years [at the Court of Rome], but in Your Holy Scriptures you shone upon me as in a certain

8. Andrea Orcagna, *St. Thomas Aquinas as the Personification of Wisdom,* ca. 1354-1357. Santa Maria Novella, Florence.

radiant mirror; whereas in my former years, in the trifles of the philosophers, you had been hidden from me as in a certain dark cloud. For previously I used to think that through the teachings of Aristotle and certain argumentations that were profound only to men profound in *vanity*, I used to think that I had penetrated to the depths of Your Truth with the citizens of Your Heaven; until You, the Solid Truth, shone upon me in Your Scriptures, scattering the cloud of my error, and showing me how I was croaking in the marshes with the toads and frogs. For until I had You the Truth to lead me, I had heard, but did not understand, the tumult of the philosophers chattering against You, the pertinacious Jews, the proud Greeks, the carnal Saracens, and the unlearned Armenians. . . . At last, O Solid Truth, You so shone upon me from above, that I burned to seize and to hold You, the Truth, Jesus promised to us in the Law and Prophets. And when in the turmoil of lawsuits a certain spell of serenity had smiled upon me, I sought You in Your sacred Scriptures, intimately and importunately, not only by reading, but also by prayer, until You came to meet me joyously in Your ways.[4]

These biographical reflections contrast the world of university philosophy and the world of late medieval spirituality. Not only do they express one of the deeply felt needs that occasioned a more vigorous exploration of the Bible within late medieval universities, but they are also a chapter in the recurring medieval theme of religious wisdom (*sapientia*) against speculation for its own sake (*contra vanam curiositatem*) based on the long-standing Augustinian and monastic contrast between wisdom generating humility (*sapientia-humilitas*) and knowledge generating pride (*scientia-superbia*).[5] The fourteenth century was a particularly volatile time for this issue. In 1344 the General Chapter of the Dominicans, presumably with Paris in mind, criticized those who in lecturing fall into the folly of vain speech and curiosity (*hanc vaniloquii et curiositatis stultitiam*), and in 1346 the attack on free-ranging study (*de scientiis vanis et curiosis*) was renewed.[6] Later in the same year in a letter to the University of Paris, Clement VI recommended that theological study be based on the text of the Bible, "where no harm of vanity and curiosity is found" (*ubi plane nulla vanitatis et curiositatis noxia reperitur*).[7]

The problem was not with terminist logic or mathematical physics per se, nor even with the use of theological *sophismata*, which became popular first in English theology (ca. 1328) and then at Paris (ca. 1340).[8] The concern was with an approach to theology that seemingly neglected the importance of orthodox doctrine, ignored the intention of scripture, or separated itself from religious and moral meaning. The sentiments expressed by Fitzralph and Bradwardine, the scriptural commentaries of Holcot and Oyta, and the spiritual writings of d'Ailly and Gerson reflect the reality of a blending of the rigorous and critical *scientia* of late scholasticism with the renewed religious sensitivity of that age. Gerson's lectures to the Parisian theological faculty in 1402, *Contra curiositatem studentium,* show the compatibility of the new critical philosophy and theology associated with nominalism and the spiritual renewal that was a principal feature of the *devotio moderna.*[9] The influence of Gerson's treatise on the treatment of *curiositas* in the *Imitatio Christi* (3.4.3) is only one of many illustrations.

Vita Contemplativa–Vita Activa

With Gerson not only have we reached the frontier between the fourteenth and the fifteenth century; we have reached a figure who, more than anyone else, seems to have combined the critical, analytical dimensions of late scholasticism with a thoroughgoing commitment to the mystical life. Like d'Ailly, Gerson was in logic a champion of terminism and nominalism against the *Modistae* and *Scotistae* of his day. Many of his theological presuppositions parallel those of Ockham and d'Ailly. Yet, at the same time, he ranks as one of the major spiritual leaders of the early fifteenth century.

How one combines or understands the blending of nominalism and mysticism in Gerson remains one of the critical problems of late medieval scholarship. Earlier in this century Walter Dress found the link in the reduced claims of Ockhamist natural theology, where the inability to prove and know God through reason and nature drove the thirsting soul of the "modern" theologian into the *via negativa* of Pseudo-Dionysian mysticism.[10] If there was no ultimate identity between divine reason and the physical and moral structure of this world, then the *vita contemplativa* was the only way of reaching God. Heiko Oberman, in contrast, developed a more positive link.[11] The theology of Ockham, with its stress on will, on human ability to reach out toward God by attempting one's best (*facere quod in se est*), and the covenantal nature of God's relation with the world and an individual's relation with God shaped Gerson's mysticism into an affective, will-focused, penitential, and nonelitist type of mysticism typical of the spiritual writers of the fifteenth century in contrast to some of those in the fourteenth. More recently Steven Ozment has reminded us that ultimately mystical experience in any form, including Gerson's, depends upon direct contact with the divine that is not satisfied with and therefore goes beyond the verbal agreements, the covenantal structure of the created world.[12] The world of God's ordained plan (*potentia ordinata*) that sufficed for Ockham is transcended in the mystical experience where one meets God face to face.

There are two questions here. One is abstract or conceptual: Can Gerson's mysticism be compatible with nominalist presuppositions and, if so, how? The second is historical: In what areas and to what degree was Gerson a nominalist? Beginning with the second question, Gerson was as much as d'Ailly a defender of terminist logic. That fact and his close attachment to his Ockhamist master, friend, and former chancellor, d'Ailly, have led most scholars to assume that Gerson was a nominalist in most aspects of his thought. The problem facing the historian, however, is that the corpus of Gerson's writings do not lend themselves as well to exploring the areas of philosophy and theology usually discussed under "nominalism" as do the writings of Ockham or d'Ailly.

Conceptually, however, there seems less of a problem with the compatibility of nominalism and mysticism than suggested by Ozment. The views of Dress and Oberman, although they stress different aspects of nominalism (the negative link of nominalist epistemology and the positive link of nominalist theology, respectively), are not mutually exclusive but, rather, reinforce each other in establishing the conceptual possibility of such a link. Moreover, the mystical experience need not take one into a form of actualized *potentia absoluta* beyond the realm of *potentia ordinata*. Inasmuch as any miraculous suspension of the normal operation of God's ordained laws as well as any *raptus* experience outside the normal course of religious experience was planned and foreknown by God, it falls within the total, foreordained will of God and is only a special ordination in contrast to the normal operation of things. There is nothing about Ockham's world view that limits a "nominalist" only to the world of everyday order or religious opportunities that are open to all.

The dimension of practical piety that is apparent throughout almost all the writings of Gerson, even the academic, magisterial works, is a dimension that is shared by most fifteenth-century scholastics. This is true of those who, like Dionysius Ryckel the Carthusian and Antoninus of Florence, follow the lead of Thomas in theology, as well as those who follow Ockham and d'Ailly, such as Gerson, Eggelinus Becker of Braunschweig and Gabriel Biel. These last two figures perhaps illustrate better than others the late medieval blending of scholasticism and spirituality. Becker, after education at Erfurt and Cologne, lectured around 1450 to the cathedral chapter at Mainz on the text of the Mass, lectures that were altered and redelivered by Gabriel Biel at Tübingen toward the end of the century. Biel's *Expositio canonis missae* was an extensive and balanced integration of nominalist theology and late medieval spirituality. Both Becker and Biel lived their spirituality outside the university setting. After his years in Mainz, Becker served as confessor and spiritual adviser to Carthusian and Dominican communities in Strasbourg. Biel, an Ockhamist in most aspects of his philosophy and theology and for a time professor of theology at the newly founded University of Tübingen, served most of his life as a noted preacher—first at

Mainz then in the Rheingau, Butzbach, and Tübingen—as well as a leader of the Brethren of the Common Life in southern Germany. Biel's dual "citizenship" in the *via moderna* and the *devotio moderna* illustrates the compatibility of these two movements.[13] Becker and Biel were, on the eve of the Reformation, two of many examples that could be given of the blending of late scholasticism and spirituality—a blending already apparent in Fitzralph and Mayronnis, expanded by the English Carmelites and by d'Ailly, and which reached full flower in the fifteenth century in the writings of Gerson, Ryckel, and Biel.

Notes

1. Beryl Smalley, *The Study of the Bible in the Middle Ages,* 196–373; idem, "The Bible in the Medieval Schools," in *The Cambridge History of the Bible,* 2:197–220.

2. On the commentaries and manuscripts of the individuals named, see Friedrich Stegmüller, *Repertorium Biblicum Medii Aevi;* for Holcot, see B. Smalley, *English Friars and Antiquity,* 133–202.

3. Thomas Bradwardine, *Summa de causa Dei contra Pelagium,* ed. Henry Savile (London, 1618) p. 308, cited in Heiko Oberman, *Archbishop Thomas Bradwardine, A Fourteenth-Century Augustinian* (Utrecht: Uitgevers-Maatschappij, 1958) 14–15.

4. Translated by L. L. Hammerich, *The Beginning of the Strife between Richard FitzRalph and the Mendicants* (Copenhagen: Kgl. Danske Viderskabernes Selskab, 1938) 20, cited from W. A. Pantin, *The English Church in the Fourteenth Century,* 132–33.

5. André Cabassut, "Curiosité," in *Dict. Sp.* 2, cols. 2654–61; H. A. Oberman, *Contra vanam curiositatem.*

6. *Chartularium Universitatis Parisiensis,* ed. H. Denifle and E. Chatelain, (Paris, 1891) 2:550 (#1091); 2:591 (#1127).

7. Ibid., 2:588.

8. On the interrelation of philosophy and theology in the fourteenth century and, in particular, on the development of a sophismatical approach to theology, see John E. Murdoch, "*Mathesis in philosophiam:* The Rise and Development of the Application of Mathematics in Fourteenth Century Philosophy and Theology," in *Arts libéraux et philosophie au moyen âge: Actes du quatrième congrès international de philosophie médiévale* (Montreal and Paris: Institut d'études médiévales and J. Vrin, 1969) 215–54; idem, "From Social into Intellectual Factors: An Aspect of the Unitary Character of Late Medieval Learning," in *The Cultural Context of Medieval Learning,* ed. J. E. Murdoch and E. D. Sylla (Dordrecht: D. Reidel, 1975) 271–348; idem, "*Subtilitates Anglicanae* in Fourteenth-Century Paris: John of Mirecourt and Peter Ceffons," in *Machaut's World: Science and Art in the Fourteenth Century,* ed. M. P. Cosman and B. Chandler (Annals of the New York Academy of Sciences 314; New York: New York Academy of Sciences, 1978) 51–86; Neal Ward Gilbert, "Richard de Bury and the 'Quires of Yesterday's Sophisms,'" in *Philosophy and Humanism: Renaissance Essays in Honor of Paul Oskar Kristeller,* ed. Edward P. Mahoney (New York: Columbia University Press, 1976) 229–57; W. J. Courtenay and K. H. Tachau, "Ockham, Ockhamists, and the English-German Nation at Paris, 1339–1341," *History of Universities* 2 (1982) 53–96.

9. Jean Gerson, *Oeuvres complètes,* ed. P. Glorieux, vol. 3, *L'oeuvre magistrale* (Paris:

Desclée, 1962) 224–49; Steven Ozment, *Jean Gerson* (Textus Minores 38; Leiden: Brill, 1969) 26–45, 82–84.

10. W. Dress, *Die Theologie Gersons.*

11. H. A. Oberman, *The Harvest of Medieval Theology,* 323–60.

12. S. Ozment, "Mysticism, Nominalism and Dissent," 67–92.

13. H. A. Oberman, *Masters of the Reformation: The Emergence of a New Intellectual Climate in Europe,* ed. D. Martin (Cambridge: University Press, 1981) 45: "The first three 'modernists' in Tübingen, Gabriel Biel, Wendelin Steinbach, and Peter Braun, were also Brethren of the Common Life and thereby at the same time members of both the *via moderna* and *devotio moderna.*"

Bibliography

Cabassut, André. "Curiosité. In *Dict. Sp.* 2, cols. 2654–61.

Dress, Walter. *Die Theologie Gersons: Eine Untersuchung zur Verbindung von Nominalismus und Mystik in Spätmittelalter.* Gütersloh: Bertelsmann, 1931.

Oberman, Heiko A. *Contra vanam curiositatem.* Theologische Studien 113. Zurich: Theologischer Verlag, 1974.

———. *The Harvest of Medieval Theology.* Cambridge, MA: Harvard University Press, 1963.

Ozment, Steven. "Mysticism, Nominalism and Dissent." In *The Pursuit of Holiness in Late Medieval and Renaissance Religion: Papers from the University of Michigan Conference,* 67–92. Edited by C. Trinkaus and H. Oberman. Studies in Medieval and Reformation Thought 10. Leiden: Brill, 1974.

Pantin, W. A. *The English Church in the Fourteenth Century.* Notre Dame, IN: University of Notre Dame Press, 1962.

Smalley, Beryl. "The Bible in the Medieval Schools." In *The Cambridge History of the Bible.* Vol. 2, *The West from the Fathers to the Reformation,* 187–220. Edited by G. W. H. Lampe. Cambridge: University Press, 1969.

———. *English Friars and Antiquity in the Early Fourteenth Century.* Oxford: Blackwell, 1960.

———. *The Study of the Bible in the Middle Ages.* Notre Dame, IN: University of Notre Dame Press, 1964.

Stegmüller, Friedrich. *Repertorium Biblicum Medii Aevi.* 11 vols. Madrid: Instituto Francisco Suárez, 1940–80.

5

Religious Women in the Later Middle Ages

CAROLINE WALKER BYNUM

THE LATER MIDDLE AGES, especially the period from the late twelfth century to the early fourteenth, witnessed a significant increase in opportunities for women to participate in specialized religious roles and saw a great proliferation in the types of roles available. The number of female saints increased markedly. Women's piety—whether monastic or lay—took on certain distinctive characteristics, which powerful males, both secular and clerical, noted, sometimes with awe and sometimes with suspicion. For the first time in Christian history, we can identify a woman's movement (the beguines) and can speak of specifically female influences on the development of piety. Indeed, that affective spirituality against which both Protestant and Roman Catholic reformations reacted—a spirituality based on effusive confidence in human capacity to imitate Christ—was in part a creation of the religious women of late medieval Europe.

New Forms of Religious Life

Being a nun was almost the only specialized religious role available to women in the early Middle Ages. (Canonesses, who appeared in the Carolingian period, were very similar to nuns but took less strict vows of poverty.) The history of early medieval nuns is complex, and recent research suggests that there was more variation over time than earlier historians noticed both in the influence of nunneries (and abbesses) on the surrounding society and in society's respect for the piety of married laywomen. But, however powerful certain ladies may have been either as abbesses or as saintly queens, specialized religious roles for women were usually restricted to the high aristocracy. In the tenth and early eleventh centuries—a grim period of war and hardship for western Europe—few female monasteries were founded and religious leaders showed little concern for encouraging women's religiosity. The major monastic reform of the period, Cluny, founded scores of male monasteries but only one house for nuns before 1100, and its purpose was to provide a retreat for women whose husbands wished to become Cluniac monks. Although we have no idea what proportion of the population of medieval Europe belonged to religious houses, we are certain that monks vastly outnumbered nuns before 1200. In the course of the twelfth and thirteenth centuries, especially in the Rhineland and the low countries, this began to change.

The proliferation in the late eleventh and twelfth centuries of wandering preachers who drew after them bands of followers determined to "imitate the apostolic life" in poverty and penitence had such a significant impact on women that contemporary chroniclers commented on the phenomenon, as much with trepidation as with admiration. Women flocked after wandering evangelists, such as Norbert of Xanten (d. 1134) and Robert of Arbrissel (d. 1116–1117), and these preachers—ambivalent about itinerant preaching even for themslves and clearly hostile to it as a form of female piety— founded monasteries for them. Double monasteries (i e., communities with both male and female houses, often side by side) emerged again in England, where there was also a significant increase in the number of female recluses (women who vowed themselves to a life of withdrawal in little cells attached to churches). On the Continent, two of the most prestigious "new orders" of the twelfth century, the Premonstratensians and the Cistercians, found the number of women's houses in their ranks growing at an alarming speed. The story of female enthusiasm institutionalized as strict monasticism repeated itself in the early thirteenth century when Clare of Assisi (d. 1253) tried to follow Francis in the mendicant life but was forced to accept a strictly cloistered role.

Women were not only followers, manipulated and circumscribed in their religious ideals by powerful clerics; they were leaders and reformers as well. In the thirteenth century, when Benedictine monasticism for men was eclipsed by the friars, an Italian woman, Santuccia Carabotti, founded a convent near Gubbio, enforced a strict interpretation of the Benedictine rule there, and later reformed and supervised twenty-four other monasteries, taking them under her direction. In the early fifteenth century, Colette of Corbie, who began her religious life as a hermit, reformed many convents of Poor Clares in France and Flanders and founded others, creating a strict group of Franciscan nuns, which survives in many parts of the world today.

The rapid growth of women's houses put strains on the resources of the new orders, which had to provide clergy for the women's spiritual direction and sacramental needs. The Premonstratensians were the first to pass legislation curtailing women's monasteries. Twentieth-century historians, among them R. W. Southern in an influential textbook, have stressed the misogyny behind their response. But recent research has shown that male reluctance and opposition did little to slow the growth of women's religious life. In eastern areas (like Franconia and Bavaria), women even continued to attach themselves to the Premonstratensian order. The Cistercian decree of 1228 forbidding the incorporation of any more convents remained a dead letter, and throughout the thirteenth century Cistercian nunneries proliferated (often with support from local Dominicans) in the low countries and the lower Rhineland. Although some monks, canons, and friars did resist taking responsibility for the pastoral care of nuns, some religious authorities from popes to local clergy, and some prominent laymen supported and endowed women's houses. Both Santuccia and Colette, for example, received significant support from popes and papal legates. In the thirteenth and early fourteenth centuries, these women's monasteries formed influential spiritual networks among themselves and produced collections of the sisters' lives and visions that were often read in both female and male houses as a form of spiritual instruction. In some parts of Europe, where male houses declined fairly steadily after the thirteenth century, both in economic base and in religious fervor, nuns were a majority of the cloistered religious by the fifteenth century.

In the twelfth and thirteenth centuries, new forms of religious life for women also appeared alongside the old Benedictine nunneries and the female monasteries of the new orders. Some of women's religious opportunities were heterodox, and historians are still debating the extent to which women were proportionally overrepresented in the major heresies of the twelfth to the fourteenth centuries: dualists or Albigensians, antisacerdotal reformers (e.g., the Waldensians and Humiliati), and those aberrant mystics commonly known as the Free Spirits. It seems clear that women were powerfully drawn to such movements, at least in their initial phases before they too developed hierarchical structures that tended to exclude female leadership. But it also seems clear that these movements, which were often initially labeled "heresies" for reasons of ecclesiastical politics—not doctrine—expressed many of the basic themes found in women's religiosity in its orthodox forms: a concern for affective religious response, an extreme form of penitential asceticism, an emphasis both on Christ's humanity and on the inspiration of the Spirit, and a bypassing of clerical authority. Thus, it may not be the case that women flocked to the heresies because they felt neglected by or alienated from the church; it may rather be that certain spiritual impulses, which characterized both heterodox and orthodox movements, appealed especially to women and were generated in significant part by them.

Indeed, the same impulses that issued in the various heretical movements produced new quasi-religious roles for women within the church. These roles were not so much novel institutional arrangements as simply ways of giving religious significance to women's ordinary lives. In the north of Europe (especially northern France, the low countries, Switzerland, and the Rhineland), we find women called "beguines." (The etymology of the word is debated, but it may be a slur, derived from "Albigensian"–that is, heretic.) These women chose to set themselves apart from the world by living austere, poor, chaste lives, in which manual labor and charitable service were joined to worship (which was not, however, rigidly prescribed as it was in convents). At least initially they contrasted sharply with traditional monasticism by not taking vows and having no complex organization and rules, no order linking their houses, no hierarchy of officials, no wealthy founders or leaders. In the south of Europe (especially Italy), paralleling the beguines, we find the "tertiaries"–individuals living in the world who affiliated with one of the great mendicant orders (usually Franciscan or Dominican) and followed a life of penitential asceticism, charitable activity, and prayer. In Spain, women in such quasi-religious statuses were known as *beatas*. All over Europe, even ordinary laywomen sometimes found, in the temporary institution of pilgrimage, a way of setting themselves off from the demands of the world in a special religious role of devotion, service, and penitence.

Early in our own century, some historians argued that the wandering evangelists of the twelfth century (heterodox and orthodox), the mendicants, tertiaries, beguines, and Free Spirits of the thirteenth and fourteenth centuries were movements of protest by the new urban lower classes. These historians saw tertiary and beguine groups as female guilds, with essentially economic functions. More recently scholars have taken the religious nature of such movements seriously and have disproved the claim of predominantly lower class membership. But it seems clear that the new groups can be associated with specific social statuses. Although the new orders and movements of the twelfth century began with aristocratic clerics and recruited from both town and countryside, thirtenth-century beguines, tertiaries, and even to some extent Cistercian nuns tended to be drawn from the new bourgeoisie or from a lower nobility associated with the towns. Thus, women who joined the new types of religious life available in the thirteenth and fourteenth centuries often came from social groups that were rising and can be shown to have felt anxiety about their new wealth and status. Their ideal—as their most distinguished historian, Herbert Grundmann, pointed out years ago—was not simply austerity but rather *renunciation*

9. Giovanni di Paolo, *St. Catherine and the Beggar,* 15th century.

of comfort and wealth. Women from the old nobility were apt to join traditional monastic establishments (Benedictine nunneries or houses of canonesses), which required large dowries from entrants.

Two explanations for the emergence of new types of female religious life have recently been popular. One suggests demographic causes: these were the daughters for whom no husbands could be found. The other argues that the women who became beguines, tertiaries, or heretics were simply a religious surplus, left on the fringes to attempt some kind of quasi-religious life after Premonstratensian and Cistercian doors closed and the friars showed reluctance to expand their pastorate to large numbers of nuns. Both explanations are plausible. There were in fact demographic factors behind all late medieval religious movements. The structure of the medieval family and of inheritance necessitated alternative roles to marriage and procreation for a large portion of the population. And in the thirteenth and fourteenth centuries, the value of dowries went sharply up, making the marriage of daughters (or even the endowing of a place for them in one of the traditional monasteries) sometimes prohibitively expensive. Moreover, there is much late medieval evidence of male resistance to the care of nuns and male suspicion of female mysticism.

Yet it seems wrong to interpret the beguines, tertiaries, and female heretics of the later Middle Ages mainly as surplus women, settling for quasi-religious roles because neither husbands nor monasteries could be found. On the contrary, the lives of individual women show many cases where beguine or tertiary status was chosen in preference to monastic life by noble women who could have afforded to enter monasteries. The recent research of John Freed has demonstrated that, far from inhibiting the growth of nunneries, friars and local clergy often encouraged them. It is not clear that there was a great shortage of places, at least in Cistercian convents. It thus appears that the beguines were less an unintended result of pastoral negligence than a new and attractive alternative because of their contrast to traditional cloistered life. Moreover, for many girls, it was the presence, not the absence, of a prospective bridegroom that activated desire for perpetual chastity. Although there were unquestionably young women who desired to leave monasteries to which they had been given, there were also many daughters forced into marriage or threatened with it who saw the convent as an escape. The dangers of childbirth and the brutality of many marriages—disadvantages pointed out by medieval moralists—led some women to prefer celibacy. But, more than this, virginity was seen by both men and women as a positive and compelling religious ideal. Set apart from the world by intact boundaries, her flesh untouched by ordinary flesh, the virgin (like Christ's mother, the perpetual virgin) was also a bride, destined for a higher consummation. She scintillated with fertility and power. Into her body, as into the eucharistic bread on the altar, poured the inspiration of the Spirit and the fullness of the humanity of Christ.

Not only did the period from 1100 to 1400 see the creation of new types of religious life for women. The number of women saints (both those canonized and those who simply acquired some reputation for sanctity) also increased—a clear indication of the growing prominence of women both in reflecting and in creating piety. There was always resistance on the part of church authorities to the canonization of women. Although the number of canonization inquiries for women rose, it was consistently the case that a smaller percentage of those women considered for canonization actually achieved it than was true for men. But recent scholarly investigations—whether they work from actual canonizations or from lists of those popularly revered—suggest that the percentage of saints who were female rose from less than 10 percent in the eleventh century to about 28 percent in the fifteenth. According to Donald Weinstein and Rudolph Bell, the big rise came between the twelfth and the thirteenth century, when the percentage of female saints doubled (from 11.8 percent to 22.6 percent), and the rise continued into the fifteenth century (to 27.7 percent), despite the fact that the total number of saints declined. In the sixteenth and seventeenth centuries, when the total number of saints turned slightly upward, the percentage of women dropped sharply (to 18 percent in the sixteenth century, 14.4 percent in the seventeenth). Not only did the percentage of female saints rise sharply between the twelfth century and the thirteenth; the percentage of married saints rose as well. And, throughout the period, women represented a consistently higher percentage of the married saints than did men, although Weinstein, Bell, and A. Vauchez suggest, on the basis of qualitative evidence, that a new ambivalence about marriage emerged in the fifteenth century. The rise in the number and percentage of women saints correlates also with a broadening of the class base of saints (although a higher percentage of saintly women than of saintly men were from the upper class) and with a rise both in the percentage of saints from urban areas and in the percentage of saints affiliated with mendicant orders (although mendicant women met with very great resistance to their canonizations). The rise of the woman saint correlates most dramatically, however, with the rise of the lay saint. Indeed, by the end of the Middle Ages, the lay male saint had virtually disappeared. Nuns (the only "non-lay" female role) continued, of course, to be canonized; but, by the sixteenth century, those males canonized were almost exclusively clerics, and the model of holy behavior offered to the Roman Catholic laity was almost exclusively a female model. According to Vauchez, women were 50 percent of the laity canonized in the thirteenth century and 71.4 percent after 1305.

Connected to the emergence of new quasi-religious opportunities for laywomen and to the increasing veneration of certain laywomen as holy were two other trends: the decline and disappearance of quasi-clerical roles for women, and the increased suspicion, from the early fourteenth century on, of exactly those prophetic and visionary powers of holy women that contrasted most sharply with male clerical authority, based as it was on ordination. In the church of the tenth to twelfth centuries, women did exercise some "clerical" roles—preaching, hearing confessions from nuns under them, bestowing blessings, and sometimes administering communion to themselves in rituals known as "masses without priests." But such practices were increasingly criticized and suppressed. The decretalist Bernard of Parma, in his commentary (ca. 1245), argued that, whatever might be found in earlier practice, women could not teach or preach, touch sacred vessels, veil or absolve nuns, or exercise judgment and that, "in general, the office of a man is forbidden to women."[1] The powerful abbesses of the early Middle Ages are seldom found in the later period. Those double monasteries over which women ruled were mostly eliminated by the thirteenth century. Although women in the world who were revered as saints were more apt than saintly men to come from the highest social ranks, those within monasteries who were revered were often not abbesses or prioresses but rather ordinary sisters, blessed with paramystical and visionary experiences. Thus, from the thirteenth century on, we find religious women losing roles that paralleled or aped male clerical leadership but gaining both the possibility of shaping their own religious experiences in lay communities and a clear alternative—the prophetic alternative—to the male role based on the power of office.

The female religious role had only to become clear to be met with suspicion. After the early fourteenth century, there was increased hostility to the forms and the themes of women's religiosity. In 1310, a woman mystic, Marguerite Porete, was accused of the Free Spirit heresy and was burned in Paris; the beguines were suppressed by the Council of Vienne (1311–1312), although the decree remained unenforced for several years and, after mid-century, the women's movement (in a far more monasticized—i.e., institutionalized form) was once again permitted. The spiritual friendships and networks of thirteenth- and early-fourteenth-century women attenuated as the fourteenth century wore on. Collective biographies of women by women disappeared. Fewer holy women wrote. Male suspicion of visionary women was articulated in a series of influential works, by John Gerson and others, on the testing of spirits. Even female eucharistic fervor was sometimes curtailed or opposed by theologians like Albert the Great, who argued that frequent communion might encourage superficiality of spiritual response in women, who were by nature given to "levity."[2] In late-fourteenth- and early-fifteenth-century hagiography, holy women appear more and more isolated and male-oriented. Their stories are now usually told by their confessors. And they both dominate these confessors as spiritual mothers and cling to them as vulnerable advisees, needful of a guarantee of orthodoxy. Although holy women were, by the fourteenth and fifteenth centuries, more likely to be lay and married and more likely to reside in the world and have opportunities for significant geographical mobility through pilgrimage, they were also more subject to male scrutiny and more in danger of accusations for heresy or witchcraft. By the time of Catherine of Siena (d. 1380), Bridget of Sweden (d. 1373) and Joan of Arc (d. 1431), the influence—even the survival—of pious women depended almost wholly on the success, in ecclesiastical and secular politics, of their male adherents.

Suspicion of prophetic women reflected the general fourteenth century suspicion of popular religious movements and of mysticism. The period was one of deep hostility to visionary and mystical males as well. But the ambivalence of church authorities and theologians about women mystics was also a reflection of virulent misogyny—misogyny that issued in both the actual witch accusations and the witch-hunting theology of the fifteenth century. By 1500, indeed, the model of the female saint, expressed both in popular veneration and in official canonizations, was in many ways the mirror image of society's notion of the witch. Each was thought to be possessed, whether by God or by Satan; each seemed able to read the minds and hearts of others with uncanny shrewdness; each was suspected of flying through the air, whether in a witches' sabbath or in saintly levitation or bilocation. Moreover, each bore mysterious wounds—whether stigmata or the marks of incubi—on her body. The similarity of witch and saint—at least in the eyes of the theologians, canon lawyers, inquisitors, and male hagiographers (who are, by the fifteenth century, almost our only source for their lives)—suggests how threatening both were to clerical authorities. (A number of women saints were suspected of witchcraft or demonic possession—e.g., Catherine of Siena, Lidwina of Schiedam [d. 1433], and Columba of Rieti [d. 1501].) Woman's religious role as inspired vessel had come to seem utterly different from man's religious role as priest, preacher, and leader by virtue of clerical office. And because it seemed so different, it titillated—and was both encouraged and feared.

Female Spirituality: Diversities and Unities

Canonesses, nuns of "old" and "new" orders, beguines, tertiaries, recluses, Albigensians, Waldensians, pilgrims, ordinary laywomen in shops and kitchens—there were many kinds of pious women in later medieval Europe.

Yet the increasingly sharp contrast between lay female saint and clerical male saint suggests that behind the wide variety of women's roles a unity can be found. We can in fact delineate some consistent differences between male and female religious experiences.

Some at least of women's forms of life (e.g., tertiaries and beguines) were less institutionalized than men's. Indeed, the tendency of later historians to try to identify pious women with a particular order has obscured the extent to which, especially in the thirteenth century, institutional affiliation and structure were, to women, unimportant or constantly changing. The thirteenth-century saint Juliana of Cornillon, for example, wandered from religious house to religious house; Christina the Astonishing (d. 1224)— despite later efforts to claim her as Benedictine, Cistercian, and Premonstratensian—was simply a laywoman seeking to follow Christ and the saints; Margaret of Ypres (d. 1237), although on the edge of Dominican circles, sought not a particular order with its articulated goals but a male protector, whom she could love and depend on. The very fact that male chroniclers felt that they ought to tell the story of the founding of the beguines as if the "order" had a leader and a rule like those of contemporary monastic or mendicant orders suggests that women's more informal arrangements for giving religious significance to ordinary life seemed odd and dangerous to male sensibilities.

Moreover, the life patterns of holy women show basic differences from those of men. In their recent quantitative study of saints' lives, Weinstein and Bell have demonstrated that, in general, women's saintly vocations grew slowly through childhood and into adolescence; a disproportionate percentage of female saints were certain of their commitment to virginity before age eight. Despite the fact that both chastity and marital status were more central themes in the *Vitae* (written lives) of women than of men, male saints were far more likely to undergo abrupt adolescent conversions, involving renunciation of wealth, power, marriage, and sexuality. Crisis and decisive change were more significant motifs in male *Vitae* than in female throughout the later Middle Ages. This was in part because medieval men had greater ability than women to determine the shape of their lives. For example, Mary of Oignies (d. 1213) and Clare of Assisi, wishing to renounce property, were virtually forced to retain income and servants; saints like Margaret of Cortona (d. 1297), Umiliana dei Cerchi (d. 1246), and Angela of Foligno (d. 1309) had to wait for the death of husbands or lovers before espousing chastity; women like the holy invalid Lidwina of Schiedam or the poets Hadewijch and Mechthild of Magdeburg were as cruelly persecuted and neglected at the end of their lives as during the childhood and adolescent stirrings of their vocations. Indeed, hagiographers operated with a somewhat inconsistent double model of the female adolescent. The virtuous girl might demonstrate her virtue either by insisting heroically on chastity (and thereby rebelling against family) or by obediently marrying at her parents' command (and thereby retreating from what the church argued to be a higher good); frequently, in saints' *Vitae*, she did both with no explanation of what the change from one behavior to the other meant to her or cost her. It is because women lacked control over their wealth and marital status that their life stories show fewer heroic gestures of casting money, property, and family away. But women's lives also seem less characterized by radical renunciations and reversals because women tended to use their ordinary experiences (of powerlessness, of service and nurturing, of disease, etc.) as symbols into which they poured ever deeper and more paradoxical meanings, and because both men and women tended to see female saints as models of suffering, male saints as models of action.

When we compare the writings as well as the *Vitae* of men and women, we find that there are no pious practices or devotional themes that are exclusively female or exclusively male, although there are certain miracles that occur only to priests (because they are connected to sacerdotal functions) and certain miracles (e.g., stigmata or bodily elongation) that occur far more frequently to women. Men and women thought in the same metaphors—for they read the same Scriptures and spiritual treatises and often heard the same sermons—and many spiritual themes that modern commentators have assumed to be gender-specific (e.g., the vision of nursing the Christ-child or of being pregnant with Jesus) are found in the visions and writings of both sexes in the Middle Ages.[3] But recent comparative study of vision literature, saints' lives, and mystical treatises by women and men suggests that there are different patterns in male and female spirituality.

Mysticism was more central in female religiosity and in female claims to sanctity than in men's, and paramystical phenomena (trances, levitation, stigmata, miraculous *inedia*, etc.) were far more common in women's mysticism. Women's reputations for holiness were more often based on supernatural, charismatic authority, especially visions and supernatural signs. Women's devotion was more marked by penitential asceticism, particularly self-inflicted suffering, extreme fasting and illness borne with patience. Women's writing was, in general, more affective, although male writing too brims over with tears and sensibility; erotic, nuptial themes, which were first articulated by men, were most fully elaborated in women's poetry. And certain devotional emphases, particularly devotion to Christ's suffering humanity and to the Eucharist (although not, as is often said, to the Virgin) were characteristic of women's practices and women's words. It was a woman, Juliana of Cornillon, who got the feast of Corpus Christi added to the liturgical calendar, and the cult of the Sacred Heart had its origins in the devotions of certain religious women in Flanders and Saxony.

Some female mystics (e.g., the Cistercian Ida of Louvain, the Vallombrosan abbess Margaret of Faenza, and the Carthusian Marguerite of Oingt) received visions of cradling or suckling the Christ-child. Some (e.g., the beguine Hadewijch, the Cistercian Beatrice of Nazareth, the Dominican tertiary Catherine of Siena, and the English laywoman Margery Kempe) united with the beautiful young bridegroom Jesus in a frenzy which they themselves described as orgasm or insanity. Some (e.g., the beguine Mary of Oignies, the English visionary and theologian Julian of Norwich, and the German nun Lukardis of Oberweimar) joined with the death agonies of the body on the cross, either by praying for disease and death or by mutilating their bodies in the form of the wounds of Christ. The description of religious women in the low countries, given by James of Vitry in the early thirteenth century, could easily be taken to characterize the piety of European nuns, beguines, and tertiaries during the next two hundred years:

> Some of these women dissolved with such a particular and marvellous love toward God that they languished with desire and for years had rarely been able to rise from their beds. They had no other infirmity, save that their souls were melted with desire of him, and, sweetly resting with the Lord, as they were comforted in spirit they were weakened in body. . . . The cheeks of one were seen to waste away, while her soul was liquified with the greatness of her love. Many had the taste of honey sensibly in their mouths because of the gift of spiritual sweetness in their hearts. . . . Another's flow of tears had made visible furrows down her face. . . . Others were drawn with such intoxication of spirit that in sacred silence they would remain quiet a whole day . . . so that they could not be roused by clamor or feel a blow. . . . Some in receiving the bread of him who came down from heaven obtained not only refreshment in their hearts but also a palpable consolation in their mouths sweeter than honey and the honeycomb. . . . [They] languished with such desire for the sacrament that they could not be sustained . . . unless their souls were frequently refreshed by the sweetness of this food.[4]

Nor did such languishing in desire for the body of God prohibit very active service of neighbor. Equally typical of female piety is the story of a woman's basket of bread for the poor which turns into roses when a husband (or father) objects to her almsgiving—a story told apocryphally of at least five medieval women, the most famous among them the saintly princess Elizabeth of Hungary (d. 1231). Indeed, women saw their very helplessness and suffering as an *imitatio Christi* that brought salvation to neighbor as well as self. Alice of Schaerbeke (d. 1250) supposedly said to her beloved companion, after losing her right eye to leprosy: "Dear sister, do not grieve [for me]; and do not think that I suffer for or expiate my own sins; I suffer rather

10. Master of Heilinginkreuz. *The Death of St. Clare,* early 15th century.

for those who are already dead and in the place of penitence [i.e., purgatory] and for the sins of the world. . . ."[5]

Recent scholarship demonstrates that differences between the sexes override all other factors (such as chronology, differences in social and economic status, etc.) in shaping women's piety. A pious peasant woman and a pious noble woman were more like each other in religiosity than either was like the male saint of her social status. But differences among women can also be delineated. Recent work, for example, suggests certain regional patterns. Scholars like Weinstein, Bell, Vauchez, and R. Kieckhefer agree that women saints in the north of Europe were more aristocratic and contemplative—more apt to be nuns or recluses and to find a basis for their sanctity in withdrawal and prayer—whereas female saints in the south of Europe, particularly Italy (which accounts for about a third of the saints of the later Middle Ages), tended to be urban, middle-class, and more active in works of charity. Recluses were more numerous in England; mystical communities in which many nuns experienced the same or similar visions were more common in the Rhineland (especially in the thirteenth century); charitable service, particularly care of the poor and sick, was especially common among Italian women affiliated with the Dominican and Franciscan orders.

Moreover, there were differences in women's spirituality that stemmed from their different religious statuses and life experiences. A study of women's own writings suggests that women who lived in the world (either as tertiaries and beguines or as laywomen) and women who converted as adults contrasted with nuns raised in convents by having a sharper sense of male/female differences, a sense of "the female" closer to the negative stereotype found in the misogynist clerical tradition, and a less intense sense of community. Women in the world or converted from the world as adults were more aware of the prohibition of sacramental functions and teaching to women, more apt to see the female as weak and vulnerable, more male-oriented (i.e., more dependent on confessors or powerful male religious leaders, not to mention husbands and fathers), and more concerned with male power and male roles (although the concern is often a critique). For example, the thirteenth-century Italian tertiary, Angela of Foligno, spoke far more frequently of her spiritual "sons" (i.e., the friars) than of any female companions. Converted as an adult after the deaths of her mother, husband, and children, Angela channeled her maternal and her spiritual impulses into criticizing and advising the local Franciscans. The German beguine Mechthild of Magdeburg, who fled her family and friends in young adulthood, directed her considerable rhetorical abilities into castigating the local diocesan clergy and friars. In the life of the twelfth-century recluse Christina of Markyate, who ran away on her wedding night, most of the visions and prophecies were for the benefit of powerful males. And in the fourteenth and fifteenth centuries, the tertiary Catherine of Siena and laywomen as different as Bridget of Sweden (later a nun) and Joan of Arc were advisers and leaders of men. In contrast, women in convents and beguinages, especially when they had been raised there, had a strong sense of spiritual networks or families of women. Michael Goodich has pointed out that mystical women in the thirteenth and early fourteenth centuries—especially in Germany and the low countries—existed in clusters, whereas male mystics were more often isolated and less influential. So common did the clustering of mystical women become by the early fourteenth century that contemporaries tended to revere houses, like Töss and Engelthal, rather than individuals. For those who had experienced such community, like the Flemish beguine Hadewijch, who was evicted from her beguinage, the grieving for lost companions was intense and never healed.

We should not, however, make too much of regional differences or of differences between nuns and quasi religious, between child oblates and adult converts. Certain towns of the thirteenth-century low countries and Rhineland produced a piety more like that of the Italian female tertiaries than the work of Vauchez, Weinstein, and Bell suggests. The sharp contrast between a more contemplative and mystical role for northern women and more active charity in southern women is blurred when we read the women's own words and find that a stress on service *and* ecstatic encounter underlay both kinds of lives. Moreover, however querulous and apologetic some medieval women occasionally seem (and this quality increases in the fifteenth and sixteenth centuries), they differed from each other relatively little in self-image, and their vulnerability seldom inhibited the confidence with which they approached God. Cloistered women were as likely as women in the world to use graphic "domestic" images for self and Christ. Women (like Gertrude of Helfta) who entered the convent as tiny girls equaled women in the world (like Gertrude van Oosten or Margery Kempe) in their maternal tenderness toward the baby Jesus and their erotic yearnings toward the beautiful young Christ. Although it is true that nuns were more likely to use imagery androgynously and to speak with self-confidence about their own advising role, tertiaries and laywomen in fact castigated, advised, and comforted others just as eagerly and effectively. Moreover, whatever their status or degree of vulnerability, religious women did not feel any necessity for acquiring metaphorical maleness in the course of their spiritual journey. Male biographers frequently praised women for "virility," and women, like Catherine of Siena, sometimes urged other women (and men) to behave "manfully." But women's most elaborate self-images were either female ("mother" to spiritual children, "bride" of Christ) or androgynous ("child" to a God who was mother as well as father, "judge" and "nurse" to the souls in their keeping).

Methodological Observations

Most of our information on late medieval women comes from male biographers and chroniclers. The problem of perspective is thus acute. Some of the stories men liked to tell about women reflected not so much what women did as what men admired or abhorred. Male biographers romanticized and sentimentalized female virtue more than male, especially by describing it (as does James of Vitry in the passage quoted above) in heightened and erotic imagery. They were also far more likely to attribute sexual or bodily temptations to women's natures than to men's (men's sexual yearnings could always be blamed on the presence of women as temptresses!) and to see women struggling unsuccessfully to overcome the flesh. It is crucial not to take as women's own self-image the sentimentalizing or the castigating of the female in which medieval men indulged. If we wish to understand what it meant to medieval women to be "brides of Christ" or symbols of either mercy or fleshliness, we must pay particular attention to what women said and did, avoiding the assumption that they simply internalized the rhetoric of theologians, confessors, or husbands.

It is therefore especially important for future historians to turn to detailed study of those works in which women wrote about their own visions and mystical experiences and about life among the sisters in their households, beguinages, and convents. Such works—letters, vision collections, nuns' books or collective biographies, hagiography, rules, religious poetry, treatises of spiritual advice, and even autobiography—proliferated, especially in the thirteenth century, as the growth of written vernacular languages gave women new access to literary expression despite their exclusion from the theological training offered in universities. Historians of late medieval religion (especially of the thirteenth and early fourteenth centuries) have a direct access to women's experiences, of which they have taken too little advantage.

Sorting out the images of woman and the experiences of women in late medieval piety, with appropriate attention to the differing vantage points from which men and women viewed these matters, is far from easy. But recent research has done much to retrieve stories of women and to describe women's spirituality. It has, however, tended to focus on the renunciation of wealth, privilege, and sexuality in women's religiosity as in men's. This is because the work has been done from two perspectives—that of the feminist and that of the traditional medievalist. Feminist scholarship has tended to concentrate on the negative stereotyping of women's sexuality and on women's lack of worldly power and sacerdotal authority. It has done so because these issues are of such pressing modern concern. The work of traditional medievalists, although attempting to start from the vantage point of medieval people themselves, has tended in fact to use male religiosity as a model. When studying women, it has tended to look simply for women's answers to the questions we have always asked about men—questions that were generated in the first place by observing male religiosity. And medieval men were deeply concerned, for themselves and for women, with the renunciation of sexual gratification and of economic and political power. Thus, recent work on medieval women has often been heavily influenced by male models and presentist issues. The religious significance of food, disease, and body—aspects of human experience that were of particular interest to women—has been neglected, while sexuality and wealth have been repeatedly explored, both as religious images and as religious renunciations. The task for future historians of women's piety is not only to devote more detailed study to texts by women but also to pay attention to the full range of phenomena in those texts, no matter how masochistic or altruistic, unattractive or heroic, peculiar, amusing, or charming such phenomena may seem, either by modern standards or by those of medieval men.

Notes

1. Quoted in Francine Cardman, "The Medieval Question of Women and Orders," *The Thomist* 42 (1978) 596.

2. Albert the Great, *Commentarii in IV Sententiarum*, dist. 13, art. 27, in *Opera omnia*, ed. August Borgnet (Paris: Ludovicus Vivès, 1894) 29:378-80, and *Liber de sacramento Eucharistiae*, dist. 6, tract. 4, chap. 3, in *Opera*, 38:432 (1899).

3. A monk of Villers supposedly received the Christ-child at his breast in a vision; see Ernest W. McDonnell, *Beguines and Beghards*, 328; and Peter Browe, *Die Eucharistischen Wunder des Mittelalters* (Breslauer Studien zur historischen Theologie, n.F. 4; Breslau: Muller & Seiffert, 1938) 106. Caesarius of Heisterbach tells of a priest who swelled in spiritual pregnancy; Caesarius, *Dialogus miraculorum*, ed. Joseph Strange (2 vols.; Cologne: J. M. Heberle, 1851) bk. 9, chap. 32, II: 189.

4. James of Vitry, *Vita* of Mary of Oignies, prologue, §§6-8, in J. Bollandus and G. Henschenius, *Acta sanctorum... editio novissima*, ed. J. Carnandet et al. (Paris: V. Palmé, 1863-), June 5 (1867) 548; translation adapted in part from Henry Osborn Taylor, *The Medieval Mind: A History of the Development of Thought and Emotion in the Middle Ages* (2 vols.; 4th ed.; London: Macmillan, 1925) 1:477-78; see also McDonnell, *Beguines and Beghards*, 330.

5. *Vita* of Alice of Schaerbeke, 3.26 in *Acta sanctorum*, June 2 (Paris and Rome, 1867) 476.

Bibliography

On religious women in the early Middle Ages, see Wemple. The works by Baker, Bolton, Elm, Freed, Grundmann, Herlihy, Lerner, McDonnell, Pontenay de Fontette, Schmitz, and Southern treat forms of religious life for women in the later Middle Ages. The most useful discussions of women saints are those that treat both sexes, which makes comparison possible; see Goodich, Kieckhefer, Vauchez, and Weinstein and Bell. For the debate over the extent of women's involvement in heresy, see Abels and Harrison, Koch and McLaughlin ("Les femmes"). Works on female spirituality include Benz, Bynum, Roisin, Thurston. On the much-discussed question of "the image of woman," which is a topic more in the history of men's attitudes than of women's, see Børresen, Bullough, d'Alverny, and McLaughlin ("Equality").

Abels, Richard, and Ellen Harrison. "The Position of Women in Languedocian Catharism." *Medieval Studies* 41 (1979) 215-51.

d'Alverny, Marie-Thérèse. "Comment les théologiens et les philosophes voient la femme?" *La femme dans les civilisations des Xe–XIIIe siècles: Actes du colloque tenu à Poitiers les 23-25 septembre 1976, Cahiers de civilisation médiévale* 20 (1977) 105-29.

Baker, Derek, ed. *Medieval Women: Dedicated and Presented to Professor Rosalind M. T. Hill.* . . . Studies in Church History: Subsidia 1. Oxford: Blackwell, 1978.

Benz, Ernst. *Die Vision: Erfahrungsformen und Bilderwelt.* Stuttgart: E. Klett, 1969.

Bolton, Brenda M. "*Mulieres sanctae.*" In *Sanctity and Secularity: The Church and the World,* 77-95. Edited by Derek Baker. Studies in Church History 10. Oxford: Blackwell, 1973.

Børresen, Kari Elisabeth. *Subordination et equivalence: Nature et rôle de la femme d'après Augustin et Thomas d'Aquin.* Oslo: Universitetsforlaget, 1968.

Bullough, Vern L. "Medieval Medical and Scientific Views of Women." *Viator* 4 (1973) 487-93.

Bynum, Caroline W. "Woman Mystics and Eucharistic Devotion in the Thirteenth Century." *Women's Studies* 11 (1984) 179-214.

———. "Fast, Feast, and Flesh: The Religious Significance of Food to Medieval Women." *Representations* 11 (Summer 1985) 1-25.

Elm, Kasper. "Die Stellung der Frau in Ordenswesen, Semireligiosentum und Häresie zur Zeit der heiligen Elisabeth." In *Sankt Elisabeth: Fürstin, Dienerin, Heilige: Aufsätze, Dokumentation, Katalog,* 7-28. Edited by University of Marburg. Sigmaringen: Thorbeke, 1981.

Freed, John B. "Urban Development and the 'Cura Monialium' in Thirteenth-Century Germany." *Viator* 3 (1972) 311-27.

Goodich, Michael. "Contours of Female Piety in Later Medieval Hagiography." *Church History* 50 (1981) 20-32.

Grundmann, Herbert. "Die Frauen und die Literatur im Mittelalter: Ein Beitrag zur Frage nach der Entstehung des Schrifttums in der Volkssprache." *Archiv für Kulturgeschichte* 26 (1936) 129-61.

———. *Religiöse Bewegungen im Mittelalter: Untersuchungen über die geschichtlichen Zusammenhänge zwischen Ketzerei, den Bettelorden und der religiösen Frauenbewegung im 12. und 13. Jahrhundert.* . . . 1935. Reprint, with additions, Darmstadt: Wissenschaftliche Buchgesellschaft, 1977. The classic account.

Herlihy, David. *The Social History of Italy and Western Europe 700-1500.* London: Variorum Reprints, 1978. Contains several articles on medieval women.

Kieckhefer, Richard. *Unquiet Souls: Fourteenth-Century Saints and Their Religious Milieu.* Chicago: University of Chicago Press, 1984.

Koch, Gottfried. *Frauenfrage und Ketzertum im Mittelalter: Die Frauenbewegung im Rahmen des Katharismus und des Waldensertums und ihre sozialen Wurzeln: 12.-14. Jahrhundert.* Forschungen zur mittelalterlichen Geschichte 9. Berlin: Akademie-Verlag, 1962.

Lerner, Robert E. "Beguines and Beghards." In *Dictionary of the Middle Ages,* 2:157–62. Edited by Joseph Strayer. New York: Scribner, 1983.

———. *The Heresy of the Free Spirit in the Later Middle Ages.* Berkeley and Los Angeles: University of California Press, 1972.

McDonnell, Ernest W. *The Beguines and Beghards in Medieval Culture with Special Emphasis on the Belgian Scene.* 1954. Reprint, New York: Octagon Books, 1969.

McLaughlin, Eleanor. "Equality of Souls, Inequality of Sexes: Women in Medieval Theology." In *Religion and Sexism: Images of Women in the Jewish and Christian Traditions,* 213–66. Edited by Rosemary Ruether. New York: Simon & Schuster, 1974.

———. "Les femmes et l'hérésie médiévale. Un problème dans l'histoire de la spiritualité." *Concilium* 111 (1976) 73–90.

Pontenay de Fontette, Micheline. *Les religieuses à l'âge classique du droit canon: Recherches sur les structures juridiques des branches féminines des ordres.* Paris: J. Vrin, 1967. The best work on the institutional history of women's orders.

Roisin, Simone. *L'hagiographie cistercienne dans le diocèse de Liège au XIII siècle.* Louvain: Bibliothèque de l'Université, 1947.

Schmitz, Philibert. *Histoire de l'ordre de saint Benoît.* 7 vols. Maredsous: Éditions de Maredsous, 1942–56. Vol. 7, *Les moniales* (1956).

Southern, Richard W. *Western Society and the Church in the Middle Ages.* Pelican History of the Church 2. Harmondsworth: Penguin Books, 1970.

Thurston, Herbert. *The Physical Phenomena of Mysticism.* Chicago: Henry Regnery, 1952.

Vauchez, André. *La sainteté en occident aux derniers siècles du moyen âge d'après les procès de canonisation et les documents hagiographiques.* Bibliothèque des études françaises d'Athènes et de Rome 241. Rome: École française de Rome, 1981.

Weinstein, Donald, and Rudolph Bell. *Saints and Society: The Two Worlds of Western Christendom, 1000–1700.* Chicago: University of Chicago Press, 1982.

Wemple, Suzanne F. *Women in Frankish Society: Marriage and the Cloister, 500 to 900.* Philadelphia: University of Pennsylvania Press, 1981.

6

Schools of Late Medieval Mysticism

ALOIS MARIA HAAS

German and Dutch Mysticism in the Fourteenth Century

AFTER THE PROLIFERATION of mendicant orders around the Mediterranean, the spiritual center of Europe was transferred with innovative energy into the Germanic lands—England, to be sure, but above all, Germany, Alsace, Austria, Switzerland, and the lowlands. There mendicant spirituality with its great stress on poverty and the naked following of Christ experienced a specific radicalization in the direction of mysticism. Following the intense disputes among Franciscans over how to live in poverty, the dominant question concerned the level and type of contemplation found in the spiritual life, and this question turned on whether the basis of contemplation in experience lay in the soul's power of will (love) or reason. That means that a theoretical interest embraced the practice of religious life and tried to transform it. Especially in Dominican circles, a strong philosophical ferment was operative in mystical theology, so that, in addition to the affective forms of love-mysticism, an essence-mysticism (*Wesensmystik*), based ever more intensively on knowledge and reason, was created. This essence-mysticism embraced the Neoplatonic mode of thinking, which was then becoming better known.

Early Female Mysticism (Frauenmystik)

It falsifies the picture if one considers so-called German mysticism apart from the spiritual interests and efforts of the early female mysticism as developed by Cistercian nuns and by beguines in Flemish and north German areas in the thirteenth century. The combination of traditional

140

Cistercian and new mystical motifs anticipates Eckhart's *Wesensmystik* with its puzzling origin and astonishing formulation. In addition, these were the women who first recorded their relationship with God in the vernacular and thereby—to a degree not yet quite clear—influenced the subsequent beguines and beghards and also late medieval bourgeois spirituality in general by supplying a vocabulary and a nomenclature for spiritual experience, which until then was usual only in monastic circles. This was audaciously novel.

Exponents of beguine mysticism in Brabant were Beatrice of Nazareth (ca. 1200–1268) and Hadewijch (mid-thirteenth century). The former died as prioress of a Cistercian convent; the latter, in all probability, belonged to a beguinage. Both have left literary testimony of their experiences of God: Beatrice in the form of an autobiography, *The Seven Ways of Loving*, and Hadewijch in poems, letters, and accounts of visions. Beatrice's basic experiences (in thematic connection with the mysticism of Bernard and the Victorines and the views on love of the courtly ethic) consist of an immeasurable experience of the love of God and a yearning for love. The soul undertakes to bear pain (*sonder enich waeromme*, or "without a why"), to die while yet living, and to let itself sink into the presence of God and there—ambivalently—to experience either a genuine "fury of love" or the calming experience of peace in God leading to fulfillment in a "breakthrough of love." Theme, vocabulary, and syntax draw upon an extremely strong mystical experience in such a theory of love.

Hadewijch, who according to her own testimony led an existence on the fringe of society, was acutely aware of her high culture and intelligence. In poetry and in prose, she presents a spirituality whose end is the divine Trinity and divine love of God, bestowed above all in the form of mystical espousals. She energetically emphasizes the unity in the Trinity of the divine persons, which is itself declared to be love: "the unity, the consummation of love and the true embrace of oneself in a person as one only love and nothing other than that. Oh, God, what a frightened being it is that unites such hate (of all division) and such love (of all unity) as a singular being in itself." But this love does not exclude the mystic; it rather appropriates her into herself in the form of a real fury (*orewoet*, a word that Beatrice already used for the ecstasy of love). The one loved by God is taken into him in a process that already anticipates the exemplaristic mysticism of Meister Eckhart—as, for example, in the fourteenth vision, where Hadewijch imagined herself on the throne of God and "acted like God." Sign and symbol of the divine source of ideas are an "abysmally deep, wide, and totally dark wheel," in which all things are contained and are shown to the seer. Thus the visibility of God is revealed to her as a visibility of herself and of creation in God. This is very similar to Eckhart, who later recognized the eye that looked into God as the eye of God himself. God's visibility to himself is the Trinity. Up until the incarnation this is nothing other than a divine self-revelation which, with both eyes (love and reason), can be perceived by humans. This does not happen without pain and resignation on the part of the mystic, because life in love is terrifying, even an experience of hell, since "the yearning lack" of pleasure "is the sweetest pleasure" (*Dat ghebreken van dien ghebrukene dat es dat suetste ghebruken*). For this experience she finds no form of clear expression; indeed, she drowns it in remarkable formulations. Her most important tool to express the paradox of experience and nonexperience is the vision, in which, in a puzzling way, she combines theology with intense imagery.

In the area to the east of the Elbe, Mechthild of Magdeburg (1207-1282) wrote her *Fliessendes Licht der Gottheit* (*Flowing Light of the Godhead*) in low German in the third quarter of the thirteenth century. It is extant today only in a Middle High German translation. This work documents a similar social predicament of its writer, who for many years lived in voluntary exile as a beguine and in advanced age only (1271) returned to the Cistercian cloister at Eisleben, where she met, in the persons of Gertrude the Great (1256-1302/3) and Mechthild of Hackeborn (1241-1298/99), a mysticism bound up with the liturgy and the church year. The Dominican Heinrich of Halle, her spiritual guide, deserves credit for showing active sympathy with her life and work. In an exclusively Augustinian sense, her work centered on God and the soul, so that she can say on the one hand *gott selber sprichet du wort* ("God himself speaks the words") and on the other hand *ez* ("the book") *bezeichent alleine mich* ("it deals with me alone"). This journal of a soul, which is divided into well-ordered biographical chapters, cannot be placed in any genre. The prose rises to lyrically independent images in which an authentic *Brautmystik* (bridal mysticism) is formed that is unique, mature, and consistent. In contrast to Hadewijch, the tones are here softer and gentler, notwithstanding that Mechthild's love of God was tested by experiences of abandonment represented as real alienation from God (*gotsvroemdunge*). The Song of Songs, with its dialogues between bridegroom and bride, is presented stylistically as events of the soul in which the immediacy of mystical union is celebrated emotionally as a "storm of love" (*minnesturm*). The theme of flowing and sinking, combined with a theology of humility, gains an autonomy of religious expression in hymnic and lyrical outbursts that are scarcely to be found anywhere else. The "expropriation" of the soul in God is finally an occurrence in hope and faith.

Marguerite Porete (d. 1310), beguine, author of a textbook of mystical love (*Mirror of Simple Souls*), was publicly burned as a heretic on 31 May

1310, in the Place de Grève in Paris. The book, composed of 139 brief chapters, portrays the life of her soul from the valley of humility to the mountain of contemplation. Her way is a way of inner liberation: as soon as the soul has become an *âme anientie* ("annihiliated soul") it becomes an *âme franche* ("free soul") that no longer needs to stand under the dictates of the law of virtue. She understands this liberation in the sense of a mystical exemplarity, as a return to the first Being, in which nothing became everything. To her inquisitors this seemed dogmatically untenable. The soul, like the flame in the fire, is turned back to its original being. The literary form used here is that of an allegorical cast of characters in which the particular speakers (Soul, Love, etc.) represent individual testimonies in monologues. Accordingly, the earlier, more lyrical passages are missing. It is interesting that Meister Eckhart must have known about Marguerite Porete from the inquisition proceedings, because he was in Paris a year after her death.

Dominican Mysticism

In the spirituality of the early Dominicans, not many characteristics that hint at mystical inclinations can be clearly ascertained. The Order of Preachers was founded in 1216 by Dominic (1170–1221) out of his missionary experience. The care of souls and the refutation of heresy by preaching and good example in the following of Christ were the determinative intentions, and so the order was scarcely directed toward the special cultivation of an "inner life." The contemplative side did play a role, though only in combination with its opposite, the active life (*vita activa*). This new model of missionary activity and life, in which the *vita contemplativa* was forced into a close connection with the *vita activa*, unleashed in time new forces for the formation of a mystical life with a new end: *contemplata aliis tradere*, or the sharing of the fruits of contemplation with others. This Thomist view of a "mixed life" gave birth, through preaching, to forms of spiritual-religious instruction that were able to integrate the old forms of contemplative mysticism with Christian practice. Instead of writing treatises on the spiritual life, the earliest Dominicans published instructions on the right kind of preaching—for example, Humbert of Romans (ca. 1200–1277) in his *De eruditione praedicatorum* (*The Instruction of Preachers*)—or exemplary hints for a holy life—for example, Jacobus of Voragine (1228/30–1298) in his *Legenda aurea* (*Golden Legend*). Since the *cura animarum* (care of souls) is almost impossible without sure knowledge of the faith, the Dominicans placed extraordinary weight on *studium*, or learning, not only in the area of biblical studies and theology but also in the field of the secular sciences (*trivium* or *quadrivium*). They transformed philosophical and theological knowledge into methodical, purposeful sciences in their own right (Albert the Great [ca. 1200–1280]; Thomas Aquinas [1224/25–1274]). They collected all knowledge available at the time in encyclopediae (Thomas of Cantimpré [1201–1263/72]; Vincent of Beauvais [1184/94–1264]). Mystical theology in such works is in the form of scholastic questions, but is scarcely discussed further with direct instructional intent. Instruction is given a new direction in the numerous Dominican collections of sermons and also in spiritual letters, as exemplified by Jordan of Saxony (ca. 1185–1237), the master general of the order after Dominic. Also important is a manner of life which, despite its adaptation to the city and its spiritual needs, was influenced by the oldest form of monasticism. This manner of life included, besides the daily prayer in choir, prayers to be said after matins and compline and daily on journeys, all of which exhibit a close connection to the old Benedictine practices. But these forms of prayer were also always at the service of a more efficient care of souls and preaching. It is, then, quite evident that the mystical theology developed by the Dominicans was based on either speculative-intellectual or pastoral concerns. When both concepts came together, a mysticism arose that had many forms and themes in common with the older monastic contemplative mysticism but that also made possible the transformation of religious experience through a heightened sense of the neighbor and the neighbor's religious needs. It thereby became a mysticism oriented to the interests of the urban culture of the later Middle Ages.

The formation of this mysticism according to its theoretical and practical sides was specified by the women's movement of the thirteenth and early fourteenth centuries, which had already begun in the earlier *Frauenmystik*. Organized in still informal communities of beguines, these groups, especially strong in Germany, sought to acquire inner and external support by affiliation with the older and newer orders of men. The mendicant orders tried at first to withdraw from this movement and to avoid the pastoral care of cloistered nuns, but in Germany the movement had become so powerful that during the 1280s it was able to make known to the papal curia in Rome its desire for pastoral care. After protracted negotiations the Dominicans and Franciscans had to acquiesce. By the end of the thirteenth century, over eighty monasteries of nuns were incorporated into the Dominican order in Germany—more than in the seventeen other provinces of the order combined and even outnumbering the monasteries of men in Germany. The Dominican communities of women were differentiated from the approximately forty small cloisters of Franciscan nuns by a rather higher population (80–100 sisters). The tendency toward and interest in mystical experience in such milieux—indeed, always present in all orders—could increase and intensify, probably because of the fact that these monasteries had a rather strict enclosure and therefore were not diverted by ecclesial or sectarian interests. It was also fortunate that the pastoral care of nuns (*cura monialium*) was entrusted to extraordinary men.

It remains to be shown in detail how this connection between Dominican nuns and friars resulted not only in a developed *cura monialium* but also in a firm interior bond due to similar interests and tendencies in the spiritual life that arose from mutual cooperation. This cooperation appeared most visibly in the translation of Latin theological works into the vernacular. Thus, works of Albert the Great, who in following Pseudo-Dionysius inaugurated a strongly Neoplatonic form of mystical theology and thereby founded speculative German mysticism, were translated into German (*On the Mass, Sermons, Sayings*). Works of others, however, were not translated into the vernacular—for example, those of Ulrich Engelberti of Strasbourg (d. 1277), who in his *Summa de summo bono* (*Summa on the Highest Good*), colored by Neoplatonism, also discussed questions concerning mystical prayer life, or those of Dietrich of Freiberg (ca. 1250–after 1310), who certainly was in personal contact with Meister Eckhart and wrote a great number of scientific, philosophical, and theological works on a Neoplatonic basis and thereby deeply influenced Eckhart. Here the high technicality of their scholastically oriented works may have been determinative. Nevertheless, these men had some pastoral influence on the nuns, especially Dietrich of Freiberg, according to the testimony of the nuns themselves.

Meister Eckhart (ca. 1260–1328)

Eckhart, born about 1260, in Hochheim (either near Erfurt or near Gotha) is above all to be seen in the framework of his life in the Dominican order and its spirituality. He finished the usual Dominican education, knew Albert the Great personally in Cologne, studied the arts in Paris (1277), became prior of the convent in Erfurt (from 1290 to 1300) and vicar of Thüringen (1293–1294). He served as bachelor again in Paris where he also twice filled a teaching position as professor (1302, 1311–1312). In 1303, Meister Eckhart became provincial of the newly founded province of Saxony, where there were forty-seven convents and a number of monasteries under his supervision. In 1307 the electors of Teutonia chose him to be their vicar, an election that the General Chapter of Naples in 1311 did not ratify because it intended to send Eckhart to Paris for further teaching. At the end of 1313, Eckhart stayed in Strasbourg, where he may well have worked, among other things, as visitator of monasteries of nuns. In 1323 he was officially spiritual director and teacher in the order's house of studies in

Cologne. He was permitted only a brief time of undisturbed, peaceful teaching, since the archbishop of Cologne, Heinrich of Virneburg, began inquisition procedures against Meister Eckhart for reasons that can scarcely be reconstructed today.

The complaint arose from the spread of heretical teachings. Probably in order to prevent the archbishop's proceedings, the order itself had tested and recognized Eckhart's orthodoxy in 1325–1326 under Nicholaus of Strasbourg, lector in Cologne and vicar of Teutonia. Beginning on 26 September 1326, the archepiscopal commission published at first one list and then a second with forty-nine and fifty-nine charges respectively against Eckhart. In his *Rechtfertigungsschrift* or *Justificatory Report*, Eckhart doubted the legitimacy of the commission judging him (since for him as a member of the Dominican Order, only the University of Paris or the Pope himself was authorized to sit in judgment), and he vigorously countered the theses charged against him. More lists (in all there must have been four or five) followed the theses thought to be heretical. On 24 January 1327, Eckhart complained to the Pope about the delay of his trial. On 13 February of the same year, Eckhart turned to the people and, in the Dominican church, declared before God that during his whole life he had always wished to avoid any error against faith and morals. No judgment was reached in Cologne. The case was heard before the curia in Avignon, to which Eckhart journeyed in person in order to present his case. There, or during the return trip, Eckhart died, toward the end of 1327 or in the spring of 1328. In his verdict, the bull *In agro dominico* (27 March 1329), Pope John XXII condemned twenty-eight theses of Eckhart. Seventeen were found to be simply heretical, and eleven were judged to be dangerous and tending toward heresy.

What can be said of Meister Eckhart's life can also be said of Eckhart's works: they are totally within the context of his existence dedicated to the life of a friar preacher. They grew out of his teaching activity or his pastoral care of nuns and the people. The extant Latin works, a project conceived by Eckhart as a three-part work (*Opus tripartitum*), comprise *Opus propositionum*, a collection of one thousand theses; *Opus quaestionum;* and *Opus expositionum*, of which only a portion remains. Extant are the prefaces to each section, several *quaestiones,* many sermon outlines, commentaries on Genesis, Exodus, Wisdom, and the Gospel of John, and the defense documents. The German works, of a pastoral nature, encompassed *The Book of Divine Consolation, Of the Nobleman, On Detachment, Counsels on Discernment* (which he delivered to his fellow Dominicans), and almost one hundred sermons, for whose written form Eckhart is probably more responsible personally than earlier research claimed.

According to his admitted intention, in his Latin publications Eckhart "explains the teachings of the holy Christian faith and of the Scripture of both testaments with the help of the principles of philosophy." [1] Written into the theological goal of the scriptural exposition is, consequently, a philosophical message in which Eckhart easily includes Neoplatonic thought of a highly developed abstract kind. Eckhart explains his intention for his treatises and sermons in the German language more as a preacher, or *Lebmeister*. The kerygmatic theme of the unity of God and humanity is monotonously developed by means of four ideas:

> When I preach, I am careful to speak about detachment and that a person should become free of self and of all things. Secondly, that one should be re-formed in the simple good that is God. Thirdly, that one should think of the great nobility which God has placed in the soul, so that a person may thereby come to God in a wonderful way. Fourthly, concerning the purity of divine nature—there is such brilliance in it that it is inexpressible. [2]

Eckhart's speech has changed here. Instead of the distancing objectification of the scientific Latin works, the directness of engaged and intentional language reigns. The presupposition, as Eckhart once asserted, is a form of understanding which is identification: the eternal truth lets itself be understood only by one who has become like it. The speaker, the Dominican Eckhart, himself speaks out of this unity with the truth. Such a form of speech, in which the speaker presents himself as an exemplary case, leads to a special mystical language, since the theme is the unity of the human being with God. The speaker understands himself as a witness of the unity to which he directs others.

Eckhart's four preaching themes are synonymous in goal. Thus, "detachment," becoming free of oneself and of all things, is nothing other than "likeness," which is the simple essence (*daz bloze wesen*) of God. This is nothing else than the detachment for which the creature yearns, so that unity is possible. Re-creation in God is the ratification of that unity which is inherent in the creaturely status of human beings. Human beings are nothing of themselves, since they receive all being from God; when they exist, they exist only in the being of God. But being is the unity between creaturely nothingness and the being of God, which works through all things (God differentiates himself from all created things in that He is differentiated from nothing!). The "nobility" in souls is God's enduring presence in them, which gives them being as well as their preexistent unity. The "purity of divine nature" (which although inexpressible must always be expressed again) is the triumphal content of Eckhart's preaching. God, as the splendor of all beings, works through them in giving being. But to maintain the secret character of this mystery requires a strongly developed negative theology in which the always greater unity of God and the rational creature will lead into the always greater difference between the two. Creatures must let God be God, so that divinity—God in the aspect of his unity—will be present. The basic affirmation in Eckhart's teaching is therefore the graciously granted unity between the all-powerful God and the "nothing" of human beings.

The individual points of Eckhart's preaching program may be better understood now as variations of the one theme.

1. Detachment is "mode-lessness" (*Weiselosegkeit*), freedom (*Ledigkeit*), spiritual poverty, selflessness, abandonment (*Gelassenheit*). The spiritual human being, in the form of an assimilation to God, should be free from all ways, exercises, and techniques to find God. God will give the right way. But then God himself is characterized by "waylessness" and "detachment." God, insofar as he *is* his own being, is the *negatio negationis*, the negation of negation, because of the power and the might of his being. Therefore, whoever is empty of all creatures is full of God and achieves the greatest similitude to God. Detachment is therefore not a certain ascetical practice but rather a total renunciation in compliance with Eckhart's recommendations to pay attention to how one is *to be* and not to what one has to do. But detachment is also no stoic virtue that human beings would practice unfeelingly against pain. On the contrary, it signifies a final defenselessness against the God who wants to make human beings one with himself. But this unity is only possible on the basis of a certain conception of the teaching on analogy. According to Eckhart, the creature is *unum purum nihil*, a pure nothing that *swebet an der gegenwerticheit gotes* ("hovers around" the presence of God). The creature "has" being only in the way of the one who "has not," because it is God who keeps giving new being. The creature is like the mirror image before the original; if the one pulls back, then the other disappears into the nothingness that it is of itself.

2. The re-creation of the human being in God is a form of image theology that must be interpreted in the sense of mirror ontology: the image is able to exist only in the return into its origin. But since there in the origin all created things rest from all eternity (as God in God), it is obvious that human beings seek to win back by means of grace this causal being (*esse causale*) from their empty formal being (*esse formale*). The mystical way (if one can so speak in the case of Eckhart) is the presently achieved *breakthrough* of the created image into its exemplar. The isolated particular being (*ens hoc et hoc*) must return to the pure being without which it is nothing. The way of existence of the creature as God in God and as created thought is, according to an old powerfully fostered Christian tradition from Neoplatonism, more noble (*eminentius*) than any falling away into earthly

existence. The outflowing (*usvliezen*) from God—as Eckhart Neoplatonically describes creation—corresponds complementarily and necessarily to the breakthrough (*durchbrechen*) into the ground, into the depth, into the river and into the well of the Godhead. Then human beings are "what they were before they were." The Christian concept of creation (*sub specie aeternitatis*) is thus deprived of its temporal dimension and reduced to the point from which the incarnation proceeds. Then, when the birth of God takes place in the human soul, the creation event and the incarnation are existentially and eternally one and simultaneous. *Creatio* and *incarnatio* are shown as two sides of the one unifying coming of God to human beings. What happened once in Bethlehem—the birth of God—happens in the human soul as a pledge of the divine gift of being. Each time this happens it is nothing other than God giving birth to God in the soul. This event, in which God himself transforms the soul, is a stepping into God's eternal dimension, wherein creation, incarnation, and human existence are lifted above their merely temporal determination. Eckhart depends strongly upon patristic teaching for his idea of the birth of God in the soul, but he radicalizes it from the perspective of his exemplarism. The unity which occurs in the re-creation of the soul in God is never a static unity, but rather a unity in fulfillment: "God and I, we are one in this work; He works and I become!" (*Got und ich wir sint ein in disem gewürke; er wirket und ich gewirde!*) God reveals himself to be an eternal God to the degree that he is a God present for the soul.

3. The "nobility of the soul" is its detachment, in whose emptiness God is present as fullness. God, the giver of being, is present in the human soul as its ground (*grunt der sêle*), as the little spark of reason (*vünkelin der redelicheit*), as "head," "man," "protector," "being," "little castle" (compare Teresa of Avila's spiritual castle), "whirlpool," "light," "power," "something" in the soul, "highest treetop," etc. The categories "createdness" and "uncreatedness," which the inquisitors applied to this flexible and dynamic understanding, are completely erroneous. Eckhart always speaks *inquantum;* that is, *insofar as* the soul is pure intellect, it is and will be divinely transformed. This is the reason for Eckhart's preference for the so-called general perfections like "unity," "being," "justice," etc. They indicate that all-embracing being, goodness, and justice of God, to which the human being has to return. Since Christ in the incarnation has assumed a human nature in general (this is also a patristic, and even an ecclesiological concept), human beings must get rid of their individual determinations to become generically human in order to be "God-formed," that is, be one with God. All this, however, occurs *sunder warum* ("without a why"), that is, finally from grace. God is more internal to all beings than they are to themselves, as Eckhart with Augustine

untiringly loved to repeat. Eckhart's ideal of the wholeness of God become human has found that spontaneity of action and being that is in accord with a mature experience of life, prudence, and practice.

4. The basis of all Eckhart's aspirations is a radical God-mysticism—more exactly, a mysticism of the Godhead. "God" is God under the aspect of his externally unfolding Trinity. "Godhead" is God under the aspect of unity. God's greatness consists in this superabundant unifying groundlessness of his dynamic and ever-intensifying oneness. But one may not take the conceptual split of God and Godhead categorically, but rather must understand them as two forms of the one presence of God. God, the Three-Personed, takes human beings into himself in the birth of God in the soul and conveys them into his unity according to the measure of each one's detachment. He is "alone one" (*das einig Ein*). From this follows the recommendation to rational creatures: study only this, to become pregnant with God (*dar ûf setze al dîn studieren, daz dir got grôz werde*)! Hence the apophatic theology which asserts the "nothingness" of God for the sake of the "superabundance of the clarity of his being" (*überswankes der lûterkeit sînes wesens*). Add to this that the ground of God (*grunt gottes*) stands in a mysterious relation to the ground of the soul (*grunt der sêle*), so that finally both grounds become a nameless and formless abyss. The key word again is the birthing: human beings are born and God gives birth to himself in the same way, but in humans this happens by grace. Thus Eckhart arrives at that beautiful sentence which serves as a summary of his teaching: "The eye, with which I see God, is the same eye with which God sees me; my eye and God's eye are only one eye and one seeing and one knowing and one love."[3]

Eckhart's mysticism reveals itself in a rare radical sense as a God-mysticism (*Gottesmystik*).

Meister Eckhart's Followers

Meister Eckhart's incomparability is attested to by an entire series of great figures in the history of spirituality who are in one way or another his spiritual heirs. Johannes Tauler, Heinrich Suso, and Nicholas of Cusa attest to this by the directness with which they connect themselves to him. Despite his ecclesiastical condemnation, a great number of Dominicans, and also Franciscans in a more or less clear way, point to the influence of Meister Eckhart. To what extent one can speak of an actual Eckhart circle or an Eckhart school is undecided. In any case, the strong, if mainly anonymous, influence of Meister Eckhart on his contemporaries and posterity may be assumed on the basis of genuine Eckhart legends and the testimonies of nuns and preachers. To designate individual figures as students and actual followers of Eckhart is justified only in a few cases. This is mainly true of the Dominicans mentioned below who stand more or less independently in the tradition of Thomism or of Neoplatonism and who give sermons in the vernacular, or have as their task the pastoral care of nuns, the *cura moni-alium*. Their circumstances were similar to Eckhart's, so that it is hard either to differentiate them from him merely according to mentality, spirituality and thought processes or simply to associate them with him. Thus, for example, Nicholaus von Strasbourg is essentially part of the circle around Eckhart and also had dealings with him as a superior, yet he was not drawn into the "school" of Eckhart. Tauler and Suso, on the other hand, are clearly connected with the Meister. They honor him and, in a critical way, follow after him.

Johannes Tauler (ca. 1300–1361). Coming from a landed bourgeois family of Strasbourg, Johannes Tauler entered the Dominican Order at an early age. He underwent the usual formation, although without achieving an academic degree, and then devoted his life entirely to the mission of preaching—probably in places in or near Strasbourg, in the numerous beguinages and Dominican monasteries. He certainly had occasional contacts with the movement of the Friends of God. Heinrich of Nördlingen testifies to this in his letters, as does a letter of Tauler to Elsbeth Scheppach and Margaretha Ebner in the monastery of Medingen. Four years of his life (1339–1343) Tauler probably spent in Basel, since the Dominicans of Strasbourg supported the papal party in the conflict between Louis the Bavarian and Pope John XXII, whereas the city supported the emperor. Journeys to Cologne, eventually to Groenendael in Belgium, and to Paris may have interrupted his life, but they did not exercise a decisive influence on him.

Testimony that Tauler was a consummate teacher appears in the works left by him and in those falsely attributed to him. His authentic writings comprise approximately eighty sermons; most of them were passed on in a set collection (in the Engelberg manuscript or the Vienna manuscript). These form the basis of the later Tauler editions of 1498, 1521, 1543, which exercised a noticeable influence on the spirituality of the young Martin Luther and the Reformation. All others that appear under Tauler's name are inauthentic.

Tauler's association with Eckhart, whom he knew either personally or, certainly, literarily, was crucial in that he recognized the precise herme-neutical point that was decisive for Eckhart. Tauler recognized the mis-understanding which Eckhart frequently encountered from his audience when he assured his own listeners that "you have not grasped the teachings of the beloved master; he spoke out of eternity, and your understanding is still time-bound."⁴ Tauler thus sees the spiritual location of Eckhart's teaching, but he also sees that there lies the difficulty for the listeners. Tauler's preaching borrowed much from Eckhart in its teaching on God and on the human person. Indeed, it is finally characterized by a turn to time and place (*zit unde stat*), to the concrete earthly existence of human beings in their temporal and local extension. Certainly, God is transcendental in comparison to all created things, "above mode, above being, above goodness" (*über wise, über wesen, uber guot!*), but the consequence for human beings is not at first to become simple like God, but is rather a firm recommendation to humility. Humility, self-knowledge, self-denial, are the decisive factors in connection with older monastic requirements. Human existence is characterized, for Tauler, by a depth (*im grunt, im gemüete*) that always has an "uncountable divinely formed place back in God." As filled with grace, "union" with God is accomplished on the basis of this intentional striving, though only when in great temptations the "created nothing" (*geschaffen nut*) has been put in its place. The Eckhartian "breakthrough" is here an essential turning, a conversion of the course of life. But it must always begin anew because it is not firmly possessed. The vision of God is surrounded by much effort, work, and sorrow. The course of life as the place to bear temptations and the proving ground for the "abandonment" (*Gelassenheit*, as detachment is termed by Tauler) takes on great importance.

A proper teaching on the stages of life, especially on the importance of the second half of life; an anthropology of a human being as composed of three parts—sense, reason, heart, and of the "inner" and "outer" human being; the mystic triple way (*triplex via*) of Dionysius the Areopagite; the model of active and contemplative life (*vita activa* and *contemplativa*); and finally also the description of mystical ecstasy stemming from Proclus—all these themes and ideas of an exemplary mystical life become ideological stages in a deep mysticism imbedded in the interconnectedness of life. Genuine theological presuppositions set forth with firmness and clarity are all the more necessary: only in faith is the experienced perception of divine truth thinkable and experiential. Jesus Christ, as the embodiment of salvation coming in history to human beings, does not become either a spiritual Christ or a "Godhead." Tauler mistrusts the mysticism of the nuns that often slips into emotionalism and drops away suddenly from the concrete insofar as, in his opinion, there is in it a pharisaical core in the self-enjoyment of their own piety. As with Eckhart, the goal, the uniting of human beings with God, comes as the vertical, inbreaking suddenness of eternity. Therefore, it is situated in the course of life. The value of guiding revelations, pious exercises, and sacramental helps is accentuated more strongly. On the other hand, the sinful entanglements of the human condition stemming from original sin and from sinful acts are more clearly classified than in Eckhart's work, for whom sin is that nothingness which can hardly be discussed, because there is nothing to say about it. Tauler's preaching is more filled with images; indeed, it is composed of chains or series of images. It is, therefore, in an immediately enlightening sense human, practical, and direct. Tauler's conception of the "ground of the soul" differs from Eckhart's "little spark" because it is drawn into an anthropologically comprehensive view of the human being which gives adequate room to the principle of reality.

Heinrich Suso (ca. 1295–1366). Heinrich Suso's life, like that of Tauler, also ran its course primarily in a single location, Constance, although he studied at the Dominican house of theology in Cologne, where he was trained as a lector of the order. During the papal interdict, 1339–1346, he also left his convent in Constance and found refuge in nearby Diessenhofen. For a time he was prior of the convent in Constance. Around 1335, after he had given up his conventual duties as lector and prior, he must have led a life dedicated purely to pastoral care, especially to the *cura monialium,* and therefore he traveled widely in Switzerland, Alsace, and the Rhineland. The final years of his life, from approximately 1348 on, were spent in Ulm. From 1336 or 1337 until his death in 1366, Suso was a close friend of Elsbeth Stagel (or Staglin), a nun of Töss, with whom he shared an interest in questions on mysticism which arose from "the sweet teaching of the holy master Eckhart."[5] Elsbeth's serious interest is a sign that the Dominican nuns were not concerned with Eckhart in a merely naïve way, as some poems suggest. In this friendship Suso was not only the leader but also often the one who was led and received instruction.

Suso left a greater number of works than Tauler. They comprise treatises, letters, and sermons, in addition to an autobiography, the so-called *Vita.* In the form of a final edition in his own hand, Suso collected and edited his writings in his *Exemplar* or *Musterbuch.* Clearly his intention was to publish his work in the most authentic way possible. Suso's spiritual profile is drawn, to a great extent, from his *Vita,* which occupies the first place in his *Exemplar.* He uses himself as an example, calling himself the "servant of eternal wisdom," an adventurer in a spiritual autobiography, a real, spiritual courtly knight. Suso describes his development from a beginner into a mature spiritual knight in an unorganized series of events described in chapters 1–32. A decisive change occurs in chapters 19 and 20, where he turns from an ascetical self-rule to suffering abandonment to the divine will (in many cases the mystic is vexed from outside by forceful human malice). In chapters 33 to 35 his spiritual daughter, Elsbeth Stagel, comes more to the fore; the text is no longer dominated by the narrative, but rather by the free, dialogic discussion of mystical problems and questions. The last chapters, 46 to 53, are like a final seal on the mystic message of Suso, a final inauguration into the perfect life.

Theory and theology of mysticism are in no way excluded by Suso; on the contrary, they are extraordinarily well developed. On the level of literary form, the theory and the practice of the mystical life are shown as two things; but in the inherent strength of their correlation they are inseparable. Suso is both a theoretician and a practitioner of the mystical life. That is evident already in the fullness of his visions and showings—in one Meister Eckhart appears to him personally (chapter 6). It is also clear from Suso's use of the desert fathers as examples of a rigorous asceticism.

Very early on, Suso shows himself to be influenced by Eckhart. In *Büchlein der Wahrheit* (*Little Book of Truth*), Suso becomes Eckhart's ardent defender when he has personified Wisdom and a disciple (Suso himself) discuss true interior abandonment in a dialogue carried on at the highest level of abstraction. A number of themes of Eckhartian mysticism—the union of the human being with God, the negativity of God, the differentiation of God/Godhead, the double being of things (in God as God, in themselves), etc.—thereby acquire a carefully weighed designation. Suso's campaign against any form of "undisciplined freedom" (as it could be perpetuated among the sectarian Free Spirits) is made vivid in the awful figure of the Nameless Wild One. Suso thus protects Eckhart indirectly from the accusation of being a Free Spirit. Such people, insofar as they refer to Eckhart, have misunderstood him.

However much Suso may have been bound to Eckhart interiorly, his path led him in other directions. The *Little Book of Eternal Wisdom,* the most successful devotional book in the late Middle Ages, contains elements of a bridal mysticism and a mysticism of suffering which are found neither in Eckhart nor in Tauler. Whatever the reason may have been (aversion to educated friars?), Suso later released the work in a new Latin version as *Horologium Sapientiae.* It has three parts. The first consists of one hundred meditations that were "revealed" before a crucifix. This is followed by an intimate discussion or private dialogue with Eternal Wisdom in two parts. The work is evidence of a practical mysticism in which the direct confrontation between the soul and the suffering Lord is not shunned but rather leads to a genuine lyrical exultation (as with Mechthild). The literary medium for the dialogue is borrowed from the Song of Songs. The "servant," who is both Suso and the Christian "faithful soul," and Eternal Wisdom, or Christ, are suspended between feminine allegory and masculine reality. The two speakers, following the pattern of a teaching dialogue between master and student, find themselves ever closer to each other and express themselves often in ecstatic language.

The basic value of *The Little Book of Eternal Wisdom* is carried over into the *Horologium* but was augmented by autobiographical features and by characteristics of the ideology of the Dominican order. In this work, Suso, unable to find satisfaction in the purely functional Christology of Eckhart, wanted to make it concrete and empirical through the use of the contemporary emphasis on the suffering and glorified Lord, presented in the sense of "wisdom" and the "philosophy of Christ," as in the old monastic view. The result was an urgent "passion-mysticism," as was depicted in contemporary art (the man of sorrows) and in visionary mysticism which an earlier generation of Dominicans might have mistrusted. From that perspective Suso comes very close to the mysticism of the nuns, even if he sometimes appears further removed from it on the basis of his important theological implications. Suso's letters are public, mystical documents, not communications of private ideas in the modern sense; they are at the service of the *cura animarum*, or pastoral care.

Suso is an excellent example of a mystic who is also a writer—and one who knows it! Eckhart and Tauler are not to be judged naïve from a literary viewpoint; Suso, in comparison to them, is even more consciously literary. He has precise knowledge of the literary-mystical genre. For the sake of knowing God, he wants to "cast out images with images"; he employs allegory, fictionalization, the literary adventures of the courtly romance; he loves the richness of genres in the development of monastic life. When it makes sense to do so, he uses the novelistic, the realistic, the suggestive-lyric mode; his language then tends toward the musical. In sum, Suso raises the mystical experience to the dignity of a complete form of literary development.

The Lives of the Nuns and Visionary Literature

Up to now we have treated the convents of nuns in southern Germany, the Rhineland, and Switzerland as beneficiaries of the Dominican *cura monialium*. That the inhabitants of these convents did not remain merely passive receivers is shown by Elsbeth Stagel, who certainly inspired Heinrich Suso in his work. The nuns were active also in a literary sense, although no longer with the spontaneous intensity of the nuns of Helfta. Their mode of literary expression is naturally not in the form of sermons and treatises, which were the specific means of the care of souls and thereby continued to be the reserve of males of the order. The nuns were strictly cloistered and therefore used literary forms that were more biographical or, indeed, autobiographical in character.

The biographical element in these texts exhibits clearly hagiographic characteristics. Basically, the books of the sisters, or the biographies of nuns—such as those extant from Adelhausen, Töss near Winterthur, Oetenbach near Zürich, Engelthal in Franconia, Kirchberg (in Sulz), Ulm, Weiler (near Esslingen) and St. Katharinental (near Diessenhofen in Thurgau) or Unterlinden (in Colmar)—furthered an old tradition of Franciscans as well as Dominicans. That tradition produced the *Acts of Blessed Francis,* the *Fioretti,* and the Dominican *Lives of the Fathers,* which promoted the hagiography of the first brothers of the order. The collections of incidents from the lives of pious and graced Dominican nuns have the same intent and purpose as the *Lives of the Fathers* for the whole order; they offer spiritual chronicles of the houses of the order and of their own heroic beginnings. Practical mysticism in legendary form is offered here through vignettes from the nuns' lives which, in a documentary format, praise their own beginnings. The individual yields to the type, as is shown by the predominance of certain general mystical themes. Accounts of visions are concentrated on the suffering and crucified Christ, on the childhood of Jesus (the playful Christ-child caressing his mother, the secret of his circumcision, motherly joys with the infant Jesus, etc.), on dialogues with Christ or the Holy Spirit, and on bridal engagement experiences with Jesus. Along with these there are also descriptions of severe ascetical practices and exercises, endurance of sorrow and pain, sickness and humiliation.

More particular mystical contents are conveyed through the individual lives from this monastic setting. Like Suso's *Life,* they undertake the daring attempt to represent simultaneously a legendary and an autobiographical account of the individual life. To this group belong *The Little Book of the Life and Revelation* by Elsbeth von Oye (ca. 1290–1340 in the monastery of Oetenbach near Zürich); *Revelations* by Margaretha Ebner (ca. 1292–1351 in Medingen near Dillingen), which was written down in 1344 at the insistence of Heinrich of Nördlingen; *Revelations* by Adelheid Langmann (d. 1375 in Engelthal); *Life of Sister Irmegard* by Elsbeth of Kirchberg—all Dominican-oriented revelation literature. Notable among the Franciscans are Agnes Blannbekin (d. 1315 in a Franciscan monastery in Vienna), Blessed Luitgard of Wittichen (1291–1348), and Elisabeth of Reute, whose life and revelations were written mainly by her spiritual advisors.

The form and purpose of these writings—that is, they are edifying accounts to be read aloud during meals—show that the writings must be interpreted as legendary literature. When the literary type and its original

11. *Virgin and Child*, German School, 15th century.

context are not taken into consideration, the texts will be completely mis-interpreted as psychologically "interesting material" concerning individuals. A "saintly life story" (*hailger wandel*) is defined precisely by its extraordinariness and so cannot be judged by standards of "normal" behavior.

Literature of the Friends of God

The phrase "Friends of God" is of biblical origin (John 25:14). In the fourteenth-century it referred to a group, often of laity, formed by a specifically religious self-consciousness: for example, groups of Friends of God formed about Heinrich of Nördlingen in Basel, where Mechthild's *Flowing Light of the Godhead* was translated from low German into high German (1343–1345) and was thus saved for posterity. These groups encouraged one another to seek the most intimate union with God. Certain members must have fostered sectarian or heretical tendencies, since the *Theologia deutsch*, or *German Theology*, differentiates true and false Friends of God. Such tendencies can be seen in the heretical exclusivity of certain later Rhineland groups called "evangelical" or "apostolic" toward the close of the fourteenth century.

"Friends of God" are to be found especially in Basel and Strasbourg, gathered around Tauler, Heinrich of Nördlingen, Margaretha and Christine Ebner, and, farther away, Suso. They developed the form of the mystical letter into a literary means of communication in which the inner dimension dominates the outer and in which a tender, genuine, and remarkable spiritual friendship between like-minded individuals could find expression.

The title Friend of God became an actual literary event when, in Strasbourg, Rulman Merswin (1307–1382) styled himself as the recipient of the revelations of a "Friend of God in the Oberland." Merswin was a wealthy merchant, and in 1347 at the age of forty, he decided, with the agreement of his wife, to buy a former Benedictine monastery in Grünen Wörth. There he established a foundation that permitted priests and laymen, knights and peasants—as long as they had the same uncompromising religious convictions—to lead a withdrawn, celibate religious life. The leadership of this foundation was held firmly by Merswin for the rest of his life, even when he had given it over to the military order of St. John. Merswin's literary interests were recorded in a series of writings that were mainly compilations, with one exception—*The First Four Years of His Beginning Life* (*Von den vier Jahren seines anfangenden Lebens* [1352]), which was autobiographical in character. The comforting fiction portrayed here is that of an intimate community gathered around the "Friend of God in Oberland" (did Oberland mean heaven or the foothills of the Alps?). The

Friend of God lived secretly, appearing in public only through letters and other writings. Among these, the *Book of the Five Men* (*Fünfmannenbuch* [1377]), written in an artificial language, played a special role. It reported details of the common life and the conversion of five men who lived in direct communication with God in the solitude of a forest under the direction of the Friend of God. These brothers comprised a man bored with marriage, a lawyer, a canon, a Jew, and the Friend of God, who like Paul found it necessary to report even about himself. He assumed a political role, worked his way to Hungary and Italy, and in his secret messages to Rulman Merswin carried on apocalyptically in the chaos of the time. After Rulman's death, nothing more was heard of the Friend of God, but the illusion remained—the illusion of lay control over a tainted world and a depraved priesthood. We must assume that Rulman's need to be important fabricated the whole strange story. Was it in order to fortify his position in Grünen Wörth in opposition to the knights of St. John, or was it out of a personal need? We do not know.

Even in the fourteenth century, the dwelling place of the Friend of God was sought out in several expeditions—in the Oberland, in Entlebuch, and in Engelberg. What seemed like a late answer came in the fifteenth century when Nicholaus of Flue (1417–1487) appeared as a lay hermit in the interior of Switzerland. From his solitude, he stood by the developing and endangered Swiss confederation in the role of a peace-loving counselor who, always beckoned by spirituality, also tried to withdraw. Like Joan of Arc (ca. 1412–1431), he typifies the lay saint challenged again and again since the fourteenth century by a clerical church. Prophetic tendencies, a personal mystical experience, a political mission—these were the emphatic convictions of a sort of piety that considered the privileges of the religious orders to be unimportant.

Theologia deutsch (or Germanica)

This treatise, stemming from the circle of writings of Tauler and Meister Eckhart and attributed to the late fourteenth century, was written by a priest whose name is unknown. He was the superior of the house of the Teutonic order at Frankfurt, that is, the foundation of the order in Sachsenhausen. Martin Luther read the text enthusiastically and published it twice, part in 1516 and the complete work in 1518. The work has had a continuous and renowned history, although John Calvin, as well as some Catholics, at times forbade it. J. Arndt, C. Schwenckfeld, P. J. Spener, and S. Franck transmitted it to the enthusiasts and pietists, where it continued to be read. The most important and central theme of the treatise is the "discernment of spirits," which centers on the question, "How and by what means can one recognize the true, just Friends of God and the unjust, false, free spirits who are harmful to the church?"[6] Such a question locates this work in the spiritual environment of the fourteenth century; the Free Spirits and the mystically oriented beguines and beghards, condemned in 1311–1313 at the Council of Vienne, tended toward quietistic and amoral teachings about divinization. Earlier, Albert the Great and Heinrich Suso had defended themselves against the Free Spirit heresies in order to support the authenticity of Christian mysticism. It can also be assumed that Meister Eckhart endeavored to give them an impartial Christian answer in his mystical teaching. But the fine line between heresy and Christian orthodoxy was difficult to maintain, especially with regard to language and expression. The discernment of spirits was not a simple matter. The treatise *Sister Catherine* (*Schwester Katrei*, written after 1317 in Strasbourg by a follower of Eckhart) is a testimony to how closely Eckhartian modes of expression could be connected with definitely heretical tendencies.

The main point of all the discussion in the *Theologia deutsch* is divinization, something that was misunderstood by the Free Spirits as amoral and pantheistic, whereas the orthodox position rested on the nature of grace. The right meaning of the concept of freedom played a central role in this. Christian freedom does not emancipate the faithful from ecclesiastical and political ordinances and laws. Therefore, the treatise stigmatizes all social, revolutionary, and libertine actions of the Free Spirits against the sexual customs and the rights and possessions of the feudal system.

The author of the *Theologia deutsch* was not exceptionally knowledgeable concerning mystical traditions. He quotes Tauler, Boethius, and Dionysius the Areopagite, uses the typical schemata of ways and steps, and acknowledges himself to be a compiler whose knowledge is eclectic. For all that, his primary emphasis is on divinization through the sole mediating exemplarity of Jesus Christ, the *Christuslebens* that, without doubt, attracted Luther. Ordinary human life is seen as purely instrumental for the *Christuslebens* and must surrender its own intentions in the total imitation of Christ. Alongside the christological principle of thought, the author places Neoplatonic principles: the differentiation of the one and the many; the emanation of the many from the one. The independence of the creature remains difficult to ascertain according to this formulation, where everything is established as emanating from the one. On the other hand, the creative activity of God *ad extra* is seen as a necessity, since God of Himself knows no beginning. That is why God makes use of the creature that gives back its individual life totally to God in Christianity. The danger from the christological, as well as from the Neoplatonic, standpoint is a radical leveling of the independence of the creature, such that only "the false light of nature" is due to the creature. On the other hand, of course, the defense of the *Christuslebens* is of unprecedented urgency and may be the basis for the appeal of the treatise through the centuries.

Franciscan Mysticism

It cannot be said that the Franciscan version of mystical teaching in Germany had the same influence as the Dominican doctrine, or even a comparable influence. Nonetheless, Kurt Ruh, the discoverer of this body of works, has been able to produce a large quantity of Franciscan writings in German in his editions and investigations of manuscripts. Some of these await further study.

Internationally, Franciscan mysticism was known as a mysticism of the imitation of Christ as taught by St. Francis of Assisi (1182–1226). The fundamental norm was the imitation of Christ as taught in the Gospel. The life of Francis, from his mystical marriage to Lady Poverty to the reception of the stigmata on Mount Alverna, remained the model. It was an ecstatic love mysticism whose themes ran through the eminent theological work of Alexander of Hales (d. 1245) or John Duns Scotus (d. 1308). Above all, these themes are present in the writings of Bonaventure (1221–1274), who in *The Journey of the Soul into God* and *The Three-fold Way* became the real theoretician of this mystical form of life. His *Life of St. Francis* and the other lives of the holy founders were soon translated into all vernacular languages, especially in Italy and in the Netherlands.

From the fifteenth century on, *Bonaventura deutsch* was a category of spirituality prominent in Germany. It was already used by Suso. The early Franciscans of Augsburg, especially David of Augsburg (d. 1272); Conrad of Saxony (d. 1279), who wrote *Mirror of the Blessed Virgin* (*Speculum Beatae Mariae Virginis*); and a century later Rudolf of Biberach (d. 1360), who wrote *Seven Paths to God* (*Sieben Strassen zu Gott*), which was long attributed to Bonaventure; Marquard of Lindau (d. 1392); and Otto of Passau (second half of the fourteenth century), who wrote *The Twenty-Four Elders or the Golden Throne of the Loving Soul*, certify the presence of a Franciscan spirituality in Germany.

In Italy, the Franciscan mystical poet Jacopone da Todi (d. 1306), created a collection of songs, *The Lauds*, which is a beautiful testimony to the *pietas franciscana*. The "Stabat Mater" is to be found in the Roman missal to this day. Blessed Angela of Foligno (ca. 1248–1309) was converted at the age of forty from a worldly life and became a Franciscan tertiary; she then lived a completely withdrawn life as a recluse. In her *Instructions* she teaches three different steps of prayer: physical, spiritual, and supernatural prayer, "in which the soul by the mercy of God . . . is made to transcend its natural condition."[7] Knowledge of God and knowledge of self are the fruits of this contemplation and lead to transformation in Christ, who is the real book of life for the blessed. Through bridal mysticism, Angela seeks to describe the final embrace with God as a mystery of love. She also uses the Pseudo-Dionysian terms demanded by an apophatic mysticism, such as "divine darkness," the inexpressibility of God, etc. Her letters drew many disciples to her.

Raymond Lull (1232-1316), a Catalan who was also a Franciscan tertiary, led an adventurous life that was finally dedicated totally to the mission that brought him to martyrdom. His *Art of Contemplation* presents a method of contemplation that uses exercises under the rubric of the three powers of the soul—knowledge, memory, and will. In his *Book of Contemplations*, he differentiates three steps in the ascent of prayer to God, and his *Book of the Lover and the Beloved* describes the ecstatic confrontation between the lovers in matchless words that intertwine life and death as a form of the innermost mystery of the cross.

Like the *Goad of Love (Stimulus Amoris)* of the Minorite James of Milan, soon translated into Italian, German, Dutch, and French, the anonymous *Meditations on the Life of Christ* is also a witness to the tender and affective Christocentric Franciscan piety and *imitatio Christi*. The birth, childhood, passion, and death of Christ become a mystical biography in this work which seeks to draw the disciple into Christ's life: "Take comfort, rejoice. Suffer with his sufferings. Through nearness, trust and love, imitate Jesus wholeheartedly and with all your strength."[8] Such a transfer of the meditative and contemplative powers into the form of an *imitatio* arranged in exercises already shows the marks of a precisely ordered *Life of Christ*, somewhat like that of Ludolph the Carthusian (d. 1370) or the *Exercises* of St. Ignatius of Loyola.

Hendrik Herp (d. 1477)—or, in the Latinized form, Harphius—is probably the most important Dutch Franciscan writer in the fifteenth century. He belongs to the tradition of Ruusbroec (Ruysbroeck, see below) and was able to exercise an extraordinary influence over the Spanish sixteenth century with his mystical genius. His personality and biography are practically unknown. His teaching may be extracted most easily from his *Spiegel der volcomenheit (Mirror of Perfection)*. This and his other works were collected under the title *Theologia mystica* (1538), which was widely disseminated far into the sixteenth and seventeenth centuries. Harphius tried to translate Ruysbroeck's speculative mysticism into an affective mysticism, and in doing so he frequently followed Hugh of Balma (thirteenth century). The mystical vision of the divine essence as the third step beyond the active and the contemplative life is designated as *superessentialis* (*ouerweselic*); it is characterized as pure gift and by passivity. The way to it is shown through affective love and the imitation of Christ, because the incarnation is not a one-time privilege reserved for the moment when Jesus became human. Rather, it is a reality in which all Christians and, to some degree, all human beings participate. Obviously, for Harphius, that moment plays a part in the mystery of the incarnation of God, which, in the generation of the Son, gives humanity sonship by adoption. The image of God is impressed in the three powers of the soul (reason, will, and memory), but the image also is found in nature, grace, and glory or is visible in the trinity of soul, spirit, and reason (*ghedanck*). In a wholly Franciscan way, human beings are incorporated into Jesus Christ by love. A mystical participation in him arises from this—one realized in the form of a method of stripping away and of introspection. This mystical way reaches its high point, fostered by unifying love. The "superessential," immediate gaze upon the divine essence is therefore a vision considered to be possible for "wayfarers" or those *in statu viae*. Harphius thereby recognizes the possibility of the light of glory (*lumen gloriae*) even during the earthly life (a doctrine opposed to the Thomist position). The influence of Ruysbroeck is particularly evident, although Harphius would not classify himself simply as an imitator of Ruysbroeck but rather as his heir, as one who made his own contribution. The influence of Harphius remained extraordinary up to the close of the seventeenth century because of the translation of his work into various vernacular languages.

Jan van Ruysbroeck (1293–1381) and Groenendael

Ruysbroeck Admirabilis, as posterity named him, was born in 1293, grew up on the land and, after the death of his father, was taken to one of his cousins, Jan Hinckaert, a canon at the collegiate church of Saint Gudula in Brussels. In 1317, Ruysbroeck became a priest and worked for twenty-five years as vicar and chaplain at St. Gudula. Apparent pseudomystical tendencies, especially ideas of a certain Bloemmaerdine, a lady from the high society of Brussels, may have moved him to concern himself with mystical questions and to treat them in the vernacular with a clearly missionary intent. Ruysbroeck, together with his cousin and another canon, Francis van Coudenberg, concluded that the clergy itself was in need of basic reform if the actualization of a more perfect life was to have a chance. The three friends decided (the exact reasons for the decision still are not known) to withdraw to a secluded place called Groenendael in the Soignes forest near

Brussels. After a few companions joined the undertaking, they decided to become canons regular and to adopt the *Rule of St. Augustine*. On 10 March 1349, the house was solemnly elevated to a priory. Coudenberg was the first provost; Ruysbroeck held the office of prior up to his death. He seldom left the monastery, but lived there meditating and working on his writings. He may have received visitors—perhaps Tauler and certainly in 1377 Geert Groote, the founder of the Brethren of the Common Life in Deventer. On 2 December 1381, he died and was beatified in 1908.

Ruysbroeck's works are all written in the Flemish dialect of Brabant, the same language used by Hadewijch for her poetry (he refers to her expressly in his *Book of the Twelve Beguines*). His language was *Dietsch,* which we designate today as Middle Dutch. The number of treatises he wrote in this language brought fame to this holy forest priest, as the Friends of God called him. It resulted in his works' being translated early on into the language of the upper Rhine. In Ruysbroeck, we find all the determining points of the Rhineland mystics: the Augustinian *imago Trinitatis* in the highest part of the soul; the spark of the soul (natural as well as divine); the eternal procession of the idea of creation from the Son; the configured distinction between God and Godhead analogous to the meeting of humans with God in concomitant experiential phenomena and in the union of love beyond all understanding; mirror ontology; exemplarity; the suddenness of the breaking through into the "divine ground"; etc. But the differences in style, form, and thought patterns are unmistakable. Ruysbroeck stands strongly in the tradition of the old contemplative mysticism of the Cistercians and the Victorines, but also in the Franciscan manner of Bonaventure. The question still remains whether he is indebted directly or indirectly (by means of translations) either to Eckhart himself or to the early women's mysticism (such as Hadewijch II, who was influenced by Eckhart) for the inclusion in his works of material that clearly has the ring of Eckhart about it. However that may be (the question appears to be yet undecided), Ruysbroeck offers an independent variant of a mystical way which, according to the *Adornment of the Spiritual Marriage,* is divided into three levels: an active life, an interior (God-seeking) life, and a "God-gazing life." This hierarchy is constructed according to its psychological presuppositions into a mysticism of introspection and according to its transcendental goals into a mysticism kbased on Christ and the Trinity. It goes without saying that the Christian means of grace—the grace of the sacraments and especially of the Eucharist, but also the "exercises"—play a role.

Ruysbroeck's mysticism is trinitarian in a consistent sense, because "Godhead" as the ground of divine unity is identified with the Father. Unlike in Eckhart's thought, the differentiation of God/Godhead is only conceptual.

Ultimately the two aspects, the unity of the essence of God and the union of the persons, are not to be differentiated from each other, since the blessed love of the persons at the same time seals the identity of the divine essence. Creaturely participation in this divine process is possible and conceivable only by grace and the imitation of Christ. Ruysbroeck sharply differentiates purely "natural" methods of meditation—like sitting still and desiring to be emptied, as practiced by the Free Spirits—from the Christian imitation of the way of the cross aided by the means of grace of the church, above all, the Eucharist. The moment of commonality in the process interior to the Godhead has been revealed in the incarnation of the Son and is accomplished from God's side as a lasting "contact"—even a "touching the ground" of the creature, while from the creature's side arises a hunger and an eager desire for God which can lead by bridal mystical intensification to a "wounding" by love and a "fury of love." From the perspective of the human capacity engaged here, Ruysbroeck speaks of *dat ghemeyne leven*, the "common" or "comprehensive" life that includes the simultaneity of active works and passive enjoyment, of intellect and affect. Mystical union has its mediate and immediate sides, most often at the same time; this union is a process of being drawn into God and of being sent out again:

> The spirit of God blows us outside so that we may practice love and virtuous deeds. But it draws us into itself as well so that we may give ourselves over to rest and enjoyment; and this is the divine life itself given graciously to human beings, principally in the seven gifts of the Holy Spirit.[9]

The influence of Ruysbroeck is noted above all in his follower Jan van Leeuwen, the "good cook" of Groenendael (d. 1374). He proposes a mystical method based on a structure of development in successive stages and thereby proves himself to be an ardent enemy of Meister Eckhart, whom he attacked repeatedly. Harphius certainly belongs to the school of Ruysbroeck. Jan van Schoonhoven (d. 1432) took certain strains of Ruysbroeck a step further, for example, his emphasis on love surpassing reason. Yet he also emphasizes simple ascetic demands—the influence of the *devotio moderna* is already evident here.

Carthusian Mysticism

The true significance of the mediating role of the Carthusians in medieval spiritual life and in medieval spirituality has in no way been properly recognized. The charterhouses were places which, precisely by their quiet and peace, invited the adoption and organization of the mystical currents and tendencies of the time. Thus they became clearinghouses in which mystical and ascetic texts were collected, copied, translated, and further distributed. This activity, however, was not merely a matter of compilation but was frequently quite creative. Its relevance is properly appreciated only when one considers the effect on Spanish mysticism of the Latin translations of the mystical writings of Tauler, Ruysbroeck, Suso by Laurentius Surius (d. 1538), or when one considers Ludolph of Saxony's (d. 1378) Latin edition of the *Life of Jesus* and its subsequent influence (perhaps on Ignatius of Loyola).

In the fifteenth century, Dennis the Carthusian (de Rijckel, d. 1471) was certainly the most eminent mystical theologian. His work is vast in scope. Aside from authoritative biblical commentaries, his work comprises commentaries on the works of Dionysius the Areopagite and other treatises that in subtle ways deal with the problems of mystical contemplation. He distinguishes between acquired and infused contemplation. The power of knowing, Thomistically speaking, takes precedence over love in mystical experience with the concession, though, that at the highest levels love stands by to assist the intuitive operations of knowledge itself. On the other hand, his dependence on Dionysius the Areopagite prevents him from giving to knowledge too much independent scope. The divine darkness, the essential and perduring final unknowability of God, is classified as the *via negationis* in discourse about God. This is a negative mysticism, which stands in opposition to bridal mysticism. Thus, de Rijckel becomes a mystical theologian of the highest order, who shows deep insight into all the ways and structures of mystical experience.

Italian Mysticism

The spiritual literature of Italy in the fourteenth and fifteenth centuries is especially rich and therefore not easily surveyed. One might usefully investigate the spiritualities of the various orders, since they provide fertile soil for different expressions of ascetical and mystical interests and tendencies. The contribution toward the formation of mental attitudes and concerns on the part of an ever more emancipated poetry and its poets cannot be overlooked. Dante's (1265–1321) *Divine Comedy* offers an intensely otherworldly perspective in the form of a visionary journey through the three realms. Nowhere else in human imagination has Christian eschatology been brought into sharper relief. Moreover, the character of Beatrice upon whom the poetic process of development in its symbolical, allegorical, and existential power is directed is finally the soul of the *ecclesia spiritualis* and embodies a mystical vision of the communion of saints. To this developing "republic of educated poets" certainly belong, among many others, Francesco Petrarch

(1304–1374) and his student, the Florentine Giovanni Boccaccio (d. 1375). If the first was compelled and fulfilled by intense religiosity, then the second was a slave to a newly discovered paganism.

The most impressive form of mystical experience in the fourteenth century in Italy is shown by Catherine of Siena (ca. 1347–1380). The life of this strong and very impressive woman developed as a whole from a religious choice. As a child, she was visited by visions and vowed to remain a virgin. Having entered the Sisters of Penance of St. Dominic at the age of fifteen, she withdrew to a life of penance and prayer at home, experienced a mystical marriage with Eternal Wisdom (ca. 1366–1367), and gathered about her a "family" of spiritual friends and dependents. Around 1370–1371 she dictated her first political letters, in which she supported the idea of a crusade. In 1374, she was cited before the general chapter of her order in Florence and asked about her orthodoxy, a test that she passed gloriously. Soon after, she journeyed to Pisa, Lucca, Gorgona, and Avignon, received the stigmata invisibly, and persuaded Pope Gregory XI to return to Rome from Avignon (1377). In the same year she began dictating her most important work, *The Book of Divine Providence* (*Libro della divina Provvidenza*); she sided with Pope Urban VI in the Great Schism and, after much suffering, she died in Rome on 29 April 1380. She was canonized in 1461.

Her work comprises almost 380 letters, the *Libro*, and two dozen prayers. Her mystical teaching, supported by manifold experiences and the stigmata, reached its climax in "Union," an experience characterized not by pure enjoyment but by suffering through the hunger and thirst of the soul with Christ on the cross. Her theological testimony centers on the redeeming blood of Jesus Christ mercifully poured out for all people, good and bad, and envisioned as a banquet laid out on the table of the cross. From this experiential insight, Catherine gained an extraordinary awareness of mission that she documented again and again with an emphatic "I will." Hunger and thirst for souls compelled her to a conception of time in which, for the sake of salvation, speed is required. To solve the problem of the short time left for salvation, patience and the ability to persevere are needed. Mystical rapture in God always gave her certitude for quick action. The image of knightly battle inspired her, and she fought against ecclesiastical decadence through criticism, instruction, and preaching about poverty and obedience, the necessity of an uncompromising knowledge of self and of God, prudence, and the renunciation of self-love and egoism. In sum, it was a unique attempt to unite action and contemplation in a life dedicated to the good of the church. Catherine's life was consumed by and offered up for the church. The church was her guarantor of the redeeming blood of Christ, the nursing mother of salvation. Her mysticism received from this a strong emphasis on the history and community of salvation. The dimension of religious subjectivity is broken through for her again and again by the common, promised salvation for all in Christ, so that she, like Augustine, was able to assign a role even to evil in the process of salvation.

Among the Franciscan mystics, Catherine of Bologna (1423-1463) is preeminent. Her life, led partly as a lady in waiting of Margaret D'Este at the court of Ferrara and partly as a Poor Clare and superior in Ferrara and Bologna, was governed by the theme of "spiritual struggle." Her trials and temptations, especially diabolical deceptions such as the devil in the guise of the Virgin Mary or Christ crucified, threw her into complete doubt. Temptations to disobedience spoiled her life in the order. Blasphemous thoughts, especially from the devil about the real presence of Christ in the Eucharist, attacked her to such an extent that she feared she would lose her mind. In opposition to this inner testing was the consolation of extraordinary mystical graces: her own death was foretold to her in a revelation. Her report, *The Seven Spiritual Weapons against the Enemies of the Soul* (1438), is at the same time an autobiography and a spiritual treatise. In it "the most excellent teacher of the interior struggle" (*peritissima militiae interioris magistra*) reports under the pseudonym "Catella" about her inner struggles and the means that led her to victory.

In fourteenth- and fifteenth-century Italy, mystical souls were found not only in the protected precincts of the orders but also among the laity. Apart from Francesca Bussa dei Ponziani (1384-1440), Catherine of Genoa (1447-1510) must be mentioned if only because of the scholarly attention bestowed on her by Baron Friedrich von Hügel in his standard work, *The Mystical Element of Religion as Studied in Saint Catherine of Genova and Her Friends* (1908). Catherine, who belonged to the famous family of Fieschi in Genoa, was married at an early age for political reasons to the worldly Giuliano Adorno. After sorrowful years in seclusion, she was able to free herself from her husband; from then on she led a life totally dedicated to prayer and discipline. But her contemplative life did not prevent her from giving extraordinary care to the poor and the sick. Even her husband was converted by these efforts of his wife and accommodated himself to these activities for twenty years until his death (1497). After that, Catherine, together with the priest Cattaneo Marabotto and a circle of friends, passed the last ten years of her life, years marked by violent interior emotions. These experiences are also the main content of the *Vita* by Marabotto, the *Dialogues,* and the treatise *On Purgatory.* In many ways, Catherine is the "Theologian of Purgatory." She experienced purgatory first of all physically in the marriage she did not desire, in her care for plague victims, and in her nervous illnesses. She then experienced it spiritually, as she says in her treatise. Her purgatorial experience was a mystical experience of sin, in which she endured what the soul must undergo painfully at the transition from life to death—the realization of one's own imperfection and sinfulness. She reflected unsystematically upon this condition by recalling her inner emotions. Her testimony is somewhat contradictory. This may be due to the complex story of the transmission of her writings, which leaves in dispute which of them may be attributed to her spiritual friends. Despite all doubt about the authenticity of her utterances, it is certain that an original mystical experience of the meaning of the history of salvation for the personal process of purification of the soul lies behind the literature attributed to her.

Theology and Mysticism

The fifteenth century is a clear illustration of the later, oft-lamented split between spirituality/mysticism and theology. The universities contributed to this split by fostering a progressively more abstract and methodically structured form of theological knowledge that separated theology more and more from religious-mystical experience. The failure to consolidate the two kinds of knowing through experiential knowledge should have meant that the universities could no longer be expected to provide spontaneous and interesting stimuli for the spiritual life. But the opposite was the case. There was, of course, a vernacular spiritual literature of edification, which continually became more weakly allegorical and ascetical, and there were also strong texts such as the *Imitation of Christ* which came out of the *devotio moderna*. But it is surprising that a number of reform movements of a spiritual and thoroughly innovative nature developed at the important universities such as Paris and Prague through men like John of Kastl and Geert Groote, the founder of the *devotio moderna*, who studied in Paris, Prague, and Cologne. Proof of a crisis in consciousness and at the same time of an inner regeneration in the fifteenth century is found in eminent representatives of the University of Paris such as Pierre d'Ailly (1350–1420), Jean Charlier de Gerson (1363–1429), and Robert Ciboule (d. 1458), who wrote an important treatise on self-awareness.

Pierre d'Ailly, the famous Cardinal Archbishop of Cambrai, turned against a false conception of mysticism in both his writings, *On False Prophets* (*De falsis prophetis*) and *Against Astronomers* (*Contra astronomos*). The "false prophets" were "wolves in sheep's clothing" and heretics; the astronomers were deceitful diviners of the future who were unmasked on the basis of a distinction of spirits, with the help of a rigid nominalism as taught by William of Ockham (d. 1347). Since from the creaturely perspective there is no absolutely binding moral obligation, because the commandments exist only because God has wished it so, the creature is duty bound to a radical union of will with the divine will. This is also the basic principle of mystical union. On the positive side, in his treatises and sermons, d'Ailly offers a theory of meditation and contemplation. Like Gerson, he granted a place of special honor to the holy patriarch Joseph. He also commented on the Song of Songs.

Jean Charlier de Gerson, a secular priest like d'Ailly, succeeded him in the important office of chancellor of the University of Paris in 1395. In this capacity he sought by peaceful means to heal the schism in the church, which had existed for seventeen years. This policy, and especially the fact that he sided with the Armagnacs against the Burgundians, embroiled him in political quarrels which made it necessary for him to flee to the German monastery of Melk (1418/1419). He then withdrew to the Celestine house at Lyons, where he became engaged in literary and apostolic activities. He died there on 12 July 1429.

Gerson was an Ockhamist to a greater degree than d'Ailly. He did not try to destroy the nominalist system; rather, he attempted to join it to a schema of mystical theology. Although familiar with the writings of Ruysbroeck, Gerson mistrusted Ruysbroeck's teaching, especially the mystical play of imagination in the *Adornment of the Spiritual Marriage*. Gerson was closer to the patristic tradition, especially to Pseudo-Dionysius and to the writings of the Victorines, of Bernard, and of Bonaventure. From these he drew the elements of his synthesis of mystical theology, *On Mystical Theology*, in which he tried to show that purely intellectual schemata could not lead to God. Instead, one is drawn to God through the intuitions of the simple intelligence, supported by the affective powers, and especially *synderesis*. The struggle to know must be bound to the emotions so that the soul is able to undergo an actual mystical experience which neither abolishes nor destroys the core of the person. Mystical experience itself is a kind of religious experience of God through unity in love (*theologia mystica est cognitio experimentalis habita de Deo per amoris unitivi complexum*). Later, Vincent of Aggsbach turned against this notion (see below). Although all are obliged to heed the call to conversion, only a few rise to fulfillment in contemplation. Gerson also reacted vehemently against the false mysticism of his time, especially against that sort which, as he understood it, was too agnostic and apophatic and easily fell into pantheism (e.g., the mysticism of Ruysbroeck). He designates the abuses of the mystical tendencies of his time by various names: the beghards, the Turlupins, certain quietistic trends, etc. Against them he refers to the promulgations of the councils (which he, as a Gallican, placed above the Pope) and to the pronouncements of the Popes, to Holy Scripture, and to tradition. In 1415, during the Council of Constance, at which Gerson as well as d'Ailly played an important part, Gerson wrote his treatise *De probatione spirituum*, at the moment when the council was concerned with the reports of visions of St. Bridget. In this work, Gerson examined the visions of mystics on the basis of the spiritual condition of the receiver and an analysis of the content. In every case reports of visions are to be met with mistrust and caution. The moral, human, and religious integrity of the mystics is the uppermost demand.

In his basic distinction between speculative and practical mysticism, Gerson made a shift that signaled an important scientific presupposition for the later preoccupation with mystical experience in the sixteenth century, especially for the Thomistically schooled Carmelites. At the same time, he bore witness to the intricate situation in which, to a certain extent, the separation between theology and spirituality became final, although in later times certain great figures were able to build bridges between them.

The second decisive impulse in the fifteenth century that had mystical experience as its goal occurred from 1451 to 1480 in the dispute over the work *On Learned Ignorance* (*De docta ignorantia*) by Cardinal Nicholas of Cusa (1401–1464). (The active life of this great churchman, his theology and political views, cannot be discussed here.) The conflict arose because in his writings Cusa appealed to Meister Eckhart, whose most important Latin and German works he possessed. Johannes Wenck of Herrenberg, professor at Heidelberg, pointed out this connection in his polemical work *On Unknown Learning* (*De ignota literatura*). In his *Apologia*, Cusa defended Meister Eckhart and referred to the entire Neoplatonic tradition which was available to him in John Scotus Eriugena and David of Dinant; indeed, he was indebted to all three. The point that Wenck considered heretical was the "coincidence of opposites" (*coincidentia oppositorum*) whose acceptance marked the beginning of the ascent into mystical theology. This point Cusa defended as unrelinquishable. Monks inspired by reform joined in the debate. The prior of the Benedictine monastery of Tegernsee, Bavaria, Bernard Waging, in his *Praise of Learned Ignorance* (1451) tried to ascertain the difference between *docta ignorantia* and *theologia mystica* (something that concerned the monks at Tegernsee), in order to define it as the scientific form of the affective connection between human beings and God. Both led to union with him. This has to do with the old question in mysticism concerning which of the two powers of the soul takes precedence in the mystical experience: knowledge or love. Kaspar Aindorffer, the abbot of the monastery of Tegernsee, posed the question to the cardinal with complete clarity:

> Whether the devout soul, without intellectual cognition or even without previous or concomitant cognition, solely by affection or through the apex of the soul called *synderesis,* can attain to God and be immediately moved or borne unto Him?[10]

The cardinal answered with reference to a certain form of concomitance of both powers of the soul:

> There is, therefore, in all such love, by which one is carried into God, a cognition, even though one remains unaware of what it is one loves. Thus there is a coincidence of knowledge and of ignorance, or a learned ignorance (*docta ignorantia*).[11]

Even if that which is loved is not known, some kind of knowledge is required, so that the power of love can set out on the way to God. Through Johannes of Weilheim, prior of Melk, who had become aware of the problem, the Carthusian Vincent of Aggsbach joined in the controversy. He was a proponent of a purely practical mysticism, a supporter of ecclesial reform and of the conciliarists. A strong emotional reaction against scholasticism moved him to call upon doctors and lectors to apply themselves to the study of practical mysticism. He turned against Gerson, who failed to teach that one could progress in practical mysticism without knowledge of God. Cusa learned about these writings from the monasteries of Melk and Tegernsee, and in 1453 he adopted a position toward them along the lines of the views he had already expressed. Some knowledge must precede a union in love, because the totally unknown cannot be loved. The principle of contradiction does not apply to infinity in any case; one must move from knowing to not knowing and see that something is and is not simultaneously (something absurd to reason). This is something of higher necessity than the importance of the principle of noncontradiction. Those from Tegernsee, whom Vincent apparently followed, proposed a compromise solution through Bernard Waging: the union of the soul with God may be without actual knowledge; but, on the other hand, it is not possible without any knowledge. Cusa rebuked them laconically by saying that the blessedness of the experience of God makes every knowing into a loving and vice versa. Finally, Marquard Sprenger of Munich entered into the discussion in his *Explanation of Mystical Theology.* He attacked Gerson's camp and that of Cusa with the Thomistic formula: knowledge with love (*cognitio cum amore*), which Nicholas approved. The controversy continued between Vincent on the one hand and Marquard Sprenger and Bernard Waging on the other.

Basically, the controversy between these churchmen points to a trend that was even more strongly noticeable in popular ascetical literature. It moved from the intellectual mysticism of a Dominican past (Meister Eckhart and his followers) toward a mysticism marked by feeling and love, ever more strongly psychologically oriented and directed to spiritual events and experience. It was a movement that would persistently characterize the sixteenth and seventeenth centuries. The *Imitation of Christ* shows the vast import of this practical path.

Notes

1. Master Eckhart, *Expositio Sancti Evangelii sec. Ioh. n. 2*, in Meister Eckhart, *Die deutschen und lateinischen Werke*, edited and published through the Deutschen Forschungsgemeinschaft, vol. 3, *Die lateinischen Werke* (Stuttgart: Kohlhammer, 1936–) 4, 5f.

2. Ibid., *Die deutschen Werke*, vol. 2, 528, 5; 529, 2.

3. Ibid., *Die deutschen Werke*, vol. 1, 201, 5–8.

4. *Die Predigten Taulers, Aus der Engelberger und der Freiburger Handschrift*, ed. Ferdinand Vetter (Dublin and Zurich: Weidmann, 1968) 69, 26–28.

5. Heinrich Seuse, *Deutsche Schriften*, ed. Karl Bihlmeyer (1907; reprint, Frankfurt am Main: Minerva, 1961) 99, 12.

6. "Der Franckforter" ("Theologia Deutsch"), critical edition by Wolfgang von Hinten (Münchener Texte und Untersuchungen 78; Munich and Zurich: Artemis Verlag, 1982) 67, 5–7.

7. *Le Livre de la bienheureuse Angèle de Foligno*, ed. Paul Doncoeur (Paris and Toulouse: Editions de la Revue d'Ascétique et de Mystique, 1925) 124, 5–7.

8. *Meditations on the Life of Christ: An Illustrated Manuscript of the Fourteenth Century*, trans. Isa Ragusa and Rosalie B. Green (Princeton, NJ: Princeton University Press, 1961).

9. *Jan van Ruusbroec, Werken III*, ed. L. Reypens and M. Schurmans (Tielt: Drukkerij-Uitgeverij Lannoo, 1947) 269, 6–9.

10. E. Vansteenberghe, *Autour de la docte ignorance*, 110.

11. Ibid., 112.

Bibliography

Sources

The Book of the Poor in Spirit by A Friend of God. Translated by C. F. Kelley. New York: Harper, 1954.

Catherine of Genoa. *Purgation and Purgatory: The Spiritual Dialogue*. Translated by Serge Hugues. Introduction by Benedict J. Groeschel. Classics of Western Spirituality. New York: Paulist Press, 1979.

Catherine of Siena. *The Dialogue*. Translated by Suzanne Noffke. Classics of Western Spirituality. New York: Paulist Press, 1980.

———. *The Prayers of Catherine of Siena*. Edited by Suzanne Noffke. New York: Paulist Press, 1983.

Eckhart, Meister. *The Essential Sermons, Commentaries, Treatises and Defense*. Translated by E. Colledge and Bernard McGinn. Classics of Western Spirituality. New York: Paulist Press, 1981.

——. *German Sermons and Treatises.* Translated and edited by M. O'C. Walshe. 2 vols. London and Dulverton: Watkins, 1979, 1981. The only complete English translation of Eckhart's German works.

——. *Parisian Questions and Prologues.* Translated by Armand A. Maurer. Toronto: Pontifical Institute of Mediaeval Studies, 1974.

——. *Teacher and Preacher.* Translated by Bernard McGinn in collaboration with Frank Tobin and Elvira Borgstadt. Classics of Western Spirituality. New York: Paulist Press, 1986. This contains the "Sister Catherine" text as an appendix.

Gerson, Jean. *Selections from "A Deo Exivit" "Contra curiositatem studentium" and "De mystica theologia speculativa."* Edited and translated by Steven E. Ozment. Leiden: Brill, 1969.

Hadewijch. *The Complete Works.* Translated by Mother Columba Hart. Classics of Western Spirituality. New York: Paulist Press, 1980.

Il Libro della Beata Angela da Foligno. Edited by Ludger Thier and Abele Calufetti. Grottaferrata (Rome): Editiones S. Bonaventurae, 1985. The new critical edition awaits translation into English.

Luther, Martin. *The Theologia Germanica of Martin Luther.* Translated by Bengt Hoffman. Classics of Western Spirituality. New York: Paulist Press, 1980.

Mechthild of Magdeburg. *The Revelation of Mechthild of Magdeburg, or The Flowing Light of Godhead.* Translated by Lucy Menzies. London: Longmans, Green, 1953.

Mediaeval Netherlands Religious Literature. Translated by E. Colledge. New York: London House and Maxwell, 1965.

Merswin, Rulman. *Mystical Writings of Rulman Merswin.* Edited by Thomas S. Kepler. Philadelphia: Westminster, 1960.

Raymond of Capua. *The Life of Catherine of Siena.* Translated by Conleth Kearns. Wilmington, DE: Michael Glazier, 1980.

Ruusbroec, Jan van. *Opera omnia.* Edited by G. de Baer et al. 2 vols. Leiden: Brill, 1981–. Two volumes of ten have thus far been published of this critical edition, which contains a facing English translation.

——. *The Spiritual Espousals and Other Works.* Translated by James A. Wiseman. Classics of Western Spirituality. New York: Paulist Press, 1985.

Suso, Heinrich. *Suso's Works.* Translated by Frank Tobin. Classics of Western Spirituality. New York: Paulist Press, 1987.

Tauler, Johannes. *Sermons.* Translated by Maria Shrady. Introduction by Josef Schmidt. Classics of Western Spirituality. New York: Paulist Press, 1985.

——. *Spiritual Conferences by John Tauler, O.P.* Translated and edited by E. Colledge and Sister M. Jane. Rockford, IL: Tan Books, 1978.

Studies

Altdeutsche und altniederländsche Mystik. Edited by Kurt Ruh. Darmstadt: Wissenschaftliche Buchgesellschaft, 1964.

Ancelet-Hustache, Jeanne. *Master Eckhart and the Rhineland Mystics.* New York: Harper, 1957. A brief, illustrated introduction.

——. "Les *Vitae Sororum* d'Unterlinden." *Archives d'histoire doctrinal et littéraire du moyen âge* 5 (1930) 317–509.

Axters, Stephanus. *The Spirituality of the Old Low Countries.* London: Blackfriars, 1954.

Deutsches Nonnenleben. Translated by Margarete Weinhandl. Munich: O. C. Recht, 1921.

Grundmann, Herbert. *Religiöse Bewegungen im Mittelalter: Untersuchung über die geschichtlichen Zusammenhänge zwischen Ketzerei, den Bettelorden und der religiösen Frauenbewegung im 12. und 13. Jahrhundert* . . . Hildesheim: Georg Olms, 1961. The second, enlarged edition of this classic study; especially important for female mysticism.

Guarnieri, Romana. "Il Movimento del Libero Spirito: Testi e Documenti." *Archivio Italiano per la Storia della Pietà* 4 (1965) 353–708. This major work contains the text of Marguerite Porete's *Mirror of Simple Souls* (there is still no complete English translation).

Haas, Alois M. *Sermo mysticus: Studien zu Theologie und Sprache der deutschen Mystik.* Freiburg: Universitätsverlag, 1979.

———. *Geistliches Mittelalter.* Freiburg: Universitätsverlag, 1984.

———. "Die *Theologia Deutsch:* Konstitution eines mystologischen Texts." In *Das "einig Ein": Studien zu Theorie und Sprache der deutschen Mystik,* 369–415. Edited by Alois M. Haas and Heinrich Stirnimann. Freiburg: Universitätsverlag, 1980.

———, and Heinrich Stirnimann, eds. *Das "einig Ein": Studien zu Theorie und Sprache der deutschen Mystik.* Freiburg: Universitätsverlag, 1980. An important collection of recent studies.

Hopkins, Jasper. *Nicholas of Cusa's Debate with John Wenck: A Translation and Appraisal of De Ignota Litteratura and Apologia Doctae Ignorantiae.* Minneapolis, MN: Arthur J. Banning Press, 1981.

Hügel, Friedrich von. *The Mystical Element of Religion as Studied in Catherine of Genoa and Her Friends.* 2 vols. London: J. M. Dent, 1961. One of the most important books ever written about mysticism.

Lerner, Robert E. *The Heresy of the Free Spirit in the Later Middle Ages.* Berkeley and Los Angeles: University of California Press, 1972.

Lossky, Vladimir. *Théologie négative et connaissance de Dieu chez Maître Eckhart.* Paris: J. Vrin, 1960. A classic work.

McDonnell, Ernest W. *The Beguines and Beghards in Medieval Culture with Special Emphasis on the Belgian Scene.* New Brunswick, NJ: Rutgers University Press, 1954.

Mommaers, P., and N. de Paepe, eds. *Jan van Ruusbroec: The Sources, Content and Sequels of His Mysticism.* Leuven: Leuven University Press, 1984.

Le mystique rhénane: Colloque de Strasbourg 1961. Paris: Presses universitaires de France, 1963.

Ozment, Steven E. *Homo Spiritualis: A Comparative Study of the Anthropology of Johannes Tauler, Jean Gerson and Martin Luther (1509–16).* Leiden: Brill, 1969.

Petroff, Elizabeth Alvida, ed. *Medieval Women's Visionary Literature.* New York: Oxford University Press, 1986.

Ruh, Kurt. *Kleine Schriften: Band II, Scholastik und Mystik im Spätmittelalter.* Berlin: de Gruyter, 1984. Collected papers of one of the major scholars in the field.

———. *Meister Eckhart: Theologe, Prediger, Mystiker.* Munich: Beck, 1985.

Stoelen, Anselm. "Denys le Chartreux." In *Dict. Sp.* 3, cols. 430–49.

Szarmach, Paul, ed. *An Introduction to the Medieval Mystics of Europe.* Albany, NY: State University of New York Press, 1984. Contains papers on several important mystics.

Tobin, Frank. *Meister Eckhart: Thought and Language.* Philadelphia: University of Pennsylvania Press, 1986.

Tugwell, Simon. *Early Dominicans: Selected Writings.* Classics of Western Spirituality. New York: Paulist Press, 1982.

Vansteenberghe, Edmond. *Autour de la docte ignorance: Une controverse sur la théologie mystique au XVe siècle.* Münster: Aschendorff, 1915.

7

Devotio Moderna

OTTO GRÜNDLER

THE DEVOTIO MODERNA was a late medieval religious reform movement that began in the Netherlands in the late fourteenth century and quickly spread into Germany. The movement originated under the impact of Geert Groote (1340–1384) of Deventer, the son of a wealthy merchant and city councilman. Groote entered the University of Paris at the age of fifteen and received his Master of Arts degree less than three years later. He remained in Paris for ten years studying canon law, medicine, and theology, supported by his inheritance as well as by two prebends at Aachen and Utrecht. In 1374, following a conversion experience, Groote resigned his prebends, turned his paternal house in Deventer over to a group of devout women who were to become the initial Sisters of the Common Life, and entered the Carthusian monastery at Monnikhuizen near Arnhem, where his friend Henry of Calcar was then prior and where Groote was to remain for nearly three years. Upon the urging of the monks to go out into the world and preach, Groote left the Monnikhuizen cloister, returned to Deventer, was ordained a deacon in the diocese of Utrecht around 1380, and quickly became an extraordinarily successful itinerant preacher. He traveled throughout Holland, preaching reform, urging his listeners to join together in leading a spiritual life, and denouncing the worldliness of the clergy. It is not surprising that the clergy reacted with protest and increasing hostility, with the result that Groote's license to preach was suspended in 1383. Geert Groote died of the plague on 20 August 1384—just before Rome rescinded the ban on his preaching and reformist activities after sympathetic supporters in the hierarchy intervened.

The Brethren of the Common Life

By the time of Groote's death, a group of his disciples was living in the vicarage of Florens Radewijns (1350–1400), a priest in Deventer. Under the latter's leadership, the group founded a community based on common property, the Brethren of the Common Life. A parallel development was that of the Sisters of the Common Life, a community that emerged from the group of devout women who had lived in Groote's house since 1374 under statutes written by Groote in 1379.

The movement expanded rapidly throughout the low countries and into Germany. The house at Deventer established new foundations in Delft, Louvain, Emmerich as well as in Münster, Cologne, and Wesel. From the house in Zwolle, new houses were founded in 's-Hertogenbosch, Doesburg, Groningen, Herderwijk, and Culm. Other settlements included houses in Herford, Marburg, Hildesheim, and Rostock. By the middle of the fifteenth century the Brethren and Sisters of the Common Life counted between them about one hundred houses in the low countries and Germany.

In contrast to the Sisters, who were laywomen, the Brethren of the Common Life were by no means a lay community. The majority of its members were priests or candidates for the priesthood (clerics). The few lay brothers, the *familiares*, usually carried out the menial tasks of cooking, cleaning, and tailoring. Like the Sisters, the Brethren held all property in common and practiced the monastic ideals of poverty, chastity, and obedience without taking solemn vows. The Brethren earned their own living by copying manuscripts and in their daily routine followed monastic patterns, including observance of the canonical hours, periods of silence and study, and the practice of meditation throughout the day. In addition, the Brethren provided pastoral care and spiritual counsel to the sister houses, and at least some of the Brethren engaged in preaching. Ever since the founding of the brotherhood, a major concern of the Brethren had been the preparation of young men for the monastic life and for the priesthood. To this end, they established hostels to provide lodging and food for schoolboys attending the city schools and served as spiritual counselors and tutors for them. Since few of the brothers had attended universities, they were, on the whole, not qualified to teach in the schools. They did, however, hold colloquies for schoolboys in the brotherhouses on Sundays after church consisting of talks on a given spiritual subject followed by discussion in groups or by individual conversations with a priest. Frequently, the Brethren recruited new members from among these schoolboys, who after completing their education at the city school joined the Brethren as clerics or entered a monastery.

The initial *consuetudines* or constitutions of the brotherhouses at Deventer and Zwolle, compiled between 1413 and 1415 and subsequently adopted by all houses in the low countries and Germany, established the daily routine of the life of the community.[1] The Brethren rose at half past three after

seven hours of sleep and prepared themselves for the praying of the canonical hours by renewing their good intentions. Immediately after the breviary,
an hour was set aside every morning for the study of Scripture, followed
by attending Mass at the parish church. From seven to ten and from noon
to three the brothers worked on copying books, and again after vespers
from five to seven until the evening meal and compline. The brothers were
allowed one hour at their personal disposal from seven to eight, and at half
past eight everyone had to be in bed.

Devotional literature was read aloud during meals, with occasional checks
by the rector to see whether the brothers were listening. On Sundays and
feast days the brothers assembled after the noon meal for collations, that is,
the reading and discussion of a passage from Scripture. Each brotherhouse
was presided over by a rector and a procurator who were elected by the
brothers.

This strong resemblance to monastic life provoked outspoken opposition
and condemnation, especially from the mendicant orders, who accused the
Brethren and Sisters of the Common Life of starting a new monastic order,
in violation of the Fourth Lateran Council's prohibition of new orders in
1215, and without taking vows. Partly in anticipation of such opposition,
Geert Groote, shortly before his death, had urged his followers to found a
monastery. The Brethren carried out his wishes by founding a monastery
for regular canons at Windesheim in 1386; several brothers from Deventer
were among the first inhabitants. Three other existing monasteries joined
together with Windesheim to form the Windesheim Congregation of
Augustinian Regular Canons in 1394–1395. Other foundations soon followed, among them Mount St. Agnes near Zwolle and St. Marienwolde at
Frenswegen, both of which joined the Windesheim Congregation. Around
1460 the historian of the *devotio moderna,* Johannes Busch, listed eighty
monasteries belonging to the Congregation. The Windesheim Congregation became noted for several significant achievements. Under its direction,
monastic reform was implemented by reintroducing strict observance of
monastic rule in the monasteries of the dioceses of Hildesheim, Halberstadt,
and Verden. Furthermore, the Windesheim canons produced standardized
liturgical texts and, most important, a new edition of the Vulgate. The
renewal of monastic spirituality was decisively influenced by such Windesheim authors as Gerlach Peters (1378–1411), Hendrik Mande (1360–1431),
and above all, by Thomas à Kempis (1380–1471), whose *Imitation of Christ*
has become a classic among spiritual treatises.

During the second half of the fifteenth century, more and more houses
of the Brethren of the Common Life applied for and received chapter status,
or entered into a union with chapter houses as in Butzbach and Königstein,

whereas most of the sisterhouses adopted the rule of the third order of St. Francis. In the wake of the Protestant Reformation, the institutions of the *devotio moderna* declined rapidly. In Protestant territories, both the brotherhouses and the monasteries were dissolved, and most of the houses of the Brethren, including the founding houses of Deventer and Zwolle, had disappeared by 1600. In Roman Catholic areas, some of the brotherhouses and houses of the Windesheim Congregation survived until they fell victim to the secularizations of the eighteenth and nineteenth centuries. The most important member of the Windesheim Congregation in Germany, St. Marienwolde in Frenswegen, held out until 1809, when it was officially dissolved by the state. The last canon, Gerhard Többe, left Frenswegen in 1815.

During the early part of the twentieth century, the *devotio moderna* has frequently been described in various studies as a radical break with medieval monasticism and as a forerunner of the Protestant Reformation. It has been credited with initiating widespread innovative changes in public education and with having influenced nearly every humanist of the fifteenth and sixteenth centuries. Evidence of the "modernity" of the movement has been found in its lay character, nonconformity, modern individualism, rejection of externals in religious practice, alienation from the church, and in its rejection of binding vows.

That the above claims do not apply to the monastic branch of the *devotio moderna*, that is, the Windesheim Congregation, is obvious. But neither do those claims, on the whole, apply to the Brethren and Sisters of the Common Life, as recent scholarship has shown.[2] On the contrary, the institutions and literature of the *devotio moderna* represent a revival of traditional monastic spirituality rather than a radical innovation.

Inner Devotion

All the adherents of the movement practiced what they called "inner devotion," and it is this cultivation of the spiritual life through inner devotion and its interrelationship with the external ordering of the community that bear a close resemblance to the spirituality of traditional monasticism.

Geert Groote, the acknowledged founder of the *devotio moderna*, developed his basic concepts of the spiritual life during his sojourn with the Carthusian monks at Monnikhuizen. Thomas à Kempis describes Groote's life in the cloister:

> Dressing in a long coarse garment of hair-cloth, totally abstaining from the use of meat and other lawful things, and passing a considerable portion of his

nights in vigils and prayer, he forced his feeble body into complete sub-
servience to the spirit.[3]

During the first period of his stay at Monnikhuizen, Groote proposed to
himself a series of resolutions regarding the ordering of his personal life:

> I intend to order my life for the glory, honor, and service of God and the
> salvation of my soul; to prefer no temporal good either of the body, or of
> honor, or of fortune, or of knowledge to my soul's salvation.[4]

He resolved never again to desire a benefice and renounced all material
possessions, including any profit he might acquire through academic pur-
suits. He proposed to abandon all manner of scholarship in any field and
to discontinue his studies in theology, medicine, and law. He declared his
intention never to write any book to enhance his reputation. He rejected
scholasticism, its method as well as its conclusions. Indeed, he renounced
every branch of academic learning as nonessential.

These resolutions reflect an attitude that lies at the heart of the *devotio
moderna* and is deeply rooted in the monastic tradition, that of contempt
for the world, *contemptus mundi*. Groote's *conclusa* are reminiscent of the
Meditations of Guigo I, fifth prior of the Carthusian charterhouse, a book
with which Groote became familiar at Monnikhuizen:

> Lack of interior vision, that is, of God . . . causes you to go outside your
> interior . . . and you spend your time admiring the exterior forms of bodies
> or the opinions of men. To gain an interior vision of God and to receive his
> benefits one must deny the world and himself. . . .
> The way to God is easy because one goes by disburdening. But it would be
> hard were one to go by taking on burdens. So, disburden yourself to the point
> where, having left all things, you deny yourself. . . . Wean yourself henceforth
> from those forms of bodies. . . . Learn to live without them, learn to live and
> rejoice in God.[5]

Groote saw a correlation between interior devotion and external works
of piety and considered both as necessary components of true spirituality.

> The work and interior exercises of religion are an intimate devotion, interi-
> ority, and submission to the will of God. Exterior works and exercises consist
> in adoration and the offering of oneself.[6]

The way to God is a life of struggle, of contempt for the world, and of
self-denial. In order to attain the goal, one must imitate the humanity of
Christ, especially Christ's passion, through meditation, prayer, and humble
self-dispossession: *crux Christi in ruminatione passionis fabricanda est* ("the
cross of Christ must be built by ruminating on the passion").[7] Imitation
means to conform one's life to the model of the *vita Christi* (life of Christ).

But the emphasis on interiority or conscious inner devotion does not exclude exterior works and exercises. For Groote, external actions and bodily gestures are symbols and signs of inward devotion. For example,

> [During the Mass] . . . our bowing at these words [the Gospel], and the bodily posture of reverence, are symbols of the reverence of our minds. . . . More-over, the outward observance is a means to induce inward reverence, but it is vain if one answers not to the other. . . . A bent posture does admirably befit devotion of mind, for the motions of spirit do bear relation to the posture of the body.[8]

Again, Groote echoes the opinion of Guigo I:

> The greatest utility of bodies is in their use as signs. For from them are made many signs necessary for our salvation . . . nor do men know the movements of one another's souls but by sensible signs.[9]

The books that Groote had copied for his personal use and to which he constantly referred included the classics of medieval devotional literature, notably the works of Cassian, Gregory I, and Bernard of Clairvaux. Groote's spirituality was thus deeply rooted in the monastic contemplative tradition, and it is not surprising that he frequently extolled the monastic life as the most perfect way of salvation: "To enter the monastery is to choose the highest state of life and that which pleases God the most."[10]

Groote's most influental disciples were Florens Radewijns and Geert Zerbolt van Zutphen (1367–1398). Radewijns, cofounder of the devotionalist movement, was the first rector of the motherhouse of the Brethren of the Common Life at Deventer from 1384 to 1400. Of his works, only two have been preserved: *Multum valet* and *Omnes inquit artes*. The former is a devotional treatise examining the goals of the spiritual life, purity of heart and love of God. Radewijns describes two ways of attaining these goals: the *via purgativa*, the practice of virtue through spiritual reading, prayer, and meditation; and the *via illuminativa*, the reflection on the benefits received from God. The second work, *Omnes inquit artes*, consists of a collection of texts from Scripture and traditional devotional writings and of a treatise on the subject matter of meditation: the passion of Christ, the four last things, humanity's sin, and the benefits received from God. The chief virtues to be practiced are love of God and love of neighbor. The brothers are admonished that among them love of neighbor consists in brotherly harmony, in giving and accepting fraternal reproof, and in obedience, which means, above all, the renunciation of one's own will. The texts for meditation selected by Radewijns are representative of monastic literature, but the one author quoted most frequently is Cassian. Almost a third of the entire text of *Omnes inquit artes* is derived from the writings of Cassian, who seems to have been the dominant influence upon Radewijns's spirituality. Scholastic learning, on the other hand, and speculative mysticism are emphatically rejected as hinderances to devotion and distractions from the eradication of faults.

Geert Zerbolt, one of the original brothers of the house in Deventer, must be counted among the spiritual masters of the *devotio moderna,* even though he died at the young age of thirty-one. His treatises, *De reformatione virium* and *De spiritualibus ascensionibus,* had a major impact on the evolving spirituality of the devotionalist movement and its later authors, including Thomas à Kempis.

The human being, according to Zerbolt, being "a noble and reasonable creature endowed with a certain greatness of mind" has a natural desire to seek and ascend to the "lofty heights" of God. But the spiritual ascent is blocked by human depravity as experienced in original sin and concupiscence, so that every human soul is now "inclined in a direction far removed from that to which God ordained it."

The restoration of the soul's powers takes place at various levels of ascent by means of self-knowledge, mortification, and humility as revealed in the *vita Christi* which is the model to be imitated. Hence, *imitatio Christi* is at the very center of Zerbolt's spirituality. Imitation of Christ is realized in three steps or ascents corresponding to appreciation of Christ's humanity, discovery of his divinity, and union with God.

To accomplish these ascents in the imitation of Christ Zerbolt prescribed four exercises: *lectio* (spiritual reading), *meditatio, oratio* (prayer), and *contemplatio,* all of them centered on Christ's passion. Meditation is explained as follows:

> By meditation is meant the process in which you diligently turn over in your heart whatsoever you have read or heard, earnestly ruminating the same and thereby enkindling your affections in some particular manner or enlightening your understanding.[11]

Zerbolt's treatise on the spiritual ascent closely resembles the *scala claustralium* of Guigo II, the ninth prior of Chartreuse.[12] Zerbolt's four exercises in achieving one's ascent in the imitation of Christ parallel those of Guigo, and, like the Carthusian prior, Zerbolt emphasizes their interrelatedness. Spiritual reading prepares for meditation, meditation for prayer, and prayer for contemplation. Reading without prayer is arid; meditation without reading erroneous. Prayer without meditation is tepid; meditation without prayer fruitless; contemplation without prayer rare or miraculous.

What had been the central theme in the writings of Groote, Radewijns, and Zerbolt became the very title of the famous treatise by the best-known representative of the *devotio moderna, De Imitatione Christi* by Thomas à Kempis, canon of Mount St. Agnes. Although the authorship of the book has been the subject of considerable dispute (e.g., parts of the work have been ascribed to Zerbolt and even Groote), tradition has always regarded Thomas as the author.

The work may well be called a *summa spiritualitatis*, the confluence of the thoughts expressed by the masters of medieval spirituality on the theme of imitation. For St. Augustine, following and imitating Christ were the very meaning of the spiritual life: as God, Christ is the goal, and as man he is the way.[13] For St. Bernard, too, the spiritual way was to imitate Christ by relating oneself both to Christ's humanity and to his divinity. One must begin with the love of Christ as man before one can ascend to the love of Christ as God, and to do so requires constant meditation on the mysteries of Christ.[14]

Thomas à Kempis reflects his spiritual predecessors when he defines imitation of Christ as the way of the cross. Christ is the model and pattern of self-knowledge, self-mortification, humility, and obedience, all of which are ranked among the key virtues revealed in the *vita Christi*.

> If you desire to be purified from your vices and to progress in the exercise of virtue, love the life and passion of Christ, whom the Father sent into the world as an example of all virtues.[15]

Echoing Zerbolt, Thomas considers self-knowledge as the prerequisite for spiritual progress. It is Christ, the perfect exemplar of humanity, who brings one to the realization of one's own condition as sinner, as one whose depravity, frailty, and incapacity to resist the temptations of the flesh have separated the sinner further and further from that true destiny which is to love and serve God in humility and obedience. Such awareness leads one to imitate Christ, to determine to bring one's life into total conformity with the pattern exhibited in the life of Christ.

Above all, Christ becomes a model of humility demanding self-mortification, self-renunciation, and contempt for the world. Guigo I had counseled his readers to "disburden yourself to the point where, having left all things, you deny yourself." Groote had called the way to God a life of struggle, of contempt for the world, and of self-denial. Thomas uses the terms "self-dispossession" and "nudity" to describe the same basic attitude. To imitate Christ means to withdraw from love of all exterior things, to become disentangled from any creature, to resist all fleshly passions.

> Strive for this, pray for this, desire this, to be stripped of all selfishness and naked to follow the naked Jesus, to die to self and live forever.[16]

This radical humility which desires nothing but to love and serve God, includes the mortification of any desire for learning which diverts one from true understanding.

> What good does it do to speak learnedly about the Trinity if lacking humility you displease the Trinity? Indeed it is not learning that makes man holy and just, but a virtuous life makes him pleasing to God. I would rather feel contrition than know how to define it. What would it profit us to know the whole Bible by heart and the principles of all the philosophers if we live without grace and the love of God? Vanity of vanities, all is vanity except to have God and serve him alone.[17]

This denigration of academic learning closely resembles the spirit of Groote's resolutions and is characteristic of the *devotio moderna*. Scholastic theology and indeed all formal theological and philosophical learning are considered worthless, superfluous, and irrelevant to the spiritual life. True understanding comes from God alone through close conformity to Christ and through attending to the words of the Gospel, which "enlighten the mind, excite contrition, and abound in consolation."

> Whoever desires to understand and take delight in the words of Christ must strive to conform his whole life to Him.[18]

Only such understanding, the source of which is Christ himself, the *magister magistrorum,* can lift the soul above itself and lead to an ecstacy of the mind in which sublime truths are understood in divinely given light and in direct communion with God. The highest point of humility in conscious imitation of Christ is the conformity of one's will to that of God. It is not only a continual source of inner peace and freedom but also the source of contemplation and ultimate unity with God.

As did Florens Radewijns and Geert Zerbolt before him, Thomas à Kempis intended most of his writings to serve as an inspiration for the Brethren's meditation or rumination on the mysteries of Christ's life and passion. For both brothers and canons, meditation was not confined to prescribed periods but was to continue without interruption throughout the day, even during manual labor. Since prayer and meditation were considered essential in fostering the inner life, aids to meditation were developed by various authors toward the end of the fifteenth century, notably the *scala meditatoria* of John Wessel Gansfort (ca. 1419-1489), a complete method of meditative prayer consisting of various steps.[19] Gansfort dedicated this work to the canons of Mount St. Agnes. It had a profound influence on John Mombaer (1460-1501), a canon of Mount St. Agnes beginning ca. 1477 and the author of the popular *Rosetum exercitiorum spiritualium et sacrarum meditationum,* published in 1494.[20] The aim of the

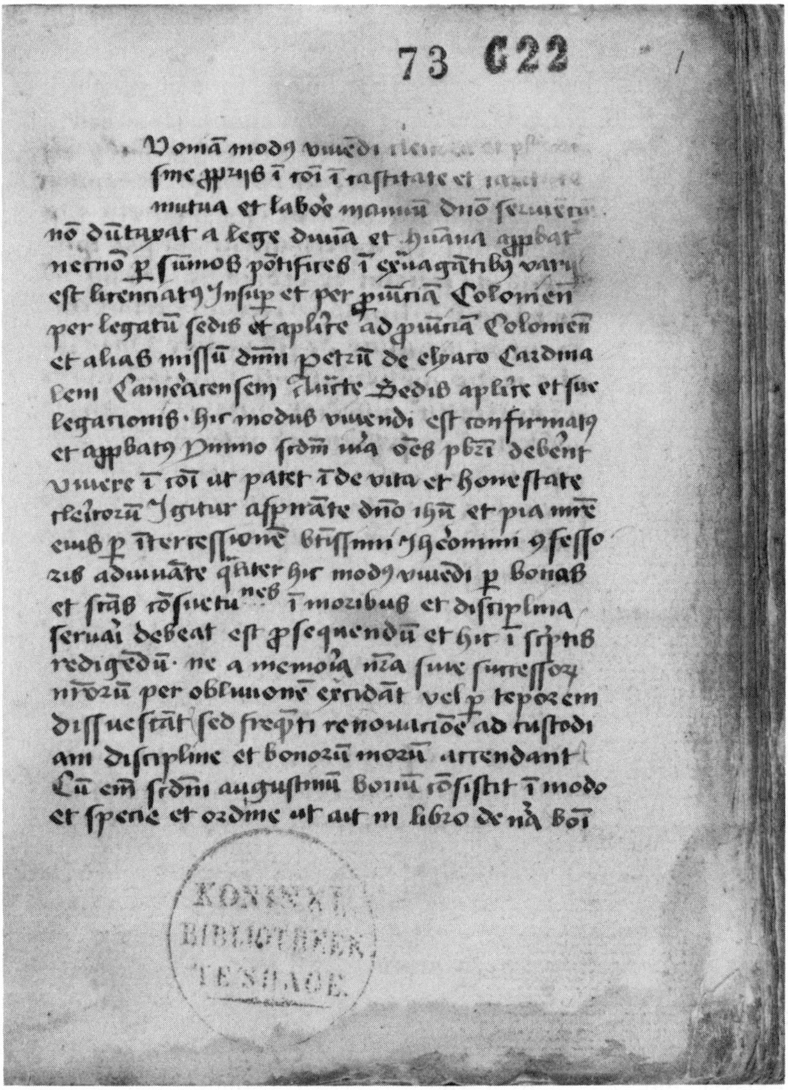

Domū modꝰ viuēdi clicoꝛū et p...
sine ꝗppbꝰ ī roī ꝓfessītate et ...
mutua et laboꝛe manuū dūo seruiēt
nō dutiuat a lege dīuīa et huāna appbat
nemō ꝑ sūmo� pōtifices ī exuagātibꝰ vary
est ferennatꝙ Insup et ꝑ pꝛūūa Coloniēn
ꝑ legatū sedis et aplīce ad pꝛūūa Coloniēn
et alias missū dīn petꝛū de elyaro Cardīna
lem Cameariensēm churte Sedis aplīce et sue
legatiōnis· hic modus viuendi est confirmatꝙ
et appbatꝰ Dūmo scdm ūa oēs pꝛī debēnt
viuere ī roī ut patet ī de vita et Honestate
rsclirozū Igitur asprāte dūo ihū et pia mꝛe
eiꝰ ꝑ ītercessioꝛē bꝛissmī tꝙ cōmūi ꝓfesso
zis adiuuāte qꝗcūꝗ hic modꝰ viuēdi ꝑ bonas
et sꝛūs cōsuetu^{nes} ī mozibus et disciplīa
seruai debeat est ꝓsequendū et hic ī scꝛūs
redigēdū· ne a memoꝛia ūa suꝛ sucessoꝛꝺ
ūꝛozū ꝑ obliuioꝛē exīdāt vel ꝑ teporem
dissuescāt sed freꝗn renouaꝛioe ad custodi
am disciplīe et bonozū mozū attendant
Cū em scdm augustinū bonū cōsisit ī modo
et spene et ozdīne ut ait ī libro de ūa bōī

12. *First Page of the Constitution of the Brotherhouse at Deventer,* MS. No. 73G22, f.1r.

Rosetum was to help his fellow brothers to tend the three most important beds in the "rose garden" of their devotional life: praying of the canonical hours, communion, and meditation. Since it is important not to let the mind be distracted while praying the hours but to reflect on events in the life of Christ, Mombaer developed a specific method called the *chiropsalterium*. While praying the psalms, the canon or brother should stroke his thumb along the inside of his other fingers, for each of which Mombaer indicated seven brief reflections or prayer intentions. These had to be learned by heart so that while stroking each finger the associated words would arouse the desired pious thoughts and intentions in the mind of the brother. In a similar way, the *scala communionis* was intended to aid in receiving communion with inner devotion and the *scala meditationis* (which Mombaer adopted in its entirety from John Wessel Gansfort) had the purpose of helping the mind to focus on the subjects of meditation. In each *scala* Mombaer employed mnemotechnical verses, a technique that was common throughout the Middle Ages. The content of every subject matter of the *scalae* was compressed into one or two points, so that the brother or canon using the *scalae* could recall it correctly. The author illustrates the various steps of the ladder and the corresponding states or activities of the mind by various examples from the life of Christ. Following the method of the *scalae* required a person's full attention, with the result that the canon or brother was totally preoccupied with the subject. Mombaer suggests that his method should be employed throughout the day, during idle moments, during work, in preparation for or as accompaniment to prayer, and during Holy Mass. It was to ensure that the devotionalists carried out their prayers, hours, study, work, eating, and any recreation in the proper devout spirit. It is possible that the *Rosetum*, with its emphasis on inner participation during the praying or singing of the hours and during the Holy Mass, and with its emphasis on a strict method during meditation, may have influenced the *Spiritual Exercises* of Ignatius of Loyola, if only indirectly.

Community Life

It appears, then, that the views and ideas of the modern devotionalists on the nature and meaning of devotion and the spiritual life were essentially monastic and derived from the masters of medieval monastic spirituality. This is true of the Brothers and Sisters of the Common Life as it is of the Windesheim canons and canonesses. Not only did their religious views completely coincide, but also the lives of their respective communities were very similar.

The Windesheim monasteries or chapterhouses differed, of course, from the brotherhouses in important ways. The property of a chapter belonged to the church; the authority of a superior was established by church law; and the singing of the canonical hours and of festival Masses as well as the taking of monastic vows was required. Although none of these stipulations applied to the Brothers and Sisters of the Common Life, their daily routine so closely resembled that of the Windesheim monks that the frequently occurring transformations of brotherhouses into chapterhouses involved no drastic change in the life of the inhabitants.

The Windesheim rules embodied in the constitution written in 1394 and approved by Pope Boniface consist of elements selected from those used in various monasteries, and the constitutions of the brotherhouses in Deventer and Zwolle, written twenty years later, contain the same traditional elements.

The stated goal was to cultivate the spiritual life through inner devotion and meditation, to live together in purity, in harmony, and in conformity with Christ.

> Our house was founded with the intention that priests and clerics might live there, supported by their own manual labor, namely, the copying of books, and the return from certain estates; attend church with devotion, obey the prelates, wear simple clothing, preserve the canons and decrees of the saints, practice religious exercises, and lead not only irreproachable, but exemplary lives, in order that they may serve God and perchance induce others to seek salvation. Since the final end of religion consists in purity of heart, without which we shall see perfection in vain, let it be our daily aim to purge our poisoned hearts from sin, so that in the first place we may learn to know ourselves, pass judgement upon the vices and passions of our minds, and endeavor with all our strength to eradicate them; despise temporal gain, crush selfish desires, aid others in overcoming sin, and concentrate our energy on the acquisition of true virtues, such as humility, love, chastity, patience, and obedience. Toward this end we must direct all our spiritual exercises: prayer, meditation, reading, manual labor, watching, fasting—in short, the harmonious development of our internal and external powers.[21]

The constitutions go on to prescribe the topics and order of daily meditation:

> Whereas the fear of the Lord is necessary to those who wish to overcome evil, it is expedient for each of us to meditate on such subjects as lead one to fear the Lord, like sin, death, judgement, and hell. But lest continued fear might engender dejection and despair, we shall have to add more hopeful subject matter for meditation, such as the kingdom of heaven, the blessings of God, the life of Christ, and his passion. These subjects we shall arrange in such a way that on Saturdays we shall meditate on sin, Sundays on the kingdom of heaven, Mondays on death, Tuesdays on the blessings of God, Wednesdays on

the final judgement, Thursdays on the pains of hell, and Fridays on the passion of Christ.[22]

It is significant that the constitutions include manual labor among the spiritual exercises as a necessary part of the harmonious development of internal and external powers. But not all kinds of manual labor were considered suitable, and those that resembled the spiritual exercises in kind, such as copying religious writings, were given preference.

Thus, the main purpose of copying books was not to provide a source of income but to "serve God and induce others to seek salvation." Guigo I had stressed the same point in his Carthusian *Consuetudines:*

> Books . . . we wish to keep very carefully as the everlasting food of our souls, and most industriously to be made, so that since we cannot do so by the mouth, we may preach the word of God with our hands. . . . For so many books that we write, it seems to us that we make so many publishers of the truth, hoping for reward from the Lord for all those who by them shall be corrected from error, or advanced in Catholic truth. . . .[23]

This spiritual dimension of manual labor is given added reinforcement in the constitutions of the brotherhouses, which exhort the brothers to accompany their labor with meditation and occasional brief prayers, called "ejaculations."

Although no binding vows of poverty, chastity, and obedience were required of the Brothers and Sisters of the Common Life, they were expected to cultivate those virtues as a matter of course. No member was to have any property of his or her own, having ceded it to the house on being admitted as a member there and having sworn before a notary public and in the presence of witnesses that he or she renounced all claim to property. All income and earnings from the brothers' or sisters' common or private labor belonged to the house and were to be spent to meet current expenses and for the relief of the poor. In case a brother was expelled for bad behavior or left the house on his own accord, he was not to take anything with him but his clothes, nor could he ever be readmitted.

The members of a brotherhouse were to observe brotherly love toward each other as equals and to maintain peace and harmony by obeying each other's wishes and admonitions. To their superior, the rector, they were to yield unquestioning obedience in all just and lawful matters. The authority of the rector, unlike that of the prior of a chapterhouse, was not established by church law but rather by the common consent of the brothers who elected him. Nevertheless, the authority of the rector was unquestioned. His rule rested less on the provisions of the constitution than on his personal authority and piety, an idea that is found also in the Benedictine and Augustinian rules regarding the authority of the superior:

> When anyone takes upon him the office of abbot, he is to instruct his disciples in two ways. That is, he is to lay before them what is good and holy, more by example than by words. . . .[24]

> Above all else, the prior should be an example of good works for everyone.[25]

This twofold exercise of authority by word and example is exemplified by Dirk of Herxen, rector of the brotherhouse at Zwolle from 1410 to 1457, and by all accounts one of the most prominent of the Brethren's rectors. He was a model rector, an extremely pious man, highly revered by both the brothers and the townspeople who came to him for advice and instruction. Rumor had it that he held daily converse with angels, and the brothers stood in such awe of him that a mere disapproving look of his would send them running with fear to their rooms.

Of Florens Radewijns, Thomas à Kempis reports that he compelled respect from everyone by his religious attitude in the choir, that he was granted visions, and that his prayers were answered in a miraculous way.

In a direct parallel to the *Rule of St. Benedict*, which refers to the abbot as one "esteemed to hold the place of Christ in the monastery,"[26] the rector Amilius of Buren on his deathbed exhorted the brothers to obey his successor as the *vicarius Christi* (vicar of Christ).[27] Thus, in his constitutional function, the rector merged with the divine figure of Christ.

Imitatio Christi

The constitutions of the *devotio moderna* reveal a striking correspondence between the mode of devotion and the mode by which the peace, harmony, and stability of the community are maintained. Both modes entail the exemplary behavior of authoritative models, carried by the medium of word and example and dependent, for their effect, upon the capacity of persons to imitate those models in attitude and deed. An essential aspect of the literature of the modern devotionalists is a clearly prescribed set of responses in its hearers and readers. The key word is *imitatio*, an internal imitation of appropriate attitudes, emotions, and self-awareness, and an external imitation of acts and gestures. Moreover, the internal attitudes of humility, self-mortification, and love of others are interrelated with the external actions of obedience, poverty, and service, since the latter both represent and shape the former.

The traditionality of this pattern is undeniable. Recent studies have shown the existence, since Gregory the Great, of a distinctive and identifiable monastic language and experience, which flowered in the works of the spiritual writers of the twelfth century, whose appeal was widespread in the fourteenth and fifteenth centuries throughout the monastic orders.[28] The framework for the various forms of this tradition—the *opus dei,* the *lectio divina,* the liturgical services and prayers, the daily meditations—was largely provided by the Gospel narratives, especially the narrative of Christ's passion. Toward the end of the Middle Ages, meditations became not only more regularized but also increasingly fixed upon the scene of the passion and upon the terms in which it was to be experienced. This late medieval focus on the passion as the paradigm of Christian experience is clearly expressed by an Augustinian contemporary of Luther, Johann Staupitz, for whom the whole of religious experience is an effective imitation of the suffering Christ:

> On the hill of Calvary he has shown us a model of all sanctity. . . . He is a model given by God, according to which I would work, suffer and die. He is the only model which one can follow, in which every good in life, suffering and death is usefully modeled. Therefore, no one can do right, suffer correctly, or die rightly, unless it happens in conformity with the life, suffering and death of Christ.[29]

It is essential to the understanding of this monastic tradition to recognize its affective nature, which determines the mode of its reception through word and example and which forms the very basis of *imitatio Christi* spirituality in that it requires a mimetic response in the hearers and readers of the sacred narrative. At its center, therefore, the monastic devotional tradition prescribes an identification of the subject with the object of devotion, a fusion of the knower and the known. For this reason, the content of knowledge cannot and must not be separated from the mechanics of its reception—hence, the rejection of all theological speculation and abstraction of meaning, and the exegetical emphasis upon the moral sense of the biblical text as the dominant level of meaning.

Clearly, the *devotio moderna* is representative of this tradition and dedicated to its reaffirmation, renewal, and conscious practice in an effort to stem the tide of spiritual deterioration and relaxation of discipline. The *devotio moderna* was "modern" not because it broke with any *devotio antiqua* but because it advocated the current practice of the latter both inside and outside the cloister. It did not, therefore, foreshadow, contribute to, nor embrace the Protestant Reformation.

Even in the thought of Martin Luther, a clear break with the monastic tradition does not become apparent until 1518, when new themes emerge in Luther's treatises that undermine the very basis of monastic spirituality.

First, Luther rejects the fourfold levels of biblical commentary and singles out the literal and historical content of the text, whose meaning is clear, precise, and independent from the processes of reception and internalization. *Meditatio* has been replaced by *explicatio*, and interior experience by external promise.[30] Second, the narrative of the *passio Christi* has lost its paradigmatic function and has acquired a theological meaning, abstracted from the narrative and its imagery, a statement about divine purpose that calls for a response of faith.

> Christ ought to be preached to the end that faith in him may be established. . . . Such faith is produced and preserved in us by preaching why Christ came, what he brought and bestowed, what benefit it is to us to accept him.[31]

Finally, faith is now defined not as a process of internalization of paradigmatic acts and gestures but as a perception of meanings and as trust in the divine word of promise.

> For faith born of this word will bring peace of conscience. . . . Whoever seeks peace in another way, for example, inwardly through experience, certainly seems to tempt God and desires to have peace in fact, rather than in faith. For you will have peace only as long as you believe in the word of that one who promised, "whatever you loose," etc. Christ is our peace, but only through faith. . . . Whoever believes this confidently has truly obtained the peace and remission of God, not by the certainty of the process but by the certainty of faith, according to the infallible word of the one who has mercifully promised.[32]

With the assertion of this notion of faith, the monastic fusion and identification of subject and object, knower and known, believer and believed have been broken, and the spirituality of *imitatio Christi* has been transformed into a dialectic of word and faith. With the adoption of this dialectic as its basis, the theology of the Protestant Reformation marks a clear break with the spirituality of the monastic tradition, which the *devotio moderna* attempted to revive.

Notes

1. R. R. Post, *The Modern Devotion*, 234.
2. Ibid., 676–80.
3. A. Hyma, *The Brethren of the Common Life*, 19.
4. Thomas à Kempis, *Opera Omnia*, ed. M. J. Pohl (7 vols.; Freiburg: Herder, 1902–1921) 7:88.
5. Guigo I, *Meditations of Guigo, Prior of the Charterhouse*, trans. John J. Jolin (Milwaukee, WI: Marquette University Press, 1951) 46–47, 13–14, 50.

6. G. Groote, *De Simonia ad beguttas*, ed. R. Langenberg (Quellen und Forschungen zur Geschichte der deutschen Mystik; Bonn: P. Hanstein, 1902) 25.

7. Groote, *Gerardi Magni epistolae*, ed. W. Mulder (Antwerp: Editricis Neerlandiae, 1933) n. 62, pp. 232–43.

8. Thomas à Kempis, *Opera omnia*, ed. Pohl, 7:97f.

9. Guigo I, *Meditations*, 46.

10. Groote, *Gerardi Magni epistolae*, ed. Mulder, n. 15, p. 50.

11. Gerard of Zutphen, *The Spiritual Ascent*, trans. J. P. Arthur (London: Burns & Oates, 1908) 26.

12. Guigo II, *The Ladder of Monks and Twelve Meditations*, trans. E. Colledge and J. Walsh (Kalamazoo. MI: Cistercian Publications, 1981).

13. *PL* 38, col. 685.

14. *PL* 186, col. 704.

15. Thomas à Kempis, *Opera Omnia*, ed. Pohl, 5:3.

16. Thomas à Kempis, *The Imitation of Christ*, trans. L. Sherley-Price (Baltimore: Penguin Books, 1975) 3:37.

17. Ibid., 1:1.

18. Ibid.

19. R. R. Post, *The Modern Devotion*, 539.

20. Ibid., 543ff.

21. A. Hyma, *The Brethren of the Common Life*, 110.

22. Ibid.

23. E. Margaret Thompson, *The Carthusian Order in England* (New York: Macmillan, 1930) 34.

24. *St. Benedict's Rule for Monasteries*, trans. Leonard J. Doyle (Collegeville, MN: Liturgical Press, 1948) chap. 2.

25. *Regula Sancti Augustini Secunda*, ed. R. Arbesmann-Hümpfner, in *Liber Vitasfratrum* (New York: Cosmopolitan Science & Art Service, 1943) 11.

26. *St. Benedict's Rule*, chap. 2.

27. R. R. Post, *The Modern Devotion*, 242.

28. Jean Leclerq, *The Love of Learning and the Desire for God: A Study in Monastic Culture* (2nd rev. ed.; New York: Fordham University Press, 1974) 33–56.

29. *Johannis Staupitii Opera*, ed. I. Knaake (Potsdam: Gropius, 1867) 1:63.

30. James Preus, *From Shadow to Promise* (Cambridge, MA: Harvard University Press, 1969); Darrell R. Reinke, "Luther, the Cloister, and the Language of Monastic Devotion" (diss., Washington University, 1972).

31. *Luther's Works*, ed. J. Pelikan (54 vols.; Philadelphia: Muhlenberg Press, 1952–) 31:357.

32. Ibid., 31:98f.

Bibliography

Barnikol, Ernst. *Studien zur Geschichte der Brüder vom gemeinsamen Leben.* Ergänzungsband zu *Zeitschrift für Theologie und Kinst;* Tübingen, 1917.

Busch, Johann. *Chronicon Windeshemense und Liber de Reformatione monasteriorum.* Edited by K. Grube. In *Der Augustinerpropst Johannes Busch.* Geschichtsquellen der Provinz Sachsen 19. Halle, 1886.

DeBeer, K. C. L. N. *Studie over de spiritualiteit van Geert Groote.* Nijmegen: N. V. Dekker & Van de Wegt, 1938.

Hyma, Albert. *The Christian Renaissance: A History of the Devotio Moderna.* 2nd ed. New York: Archon Books, 1965.

———. *The Brethren of the Common Life.* Grand Rapids: Eerdmans, 1950.

Iserloh, Erwin. "The Devotio Moderna." In *Handbook of Church History.* Vol. 3, *From the High Middle Ages to the Eve of the Reformation.* Edited by Hubert Jedin and John Dolan. Translated by Anselm Biggs. New York: Herder & Herder, 1970.

Janowski, H. J. *Geert Groote, Thomas von Kempen, und die Devotio Moderna.* Olten and Freiburg: Walter, 1978.

Persoons, Ernest. *Recente publicaties over de moderne devotie 1959–72.* Leeuwen: Institute voor Middeleewse Studies, 1972.

Pohl, M. Josef, ed. *Thomae Hemerken a Kempis Opera Omnia.* 7 vols. Freiburg: Herder, 1902–1922.

Post, Regnerus R. *The Modern Devotion.* Leiden: Brill, 1968.

Spitz, Lewis. *The Religious Renaissance of the German Humanists.* Cambridge, MA: Harvard University Press, 1963.

Stupperich, Robert. *Das Herforder Fraterhaus and die devotio moderna.* Münster: Aschendorff, 1975.

Van Zijl, Theodore P. *Gerard Groote: Ascetic and Reformer, 1340–1384.* Washington, DC: Catholic University of America Press, 1963.

Zerbolt, Gerard. *The Spiritual Ascent.* Translated by J. P. Arthur. London: Burns & Oates, 1908.

8

The English Mystics

BERNARD McGINN

THE ENGLISH MYSTICS and spiritual writers of the fourteenth and fifteenth centuries are too varied to form a school. A certain individuality—in some cases we might even say English eccentricity—marked the four great writers of the fourteenth century, Richard Rolle, Walter Hilton, the anonymous author of *The Cloud of Unknowing*, and Julian of Norwich. Nonetheless, these mystics shared common values and approaches, as well as a typical late medieval desire to express traditional Latin spirituality in the vernacular. They are perhaps the greatest English prose writers of their age, and their masterpieces remain unsurpassed among spiritual works written in the English language.

There had, of course, been earlier English contributions to medieval spirituality in the Latin writings of Bede and Aelred of Rievaulx or in such vernacular works as the eighth-century poem "The Dream of the Rood" and the *Ancrene Riwle*, a thirteenth-century guide for women recluses. The remarkable flowering of spiritual literature in late medieval England was part of a European-wide phenomenon, but there is no evidence that the major English authors were influenced by their continental contemporaries in any decisive way.

The historical roots of this English "Golden Age" are too complex to be easily summarized. Some were shared with the continental movements, especially the important new role taken by the laity. The fourteenth century was the first time in the history of medieval spirituality when the possibility that lay people living in the world could reach the heights of perfection was seriously entertained. Another important factor was the role of the religious orders, especially the Carthusians, in both the guidance of souls and in the production and dissemination of religious literature. A factor distinctive of England was the special role played by the eremitical or solitary life. By and large, however, the English writers were shaped by the same situation and drew upon the same rich background of Augustinian, Cistercian, Victorine, mendicant, and modified Dionysian piety that the continental mystics did. The English originality lies in what they did with this heritage.

The mystical writers who will be our concern here are the best-known part of a large body of spiritual literature produced in late medieval England. This involved not only translations of the Bible into the vernacular (unfortunately closed off in the wake of the condemnation of Wycliff) and a wealth of sermonic material but also important instructional manuals for parish priests. The practical character of the English mystics is not unrelated to this emphasis on the importance of sound instruction in living the Christian life. A wide range of vernacular devotional literature, both in prose and in poetry, demonstrates the spread of concern for spirituality on every level of society. Perhaps the greatest monument of this literature is the late-fourteenth-century poem "Piers Plowman," whose central message of redemption through the love of Christ is not different from that of the mystics:

"Conseille me, Kynde [Nature]," quod I, "what craft be best to learn?"
"Lerne to love," quod Kynde, "and leef alle othere."
B Text, Passus XX, lines 207–8

Since all the English mystics place love at the heart of their message, it has been customary to speak of affectivity as one of the distinguishing features of English mysticism. Similarly, the mistrust of contemporary scholastic theology expressed by Rolle and the author of *The Cloud* (and even Hilton) and the "unlearned" nature of the teaching of Julian and later of Margery Kempe have led to English mysticism's being described as anti-intellectual. Such broad terms are not really very helpful, however, in grasping the distinctive teaching of the English mystics. No Christian mystic has ever denied love a crucial role in the path to God (however differently they may have conceived this), and almost all the great mystics of the fourteenth century could be described as affective mystics. Likewise, mystics have always been in the forefront of those who are most conscious of the limitations and pretensions of academic speculation about God. The following account will try to get at something of the special nature of the English mystics not only by highlighting the individual major themes of each author but also by comparing their attitudes on some issues that are central for the history of Christian mysticism: the role of Jesus in his humanity; the place of the "dark night," or the experience of the withdrawal of God; the relation of love and knowledge in the mystical life; and the connection between action and contemplation.

Richard Rolle

Rolle was born in Yorkshire about 1300 and spent time at Oxford before he rejected the world in rather bizarre fashion by cutting up two of his sister's tunics and his father's rainhood to construct a makeshift hermit's garb. The wandering young hermit's acerbic personality is at times a disconcerting presence in his early writings. Nevertheless, he persevered in the life, and the interior and exterior difficulties he underwent brought him a mature wisdom and discretion that allowed him to serve as a valuable spiritual guide in later life. He was a prolific author both in Latin and in the vernacular and was widely read in the late Middle Ages. Rolle died in 1349, probably a victim of the Black Death. Although he wrote a number of poems, the Yorkshire hermit is more distinguished as a prose writer. Rolle was one of the first major English translators of the Bible, but it is in the Latin works that we find the essence of his teaching.

In his exuberence, dedication to the language of love, and innocence of apophatic mysticism, Rolle is reminiscent of a near contemporary whose works he seems not to have known, Ramond Lull (1232–1316). Rolle is controversial both to his immediate successors and to his modern interpreters. Both Hilton and the *Cloud* author felt that his emphasis on manifestations of God's presence through physical experiences was at best ambiguous and sometimes even a dangerous confusion of the true meaning of mysticism.[1] Modern scholars like David Knowles have agreed in judging that "of purely mystical prayer and experience Rolle knows little or nothing."[2] But Thomas Merton has questioned whether Knowles's definition of mysticism based on John of the Cross is adequate for appreciating a witness like Rolle, who shows more parallels with the hesychast experience of divine light or with aspects of the patristic tradition common to East and to West than to the Spanish Doctor.[3]

Rolle's *The Fire of Love* and *The Mending of Life* provide us with the most direct access to his thought. He is far from being a systematic thinker; most of his works are discursive meditations on the experience of loving God. *The Mending of Life* was his most general and best-known book. The first ten chapters discuss such essential ascetical values and practices as poverty, tribulation, prayer and meditation—the means by which the converted soul is led to the love of God and contemplation (chaps. 11–12). The treatment of divine love is based upon a distinction of three stages of the love of Christ adapted from Richard of St. Victor—insuperable love, inseparable love, and singular love.

Rolle's love for the incarnate Jesus shines through all his works. "Therefore, may Jesus Christ, whom we love for his own sake, be the beginning of our love, and may he be its end" (*The Mending of Life*, chap. 11).[4] In *The Fire of Love*, his most powerful work, Rolle declares, "I have found that to love Christ above all things will involve three things: warmth, song and sweetness" (chap. 14). Rolle considered these three experiences, especially the last, as the height of Christian perfection, a foretaste of the vision of God, which he insisted could only be fully enjoyed in heaven. His lyrical descriptions of the physical manifestations of heat, melody, and sweetness (e.g., *The Fire of Love*, chaps. 15, 19, 22, 31, 33–34, and 40; and *The Melody of Love*, *passim*) were the source of later suspicions about the authenticity of his mysticism, although in *The Mending of Life* he insists "that sanctity is not in the roaring of the heart, either in tears or in external acts, but in the sweetness of perfect love and heavenly contemplation" (chap. 12). Because of the absence of anything corresponding to the terrible ordeal of the "dark night" of divine withdrawal, Rolle has frequently been denied the title of true mystic, but his teaching regarding the divinely infused nature of the higher stages of the experience of love and his distinction of two kinds of rapture (*The Fire of Love*, chap. 37) argue that it is more just, with Thomas Merton, to see him as a different kind of mystic.

The Yorkshire hermit so concentrates on the language of love that he gives little consideration to the role reason plays in the path to God. He is also less than clear on the relation of action and contemplation in the life of Christian perfection. *The Fire of Love* (chap. 21) denies that the active and contemplative lives can really be combined, but *The Mending of Life* (chap. 12) seems to suggest that they can. One does not go to Richard Rolle for careful discriminations about difficult issues, but for the forcefulness and tenderness of his language of love.

Walter Hilton

Hilton, who died in 1396, lived as a hermit before becoming an Augustinian canon. Theologically, he was the most careful of the English mystics. Although he differed from Rolle in many ways, he shared with him the insistence that all true experience of God in this life can come only through the love of Jesus. Hilton wrote his major works in the vernacular; his masterpiece is *The Scale* (or *Ladder*) *of Perfection*. He was also a translator (his free rendering of a popular work of Franciscan piety known in English as *The Goad of Love* is another major source of his thought). Hilton lived in the troubled times of the Lollard heresy, and his sharp reaction to theological error must be seen in this light.

A return to Augustine was one of the major movements in fourteenth-century thought, and Hilton is a good example of this in mystical theology.

No other mystic of the late Middle Ages is so Augustinian, especially in the central role that he gives to the restoration of the damaged image of God in each human person. The first book of *The Scale* takes as its announced theme the three degrees of the contemplative life: "knowledge of God and of spiritual matters . . . through the use of reason"; "loving God that does not depend on intellectual light"; and "the third degree of contemplation, which is the highest attainable in this life, . . . of both knowledge and love" (*The Scale* 1.4–8). In the third stage "the soul becomes united to God in an ecstasy of love and is conformed to the likeness of the Trinity" (1.8). The major theme of the latter part of book 1, however, shifts to the contrast between the image of Christ and the image of sin in the human soul. Book 2 differs in audience and in depth of theological tone, taking as its explicit theme the two stages in the reformation of the divine image: reformation in faith and reformation in faith and in feeling (e.g., 2.13–20, 28–35). Hilton consistently opposed giving rapturous experiences like those of Rolle any essential role in the path to perfection; the "feeling" in his reformation in faith and in feeling is fundamentally "God's gracious presence revealed to a pure soul" (2.41). Hilton also insists that the process of reformation is the joint work of both love and knowledge: "love derives from knowledge and not knowledge from love; consequently the happiness of the soul is said to derive chiefly from this knowledge and experience of God, to which is joined the love of God . . ." (2.34). In the highest stage of the reformation in faith and in feeling, "the soul, as far as it may be in this life, contemplates the Godhead united to manhood in Christ" (2.30). Recollection of the "precious Humanity and Passion of Jesus Christ" (1.92) is the necessary way to God, and mystical experience in this life is never possible apart from the person of the God-man. Thus, the reformation of the image is its conformity to the likeness of Jesus (e.g., 1.51–53, 86; 2.24).

Despite his emphasis on the mutuality of love and knowledge in the path to God, Walter Hilton stressed the language of love and longing for Jesus throughout his works, though usually without the erotic imagery found in Rolle.[5] Like Rolle, but with far greater theological precision, he emphasized the infused character of the higher stages of the contemplative life (e.g., 2.35). Unlike Rolle, he had a place for the painful experience of the "dark night," in which sin and its vestiges are purged by the action of grace (e.g., 2.24, 28), and he at times used apophatic expressions (e.g., 2.27, 40).[6] In general, however, Hilton remained strongly in the Augustinian camp in his emphasis on positive language in describing the love of Christ and in his preference for speaking of the experience of the immediate presence of God in Christ as the height of perfection (e.g., 1.89; 2.21, 27, 41).

The first book of *The Scale* implies that someone involved in the active life cannot be expected to reach the heights of perfection; but the second book (e.g., 2.18, 40) and other works of Hilton, especially *The Goad of Love* (chap. 16) and *The Epistle on the Mixed Life,* show that this does not represent his mature thought, which held that contemplation, as the growing expression of the love of God, marks all the stages of the Christian life and that true perfection is possible in any state.[7] In advancing this new and more democratic notion of Christian perfection, Walter Hilton takes his place beside such other fourteenth-century mystics as Meister Eckhart and Julian of Norwich in marking a new stage in the history of Christian spirituality.

The Cloud Author

Some have claimed that Hilton was the author of the treatise known as *The Cloud of Unknowing* and its related shorter works, but theological and stylistic differences make this unlikely.[8] All we can say about the unknown author is that he was a contemporary of Hilton who lived as a solitary, possibly a Carthusian. He had received a good theological education, and of his genius as a guide to the spiritual life there can be no question. Besides *The Cloud* itself, his corpus includes *The Book of Privy Counselling* (a major work on mystical union), *The Epistle of Prayer, The Epistle of Discretion, Of Discerning Spirits,* and two translations, *Hid Divinity,* a version of Pseudo-Dionysius's *Mystical Theology,* and an adaptation of Richard of St. Victor's *Benjamin minor.*

The author's praise for Pseudo-Dionysius (e.g., *Cloud,* chap. 70) has sometimes obscured the true nature of his relation to his sources. It is true that the anonymous Englishman makes much use of the Dionysian writings, but his Dionysianism is of a special western type that was primarily dependent on Thomas Gallus (d. 1246) and the Carthusian Hugh of Balma (d. 1340). This form of Dionysianism reinterpreted language about the limitations of reason in terms of the supremacy of affectivity to all forms of knowing in the ascent to God. Of course, the *Cloud* author is a man of more than one book, as his use of Bernard of Clairvaux and the fathers shows, but his affective Dionysianism is important for understanding his differences from the other great English mystics.

The Cloud of Unknowing is a specialist document, addressed to a young man pursuing the contemplative life under monastic obedience. It takes its name and central theme from the author's insistence upon "a sort of cloud of unknowing . . . [which] is always between you and your God, no matter what you do, and it prevents you from seeing him clearly by the light of understanding in your reason, and from experiencing him in sweetness of love in your affection" (chap. 3). Although this cloud of unknowing can never be dispersed, this does not prevent loving union with God in this life. The path to God must follow the dark road of unknowing and of inner suffering. The "dark night" experience is central to the *Cloud* author, albeit differently expressed from the later formulations in the Spanish mystics.

The *Cloud* author does not disparage the preparatory roles of reading, reflecting, and praying (e.g., chap. 35), but these practices do not really penetrate the cloud. The lower stage of the active life, which consists of good works, and the higher stage, which is concerned with meditation, are both merely preparatory (see chaps. 8, 21). Real progress begins only in the higher stage of contemplation and consists in a twofold strategy: first, in invoking another cloud, the "cloud of forgetting," which one must put between oneself and all creation (chaps. 5, 43); and second, in smiting "upon that thick cloud of unknowing with a sharp dart of longing love" (chap. 6).

This "sharp dart of longing love" is central to the *Cloud* author's teaching. As a "blind impulse of love" (chap. 12), it finds expression in prayers of simple ejaculation that surpass any form of discourse (chaps. 39–40). The union that such prayer leads to is the result of a strictly operative grace—God's work and not our own (chaps. 26, 34). In this the *Cloud* author—and, indeed, all the fourteenth-century English mystics—stands in line with a generally Thomistic understanding of the nature of grace. *The Cloud* attempts to express the mystery of union with God in the form of paradoxes and apophatic language unusual for the English mystics (e.g., chaps. 68–69). Chapter 71 judiciously distinguishes between two kinds of union possible in this life: one of intermittent rapture; the other of the permanent possession of God.

The Book of Privy Counselling analyzes the "naked intent" that leads to God and the nature of the union possible in this life. Noting that pure existence is the most proper name of God, the author insists that God is the being of the soul, "evermore saving this difference between you and Him, that He is your being and you are not His."[9] Some of the language used here is reminiscent of the Rhineland mystics,[10] but the *Cloud* author, like the other English mystics, never allows abstract terminology to dominate, as when he orders his reader: "Take good, gracious God as He is, plat [flat] and plain as a plaster, and lay it to your sick self as you are."[11] What *The Book of Privy Counselling* adds to *The Cloud*'s teaching is a detailed reflection on the cloud of forgetting as the oblivion of our own being in order to center on the being of God: the work of love is total forgetfulness of self.

The contrast sometimes asserted between the Christocentric Hilton and the theocentric *Cloud* author is a dangerous half-truth. Christ plays an essential role in the *Cloud* author's works; meditation on Jesus' passion begins the way to God. *The Book of Privy Counselling*'s claim that thoughts

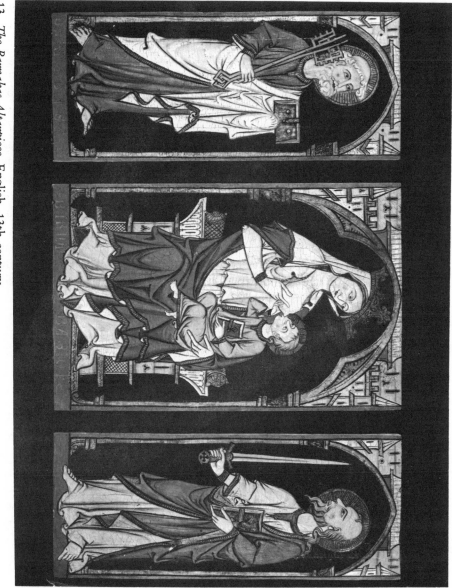

13. The Barnabas Altarpiece, English, 13th century.

on the passion pertain to common grace, not to the higher special grace of contemplation, needs to be understood in the light of the traditional distinction between the "carnal" love of Christ's humanity and the higher "spiritual" love of the Godhead made manifest in him.[12] Still there is a difference in tone and emphasis between the language about Christ found in the *Cloud* author and that of the other great English mystics, and his emphasis on the "naked intent" seems to have been criticized by Walter Hilton.

On the relation of love and knowledge in the path to God, the dominant note of the *Cloud* author is well expressed in this statement: "it is love alone that can reach to God in this life, and not knowing" (*Cloud*, chap. 8). But the anonymous mystic did not lack all appreciation of the role of rational knowledge; there are passages in *The Book of Privy Counselling* and *The Epistle of Prayer* that show he agreed with a long tradition in Christian mysticism that recognized a form of transcendent knowledge in the experience of loving union, however much he weights the balance on the side of love.[13] Where he does differ from earlier authors is in his failure to stress the subsuming power of love to draw up all human knowing into the higher awareness of God.

The *Cloud* author's teaching on union with God is eminently orthodox, carefully avoiding any suggestion of union of identity or indistinction and adhering to traditional formulas based on the notion of *unitas spiritus* found in 1 Cor 6:17. For him, the mystical union was achieved by Moses who entered the dark cloud "to feel in experience the presence of Him that is above all things."[14] This experience, however, seems open only to those who lead the contemplative life under a religious rule (*Cloud*, chap. 21).

Julian of Norwich

On the night of 13 May 1373, a thirty-year-old dying woman received fifteen "showings" or revelations from God. Later that day she was granted one further revelation confirming the truth of the previous manifestations. The young woman became an anchoress in a cell attached to St. Julian's church in Norwich, and she based her long life of prayer, contemplation, and spiritual teaching on these visions. Twice she either wrote or dictated accounts of the visions and their meaning, so her *Book of Showings* comes down to us in an early "Short Text" and a theologically more developed "Long Text," which was finished about 1393. Julian was still alive as late as 1416.

Dame Julian is the great original among the English mystics. However much she may have been familiar with earlier spiritual authors, her message is an intensely personal one based on her efforts to understand the meaning of her visions.[15] The conclusion of the Long Text summarizes the central message:

> And from the time that it was revealed, I desired many times to know in what was our Lord's meaning. And fifteen years after and more, I was answered in spiritual understanding, and it was said: What, do you wish to know your Lord's meaning in this thing? Know it well, love was his meaning. Who reveals it to you? Love. What did he reveal to you? Love. Why does he reveal it to you? For love.

Julian was the most Pauline of the fourteenth-century mystics; her essential concerns, like Paul's, were rooted in the mystery of sin, grace, and redemption in the love of Jesus. Like the apostle, she found a key to some grasp of the mystery in the solidarity of all humanity in Christ.

Julian wrestled long with the meaning of her visions, not least because she sensed a conflict between the message of universal love revealed to her in the figure of the crucified Jesus and the "common teaching" of the church regarding sin, divine wrath, and damnation. Over and over again she pondered the meaning of the words "I may make all things well, and I can make all things well, and I shall make all things well; and you will see yourself that every kind of thing will be well" (Long Text, chap. 31; cf. Short Text, chap. 14). For Julian the solution to the dilemma was given in the vision of the lord and the servant (Long Text, chaps. 51–63). In this allegorical parable she sees a loving lord send out a dutiful servant on a mission. Despite his good intention, the servant falls into a ditch, suffers grave injury, and is unable to fulfill his lord's wishes, though the lord never ceases to look upon him "with great pity and compassion." Julian goes on to explain that the servant is, first of all, Adam, but from another perspective Christ himself who "fell into" human nature and in whom all humanity will be restored to God. The anchoress's shifting perspectives in the parable do not provide us with a simple rational solution to the paradox of divine goodness and human sinfulness; nor are they meant to. They are a mystical revelation that God's ways are not our ways (Long Text, chap. 32). Julian does not engage in theoretical discussions of the relation of love and knowledge, like Hilton and the *Cloud* author, but her teaching is that the mystery of love surpasses the antinomies of reason.

It is from this point of view that two difficulties in Julian's thought must be approached. The first is the universalism that seems implied in the revelation that God will make all things well. Julian carefully avoids asserting that all human beings will be saved. She does say that God performs two great deeds which will fulfill his promise: a deed that is begun in this life but completed in the next (Long Text, chap. 37), and a hidden, eschatological deed "which the Blessed Trinity will perform on the last day" (Long Text, chap. 32).[16] The second problem area is related to this—the issue of the meaning and seriousness of sin. The anchoress had a clear sense of the shamefulness of sin, and she insisted that in some way it clouded the whole course of human life. How then could she assert that "synne is behouely," that is, necessary (Long Text, chap. 27), or claim that "in every soul which will be saved there is a godly will which never assents to sin" (Long Text, chap. 37)? Again, the answer seems to be one of perspective. Sin separates us from God, but, from the viewpoint of divine love, the pain that sin causes in us is a necessary part of the purgative process of falling and rising that we must undergo throughout this life.[17] As the parable of the lord and servant suggests, from the perspective of the Father's good pleasure in his Son, who has taken all humanity to himself, there is indeed a godly will that has never consented to sin: "we have all this will whole and safe in our Lord Jesus Christ" (Long Text, chap. 53; cf. Short Text, chap. 23).[18]

Julian expresses her theology of love in terms of a threefold distinction: "The first is uncreated charity, the second is created charity, the third is given charity" (Long Text, chap. 84). The uncreated charity that is God is the source and goal of all. Julian's thought has a strong trinitarian dimension, though she insists that all that we can know about God is revealed to us in the person of Jesus. This means that the mystical life here on earth can never depart from the image of the crucified Jesus.[19]

Created charity is our soul in God, that is, the mystery of how we are "oned" in Christ to become partakers of the divine nature. This theme draws us back again to the central vision of the lord and the servant. In seeking to express the bond between the uncreated charity manifest in Jesus and the created charity of the soul, Julian turned to the image of the motherhood of God, especially the motherhood of Christ as God (Long Text, chaps. 52–63).[20] Julian did not invent this language, which had a long tradition, but she brought it to a height of theological sophistication beyond anything found in earlier literature. Christ is our mother not only because the image of a mother's love helps us to overcome our fear of God, but more fundamentally because it explains the nature of our bond with Christ and the source of his constant solicitude for us.

Julian's "given charity" is the life of virtue by which the Christian returns love for love given. Her teaching here centers on the great values of faith and charity, prayer and contemplation, contrition and compassion, and not on particular practices or forms of life. Despite her life as an enclosed contemplative, Julian, like Hilton, does not restrict her teaching to a group of contemplative adepts. One might argue that she goes beyond Hilton and others, quietly leaving to one side the traditional distinctions between the active and contemplative lives in directing her message to all who form one body in Christ.

Later Stages

The flood of English spiritual literature did not dry up at the end of the fourteenth century, though later productions do not reach the level of Julian, Hilton, or the *Cloud* author. The most interesting (and sometimes disconcerting) work is *The Book of Margery Kempe*, the first autobiography in English. Margery (ca. 1373–ca. 1440) was a wife and the mother of fourteen children; her call to a higher life led her not out of the world but to special ascetical and devotional practices, including a mutual vow of chastity with her husband, the gift of tears, and much ecstatic groaning and shouting. Her dictated *Book* is a lively, if disjointed, account of her pilgrimages, visions, and interior and exterior trials. Margery's devotional life centered on Jesus in his passion and was enriched with considerable erotic imagery. Recent studies have highlighted the difficulties that Margery faced in trying to live a life of perfection as a married woman in the world and have shown that the models for her piety must be sought among the ecstatic women saints of the Continent.

Among the other important spiritual works of the fifteenth century were the Carthusian Nicholas Love's *The Mirror of the Blessed Life of Jesus Christ* (ca. 1410), an influential rendering of *The Meditations of the Life of Jesus Christ* falsely ascribed to Bonaventure. Another Carthusian, Richard Methely, translated *The Cloud* into Latin and wrote several independent treatises.

The great age of English spiritual literature was largely over by 1500, though both John Fisher and Thomas More produced ascetical and devotional works of merit. The story of Anglican and Puritan spirituality will be told in another volume. After the Reformation, the English Recusant Catholics kept the earlier literature alive, both in England and on the Continent, by copying manuscripts—and, in the case of Augustine Baker (1575–1641), even of writing a commentary on *The Cloud*. The Recusants produced a valuable spiritual literature of their own, of which *The Rule of Perfection* by Benet of Canfield (1562–1610) is the most notable example. In summary, the great English mystics of the fourteenth century and their successors form a distinct and important moment in the history of Christian spirituality, not only for their linguistic descendants, who make use of the English language in trying to express the mystery of God, but also for all their spiritual descendants throughout the world.

Notes

1. Walter Hilton, *The Ladder of Perfection,* trans. Leo Sherley-Price (Baltimore, MD: Penguin Books, 1957) 1.10–11, 26; 2.29 (all subsequent quotations from *The Scale, or Ladder* will be taken from this edition). *The Cloud of Unknowing,* ed. James Walsh (The Classics of Western Spirituality; New York: Paulist Press, 1981) chap. 48 (all subsequent quotations from *The Cloud* will be from this translation).

2. David Knowles, *The English Mystical Tradition,* 64.

3. Thomas Merton, "The English Mystics," in *Mystics and Zen Masters,* 147–50.

4. All quotations from Rolle are taken from *The Fire of Love and The Mending of Life,* trans. M. L. del Mastro (Garden City, NY: Image Books, 1981).

5. Erotic imagery is found in *The Goad of Love,* chaps. 4, 6, 11, 26, 30. See Walter Hilton, *The Goad of Love,* an unpublished translation of the *Stimulus Amoris,* formerly attributed to St. Bonaventure, now edited from manuscripts by Clare Kirchberger (London: Faber & Faber, 1952).

6. See J. P. H. Clark, "The 'Lightsome Darkness'—Aspects of Walter Hilton's Theological Background," *Downside Review* 95 (1977) 95–109; idem, "The 'Cloud of Unknowing,' Walter Hilton and St. John of the Cross: A Comparison," *Downside Review* 96 (1978) 281–98.

7. See J. P. H. Clark, "Action and Contemplation in Walter Hilton," *Downside Review* 97 (1979) 258–74.

8. For a comparison of styles, see Janel M. Mueller, *The Native Tongue and the Word* (Chicago: University of Chicago Press, 1984) 53–73. J. P. H. Clark, in his article "Sources and Theology in 'The Cloud of Unknowing,'" *Downside Review* 98 (1980) 108–9, discusses the relation of *The Cloud* and *The Scale.*

9. The quotations from *The Book of Privy Counselling* are my translations from *The Cloud of Unknowing and Related Treatises,* ed. Phyllis Hodgson (Analecta Cartusiana 3; Exeter: Catholic Records Press, 1982) 75, lines 36–37.

10. Illuminating comparisons between the language of the English mystics and that of their continental counterparts may be found in Wolfgang Riehle, *The Middle English Mystics.*

11. *The Book of Privy Counselling,* ed. Hodgson, p. 77, lines 27–28.

12. See especially *The Book of Privy Counselling,* ed. Hodgson, 94, 98. On this see William Johnston, *The Mysticism of the Cloud of Unknowing,* 67–79.

13. See *The Book of Privy Counselling,* ed. Hodgson, p. 82, lines 4–19; and *The Epistle of Prayer,* ed. Hodgson, p. 104, lines 28–34.

14. *Hid Divinity,* ed. Hodgson, p. 123, lines 20–21.

15. Julian's classification of her various kinds of showings (e.g., Short Text, chaps. 4, 7, 23; Long Text, chap. 1) show her acquaintance with the Augustinian tradition.

16. See Brant Pelphrey, *Love Was His Meaning,* 301–5.

17. This is as close as Julian comes to something like a "dark night" (see Long Text, chap. 64).

18. On sin in Julian, see Pelphrey, *Love Was His Meaning,* 152–62, 179–84, 199–204, 266–79.

19. In chap. 19 of the Long Text, Julian resists the temptation to look above Christ crucified toward the naked Godhead.

20. Julian speaks of the Trinity as our mother (Long Text, chap. 54), and of God in general as mother (Long Text, chaps. 52, 62), but the dominant theme is Christ as mother. See Paula Barker, "The Motherhood of God in Julian of Norwich's Theology," *Downside Review* 100 (1982) 290–305.

Bibliography

Allen, Hope Emily. *Writings Ascribed to Richard Rolle, Hermit of Hampole, and Material for His Biography.* London: Oxford University Press, 1927.

Atkinson, Clarissa W. *Mystic and Pilgrim: The Book and the World of Margery Kempe.* Ithaca, NY, and London: Cornell University Press, 1983.

Clark, J. P. H. The best studies on Walter Hilton may be found in the series of articles by J. P. H. Clark published in *Downside Review* from 1977 on.

Colledge, Eric, ed. *The Medieval Mystics of England.* New York: Scribner, 1961. An anthology with a good introduction.

Johnston, William. *The Mysticism of the Cloud of Unknowing.* Wheathampstead: Anthony Clarke Books, 1978. The second edition of this classic work.

Knowles, David. *The English Mystical Tradition.* London: Burns & Oates, 1961. Despite limitations of perspective, this is still the best introduction to the English mystics.

Lagorio, Valerie Marie, and Ritamary Bradley. *The 14th-Century English Mystics: A Comprehensive Annotated Bibliography.* New York and London: Garland, 1981.

Merton, Thomas. "The English Mystics." In *Mystics and Zen Masters,* 128–53. New York: Dell, 1967. An insightful essay.

Molinari, Paul, S.J. *Julian of Norwich.* London: Longmans, 1958.

Pantin, W. A. *The English Church in the Fourteenth Century.* Cambridge: University Press, 1955. Best background study.

Pelphrey, Brant. *Love Was His Meaning: The Theology and Mysticism of Julian of Norwich.* Salzburg: Universität Salzburg, 1982.

Pepler, Conrad, O.P. *The English Religious Heritage.* St. Louis, MO: Herder, 1958.

Riehle, Wolfgang. *The Middle English Mystics.* London and Boston: Routledge & Kegan Paul, 1981. An important study concentrating on language.

Walsh, James, S.J. ed., *Pre-Reformation English Spirituality.* London: Burns & Oates, n.d.

9

Spiritual Life in Palamism

GEORGE MANTZARIDIS

The Saint

ONE OF THE MOST PROMINENT FIGURES in the history of Eastern Orthodox spiritual life is St. Gregory Palamas (1296–1359), a monk of the "holy mountain" of Athos, a great theologian, and archbishop of Thessalonica (from 1347 to 1359). The Eastern Orthodox church has dedicated two days of the year to his memory: 14 November, which commemorates his passage from life, and the second Sunday of Great Lent, which celebrates the victory of his teaching over his opponents. This double commemoration shows the particular interest which the Orthodox church has shown in this saint of Thessalonica. More specifically, by celebrating his memory on the second Sunday of Lent, the Orthodox church proclaims the triumph of his teaching as a second triumph of Orthodoxy.

At the cathedral of Thessalonica, which is dedicated to St. Gregory Palamas and in which his holy relics are preserved, these two days are observed with great splendor, especially the second Sunday of Lent, when the saint's relics are carried along the streets of the city he served as archbishop.

As a great ascetic, a formidable theologian, and a distinguished hierarch, Gregory Palamas formulated a harmonious synthesis of the spiritual wealth of Orthodoxy, as it has been handed down by the fathers of the church and as it was actually lived out during the Byzantine and late Byzantine periods. Like all the fathers of the church, Gregory Palamas did not try to put forward his own opinions. His frequent references to the patristic tradition and the manifold support he sought for all his theological positions in the biblical and patristic texts demonstrate the close link between his teaching and the biblical and patristic tradition. Furthermore, the new manner in which he expressed the tradition within the context of his particular time shows the authentic and experiential character of this tradition.

Palamite Spiritual Life

The spiritual life is, according to Gregory Palamas, founded on three premises: (1) the creation of man and woman "in the image and likeness of God"; (2) the renewal and deification (*theōsis*) of human nature in Christ; and (3) the human person's potential to share in this renewal and deification. Creation in the *image* of God is a common attribute of all human beings because all come from God and all express God in their existence, but the same is not true of the likeness, which is offered to each person as a potentiality. As Gregory Palamas typically observed, "Every person is in the image of God, and perhaps also in the likeness" (*Second Letter to Barlaam* 48).[1] The likeness was not imposed on human beings as a necessity, but was left to depend on their free disposition. The fall, as a freely chosen separation from God, darkened the image of God in human beings and made the likeness unattainable. But the renewal and deification of human nature in the incarnation of God opened once again to humanity the way toward the "likeness of God" and, therefore, to personal deification. This gift is communicated to each believer by the Holy Spirit. The Holy Spirit does not perform the saving work but makes accessible to all the unique restoring act of Christ. This is realized within the church in the sacraments, especially baptism and the Eucharist.

In baptism, a person dies with Christ and is raised with him to the new life of the future age. The mystery of baptism joins death and life, burial and resurrection. While dead in sin, a person enters the sphere of life and grace which is revealed by the seal of the gift of the Holy Spirit—that is, Chrismation, which is directly linked with baptism. The devil has no home in the baptized person; however, the baptized person is still subject to the external attacks of the devil and continues to be weighed down by the burden of corruption. This is not due to any imperfection in baptismal grace, but is allowed by God so that human beings can cooperate in the work of their salvation.

The other great mystery for life and perfection in Christ is the Holy Eucharist. This sacrament presupposes baptism: it is baptism that enables a person to receive the body and blood of Christ. Baptism washes the "image" and is the beginning of a person's imitation of Christ, but the Eucharist empowers the Christian's progress toward the "likeness" and the fullness of union and identification with Christ.[2] This union of Christ with believers in the Eucharist is, of course, not the same as the union of the Word with the human nature which Christ assumed, but neither is it simply a moral union. Christ is truly, and not only morally, united with each believer, yet not in a way that brings the two into a single hypostasis. This happened only in the union of the Word with his assumed human nature. The sacramental union is a true union with the renewing and deifying grace of Christ. For this reason, Christ remains always one, as having "one and, in all circumstances, undivided hypostasis," but the many become "Christ-like" (*Antirrhetic against Akindynos* 3.6.13).[3]

For the grace of the sacraments to bring forth fruit, however, human cooperation is necessary. Without this cooperation (synergy) the grace of God remains barren. For this reason, believers are called to use all their powers to work and cooperate with God toward the completion of their renewal and deification. The monk does not pursue anything more than what every believer living in the world ought to pursue. What sets the monk apart is that he lives far from the cares and worries of life, and so he becomes the model of the spiritual life to those believers who live in the world.

Gregory Palamas was a hesychast, and he lived a great part of his life in absolute silence. In particular, during his stay in Beroea (1326–1331), as also during his sojourn at the hermitage of St. Sabbas, he remained alone in his cell for five days of the week and came out only on Saturday and Sunday to participate in the divine liturgy.[4] He would have remained in his silence—and therefore would have perhaps been totally unknown as a writer—had he not been provoked by the monk Barlaam from Calabria, who fought against the hesychast tradition of the Athonite monks. In this regard, we are indebted to Barlaam, for with his challenge he brought to the forefront the greatest Byzantine theologian of the fourteenth century and one of the most prominent theologians of any age.

Hesychasm is not a marginal phenomenon in the history of monasticism, but it is rather in direct continuity with the most ancient tradition of Eastern monasticism. The word *hēsychia* (silence) itself, from the time of Origen, had already taken on the meaning of isolation and a life far from the world: "If a person wonders about doctrine, or is miserable, and suffers and is hated for his convictions, he often asks, Should I not rather escape to the desert and keep silence?" (*Homily on Jeremiah* 20.8).[5] For Palamas, *hēsychia* is a sign of a soul reaching its true balance. It bestows "stability of mind and of the surrounding world, abandonment of things below, initiation to things above, concentration of thoughts on that which is good. *Hēsychia* is indeed an action, leading to true contemplation, or the vision of God" (*Homily* 53.33). Palamas presents the Virgin Mary as a prototype of the hesychast, and he likens the monks to the disciples of Christ who waited in the upper room for the descent of the Holy Spirit.

To be sure, with the evolution of monastic life great monastic communities developed where the monks did not live alone but in organized groups. But there always continued to exist anchorites who lived alone in the desert and there sought to return to themselves and to find a closer knowledge and communion with God. Fleeing to the desert, they gave themselves to asceticism and prayer, and so prepared themselves to receive God's visitation and to see his glory.

The Problem

At the time of Gregory Palamas, monasticism on the holy mountain of Athos had already flourished for nearly four centuries and had established a tradition of intense spiritual life which was now seeking a theological framework and expression. Because the Athonite monks were also practicing new ascetical methods connected with specific spiritual experiences, the theological defense of these against misinterpretations and outside attacks became necessary. Specifically, the Athonite hesychasts of the fourteenth century connected the effort of self-recollection and unceasing prayer with a particular discipline of breathing and concentration. According to this method, the monks would keep their chin pressed against their chest and their eyes fixed downward while repeating inwardly the simple prayer "Lord Jesus Christ, Son of God, have mercy on me." By the continual practice of this prayer, the hesychasts were guided into the vision of the uncreated deifying grace of God. But a few simpleminded monks, not understanding correctly the meaning of the method, may have distorted it, interpreting it as an automatic system for reaching the divine light. Thus, they gave cause for the attacks of their opponents. Palamas himself, although a defender of the hesychasts, had reservations concerning the use of this method. He considered its use beneficial mainly for beginners, and he regarded the book of Nicephorus, in which this method was described, as "naïve" and "artless."[6] According to Palamas, the position of the body and the words of the prayer do not have a magical power, but they are useful in guarding the concentration of the mind in its yearning for undisrupted communion with God and the vision of his glory. The elucidation and defense of this communion with God and vision of his glory are, in the final analysis, the aim of all Palamite theology.

But inevitably questions arose: Is it possible for the invisible and transcendent God to become participable and visible to human beings? If he really becomes participable and visible, how can he also remain transcendent and unapproachable?

The answer of the Greek fathers to this problem is clear. God is not only unapproachable but also approachable; he is not only invisible but also visible. The possibility of communion with God and the vision of his glory rests on the approachability and knowability of the divine. God, who is invisible and nonparticipable in his essence, becomes visible and participable in his energies. This distinction between the essence and energies of God is known to the entire patristic tradition. As early as the apologist Athenagoras, we find the distinction between the essence and energies of God (*On the Resurrection* 1), and Irenaeus speaks of the divine energies as the creative and foreknowing cause "of all times and places and of every nature" (*Fragments* 5 [*PG* 7, col. 1232B]). But a more complete expression of this distinction developed from the fourth century on. The Greek fathers were guided into a fuller formulation by the need of a theological definition and defense of the real communion between God and human beings experienced within the church—something that was disputed by Arius—and by the need to preserve the theological truth of the unknowability of God against the opposite teaching of Eunomius. Human beings see and recognize the energies of God as power, as light, as majesty, and in countless other ways. Therefore, the vision of God, not only by human beings but also by the angels, does not have as its object the divine essence, but the divine energies. These appear sometimes without mediation, sometimes through the medium of creation.

St. Isaac of Syria, summing up the tradition of the older mystical theologians, says that human beings have two different inner eyes, so that there are two types of vision: the "natural vision," by which one is lifted toward the Creator by way of nature, and the unmediated vision of the divine glory, which the Evagrian tradition calls "theology" (*theologia*). "With one eye," notes Isaac, "we see the glory of God that is hidden in all the things of nature; that is, his power and wisdom, and his co-eternal providence for us. With the same eye we also see the heavenly orders who are God's co-servants with us. With the other eye, we see the glory of his holy nature, for it is God's good will to initiate us into the spiritual mysteries and to open to our understanding the ocean of faith" (*Discourse* 72).[7]

Interpreting the thought of Isaac, Gregory Palamas notes that even in the case of the unmediated vision, human beings do not see the nature of God. Rather, they only have the experience of his glory, similar to that which the disciples of Christ had at the transfiguration on Mount Tabor. The event of the transfiguration of Christ, which holds a central place in the thought and teaching of Palamas, reveals the character of deifying grace and certifies the renewal and recreation which grace effects in human beings. As he appeared then to the chief of the disciples, so does the Son of God always appear to those who love him, "not revealing his essence—for it is invisible and appears nowhere, even though it is present everywhere. He is not experienced in his essence, he does not reveal it, nor does he bestow it—it would be blasphemy to think it—but in a most mysterious manner, he shines upon them the radiance of his proper nature and grants them to participate in it" (*Antirrhetic against Akindynos* 4.14.36).[8] Furthermore, since the glory of God is not created but is a physical reflection of the divine essence, the vision of it is not symbolic but real. In this way, Palamas, following the tradition of the Greek fathers, was able to defend the possibility of a real vision of God while excluding any notion of knowing or participating in the divine essence.

In contrast to Palamas, the monk from the West, Barlaam, was not able to understand correctly the spirit of hesychasm. Provoked by the practice of the hesychasts, which he regarded as monstrous and unacceptable, he directed his attacks not only against those practicing this method but also against essential positions of Orthodox monasticism and theology. By treating unceasing prayer as purely intellectual, he was destroying its very reality. Under the influence of Platonic philosophy, he thought it impossible for the human body to participate in spiritual blessings. Finally, by rejecting the existence of God's uncreated energies, which he, together with the theology of the West, identified with the divine essence, he was denying the possibility of seeing God and the Christian's union with God and deification.

In facing the polemics of Barlaam and other like-minded people, Palamas was, in reality, fighting to preserve basic principles of the monasticism and theology of the Orthodox church. The new form in which hesychasm was being lived out during his time did not in the least shock him. The use of methods unknown to the ancient tradition, or even foreign to it, was not considered by him as unacceptable, since these methods did not distort the essence and purpose of hesychasm, which is the person's self-recollection and communion and union with God.

But the debate raised another question: Can a Christian strive for the vision of God in this life and not, rather, wait for it in the future age? The answer of Palamas is clear. Since the vision of God is connected with deification, which is the heart of a person's "likeness of God" and union with him and which begins in the present life, it follows that the possibility of seeing God should increase with growth in deification. Of course, this vision cannot be perfect, nor can it have the fullness of the vision of the future age. It is real, however, even in the present age, because it has as its object the uncreated glory of God and it manifests itself in degrees, "according to the purity each person attains from the practice of God's commandments" (*Triads* 2.2.19–20; 3.3.15).[9] This means that the vision of God is not only

God's gift to believers; it is also the fruit of their personal effort and cooperation in the process of their own perfection. For this reason, not all believers
reach the vision of God in the present life.

The vision of God, although in the final analysis God's gift, does not cease
to have the character of a reward for a person's effort toward spiritual
growth and perfection. Indeed, to gain this vision one has to labor hard. The
vision of God presupposes ascetical effort in the sense of purification and
one's return to oneself and to God. Attachment to the desires of the flesh
and the deceptive elements in creation separate one from God. To "see" God,
Christians have first to return to themselves, to redirect their existence
toward God, and to transform their passionate proclivities toward themselves and the world into disinterested love and "divine eros."[10] The passionlessness of which the ascetics and mystics constantly speak and which they
connect with the vision of God has a positive, not a negative, character.
Passionlessness is not the mortification of the passions, but their redirection
toward God. The desert offers the most suitable environment for a person's
effort at self-recollection and for the practice of passionlessness and perfect
love. This does not mean that the faithful who live in the world are excluded
from the path of perfection. "It is possible," says Gregory Palamas, "for those
living in marriage to attain a similar purity, but with much more difficulty"
(*To Xene* [*PG* 150, col. 1056A]).

Unceasing Prayer

The human life that separates itself from material concerns and turns to
God is joined with God in prayer. Prayer is not a magical means of compelling God, but a spiritual means of raising human beings to a personal
encounter with God. "For this is the nature of prayer, that it raises one from
earth to heaven, higher than every heavenly name and dignity, and brings
one before the very God of all" (*Homily* 2 [*PG* 151, col. 20C]). Dionysius
the Areopagite uses the following analogy: Just as a man in a rowboat pulling on the rope tied around a rock does not move the rock but is himself
with his boat drawn to the rock, so also the man who prays does not lower
the omnipresent God to himself but is himself raised in spirit to him.
Through prayer, the mind gains its proper orientation. Shedding every
material and passionate desire, the person is raised to the sphere of God's
grace. The person who has forgotten God and is separated from him because
of sin will, through prayer, remember him and draw near to him. The
human aversion to sin and the desire to return to God find in prayer their
highest and most spiritual expression. For this reason, the life of the Christian, and especially of the ascetic, in opposition to the course of the fall and

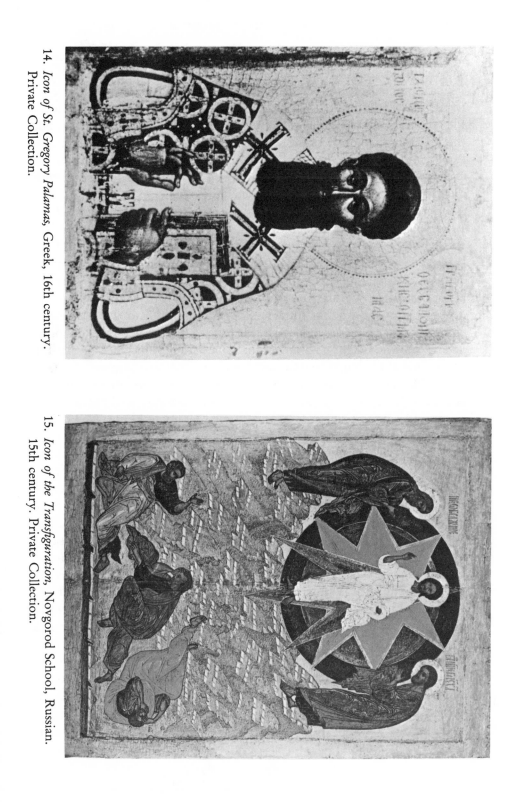

14. *Icon of St. Gregory Palamas*, Greek, 16th century. Private Collection.

15. *Icon of the Transfiguration*, Novgorod School, Russian. 15th century. Private Collection.

as a journey of return to God, has, as its most important and highest spiritual expression, prayer.

The command to pray continuously and without ceasing was always at the center of the fathers' teaching. No Orthodox commentator ever saw hyperbole in this command. Different opinions were expressed only about the manner of understanding unceasing prayer.[11] This was natural, since experience shows that, not only for the faithful in the world but also for those who leave the world and its cares, certain basic needs arise that make the active practice of unceasing prayer impossible.

Origen was the first to examine this subject in his book *On Prayer*. According to him, unceasing prayer can be understood only as the combination of what is usually meant by prayer and the Christ-like conduct of each believer. The entire life of the saint is a single prayer, and what is commonly called prayer is only one aspect of the contemplative life. This view of Origen had a great influence upon later theologians. Despite this, many other ascetics and mystics sought to be more faithful to the letter of the commandment. There were those who increased the frequency of prayer and others who taught its uninterrupted practice—for instance, St. Basil the Great: "All of life ought to be a time for prayer" (*Ascetic Discourse* 4 [*PG* 31, col. 877A]). According to other monastic writers, whoever prays only at the appointed hours does not pray at all. There is no measure of prayer for the monk: "It is good to bless God at all times" (Hyperechios *Exhortations to the Ascetics* 95 [*PG* 79, col. 1481D]).[12] Strict adherents of "unceasing prayer" among heretics were the Messalians or Euchites. They scorned the liturgical life and sacraments of the church and insisted that they were following St. Paul's command to "pray without ceasing." For them, prayer is the only means of salvation and the deliverance of human beings from the evil spirits indwelling them.

At the time when Palamas stayed in Beroea, there lived in the area—we are informed by Gregory's biographer, Philotheos of Constantinople—a simple but renowned old ascetic named Job. This old man used to visit Gregory frequently in order to converse with him and to be taught by his wisdom. During one conversation he heard Gregory say that unceasing prayer is not only for monks but for all Christians. Not only the monks who forsook the world, but also all the faithful in general, men and women and children, the simple and the wise, ought to be taught in these things and instructed with great attention. When he heard this, the monk Job reacted violently and insisted that unceasing prayer is only for the anchorites and not for those living in the world. Palamas attempted to convince him with various passages from Scripture and the fathers, but he remained adamant and brought the conversation to an end. When they parted and each went to his cell to pray, an angel appeared to Job and told him not to think differently on this matter from the holy Gregory. The old man immediately went to Gregory to tell him of this and to ask his forgiveness for his opposition (Philotheos *Encomium on St. Gregory Palamas* [PG 151, cols. 573B–74D]).

The representatives of the two sides in the hesychast controversy did not disagree about the necessity of unceasing prayer, but they understood it in two different ways. Barlaam believed that Christians pray unceasingly when they acquire the habit of prayer, and the habit of prayer for Barlaam is the same as the conscious knowledge that nothing can be done without the will of God. When Christians know that they can do something only if God wills it, then they are praying unceasingly. Thus, Barlaam gave unceasing prayer a passive and ultimately intellectual character, and he naturally attracted the opposition of Palamas. If unceasing prayer were nothing more than this, then the devil, who never prays, would also be practicing it, since he, too, knows that it is impossible to do anything without God's concession. Of course, Palamas used the example of the devil as exaggeration, but his purpose was to underscore the active and existential nature of prayer.

The belief that one cannot do anything without God is not prayer itself, but the presupposition for prayer. Prayer is an active expression of the whole human existence, when, inflamed by divine love, it forsakes everything to find God. Unceasing prayer for Palamas is, therefore, nothing else than the continuous and living communion of a human being with God. This communion becomes possible when a person receives the gift of prayer. This gift, granted by God to those who are vigilant in prayerful asceticism, remains unceasingly within them, sometimes drawing them to communion and union with God, other times praying with them (*Triads* 2.1.30–31).[13] Thus, unceasing prayer is not seen as a one-sided human spiritual activity, but as the fruit of cooperation with the spiritual gift that is secretly active within those who pray.

Another characteristic of genuine Christian prayer is purity. Purity of prayer corresponds to the purity of the heart and mind of those who pray. When minds are ruled by passion, persons cannot approach God and receive his grace. Separated, however, from the cares of life and returning to themselves, they become open to the divine mercy. Then believers feel their sickness and mourn. Christ blessed those who mourn for their sins and for the salvation that they have lost on account of their sins. For this reason, such mourning is called blessed. In the ascetical tradition, blessed mourning is seen as the fruit of God's grace, but it also presupposes human cooperation through humility, self-reproach, hardship, fasting, vigil, and, especially, prayer. Such mourning does not lead to morbidity or despair, but on the contrary acts as a renewing force upon human beings and brings to their souls peace, comfort, and joy. The tears that flow from this mourning give wings to prayer and, united with prayer, they illumine and purify the minds of the faithful. In this manner, real prayer is both mother and daughter of tears, and progress in the Christian moral life becomes a synthesis of personal effort aided by prayer and prayer that is perfected and purified by continuous interior renewal and release from passions.

In accepting passionlessness as the major condition for achieving perfect prayer, Barlaam was in agreement with Palamas and the hesychast tradition. But, as noted already, the two men disagreed fundamentally on the meaning of passionlessness, and this because of their different anthropological assumptions. Barlaam, as a follower of a dualist anthropology which regards the body as a base instrument of the soul, understood passionlessness as the total mortification of the passible part of the soul, and he rejected any participation of the body in prayer. In contrast, Palamas, following an integral Christian anthropology, accepted passionlessness as a transfer of the passions from the world to God and insisted that each human being participates in the "spiritual worship" of prayer as a single psychosomatic entity.

Since the Word of God became perfect man and deified the entire human nature, so each person needs to cooperate with God to become deified as a single psychosomatic hypostasis. The kingdom of God is found within. The Spirit of God comes into the heart of each Christian and cries out, "Abba, Father." Why, then, should one seek to expel the mind from the body and not work to concentrate it in the heart where it can pray with the Spirit of God?

Here lies the source of the hesychasts' psychosomatic method of prayer. For a fuller concentration of the mind in the heart and a more effective practice of prayer, they sat for hours holding their chin pressed against the chest and their eyes drawn down while they prayed inwardly using the single-phrase prayer, "Lord Jesus Christ, Son of God, have mercy on me" (*Synodical Tome* 1.47 [*PG* 151, col. 689A]). At the same time, they sought to restrain their breathing to prevent the distraction of the mind and to help its concentration within the heart. By the practice of this prayer, the hesychasts were guided into the vision of God, which is the summit and the confirmation of the desired meeting with God.

The vision of God is realized within an atmosphere of mutual ecstasy of God and one who prays. In it, persons transcend themselves and behold in the Spirit the glory of the Creator. God, also, undergoes an ecstasy in order to reveal himself to his creature. Thus, in this transcending ecstasy of the person praying and the condescending ecstasy of God, their personal meeting and union are fulfilled: "Our mind, then, comes out of itself and becomes united with God after it has transcended itself. God also comes out of himself and becomes united with our mind by condescension" (*Triads* 1.3.47).[14] This vision of God has a beginning and a consequence, but no end. Its beginning is the simple illumination by the divine light, and what follows is the lasting vision of the glory of God, which is completed and perfected in the future age. But even then the vision of God will not have a static character. Participating in the grace of God and becoming increasingly more receptive to his glory, the saints ceaselessly enjoy grace upon grace (*Triads* 2.3.35; 2.2.11).[15]

Here and Hereafter

The vision of God in the present age has an eschatological character. If one is deemed worthy to see the glory of God in the present life, this is because one is already in communion with God's kingdom and already enjoys a foretaste of the final beatitude. The vision of God in the present life is the pledge of the vision of God in the heavenly kingdom. The just, observed Gregory Palamas, will be illumined by the divine light in the kingdom and, as offspring of this light, they will be able to see the divine splendor of Christ (*Homily* 34 [*PG* 151, col. 432C]). So the vision of God "face to face" does not, for Palamas, mean a vision of the essence of God, but of his splendor. This divine splendor, having been fully communicated to the human nature which was hypostatically united to the Word, is made participable and visible to human beings by the Holy Spirit. Reborn in the sacrament of baptism and becoming concorporeal with Christ in the communion of his deified flesh, Christians become partakers of the new life in Christ and citizens of the kingdom of God. When living a life that preserves its link with the source of real life, Christians neither fear death nor feel threatened by its power. The uncreated life and energy of Christ become common to each person united with him. In such persons Christ himself lives and acts. The needs and temptations of life do not lead such persons into falls and compromises with sin, but into spiritual effort and exaltation of God. The chief concern in these persons' earthly lives is to preserve an uninterrupted communion with God through prayer and the sacramental life. Their only rest is in the mystical union with God, from which they also gain knowledge concerning the end toward which they are proceeding. The vision of the uncreated divine light extends to them the experience of the final glory and the "face-to-face" vision of God.

The event of Christ's transfiguration is the pledge of the "face-to-face" vision of God by human beings in the future age. Such a vision becomes possible because God as a person acts personally. The uncreated light that shone forth from Christ in the transfiguration did not represent an undefined or impersonal power, but a particular personal activity of the Word of God. The hesychasts, in their mystical experiences, see the light of Tabor, and so will all the saints in the future age.

The transfiguration of Christ as a pledge of the "face-to-face" vision of God contained for Palamas, as also for the ancient fathers of the church, a most profound eschatological significance. Following the teaching of earlier fathers, Palamas found in this event the fulfillment of Christ's promise about his quick coming in glory (Matt 16:27–28; Gregory Palamas *Homily* 34 [*PG* 151, col. 425B]). Using the terminology of modern scholarship, we may say that the fathers saw in the transfiguration of Christ an instance of "realized eschatology." Since the light of the transfiguration is the same as the light of the kingdom of God, was revealed by Christ, and is now communicated to all human beings by the Holy Spirit, then truly the kingdom of God is already present in the world. On the other hand, notes Palamas, the coming of the kingdom of God is not a matter of locative movement, but of revelation. The kingdom of God is present everywhere. When a Christian is appropriately prepared, he or she receives by the grace of God the revelation of the glory of the kingdom.

Commenting on the words of Christ, "there are some standing here who will not taste death before they see that the kingdom of God has come with power" (Matt 16:28), Palamas noted the following:

> Everywhere is the king of all, and everywhere is his kingdom, so that the coming of his kingdom does not mean its transfer from one place to another, but its revelation in the power of the Holy Spirit. This is why he said, "has come with power." And this power does not come upon anyone, but upon those who have stood with the Lord, that is, those who are anchored in his faith, like Peter, James and John. But even these three were first brought by the Word to a high mountain, in this way to symbolize those who transcend our low estate. For this reason, Scripture shows us God descending from his supreme dwelling-place and on a mountain elevating us from our lowly condition, so that he who is infinite may be surely but within measure encompassed by created nature. (*Homily* 34 [*PG* 151, cols. 428C–29A]).

So the Christian can, in the present life, already become a communicant of the eschatological glory of the kingdom of God and can receive the pledge of the "face-to-face" vision.

Thus, the "face-to-face" vision of God by human beings, which begins in the present age, awaits its fulfillment and perfection in the kingdom of God. But the vision of the saints in the future age will not have a static character. Participating in the grace of God and, through this communion, becoming increasingly receptive to the divine splendor, the saints will continuously receive grace upon grace from God, who is its infinite and inexhaustible fountain.

Certainly, as a strict discipline, hesychasm can only be practiced by a few, but, despite this, it reflects the deepest truths of authentic Christian ethics and Orthodox spiritual life according to the spirit of the fathers' teaching. Hesychasts seek to live within the gift which the incarnate Son of God has offered to human beings. They do not desire to win the grace of God through the works of hirelings, since grace is freely extended to human beings, but to remain at the height of their calling, to appropriate in their own lives and mystical experiences Christ's victory over the powers of evil, corruption, and death, and to remain within the sphere of Christian freedom. This, however, is the proper goal of the spiritual life for every true Christian.

Notes

1. See Gregory Palamas, *Works*, ed. P. Chrestou (Thessaloniki, 1962–72) 1:287.

2. See Gregory Palamas, *Homily* 56, in *Gregory Palamas, Archbishop of Thessaloniki, 22 Homilies*, ed. S. Oikonomos (Athens, 1861) 206–8.

3. See *Works*, 3:170–71.

4. See Philotheos of Constantinople, *Encomium on St. Gregory Palamas*, in *PG* 151, cols. 571C, 547D.

5. For more about *hēsychia*, see I. Hausherr, "L'hésychasme: Étude de Spiritualité," *Orientalia Christiana Periodica* 32 (1956) 5–40, 247–85.

6. See *Triads* 2.2.2–3, in *Works*, 1:509.

7. Ed. I. Spetsieris (Athens, 1895) 281.

8. See *Works*, 3:267.

9. See *Works*, 1:692–93.

10. For more on this subject, see J. Meyendorff, "Le thème du retour en soi dans la doctrine palamite du XIVe siècle," *Revue de l'Histoire des Religions* 145 (1954) 188–206.

11. I. Hausherr, "Comment priaient les Pères," *Revue d'Ascétique et de Mystique* 32 (1956) 33.

12. See I. Hausherr, "L'hésychasme," 36–37.

13. See *Works*, 1:490–92.

14. See *Works*, 1:458.

15. See *Works*, 1:569, 517.

Bibliography

Behr-Sigel, E. "Reflexion sur la doctrine de Grégoire Palamas." *Contacts* 12 (1960) 118–25.

Chrestou, P. "Gregory Palamas." In *Festschrift Honoring the Six Hundredth Anniversary of the Death of St. Gregory Palamas*, 255–71. Edited by P. Chrestou. Thessaloniki, 1960. In Greek.

Florovsky, G. "Gregory Palamas and the Patristic Tradition." In *Festschrift Honoring the Six Hundredth Anniversary of the Death of St. Gregory Palamas*, 240–54. In Greek.

Hausherr, I. "L'hésychasme. Étude de spiritualité." *Orientalia Christiana Periodica* 22 (1956) 5–40, 284–96.

Ivánka, E. von. "Hesychasmus und Palamismus: Ihr gegenseitiges Verhältnis und ihre geistesgeschichtliche Bedeutung." *Jahrbuch der Österreichischen Byzantinischen Gesellschaft* 2 (1952) 23–24.

———. "Palamismus und Vätertradition." In *L'Église et les Églises*, 2:29–46. Chevetogne, 1955.

Kiprian, C. *Antropologija sv. Grigorija Palamy.* Paris: YMCA-Press, 1950.

———. "Duchovnye predki sv. Grigorija Palamy." *Bogoslovskaja Mysl'* 3 (1942) 102–13.

Krivochéine, B. "Asceticeskoe i bogoslovskoe ucenie sv. Gregorija Palamy." *Seminarium Kondakovianum* 8 (1936) 99–154.

Lossky, V. "La théologie de la lumière chez saint Grégoire de Thessalonique." *Dieu Vivant* 1 (1945) 95–118.

———. *Vision of God.* London: Faith Press, 1963.

Mantzaridis, G. *Palamika.* Thessaloniki, 1973. Reprint, Crestwood, NY: St. Vladimir's Seminary Press, 1983. In Greek.

———. "Tradition and Renewal in the Theology of St. Gregory Palamas." *Eastern Churches Review* 9 (1977) 1–18.

Meyendorff, J. *St. Gregory Palamas and Orthodox Spirituality.* Crestwood, NY: St. Vladimir's Seminary Press, 1974.

———. *A Study of Gregory Palamas.* 2nd ed. Crestwood, NY: St. Vladimir's Seminary Press, 1974.

Monk of the Eastern Church. *Orthodox Spirituality: An Outline of the Orthodox Ascetical and Mystical Tradition.* London: SPCK, 1961.

Romanides, J. "Notes on the Palamite Controversy and Related Topics, I-II." *Greek Orthodox Theological Review* 6 (1960–61) 186–205; 9 (1963–64) 225–70.

Staniloae, D. *Viatsa si invatsatura sf. Grigorie Palama.* Sibiu, 1938.

Ware, K. "The Debate about Palamism." *Eastern Churches Review* 9 (1977) 45–63.

10

Late Medieval Russia: The Possessors and the Non-Possessors

Sergei Hackel

THE RUSSIAN CHURCH COUNCIL OF 1503 had completed its agenda by the early days of September and was about to disperse when it was suddenly confronted by an additional, unscheduled and yet all-important item of business. Should the monasteries own land? Or, rather, should they not be deprived of it? It was the revered monastic elder Nil Maikov (1433–1508) who rose to his feet with the assertion that "monasteries should own no villages, that monastics should live in deserted places, and that they should gain their sustenance by the work of their own hands."[1]

The Council's Debate

It is difficult to reconstruct the Council's debates. No minutes have survived, and most accounts of it were composed some decades later. Nil's own role is variously represented, most frequently (and convincingly) as one subordinate to that of Ivan III, the grand prince of Moscow. Certainly, it was the Muscovite state that stood to gain most from such secularization of church lands as was implicit in Nil's proposal. Thus, it is not surprising to learn from a distinguished contemporary, Vassian Patrikeev, that it was Ivan III who made every effort to ensure Nil's attendance at the Council. Ivan's own (already well-known) views on the subject could be expected to have much less effect on a recalcitrant Council than those of a churchman with Nil's reputation for integrity and unworldliness. Indeed, had there not been a Nil at the Council, it would have been prudent to invent one; and some historians have actually argued that this may have happened.

Be that as it may, Nil was the appropriate person to use as a front. Admittedly, his surviving works do not touch on the political and economic grounds for ending the monastic ownership of land. But the whole of his spirituality is based on the freedom to be gained from personal and collective poverty, the complete absence of avarice or possessiveness of any sort.

The question of church property had not been approached with quite such rigor or such reservations in earlier times. On the contrary, Nil's opponents were able to demonstrate that Russian (as well as Byzantine) precedent provided plenty of arguments against him. Yet he was not alone. No less an authority than Metropolitan Cyprian of Kiev and all Rus' (d. 1406) had once issued a statement to Abbot Athanasius of Vysotskoe to the effect that "the possession of villages and personnel by monastics does not form part of the tradition passed on by the holy fathers." Was it possible, he asked, "for those who have once renounced the world and the things of the world to engage themselves once more in worldly affairs?" The ownership of villages or other property could be seen only as a weakening of the rules, a decline.[2] Similarly, St. Cyril of Beloozero (1337–1427) was (unjustifiably, but no doubt credibly) represented by Nil's contemporaries as someone who was reluctant to accept inhabited land for his monastic foundation. On one occasion he is said to have preferred a donation of grain. On another he stated, somewhat ambiguously, "I require no villages during my lifetime. But when I depart from you, do as you will."[3]

Furthermore, there were Russian heretical movements—whose cause Ivan III himself had espoused for a time—which openly preached against monastic ownership of land, though in their case this followed from a more brazen dismissal of monasticism as such. They could thus not only draw attention to the problem, but also inadvertently provide Nil's opponents with ammunition against him.

Yet Russian precedents were not necessarily to the point, since the Russian situation had changed considerably in the century which preceded Nil's birth.

The Mongol invasion of the thirteenth century, with its attendant destruction and demoralization, had seriously disrupted the established norms of monastic life. Previously the monasteries had almost invariably been urban foundations, under the patronage of the local prince. Thus subsidized and endowed, they were expected to play a positive part in the social life of the realm. But in the course of the fourteenth century there was an extraordinary revival of the monastic life, which at the same time involved the exploration of new ways. Many dozens of new communities were to be established away from the existing centers of civilization in the unpopulated or as yet sparsely populated wilderland, to which the Russian monks gave the picturesque designation "desert." Moreover, these were initially to be self-supporting and in any case economically independent entities. It was a revival that was closely associated with the name of one man in particular, Sergii of Radonezh (ca. 1314–1392).

St. Sergii of Radonezh

Sergii left no writings, and his outlook must be reconstructed largely from the biography composed by one of his immediate successors. Through the filter it provides, Sergii may be seen as virtually recapitulating the stages of monastic history within the span of a few years. Initially he proceeded with his brother into the "desert" in search of separateness and silence. Abandoned by his brother, Sergii underwent all the trials and temptations of the hermit's calling over several years. Only then did he unwillingly accept the company of fellow monks, and a loosely structured community or "skete" grew up around him. Eventually he was persuaded, supposedly at the insistence of the patriarch of Constantinople himself, to introduce the *Studite Rule* and thus to transform his Trinity monastery into a cenobitic community. From dedicated poverty it was about to move toward unwonted and, at first, involuntary affluence.

It remains unclear whether Sergii himself remained basically a nonpossessor: it may well be that his monastery owned no villages in his lifetime, however much this was to change in the years to come. In any case, the growth of the community and its corresponding growth in public esteem were not in any way achieved at the expense of Sergii's personal simplicity, humility, and grace. Certainly the record of his mystical experiences locates these in his later years.

The reader of Sergii's biography is left unclear about the nature and the framework of these experiences, the first to be recorded of any Russian saint. The most striking of them involved a vision of the Mother of God, who undertook to be the heavenly patron of the Trinity monastery. But virtually all of them involved some vision of light, and it is this that suggests that they may be the fruit of hesychast concerns and prayer. It is certainly not surprising to discover that the monastery's library contained not only fifteenth-century but also, and more important, fourteenth-century Slavonic translations of works by such hesychast masters as Symeon the New Theologian and Gregory of Sinai.

It was by means of translations like these (and the number of Byzantine texts translated into Slavonic languages was to double in the period 1350 to

1450) that hesychasm began to penetrate the Russian world. Such translations issued from Mount Athos, possibly Constantinople, most certainly Bulgaria. Even more important were the personal carriers of the teachings which the texts purveyed, among them the same Metropolitan Cyprian, himself a Bulgarian translator with Athonite experience.

By the time of Nil, the best part of a century later, the precarious balance maintained between the different elements in the composition of the communities—their original eremitic spirit and their subsequent cenobitic practice—was no more, nor could it be restored. The spiritual leaders at the Council of 1503 were faced with apparently stark alternatives. And Nil's personal stance ("monasteries should own no villages") was the expression of what one of these seemed to imply and require.

St. Nil Maikov

Nil himself was a personal carrier of Byzantine hesychast teaching and experience. Details of his life are lacking, but it is known that he visited not only Constantinople but also Athos—and this in the aftermath of its great flowering at the time of the fourteenth-century hesychast elders. It may even be that he ventured further—to Palestine, if not to Sinai itself, thus uncovering *in situ* what, in any case, he must have perceived in the living tradition of the Orthodox church: the early norms of monasticism as enshrined in the *Rule of St. Sabbas* (d. 524) or the writings of St. John Climacus (580–650), abbot of Sinai.

Nil returned to his native land not only to write about the monastic life but also to work for its renewal. Yet the mere fact that he wrote at all was already significant. In the already long history of Russian Christianity (the conversion of Kievan Rus' was begun at the end of the tenth century), his were to be the first writings to deal explicitly and at length with the spiritual life.

This is not to say that their contents are original. He remained ever the faithful exponent and unassertive mouthpiece of his spiritual masters. Principal among these were John Climacus, John Cassian "the Roman," Isaac of Syria, Symeon the New Theologian, and Gregory of Sinai. These were writers whose works Nil himself transcribed, as did his follower and correspondent Gurii Tushin of Beloozero (ca. 1452–1526). Yet those works to which Nil attached his own name may also be said to bear the stamp of his personality. The patina that they bear is the product of his insight, experience, and discrimination.

Nil began his own monastic career at the monastery of St. Cyril at Beloozero, and he was to return there after his travels abroad. Those travels had

16. *Icon of St. Sergius
of Radonezh,* Russian,
twentieth century.
Community of St. Denis
and St. Seraphin, Paris.

17. left to right: Annunciation Cathedral (1482–1490); Dormition Cathedral
(1479); and Archangel Cathedral (1505); Moscow.

evidently convinced him that a complex, well-populated, and ever more prosperous monastery such as St. Cyril's was not sufficiently conducive to inner silence and therefore prayer. It was then that he made the move to an inhospitable location some miles away, which was "difficult of access to the worldly."[4] There he established himself at some time during the 1470s or 1480s in an Athonite skete. Nearby was the river Sora—hence his usual sobriquet, "Sorskii," Nil of Sora. A few followers were to be carefully admitted to this skete; rather more were refused. All were to live in a loosely coordinated fellowship, the basic and independent unit of which consisted of two or three monks. Each might select an elder and would be encouraged to do so, but there was no question of any abbot or hierarchy whatsoever. Nil preferred to speak of his companions as "brothers." "I give you this name, rather than 'disciples,'" he wrote, "since we have but one teacher, the Lord Jesus Christ, Son of God."[5] The latter's will was to be sought in the sacred Scriptures, even when (or especially when) no ordinary spiritual guide might be at hand.

Nil urged that even the apparently well-established Scriptures should be carefully scrutinized, for "writings are many, but not all are divine."[6] Thus spoke the contemporary of the "Novgorod-Moscow" heresy, also the curiously modern yet utterly orthodox editor of the sacred texts which passed through his scriptorium. It was his obligation, as he put it, to distinguish authentic readings from among the variants.[7] But it was not for him in any way to set himself up against the church or to manipulate her tradition, only to ensure its optimum expression.

The life of the skete was necessarily concerned with combatting sin, and Nil compiled a manual of spiritual combat to this end. In it he listed eight principal temptations: gluttony, fornication, avarice, anger, sadness, accidie (morbid depression or despair), vainglory, and pride. Under each heading he provided detailed advice on how to counteract them. In all cases, perpetual vigilance is required, sustained by consistent, if moderate, asceticism. Such vigilance should involve the deflection of thoughts that might ultimately develop into temptations and that in any case act as distractions. Beyond this, the heart needs to be kept clear of any thought, whether good or evil. Such elimination of thoughts, however imperfect it may be, is the necessary preliminary to that inward peace (*hēsychia*) out of which, and only out of which, authentic prayer may proceed. The practice of authentic prayer may be accompanied by the "gift of tears," a gift from God, as Nil stresses, not merely the result of compunction; this "exalts the mind, it generates comfort and joy from within."[8]

Nil urged the use of the Jesus prayer. He did not introduce it to his Russian readers for the first time; Russians had been familiar with it since at least the middle of the eleventh century. In conformity with his hesychast masters, Nil was able to provide it with a new context. The formula is less important than the way in which it is used. Nil did not express a preference for any one of the forms that he quoted: "Lord Jesus Christ, have mercy on me"; "Lord Jesus Christ, Son of God, have mercy on me"; or "Lord Jesus Christ, have mercy on me, a sinner." Rather, he tolerated some variation between them. Nor did he give preference to any one posture for its performance; the main thing, he pointed out, is to recite the prayer "as is most convenient." It was above all when he referred briefly to the control of the practitioner's breathing and urged him to "contain the mind in the heart" that it became perfectly clear that he was no longer speaking of one ejaculatory prayer among others, but of a deeply interiorized prayer, an important and immutable stepping-stone on the way to *theōsis*, divinization.[9]

We can do no more than speculate about whether Nil himself was able to enjoy some foretaste of *theōsis*. It is not that he avoided the question. But it is typical of him that he preferred to hide behind one of his usual sources, and his use of the first person singular must therefore be carefully qualified by the addition of quotation marks. And yet, in seeking to express the ineffable ("What tongue can express it? what mind encompass it?"),[10] might he not have been grateful to borrow the ready vocabulary of others, even though he himself may have passed through a comparable experience? At least it may be said that his confident use of the borrowed vocabulary, which belongs entirely to Symeon the New Theologian, suggests that this should not be too readily discounted. In any case, Symeon's vision of light must have corresponded to Nil's deepest aspirations:

> Seated in the middle of my cell, I see a light which is not of this world. Within me I perceive the creator of the world. I converse with him, love him, and am nourished amply by this single vision. I unite myself to him and so am raised above the heavens. With all clarity and certainty, this I know. But I do not know where the body is at such a time [. . .]. For God loves me, he has received me into his very being and hides me in his embrace [. . .]. Not only is there no desire to leave one's cell in such a state; there is a longing to hide deep in some burrow down below the ground and there, separated from familiar worlds, to gaze on my immortal Lord and maker.[11]

Nil's inward path left little room for any public mission. On rare occasions ("if a brother seeks to receive some communication from us, if he genuinely demands the word of God and we possess it") the monk may act as teacher; indeed, we must give him not only the word of God [. . .] but our very soul."[12] But in general, the contemplative's role is that of a reminder, a model, a signpost. Even with regard to heretics, the contemplative's role must be essentially passive. For if one is not to have dealings with the possessors, "ordinary friends and worldly-wise men and those who are concerned with vain worries such as the increase of monastic wealth or the ownership of land,"[13] and if one is not even to reprove or correct such misguided fellow churchmen, how much less should the heretics detain the contemplative. Least of all should one pursue or oppress them. On the contrary, as Nil's close associate Vassian Patrikeev was to write in their regard, "We truly know the mercy of God, and that God wishes to save all and to bring every sinner to an understanding of the truth by way of repentance."[14]

If the monastic skete is not to engage in any public mission, neither is it to engage in charitable works. It was again Vassian who gave expression to the nonpossessor view on this question. "Monks should live in the complete absence of possessions, in poverty and without any refinements," he wrote. "Neither should they amass wealth, nor should they have superfluous [funds for] alms. They should keep only what is needed for the church [. . .]."[15] Yet even here there were unusual restrictions, untypical of Russian monasticism. For instance, gold and silver were to be avoided, even for sacred vessels. Investment in such objects and materials was misplaced, for, according to St. John Chrysostom, notes Nil, it should have been directed to the needy in the first place. Nil takes evident pleasure in quoting Chrysostom's rider to the effect that "no one was ever condemned for not decorating a church."[16]

Nil's conscientious reluctance to concern himself with social problems set him aside most clearly from his opponents, and it marked a deviation from a well-established Russian trend. The memory of St. Theodosius (d. 1074) and his weekly visitation of Kiev's prisons with a cart of bread was impressed on the memory of Russian Christians from much earlier days. Thus, Theodosius's admonition—"It would be good for us to feed the poor and the wanderers with the fruit of our labours and not to dwell in idleness, strolling from cell to cell"[17]—was to find its most sonorous echo among Nil's antagonists, both at the Council of 1503 and in its aftermath.

At the Council itself, Nil was supported by a number of elders from the Beloozero region, as well as by two bishops. The unhappy occasion brought the Russian hesychasts momentarily to the attention of the general public and linked them to an untoward degree with the principle of nonpossession, subordinate though this was to their main concern for prayer. Yet it was at least partly their nonpossessor position, as well as the moderation of their attitude to the heretics (which was to lead to accusations that they not only sheltered but also supported them) which led to the harassment, peripheralization—if not actual suppression—of the Nilite sketes by the new establishment from the 1530s on. Among Nil's most eminent followers or associates to suffer were Vassian Patrikeev, who died prematurely in 1546 as the result of his confinement in the possessor monastery at Volokolamsk, and Maksim Trivolis "the Greek" (ca. 1470–1556). The latter, much maligned and misused by his Muscovite hosts and imprisoned for almost a quarter of a century, was ultimately to be venerated for his innocent suffering, above all at St. Sergii's monastery, which served as his final refuge.

Nil himself had long before spoken of suffering as the way of purification. It was impermissible to kill for the truth, as he would have argued in defense of the heretics; but one should ever be ready to die for it. He reminded a politically disgraced disciple that it was "a sign of God's love that anyone should suffer as the result of furthering the truth. For it causes him to participate in Christ's passion when he undergoes sorrow for his sake, and it likens him to the saints. Indeed, God does not favor those who love him other than by proving themselves through sorrow."[18]

The movement represented and nourished by Nil was barely to survive as an undercurrent in Russian church life during the succeeding centuries. Only toward the end of the eighteenth century was it to experience a dramatic revival. Not until then was Nil himself unobtrusively to be listed among the saints.

St. Joseph Sanin

As a result of the 1503 Council, the Muscovite state reluctantly accepted that monastic and other church property was inalienable or at least not yet alienable from its owners. In this respect the Russians were soon to be overtaken by Sweden (1527), Denmark (1536), and England (1536–1539), where secularization of church lands proceeded apace as part and parcel of the Reformation. In contrast, those Muscovite monastics who argued forcibly against such secularization—the majority at the Council of 1503—were to gain increasing and unexpected prominence in church and state alike, binding the one ever more firmly to the other. Most remarkable among them was St. Joseph Sanin (1439–1515), abbot and founder of Volokolamsk.

At the very moment of its foundation in October 1479, the monastery of Volokolamsk was already endowed with three villages. By January of the following year, several more were to be added to its holdings, and over the years to come there was to be an unimpeded and consistent increase in its acquisitions. Never was there to be any doubt about where Joseph stood on this question. But a landed, busy, and efficient monastery, unlike Nil's skete, needed a *Rule* to regulate its affairs. Two *Rules* of Joseph have survived, the earlier and shorter of which seems to have served the community for most of his life, while the second was prepared as an elaboration of it in his final years. Each speaks in similar terms of that good order which Joseph prized above all and promoted.

The very first sentence of his shorter *Rule* already expresses his concern that "everything in the common life be done decorously and in accordance with the regulations."[19] Even more explicitly, he later stresses the primacy of well-regulated behavior over understanding: "Let us concern ourselves first of all with the proper aspect and the proper ordering of things, and then with inner attentiveness and obedience."[20] Joseph thus inverted the attitude of Nil, for whom the external ordering of life could never assume comparable importance, let alone precedence. Joseph sought to regulate the very posture of his monks at public prayer. "Press your hands together and join your feet," he told them, "close your eyes and concentrate your mind."[21] He also urged promptness and precision in the fulfillment of liturgical requirements. All this is to be upheld by fear of God. For "salvation, my brothers, is impossible for those who do not fear the awesome threats of God and his just wrath."[22] It is for the abbot to mediate God's will; resistance to the one must be interpreted as resistance to the other, and it is the devil who tempts by way of independence. A proportion of Joseph's formulations undoubtedly speak of that which G. P. Fedotov once designated as Phobos religion. The system, even where it curiously allows for different well-defined categories of monastic garb or diet, as does the later *Rule,* is finite, inflexible, and relentlessly demanding.

It deals curiously little with the inner life. Here there is no evident expectation of, and certainly no stress upon, any kind of mystical experience. Nevertheless, it would seem that Joseph recommended the Jesus prayer and, according to his *Life,* practiced it. A text that is usually ascribed to him contains a striking testimony to its universal application:

> Wherever you are, my beloved, whether you are traveling by sea or by land, whether you are at home, walking or seated or asleep, in whatever place you are, ceaselessly pray with your conscience clear, saying, "Lord Jesus Christ, Son of God, have mercy on me," and God will hear you: for his is the earth and the ends thereof.[23]

However, the alternative ascription of this text to Nil Sorskii must serve to restrict its importance in the present context.

More obviously and indisputably important for Joseph was communal worship, which provided the foundation and the motivation for all the community's activities. In contrast to Nil's attitude to such things, there was a ready acceptance of church decoration, and Joseph did not hesitate to use ecclesiastical objects made of "gold and silver and pearls."[24] These would all express the glory of God, but they would also form part of the community's investments, as is clearly suggested in one of Joseph's letters.[25] For this community is unashamedly and advisedly a possessor.

Not that its individual members should benefit from communal possessions. Indeed, according to the shorter *Rule*, later to be somewhat modified, they should possess nothing of their own. There was to be no talk of "yours" or "mine," of "this person's" or "another's": not for nothing was this called the common life, wrote Joseph, "since everything is held in common."[26] In this first *Rule* he quoted the remark of the monk Evagrius to the effect that "a certain brother possessed only the Gospels, which he sold and gave [the proceeds] to the needy with the words, 'I sold that which ever said to me: sell what thou hast and give to the poor.'"[27] But whereas the principle of Nil would have been to begin the monastic life with one such distribution of all worldly goods, the Josephite intention was to perpetuate it. In this way, he paid deference to the model provided not only by St. Theodosius but also, and more recently, by St. Sergii, the same who had firmly urged his disciples "to entertain strangers" (Heb 13:2).

No one more than Joseph was to place the established church at the disposal of the needy. In one letter he speaks of feeding six or seven hundred people daily; in periods of famine his monastery became a refuge for thousands. At all times it sought to be a source of economic aid, a support for development, a haven for the deprived. Did not Christ manifest himself in the person of the hungry, the thirsty, the homeless, the sick, and the imprisoned? In his shorter *Rule*, Joseph reminded the reader of the relevant Gospel imagery (Matt 25:35–40). The implication was obvious, and there was no need to belabor it: their service was an integral part of the Christian, therefore of the monastic, way of life. Joseph's spirituality therefore had its necessary, visible, and laudable application.

But there was a dark side to his spirituality which set a limit even on the apparently broadcast nature of his charity. Moreover, it involved more than the mere withholding of it. When faced with heretics, there could certainly be no question of sharing food with them; for this restriction Joseph could at least refer to apostolic and patristic sanction. But more than this was required: it was as much a question of suppression as of segregation.

Not uninfluenced by favorable reports of the contemporary Spanish Inquisition (and in this respect in one accord with his former bishop, Gennadius of Novgorod), Joseph insisted that the ultimate extirpation of heresy could result only from the physical extermination of the heretics. Furthermore (and in this his severity showed itself in its most extreme form), any pleas of repentance that the heretics might make were to be distrusted and ignored.[28]

The executions that finally took place after a further Council in 1504 marked yet another victory for the Josephite cause. But the cold rigorism and the devious rhetoric that paved the way for them were hardly to Joseph's credit, and the elders of Nil's persuasion were not slow to say so. Surely, they argued, Christ himself had required his apostle to forgive not merely seven but seventy times seven (Matt 18:21–22). Such mercy could only be praised and emulated.[29]

Nevertheless, the painful division between the schools of Nil and Joseph was not absolute and all-inclusive. Even the scribes of the Volokolamsk monastery could be found at work on copies of Nil's texts. Moreover, Nil himself copied the writings of Joseph and, at least to this extent, gave them his approval. Even though those disparate strands of Russian spirituality that once might have been reconciled by someone of Sergii's caliber were now destined to evolve apart, there were yet some vital convictions that were shared by representatives of each. Thus, on the vexed question of personal possessions, they could be at one, and the injunction that a monk ought "neither to own possessions or even to desire them" finds its place in the writings of Nil and Joseph alike.[30] Again, when Nil urged Vassian Patrikeev, "Treat every brother as a saint,"[31] he was not far removed from the Joseph who was able to urge his reader that he should never be ashamed "to bow down before every man who is created in the image of God."[32] Each might well have subscribed to the judgment of Nil's favored and familiar author, Gregory of Sinai. "The work of silence is one thing," he wrote, "and that of a cenobite another. But each abiding in that to which he has been called shall be saved" (*PG* 150, col. 1333D).[33]

Notes

1. *Polaniia Iosifa Volotskogo*, ed. A. A. Zimin and I. S. Lur'e (Moscow and Leningrad, 1959) 367.

2. *Russkaia istoricheskaia biblioteka* (St. Petersburg, 1880) vol. 6, col. 263.

3. Quoted in I. U. Budovnits, *Monastyri na Rusi i bor'ba s nimi krest'ian v XIV–XVI vekakh* (Moscow, 1966) 170.

4. Nil Sorskii, Letter to German Podol'nyi, "Poslaniia Nila Sorskogo," ed. G. M. Prokhorov, *Trudy otdela drevnerusskoi literatury* 29 (Leningrad, 1974) 142.

5. M. S. Borovkova-Maikova, ed., "Nila Sorskago Predanie i Ustav [. . .]," *Pamiatniki drevnei pis'mennosti i iskusstva* 179 (St. Petersburg, 1912) 1–2.

6. Nil Sorskii, Letter to Gurii Tushin, "Poslaniia Nila Sorskogo," 140. See also Nil's remarks on his editorial principles, quoted in G. M. Prokhorov, "Avtografy Nila Sorskogo," *Pamiatniki kul'tury: Novye otkrytiia, 1974* (Moscow, 1975) 46.

7. Nil Sorskii, Letter to Gurii Tushin, "Poslaniia Nila Sorskogo," 140.

8. Borovkova-Maikova, *Pamiatniki*, 77.

9. Ibid., 21–22.

10. Ibid.

11. Ibid., 28–29.
12. Nil Skorskii, Letter to Gurii Tushin, "Poslaniia Nila Sorskogo," 140.
13. Ibid.
14. N. A. Kazakova, *Vassian Patrikeev i ego sochineniia* (Moscow and Leningrad, 1960) 277.
15. Ibid., 280.
16. Quoted in G. P. Fedotov, *A Treasury of Russian Spirituality*, 93.
17. Quoted in G. P. Fedotov, *The Russian Religious Mind*, 1:133.
18. Nil Sorskii, Letter to Vassian Patrikeev, "Poslaniia Nila Sorskogo," 138.
19. *Poslaniia Iosifa*, 297.
20. Ibid., 300.
21. Ibid., 299–300.
22. *Velikiia Minei Chetii (sentiabr' 1–3)* (St. Petersburg, 1868) col. 508.
23. N. A. Kazakova and I. S. Lur'e, *Antifeodal'nye ereticheskie dvizheniia na Rusi XIV–nachala XVI veka* (Moscow and Leningrad, 1955) 356.
24. Kazakova, *Vassian*, 355.
25. *Poslaniia Iosifa*, 182.
26. Ibid., 308.
27. Ibid.
28. Ibid., 179, 231.
29. Kazakova and Lur'e, *Antifeodal'nye dvizheniia*, 513.
30. Borovkova and Maikova, *Pamiatniki*, 479 (Nil); *Poslaniia Iosifa*, 307 (Joseph).
31. Nil Sorskii, Letter to Vassian Patrikeev, "Poslaniia Nila Sorskogo," 137.
32. *Prosvetitel' Iosifa Volotskago* (Kazan', 1904) 367.
33. Trans. G. A. Maloney, *Russian Hesychasm*, 140.

Bibliography

Fedotov, G. P. *The Russian Religious Mind.* Vol. 1, *Kievan Christianity: The Tenth to the Thirteenth Centuries.* Vol. 2, *The Middle Ages: The Thirteenth to the Fifteenth Centuries.* Edited by J. Meyendorff. Cambridge, MA: Harvard University Press, 1966.

Fedotov, G. P., ed. *A Treasury of Russian Spirituality.* New York: Sheed & Ward, 1948.

Maloney, G. A. *Russian Hesychasm: The Spirituality of Nil Sorskii.* The Hague: Mouton, 1973.

The Rule of Iosif Volotsky. Translated by D. Goldfrank. Kalamazoo, MI: Cistercian Publications, 1983.

Špídlik, T. *Joseph de Volokolamsk: Un chapitre de la spiritualité russe.* Orientalia Christiani Analecta 146; Rome, 1956.

The 'Vita' of St. Sergii of Radonezh. Translated by M. Klimenko. Houston, 1980.

11

Humanism

I. *The Spirituality of Renaissance Humanism*

WILLIAM J. BOUWSMA

ENAISSANCE HUMANISM, considered formally, was a movement, originating in the towns of Italy and eventually spreading across the Alps, that aimed at a major shift within the standard educational curriculum of the later Middle Ages. It proposed to substitute for dialectic, the art fundamental to scholastic discourse, a primary emphasis on grammar, the art of reading and interpreting texts, and, above all, on rhetoric, the art of eloquent and persuasive discourse. The scholastic curriculum had been primarily concerned with generating and systematizing the general, supposedly objective and immutable truths of natural philosophy (i.e., science), metaphysics, and dogmatic theology. But what was described by the later fourteenth century as the *studia humanitatis* had a quite different focus. It was more concerned with individual human beings, with their changing thoughts, values, and feelings, and with human interaction in society. The ancient texts that chiefly inspired the humanists were not the works of the ancient Greek philosophers but those of the Latin orators (above all Cicero and Quintilian), and of the ancient poets and historians. As this emphasis suggests, therefore, Renaissance humanism also had more than formal importance. Promoted on the ground that it was better suited to the needs of the laity and of life in society, humanistic education had profound epistemological and anthropological implications that pointed to an evangelical spirituality significantly different from the more intellectual spirituality of the previous period.

The Humanists

The most influential early Italian humanist was Francesco Petrarca (1304–1374), known to posterity as Petrarch. First renowned for his Italian lyric

236

poetry, he also attempted to master Latin literature as a whole. He collected the manuscript works of both classical and Christian antiquity, improved texts, and modeled his own style on the great Latin writers, with marked benefits for the clarity and—since his interests were broad and touched on the most concrete and vivid aspects of human experience—the expressive range of both Latin and the vernacular. Thus Petrarch moved through the literary studies of a grammarian to become a skilled rhetorician. By converting language into an increasingly creative, flexible, and versatile instrument, he seemed to have restored to it some of the power to please and influence human beings that it was believed to have possessed in antiquity. At the same time he attacked the scholastic discourse of his time, especially its natural science, because, he believed, in its effort to open up the abstract order of the intelligible universe to human understanding, it had diverted attention from both God and humanity to nature. Thus, Petrarch articulated for later humanists what might be described as a layman's perception of the abstract formulations of scholasticism as irrelevant to the daily experience of human beings, perhaps especially to those living in towns.

Petrarch's influence spread rapidly at the princely courts of Italy and among the ruling circles of the republican city states; among the most famous of Italian humanists were two chancellors of Florence, Coluccio Salutati (1331-1406) and Leonardo Bruni (1369-1444). Eloquence acquired by training in rhetoric was especially prized for its persuasive power. It was believed capable, as the humanists thought that scholastic formulations were not, of penetrating the hearts of human beings, transforming the will, arousing the emotions, and accomplishing the world's work by inspiring action. As Petrarch wrote, "To accuse, to excuse, to console, to irritate, to placate souls, to move to tears and to remove them, to light fires of anger and to extinguish them, to color facts, to avert infamy, to transfer blame, to arouse suspicions—these are the proper work of orators."[1] Words, he declared, "can sting and set afire and urge toward love of virtue and hatred of vice."[2]

The tendency of humanists to reject logical discourse directed toward intellectual conviction in favor of persuasive discourse colored by all the strategies of rhetorical art also suggests a change in the understanding of the human personality. For Petrarch, who had been deeply influenced by his reading of Augustine's *Confessions*, a human being could no longer be understood as primarily intellectual—in short as *homo sapiens,* all of whose faculties should be ruled by "higher" mental powers—but a complex and mysterious unity.

One consequence of this conception was a remarkably positive view of the human body. One of Petrarch's fifteenth-century followers, Giannozzo

Manetti, celebrated the intricate wonders and external beauty of the body in a typical humanist treatise *On the Dignity and Excellence of Man,* which drew equally on Lactantius and Cicero. Thus, Renaissance humanism tended to subvert the kind of asceticism that sought spiritual fulfillment by mortifying the body. Indeed, the originality of Renaissance Christianity, now that Christ's divinity had been fully acknowledged, was its tendency to emphasize the humanity of a God who had become flesh in every way. Renaissance artists were giving expression to this impulse in humanism not only by dramatizing the most humanly poignant episodes in the life of Christ but also by depicting his body nude, thereby giving a kind of ultimate proof of the full humanity implied by the incarnation. The honor that humanists attributed to the nonintellectual dimensions of the personality also implied that the best or most blessed life is not necessarily a life of contemplation, even of monastic contemplation. Christian spirituality, this anthropology suggested, might find full expression in a lay life of active service to others.

This change in the understanding of the personality was also accompanied by a changing conception of what it means to "know" something. The humanist position on this matter was often expressed negatively as an attack on what passed for knowledge among scholastic thinkers. Humanists, for the most part laymen, objected to scholastic discourse because its abstractions seemed irrelevant to their experience in the constantly changing and increasingly vivid urban or courtly world they inhabited and because, in the words of the most profound thinker among the humanists of fifteenth-century Italy, Lorenzo Valla (ca. 1406–1457), "they impede our knowledge of better things."[3] Underlying such charges was also a sense of the limits of the human mind and the fragility of all merely human claims to knowledge. As Petrarch wrote:

> This prattling of the dialecticians will never come to an end; it throws up summaries and definitions like bubbles, matter indeed for endless controversies; but for the most part they know nothing of the real truth of the things they talk about.[4]

Back of such objections, however, was a changed conception, corresponding to the humanist understanding of human nature, of what knowledge should be. Instead of localizing knowledge in the intellect, the humanists understood it as a total experience involving the feelings, penetrating the heart, shaping the will, and stimulating the whole person to some active response. Knowledge, in this conception, had to be subjectively appropriated in order to constitute, as we might say, "really" knowing. Against what he considered the excessive attention given by the schoolmen of his time to nature, Petrarch recommended that we look within ourselves and, in considering what we discover there, "be particularly honest and exacting in passing judgment." A further consequence of this view of knowledge was a disposition among humanists to accept contradiction and paradox as a source of insight. Although it emerged fully only with Erasmus, hints of a willingness to praise folly may be discerned as early as Petrarch's ironic contrast between his own "ignorance" and the pretentious "wisdom" of his scholastic critics.

In its earlier stages the dynamic possibilities of humanism were somewhat obscured by its tendency to idealize the ancient past, pagan or Christian, as a model of perfection for the reformation of a decadent present. Earlier humanists had aimed at a *restoratio* of the virtue and piety of the past through the *imitatio* of what was displayed in ancient documents. But, having little sense of historical and cultural distance, they assumed that the reading and comprehension of texts was a relatively simple task. A sensitive reader like Petrarch, to be sure, was already aware that genuine imitation depended on grasping the inner reality of the model so that the imitation would have something of the life of the original. His own ideal of human existence was dynamic, and he attacked the scholastic dialecticians because of what seemed to him their inability, stuck at an immature stage of life, to progress toward wisdom. "Who of us," he asked, "is not a traveler? We all have our long and arduous journey to accomplish in a brief and unfavorable time—on a short, tempestuous, wintry day, as it were."[5]

Lorenzo Valla initiated a new stage in the development of humanism with his deeper understanding of the philological resources necessary to grasp the spirit of the past. Valla realized that to understand a text it is necessary to understand the culture from which it has come, and that this in turn required proficiency in the language of that culture. He recognized that genuine *imitatio* had to be based on *eruditio*. Implicit in this insight was a sense of the distance between past and present and of the individuality of historical moments—what we would call historical perspective. The awareness of time and change in this perception contributed to an understanding of the life of the spirit not as conformity to a static ideal, much less a set of defensive strategies against the contamination of spirit by the world, but as a process, a progress, or a journey.

The affinities between this general culture of Renaissance humanism and the cultural assumptions underlying the Judeo-Christian Scriptures were close. They ranged from the humanists' sense of the power of language, through their anthropology and epistemology, to their dynamic view of existence and their sense of history. The rhetorical Christianity of the humanists was directed rather to the hearts and feelings of human beings than to their intellects, and it aimed to promote not the contemplation of holy mysteries but active works of love in the service of one's neighbors.

This was not altogether new; it was an extension of a sense of obligation to the love and service of others that had been intensifying in Western Christendom at least since the eleventh century. What humanists chiefly added was an insistence on the special utility of language for meeting the obligation. Only language, they argued, enabled persons to share with each other their most delicate feelings and indeed the whole quality of their inner lives. Thus, they believed, only the persuasive power of language could dissolve the barriers of hatred and pride between human beings, resolve conflicts, and heal social division. Furthermore—in this respect the humanists often shared in the anticlericalism of the later Middle Ages—they believed that, since language is the common possession of all human beings, its use for these excellent purposes could not be restricted to clerical experts.

Humanist spirituality was thus very much a lay phenomenon that testified to a growing sense of the dignity of the lay estate; the humanists were, for the most part, faithful Catholics but little concerned with the finer points of theology. Indeed Petrarch considered genuine piety easier for ordinary folk than for clerical intellectuals, and Valla belligerently rejected the superiority attributed to the "religious" in an earlier tradition of spirituality. He asked pointedly of the defenders of that tradition:

> When the layman and the religious differ from each other in no quality of mind or body and lead identical lives, is a greater reward owed by God to him who has entered that sect which you call "religion," so that you call yourselves "religious," than to him who belongs to no sect?[6]

The general sense of lay social obligation central to humanist spirituality was given particular urgency and converted into a movement of active reform by the sense, widespread among humanists, that their own time was one of special moral and religious crisis. This conviction was nourished by an accumulation of historical catastrophes that left a similar impression on other figures who were not humanists, for example, Catherine of Siena. Petrarch, during the middle decades of the fourteenth century, reviewed them: the pope had abandoned Rome for a "shameful exile" in Avignon; the emperor had lost all sense of universal responsibility and sought only to strengthen his position in Germany; France and England were embroiled in an endless war; the Turks were reducing Christendom in the East; the Black Death was decimating the population of Europe. He also noted more general problems: the corruption of princely courts, notably that of the pope; the degeneracy and disagreements of the rulers of Europe; political disorders in the towns. He believed, however, that all these evils could be reduced to a single cause: the world was in so perilous a state because "everybody seeks his own interest, no one that of Christ."[7] Later humanists regularly repeated this lament, sometimes shifting the emphasis or adding further particulars, as disasters continued to accumulate during the next centuries—notable among them, the Great Schism.

In the context of this sense of crisis, the rivalry between humanist rhetoricians and scholastic dialecticians for religious and cultural influence takes on its full significance. From the standpoint of the humanists, the lifeless abstractions of scholastic discourse might in some remote sense be "true," but they were incapable of moving human beings to reform their own lives and devise remedies for the general evils of their age in a situation in which any delay invited catastrophe. But what dialectic could not bring about, they were convinced, rhetoric could, with God's help, accomplish. Humanist orthodoxy, much influenced by the Augustine of the *Confessions*, generally included a deep sense of the inability of sinful human beings to extricate themselves, without divine assistance, from this terrible predicament. Their sense of dependence on grace also attracted them to the Bible. Humanist spirituality from the beginning invites a label that historians have reserved for the later, Erasmian stage in its history: evangelism.

Humanist Spirituality

It has seemed necessary to say this much about Renaissance humanism as a historical movement in order to explain the spirituality that it nourished, and we will now turn to that spirituality itself. Because of the tendency of Renaissance humanists to reject intellectual system building in favor of human perceptions and responses, an account of humanist spirituality can appropriately begin with the humanists' view of the condition of fallen humanity. Some humanists, to be sure, on the basis of human creation in God's image and likeness, celebrated human creativity and accomplishment in the world. But they rarely forgot the fragility of this accomplishment because of sin. For Petrarch, the most virtuous of human beings "endure continually the most cruel conflicts with temptation, lie always open to many grievous perils, and are never secure before they die."[8] He imagined himself confessing to St. Augustine:

How many times I have pondered over my own misery and over death; with what floods of tears I have sought to wash away my stains so that I can scarce speak of it without weeping, yet hitherto all is in vain. God indeed is the best: I the worst. What proportion is there in such great contrariety? I know how far removed envy is from that best one, and on the contrary I know how tightly iniquity is bound to me. Moreover what does it matter that he is ready to benefit when I am unworthy to be treated well? I confess the mercy of God is infinite, but I profess that I am not fit for it, and as much as it is greater, so much narrower, indeed, is my mind, filled with vices. Nothing is impossible to God; in me there is total impossibility of rising, buried as I am in such a great heap of sins.[9]

Petrarch and Valla were in agreement, against the Stoics, that only our sins are our own; our virtues come from God.

God, for the humanists, was thus infinitely different and, in this sense, remote from human creatures. Petrarch emphasized God's absolute transcendence:

Between heaven and earth, certainly, there is a great distance, I admit, but it is finite; between God and man the distance is infinite. Man is certainly earth, whence he received his name, from earth born, on earth living, into earth returning. God, moreover, is not heaven but the creator of heaven, as much higher than heaven as heaven than earth.[10]

But God's spatial distance was also a figure here of his inaccessibility to human understanding; there was no possibility of comprehending such a God, even granted a far higher estimate of human intellectual capacity than was common among humanists. As Salutati remarked, paying tribute at the same time to the mysteries of human behavior:

Therefore human garrulousness should cease to seek the reason of the divine will in its effects unless it thinks it worthy for the creature to ask of the Creator that which we do not know how to explain in what we ourselves will to do.[11]

God, for Salutati, could be experienced only through his actions, in his mysterious power at work in the universe. "Although men are not able to apprehend God directly," he observed, "they are able to notice many of his effects, and thus have been able to know him solely by effects, that is, indirectly."[12] Bruni's sense of divine transcendence led him to question the power of language, however competent elsewhere, to deal with God, "whose glory and magnificence the speech of the most eloquent man cannot capture even in the smallest degree."[13]

But this remote and awesome deity was at the same time felt as a loving father, on whose mercy human beings could depend; and an ever-closer relationship and finally union with God was, for humanists, the purpose of Christian devotion. God's love for us, Valla declared, "is so great that what we are constrained to hope from it is inexpressible." He quoted Paul: "The eye has not seen, nor the ear heard, nor the heart of man ascended to what God has prepared for those who love him" (1 Cor 2:9).[14] It was of the essence of humanist spirituality that it understood Christianity not as a

18. Raphael Sanzio, *The School of Athens*, 1509-1511. Stanza della Segnatura, Vatican City.

body of doctrines, a conception that humanists were inclined to attribute
to the schoolmen, but as the development of an ever-deepening relationship
first to God and then, through him, to other persons.

The dependence of human beings on God also meant that the nature of
this relationship and the manner of its establishment could not be discovered by human effort but only through divine initiative. This pointed
to the absolute necessity of divine revelation, in the biblical word and
ultimately in Christ as Word. Here the humanists looked to the example
of the ancient fathers, their models for religious discourse, whom they
regularly contrasted with the schoolmen. Valla made the point:

> [The fathers] held that one ought not mix sacred doctrines with the tricks
> of dialectics, nor with metaphysical quibbles, nor with the futilities of the
> modes of signification; and they did not base their treatises on philosophy
> because they had read Paul, who declared, "not by philosophy and empty
> deceit." We know that he was faithful to this affirmation.[15]

The fathers, in a word, were biblical theologians. They had practiced not
a dialectical but a grammatical and rhetorical mode of theology.

The father who impressed them most, at least until Valla's demonstration
of the importance of *eruditio* increased respect for Jerome, was Augustine.
For Petrarch, Augustine had been "the greatest in an age of fertile minds,"[16]
and he imagined himself telling Augustine that in reading the *Confessions*
he seemed to be reviewing "the story of my own self, the story not of
another's wandering but of my own."[17] Whereas medieval theologians had
chiefly relied on Augustine as an authority on doctrine, Petrarch suggested
that the humanists were rediscovering Augustine as a human being whose
life had been a model spiritual journey; they sought to absorb not so much
his doctrine as his spirituality. Nor were they unaware of his career as a
rhetorician; they relished the contrast between his spirited prose and the
abstract language of the schoolmen.

The fathers directed the humanists back to the Bible as the immediate
foundation of patristic faith. As Petrarch remarked in connection with a
famous passage in Augustine's *Confessions:*

> If the Scriptures infused true faith into Victorinus when he was an old pagan,
> God speaking through them and softening the hardest breast, why should
> they not infuse into me, a Christian, a firmness of true faith and works and
> love of a happier life?[18]

The humanists' encounter with Scripture was characterized by two innovations, both connected with their experience as students and connoisseurs
of classical literature. The more important was the application of techniques
of philological criticism already employed in the study of secular writings

to the sacred texts. Valla notably recognized the need, if the Bible was to be accepted as the source of Christian belief, for an authentic text. He made a start toward developing such a text by compiling a series of notes, mostly grammatical, though occasionally with exegetical significance, on the New Testament (1442). He engaged in this task in the conviction that, since Christian belief depends on the language of sacred texts and since rhetoric is the key to the proper use and interpretation of language, rhetoric must be the basis of theology and the Christian life. He also recognized the importance of dealing with the text in its original languages, a conception that implied an awareness that all translations are problematic, notably including the Vulgate. Noting Jerome's testimony to the corruption of biblical manuscripts already in his time, Valla remarked:

> If after only four hundred years the river had become too murky, need we be surprised that after a thousand years—for we are separated from Saint Jerome by that many years—that river, never having been cleansed, carries both mud and refuse?[19]

Humanist pressure for better biblical texts would produce notable results in the sixteenth century.

Only slightly less important was the discovery by the humanists—a discovery related to their openness to the emotional impact of the Gospel—of the literary merit of the Bible. They were also assisted in this direction by decades spent in sharpening their sensitivities to the nuances of language in studying the pagan classics. Petrarch emphasized the fact that much of the Bible was poetry, a point that would eventually have implications for understanding the varying intentions of the text. The discovery also pushed him toward a more spiritualized conception of theology. "One might say," he wrote, "that theology is actually poetry, poetry concerning God."[20]

This view is also related to the emotionality that is characteristic of humanist spirituality. A sense of the central importance of feeling in Christian piety is implicit in Petrarch's special appreciation for the Psalms, which he kept always near him when awake and under his pillow when he slept. It is also apparent in Valla's response to the Gospels. "When we read them," he wrote, "our souls are transported into I know not what higher place, and we are seized by a kind of ineffable sweetness."[21] Humanists often attacked the Stoic ideal of *apatheia* because it rejected what they saw as the most precious aspects of the personality. As Cardinal Sadoleto, a leading humanist of the sixteenth century, wrote in his famous open letter to Calvin, God's Word is effective because it is affective, persuasive because it penetrates the heart; in short its mode of communication is essentially rhetorical.[22]

Humanists had similar requirements for preaching. As Valla asked, immediately responding to his own question:

> Can anyone move an audience to anger and mercy unless he is first moved by these affects himself? It cannot be. So no one will kindle a love of divine things in the minds of others who is cold to that love himself.[23]

But, in its recognition that the divine initiative had found supreme expression in the incarnation, humanist spirituality was also markedly Christocentric; it emphasized human dependence for salvation on faith in the work of Christ and the source of this faith in grace. Petrarch contrasted his own piety with the naturalism he discerned in scholastic science by proclaiming himself a follower of Christ rather than of Aristotle. Christ, he explained, "does not promise me empty and frivolous conjectures of deceitful things which are of use for nothing and not supported by any foundation," but rather "the knowledge of himself," a knowledge that makes it "superfluous to busy myself with other things created by him."[24] Both the utilitarianism and the skepticism of Renaissance humanism are evident in this passage, but there are also hints of the inwardness of humanist spirituality. Petrarch celebrated "the clarity of the internal light" by which "devoted souls see Christ."[25] Valla held out Christ's willingness "to assume the humility of human flesh and to accept the punishment of death (and what a death!)" as the guarantee of every good we might desire.[26] One of the greatest biblical scholars among the humanists of the fifteenth century, Giannozzo Manetti, celebrated Christ's saving work as he elaborated on the dignity of the human condition honored in the incarnation:

> Although that first ancestor of ours transgressed the divine commands and through this he and all his descendants earned the eternal punishment of damnation, in order that they might be redeemed, since it could not be accomplished in any other way, he caused his own son to take on human flesh and to undergo the shameful death of the accursed cross. . . .[27]

The humanists wrote often about the necessity of grace for salvation. Hope, Petrarch declared, is possible only through the mercy of God: "the merit of man does not liberate, but the grace of God alone." He thanked God for freeing him from his sins. Augustine had taught him that human help is worthless in matters of this kind and that he must implore God for grace, "often it may be with tears."[28] Nevertheless, the humanists did not usually believe in an effortless or "imputed" righteousness. Even as he argued that virtue "cannot be achieved outside the doctrine of Christ and without his help," Petrarch agreed that the great Latin moral philosophers, also effective rhetoricians, could be "a great help to those who are making their way to this goal."[29] Salutati was typical in his insistence on the need to purify scrupulously the "temple" of one's life. "Purge your temple, my Peregrino," he exhorted the chancellor of Bologna.[30] But the humanists rarely felt the need to describe precisely the relation between faith and works; this was the sort of "useless" operation for which they criticized the schoolmen. "This is the task, this the work," wrote Salutati: "to gain merit or drive away sin with the aid of divine grace. And, merit driving away sin, we are certain never to lack grace in action."[31]

The humanists nevertheless emphasized faith as basic to the Christian life. "Since this foundation stands, that God is omnipotent and all-benevolent," Petrarch wrote, "nothing can be imagined so magnificent that he cannot do it, so beneficent that he does not wish it." This, for him, was the essence of faith; it could be depended on as "solid, and unshaken by all the undermining and battering rams of the enemy." Faith, he declared, makes everything plain, and he elaborated on its substance by repeating as his own *credo* the articles of the ancient creeds on the second person of the Trinity:

> God has come among men born of a virgin and dwelt among us, taught us the way of life; having been crucified he suffered and died, descended to the lower regions, despoiled hell, ascended to heaven and is awaited for judgment.[32]

He contrasted this simple faith of the Christian with the "haughty ignorance" of philosophy.[33] Valla attributed faith, since it could not come by demonstration, to rhetorical persuasion; this made it something deeper and more effective than rational conviction.

Humanism tended, therefore, to a kind of Christian fundamentalism; and, like other expressions of fundamentalism, it associated more intellectual approaches to belief with the dangers of heresy. Its deep conservatism was expressed by Salutati in his reply to a critic of humanistic literary studies. Salutati denied the intent "to affirm anything opposed or proposed against faith." God had given him, he asserted, "this grace, that never in anything have I felt opposed to faith or even lightly hesitated concerning it." How, he asked, "should my intellect presume to disagree with the Holy Scriptures or to doubt in those matters which the community of the faithful has determined?"[34]

Activity in the World

But all these elements in humanist Christianity—its insistence on a God at once transcendent and benevolent, an anthropology that combined a sense of the creatureliness and sinfulness of the human being with confidence in its potentialities, a Christocentric theology of grace and faith—pointed finally, in humanist spirituality, to activity in the world. Petrarch's own capacity for action was often impeded by times of anxiety, apathy, and depression; for him the Gospel meant the recovery of confidence and creative vitality. Valla played on the ambiguity of "virtue" as both vigor and righteousness; he emphasized the centrality of the passions and the will in the human personality and identified spirit with the capacity to perform effectively in every aspect of life. Repelled by the Aristotelian conception of God as unmoved mover, he insisted that God must be conceived, by Christians, as constantly and spontaneously active.

The first clear identification among the humanists of the Christian life with activity in the world was made (though with some ambivalence) by Salutati as an assertion of the value of lay piety, in words that suggest the influence of the *Divine Comedy:*

> Since our supreme end is not [merely] to know God, but that supreme beatitude which is to see God just as he is, and also to enjoy that vision and to love what is seen, and to adhere to him eternally through a love that so unites lover and beloved that whoever clings to God is one spirit with him; and since we are not able to gain this by science or human speculation but only by the grace of God through virtues and other actions, certainly it is the active life whose principle is the will, not the speculative, perfected by intellect, which pertains to that true happiness. And in that very beatitude, the act of the will, which is joy, is nobler and more beautiful than the act of intellect which can be called contemplation or vision.[35]

Leon Battista Alberti, a humanist and architect in the next century, shared this position:

> Intelligence, intellect, judgment, memory, appetite, anger, reason, and discretion—who would be so unreasonable as to deny that these divine forces by which man outdoes all other animals in strength, in speed, and in ferocity, were capacities given to us to be amply used?[36]

Such sentiments have been interpreted as a middle-class justification for work against aristocratic and clerical ways of life, but as a component of humanist spirituality they pointed to the loving service of others. Petrarch honored such service:

> There have been and perchance still are very active men of saintly nature who themselves go the way of Christ and lead straying souls along the same path. When this happens, it is a great and immeasurable good, a double blessing. For what is there more blessed, more worthy of a man, and more like a divine goodness than to serve and assist as many as require help?[37]

Salutati contrasted his own social ideal with that of philosophy:

You may be full of speculation, but I would abound in the goodness by which I may be made good. I would always be engaged in doing things, I would consider the final end: whatever I do, am I helping myself, my family, my relatives, and above all my friends, am I useful to my country? And I would so live as to contribute both by example and works to human society.[38]

He thus proposed to express this active spirituality in a series of ever-widening social circles. The realistic and more aggressive Valla extended the humanist ideal of Christian activity in still another direction. He saw himself as a *miles Christi,* and the Christian life as a joyful struggle with successive challenges along the path of life.

But perhaps the most original expression of the conception of an active spirituality among the humanists was its association with creativity. This originated in their fascination with the implications of the creation of human beings in the image of God, which suggested that human beings, their energies replenished and sanctified by grace, could realize the divine potentiality in themselves by creative activity. Such activity would draw not only on the intellect but on all the capacities of the rich and complex human personality, notably the imagination. As Valla observed, the human spirit "is painted in the image of God"; this meant, for him, that it possessed a Godlike creativity of its own:

Just as a flame seizes and devours and reduces to ashes the material by which it is fed, so the spirit is nourished by learning and hides what it absorbs within itself and transmutes it into its own heat and light. Hence it paints others rather than being painted by them. The spirit, advancing onto them by its own light, projects and paints upon them an image of its own memory, intellect, and will.[39]

In this way, freely, out of the resources of their own God-given spirituality, human beings might create for themselves a human world, just as God had created the natural world. So Manetti wrote, as part of his demonstration of the dignity of human being:

Everything that surrounds us is our work, the work of man: houses, castles, cities, magnificent buildings over all the earth. They resemble the work of angels more than of man; nevertheless they are the work of man. There are pictures, sculpture, science, and doctrine. There are inventions and literary works in many languages, and finally machines. And when we see these marvels, we realize that we are able to make better things, more beautiful, better adorned, more perfect than those that we have made until now.[40]

Passages like this, with its hint of indefinite progress, might be taken to suggest that individual humanists, stimulated by the exuberant creativity of Renaissance culture, were tempted to engage in radical experiments with the balance between human limitation and divine potentiality. But the demonic spirituality that deifies an autonomous humanity was still far in the future. Manetti illustrates, perhaps, the excess into which all rhetorical celebration can be tempted. But the spirituality of Renaissance humanism remained essentially evangelical.

Notes

1. Quoted in Charles Trinkaus, *The Poet as Philosopher: Petrarch and the Formation of Renaissance Consciousness* (New Haven: CT: Yale University Press, 1979) 106.

2. *On His Own Ignorance and That of Many Others,* trans. Hans Nachod, in *The Renaissance Philosophy of Man,* ed. Ernst Cassirer, Paul Oskar Kristeller, and John Herman Randall, Jr. (Chicago: University of Chicago Press, 1948) 104.

3. *Encomion Sancti Thomae Aquinatis,* in Lorenzo Valla, *Scritti filosofici e religiosi,* ed. Giorgio Radetti (Florence: Sansoni, 1953) 465.

4. *Petrarch's Secret,* trans. William H. Draper, 29–30.

5. Letter to Tommaso Caloiro of Messina, ca. 1351, in *Petrarch, a Humanist among Princes: An Anthology of Petrarch's Letters and of Translations from His Works,* ed. David Thompson (New York: Harper & Row, 1971) 25.

6. Quoted in Charles Trinkaus, "Humanist Treatises on the Status of the Religious: Petrarch, Salutati, Valla," *Studies in the Renaissance* 11 (1964) 36.

7. Quoted in Charles Trinkaus, *Image and Likeness,* 1:20.

8. Quoted in Trinkaus, *Poet as Philosopher,* 126.

9. *Petrarch's Secret,* 15; and Trinkaus, *Poet as Philosopher,* 87.

10. Quoted in Trinkaus, *Image and Likeness,* 1:36.

11. Ibid., 1:96.

12. Quoted in Nancy S. Struever, *The Language of History in the Renaissance: Rhetoric and Historical Consciousness in Florentine Humanism* (Princeton, NJ: Princeton University Press, 1970) 88.

13. *Laudatio* in *The Earthly Republic: Italian Humanists on Government and Society,* ed. Benjamin G. Kohl and Ronald G. Witt (Philadelphia: University of Pennsylvania Press, 1978) 135.

14. Quoted in Trinkaus, *Image and Likeness,* 1:143.

15. *Encomion,* in *Scritti,* 465.

16. Letter to Boccaccio, 28 April 1373, in *Petrarch,* 236.

17. *Petrarch's Secret,* 21.

18. Quoted in Trinkaus, *Poet as Philosopher,* 105.

19. Quoted in Eugenio Garin, *Italian Humanism: Philosophy and Civic Life in the Renaissance,* trans. Peter Munz (Oxford: Blackwell, 1965) 16.

20. Letter to his brother Gherardo, 2 December 1348, in *Petrarch,* 90.

21. Quoted in Trinkaus, *Image and Likeness,* 1:143.

22. *John Calvin and Jacopo Sadoleto: A Reformation Debate,* ed. John C. Olin (New York: Harper & Row, 1966) 32.

23. *De vere bono,* in *Scritti,* 165–66.

24. *On His Own Ignorance,* 101.

25. Quoted in Trinkaus, *Image and Likeness,* 1:33.

26. Ibid., 1:134.

27. Ibid., 1:252–53.

28. *Petrarch's Secret,* 79.
29. *On His Own Ignorance,* 104–5.
30. Letter to Peregrino Zambeccari, in *Earthly Republic,* 108.
31. Quoted in Trinkaus, *Image and Likeness,* 1:97.
32. Ibid., 1:32.
33. *On His Own Ignorance,* 76.
34. Quoted in Trinkaus, *Image and Likeness,* 1:55.
35. Ibid., 1:68.
36. *I libri della famiglia,* quoted in the translation of Renée Neu Watkins, *The Family in Renaissance Florence* (Columbia: University of South Carolina Press, 1969) 133.
37. *De vita solitaria,* in *Petrarch,* 63.
38. *De nobilitate legum et medicinae,* ed. Eugenio Garin (Florence: Edizione nazionale dei classici del pensiero italiano, 1947) 180.
39. Quoted in Charles Trinkaus, *The Scope of Renaissance Humanism* (Ann Arbor: University of Michigan Press, 1983) 443.
40. Quoted in Marvin B. Becker, *Florence in Transition: Studies in the Rise of the Territorial State* (Baltimore, MD: Johns Hopkins University Press, 1968) 6.

Bibliography

Representative texts of Italian humanism, several relevant to its spirituality, are available in Cassirer et al., eds. A key work is Petrarch's *Secretum,* available in a translation by William H. Draper. Much that is relevant to this article may be found in Trinkaus and Oberman. For the medieval backgrounds of humanist spirituality, see Bynum. The most valuable general studies of the religion of the humanists have been done by Trinkaus, especially *"In Our Image."* On the importance of the incarnation in Renaissance culture, see Steinberg, which includes a valuable epilogue by John W. O'Malley, S.J. The most suggestive recent studies of Lorenzo Valla have been made by Salvatore I. Camporeale, O.P. On humanism and the papacy, see, generally, D'Amico; more specifically focused on rhetoric, see O'Malley.

Bynum, Caroline Walker. *Jesus as Mother: Studies in the Spirituality of the High Middle Ages.* Berkeley and Los Angeles: University of California Press, 1982.
Camporeale, Salvatore I., O.P. "Lorenzo Valla tra Medioevo e Rinascimento: Encomion S. Thomae–1457." *Memorie Domenicane* n.s. 7 [Rome] 1976.
Cassirer, Ernst, et al., eds. *The Renaissance Philosophy of Man.* Chicago: University of Chicago Press, 1949.
D'Amico, John F. *Renaissance Humanism in Papal Rome: Humanists and Churchmen on the Eve of the Reformation.* Baltimore, MD: Johns Hopkins University Press, 1983.
O'Malley, John W., S.J. *Praise and Blame in Renaissance Rome: Rhetoric, Doctrine, and Reform in the Sacred Orators of the Papal Court, c. 1450–1521* Durham, NC: Labyrinth Press, 1979.
Petrarch. *Secretum.* Translated by William H. Draper. London: Chatto & Windus, 1911.
Steinberg, Leo. *The Sexuality of Christ in Renaissance Art and Modern Oblivion.* New York: Pantheon Books, 1983.
Trinkaus, Charles. *In Our Image and Likeness: Humanity and Divinity in Italian Humanist Thought.* 2 vols. Chicago: University of Chicago Press, 1970.
——, and Heiko A. Oberman, eds. *The Pursuit of Holiness in Late Medieval and Renaissance Religion: Papers from the University of Michigan Conference.* Studies in Medieval and Reformation Thought 10. Leiden: Brill, 1974.

II. *Ad Fontes: The Humanist Understanding of Scripture as Nourishment for the Soul*

JAMES D. TRACY

READERS OF THIS VOLUME may be surprised to encounter a chapter on the northern humanist movement. In fact, scholars long assumed that Renaissance humanists propounded a secular view of the world, and the more recent discovery of humanist religious thought is better known among specialists than among the reading public at large. While Jacob Burckhardt's famous *Civilization of the Renaissance in Italy* (1860) presented an epoch in which cultivated men and women showed little interest in traditional religion,[1] the scholarship of the last few decades has substantially rehabilitated the role of orthodox Christian belief in the life and thought of major Italian humanists (see the first part of this article by William Bouwsma). Paul Oskar Kristeller, in a general interpretation of the humanist movement that is now widely accepted, argued that what the humanists had in common was not a set of philosophical beliefs, but rather a set of intellectual interests, relating to the rhetorical tradition of classical antiquity. Thus, Lorenzo Valla, who on religious grounds called human freedom of the will into doubt, was no less a "humanist" than the many others (like Giovanni Pico della Mirandola) who extolled the freedom of humans to shape their own destiny.[2] Charles Trinkaus and others have shown that humanist writers, once thought to exhibit a strictly "rationalist" point of view, are better understood as professing a Pauline Christianity, with emphasis on the sinful human will and its need for the redeeming power of divine grace. To be sure, texts like Valla's *De Voluptate* or Coluccio Salutati's *De Nobilitate Legum et Medicinae* are indeed critical of the Thomist synthesis of Christian faith and Aristotelian logic, but not from the standpoint of a presumed secular alternative. Rather, these humanists, like the contemporary "nominalist" school of late medieval theology, viewed Thomist metaphysics as excessively rationalistic in its view of human nature and presumptuous in subjecting God's will to laws of human devising.[3]

Humanist Interpretation of Scripture

Meanwhile, students of northern European humanism were engaged in a parallel process of reinterpretation. Here Erasmus of Rotterdam had been claimed by secular-minded *philosophes* of the Enlightenment as one of their own, while both he and Philip Melanchthon had been repudiated by their respective coreligionists, as being (at best) weak-minded moralizers and compromisers, incapable of a firm grasp on the principles of orthodox Christianity. Though shades of opinion may still differ significantly, it is now recognized that both men took matters of doctrine seriously and did not reduce religion to ethics. It hardly needs adding that a more ecumenical age can better appreciate the efforts of humanists like Erasmus and Melanchthon to achieve an honest understanding of the adversary's point of view.[4] It has also become clear that the northern humanist movement had important points of contact with religious reform movements of a more traditional sort, particularly in the decades just prior to the Reformation. In Paris during the 1490s, both Erasmus and Jacques Lefèvre d'Étaples were on friendly terms with monastic reformers, including a group of monks from the north-Netherlandish congregation of Augustinian canons to which Erasmus himself then belonged. In Strasbourg, the earnest and popular reform preacher Geiler von Kaiserberg was a close friend of Jacob Wimpheling, a devout humanist of the older school and mentor to a whole generation of younger scholars.[5] Partly because of these connections, humanists of Erasmus's generation, building on the intellectual achievements and the moral insights of their Italian predecessors, became spokesmen of a movement for religious renewal.

For more traditional reformers, like Geiler in Strasbourg or the Netherlandish Augustinians in Paris, reform meant stricter enforcement of canon law or of the constitutions of religious orders. But humanists like John Colet in England or Lefèvre in France believed that genuine reform depended on a new kind of Christian education whose fruits could be shared by laity and clergy alike. Erasmus's *Enchiridion Militis Christiani* may be regarded as a charter for the humanist vision of reform: "There is no temptation so strong, no onslaught of the enemy so vehement, that the ardent study of Sacred Scripture does not easily repel, no adversity so full of grief that it does not render bearable." The image of Scripture as a weapon in the warfare against temptation is, of course, commonplace in spiritual writing. What is new is the suggestion that prevailing methods of study and reflection on Scripture must be swept away before the healing power of

God's word can be felt: "If you wish to grow stronger in spirit rather than better armed for debate, if you wish nourishment for the soul instead of a mere scratching of the intellect, you will particularly study the ancients," that is, patristic commentators on Scripture, rather than scholastic interpreters of the thirteenth and fourteenth centuries.[6] At a distance of centuries it may be difficult to recapture the innocent and vibrant hope that this vision of a return "to the sources" (*ad fontes*) of Christian faith could inspire, not just among clerics and scholars but also among the cultivated, Latin-reading public all across Europe. Erasmus himself had no idea how famous he had become until, en route down the Rhine to Basel in 1514, he was wined and dined by the town government in Strasbourg, the city of Geiler and Wimpheling, where it was, above all, the religious message of his *Enchiridion* that made him so popular. In a word, the humanists had become reformers.[7]

Even if one grants the validity of these newer interpretations of the humanist movement, however, one may still find the notion of "humanist spirituality" somewhat problematic. When humanists engaged in that reading and study of Scripture which was believed capable of changing a person's life for the better, their methods were quite lacking in originality. Thomas More's Tower-of-London writings, the *De Tristitia Christi* and the *Treatise on the Passion,* are much influenced by Jean Gerson's *Monotesseron* and by the *Catena Aurea* of Thomas Aquinas, and probably owe more to his four years as a Carthusian novice than to his humanist interests and training.[8] Erasmus's *Enchiridion* proposes for meditation on Scripture the traditional allegorical exegesis expounded by Origen, whose writings were recommended to him by a learned and devout Franciscan friend in the low countries, Jean Vitrier.[9]

Ad Fontes

But there is a particular area in which humanist writings about Scripture (particularly the New Testament) have a better claim to originality and thus a proper place in the evolution of European Christian spirituality. "Spirituality" implies not only a regimen of prayer but also a notion of personal spiritual growth to be achieved through prayer. It is here that the characteristic intellectual preoccupations of the humanist movement offer a new perspective. First, the humanist program of a return *ad fontes* provides elements not found in earlier reflections on the theme of Scripture as food for the soul. The modern science of philology is a specific creation of the humanist movement, with the main line of development running from Lorenzo Valla through Erasmus's Greek New Testament (1516) and

Guillaume Budé, author of historical commentaries on the *Corpus Juris Civilis*. The term *philologia*, as these men employed it, combines the modern notions of text criticism, literary analysis, and much else besides.[10]

As applied to the New Testament, humanist *philologia* required treating texts as literary products, that is, as the works of individual authors. Humanists were particularly drawn to the figure of St. Paul. Erasmus completed "four volumes" of a commentary on Romans, but they were never published and are now lost. Later he began his *Paraphrases* with the same epistle (1517). John Colet wrote commentaries on Romans and 1 Corinthians, Jacobo Sadoleto on Romans, and Lefèvre d'Étaples published a French translation (1512) of the Vulgate text for all the epistles.[11] In regard to the Gospels, the humanist sense of text meant treating them as separate works rather than weaving them all into a continuous narrative, as Jean Gerson's *Monotesseron* had done. In late medieval spiritual writing, the focus was on the life of Christ and not on the texts through which it was conveyed; Ludolph the Carthusian's *Vita Christi* and the *Rosetum Spiritualium Exercitium* of Johannes Mauburnus (insofar as it treats the life of Christ) dwell on particular incidents in such a way that it is a matter of indifference which Gospel text is cited (Mauburnus, incidentally, was one of the Netherlandish monastic reformers active in Paris in the 1490s, and a correspondent of Erasmus).[12] Thomas More's Tower treatises follow in the same vein as Ludolph and Gerson, but he seems rather an exception among the humanists in this respect. Jacques Lefèvre d'Étaples's *Commentarii Initiatorii in Quattuor Evangelia* (1527) are, as the title indicates, commentaries on each successive Gospel, as are the more celebrated *Paraphrases* of Erasmus, who began with the Pauline letters and then turned, in 1522, to the Gospels. Ulrich Zwingli, the reformer of Zurich, showed his humanist background when he began his preaching career at the Grossmuenster (1519) with a sequence of sermons on the Gospel of Matthew, rather than following the cycle of Gospel texts prescribed for the Sunday liturgy.[13]

Treating the sacred text as a literary product, even while preserving the traditional doctrine of divine inspiration, had some fairly specific implications. Unlike scholastic exegetes, humanists approached a text with a certain curiosity about the distinctive personality and style of each author. Thus, Erasmus, in his notes to successive editions of the Greek New Testament, revived ancient skepticism about the Pauline authorship of Hebrews and braved controversy by defending Jerome's view that Paul's Greek was sprinkled with solecisms and was not to be compared with the elegant diction of Lucian or Isocrates. One also notices among the humanists a greater willingness to admit the problematic nature of passages that are either difficult to understand or seem to conflict with the believer's expectations. For example, Lefèvre d'Étaples, commenting on the text (Matt 16:28) where Jesus says that some of those present "will not taste death" until he comes again, acknowledges that it would be "forced" to refer this phrase to Jesus' transfiguration (rather than to his second coming), although he himself had previously favored this interpretation as a way out of the difficulty. One knows only, says Lefèvre, that, however this passage is to be understood, its meaning is most true and certain.[14] Finally, the humanists seem to exhibit a greater interest in the personality of the actors in the New Testament drama, especially the personality of Christ himself. As Jacques Chomarat points out, even though the unfailing prescience of Jesus is a "weakness in the presentation of his character" in the Gospel *Paraphrases,* Erasmus was still prompted to explore Jesus' motivation, since consideration of motive was one of the standard techniques of "amplification" or paraphrase. Some years previously, Christ's human motivation had been the focal point of a noted debate between Colet and Erasmus, in which Colet defended Jerome's assertion that the fear and anguish Jesus expressed at Gethsemane ("Father, if it be possible, let this chalice pass from me") refer not to a fear of his own death, but to fear of what would happen to the Jewish people in consequence of their rejection of him. Colet's position was "humanist" in the sense that his position had strong, if not unanimous, support among the fathers, whereas the *neoterici,* or scholastic theologians of the High Middle Ages, were agreed that Christ in his human nature had a normal fear of death. Erasmus this time consciously sided with the *neoterici,* and it was clearly important to him that (as Bonaventure and others put it), apart from sin, Christ experienced all the weakness of human nature. Thomas More in his Tower treatises tactfully allowed room for the interpretations of both his friends, but clearly favored that of Erasmus, and Lefèvre adopted the same view in his *Commentarii Initiatorii.* One may summarize by saying that even though the humanists did not, by and large, reject the traditional allegorical exegesis by which awkward or peculiar details could be explained away, they still tended to grant human motivation and human idiosyncracies a greater degree of autonomy as an integral component of God's revealed truth. At a different level, as the controversy between Erasmus and Colet suggests, they were able to combine the christological insights of the scholastics with the literary and rhetorical sensitivity of their admired church fathers.[15]

Apart from *philologia,* rhetoric was the other great preoccupation that provided the diverse and multifarious humanist movement with a common framework, and rhetoric, too, had special implications for the understanding of Scripture. The reason that humanists so admired the fathers as expositors of the Bible was that the fathers, themselves products of an education centered on the art of persuasion, understood the expositor's task as homiletic rather than speculative in character; its purpose was to make God's word come alive in the hearts of readers and listeners—hence, the barbed quality of Erasmus's contrast between "nourishment for the soul" (to be found in patristic commentaries) and a "mere scratching of the intellect" (scholastic commentaries). Erasmus's own writings, like those of Lefèvre, are filled with exhortations to the reader to "transmit into your vitals" the teachings of Scripture, exhortations that have a distinctive patristic resonance both in theme and language. Humanists also imitated the patristic technique of allowing Scripture to interpret itself by constructing comments that consisted of parallel or related passages from other books of the Bible.[16] But in assimilating, as they did, the classical discipline of rhetoric, humanists also imbibed certain themes or assumptions that in the end made their exegesis somewhat different from that of the fathers.

In the first place, ancient rhetoric, in its beginnings and early development, had a civic context, which the humanists were able to recapture through their studies. In the theoretical treatises of Cicero and Quintilian, the ideal orator was not merely an expert in forensic techniques, but a *vir bonus*, able and willing to speak unpleasant truths where the speaking of them might do some good.[17] When humanists sought to delineate the meaning of Scripture for the world in which they lived, they had only a limited interest in the allegorical references to the church (e.g., Peter's bark, the house of Peter's mother-in-law) that were so common in patristic and medieval exegesis. Instead, they tried, at least on occasion, to make Scripture relevant to the larger civic concerns of their society. Here, too, the personal relationship between Colet and Erasmus is of considerable interest. Erasmus knew that Colet had for a time lost favor with his patron, Henry VIII, by daring to criticize, in a sermon before the court, the king's plans to embark on a war across the channel. Erasmus greatly admired his friend's forthrightness, but preferred to imitate it indirectly, in his Latin writings, including his *Paraphrases* on the New Testament. That Scripture rightly understood could transform the lives of communities, not just individuals, was part of that traditional understanding of the unique power of God's word which the fathers bequeathed to subsequent ages. But only a humanist could write, as Erasmus did in one of the introductory writings to his 1516 New Testament, that "if the Gospel were truly preached, the Christian people would be spared many wars."[18]

Classical rhetoric also had a pedagogical context, in that ancient treatises "on education" by Cicero, Quintilian, or Isocrates were really treatises on the education of an orator. Certainly in the form of Hellenic culture that was transmitted to Rome, pride of place was given not to the Socratic ideal of education but to those very rhetoricians whom Plato so often attacked in his dialogues. Both as a mode of civic discourse professing to appeal to the better instincts of hearers and as a means of "drawing out" (e-ducare) the talents of young pupils, the theory of persuasion rested on fundamentally optimistic assumptions about human nature. Even granting Kristeller's point that the humanist movement is not unified by any single philosophical doctrine,[19] it cannot be accidental that writers of humanist background and training so often line up on the same side of that great debate between free will and predestination that runs through the religious history of the sixteenth and seventeenth centuries. In his defense of free will against Luther, Erasmus was to be joined by Melanchthon, who in the 1530s makes room in his doctrine of justification for an act of assent by the human will; by the Arminians, who battled strict Calvinism in the Netherlands; and by the Jesuits, who warred against Jansenism all over Catholic Europe. As applied to the understanding of the New Testament, the optimistic bent that seems to be linked with humanist classical training finds its clearest expression in Erasmus's reluctance to find in Scripture a clear statement of the doctrine of original sin, particularly in his notes to Romans 5:12–14. Conversely, if the great French scholar Guillaume Budé, in his later writings, minimizes the capacities of the human will *coram Deo* (to use Luther's phrase), he also calls into question the moral value of classical culture, or *philologia*, which in earlier works he so ardently defended.[20]

In sum, from what has been said, one would expect to find in humanist writings on the New Testament a more honorable place for the human world, with its endless diversity, its mundane motives and concerns, than would be true for works of the patristic or scholastic era. The concept of spiritual growth through the prayerful study of Scripture, as the humanists formulated it, would be more attuned to the daily life of ordinary mortals, less influenced (note that it is a question of degree) by the traditional ascetic ideal whereby the soul strives ever upward, to escape the dross of earthly cares. It would be well to illustrate this argument by briefly examining a particular humanist text.

Erasmus's *Paraphrases*

For present purposes, the focus will be on the first half (chaps. 1–12) of Erasmus's *Paraphrase* of the Gospel of Luke, published in 1523, with a dedicatory preface to King Henry VIII. No humanist text can be labeled "typical," but Erasmus's *Paraphrases* have at least the merit of having enjoyed a certain vogue as spiritual reading for lay folk in the later sixteenth century, through the medium of translation into English (by Mary Tudor among

19. Dieric Bouts, *Holy Sacrament Altarpiece,* central panel: *Institution of the Eucharist,* 1464–1468. Collegiate Church of St. Peter, Louvain.

others) and other languages as well. Luke is chosen as a mean between Mark, for which, as Erasmus complains, there are no patristic commentaries to guide the modern expositor,[21] and Matthew and John, for which there is a plethora of commentaries both ancient and medieval. For Luke, there is a fairly precise number of sources which Erasmus is known to have consulted (Origen, Chrysostom, Ambrose, Theophylact, and the *Catena Aurea*),[22] so that, by comparing his text with these others, one can form at least preliminary conclusions about those aspects of the commentary, or paraphrase, which Erasmus himself supplies. (For a more thorough examination than is possible within these pages, one would also have to check the voluminous commentary literature for synoptic pericopes parallel to those given in Luke.) One further caveat is that the object of this discussion is not to demonstrate influence,[23] but rather the opposite—that is, to isolate those instances where Erasmus's thought appears to be original. For this purpose, a given passage can be treated as derivative even if there is only a general resemblance to what, for instance, Ambrose says, without the precise verbal echoes that would be needed to demonstrate a positive influence.

When the question is posed in this way, it becomes clear that far the greater part of Erasmus's elaborations on the Gospel text are, at the very least, parallel to the observations of earlier writers. This finding is hardly surprising, since Erasmus would have regarded conformity with the teaching of "the ancients" as a virtue and would not have boasted of originality. His dependence on the fathers is most clear when he finds in certain passages "types" of the old law and the new, or of the synagogue and the church. Thus, as in Ambrose, the demoniac in the synagogue at Capharnaum (4:34) is a "type" of the vices with which the Jewish people was afflicted. As in Ambrose again, the woman who anoints Jesus' feet with precious ointment is a type of the new law, while the envious, stay-at-home elder brother of the prodigal son is a type of the old law.[24] Equally traditional are specific references to the life of the church, such as that Christians must dutifully obey their bishops, just as the child Jesus obeyed his parents, or that the shepherds keeping watch on the hillside at Bethlehem are types of the faithful bishop.[25] One also finds echoes of a nearly vanished patristic soteriology in statements that this or that aspect of the Gospel story (such as the choice of Mary to be the mother of Jesus) was ordained by God in his wisdom so as to deceive his adversary, the devil, who was to be tricked into releasing humanity from bondage.[26] It often happens, too, that interpretations not clearly grounded in the text, which might thus seem to be novel, are, in fact, parallel to earlier interpretations. Thus, Ambrose seems to be the source for the view that it was the angel, not her mute husband, Zachary, who told Elizabeth that her son's name was to be John, whereas

Origen provides the explanation, emphasized more strongly by Erasmus, that Elizabeth hid herself from the world during her pregnancy out of shame, because others would know that she and her husband, at their age, were still having sexual intercourse.[27]

Erasmus's interest in delineating the motives of persons figuring in the Gospel story is less traditional and more pertinent to the present discussion. Like Theophylact, he notes that Zachary, taking his turn at the altar, offered prayers not for any intentions of his own but for the sins of the people; but then he adds, in the angel's words, a description of Zachary's state of mind: "Not only has what you asked been obtained, but divine goodness has also added, for the culmination of your prayers, that which you dared not ask, because you despaired of its possibility. You asked for a redeemer, now accept also a forerunner for the redeemer." Later, at 2:17, he makes a seemingly gratuitous comment to the effect that the shepherds recounted to others what they had seen in the stable with their own eyes, not relying simply on the word of the angel, for "piety has its own *prudentia* among men and women, however lowly they might be." At 9:49, where John tells Jesus how the disciples squelched someone not of their company whom they found expelling demons in Jesus' name, Ambrose thinks John acted out of love for the Lord in so doing, but Theophylact believes "he began to fear they perhaps did something wrong because through arrogance and pride they had commanded the man to cease." Erasmus elaborates on Theophylact's suggestion:

> Because they heard [9:48] that even little children were to be received in Jesus' name, it occurred to John that they had excluded someone from the fellowship of the Gospel. He wondered, therefore, whether all were to be admitted to the office of preaching the Gospel and working miracles, just as all were to be admitted to the fellowship of Gospel salvation. For a certain silent feeling of envy was just beneath the surface.[28]

Perhaps the clearest example of Erasmus's attempt to harmonize his humanist understanding of classical values with the Gospel comes in his portrayal of Jesus as a perfect exemplar of *humanitas* and *mansuetudo*, the gentle virtues of the eager pupil and the dutiful citizen, as distinct from the combative virtues of the warrior noble, or of the scholastic doctor relishing victory in debate. Thus, the child Jesus, even when expounding Scripture to the scholars in the temple, was wholly lacking in "arrogance, boldness, and boasting, the vices usually found in boys of precocious native ability"; the scholars "marvelled greatly, not only because of the uncommon modesty of countenance, gesture, and speech, which adds grace to intelligence." The Jesus of Erasmus displays the same qualities in manhood. To the simple phrase, "Et reversi Apostoli, narraverunt illi quaecunque fecerunt" (Luke 9:10), Erasmus adds a brief homily, in which "Jesus recalled them to modesty, lest they become insolent because of their successes; for miracles are worked by the power of God, not of men, and are sometimes effected through men not destined for eternal life."[29]

The *modestia* of Jesus is parallel to a theme that recurs again and again in Erasmus's exposition of the Gospel message, namely, that the spread of God's word is in no way dependent on human strength and power, or *praesidia humana*. To Simeon's brief comment that Mary's heart will be pierced by a sword of grief, Erasmus adds a prophecy about how the mighty in religion shall be brought low and the humble exalted:

> Publicans, prostitutes, and sinners are excluded from worship by those hypocrites in religion [the Scribes and Pharisees], but these God shall receive first in the kingdom of heaven. Nations sworn to idolatry, by a sudden change of life, shall embrace the teachings of true piety; Pharisees and high priests [*Pontifices*], who had the highest repute in religion and the Law, shall oppose the Author of the Law.[30]

In light of this contrast between *praesidia humana* and the *modestia* of Jesus' true followers, Erasmus feels at liberty to include in his *Paraphrase* animadversions on the princes and high priests of his own day. Where Herod's wickedness is noted in Luke 3:19, Erasmus makes the interesting suggestion that a ruler like Herod would have his own reasons for seeking the advice of a saintly man like John the Baptist:

> Of this sort are the souls of many princes, whom evangelical wisdom has not freed from the control of shameful vices. They command over others, but are themselves in servitude to their own violent passions, and think themselves kings precisely in this, that they can with impunity live in bondage to wickedness. Sometimes they summon to themselves men noted for sanctity of life, sometimes they converse with them, and do certain things on their advice: not because they care for true piety, but because by this deceit they gain for themselves the reputation of honesty, and mollify resentment of their evil deeds, so that when they fleece the people, or launch impious wars, or rage against those who wish well to the commonwealth, these things, too, may seem to be done by the advice of the most upright men.

Elsewhere, when the text (8:3) mentions wealthy women serving the needs of Jesus, Erasmus remarks that Christ "never importuned anyone, nor do we read that he ever asked for anything, so that those men should be all the more ashamed of their impudence, who, though they do labor for the Gospel, nonetheless use the name of the Gospel to extort from the unwilling not merely what suffices for necessity, but even what abounds unto luxury."[31] In one sense the themes of these passages—Erasmus's running critique of the mendicant friars and of warlike princes—are clear enough. What is worth noting here is that the reform of Christian society is part and parcel of Erasmus's understanding of how Scripture is to be read for spiritual profit.

Finally, Christ (as Erasmus understands him) is *modestus* even and especially in the display of his divine power, lest human nature be simply overwhelmed by a force beyond its ken. Apropos of the fact that the preaching of the cured Gerasene demoniac was fruitful, since many believed, Erasmus notes "by this image the Lord Jesus taught us that anyone however impious is to be offered the grace of the Gospel, and it is not to be forced upon the unwilling and scornful, but we are to withdraw from them, leaving behind a certain spark of true piety, that will perhaps shine forth on a later occasion." During the parable of the sower (4:4) he pauses to explain the function of Christ's miracles:

> It belongs to magicians and wonder-workers to effect or simulate marvellous deeds for mere ostentation, or to tickle the idle curiosity of spectators, whence there is no praise for the glory of God, nor any utility for our neighbor. . . . Jesus never worked any miracle, except when by so doing he both glorified the power of God, and succored the needs of men: or for a time to challenge human incredulity.

In general, says Erasmus, "it seemed good to the Lord Jesus so to temper all his words and deeds, so that he now brought forth certain sparks of his divine power, now lowered himself to human lowliness." He gives expression here to the theme of *accommodatio*, borrowed from patristic theology, whose importance in Erasmus's writings has been stressed by Georges Chantraine.[32] A bit further along in the same passage, in language that might owe something to the influence of Italian Neoplatonists like Marsiglio Ficino, he says that just as "the common crowd" (*vulgus hominum*) must first be drawn by physical beauty before coming to love the soul of the beloved, "so for us [Jesus'] sharing in our human nature was as it were an enticement to engender love for the Lord Jesus, from whence we go forward to the love of his divine power."[33]

This brief look at a single work has suggested that, even where there may not be precise parallels to the works of earlier commentators on Scripture, humanist reflections on Scripture were very much part of a theological and exegetical tradition that was largely if not exclusively patristic. Yet one does not find in the fathers anything quite like Erasmus's notion that Christ worked miracles only in the service of human need. If the Greek fathers constructed their exegesis around a vision of God's majesty and the exaltation of humanity through the incarnation, Erasmus's *Paraphrase* hints at a

new symmetry based on recognition of human weakness and God's wondrous accommodation to it. The foibles of Jesus' disciples are highlighted
more than was customary, but he consistently emphasizes the *mansuetudo*
by which Jesus renounces all grandeur, even to the point of glossing over
passages that are dominated by Jesus' anger.[34]

Finally, the distinctive humanist blend of text criticism and literary sensitivity brings a subtle but important change in the state of mind prescribed
for pious reading of the Gospel. The difference can best be brought out by
citing two brief descriptions of the technique of *meditatio,* the first from
Ludolph the Carthusian, the second from Erasmus's *Paraphrase* of Luke.[35]

> Do not believe that everything which Christ did or said, and which we can
> meditate on, has been written down. To make a greater impression, I will
> recount things to you according to certain imaginative representations, either
> in such wise as they happened, or as it may piously be believed that they
> happened . . . ; thus you may make yourself present for those things which
> Jesus did or said.
> Now if we stay a while before sculptures or paintings, considering each of
> the parts of the work, we always notice something new which previously
> escaped our eyes: likewise, I think it will be pertinent to pause a while before
> this remarkable spectacle [the cure of the paralytic lowered through the roof],
> and let our minds play over all its details in pious curiosity.

What is important for Ludolph is the immediacy with which one can represent to oneself what Christ said or did; the distinction between what the
Gospels actually record of him and what may piously be imagined is
secondary. For Erasmus, it is not Jesus himself who is the direct focus of
reflection but rather the inviolable text through which he may be glimpsed.
Like a work of beauty, it must be savored by dwelling on its details. Historians of spirituality will differ in their appreciation of these two approaches,
and some will no doubt prefer the directness and spontaneity of Ludolph
to Erasmus's self-consciously aesthetic ruminations. But, like the human
weakness of Christ's disciples, the critical faculties of the human mind have
a legitimate place in the understanding of Scripture, and it is above all in
this respect that humanists like Erasmus made a distinctive contribution to
the development of Western spirituality.

Notes

1. See Wallace Ferguson, *The Renaissance in Historical Thought* (Boston: Houghton
Mifflin, 1948).
2. Charles G. Nauert, Jr., "Renaissance Humanism: An Emergent Consensus and Its
Critics," *Indiana Social Studies Quarterly* 23 (1980) 5–20.

3. Charles Trinkaus, *Image and Likeness;* idem, *The Scope of Renaissance Humanism* (Ann Arbor: University of Michigan Press, 1983).

4. James D. Tracy, "Humanism and the Reformation," in *Reformation Europe: A Guide to Research*, ed. Steven Ozment (St. Louis, MO: Center for Reformation Research, 1982) 33–57.

5. Augustin Renaudet, *Préréforme et Humanisme à Paris pendant les premiers Guerres d'Italie (1494–1517)* (2nd ed.; Paris: Librairie d'Argences, 1952); Otto Herding, ed., *Jacob Wimpheling, Beatus Rhenanus, Das Leben des Johannes Geiler von Kaysersberg* (Munich: Wilhelm Fink, 1970). For a brief life of Erasmus by the same Beatus Rhenanus, see P. S. Allen, *Opus Epistolarum D. Erasmi* (12 vols.; Oxford: Clarendon Press, 1906–58) 1:56–71.

6. *Enchiridion Militis Christiani*, in *D. Erasmi Opera Omnia*, ed. Jean Leclercq (10 vols.; Leiden: Leclercq, 1703–1706) 5:6EF, 8CE.

7. James D. Tracy, "Erasmus Becomes a German," *Renaissance Quarterly* 21 (1968) 281–88.

8. *The Yale Edition of the Complete Works of St. Thomas More*, vol. 13, *Treatise on the Passion*, ed. Garry E. Haupt (New Haven, CT: Yale University Press, 1976); and *De Tristitia Christi*, ed. Clarence H. Miller (New Haven, CT: Yale University Press, 1967).

9. Andre Godin, *Erasme, Lecteur d'Origène* (Geneva: Droz, 1982) 22–116.

10. Jerry H. Bentley, *Humanists and Holy Writ;* L. Delaruelle, *Guillaume Budé: L'Origine et Développement de sa Pensée* (Paris: H. Champion, 1907); Salvatore Camporeale, *Lorenzo Valla: Umanesimo e Teologia* (Florence: Istituto Nazionale di Studi di Rinascimento, 1972).

11. Erasmus's *Paraphrases* occupy vol. 7 of the Leiden *Opera Omnia*, printed in the same sequence as the books of the New Testament, though Erasmus began with the Pauline letters, starting in 1517 with Romans. Lefèvre d'Étaples, *S. Pauli Epistolae XIV* (Paris: Estienne, 1512); Sadoleto, *Commentaria in Epistolam S. Pauli ad Romanos* (Lyons: S. Gryphius, 1535).

12. Ludolphus de Saxonia, *Vita Jesu Christi* (Paris: F. Regnault, 1510). Johannes Mauburnus, *Rosetum Exercituum Spiritualium* (Paris: J. Petit, 1510). Ludolphus treats each episode in Christ's life in sequence; Mauburnus, in his far more diverse work, applies to selected incidents in Christ's life charts based on the hours of the Divine Office, and topics on which the reader is invited to meditate.

13. Roland Bainton, "The *Paraphrases* of Erasmus," *Archiv für Reformationsgeschichte* 57 (1966) 67–76; Lefèvre, *Commentarii Initiatorii in Quattuor Evangelia* (Basel: Cratander, 1526); Emil Egli, *Schweizerische Reformationsgeschichte* (Zurich: Zürcher & Furrer, 1910) 52.

14. *D. Erasmi Opera Omnia*, 4:1023C–1024F, 673EF; Lefèvre *Commentarii Initiatorii in Quattuor Evangelia* 75ᵛ. Implications of the humanist interest in grammar (as distinct from the scholastic interest in logic) for the treatment of texts are spelled out in Richard McKeon, "Renaissance and Method in Philosophy," *Columbia University Studies in the History of Ideas* 3 (1935) 36–144.

15. Jacques Chomarat, "Grammar and Rhetoric in the *Paraphrases* of the Gospel by Erasmus," *Erasmus of Rotterdam Society Yearbook* 1 (1980) 30–68. James D. Tracy, "Humanists Among the Scholastics: Erasmus, More, and Lefèvre d'Étaples on the Humanity of Christ," forthcoming in *Erasmus of Rotterdam Society Yearbook*.

16. E g., *Enchiridion Militis Christiani*, in *Erasmi Opera Omnia*, "Si non concoctum in viscera trajicit, evidens habeas argumentum valetudinariam esse animam" (4C), and "Manna tibi putrescat, nisi viscera adsectus trajeceris" (8BC).

17. For classical and humanist references to the quasi-magical power of speech to calm

turbulent passions (like Neptune calming the waves in book 1 of the *Aeneid*), see James D. Tracy, "Against the Barbarians: The Young Erasmus and His Humanist Contemporaries," *Sixteenth Century Journal* 11 (1980) 1–22.

18. *Opus Epistolarum D. Erasmi*, Letter 1211, 1:558–616, 4:524–526; *Paraclesis*, in *Desiderius Erasmus Ausgewählte Werke*, ed. Hajo Holborn (Munich: Beck, 1933) 143–44.

19. The philosophical implications of the humanist appropriation of classical rhetoric are discussed in Nancy S. Struever, *The Language of History in the Renaissance: Rhetoric and Historical Consciousness in Florentine Humanism* (Princeton, NJ: Princeton University Press, 1970).

20. *Erasmi Opera Omnia*, 6:585B–590B; Budé, *De Transitu Hellenismi ad Christianismum* (Paris: Estienne, 1535).

21. Preface to *Adnotationes* on Mark, *Erasmi Opera Omnia*, 6:151–52, "In hunc nihil habemus, quod equidem sciam, vetustum."

22. Origen *Homeliae in Lucam* (*PG* 13, cols. 1801–1900); Chrysostom *Homeliae XXV in Quaedam Loca Novi Testamenti* (*PG* 51); Theophylact *Enarratio in Evangelium S. Lucae* (*PG* 123, cols. 683–1126); Ambrose *Expositio in Lucam*, in *Corpus Christianorum, Series Latina*, vol. 14 (Turnhout: Brepols, 1957); Thomas Aquinas, *Catena Aurea in Quattuor Evangelia*, in *Opera Omnia*, vols. 11–12 (reprint, New York: Musurgia, 1948–1950). The frequency of citations of these and other commentators in Erasmus's *Adnotationes* to the New Testament is discussed by Godin, *Erasme, Lecteur d'Origène*, 143–45.

23. Godin (*Erasme, Lecteur d'Origène*) is unsurpassed in the subtleties of tracing influence, in this case of Origen on Erasmus.

24. *Erasmi Opera Omnia*, 6:330C, 409EF (cf. Ambrose *Expositio* 120, 296–97).

25. *Opera Omnia*, 6:308AV (cf. Origen *Homeliae* 1852C–1853A); 6:299AB (cf. Ambrose *Expositio* 50, 53).

26. *Opera Omnia*, 6:290B (cf. Ambrose *Expositio* 31).

27. *Opera Omnia*, 6:294CD, 288BC, 284E–285A (cf. Ambrose *Expositio* 44; Origen *Homeliae* 1814A; and Ambrose *Expositio* 15–16).

28. *Opera Omnia*, 6:285D–268B (cf. Theophylact *Enarratio* 698); 6:300B, 372EF (cf. Theophylact *Enarratio* 826).

29. *Opera Omnia*, 6:306C, 368AB.

30. *Opera Omnia*, 6:303DF; cf. 323E: Christ began his preaching in Galilee "partim, ut ne quid Euangelici successus hujus mundi praediis imputaretur, si per eruditos, si per opulentos, si per potentes proditum fuisset Euangelium, si a celebri regione exortum."

31. *Opera Omnia*, 6:314DE, 360EF. One wonders if, in a work dedicated to Henry VIII, Erasmus may have been remembering how the warlike young prince occasionally liked to have the upright John Colet preach at court (above, n. 18).

32. *Opera Omnia*, 6:365A, 319F; cf. Erasmus's treatment of Jesus' passing through the midst of the hostile crowd (Luke 4:30) in 329B, "Non se vertit in avem, aut serpentem, aut aliud praestigii genus, ut elaberetur," in contrast to Bede as cited in *Catena Aurea* 2:54, "Sed illorum mente mutata subito, vel obstupefacta, decendit." Georges Chantraine, S.J., *"Mystère" et "Philosophie du Christ" dans de Ratio Verae Theologiae d'Erasme* (Namur: Duculot, 1971); idem, *Erasme et Luther: Libre ou Serf Arbitre: Erasme contre Luther* (Paris: Lethielleux, 1982).

33. *Opera Omnia*, 6:307E–308A; Paul O. Kristeller, "Erasmus From an Italian Perspective," *Renaissance Quarterly* 14 (1961) 1–15, documents on important borrowing from Ficino in Erasmus's *Moriae Encomium*.

34. The theme of *mansuetudo* occurs in Erasmus's debate with Colet (above, n. 15), *Disputatiuncula de Taedio Jesu*, in *Opera Omnia*, 5:1289DE: "Imo totam Christi vitam

ab incunabulis relege, multa reperies mansuetudinis ac patientiae documenta, alacritatis nulla." Chomarat is right in saying that Erasmus sometimes "palliates or extenuates what may be hard or severe" in the words of Christ, but one may question whether this "softness" is to be explained psychologically, by suggesting that "in his Christ Erasmus projects unconsciously his own, idealized image," rather than by reference to the humanist and/or Netherlandish milieu of Erasmus ("Grammar and Rhetoric in the *Paraphrases* of the Gospel by Erasmus," 51–52, 65–66). One thinks, for example, of the conventional Christ of Netherlands painters like Dirk Bouts or the Master of Alkmaar, meek to the point of seeming passive and sharply different from the heroic Christ of contemporary Italian art.

35. *Opera Omnia,* 6:172B; Ludolphus de Saxonia, *Vita Jesu Christi,* iii–iv.

Bibliography

Bentley, Jerry H. *Humanists and Holy Writ.* Princeton, NJ: Princeton University Press, 1984.

Chomarat, Jacques. "Grammar and Rhetoric in the *Paraphrases* of the Gospel by Erasmus." *Erasmus of Rotterdam Society Yearbook* 1 (1980) 30–68.

Erasmus. *Collected Works of Erasmus.* Vol. 42, *New Testament Scholarship: Paraphrases on Romans and Galatians.* Edited by Robert D. Sider. Translated by John B. Payne, Albert Rabil, Jr., and Warren S. Smith, Jr. Toronto: University of Toronto Press, 1984.

Hughes, Philip Edgcumbe. *Lefèvre: Pioneer of Ecclesiastical Renewal in France.* Grand Rapids: Baker, 1984.

More, Thomas. *The Yale Edition of the Complete Works of St. Thomas More.* Vol. 13, *Treatise on the Passion.* Edited by Garry E. Haupt. New Haven, CT: Yale University Press, 1967.

Smalley, Beryl. *The Study of the Bible in the Middle Ages.* 2nd ed. Oxford: Oxford University Press, 1952.

Trinkaus, Charles. *In Our Image and Likeness: Humanity and Divinity in Italian Humanist Thought.* 2 vols. Chicago: University of Chicago Press, 1970.

12

Luther and the Beginnings of the Reformation

MARC LIENHARD

Martin Luther: Journey and Influence

AT THE JUNCTURE BETWEEN THE MIDDLE AGES and modern times, Luther and his message had considerable impact on Christianity.[1] Luther was born in 1483 at Eisleben, in the heart of Germany.[2] In 1505, he entered the convent of the Erfurt Augustinians. Drawn toward teaching, he became a doctor of theology in 1512 at Wittenberg. He commented successively on the Psalms, the epistles to the Romans, to the Galatians, to the Hebrews, and at the same time he presided over and inspired important academic disputes. In 1517, the debate regarding the question of indulgences became known to the general public. By 1521, the conflict with Rome led to Luther's excommunication, and he was placed under the ban of the empire. But the impact of his writings and of his action was already considerable in Germany and beyond.

Between 1521 and 1525, Luther kept his distance from the radical tendencies represented by Carlstadt and Thomas Müntzer, and he wrote savagely against the peasants' revolt in 1525. In the same year, during his debate with Erasmus, Luther proclaimed the bondage of the human will and asserted that salvation is the work of God alone. In his disagreements with the Swiss reformer Zwingli, he maintained the traditional faith in the real presence of Christ in the Lord's Supper (1527–1529). Having married Katherine von Bora in 1525, the former monk knew the joys and pains of family life. Until his death in 1546, he taught at the University of Wittenberg and produced a number of writings on the most diverse subjects. At the end of his life, nearly half of western Christendom had been detached from Rome. Another way of living the Christian faith was born.

Life in the convent had not appeased Luther's spiritual anxiety: "I made

a martyr of myself through prayer, fasting, vigils, cold . . . ; what was I looking for in all that if not God? He knew how well I observed my rules and
what a severe life I led. . . . I no longer believed in Christ, rather I took him
for a severe and terrible judge, the painted kind that one sees in paintings
sitting on a rainbow" (WA 45, 482, 9–17).

Luther seemed to have experienced in a more radical manner the fears
experienced by numerous believers at the end of the Middle Ages with
regard to God as judge. It was in vain that he fled to mediators such as the
Virgin and the saints. At the same time he butted up against the limits of
a spirituality and a theology. His ascetical exercises and his contrition gave
him no certitude. Had he done enough to conciliate God, the judge? The
question remained without answer for him, or rather the permanence of sin
drove him to despair. In 1507, at the moment of celebrating his first Mass,
Luther was nearly overcome with fear and asked, "What sort of person is
it with whom you speak?" (WA Tr. 5, 86 no. 5357). He had to be restrained
at the altar because he feared he would run away.

To his anxiety before God the judge and to the obsession of not being able
to make sufficient satisfaction for his sins was added the feeling, experienced
as a temptation by believers in all times, of being abandoned by the grace
of God.

Certain historians today have tried to explain the anxiety of Luther either
by psychoanalysis (father complex) or by collective mentalities (the fear
spread in the West). In fact, it is possible to show that, from biblical witnesses through the saints of all times, fear before the holiness of God played
an integral part in the experience of faith. But another element increased
Luther's torment—namely, the Ockhamist theology in which he had been
formed. It encouraged an individual, by the natural strength that one had
in one's own power, to try to merit the attribution of grace. This theology
left Christians uncertain. Luther's combat led him toward the definition of
another certitude, founded on Christ and the promise of God received in
faith. It led also to another definition of the justice of God by which the
believer lives—no longer that of a judge keeping accounts of works but that
of a merciful God, imputing to believers the justice of Christ.

In 1545, looking back to the moment of his new understanding, Luther
wrote:

> I have begun to understand that the justice of God is that by which the just
> person lives by the gift of God, that is to say by faith. This means that the
> gospel reveals to us the justice of God, that is to say that passive justice by
> which God, in his mercy, justifies us by faith, as it is written: the just one
> lives by faith. I felt then reborn and I entered into the wide-open gates of
> paradise itself. (WA 54, 186, 5–9)

Scholars disagree concerning the exact date of this "breakthrough," which occurred sometime between 1513 and 1518.

The Emergence of a Theology

The interior journey of Luther, although attested to by his own memories of the years 1530–1545, still remains something of an enigma. One is on more certain terrain when one describes the emergence of his theology between 1513 and 1518.[3] It was an impassioned effort so that "the pure study of the Bible and of the Holy Fathers might be returned to honor" (WA Br. I, 170, 36–37). "It is impossible to reform the church," Luther wrote, "unless one uproots radically the canons, the decretals, scholastic theology, philosophy, logic, as they are taught today" (ibid., 170, 33–35).

Luther concentrated therefore on the Scriptures and developed a new hermeneutic. With Augustine, he applied the Psalms to Christ, but he went further in applying to him even the Psalms where the psalmist cries out that he has been abandoned by God (e.g., Psalm 22). In addition, he insisted that the exegetical tradition (which distinguished four meanings) appeal to the tropological meaning. Luther did not mean the moral sense, but rather an appropriation of Christ by the believer so that what Christ is in his person—that is to say, justice, truth, power—is applied to the believer. It is therefore Christ who makes one just, true, powerful in the faith. The gospel's theme was justice, a justice given by God to Christ and, in Christ, to the believer.

Luther was strongly opposed to scholastic theology, in particular to that at the end of the Middle Ages (Ockham, Biel, etc.). He criticized the idea "that the whole of original sin as well as actual sins could be removed, as if it had to do with things which one could remove in an instant, as shadow is chased away by light" (WA 56, 273, 4–6). He called Pelagian the opinion that grace could be obtained automatically "by doing what one is able to do." In a dispute against scholastic theology in 1517, he affirmed: "To love God naturally above all things is a fiction, something like a chimera" (WA 1, 225, 3). With Augustine he proclaimed: "Whoever is outside of grace sins constantly" (ibid., 227, 14). He rejected the scholastic and Aristotelian concept of *habitus*. He taught that one must avoid the impression that by means of exercises Christian life could become a sort of habit and that a person, more and more sanctified, would no longer have need to implore God's pardon. A passage from a letter of 1516 admirably expresses the conviction at which Luther had then arrived: "Learn to know Christ and Christ crucified; learn to sing his praise, to despair of yourself and to say: You, Lord Jesus, you are my justice, but I, I am your sins; you have assumed that which is mine, and you have given me that which is yours. . . . In effect, Christ lives only with sinners. . . . Think of this great love and you will see there the sweetest consolations. In effect, if it is possible to come to a quiet conscience by our efforts and our trials, why, then, did Christ die?" (WA Br. 1, 35, 24–27; 29; 31–33).

This journey was a return to the apostle Paul, in particular to justification by faith. Certain witnesses of the Christian tradition helped Luther in his rereading of Scripture. There are references to mystical themes in Luther's early works, such as the love of the true theologian for silence, the rapture and ecstasy (WA 3, 372, 13–27). Luther was enthusiastic about the Rhenish mystic Tauler and for that writing typical of German mysticism: *Eine Theologie deutsch*. Like Tauler, Luther placed the root of sin in the will and in the self-affirmation of the person. When Tauler preached reduction to nothing, *ad nihil*—that is to say, the self-abasement of a person—Luther responded in his course on the epistle to the Romans that one must search for God through humiliation. A meeting with God comes about even through a journey that takes one through the pains of hell.

With Augustine, Luther spoke of a veritable corruption of a person. But he went further. The bishop of Hippo found nothing in himself after his conversion but a remnant of the weakness of the flesh. Luther, on the contrary, situated sin as a permanent reality in the will itself, in the tendency of human beings to affirm themselves over against God. But it was in Augustine that Luther discovered a hymn to the omnipotence of grace. Salvation was conceived entirely as the work of the grace of God. The virtue of pagans was denied as well as the ability of sinners to prepare themselves for grace and to acquire any merit whatsoever. But there again, a difference appears: for Augustine, grace was a gift of God, a reality infused in persons which conferred on them qualities and new strengths; for Luther, grace was an attitude of God and not an objective quality susceptible of being detached from God—that is to say, Luther remained in some way a debtor to Ockhamism. It was also typical of Ockhamism to underline the revelation of God in Holy Scripture. It is there that one finds God, not through reason.

Conflict with Rome

According to certain Roman Catholic theologians, the message of the young Luther could be received today by the whole of Christianity. Why, then, was there a rupture in the sixteenth century?[4] Besides social and political factors (e.g., opposition of the Germans to Rome), three elements in the career of Luther create a problem. There was, first of all, the novelty of his language and of his behavior. Luther no longer considered persons in themselves as bearing a certain number of properties, but only persons in relation with God. Instead of speaking in terms of moral categories, of persons in the process of sanctifying themselves by their actions under grace, he described the human being in relation to Christ. His language was more existential than ontological, more biblical than philosophical, marked by care to liberate theology from the domination of philosophy, in particular from that of Aristotle, and to return to the very source—to the revelation of God in Jesus Christ, which breaks natural ways of speaking of God.

In the second place, Luther's actions imply, from before 1517, criticism of the life of the church. These criticisms were reinforced by the indulgence affair. Certainly, the criticisms of Rome and of the clergy were scarcely new, but Luther gave them a more deeply religious foundation. He rose up against the practice of indulgences because, according to him, they led Christians to a false security. Christians might rest on them, forgetting their penitence and forgetting that "our Lord and Master Jesus Christ wished that all the life of the faithful should be one of penitence" (the first of the ninety-five theses). After 1517, other criticisms emerged in the writings of Luther bearing, for example, on votive Masses, pilgrimages, the distinction between clergy and laity. The official church did not accept his criticisms; some of them were not taken up until Vatican Council II, but in the sixteenth century they led to conflict.

Behind all of Luther's efforts to reform the church lay the fundamental conflict of authority. Following the ninety-five theses of 1517, Luther had been accused of *lèse-papauté*. During the interview with Cardinal Cajetan in October 1518, Luther begged in vain to be convinced by biblical arguments instead of being opposed by the inerrancy of the pope and the supreme magisterium of the church. According to Luther, "divine truth is mistress (*domina*] even of the pope" (WA 2, 18, 2). The magisterium of the church (which he did not exclude) did not have authority except in reference to the gospel. His adversaries, on the other hand, were of the opinion that Luther neglected the assistance of the Holy Spirit promised by Christ to the apostles and to their successors. They thought that Luther raised his interpretation of the Bible over against tradition and the magisterium.

The rupture was a source of suffering for Luther. He wished to act within the church and favored a renovation of preaching and of faith. In 1522, he could still write: "I ask that one be careful not to cite my name, and not to say that one is a Lutheran, but a Christian. For what is Luther? This doctrine does not belong to me at all. I was not crucified for anybody. . . . I am not, and I do not wish to be, the master of anybody. I share with the community this unique common teaching of Christ who is our only master" (WA 8, 685, 4–15).

In fact, he exercised a considerable impact by his writings, his action, the counsels of every kind that he was called upon to give, and by his diverse positions. His literary work includes more than six hundred different titles (gathered in one hundred volumes). Even his biblical commentaries, not to mention his numerous controversial writings, were always done for the edification of Christians, as were the numerous treatises (such as the *Declaration to the Nobility*, the *Treatise on Christian Liberty* of 1520) and the works of edification properly understood, such as his sermon "On the Contemplation of the Holy Suffering of Christ"(1519) and that on preparation for death, his little book of prayer (*Betbüchlein*) of 1522, or his introduction to prayer of 1535 (*A Simple Way to Pray*). His two catechisms of 1529 and his thirty-six hymns would remain influential even until today. But the major work was surely his translation of the Bible into German (the New Testament in 1522; the complete Bible in 1534). Luther succeeded in an admirable manner in transcribing the biblical text into the everyday language of his contemporaries without sacrificing thereby the poetry and other particularities of the original version. It was, to be sure, the same biblical text, but seized upon and rewritten in a manner that revealed the religious experience of Luther. It is truly this translation that spread the message of Luther among the people and that would impregnate for centuries both German culture and religious faith.

But whoever would like to see the work of Luther as a spiritual director should plunge also into the 2,650 letters written between 1501 and 1546; there one can discover in this very special way Luther the man, turn by turn engaged in play and polemics, taking a very personal part in the joys and pains of his correspondents, knowing always how to exhort and edify them with firmness and sweetness.

The Affirmation of the Faith

Luther the theologian accented two themes of the faith: "The proper subject of theology is the man accused for his sin and lost, and the God who justifies and saves the sinner. In theology, whatever outside of this subject is researched or disputed is error and poison" (WA 40, II, 328, 17–20).[5]

Let us make precise the manner in which Luther defined the sinner. At the base of a sin there is, according to Luther, a tendency to curve in upon oneself (*incurvatio hominis in se ipsum*). Insofar as one is a sinner, one cannot do otherwise than to love oneself above all. That is the fundamental sin and not the reign of instincts or tendencies. A person turned in on oneself: that concerns one's intellectual capacities as well as one's senses and desires. It is the total person who is the sinner, in the measure in which one closes in upon oneself in place of attaching oneself by faith to the word and of abandoning oneself to God. Sin is opposition to this "eccentric" orientation. This opposition can also manifest itself in libertinist antinomianism, which wants to live without reference to a law except by pious words through which one intends to affirm one's autonomy.

Insistence on sin, on its permanence, even though it may be pardoned without cease, is characteristic of Luther. All perfectionism is thereby excluded from Christian life, where the spiritual pride of the Pharisees has always to be ousted.

It is, first of all, a very deliberate act on Luther's part to privilege the God of biblical revelation and of the history of salvation over against the God of the philosophical tradition. Luther's theology speaks of the God who saves people in Jesus Christ. Justification by faith alone always implies that God does not treat people as a function of moral and metaphysical justice, but rather in function of another justice, which is that of the gospel, that of grace. It implies that people may subsist before God because of Christ and in the measure in which they are united to Christ in faith. All human merit, every form of a religion of works, is therefore excluded by this triple *solus:* grace alone, Christ alone, faith alone.

Luther taught that this message ought to determine the whole of the life of the church; the article of justification is "master and prince, lord, guide and judge over all forms of doctrine. It guards and governs all ecclesiastical doctrine and brings our consciences before God. Without this article, the world is only death and shadows" (WA 39, I, 205, 2–5).

Law and Gospel

The central message of the church consists, then, in announcing salvation. But Luther makes a precise distinction characteristic of his thought. He came to speak of the law and the gospel without separating them and without confusing them. Law is the word that accuses the sinner and reveals the sin. To the humbled person, powerless and anxious, is announced the liberating word of God which is the gospel. If the law alone is announced, the sinner is led to despair or to pride. If the gospel alone is announced it risks becoming cheap grace. Indeed, it is necessary to distinguish well the gospel from the law in order to make clear the gratuitous character of salvation and to distinguish clearly Jesus Christ from Moses and the biblical God from the God of Aristotle. But the law is also at the service of the gospel in the measure in which it prepares the sinner to receive with empty hands the promise of salvation.

The Word, Faith, and the Sign

"The soul can pass up everything with the exception of the word of God" (WA 7, 50, 39). There is no faith without the word. "There where there is no promise of God there is no faith" (WA 6, 364, 8-9). The word is the "means of salvation" to the same degree as the sacraments. In addition, the sacraments are only another form of the word, a sign joined to the promise of God. Luther criticized everything in the sacramental practice of his time that tended to hide this element, transforming the sacrament, sign of the grace of God, into a work carried by people to God. "In order to constitute a sacrament, there is required above all a word, a divine promise, by which faith may be exercised. . . . We have said that in every sacrament, there is a word of divine promise. Whoever receives the sign must believe this promise: but the sign alone cannot be the sacrament" (WA 6, 550, 9-25).

But in his great goodness, God has joined to his word "a sign and a seal" (WA 7, 323, 5) in order to reinforce the certitude of faith. Two things constitute the sacrament: the visible sign and a word—that is to say, a promise of grace. In function of this criterion, Luther retained only three of the traditional seven sacraments: baptism, the supper, and penance. In the other sacraments, there was not, according to him, a promise of grace. In distinction to those who would later become Protestant, Luther did not privilege preaching at the expense of the sacraments. In 1537, he wrote thus in the Smalkald Articles:

> The gospel brings us help against sin, and does so in many ways because God is rich in mercy. The gospel comes to our help primarily by the oral word which preaches in the entire world the remission of sins, which is the proper office of the gospel; secondly by baptism; thirdly by the holy sacrament of the altar; fourthly by the power of the keys as well as by the conversations and consolations of the brothers."

But if faith is necessary for one to benefit from hearing the word and using the sacraments, it is itself elicited by these and the action of the Holy Spirit which is joined to them. That is why Luther was opposed to Carlstadt and others whom he qualified as "Schwärmer" (enthusiasts, illuminists). He reproached them for devaluing the exterior word (and the sacraments) in relation to the Spirit. Carlstadt would like "to enter first into the Spirit" (WA 18, 136, 31). According to Luther, on the contrary, God "does not wish to give anyone the Spirit or faith, without the exterior word and the sign" (1Bw, 136, 17). One must first hear the gospel and receive the corporal signs which are baptism and the supper, "and then come mortification, the cross and the works of love" (ibid., 139, 24-25).

Authority and Holy Scripture

The gospel is "a loud cry" before being a text. It is a living message first con-
fided to the apostles, then transmitted throughout the ages, but always in
reference to the apostolic message. Nevertheless, the writing of the gospel
became necessary because of the heretical deformation in preaching. It constituted, in addition, an instrument of criticism for the community, a
counterweight in regard to pastors. Scripture is not, for Luther, a moral or
doctrinal code. He did not intend to replace the Roman pope by a "paper
pope." The Scriptures have authority because their center is Jesus Christ. It
is around this center that the Scriptures gather in all their diversity. To be
more precise, it is Christ as the salvific reality and not Christ the legislator
or example who is at the heart of Holy Scripture. It is to this central message
that the promises of the Old Testament look. It is to Christ that the
different laws and exhortations lead. They guide believers toward him who
is the only one to have fully accomplished the law and who liberates from
the accusation of the law.

With regard to the original and authentic witness rendered by the apostles
to Christ, the Scripture is preeminent in relation to the tradition that
followed, preeminent also with regard to the magisterium. The bishops, the
councils, and the popes can err and have erred. One must not follow their
teachings unless they clearly conform to Scripture. Luther was persuaded
that "the Scripture is its own light" (WA 10, III, 238, 10) and that it is easy
to understand, at least with regard to that essential which is faith. This
breaks with the principle that, in case of doubt, the ecclesiastical
magisterium ought to decide on the proper interpretation of Holy Scripture. Holy Scripture can be understood by every Christian. But the authority of the Scripture is also opposed to illuminists, to all those who wish to
join to the biblical witness a spirit taken from elsewhere, in particular from
their own proper inspiration.

Luther did not, however, set Scripture in radical opposition to tradition.
He himself took into consideration the confessions of faith of the ancient
church, as well as the liturgical and hymnological tradition of the church,
in the measure in which these were not contrary to the message relative to
Christ and to justification by faith inscribed at the heart of Scripture.

The Union of the Believer with Christ

According to Luther, Christ is not only the distant object of faith, but he
is present in faith. He often employs, in this regard, the term *fides Christi*.
In the treatise *On Christian Liberty* he speaks, following Ephesians 5:30, of

the mystical tradition (St. Bernard), of the marriage between the soul and Christ. "Christ is become with us one sole body and one sole flesh, . . . so that he is essentially and truly in us" (WA 33, 232, 26–28). Nevertheless, there is no absorption of the individual in God, as certain mystics affirmed, but rather an exchange "between Christ who gives to man justice and man who gives his sin to Christ." In addition, the "Christ in us" is not the result of ascetic efforts or of meditations, but rather is bound to the word, which offers Christ as a salutary gift before it holds him up as an example. But the Christ "for us" is truly present in believers, here below. Luther was opposed also to "the speculation of the Sectarians with regard to the faith when they dream that Christ is in us spiritually, that is to say, speculatively, but that he is in reality in heaven. . . . Christ and the faith must be entirely bound together; it is necessary simply that we turn toward heaven, and that Christ be, live and act in us" (WA 40, I, 546, 24–27).

This union with Christ frees the conscience accused because of sin. "It is necessary that Christ and my conscience be made one unique body, so that nothing offers itself to my view but Christ crucified and risen. But if I look only to myself, excluding Christ, that is my doing" (WA 40, I, 282, 21–23).

But Luther spoke of Christ not only as the cause of salvation. He repeated the Augustinian formula of Christ as "sacrament and example." Christ draws the believer toward other people. Luther could also speak of Christ as the image according to which God leads believers through the cross toward glory.

The Priesthood of All Believers

If we are united to Christ, "we are given the dignity to present ourselves before God, to pray for others, and to instruct each other mutually in the things of God" (WA 7, 57, 26–27). In affirming that all Christians are priests, Luther put an end to the traditional distinction between the state of the priest and the state of the laity. It is a considerable valorization of the place of laity in the church, an effort to make them adult and responsible, in particular on the level of piety and witness. According to Louis Bouyer, Luther was "the first, at least after the patristic period, to affirm so clearly the priesthood of the faithful, to propose concretely a properly lay spirituality."[6] But, for all that, he did not exclude the particular ministry in which a man is called by a community to announce the gospel and to give the sacraments. This would be forevermore one function among others and not a state that puts the minister above others.

In addition, it is appropriate to note that, according to Luther, Christian faith would not know how to go beyond the church. Certainly, he entered into conflict with the church of his time, more precisely, with the church of Rome. But, for all that, he did not oppose the individual to the church taken as the gathering of believers around the word and the sacraments:

> Who wishes to find Christ, must first find the church . . . , but the church, that is not something of wood and stone, but the gathering (*der Hauff*) of people believing in Christ. We must hold to this and see how those who believe in Christ live and teach. They certainly have Christ with them, because outside of the church of Christ, there is no truth, no Christ, no salvation. (WA 10, I, 1, 140, 8–9, 14–17)

There is a church because people participate in the goods dispensed by Christ and share in them. And again, as long as one lives in the flesh, relation to God comes only through those exterior means, preaching and the sacraments.

The Setting of Christian Life and Vocation

In many writings, Luther values three states (*Stände*) or foundations instituted by God, in which the Christian is called to act: the charge of priest, the state of marriage, and temporal authority. As witnessed by many biblical passages, these states correspond well to the will of God. The Christian, therefore, does not run from them, but lives in them in obedience to God, knowing that by these states God continues his creative work and combats the reign of Satan. Willed by God, these states have as their end the service of the neighbor, but there are also states that do not serve the neighbor and are not willed by God. He thinks in particular of the hierarchy and of monks in the measure in which they do not announce the word of God, or again of the secular states such as begging, "robbery, usury, and prostitution" (WA 10, I, 1, 317, 22).

It is not a matter, then, of accepting everything with fatalism. Spirituality does not fall into quietism. The Christian ought, when the opportunity occurs, to change the existing structures or to abandon them if they contravene the will of God and are a disservice to the neighbor.

A characteristic term ought to be mentioned: "vocation" (*Berufung*). As used in German mysticism, this typical term of Lutheran spirituality points to the call that each one receives from God in the state (or the states) in which one finds oneself. In the Middle Ages, the monastic state had taken over for itself the term "vocation" in its fullest sense, with the idea that by the monastic vows, the religious broke totally with the world and offered himself or herself totally to God. Luther developed another medieval tradition which revalorized the secular functions at the heart of society. Here are the farmer and the artisan, and they are in direct relation with God. The German mystics spoke in this manner of *Ruf*. Luther subscribed to this tradition and, in developing it, opposed it to monasticism.

In addition, he felt he must criticize a piety built upon works considered to be more holy than other works. He continually set the works required by God in these various states and by vocation against those which a person chose for oneself, as, for example, pilgrimages. Having said that, the action of the Christian is not contained in the sphere of one's state and vocation. "Beyond these three institutions and orders, there is now a common order of Christian love in which one serves not only the three orders, but also and in common, by all sorts of benefits, each person who has need" (WA 26, 505, 11–13).

The Edification of Christians or How Spirituality is Nourished

The Lutheran reform is an immense effort to put the faithful into contact with the word of God in the most diverse forms. The base is evidently familiarity with the Bible, read and reread, commented upon, illustrated in paintings and in theater.[7] Humanism and the Reformation advocated the return to the sources, in particular, biblical sources. Luther's genial translation popularized the Holy Book of Christians. Up until his death, more than 430 editions of the Bible translated by Luther or extracts from this Bible were published. It is possible to calculate that, in 1535, one German in seventy was in possession of a New Testament, but not everyone knew how to read, and Luther himself considered the Bible to be an oral message rather than a written work. That is why, with regard to the Bible, other forms of transmission of the gospel ought to be considered.

Preaching and Catechesis

The multiplication of preaching in the churches of the Reformation is a well-known fact.[8] Daily Mass was suppressed and replaced by offices of the word. They are described in *The German Mass* of 1526:

> On Monday and Tuesday morning, one lectures in German on the Ten Commandments, the faith, the Our Father, baptism and the sacrament. . . . On Wednesday morning . . . , the whole of the gospel of Matthew is to be read, and on Thursday and Friday morning, we have the daily lessons of the week in the epistles of the apostles and whatever is left in the New Testament. . . . Outside of the service, there are also lessons at the University for those who are learned. (WA 19, 79, 17–80, 3)

On Sunday, the faithful can hear three different preachings: at five or six in the morning on the epistle of the day; at the Mass at eight or nine there is a sermon on the Gospel; and in the afternoon at vespers, on the Old Testament. The traditional order of the pericopes has been preserved. Ministers not yet capable of preaching by themselves had to utilize *postils*, or summaries of sermons that Luther had prepared, and read the sermon of the day. This was only a provisory solution, since the pastors in the future would be formed as preachers. Outside of the sermon properly speaking, exhortations were multiplied in the different liturgies, for example, at the moment of the Lord's Supper.

In fact, for Luther, the courses at the university as well as the instruction of children were forms of preaching. The efforts invested in catechesis were remarkable. Even before Luther's catechisms of 1529, other catechisms had appeared.[9] The transmission of the faith to children was no longer confined to the family but had to be done in the schools as well as the churches. The children were familiarized with the Bible and, while exercising their memories, they also learned material relevant to faith, prayer, and the sacraments.

In the value it gave to preaching, the Lutheran reform took up certain earlier tendencies. The preaching orders were steadily at work in the church at the end of the Middle Ages. Some cities like Strasbourg had founded prebends for preachers, and the humanists insisted on the formation of the faithful by the word rather than by ritual. But Luther was not content simply to give value to preaching as such; he fought equally for its renewal. Preachers ought not to be content with promoting a simple historical knowledge of Christ, nor should they seek to stimulate emotions (to become tender over Christ or to be enraged against the Jews). They ought "to excite faith in Christ so that he may not be simply Christ, but Christ for you and for me so that he may work in us that which is said of him and that which his name signifies" (WA 7, 58, 39). However great had been the part of teaching in Luther's sermons that have been preserved, preaching was not, for him, a discourse on Jesus Christ, but a word in which Jesus Christ was present and through which he acted.

Baptism and the Lord's Supper

Baptism and the Lord's Supper retained their full importance.[10] The altar remained at the center of Lutheran churches and was not replaced by a simple table as was the case in Zurich and Geneva. At the time of Luther, the Lord's Supper was celebrated every Sunday at Wittenberg. The heated battle against Zwingli shows that for Luther the questions of the Lord's

Supper and of the real presence of Christ were found at the very heart of the faith.

There is the sign (the water) and the promise: "Whoever believes and is baptized will be saved."[11] For Luther, baptism is an expression of the grace of God; it can therefore be conferred on infants. But faith is necessary for it to be efficacious. Expressing the grace of God at the beginning of a Christian life, baptism contributes to the certitude of Christians. *"Baptizatus sum"* (I am baptized) wrote Luther on his work table to console himself in moments of doubt and temptation.

Insofar as it is the word of God, baptism is not without effect even in the life of a child, giving at the same time new life and faith. "If he [Christ] is present, if he speaks himself and if he baptizes, why should not the faith and the Spirit come into the child through the words and through the baptism which he gives, just as much as in the case of John the Baptist?" (WA 26, 156, 38–40).

Luther also made explicit the action of baptism: "It brings about the remission of sins, frees from death and the devil and gives eternal happiness to all those who believe that which the words and the promise of God express." (*Small Catechism*). It is to be noted that, in the baptismal formula translated into German in 1523 and above all in the revised version of 1526, Luther abandoned many of the traditional symbolic gestures such as breathing on the infant and the use of salt and oil, but he retained the exorcism— that is to say, the word against Satan: "The minister who baptizes will say: Go out, impure spirit and make place for the Holy Spirit. . . . I conjure you, impure spirit, in the name of the Father (sign of the cross) and of the Son (sign of the cross) and of the Holy Spirit (sign of the cross) to go out and to leave this servant of Jesus Christ" (WA 19, 540; cf. WA 12, 44).

We ought also to emphasize the bond between baptism and penance. Baptism signifies death and resurrection. To believe is to realize throughout the whole of life that which baptism signifies. "From the moment we begin to believe, we begin at the same time to die to this world and to live for God in the life to come, so that faith may truly be death and resurrection" (WA 6, 534, 15–16).

Penance is nothing else than a way of killing the old human in daily repentance and thereby pursuing the work of baptism. It is also a continually repeated return to the assurance conferred by baptism. "For I have said that the sacrament of penance is nothing else than a way toward baptism, and a return to baptism" (WA 6, 572, 15–17). Baptism holds an eminent place in Lutheran spirituality.

The liturgy of the Lord's Supper in Lutheran churches follows the traditional order of the Mass such as it was established in the West in the Middle

Ages.[12] Some changes were made, however, in the practice and in the liturgical texts, according to the theological options of Luther.

Communion under both species was reestablished because Jesus had given
the cup to his disciples and the church had no authority to act contrary to
the institution of Christ. In addition, Luther energetically fought all that
might make one think that the Mass was a good work and a sacrifice
brought by people to God. To celebrate the Mass is not to bring God a
sacrifice but to receive something from God. In 1520, Luther defined the
Lord's Supper as Christ's testament—that is to say, as the promise of pardon
for sins and of life eternal left by a dying person and confirmed by his death.

Votive Masses were therefore suppressed because they were ordinarily
celebrated by the priest alone in the absence of any community. "The Mass
is not a work communicable to others, it is the object of faith destined to
nourish and to fortify faith for each individual" (WA 6, 523, 6). The essential
in the Mass is the promise of grace and faith that is attached to it; therefore,
it is important that the words of institution which announce pardon of sin
be pronounced in a loud voice and, of course, in the language of the people.
Luther suppressed all references to sacrifice in the canon of the Mass: the
words of institution "make no mention of either a work or a sacrifice"
(WA 6, 523, 20).

It is also necessary to remember the conflict between Luther and Zwingli.
With the tradition, Luther affirmed the real presence of Christ in his body
and his blood under the species of bread and wine in the Supper (at the same
time he denied the theory of transubstantiation). Zwingli, on the other
hand, taught a symbolic concept: *est* really means "signifies." Christ is therefore present spiritually, not corporally. The Supper recalls that which was
done one time for everyone and which through the "contemplation of faith"
(*contemplatio fidei*) is eternally present. Flesh is good for nothing, said
Zwingli, and included in "flesh" the historical flesh of Christ. The bread and
wine are perishable elements of the Supper and so are opposed to the spirit.
Luther, on the contrary, did not devalue that which is physical and visible.
In the Supper, the incarnation of Christ is continued in a certain manner.
The word never acts alone; God always joins to it a sign.

The conflict emphasizes the meaning of the Supper for Luther. It is part
of those elements which by their "objectivity" give a foundation to the faith,
in particular, in moments of doubt. That is why it is especially to be given
to the sick at home or to the dying. For Zwingli, the Supper has more of
a community orientation; it allows people to manifest their common
belonging to Jesus Christ and the will to serve him. One might ask if the
Lutheran approach does not give too much privilege to the pardon of sins
to the detriment of other elements in the eucharistic celebration (for

20. Lucas Cranach the Elder, *Portrait of Martin Luther*, 1529.
Galleria Uffizi, Florence.

example, doxology, ethical and community dimensions), and if the numerous exhortations and instructions inserted in the celebration of the sacraments have not taken over too much the place of prayer. Does not the pedagogical orientation alter the liturgical process?

Confession

Penance, composed of contrition, confession, and satisfaction, was traditionally part of the seven sacraments. Sins were confessed to the priest, who gave absolution and imposed penances. The priest asked questions based on the five senses, the seven capital sins, the ten commandments, and this questioning often had a detailed and scrupulous character. But recourse to the various dispensations could also lead to laxism. After Lateran Council IV (1215), it was necessary to confess at least once a year. At one point, Luther underlined that the central element of confession was absolution— that is to say, the word of pardon personally announced to the Christian by the pastor. But he did not bring into question the necessity of confession. Between 1520 and 1522, he vigorously denounced the tyranny exercised by the popes over consciences. In a treatise on confession in 1521 (*Von der Beicht*, WA 8, 129–185), he thought that it was necessary only to confess sins that weighed on the conscience, that everything that had been forgotten was already pardoned. Nor was it necessary to confess one's sins to a priest or a monk; any brother could hear confession and give absolution. But there were two reasons that impelled Christians to confess their sins: the shame of confession is a manner in which Christians can carry the cross, and through absolution they receive the unconditional assurance of pardon.

Two facts must be weighed in the development of confession in the Lutheran churches.[13] At Christmas 1521, in the absence of Luther, Carlstadt celebrated an evangelical Mass at Wittenberg without the confession that would normally precede it, and this provoked the hostility of Luther. In addition, in the communities that had joined the evangelical movement, individual confession was used less and less. It was considered a typical institution of the papacy from which Luther had freed Christians. People were content with a collective confession and absolution.

Then, in 1523, Luther introduced an examination of conscience before communion. In order to preserve communicants from superficiality and because of the holiness of the sacrament, each one had to be questioned on faith and life before communion. This practice, at first used at Wittenberg, spread to most of the Lutheran churches in spite of resistance. In fact, confession was thus bound to the Supper; it became an obligatory preamble. More and more it took the place of a catechetical examination for the communicants, to which was added moral exhortation. At the end of the seventeenth century, under the influence of pietism, this practice fell into disuse in Lutheran churches.

Hymns and Images

In order to transmit the gospel in the best manner possible, Luther did not hesitate to use singing and pictures. "I would rather see all the arts, in particular music, in the service of him who gave and created them" (WA 35, 475, 4–5). Singing in particular would be characteristic of Lutheran spirituality.[14] Luther himself composed (or adapted) thirty-six hymns, "so that through this means the word of God and Christian doctrine might be spread and practiced under as many diverse forms as possible" (WA 35, 474, 8). He translated Latin hymns into German or provided new strophes for German hymns already in existence. Two innovations of the Lutheran reform ought to be particularly underlined: the transformation of Psalms into hymns (for example Psalm 130) and the constitution of a hymn book, the first of which appeared in 1529 in Wittenberg. From 1524 on, other composers such as Paul Speratus, Elisabeth Kreuziger, and Lazarus Spengler joined their works to Luther's. Besides the Bible, the hymn books played a central role in the piety of Lutheran Christians. Certain hymns by Luther, published at first under the form of leaflets, served particularly for the diffusion of evangelical themes. This is the case notably of "Ein neues Lied wir heben an," "Nun freut euch, lieben Christen gmein," "Ein feste Burg ist unser Gott," "Erhalt uns, Herr, bei deinem Wort," "Ach Gott vom Himmel sieh darein." Other hymns, such as those on the Decalogue were used especially during catechetical instruction, and others were used during the liturgy.

Under this popular form, the essential themes of the Lutheran message were diffused: justification by faith; Christ incarnate and victorious over sin, death, and the devil; confidence in God, who is the only fortress of his church. Many hymns were invocations to the Holy Spirit. In contrast to the later evolution of Lutheran hymnology (Paul Gerhard, for example), none concentrated on the suffering Christ. Piety was drawn more by the incarnation and Easter joy. On the other hand, the great facts of the history of salvation were celebrated and at the same time were applied to individual believers through the work of Christ. But it is especially the work of God (for us) that is evoked, and not the states of the believing soul, a notable difference from the hymns of pietism.

To transmit the gospel and to make it more concrete for simple people, Luther wished to use pictures also.[15] It is well known that numerous representatives of the evangelical movement—in particular Zwingli, Carlstadt, and Calvin, as well as the Anabaptists—banished all paintings and sculptures from the churches. Luther understood just as well what risks were involved in allowing images to remain. Obviously, they are not to be adored. Any illusion that a person who presented an image to a church accomplished a good work also had to be avoided. Preaching had to combat the false confidence placed in images.

But Luther seems to have evolved toward a more and more positive appreciation of images. At first he rejected the idea that images were forbidden by the Decalogue and by the Old Testament in general. He opposed Carlstadt when Carlstadt wanted to remove the images by force. The Christian is not only free to use or not use such images; Luther went so far as to consider images desirable. "May it please God that I can convince the lords and the rich to have the interior and the exterior of their houses painted with biblical scenes. That would be a Christian work. . . . Images are preaching for the eyes" (WA 18, 83, 3). "If images come forth from the heart, they cannot do evil to the eyes" (WA 18, 67, 12ff.). He thus allowed that one might have a crucifix, an image of a saint or of the Virgin "to look at them, as witnesses, as a help to the memory, as a sign" (WA 18, 80, 7).

Nevertheless, changes would occur. Luther rose up against images that showed anxious people seeking shelter under the mantle of the Virgin Mary. He criticized images of St. Barbara or St. Christopher, those which represented the church as a ship in which only the clergy were welcomed. Reforming themes ought to be the subject of pictures. Pictures of justification of the sinner and of the fall and redemption, illustrated notably by Cranach, were widely diffused as well as pictures of the meeting between Christ and the adulterous woman or again the welcoming of children by Jesus.

Catechisms, hymn books, and Luther's translation of the Bible into German were the books most often illustrated. Images concretized the text, and the text explained the images. Thus, even if the Lutheran reformation led to a more simple piety and to changes with regard to images, it nevertheless remained indebted to the visible.

Prayer

Faith, based on hearing the gospel and the reception of the different means of grace, manifests itself normally through word and action, through invocation and praise.[16] What is the faith if not "pure prayer," cried Luther.

He spoke against "the prayers of monks and of priests who night and day mumble without any of them dreaming in the least of asking something. . . . Not one of them has ever advised prayer through obedience to God or to express faith in his promise, or to seek help in some pressing necessity; on the contrary they have thought of nothing else than of doing a good work so that they might pay God, because they do not intend to receive anything from him but only to give to him" (WA 30, I, 196, 23–30).

There are three fundamental reasons for prayer. First, "God wishes us to pray, and he should not have to wait on our good pleasure" (ibid., 193, 34). In addition there is a promise attached to prayer: "God has promised that our prayer will be heard in all certitude" (ibid., 195, 30). Finally, on the road to sanctification, when the Christian is confronted by the devil, the world, and one's own flesh, "nothing is more necessary than to beat unceasingly on the ears of God, to invoke him and to ask him to give us what we need, to save us and to increase in us faith and obedience to the Ten Commandments" (ibid., 193, 8–9).

In this perspective, Luther was preoccupied as much with community prayer as with personal prayer.

Community Prayer

The community was manifested in three types of gatherings. During the week smaller groups composed of the pastor and of scholars ought to pray together in the morning and in the evening. There was also the domestic community, to which Luther addressed counsels in his small catechism. The third was the whole community gathered on Sunday, principally to celebrate the Mass.

In the liturgy of the Mass, Luther preserved all the elements from tradition that he considered were not opposed to Holy Scripture—in particular, the Psalms, which make up the greater part of this liturgy. But even the non-biblical texts such as the Kyrie, the Gloria, the Benedictus, and the Agnus Dei were preserved. Luther considered them to be praise of God in accord with the gospel. Beyond these, they manifest continuity with the ancient church. As for the traditional collects, he expurgated all of them that seemed to him contrary to the gospel, while preserving relation with the ecclesiastical year and the use of the "we" to express community prayer.

Around 1529, the litany reappeared in the liturgy of Wittenberg (in the Mass earlier), but purified of invocations addressed to saints. Luther was inspired by a text from the tradition, but he added to it new requests. The litany favored, according to Luther, the active collaboration of the community, and insofar as it enumerated the different distresses of humankind it could be appropriated.

The daily offices celebrated with the students were based, above all, on the Psalms (still often sung in Latin). Besides the biblical readings, there were hymns and the recitation of the Our Father; then the pastor or chaplain pronounced a collect, and the office ended with the Benedicamus Domino.

There was also prayer in the family. The head of the family had the duty of instructing both children and domestics in their personal morning and evening prayer as well as the *Benedicite* and the graces to be said before and after meals. But home life also included offices, daily if possible, that were more developed and composed of a hymn, a reading, a prayer, and a part of the catechism.

Personal Prayer

Luther believed that "a strong and good reformation" (WA 10, II, 375, 11) of traditional books of prayer was necessary, because these prayers did not lead people truly to recognize their sins but instead led them to seek justification from works. How better to incite the people to true prayer than through the commandments of God, the apostolic faith, and the Our Father? In commenting on these texts in his *Betbüchlein* (WA 10, II, 331–501), Luther proposed at the same time to give an instruction on prayer and an introduction to the faith. In order to pray, Christians ought not only to recite preestablished texts but also to enter into a good attitude for prayer. The only text for prayer that is given to be repeated is the Our Father. "A Christian has prayed profusely if he has prayed well the Our Father" (ibid., 376, 1–2). During the whole of his life, Luther forced himself to teach true prayer by commenting on the Our Father. Other biblical texts that he used included, above all, the Psalms. The *Betbüchlein* of 1522 contains a choice of Psalms, with titles indicating which one is appropriate to pray in which circumstances.

It is especially in a writing of 1535, *Eine einfältige Weise zu beten* (*A Simple Way to Pray*, WA 38, 351–375), that Luther gave numerous counsels for prayer. He did not reject the sentence attributed to Jerome, "All the works of believers are a prayer," nor the proverb "He who works faithfully, prays doubly." He interpreted them thus: "A believer fears and honors God in his work and keeps in memory his commandments" (WA 38, 359, 14–15). But "they must also watch lest they lose the habit of true prayer, . . . lest they become lax and lazy, cold and disgusted with regard to prayer. For the devil is neither lazy nor lax with regard to us; in the same way our flesh is still far too lively, much too disposed to sin and drives us contrary to the spirit of prayer" (ibid., 359, 30–35). It is not a matter of multiplying words "in long empty verbage" (ibid., 362, 38), but of having "a free heart disposed to pray" (ibid., 363, 17).

Regular prayer is recommended morning and evening, and even an exterior

attitude (on one's knees or standing, hands crossed, eyes toward heaven) is
a help if the heart is disposed to prayer. In the same manner, recitation aloud
is useful:

> When I feel preoccupied or that strange thoughts have made me cold and
> have taken from me the desire to pray . . . , I take my little psalter. I run into
> my room or, if it is the proper day and hour, to the church among the
> multitude and begin to recite in a loud voice, for myself, the Ten Command-
> ments, the Creed, and, if I have the time, some words of Christ, of Paul, or
> the Psalms, just as do little children. (WA, 358, 5–359, 3)

Luther advised the following use of the Ten Commandments for prayer:
"I take each commandment, in the first place, as a teaching, which in fact
it is, and I imagine what in that commandment our Lord God demands so
gravely of me; in the second place, I thank God; thirdly, I make confession;
fourthly, a prayer [of petition]" (ibid., 365, 1–4).

A recent work by Martin Nicol on Luther's meditation has shown how
Luther changed the traditional *lectio, meditatio, oratio, contemplatio* into
oratio, meditatio, tentatio.[17] Prayer, with regard to recollection and illumination, precedes reading of the Bible. Bible reading should be inserted into
meditation, which actually goes on always on a biblical basis. The most
radical change is in the orientation of prayer: it is no longer to seek the
mystical vision of God but to remain firm against trials and temptations.
Prayer flows out, therefore, into daily life.

The Communion of Saints

Luther put an end to the invocation of saints.[18] Christ is the only mediator
between God and people, so that it is not necessary to pass through other
intermediaries. All people, including the most holy, have lived from the sole
merit of Christ. Luther openly criticized the idea that there were protector
saints for particular situations in life (Christopher for trips!). Christians
must expect help from God alone.

In consequence, prayer is addressed always to God through Christ. The
invocation of the saints, including Mary, disappeared. The accent is placed
on the personal prayer of the Christian. No one can replace an individual
in this office, just as no one can believe in another's place. "We are all
doomed to death and none of us can die for another, but each of us must
be armed and equipped for our own proper selves. . . . Each one must watch
over one's own proper fortress, and engage personally in the battle with
one's enemies, with the devil and with death, and engage in single combat
against them" (WA 10, III, 1, 7ff.).

It is also important to note how often Luther spoke of the communion of saints. It was for him an existential reality of the greatest importance not to be alone, but to live and to believe and to pray with other Christians, whether living or dead. But what did he mean by "saint"? In fact, the saints are the believers—not necessarily those who have accomplished extraordinary things, but those who in daily life lived (and live) in the faith and grace of Christ. In this perspective, "one must remember the saints, in order to strengthen one's own faith, when we see how they have obtained grace and how they have been helped by faith. And what's more, we ought to take their good works for an example" (*Augsburg Confession*, article 21).

Numerous passages from Luther show the importance that he attached to the intercession of the saints:

> That is why, when I suffer, I no longer suffer alone, Christ and all Christians suffer with me. . . . The faith of the Church comes to help me in my fear, the chastity of others undergirds me in my carnal temptation, the fasts of others are a gain to me, the prayer of another is solicitous for me. . . . Who, therefore, should despair in sins . . . [when] one is helped by so many holy children of God; and finally by Christ himself? Such is the grandeur of the communion of saints and the Church of Christ. (WA 6, 131, 14–19; 26–29).[19]

Luther took special pains to instruct the faithful in a good way to pray and, through paraphrases of the Our Father, to help them to appropriate for themselves this prayer, which is the prayer *par excellence*. The first books of evangelical prayers were those spread from Strasbourg by Brunfels (*Biblisch Betbüchlin*, 1528), anthologies of biblical prayers, particularly of the psalms.[20] Very early, some close workers with Luther such as Amsdorf and Spalatin also drew passages from Luther's writings and turned them into prayers. A little book of such prayers was widely distributed, published in 1579 by Treuer: *Beteglocklin Doctoris Martin Lutheri.*

Around 1530, collections of prayers that transmitted both biblical and nonbiblical texts of diverse origins but were inspired by Lutheran ideas began to appear. Some were intended for the sick and the dying; others for those who were preparing for communion, others for children. This effort is observable in collections of hymns and of books like those of J. Otter (*Betbüchlein für allerlei gemein Anliegen der Kirchen . . . 1537*), in order to bind personal piety to the community liturgy. Even in 1550, the texts are concise, marked by the biblical message relative to salvation and by a concern to instruct the faithful. The books of prayer in the second half of the century began to draw on other sources, including the spirituality from the end of the Middle Ages as well as from contemporary Roman Catholic authors (in particular, the Jesuits). The prayers are more individualized, according to different professions and situations. The subjective element, as well as the emotional expression, begins to take the upper hand. Interest in eschatology, in particular the nostalgic anticipation of the glory of heaven, is striking.

Lines of Strength of Lutheran Spirituality

Earthly Life

Luther criticized the orientation of an ascetical piety that turned away from creation and cast suspicion on the body and on marriage.[21] The yes of Luther to God the Creator found its classical expression in his explanation of the first article of faith:

> I believe that God created me as well as all creatures. He gave me and preserves for me a body and a soul, eyes, ears, and all my members, reason and all the senses. Every day he gives me abundantly clothes and shoes, nourishment and drink, a house, a wife and children, fields, beasts and all my goods, thus all things necessary unto this life. (*Little Catechism*)

When God sees the happiness of two spouses, "he smiles and rejoices" (WA 34, I, 62, 20). Many texts show Luther's admiration for the conception and birth of a child, his gratitude for family happiness, and also his positive attitude toward eating and drinking, playing, dancing, and the arts. The continual action of God the Creator at all levels of terrestrial life ought to incite an individual to praise God and to obey Him: "For all these benefits I must thank God and praise Him, serve Him and obey Him" (end of the explanation of the first article of faith). Rooted in the terrestrial life, received as a gift from God, Lutheran spirituality promotes joy in life; the smile of the person responds to that of God the Creator. And because God concerns himself with his creatures even on the corporal level, they in turn must serve him even in the most ordinary things. "Faith opens the eyes, considers in the spirit all these humble works, unpleasant or despised, and it tells us that the divine favor adorns them with ornaments made of gold and precious diamonds" (WA 10, II, 295, 27–296, 2).

Nevertheless, besides the joyful yes to creation, Lutheran spirituality is also aware of a suffering world, of life stretched out toward the accomplishment of the last day. It is aware of the sighs of creation, the incessant activity of Satan, the great adversary of God, who tries to pervert the proper use of creation. It is therefore not possible to install oneself in this world, which is nothing but a "stable full of rascals."

> In all ages, saints live in the world in the following manner: they occupy themselves with domestic affairs and the temporal domain, they carry on

public business, they build families, they cultivate fields, they engage in commerce or in some other career. They recognize, nevertheless, with their fathers, that they are strangers in exile; they use the world (only) as a place of passage. (WA 42, 441, 40ff.)

Luther also knew the nostalgia of the "dear last day," which was so late in coming. For him, the Christian is a guest in a disagreeable inn. "We serve here below in an inn where the master is the devil, the world the mistress of the house, and (where there reign) all sorts of evil passions" (WA 2, 329, 22). One must not "settle down"; one must certainly utilize the goods given by God but not make idols of them, and remain ready to abandon them if God asks it, and to continue to look toward the last day.

The Life of Faith

"Christ-like sanctity or common Christian sanctity occurs when the Holy Spirit gives to people faith in Christ and through that faith sanctifies them" (WA 50, 626, 15). *Faith* is evidently the key word in Lutheran spirituality.[22] It is by faith alone that Christians have access to God; thus, Luther's struggle for an authentic Christian spirituality is the struggle for true faith. This last is always defined by the attachment of a person to the word of God (and, through it, to Christ). To believe is to believe God on his word. It is "the confidence which attaches to God alone" (*Large Catechism*). But faith is not an act that a person realizes by one's own strengths. "I believe," confesses the believer with the explanation of the third article of the Creed. "What I cannot do, by my reason and my own strength, is to believe in Jesus Christ my Lord, or come to Him. But it is the Holy Spirit who calls me by the Gospel" (*Small Catechism*). Luther did not cease to fight against an illusory faith, a faith produced by human effort or a faith of simple credulity. True faith is a gift and the believer attributes its origin to the word and to the Holy Spirit. Only this faith resists temptation. To live in the faith is to experience without ceasing that the word of God rules believers, giving them interior certitude, and this is a completely personal assurance. The Lutheran reform heightened the value of the individual and that individual's own journey.

In the measure in which the word to which this faith is attached concerns a hidden reality (God, Christ), faith is opposed to the experience of the visible. The believer experiences a hostile world, a hidden God, with a reality opposed to the faith. It is "so that we do not follow our own thoughts nor the counsel of men . . . but that we remember to seek Christ in all things that draws us back to the Father, and that we hold ourselves simply and uniquely to the word of the Gospel which shows us Christ clearly and makes Him known to us" (WA 17, II, 25, 20–24).

Lutheran spirituality leaves much room for the trials and doubts of the believer. The believer suffers the trials of a life that seems to contradict the love of God. The believer is accused by the divine law and can no longer perceive anything but the anger of God. At that point the believer must believe against experience—that is to say, against God. Faith then becomes heroic, fighting to discern the yes of God beyond God's no. It is consoling for the believer to know that such a trial corresponds to the will of God in order to avoid falling into a deceiving security and so that the believer will continue reaching toward God and his word. That is why God "consoles only the sad, he does not bring to life any except those who are dead, and he justifies only sinners" (WA 42, 254, 6–8).

Nevertheless, even if the faith rests, above all, on the word, it is translated through experience. Luther took up mystical terms to express the fact that believers "feel" God and what he has promised them. The believer experiences not only abandonment, doubt, and trial but also consolation and joyful assurance because of the effective presence of God and his action.

Christian Battle

The believer is never at rest, but is in incessant combat against the "flesh," the "world," the "devil." These three powers are opposed to God and his word. It is not always possible to distinguish them at the level of their action on Christians. The evocation of the devil by Luther was something more than a simple medieval heritage.[23] If he spoke of the devil so often (and more deeply than was done in the Middle Ages), it is because he understood the whole of the history of the world as a battle of a demonic power against God the creator and redeemer. Evil is not simply moral or a weakness of people, but transpersonal, bound to that mysterious power which Luther called, with the tradition, Satan or devil. The will of human beings is between God and Satan, "like a beast of burden. When it is God who mounts it, it goes there where God wants it to go. . . . When Satan mounts it, it goes there where Satan wants it to go" (WA 18, 635, 17). A person is freed from Satan by baptism, which unites to Christ, but this liberty ought to be preserved through an incessant combat during the whole of life. In this combat, the Christian rests on "the true man (who) fights for us . . . , Jesus Christ . . . who remains master of the terrain" (strophe 2 of the celebrated hymn of Luther, "A Mighty Fortress"). From another angle, the individual Christian fights, as does the church, against Satan through the word of God. One must "kill the devil through the strength of teaching (the gospel)" (WA 30, I, 129, 2–3).

The frequent evocation of the devil (and of the "world," which is in some way the ensemble of his instruments) gives to Lutheran spirituality a cosmic orientation. Believers do not live only for themselves, even for their own salvation. By their faith, their prayer, their proclamation of the gospel, they participate actively in a much vaster history; they are instruments of God the creator and redeemer, who fights against the outbreak of chaos.

Very often, Luther was also content to describe the combat of the faithful against their own flesh. The Christian, of course, does become "a new man" by baptism and faith, but the "old man" and his tendencies subsist. We have seen that the Lutheran reform has clearly underlined the permanence of sin. The Christian lives, then, from two realities; the Christian is a double being. During all of life the Christian is "at the same time just and a sinner."[24] That signifies that believers are totally just by the alien justice of Christ which God imputes to them, but also totally sinners by that which they are in themselves and through themselves. The pardon of God to which Christians must always return concerns the whole person.

But there is another angle: Christians are double in themselves. They live in the faith and also in the flesh. The person is the place of an incessant combat between the faith and the flesh. By "flesh" Luther understood that in a person which is opposed to God and not that particular part of a person judged inferior (such as instincts, body, senses).

Christian existence is manifested precisely in this combat, which begins with baptism, whereas nonbelievers are slaves of their flesh. God promises to give the "old man" over to death during all of the baptized person's life. On the other side, the baptized promise to lend themselves, through works and suffering, to this operation begun and signified by baptism.

God gives to each person the places and occasions of combat which are works (in particular those belonging to one's vocation in various states and institutions) and suffering. To battle against the "old man," in particular against pride, the believer needs the cross. The believer is called to battle through fasts, vigils, prayer, and work. Luther is sometimes reproached for being too accommodating to sin and denying the possibility of making progress in sanctification. It is true that until the end of life the believer remains, according to Luther, in need of pardon. But the believer is also called to an incessant combat against the flesh, and relative progress in this area is not excluded.

Spirituality and Ethics

In the face of misunderstandings, Luther did not cease proclaiming that "faith in Christ does not free us from works but from the opinion that we have about them" (WA 7, 70, 14).[25] Since salvation is a free gift, the action of the Christian will be under the sole sign of gratitude toward God and of obedience to his will. One can speak in this regard of the inspiration of works. The object of works is the needs of the neighbor. "Every work which has not as its sole end to serve another . . . is not a good or Christian work" (WA 7, 37, 18-20). The Christian has no further need to be preoccupied with self, even with one's own proper salvation. The Christian is now totally at the disposal of the neighbor.

Accepted by God in spite of the permanance of sin and, therefore, of the imperfection of their works, Christians know a double liberty. On the one hand, they are free to do the most humble works that God expects of them in concrete situations where they find themselves and which touch the needs of the neighbor. They no longer run after particularly religious works. On the other hand, they are free from the obsession of perfection. As pardoned sinners, they dare to commit themselves in spite of their weaknesses and their failures.

Accepted and loved by God, drawn by the Holy Spirit, Christians manifest in their lives the love from which they live. The good tree bears good fruit. "This is what springs forth from faith, love and joy in God and the love of a free existence, spontaneous, joyful, which devotes itself freely to the service of the neighbor" (WA 7, 36, 3-4). Along Augustinian lines, Luther had frequently insisted on the spontaneity and the liberty of the new life and of love. Insofar as they are "new," Christians have no need of a law that constrains them. They accomplish of themselves good works that are imposed on them. Lutheran spirituality is opposed to legalism and to casuistry.

A particular problem comes up with regard to the interpretation of the Sermon on the Mount. How can the needs of civil and family life be reconciled? Luther rejected the monastic option on one side and that of the Anabaptists on the other. According to the first, only the elite (the monks) could live according to the Sermon on the Mount. The common people would have to content themselves with the Decalogue. The Anabaptists, on the other hand, pleaded for an integral application of the Sermon on the Mount and advocated Christian abstention from civil functions and from war. According to Luther, the Sermon on the Mount should be applied to all Christians. It should guide them, for example, to an interior distance with regard to property, even if they ought to use it on the level of their careers and family. In the same way, the individual Christian ought to practice nonviolence. But love for one's neighbors ought, when the occasion occurs, to draw the Christian to take up arms to protect them. In fact, one could ask if the radicalism of the Sermon on the Mount was properly perceived by Lutheran Christians, so often overwhelmed by their insertion, pure and simple, in the existing order.

God the Judge and Redeemer: History at the End of Time

Believers know that God the judge and redeemer is at work in history. He imposes his reign against that of Satan. But this action of God is still hidden, in particular in the weakness of Christ and of his word. Christians wait, then, with patience for the revelation of his glory at the end of time.[26] While waiting, they notice with fear and confidence the present action and the coming of God. Luther had excluded the Origenist idea of a universal redemption. Rather, he maintained the affirmation that there would be a judgment according to works. He did not cease putting his contemporaries on guard against infidelity and disobedience to the commands of God.

As A. Peters has underlined, "fear before a jealous and holy God remains a decisive theme in Lutheran piety."[27] The explanation of the Ten Commandments in the *Little Catechism* ends thus: "God threatens with punishments all those who transgress His commandments: that is why we ought to fear His anger and do nothing contrary to His laws."

But fear is not terror, because it is bound to confidence in the Father, who "promises His grace and every kind of good to those who observe His commandments; that is why we ought to love Him, entrust ourselves to Him and do with a good heart that which He commands us" (ibid.).

God fights for his honor at every moment, opposing not only those who attack the gospel but also those who destroy creation or natural bonds, such as that of marriage. But the decisive intervention of the judge and of the redeemer will take place at the last judgment and by the events at the end of time. Faith awaits these events with fear and with confidence. To suppress the last horizon would be to suppress God himself. "Negatio enim futurae vitae tollit simpliciter Deum" (WA 43, 363, 21).

Notes

1. The scholarly edition of the works of Luther, called the Weimar edition (1883ff.), contains at this writing 100 volumes. It is cited under the sign WA (Weimarer Ausgabe). The translation is taken from *Luther's Works* (55 vols.; St. Louis, MO: Fortress, 1955ff.). The *Small Catechism* that is cited frequently here is found in WA 30, I, 239–339.

The subject of our study is based on the following works: Werner Elert, *Morphologie des Luthertums* (2 vols.; Munich: Beck, 1931 [Eng. trans., *The Structure of Lutheranism:*

The Theology and Philosophy of Life of Lutheranism, 16th and 17th Centuries (St. Louis, MO: Concordia, 1974)]); Paul Althaus, *Die Theologie Martin Luthers* (Gütersloh: Mohn, 1962 [Eng. trans., *The Theology of Martin Luther* (Philadelphia: Fortress, 1966)]); idem, *Die Ethik Martin Luthers* (Gütersloh: Mohn, 1965 [Eng. trans. by Robert C. Schultz, *The Ethics of Martin Luther* (Philadelphia: Fortress, 1972)]). Louis Bouyer, "La spiritualité protestante et anglicane," in *Histoire de la spiritualité chrétienne* (Paris: Plon, 1965) 3:81ff.; Jared Wicks, *Man Yearning for Grace* (Wiesbaden: F. Steiner, 1968); idem, "Luther" in *Dict. Sp.* 9, cols. 1206–43; idem, *Luther and His Spiritual Legacy* (Wilmington, DE: Michael Glazier, 1983); Peter Manns and Harding Meyer, eds., *Luther's Ecumenical Significance* (Philadelphia: Fortress, 1982); Marc Lienhard, *Luther, témoin de Jésus-Christ* (Paris: Cerf, 1973 [Eng. trans., *Luther, Witness to Jesus Christ: Stages and Themes of the Reformer's Christology* (Minneapolis, MN: Augsburg, 1982)]); idem, *Martin Luther, Un temps, une vie, un message* (Paris: Centurion; Geneva: Labor et Fides, 1983); Helmar Junghans, ed., *Martin Luther 1526–1546: Leben, Lehre und Schriften* (2 vols.; Berlin: Evangelische Verlagsanstalt; Göttingen: Vandenhoeck & Ruprecht, 1983); Albrecht Peters, "Die Spiritualität der lutherischen Reformation," in *Lutherische Kirche in der Welt: Jahrbuch des Martin Luther-Bundes* 31 (Erlangen: Martin Luther Verlag, 1984) 18–41.

2. See on this subject the different biographies of Luther, such as Roland H. Bainton, *Here I Stand* (New York: Abingdon, 1950); Martin Brecht, *Martin Luther: Sein Weg zur Reformation 1483–1521* (Stuttgart: Calwer, 1981); Walter V. Loewenich, *Martin Luther: Der Mann und das Werk* (Munich: List, 1982; Minneapolis, MN: Augsburg, 1983); Marc Lienhard, *Martin Luther.*

3. One should consult here the work of Leif Grane: *Contra Gabrielem: Luthers Auseinandersetzung mit Gabriel Biel in der Disputatio Contra Scholasticam Theologiam 1517* (Acta Theologica Danica 4; Gylgendal, 1962); idem, *Modus loquendi theologicus: Luthers Kampf um die Erneuerung der Theologie (1515–1518)* (Leiden: Brill, 1975); Karl Heinz Zur Muhlen, *Nos extra nos: Luthers Theologie zwischen Mystik und Scholastik* (Tübingen: Mohr-Siebeck, 1972).

4. Wilhelm Borth, *Die Luthersache (causa Lutheri), 1517–1524: Die Anfänge der Reformation als Frage von Politik und Recht* (Lubeck: Matthiesen, 1970); Daniel Olivier, *Le procès Luther 1517–1521* (Paris: Fayard, 1971 [Eng. trans., *The Trial of Luther* (St. Louis, MO: Concordia, 1978)]); Scott H. Hendrix, *Luther and the Papacy* (Philadelphia: Fortress, 1981).

5. Besides the works of Paul Althaus and of Marc Lienhard (see n. 1), see Gerhard Ebeling, *Luther: Einführung in sein Denken* (Tübingen: Mohr-Siebeck, 1964 [Eng. trans., *Luther: An Introduction to His Thought* (Philadelphia: Fortress, 1970)]); Daniel Olivier, *La foi de Luther: La cause de l'Evangile dans l'Eglise* (Paris: Beauchesne, 1978 [Eng. trans. by John Tonkin, *Luther's Faith: The Cause of the Gospel in the Church* (St. Louis, MO: Concordia, 1982)]); Otto Hermann Pesch, *Hinführung zu Luther* (Mainz: Grünewald, 1982).

6. Bouyer, "La spiritualité," 107.

7. Wilhelm Walther, *Luthers Deutsche Bibel* (Berlin: E. S. Mittler and Son, 1917); Heinz Blum, *Martin Luther–Creative Translator* (St. Louis, MO: Concordia, 1965); Bernhard Lohse, "Die Aktualisierung der christlichen Botschaft in Luthers Bibelübersetzung," *Luther* 51 (1980) 9–25.

8. Emmanuel Hirsch, "Luthers Predigtweise," *Luther* 25 (1954) 1–23; Alfred Niebergall, "Die Geschichte der christlichen Predigt," in *Leiturgia: Handbuch des evangelischen*

Gottesdienstes (Kassel: Stauda, 1952–) 2:257–75.

9. Karin Bornkamm, "Das Verständnis christlicher Unterweisung in den Katechismen von Erasmus und Luther," *Zeitschrift für Theologie und Kirche* 65 (1968) 204–30; Albrecht Peters, "Die Theologie der Katechismen Luthers anhand der Zuordnung ihrer Hauptstücke," *Lutherjahrbuch* 43 (1976) 7–35; Gerald Strauss, *Luther's House of Learning: Indoctrination of the Young in the German Reformation* (Baltimore, MD: Johns Hopkins University Press, 1978).

10. To understand the liturgy for Luther, see Vilmos Vajta, *Die Theologie des Gottesdienstes bei Luther* (3rd ed.; Göttingen: Vandenhoeck & Ruprecht, 1959). For Luther's conception of the sacraments, see Wolfgang Schwab, *Entwicklung und Gestalt der Sakramentstheologie bei Martin Luther* (Frankfurt and Bern: Lang, 1977); Frieder Schulz, "Der Gottesdienst bei Luther" in *Martin Luther 1526–1546,* ed. H. Junghans, 1:297–302, 2:811–825.

11. Lorenz Gronvik, *Die Taufe in der Theologie Martin Luthers* (Acta Academica Aboensis; Åbo, 1968).

12. Hans Bernhard Meyer, *Luther und die Messe* (Paderborn: Bonifacius, 1965); Albrecht Peters, *Realpräsenz* (Berlin: Lutherisches Verlagshaus, 1960); Marc Lienhard, *Luther, Witness to Jesus Christ,* 195–251.

13. Leonhard Fendt, "Luthers Reformation der Beichte," *Luther* 24 (1953) 121–37; Laurentius Klein, *Evangelisch-lutherische Beichte: Lehre und Praxis* (Paderborn: Bonifacius, 1961).

14. Christhard Mahrenholz, *Luther und die Kirchenmusik* (Kassel: Barenreiter, 1937); Marc Lienhard, "Les cantiques de Luther et leur témoignage christologique," *Positions luthériennes* 20 (1972) 235–49; Patrice Veit, "Martin Luther, chantre de la Réforme. Sa conception de la musique et du chant d'église," *Positions luthériennes* 30 (1982) 47–66. For a study of religious sensitivity, see P. Veit, "Le cantique luthérien et ses prolongements jusqu'à l'époque de J. S. Bach (XVIe–XVIIe siècles)," in *Bulletin de la Soc. d'Hist. du Prot. français* (1983) 23–46; Markus Jenny, "Luthers Gesangbuch" in *Martin Luther 1526–1546,* ed. H. Junghans, 1:303–22, 2:825–32.

15. Margarete Stirm, *Die Bilderfrage in der Reformation* (Gütersloh: Mohn, 1977); Carl C. Christenson, *Art and the Reformation in Germany* (Athens, OH: Ohio University Press, 1979).

16. Ingetraut Ludolphy, "Luther als Beter," *Luther* 33 (1962) 128–41; Horst Beintker, "Zu Luthers Verständnis vom geistlichen Leben des Christen im Gebet," *Lutherjahrbuch* 31 (1964) 47–68; Jean-Paul Cazes, "Martin Luther Commentateur du Notre Père, Le Commentaire de 1519," *Positions luthériennes* 28 (1980) 97–116.

17. Martin Nicol, *Meditation bei Luther* (Göttingen: Vandenhoeck & Ruprecht, 1984).

18. Paul Althaus, *The Theology of Martin Luther,* 254–78; Marc Lienhard, "La communion des saints," *Positions luthériennes* 30 (1982) 119–35; Vilmos Vajta, "The Church as Spiritual-Sacramental Communion with Christ and His Saints in the Theology of Luther," in *Luther's Ecumenical Significance,* ed. P. Manns and H. Meyer, 111–21.

19. In the same sense, see WA 28, 150, 2ff.; WA 38, 362, 32.

20. Paul Althaus, Sr., *Forschungen zur evangelischen Gebetsliteratur* (Gütersloh: Bertelsmann, 1927) 1–142 (reprint with additions, Hildesheim, 1966); Frieder Schulz, "Gebetbücher III: Reformations- und Neuzeit," in *Theologische Realenzyklopädie* (Berlin and New York: de Gruyter, 1984) 12:109–19.

21. Werner Elert, *Morphologie des Luthertums;* see esp. "Erdverbundenheit" (pp. 393–406) and "Kreuz und Jammertal" (pp. 407–18).

22. Paul Althaus, *The Theology of Martin Luther.*

23. Heiko A. Oberman, *Luther, Mensch zwischen Gott und Teufel* (Berlin: Severin & Siedler, 1982).

24. Otto Hermann Pesch, *Hinführung zu Luther,* 189–202.

25. Paul Althaus, *Die Ethik Martin Luthers.*

26. Albrecht Peters, *Glaube und Werk: Luthers Rechtfertigungslehre im Lichte der Heiligen Schrift* (2nd ed.; Berlin: Lutherisches Verlagshaus, 1967); idem, "Die Spiritualität der lutherischen Reformation," 29–31; Ilrich Asendorf, *Eschatologie bei Luther* (Göttingen: Vandenhoeck & Ruprecht, 1967).

27. Peters, "Die Spiritualität," 30.

13

The Spirituality of Zwingli and Bullinger in the Reformation of Zurich

FRITZ BÜSSER

THE REFORMATION IN GENERAL cannot be equated simply with Luther, and Reformed Protestantism does not mean "Calvinism" only. As a historical process and in its effects it was much more complex. With regard to its historical classification it is not an isolated epoch, but rather must be seen in connection with the late Middle Ages and with the Renaissance. The Reformation itself was a complex of many theological and ecclesial factors. At least as important as these are the political, societal, economic, and cultural influences, not to mention the varied personalities who determined the course and character of the Reformation.

The Zurich reformation was equally complex. This is particularly the case with Huldrych Zwingli (1 January 1484–11 October 1531). Just twelve years were granted Zwingli for his activity in Zurich, yet the brief time sufficed at least to lay the foundation for a reform of the church with its own distinctive stamp (and likewise its own spirituality), which set it apart from that of Luther and Calvin. This reformation was continued and achieved worldwide significance under the leadership of Heinrich Bullinger (4 July 1504–17 September 1575). For more than forty years Bullinger was not only "chief pastor at the Grossmuenster" and "wise leader of the church in Zurich" but also "counselor of all Reformed churches" and "paternal patron and protector" of countless evangelical Protestants. His imposing theological labors and his enormous correspondence, which extended throughout Europe, were at least equal to if not more far-reaching than those of Calvin.

Not the fact of spirituality, but rather the idea of it, is relatively recent in Protestantism. Even today in German-speaking areas there is still no satisfactory definition of spirituality in theological and church lexicons. Therefore I begin with the definition given in the (secular) *Brockhaus Encyclopedia*. There, "spirituality" is understood as "the completed work of the Spirit of God in cooperation with human beings," but "spirituality" is then reformulated in somewhat more detailed terms as "personal appropriation of the message of salvation." The Brockhaus article continues:

> Through such an unfolding spiritual life human beings enter into an ever deepening and maturing personal relationship with God in Christ which shows itself not only in prayer and worship, but also in service to the church and to others. With the development of such attitudes, spirituality also can at times transform even secular vocations. At present it seems a new form of spirituality is developing. It is characterized by a return to the sources and by a growing openness for the tasks of the world arising from a deepened inner sensitivity.[1]

This definition has great merit in that, to a great extent, it matches what can be said about spirituality in the Zurich reform. Zwingli and Bullinger understood their work from the very beginning as a return to the original form of the church, a renewal of the church. Connected with this process—in contrast to Luther, but not to Calvin—was the renewal of society as well. This can be explained in that their reform had been sparked not by the spiritual anguish of a monk struggling with his salvation but rather by the concerns of pastors who knew themselves to be responsible for their communities, in which church community and political community coincided. Zurich understood itself as a *respublica christiana*. The Zurich reformation encompassed both spiritual and secular realms from the very beginning, since it applied not only to liturgy and worship in the narrow sense but also to the problem of the individual's service to the community in the exercise of his or her calling.

Nevertheless, the spiritual aspect remains more important. The reformers of Zurich understood their work always as the work of the Holy Spirit. Even if today spirituality in Protestantism is being discovered for the first time[2]—and in this connection the lack of pneumatology is lamented (most emphatically by Hendrik Berkhof in his "theology of the Holy Spirit")[3]—it should have been better known. There never was such a deficiency of pneumatology in Zurich! On the contrary, Luther had identified Zwingli and the Zurich reformers with the so-called Schwärmer, Baptists, followers of Carlstadt, Schwenckfeldians, and others; for him they were "spiritualists." Luther's characterization, which grew out of the conflict over the Lord's Supper, is not correct in this exclusive form; yet as a designation it is not wholly off the mark. Zwingli and Bullinger's theology has an explicit pneumatological content. In considering this, one should recall the work of

A. E. Burckhardt and Fritz Schmidt-Clausing, who represented Zwingli expressly as a pneumatologue and not as a spiritualist. Gottfried W. Locher also asserts: "Spiritualism has been discussed often in Zwingli's thought. . . . We prefer to speak of the *pneumatological* character of Zwingli's theology."[4] The same can be said of Bullinger; indeed, one need only consider the basic fact that, for Zwingli's follower, the central doctrine of the covenant is full of pneumatology.[5]

Roots and Sources

What were the *roots* and *sources* of the spirituality in the Zurich reformation? The *Second Helvetic Confession*, which, next to the *Heidelberg Catechism*, is the most important confession of Reformed Protestantism, has the title: "Confession and simple clarification of the orthodox faith and of the general teaching of the pure Christian religion by the servants of the Church of Christ in the Swiss Confederation . . . , unanimously published with the intention to convince all believers that they are in unity with the old true church, that they spread no new and false teachings and therefore have nothing in common with various sects or false doctrines." It thus decisively underlines (in 1566) that the Zurich Reformed church understood itself as a member of the one holy universal Christian church. It sought no break with the Western Christian tradition but rather a radical return to the sources, to the real wealth of the catholic church and its tradition.

The first chapter of the *Confession* shows immediately where the true roots and sources of the Zurich reformation lie, and with it also its spirituality: *only* in the Sacred Scriptures, in the word of God. The church and spirituality exist only from the hearing of the word of God. In this sense especially, Zwingli describes the existence of the church by the parable of the Good Shepherd (John 10). There Christ teaches "that the sheep hear the voice of the shepherd, if he is a shepherd, and that they follow him. . . . Finally, only that church cannot lapse and err which hears the voice only of its shepherd, God; for only his voice is from God" (*Commentarius de vera et falsa religione* [Z III 258f.; LW III III 372]).[6] Already in the *Sixty-seven Articles* Zwingli had stressed his adherence to the traditional concept of the church as the body of Christ. On Christ as salvation and head depend all believers.

> First, that all who live in the Head are His members and children of God. And this is the Church or fellowship of the saints, the bride of Christ, *ecclesia catholica*. Secondly, that, just as the members of a physical body can do nothing without the guidance of the head, so now in the body of Christ no one can do anything without Christ, its head. (Z I 459, art. 8, 9; Cochrane, 37)

This understanding of church was never merely a theoretical matter in the Zurich reform. It showed itself much more in practice and in turn also determined practice. Zwingli and Bullinger understood themselves first and foremost as prophets, that is, shepherds, preachers. As such, they had the unimaginably difficult task of making the written biblical word of God the existentially appropriate word of God verbally proclaimed, attuned to time and audience. Bullinger expressed this belief in a classical formulation:

> For the Lord himself has said in the gospel, "It is not you who speak, but the Spirit of my Father speaking through you"; therefore "he who hears you hears me and he who rejects me rejects him who sent me" (Matt 10:20; Luke 10:16; John 13:20). *The preaching of the Word of God is the Word of God.* Wherefore when this Word of God is now preached in the church by preachers lawfully called, we believe that the very Word of God is proclaimed, and received by the faithful. (CH II, chap. 1; Cochrane 224f.)

As prophets, Zwingli and Bullinger were well aware that they could not do this work without the action of the Holy Spirit. On the one hand, it gave them courage, confidence, and consolation. Already in 1522, Zwingli was so convinced "of the clarity and certainty or infallibility of the Word of God" (Z I 338–84) that he could write this summary:

> Do you feel that the Word of God is renewing you, that God begins to be dearer to you than before when you harkened to human teachings? Then be sure that God has brought this about in you. Do you feel that it makes you certain of the Grace of God and of eternal salvation? Then that comes from God. Do you feel that it makes you small and insignificant, whereas God is great in you? Then that is a work of God. Do you feel that the fear of God begins to make you more happy than sad? Then that is a certain work of the Word and Spirit of God. May God give us these feelings. Amen. (Z I 384)

On the other hand, the prophetic task meant a powerful obligation. Zwingli and Bullinger took the proclamation of the word of God so seriously that the study of the Bible and the proclamation of the gospel had absolute priority in their lives. *Sola scriptura*—this principle led immediately to concrete developments and results in Zurich. Already in 1525, the Prophezei, the first theological seminary of Reformed Protestantism, was founded in Zurich. Under its auspices, not only Zwingli and Bullinger but also other important theologians (Conrad Pellikan, Theodore Bibliander, Rudolph Gwalther, Peter Martyr Vermigli) edited a plethora of commentaries on the Old and New Testaments of the highest quality, which were distributed all over Europe. Above all, out of the exegetical work of the Prophezei arose the Zurich translation of the Bible, which not only was completed before that of Luther but by comparison achieved its own rank. According to expert judgment, "Luther translated the Bible into German as a skilled poet. Zwingli and the Zürich School translated the Bible as knowledgeable philologists."[7]

Out of this intensive work on the Bible necessarily arose a deeply biblical theology in the basic systematic works of the Zurich reformers: Zwingli's *Auslegen und Gründe der Schlussreden* (*Exposition and Bases of the Conclusions or Articles*, 1523) and *Commentarius de vera et falsa religione* (*Commentary on True and False Religion*, 1525), Bullinger's *Sermonum decades quinque* (1552), published in England as *Fiftie godlie and learned Sermons, divided into five Decades* (1577) and the *Confessio Helvetica posterior* (*A Confession of Faith* or *The Second Helvetic Confession*, 1566).[8]

That the Scriptures were the word of God demonstrates the roots and sources of Reformed spirituality in yet another easily connected aspect. Zwingli and Bullinger were always aware that no human being could control God's Spirit. There are few biblical verses more frequently quoted by Zwingli than John 3:8, "The wind blows where it wills," and John 6:44, "No man can come to me unless he is drawn by the Father who sent me." As a pneumatologist, he, no less than Bullinger, drew two conclusions from this fact. The first was that, contrary to the teaching of Luther, the Spirit of God is bound neither to the Bible nor to the sacraments: "For in this way the liberty of the divine Spirit which distributes itself to individuals as it will, that is, to whom it will, when it will, where it will, would be bound" (Z III 761.4f.; LW III 183). And: "It is clear, then, that we are rendered faithful only by that word which the heavenly Father proclaims in our hearts, by which also he illumines us so that we understand, and draws us so that we follow" (Z III 752.17-19; LW III 376).

In the Zurich reform another consequence arose out of their teaching that the Spirit of God was not at the disposal of just anyone. This Spirit is also not bound to the word of the Bible and to "salvation history." As was emphasized first by Zwingli and to a lesser extent by Bullinger—but above all by Theodore Bibliander—there is also "salvation of elected heathens." "Thus the law of nature, too, comes solely from God and is nothing other than the pure Spirit of God, who inwardly draws and illumines" (Z II 327.5-7; *Writings, 1:265). Especially in his Fidei expositio,* dedicated to King Francis I of France, Zwingli wrote that some day in heaven the king will meet not only all God-fearing men and women of the Old and New Testaments but also, along with many of his royal ancestors, Hercules, Theseus, and Socrates. Indeed, Luther had completely misunderstood Zwingli on this point when he said that Zwingli teaches that a human being could come to the knowledge of God and could gain salvation through his own efforts. Zwingli said exactly the opposite. With regard to the heathens, his doctrine of the elected heathens shows that the Spirit of God is free to act. There was an incipient universalism in the theology of the Zurich reformation, and there was an openness to other world religions, which again appeared during the Enlightenment and for the first time was taken up by the major churches in the twentieth century.

The Center of Spirituality: Christ

What was the practice of spirituality in Reformed Zurich? From the previous description arises necessarily the most important difference in contrast to the Middle Ages: whereas the center of the worship of God had been the Mass, from 1519 on it was preaching. Zwingli himself probably preached every day. Bullinger certainly preached every Sunday for over forty years and probably two or three times each week. In 1532, the "Prediger- und Synodalordnung" determined that every pastor had to preach twice on Sundays and once during the week and also on the feasts of the apostles. Since the Zurich reformers wanted their listeners to be completely familiar with the entire Bible, they, in contrast to authorities in Rome and Wittenberg, did not follow the medieval arrangement of set texts, but rather followed the practice of the church fathers in a continuous exposition of individual books of the Bible. In their preaching they expounded successively on practically all the books of the Old and New Testaments—a practice that would become typical of all of Reformed Protestantism. Regrettably, we know no more of Zwingli than the order of the texts on which he preached in a well thought-out arrangement. On the other hand, we have hundreds of published and unpublished sermons by Bullinger, thousands of preaching ideas—a source material not put on record until recently.[9]

It followed from *sola scriptura* that the spirituality of reformed Zurich should be absolutely *solus Christus*. Nevertheless, more than in any place and at any time, real Christian spirituality developed in Zurich—spirituality in the sense of the Brockhaus definition, that is, a "personal appropriation of the message of salvation" as "an ever deepening and maturing personal relationship with God in Christ." Belief in God's gracious actions in the crucified and risen one resulted in imitation based on faith, through active love of God and neighbor. The hope in the coming of God's kingdom was actually the content of the Reformed gospel in Zurich. This is not difficult to prove. *Solus Christus* is demonstrated by the biblical citations Zwingli and Bullinger placed on the title pages of all their published works. For Zwingli it was Matt 11:38: "Come to me, all whose work is hard, whose load is heavy; and I will give you relief." For Bullinger it was Matt 17:5: "This is my Son, my Beloved, on whom my favour rests; listen to him."[10]

The content of the preaching in any case permits a more exact definition. Thus, Zwingli writes at the beginning of the *Conclusions:* "The sum of the Gospel is that our Lord Jesus Christ, the true Son of God, has made known to us the will of his heavenly Father, and by his innocence has redeemed us from death and reconciled us unto God" (Z I 458.2).[11] Zwingli provides an accompanying explanation:

> With this statement, I intended to show that Christ has not only come to save us but also to teach us the true love of God and the works which God demands of us. . . . All the evangelists' writings are full of this; the loveliest expressions, however, concerning Christian conduct toward the neighbor are all contained compactly in Mt. 5, 6 and 7; those concerning the adoration of God, Jn. 5 and 6 and thereafter in the teaching which Christ delivered after the Supper, beginning with Chapter 14. (Z II 28f.; *Writings,* 1:15)

This completely agrees with Zwingli's statement in his influential sermon "The Shepherd" at the Second Zurich Disputation of October 1523.

> Therefore the shepherd is to bring his charges to an understanding of their infirmity. If they understand that and perceive that they cannot be saved out of their power, then he should point them to the grace of God so they let themselves trust fully in it. For God has given us for a certain assurance of his grace his only begotten son, Jesus Christ our Lord, through whom we have forever a certain entry to God (cf. Rom 5:2). If they, who were previously of the flesh and damnation, have believed the salvation and assurance of the grace of God and have now become God's, then they are also now obligated henceforth to live according to the will of God from now on—for they are a new creation. (Z III 22; *Writings,* 2:92)

As with Zwingli, Christ is also the core of Bullinger's preaching. His Christology is found already in seminal form in an incomparable formulation in the *Ratio Studiorum* of 1527 or 1528:

> I read that Christ was affixed to the cross; I believe that Christ is the satisfaction for all believers. I read that Christ raised up the dead, etc.; I teach that Christ alone should be invoked in all dangers. I read that Christ spurned worldly things, that he taught innocence and charity; I conclude therefore that true worship of God consists in purity of life, in innocence and charity and not at all in external sacrifices, feasts, vesture, etc.

In its full form Bullinger's teaching is revealed in his commentaries, sermons, and confessions. In the commentaries this is shown most emphatically in the exposition of the four Gospels. As Bullinger announces in the corresponding dedicatory prefaces, for example, Matthew wanted to show and does show, "that the Lord Jesus Christ did not burden his Church, and what are the enumerated sources of true piety" (1542).[12] John treats of "the true justification of the Christian, and the true and just conception of good works" (1543). Mark deals with "Jesus Christ the Great High Priest and King of his faithful people, who reigns in the Church of the saints" (1545). And finally, Luke's thesis is "that God the Father gave to his church in his only begotten Son and Our Lord Jesus Christ all things which pertain to the life and salvation of humans, so that it is not necessary to seek them from any other source" (1546).

That the sermons basically follow the same direction is impressively demonstrated in the *Decades*, those fifty didactic sermons (1549–1551) that are to be considered equally valuable counterparts to Calvin's *Institutio* and which have contributed decisively to the expansion of the wealth of Reformed thought throughout Europe. Here Bullinger places Christology in the obvious core of his teaching on God; at the same time, he brings it into the closest connection with pneumatology. Bullinger treats first of the triune God, of God, creation, providence, predestination (sermons 33 and 34). Then follow the expositions on Christ as sole mediator (35), the Son of God (36), Christ as king and priest (37), and then the power and operation of the Holy Spirit (38). Another aspect typical of Bullinger that differentiates him from Zwingli is stressed by article 10 of the *Second Helvetic Confession*, concerning "the Predestination of God and the Election of the Saints." Here Christ appears as the means but also as the goal of election: "We are elected or predestinated in Christ," and "the saints are chosen in Christ by God for a definite purpose. . . . 'He chose us in him for adoption that we should be holy and blameless before him in love' (Eph 1:4)" (Cochrane, 240). [13] Without entangling himself, like Calvin, in the abyss of predestination, Bullinger called to attention the mystery, ultimately the otherness, of God. He quoted Matt 11:28, with a clear inclination to universal salvation: "Come to me all who are weary and overburdened, and I will give you rest" (Zwingli's motto); and John 3:16: "God loved the world so much that he gave his only Son, that everyone who has faith in him may not die but have eternal life"; and Matt 18:14: "In the same way, it is not your heavenly Father's will that one of these little ones should be lost"; and finally Phil 2:12: "So you too, my friends, must be obedient, as always; even more, now that I am away, than when I was with you. You must work out your own salvation in fear and trembling" (CH II, chap. 10; Cochrane, 240–42).

Spirituality in Prayer and Liturgy

Preaching formed the focal point but not the whole of the service of God. It was part of a comprehensive liturgy that was likewise in its organization a liturgy reformed according to the New Testament. This was far richer than that which was produced and accepted in general. According to the preface to the *Church Order* of 1535, the following basically applies: "The Zurich church follows the usages of the primitive church."[14] In fact, this *Church Order* contained detailed liturgies for the preaching service on Sunday and workdays, for the sacraments (baptism and the Lord's Supper), marriage, and burial. These had been drafted by Zwingli and later revised by Bullinger (Z IV 695–717). Seen in their entirety these conformed to the Bible, but Zwingli and Bullinger also retained many texts and prayers from the traditional liturgy. Thus, not only the three traditional parts of the catechism—the Our Father (with the Hail Mary), the Decalogue, and the Apostles' Creed—belonged to the preaching service, but also the prayers of intercessions, the public confession, the prayer for the church, and the *Commemoratio pro defunctis* (Remembrance of the Dead).

Even more clearly than in the *Order* for the preaching service of God, the liturgy of the Lord's Supper shows the dual dependence on Scripture and early Christian traditions. Indeed, the number of celebrations of the Lord's Supper was reduced drastically in the Zurich reform to Christmas, Easter, Pentecost, and the commemoration of the dedication of the church. According to Zwingli's own words, the Supper was held in Zurich:

> I preserve entire in the supper the things that ought to have been preserved in the Mass, namely, prayers, praise, confession of faith, communion of the Church or the believers, and the spiritual and sacramental eating of the body of Christ, while, on the other hand we omit all those things which are not of Christ's institution, to wit, "We offer efficaciously for the living and the dead": "We offer for the remission of sins," and the other things that the Papists assert not less impiously than ignorantly.[15]

The decisive difference from the Roman Mass was that the Zurich reformers replaced transubstantiation by asserting that the community of believers was transformed into the body of Christ through the work of the Holy Spirit. The Lord's Supper was a service of remembrance, thankfulness, and joy, but above all a binding symbol and a necessary sign of the community of believers.

Solus Christus—that is the content of the preaching in Zurich, especially during the Service of God. Both preaching and the Service of God hinge on the recognition of human sinfulness, God's grace in Christ, and its positive effect upon the Christian life. This is not the place to establish that Zwingli and Bullinger have given a decisive impulse to the spirituality of Reformed Protestantism with these three elements. Before the secular—that is, political—consequences of this spirituality are treated below, a few special factors need to be stressed in order to enable us to make the transition to a consideration of certain elements in the spiritual sphere. First, let us

21. *Portrait Medallion of Huldrych Zwingli at 48.*

enumerate a few characteristics and themes of Zurich's Christocentric spirituality.

For Zwingli it is necessary above all to recall his idea of Christ as "leader and captain," as found, for example, in article 6 of the *Conclusions*. G. W. Locher has pointed out that this idea goes back to Scripture (Eph 6; Heb 12:2f.), on the one hand, and to Zwingli's experiences as a military chaplain, on the other.[16] Zwingli has before his eyes the captain who not merely commands his troops but who leads them even unto death. Christ is "Our Captain," who stands for obedience, struggle, sacrifice, and, under certain circumstances, death, but also consolation through the internal solace of the Spirit who receives our faith. Supported by this faith, Zwingli was killed at Kappel.

Bullinger treats of the same thing when he comes to speak about the daily demands of true Christian existence—in particular when he talks about the temptations that assail Christians from all sides. Bullinger knew as well as Zwingli (and naturally Luther) that the cross belongs to the life of a Christian, but also that God always sends the power to bear it with all its burdens. This belief was impressively represented by Bullinger in two works that arose immediately from contemporary occurrences, but contained "eternal" truths and, in that regard, found an extraordinarily wide acceptance. In 1557, he released one hundred sermons on the Apocalypse, *the* great book of comfort of the Christian church, and dedicated these to all who would be persecuted in Europe for the sake of the faith.[17] In the wake of the St. Bartholomew's Day massacre, he wrote *On the Severe Persecution of the Christian Church*, which not only treated the reasons for the persecution and called for patience and perseverance but also attempted to represent the whole of church history as a history of general persecution.[18]

This indicates that a series of pastoral writings belongs to the characterization of the spirituality of the Zurich reform. For Zwingli, pedagogical interests take precedence. Foremost is the educational work *Quo pacto ingenui adolescentes formandi sint.*[19] As a gifted teacher, the reformer writes to his stepson in the dedication:

> The first part of these instructions treats of the lessons in godliness and of the tender disposition of the noble Christian; the second concerns self-discipline, and the third is about relations with one's neighbors. My intention is not to begin from the cradle, also not from the first lesson; no, I hold for the age in which reason is present, when he can swim without a life-jacket. You are now at that age. I hope you will read the instructions carefully and that you will conform your life to them in order to be able to be a living example for others. May Jesus reign! Amen! (Z V 431)

To the same area also belongs his pastoral theology: *Der Hirt* (*The Shepherd*),[20] the work entitled *Von dem Predigtamt* (*On the Preaching Office*),[21] even his *Plan über einen Feldzug*, in which, among other things, he also describes "How a Captain should be,"[22] and finally his three songs, the "Plague Song," a reworking of Psalm 69, and the "Song of Kappel."[23] These songs support indirectly the claim that Zwingli was *not* an opponent of church songs.

That Bullinger was a great spiritual advisor and as such contributed decisively to the spirituality of the reform in Zurich is demonstrated by his concept of preaching. This should follow the New Testament model of *docere, hortari, consolari* ("to teach, to exhort, and to console"). Next to the consoling works mentioned above, the same goal is served by the corresponding treatment in the *Decades* and in the *Second Helvetic Confession*, but above all in writings that were distributed far and wide by reason of their effectiveness: *Der christliche Ehestand* (*Christian Marriage*)[24] and *Bericht der Kranken* (a guide for those who care for the sick, in the style of the medieval "art of dying," *ars moriendi*).[25] For Bullinger, one also thinks of the numerous letters to rulers, friends, colleagues, and students, in which the Zurich spirituality found its most immediate and stirring expression.

Spirituality in Service to the World

Spirituality was in no way limited to cult and prayer in the Zurich reform. Preaching, liturgy, sacraments, public and private prayer—all formed the necessary core of Christian existence. For Zwingli and Bullinger, Christian existence required something more: the "personal appropriation of the message of salvation," the "ever deepening and maturing personal relation to God in Christ" extended into everyday life. For the Zurich reformation, service to the church and to neighbor achieved its goal in the realm of public life, in actions in the political and social spheres. Expressed in modern terms, spirituality in the Zurich reformation is really "secularization." Christendom becomes the world not in the sense of a process of Christianity's becoming worldly, but rather a Christianization of the world. It is the attempt to actualize God's will in the world.

This aspect of evangelical-Reformed spirituality clearly differed from that of Luther and is closely connected with the ecclesiology and pneumatology of Zwingli and Bullinger. For them, the church was always very real, precisely as a universal worldwide community of believers. As the body of Christ, the church was incarnated in individual church communities and thus as a universal church of all peoples. It is also not the place here to consider in more detail the theological, political, and social backgrounds and consequences of this view, although we should allude to them. On the one hand, the idea of *corpus christianum*, which went back to Constantine and

Augustine, survived in the Zurich reform. This means that the Zurich community was conceived as a *respublica christiana;* the Reformation was the crowning act of the communalization of the church. It brought about, according to R. C. Walton, the "completion of the institutionalization of the city magistracy's authority over all aspects of the external affairs of the church. In this sense the Reformation marks the end rather than the beginning of the process."[26] On the other hand, the Zurich model lived on and had an international impact. It influenced heavily the form of the English state church and influenced directly many political, social, and economic developments of the modern world.

Precisely here the question of the content of the secularized spirituality of the Zurich reformation must be posed with double urgency. As in the area of individual spirituality, it is here correct to infer that the Zurich reformers did not, like Luther, place law and gospel in opposition to each other; rather they understood them as being in each other. Or as H. R. Lavater has formulated it briefly in a commentary on Zwingli's letter to A. Blarer:

> Reformation is a political matter, a Christian state is the political form of a Christian community, a good Christian is a good citizen. In this the kingdom of Christ is not only something internal within the heart of the believer, but it is also something external because it commands that the world changes (Regnum Christi *etiam* externum). No area is excluded from the claims of the sovereignty of Christ! The word *etiam* means that the distinction between interior and exterior is finally abolished. There is only the concrete actualization of the kingdom of Christ.[27]

The idea of the state as Christian community is most clearly expounded in Zwingli's *Von göttlicher und menschlicher Gerechtigkeit (On Godly and Human Righteousness).*[28] Proceeding from the distinction between as well as the correlation of spirit and matter, soul and body, Zwingli discovers the tension between idea and reality. The ideal goal that Christians of all times seek to achieve again is the "divine justice," that is, God's sovereignty. This exhorts us to be perfect as is our heavenly father. Measured against this divine justice, expressed in the teachings of the Sermon on the Mount and according to the norms of the fulfillment of the love of God and neighbor, we are and remain sinners. We are, therefore, above all else, always in need of God's grace. Precisely because of our sinfulness, God in his mercy has given to us humans a human justice, that is, a civil order, administered by the civil authorities, who serve as "schoolmasters" and discipline and punish us by means of human laws. Measured against divine justice, this human justice is relative, scarcely worthy of being called justice at all. Nevertheless, it is necessary. First of all, it makes possible a communal life on all levels.

Because human justice is always imperfect, it is always open to improvement through the standards of divine justice.

Bullinger's ideas with regard to the identity of the ecclesial and civil communities proceeded from the same premises as Zwingli's but with far greater effect. Recent research on Bullinger most clearly proves that his theology—in the exegetical works, in the *Decades*, in the *Second Helvetic Confession*—sometimes explicitly, sometimes implicitly, always centers on the concept of the covenant. Therefore Bullinger is rightly known as the founder of Reformed "federal" theology (*Föderaltheologie*), that is, another Reformed tradition *not* begun by Calvin. What is especially interesting in this connection is that, as G. W. Locher has observed, this federal theology is filled with pneumatology. Federal theological and pneumatological claims run parallel to each other, so that we must recognize a certain identity of both. "The Spirit lives in the covenant; the covenant lives in the Spirit."[29]

It is evident that the concept of a single and eternal covenant made in Christ with humanity had not only individual but also social and ethical implications. Thus, in the *Decades* Bullinger describes a well-ordered type of Christian state:

> What is, I pray you, more to be delighted in, than the good platform of a well-ordered city, wherein there is (as one did say) the church well grounded; wherein God is rightly worshipped; and wherein the word of God in faith and charity is duly obeyed, so far forth as it pleaseth God to give the gift of grace; wherein also the magistrate doth defend good discipline and upright laws; wherein the citizens are obedient and at unity among themselves, having their assemblies for true religion and matters of justice; wherein they use to have honest meetings in the church, in the court, and places of common exercise; wherein they apply themselves to virtue and the study of learning, seeking an honest living by such sciences as man's life hath need of, by tillage, by merchandise, and other handy occupations; wherein children are honestly trained up, parents recompensed for their pains, the poor maintained of alms, and strangers harboured in their distress?[30]

It would be too much here to consider in detail how carefully Bullinger has outlined a comprehensive social ethic in his complete works—especially in the sermons of the Second and Third Decades. These sermons consider practically all problems of a political, social, and economic nature which concerned human beings then and continue to concern them now.

In conclusion, we stress the effectiveness demonstrated in the history of this typically Reformed spirituality which is open to the world. Without any doubt, Zwingli and Bullinger's secularized Christian faith not only created Reformed Switzerland, but had directly and indirectly a worldwide effect as Reformed Protestantism. Thus, "covenant" theology with its ethical implications not only found an echo in corresponding political ideas but also influenced decisively their actualization in the modern democratic and social constitutional states of the West. In an essay entitled "The Idea of Covenant and American Democracy," H. R. Niebuhr wrote about the meaning of the covenant idea: "The world has this fundamental moral structure of a covenant society and that what is possible and required in the political realm is the affirmation and reaffirmation of man's responsibility as a promise-maker, promise-keeper, covenanter in universal community."[31]

Notes

1. *Brockhaus Enzyklopädie* (20 vols.; 17th ed.; Wiesbaden: Brockhaus, 1973) 17:748.

2. *Breaking Barriers: Nairobi 1975: The Official Report of the Fifth Assembly of the WCC, Nairobi, Kenya, 23 November–10 December 1975*, ed. David M. Paton (Geneva: World Council of Churches, 1976); and *Nairobi to Vancouver, 1975–1983: A Report of the Central Committee to the Sixth Assembly of the World Council of Churches* (Geneva: World Council of Churches, 1983) 199ff.

3. H. Berkhof, *The Doctrine of the Holy Spirit* (Richmond, VA: John Knox, 1964).

4. A. E. Burckhardt, *Das Geistproblem bei Huldrych Zwingli* (Quellen und Abhandlungen zur Schweizerischen Reformationsgeschichte 9; Leipzig: M. Heinsius Nachfolger, 1932); F. Schmidt-Clausing, *Zwingli* (Berlin: de Gruyter, 1965); G. W. Locher, *Die Zwinglische Reformation im Rahmen der europäischen Kirchengeschichte*, 208; see also Locher, "Die Lehre vom Heiligen Geist in der Confessio Helvetica Posterior," in *Glauben und Bekennen: Vierhundert Jahre Confessio Helvetica Posterior*, ed. Joachim Staedtke (Zurich: Zwingli, 1966).

5. *Confessio et expositio simplex orthodoxae fidei ... qui sunt in Heluetia, Tiguri, Bernae, ...* (Tiguri: Christophorus Froschouerus, 1566); Microfiche EPBU-226. Modern English edition, "A Simple Confession and Exposition of the Orthodox Faith: The Second Helvetic Confession of 1566," in *Reformed Confessions of the 16th Century*, ed. Arthur C. Cochrane.

6. The following abbreviations of source materials are used in this article; for full citations, see the bibliography below. Z=*Huldreich Zwinglis samtliche Werke;* LW=*The Latin Works of Huldreich Zwingli;* Cochrane=*Reformed Confessions of the 16th Century;* CH II=*Second Helvetic Confession; Writings*=Zwingli, *Writings,* trans. E. J. Furcha and H. W. Pipkin. Microfiche EPBU=*Reformed Protestantism.*

7. Adolf Fluri, "Luthers Uebersetzung des neuen Testamentes und ihre Nachdrucke in Basel und Zürich," in *Schweizerisches Evangelisches Schulblatt* 37 (1922) 294: "Luther übertrug die Bibel ins Deutsch als sprachgewaltiger Dichter. Zwingli und die Zurcher übersetzten sie als sprachenkundige Philologen" (cited in Hans Rudolf Lavater, *Die Froschauer Bibel 1531–Das Buch der Zurcher Kirche* [Faksimile-edition of Die Zurcher Bibel von 1531; Zurich: Theologischer Verlag, 1983] 1386).

8. *Usslegen und grund der schlussreden oder articklen ... 1523.* (Z II, 1–457). Latin, *Opus articulorum sive conclusionum ... a L. Judae in Latinam versum ...* (Zurich: Christoph Froschauer, 1535; Microfiche EPBU-476, edition of 1544–45); English, *Huldrych Zwingli Writings,* vol. 1, *The Defense of the Reformed Faith,* trans. Edward J. Furcha (Allison Park, PA: Pickwick Publications, 1984). *De vera et falsa religione, Huldrychi Zuinglii Commentarius* (Z III, 590–912); English, *Commentary on True and*

False Religion, ed. Samuel Macauley Jackson and Clarence Nevin Heller (Durham, NC: Labyrinth Press, 1981). *Sermonum decades quinque, de potissimis Christianae religionis capitibus . . . authore Heinrycho Bullingero . . .* (Zurich: Christoph Froschauer, 1552; Microfiche EPBU-159); English, *The Decades of Henry Bullinger, Minister of the Church of Zürich,* trans. H. I.; ed. Thomas Harding for the Parker Society (Cambridge: University Press, 1949–52). *Confessio Helvetica posterior;* see n. 5.

9. Fritz Büsser, "Bullinger–der Prediger," in Fritz Büsser, *Würzeln der Reformation in Zürich,* 143–58; idem, "Bullinger, Heinrich," in *Theologische Realenzyklopädie,* 7:375ff.

10. Quotations according to *The New English Bible* (Cambridge: University Press, 1972).

11. "Summa des euangelions ist, das unser herr Christus Jhesus, warer gottes sun, uns den willen sines himmlischen vatters kundt gethon unnd mit siner unschuld vom tod erlost und gott versunt hat" (Cochrane, 36).

12. These dedicatory prefaces are found in the following works: *In sacrosanctum . . . Euangelium secundum Matthaeum, Commentariorum libri XII. per H. Bullingerum* (Zurich: Christoph Froschauer, 1542), fol. 2a: "Dominum Iesum Christum non onerasse Ecclesiam suam, & quae sint numerata illa uerae pietatis capita . . ."; *In divinum Iesu Christi . . . Euangelium secundum Ioannem, Commentariorum libri X. per H. Bullingerum* (Zurich: Christoph Froschauer, 1543), fol. 2a: "De uera hominis Christiani iustificatione, uera item & iusta bonorum operum ratione . . ."; *In sacrosanctum Euangelium . . . secundum Marcum, Commentariorum lib. VI. per H. Bullingerum* (Zurich: Christoph Froschauer, 1545), fol. 2a: "De Iesu Christo Pontifice Maximo & Rege fidelium summo, regnante in ecclesia sanctorum, . . ."; *In luculentum et sacrosanctum Euangelium . . . secundum Lucam, Commentariorum lib. IX. per H. Bullingerum* (Zurich: Christoph Froschauer, 1546), fol. 2a: "Deum patrem in filio suo unigenito domino nostro Iesu Christo omnia dedisse ecclesiae suae, quae ad vitam & salutem hominis pertinent, ita ut non sit necesse illa aliunde petere. . . ."

13. Peter Walser, *Die Prädestination bei Heinrich Bullinger im Zusammenhang mit seiner Gotteslehre* (Zurich: Zwingli-Verlag, 1957); J. Wayne Baker, *Heinrich Bullinger and the Covenant.*

14. Ludwig Lavater, *De ritibus et institutis ecclesiae Tigurinae* (Zurich: n.p., 1559).

15. *Christianae fidei a H. Zuinglio praedicatae brevis et clara expositio . . .* (1531), in *Huldrici Zuinglii opera,* ed. Melchior Schuler and J. Schulthess (Zurich: ex officina Schulthessiana, 1841) 4:74; LW II 286f.

16. G. W. Locher, "Christus unser Hauptmann," in *Zwingliana* (Zurich: Berichthaus, 1950) 9:121–38.

17. *In Apocalypsim Iesu Christi . . . Conciones centum: authore H. Bullingero* (Basel: Johannes Oporinus, 1557; Microfiche EPBU-196); English, *A hundred Sermons upon the Apocalips . . .* (London: John Day, 1561; Microfiche EPBU-201).

18. *Veruolgung. Von der schweren langwirigen veruolgung der Heiligen Christlichen Kirchen . . . durch H. Bullingern* (Zurich: Christoph Froschauer, 1573; Microfiche EPBU-248); Latin, *De persecutionibus ecclesiae Christianae, liber ab H. Bullingero . . . conscriptus . . .* (Zurich: Christoph Froschauer, 1573; Microfiche EPBU-249); English, *The tragedies of tyrantes. Exercised upon the church of God, from the birth of Christ unto this present yeere. 1572. Written by H. Bullinger, and now Englished* (London: William How, 1575; Microfiche EPBU-251).

19. *Quo pacto ingenui adolescentes formandi sint . . . H. Zuinglio autore . . .* (Basel: Johannes Bebelius, 1523; Z II 526–551); German, *Wie man die jugendt in guten sitten und christenlicher zucht uferziehen unnd leeren solle, ettliche kutze underwysung durch H. Zuinglin beschriben* (Zurich: Christoph Froschauer, 1526; Z V 427–447).

20. *Der Hirt*... (Zurich: Christoph Froschauer, 1524; Z III 1ff.); English, "The Shepherd" *Writings*, 2:77ff.

21. *Von dem Predig Ampt*... (Zurich: Christoph Froschauer, 1525; Z IV 369–433); English, "The Preaching Office" (*Writings*, 2:147ff.).

22. *Plan zu einem Feldzug*, 1524/25 (Z III, 579).

23. Markus Jenny, *Luther, Zwingli, Calvin in ihren Liedern* (Zurich: Theologischer Verlag, 1983).

24. *Der Christlich Ehestand... durch H. Bullingern beschriben* (Zurich: Christoph Froschauer, 1540; Microfiche EPBU-137); English, *The golden boke of christen matrimonye... set forthe in English by Theodore Basille*... (London: John Mayler, 1542; Microfiche EPBU-138).

25. *Bericht der krancken... Heinrychen Bullingers* (Zurich: Christoph Froschauer, 1535; Microfiche EPBU-126); Latin, *Quo pacto cum aegrotantibus ac morientibus agendum sit*... (Zurich: August Fries, 1540; Microfiche EPBU-127).

26. R. C. Walton, "The Institutionalization of the Reformation at Zürich," in *Zwingliana*, 13:497.

27. H. R. Lavater, "Regnum Christi etiam externum – Huldrych Zwinglis Brief vom 4. Mai 1528 an Ambrosius Blarer in Konstanz,"in *Zwingliana* 15:338f.

28. *Von gottlicher und menschlicher Gerechtigkeit, wie die zemen sehind und standind. Ein predige Huldrych Zuinglis*... (Zurich: Christoph Froschauer, 1523; Z II, 458–525); English, "Divine and Human Righteousness" (*Writings*, 2:1–41).

29. G. W. Locher, "Die Lehre vom Heiligen Geist in der Confessio Helvetica Posterior," 335.

30. *The Decades of Henry Bullinger, Minister of the Church of Zürich*, 276.

31. H. R. Niebuhr, "The Idea of Covenant and American Democracy," *Church History* 23 (1954) 130.

Bibliography

Sources

The Creeds of Christendom. Vol. 3, *The Evangelical Protestant Creeds*. Edited by Philip by Schaff. New York and London: Harper & Row, 1931. Reprint. Grand Rapids, MI: Baker, 1983.

The Latin Works of Huldreich Zwingli. Edited by S. M. Jackson, W. J. Hinke, and C. N. Heller. Vol. 3. Philadelphia: Heidelberg Press, 1929.

Reformed Confessions of the 16th Century. Edited by Arthur C. Cochrane. Philadelphia: Westminster, 1966.

Reformed Protestantism. Sources of the 16th and 17th centuries on microfiche, 1. Switzerland, A. Heinrich Bullinger and the Zürich Reformation. Inter Documentation Company AG (IDC), Poststrasse 14, 6300 Zug, Switzerland.

Zwingli, Huldrych. *Writings.* Translated by Edward J. Furcha and H. Wayne Pipkin. 2 vols. Allison Park, PA: Pickwick Publications, 1984.

——. *Huldreich Zwinglis samtliche Werke. Edited by E. Egli. Corpus Reformatorum. Zurich: Theologischer Verlag. 1905–.*

Studies

Baker, J. Wayne. *Heinrich Bullinger and the Covenant: The Other Reformed Tradition.* Athens, OH: Ohio University Press, 1980.

Büsser, Fritz. "Bullinger, Heinrich." In *Theologische Realenzyklopädie*, 7:375ff. Berlin and New York: de Gruyter, 1981.

———. *Würzeln der Reformation in Zürich: Zum 500. Geburtstag des Reformators Huldrych Zwingli*. Studies in Medieval and Reformation Thought 31. Leiden: Brill, 1985.

Gabler, Ulrich. *Huldrych Zwingli im 20 Jahrhundert: Forschungsbericht und annotierte Bibliographie 1897–1972*. Zurich: Theologische Verlag, 1975.

Herkenrath, Erland. *Heinrich Bullinger: Bibliographie*. Vol. 2, *Beschreibendes Verzeichnis der Literatur über Heinrich Bullinger*. Zurich: Theologischer Verlag, 1977.

Locher, Gottfried W. *Die Zwinglische Reformation im Rahmen der europäischen Kirchengeschichte*. Göttingen and Zurich: Vandenhoeck & Ruprecht, 1979.

———. *Zwingli's Thought: New Perspectives*. Studies in the History of Christian Thought 25. Leiden: Brill, 1981.

Staedtke, Joachim. *Heinrich Bullinger: Bibliographie*. Vol. 1, *Beschreibendes Verzeichnis der gedruckten Werke von Heinrich Bullinger*. Zurich: Theologischer Verlag, 1972.

14

The Spirituality of John Calvin

WILLIAM J. BOUWSMA

ALVIN'S SPIRITUALITY HAD ITS ORIGINS in the rhetorical tradition represented in the fifteenth and sixteenth centuries by Renaissance humanism. He acknowledged Lorenzo Valla not only as a distinguished scholar but also as an ally in the doctrine of predestination. His first published work was a commentary on Seneca, composed in a deliberate effort to outshine Erasmus. He knew the biblical scholarship of Erasmus well, and, unlike Luther, he generally avoided direct criticism of the great northern humanist.

That Calvin's religion has not been generally treated as "spirituality" is largely a result of the widespread notion of Calvin as a systematic and dogmatic theologian, a conception that probably says more about later Calvinism than about Calvin. Calvin thought of himself as an exclusively biblical theologian, and he was well aware of what this implied about all human theologizing. He valued system and expressed himself systematically only for limited, practical, and pedagogical purposes. Otherwise he distrusted the all-too-human impulse to systematize, above all in religious matters. "Anyone who does not allow God to be silent or to speak as he alone decides," Calvin declared, "is striving to impose order on God, a thing disgraceful and repugnant to nature itself." He contrasted the "beautiful dispensation of Scripture" with philosophical system building, noting with some irony that the Holy Spirit, "because he taught without affectation, did not adhere so exactly or continuously to a methodical plan."

The Humanist

Calvin also insisted that Christianity is essentially paradoxical. Because the principal articles of theology are paradoxes, he noted, "they are contemptuously rejected by the common understanding of men." He listed these

318

paradoxes with something like defiance: "That God became a mortal, that life is submissive to death, that righteousness has been concealed under the likeness of sin, that the source of blessing has been subjected to the curse." As a biblical theologian, Calvin was always ready to sacrifice systematic order in order to introduce into his discourse an unexpected imaginative insight, rhetorical elaboration, digressions, and repetitions that might serve persuasive, polemical, instructional, or other practical purposes.

He held rhetoric in high esteem; thus, he was concerned lest St. Paul's repudiation of *sapientia verbi* (1 Cor 1:17) be interpreted as authorizing a general attack on the arts of verbal discourse, which he defended as "noble gifts of God that men put to good use." He emphasized the capacity of rhetoric to infuse words with power, both in writing and in preaching, so that they could penetrate the human heart and transform the personality from within. In reply to a complaint against the use of figurative language in religious communication, he gave, as he put it,

> the only answer becoming to a theologian: that although a figurative expression is less precise, it expresses with greater significance and elegance what, said simply and without figure, would have less force and address. Hence figures are called the eyes of speech, not because they explain the matter more easily than simple ordinary language, but because they win attention by their propriety and arouse the mind by their luster, and by their lively similitude so represent what is said that it enters more effectively into the heart.[1]

He particularly admired the rhetorical gifts of the Old Testament prophets, and he recognized the importance, in order to appreciate fully the art as well as the substance of the biblical texts, of studying them in the original Greek and Hebrew. Calvin thus combined the ideal of *persuasio* central to earlier humanism with Valla's appreciation of *eruditio*.

As this characterization will already have implied, Calvin shared in the anthropological and epistemological assumptions underlying Renaissance humanism that shaped its spirituality. He too saw the human personality as a complex and mysterious whole in which the feelings and the will are central, and the intellect peripheral. This explains his frequent attacks on Stoic *apatheia* as a "mad philosophy" that requires one "to be utterly stolid in order to be wise." The feelings "that God has placed in human nature," he wrote, "are in themselves no more corrupt than their author himself." He admired, too, as much as any other humanist, the workmanship that had produced the human body, and David's dance before the ark of the covenant (2 Sam 6:16) elicited from him a remarkable defense of the involvement of the whole person in worship: "We need to exercise and employ in it all our senses, and our feet, and our hands, and our arms, and all the rest, that all may serve God and magnify him." Although he believed that fasting had more value in the Christian life than some of his Protestant brethren were prepared to recognize, the mortification of the flesh had little place in his spirituality and his attitude to bodily pleasure was benign. He argued, for example, that "the legitimate use" of food includes more than nourishment, "for it is not beside the point that food has savor as well as vital nutriment; thus our heavenly Father sweetly delights us with his delicacies." He suggested, perhaps recalling a famous colloquy of Erasmus, that "holy men" might properly invite their friends, "giving thanks to God together, to the mutual enjoyment of feasting with uncommon hilarity." Nor did Calvin discern spiritual value in celibacy; indeed, he defended and even celebrated sexual attraction, excusing Jacob's preference for Rachel over Leah with the reflection that "he who shall be induced to choose a wife because of the elegance of her shape will not necessarily sin." He had little sympathy for the ascetic strand in the tradition of Western spirituality.

His conception of the human personality as both more and less than intellectual carried with it, as for other humanists, doubts about the adequacy of the mind to attain certain knowledge, especially about spiritual matters. Like other humanists, he attacked what he interpreted as merely human claims to religious knowledge. As he remarked in the case of predestination, "Of those things which it is neither given nor lawful to know, to remain ignorant is to be learned; the craving to know a kind of madness." Among other consequences this position democratized the spiritual life. "There are many poor dunces today," Calvin declared, "who, though ignorant and unskilled in the use of language, make Christ known more faithfully than all the theologians of the pope with their lofty speculations." But his more profound point was that spiritual knowledge is different in kind from the sort of knowledge that, as he observed, "is perceived by the mind only and afterwards quickly disappears because it is not fixed in the heart." Spiritual knowledge, for Calvin, is always affective. This is why faith, as he argued, cannot be simply "a common assent to the gospel history, for genuine faith is more of the heart than of the brain, and more of the disposition than of the understanding."

An even more serious weakness of merely intellectual knowledge, for Calvin, was its uselessness. Utility, indeed, came close to being his major criterion for truth. "God's teaching results in practice," he argued; "Scripture is the school of the Holy Spirit, in which, as nothing is omitted that is both necessary and useful to know, so nothing is taught but what is expedient." Accordingly, he defended predestination primarily on the ground that "no doctrine is more useful, provided that it is handled properly and soberly." Conversely, he attacked the notion of merit not only as erroneous but because it inflated human pride. Calvin generally retained a rhetorician's concern for the practical consequences of what he taught, and much in his religious discourse must be interpreted in the light both of his doubts about the certainty of all human knowledge and his primary interest in practicality.

Among the considerations that shaped his doctrine was always its impact on the community, both secular and sacred. Calvin's individualism has been much exaggerated; it was balanced by an insistence, Aristotelian and Stoic as well as biblical, on the sociability and solidarity of human beings. "Since man is by nature a social animal," he wrote, "he tends through natural instinct to foster and preserve society. Consequently, we observe that there exist in all men's minds universal impressions of a certain civic fairness and order." "To keep us in a fraternal bond of love," he insisted, "God testifies that our neighbors are mankind in general, for the common tie of nature unites us."

What was needed for society in general was, for Calvin, peculiarly required by the church, which he saw as a community of comprehensive mutual assistance. "God does not stretch forth his hand to us to lead each on his own course," he remarked, "but in order that we should assist others and advance their spiritual progress." Public worship was mandatory for him because "everyone should publicly celebrate his experience of the grace of God as an example to others to confide in him," or, as he put it elsewhere: "In the church of God, where unity of faith ought to prevail, there is nothing more offensive or even detestable than for each to make up his own mind about what he should follow."[2] He valued the sacrament as "the bond of charity" and therefore a symbol of the unity of the church, "for as the bread there sanctified for the common use is made of many grains so mixed together that one cannot be discerned from another, so we ought to be united in one indissoluble friendship." Calvin's spirituality was social and inclusive; he took pains to dissociate it from monastic spirituality because of what he took to be the latter's exclusiveness. "Do they not separate themselves from the lawful society of believers," he asked rhetorically, "in adopting a peculiar ministry and a private administration of the sacraments?"

Calvin also resembled the Italian humanists in his sense of the urgency of reform in a time of special moral and religious crisis. Driven by an anxious concern to bring the world into conformity with God's will, he often denounced contemporary wickedness and vice:

> How many are the distresses with which Europe has been afflicted for the last thirty or forty years! How many are the chastisements by which she has been called to repentance! And yet it does not seem that these have done any good. On the contrary: luxury increases every day, lawless passions are still inflamed, and men persist more shamelessly than ever in their crimes and profligacy! (Commentary on Isa 9:10; OC 36, col. 202)

But he was most of all troubled by what he saw as the corruption of the sacred community. He often attacked it in Erasmian terms as externalism and superstition, which he attributed to erroneous doctrine. The papal church, he believed, had departed from the gospel message of salvation by grace alone into a works-righteousness that cut off the possibility of genuine sanctity, so that the teaching of the church had become not merely erroneous but deeply *unprofitable*. He attributed this error, however, not to a misreading of Scripture or to intellectual failure but to the *libido dominandi* of the upper clergy for whom the administration of a kind of commerce in good works with the deity for the salvation of souls promised vast power in this world: "These sacrilegious men, wishing to impose an unbridled tyranny under the cover of office in the church, are indifferent to the absurdities with which they ensnare themselves and others, if only they can force this one idea upon the simple: that the church has authority in all things."[3] The result, for Calvin, was the destruction of the kind of community God had ordained for his people.

His spirituality, then, was designed to rebuild the shattered sacred community; and he proposed to do so by adapting to this purpose the power of language on which the humanists of the Italian Renaissance had relied to reconstruct their own, for them scarcely less sacred, political communities. For the eloquence of human words Calvin proposed substituting the power of God's word to bring light out of medieval gloom. The novel historical perspective of the Renaissance shaped his understanding of the situation of the church, and to it Calvin added the militancy of the second generation of the Protestant Reformation:

> Although God's loving kindness to us was wonderful when the pure Gospel emerged out of that dreadful darkness in which it had been buried for so many ages, our affairs are still troubled. The impious still ceaselessly and furiously oppose the unhappy church, both by the sword and the virulence of their tongues. Internal enemies use covert arts in their schemes to subvert our edifice; wicked men destroy all order and interpose many obstacles to impede our progress. But God still wishes in these days to build his spiritual temple amidst the anxieties of the times. The faithful must still hold the trowel in one hand and the sword in the other, because the building of the church must still be combined with many struggles. (Commentary on Dan 9:25; OC 41, col. 184)

Experiencing God

Except for this militancy appropriate to a new historical situation, Calvin's spirituality resembled that of the Italian humanists, beginning with its recognition both of God's transcendence and the total dependence of

human beings on him, each illuminating the other. Calvin himself acknowledged that, "while joined by many bonds, which one precedes and brings
forth the other is not easy to discern."

It was consistent with his reservations about human knowledge, however,
that Calvin insisted on the total inability of human beings to know God
as he is. For Calvin, believers *experience* God–this is a better word for con-
veying Calvin's meaning than the more specific and limited "know"–only
indirectly, through his mighty acts and works in the world, the effects
primarily, at least as they are apprehended, of God's *power.* Believers experience God as they experience–but can hardly be said to "know"–thunder,
one of Calvin's favorite metaphors for religious experience. It pointed to the
power of even a dim apprehension of divinity that, if it were more vivid,
could not be endured: "If we simply listen to natural thunder, we are seized
with fear. Yet nothing is put into words; God only produces an indistinct
rumbling. How would it be, then, if he should speak to us and reveal his
glory? A human being cannot see God without dying or being consumed"
(Sermon 43 on Deuteronomy; OC 26, col. 399). Calvin's spirituality was
suffused with a numinous awe that characteristically found expression in
figures drawn from the energies operating in nature.

But even our experience of God *in actu* is limited to what is useful. The
faithful are to derive from this experience, Calvin held, only such knowledge "as is necessary to glorify God," for "we only praise God aright when
we are filled and overwhelmed with an ecstatic admiration of the immensity
of his power." But for another reason too one should look first to God's
power: confidence in God's power is the only basis for confidence in his
ability to aid one and so "to prevent those anxious thoughts that might
otherwise rise in our minds."

Calvin's emphasis on the transcendence and power of God–his biblicism
to the contrary notwithstanding–was as much a speculative inheritance
from Ockhamism as a product of his spiritual experience. More clearly
biblical was his insistence on God as loving father, although he was clear
that God's fatherhood was metaphorical (this kind of sensitivity was probably also intensified by his rhetorical culture). Scripture, Calvin explained,
compared God to earthly fathers "not because he is similar to them, but
because his incomparable love for us could not be expressed otherwise." At
other times, Calvin, so often identified with the most patriarchal type of
religion, could recognize biblical authority for experiencing God as a
mother. He stressed this in a sermon to his congregation in Geneva: "Our
Lord makes himself uniquely familiar; he is like a nurse, like a mother; he
does not compare himself only to fathers, who are so benign and humane
toward their children, but he says that he is more than mother, more than

nurse" (Sermon on Job; OC 34, col. 316). He responded with deep feeling to the words of the Lord in Isaiah, "I will cry out like a woman in labor, I will gasp and pant" (42,14): "[God] compares himself to a mother who singularly loves her newborn child, though she brought him forth with extreme pain. It may be thought that these things are not suitable to God; but in no other way than by such figures of speech can his ardent love towards us be expressed" (Commentary on Isa 42:14; OC 36, col. 69). Whatever Calvin may have felt compelled to say in his more embattled moments or for rhetorical purposes, he denounced those who represented the deity as "a dreadful God from whose presence all must fly." Calvin's God was "mild, kind, gentle, and compassionate, so that he will not drive the weak harder than they are able to bear." "We will never spontaneously and heartily sound forth his praises," Calvin declared, "until he wins us by the sweetness of his goodness."

Calvin's doctrines of providence and predestination can be understood only in the context of his positive mode of experiencing God. Providence, to be sure, is for Calvin an expression of God's power; but it is precisely God's power that makes his love efficacious. Providence displays God's ceaseless concern and activity on behalf of the world and especially of humanity. This is what distinguishes the Christian God from the god of the philosophers, his providence from the providence of the Stoics. "God," Calvin insisted, "can never rest; he sustains the world by his energy, he governs everything, however remote." God's "virtue," a term whose ambiguity as both strength and righteousness Calvin often exploited, might be conceived abstractly, as he put it, in "motion and action"; but what providence meant to Calvin emerges most vividly when he associates it with events that had special emotional significance for him, such as the birth and nourishment of a child.

> [In such events] the wonderful providence of God brightly shines forth. This miracle is less noticed by us because of its ordinariness. But if ingratitude did not obscure our eyes with stupidity, we would be ravished with admiration at every childbirth in the world. What prevents the child from perishing a hundred times, as it might, before the moment for bringing it forth arrives, but that God, by his secret and incomprehensible power, keeps it alive in the womb? And after it is brought into the world, seeing it is subject to so many miseries and cannot stir a finger to help itself, how could it live even for a single day, did not God take it up into his fatherly bosom to nurse and protect it? (Commentary on Ps 22:10; OC 31, col. 226)

Again, it is only because God's power is sufficient absolutely to control the world that, as Calvin repeatedly insisted, predestination is not a terrifying but a comforting doctrine for believers.

IOANNES · CALVINVS ·

22. *Portrait of John Calvin, called The Portrait of Rotterdam*, French,
16th century. Musée Bymans, Rotterdam.

The Human Condition

Calvin also resembled the humanists in his treatment of the human condition. Like them, he combined a keen interest in the creation of human beings in God's image and likeness with a deep sense of the result of the fall. He often referred to the original God-likeness of humanity, seeking to locate it precisely in one or another aspect or function of the personality. His results were inconsistent, but the attempt indicates the importance of the doctrine for him.

His emphasis on what was lost by the fall has encouraged the belief that, for Calvin, the divine image was totally obliterated by it, but other evidence suggests that his denunciations of fallen humanity were often as much rhetorical as descriptive and were intended more to discourage presumption and strengthen humility than to state general truths. Like Augustine, Calvin celebrated human achievement with remarkable enthusiasm for one to whom so harsh an estimate of the effects of the fall has been attributed. He often suggested that he cherished what had survived of the original image and likeness of God. Indeed he insisted on it. He rebuked Job, for example, for cursing the day of his birth and so, in effect, rejecting the gift of life: "It is necessary to hold to this rule: that is, to know that human life is in itself a gift of God so precious and so noble that it deserves to be highly prized. For it is always necessary to come back to this: that God never created a man on whom he did not imprint his image" (Sermon 11 on Job: OC 33, col. 145).

That there was also a negative side to Calvin's perception of the human condition in historical existence hardly requires elaboration. Many passages in his works make the point, for example: "Let us hold this, then, as an undoubted truth that no opposition can ever shake, that the mind of man has been so estranged from God's righteousness that it conceives, desires, and undertakes only that which is impious, perverted, foul, impure, and infamous. The heart is so steeped in the poison of sin that it can breathe out nothing but a loathsome stench" (*Institutes* 2.5.19). But this passage, and many others like it in Calvin's works, appears in a polemical context that helps to explain its lack of qualification, and what is most interesting about the passage is less its vehemence than its identification of sin with the mind and heart rather than with the "lower" dimensions of the personality. This emphasis also helps to explain the conception of total depravity especially identified with Calvin. It means not that there is nothing good left in human beings but that no part of the personality has been left untouched by sin and thus that no area of the self can be depended on for human salvation. The practical effect of the doctrine—utility always being of primary importance for Calvin—was to compel human beings to depend wholly on Christ.

Calvin's understanding of sin was also closely related to the medieval conception of *acedia,* that vague spiritual malaise of monastic existence which, by the thirteenth century, had also spread among the laity. Petrarch, too, had suffered from it. So, for Calvin, death, which had entered the world through sin, had already seized on all human beings. We experience it as drowsiness when we should be alert, as apathy when we should feel concern, as sloth when we should be diligent, as coldness when we should be warm, as weakness when we need strength. In short, the effect of sin was, above all, evidenced in the absence of the various manifestations of energy that Calvin associated with God's power and that were, for him, identified with Spirit. He gave particular attention to the various symptoms of its absence in his sermons; it was for him especially a pastoral problem.

This understanding of Spirit, its presence and its absence, had various reverberations for Calvin. For example, since the devil, who seeks always to drain one of one's God-given spirituality, amuses himself by lulling his victims to sleep, God must employ various stratagems to awaken the victims. He threatens, chastises, compels them to remember him by causing their lives to go badly. Again, in the absence of the power of the Spirit, the faithful cannot react with appropriate wonder to the marvels of the world, and so they fail to perceive it as God's creation and to glorify him for it. Failure of spirituality was thus the primary obstacle to movement from a shallow intellectual knowledge to the affective awareness than can move the whole personality. Calvin, in thinking about the effects of sin, attached particular importance to the ways in which it deadened the feelings, notably in worship. Sometimes he contrasted his own followers unfavorably in this respect with infidels or Roman Catholics: "Let us be ashamed, I say, that we are so negligent, and cold, and even freezing, when the worshipers of idols are so ardent!" He objected to contemporary scholastic theology as a set of "frigid speculations"—in this respect another symptom of original sin— incapable of inducing a spiritual response. Sin makes us "so lazy that instead of taking only a minute to move our foot, we need an hour before we can stir; for every step we take forward, we stumble and fall back two, or suffer some pitiful setback." The lack of spirit, in short, could deprive human beings of the capacity for any accomplishment.

Two further points may be made about Calvin's treatment of sin. One is a subtlety that must have made him singularly acute as a spiritual director, a role he served for many in the course of the heavy pastoral responsibilities that, it is often overlooked, were an important aspect of his life. He recognized how, in responding to what God requires of believers, "just as the branches of a tree are entangled and intertwined," so their thoughts "are bent and mingled together in confusion and contradiction." He was fully aware of the distinction between repression, the force that bottles up those vicious impulses that most of us would otherwise "wantonly indulge," and an authentic holiness; but he also understood that, although hiding sins by repression makes genuine righteousness impossible, it is nevertheless "necessary for the community." He noted too, as a rhetorician well might, the abuse of language to cover sin: "Craftiness and a perverse cunning are called prudence; and he is described as provident and circumspect who cleverly cheats others, who deceives the simple, and who insidiously oppresses the poor." He understood that turning the other cheek can be a form of aggression, and he noted that the sacrifices people make are often "not so much to God as to themselves."

A second point is that, although Calvin was clear enough that to know the good, in the traditional sense in which "knowing" had been understood, is not enough to do the good, his own conception of "really knowing" reestablishes the broken connection between knowledge and action. "We are indeed aware," Calvin remarked, "that when God is really known, the fear of him must necessarily affect our hearts, and we spontaneously and willingly worship and serve him." This is so because when knowledge is a function not simply of the mind but of the whole personality, it cannot be dissociated from a practical response. The position also suggests Calvin's recognition that sin is finally not a moral but a religious problem, the product, in the first instance, not of lawlessness or wicked desires, but of a broken relationship with God. To know *the good* is insufficient to avoid sin; for that one must, in a biblical sense, know *God*.

Calvin's skill in laying bare human sinfulness combined with the familiar Calvinist practice of self-examination to break down those attachments to self-image that have often been identified, in the tradition of Christian spirituality, as the greatest obstacle to spiritual growth. Self-examination, then, which had for Calvin the ostensible purpose of bringing to conscious attention the whole of one's sinfulness so that it could be perceived in all its ugliness, was also a kind of therapy, revealing a truth that could bring one to freedom. Calvin knew in advance what must emerge from self-examination and would have seen any result except self-accusation as failure. But this only means, once more, that Calvin's kind of self-examination was not an exercise in idle curiosity but had the most practical of purposes. "Once we have carefully examined all that is in us," he maintained, more concerned with the result he aimed at than with a balanced description of human nature, "we will find nothing but corruption and damnable vice." The essential purpose of the exercise was to dissolve the defensive strategies in which human beings engage, in order to open the way for an authentic spirituality, and in this way to engender "a tranquil mind" and "a happy peace" such as "can find no place in a double heart." Calvin aimed, in short, at wholeness. The alternative to this could only be "an anxiety that must tremble before any shadow or breath of wind."

He could also state this in simpler, more evangelical terms: "The rigor of this examination ought to proceed till it casts us down into complete consternation, in this way preparing us to receive the grace of Christ." He sometimes used language such as would be later employed by Montaigne: self-examination, he declared, "strips men naked," leaving them open to intimacy with God. It took the place, for him, of the confessional; he could demand for it that individual privacy he repudiated in worship. "Solitude," he observed, "helps men to compose themselves, to examine themselves thoroughly, and to commune with themselves freely and in good earnest." Privacy aids believers to discover that what they lack in themselves "may be recovered in God." This discovery was thus the first step in restoring the relationship with him destroyed by sin.

Divine Initiation and Christian Response

The spiritual limitations of human beings also meant, for Calvin as for other humanists, that only a divine initiative could cross the gulf dividing God from themselves: hence the necessity of revelation. But his approach to Scripture differed from theirs in several particulars that are relevant to his spirituality. Partly because he came later in the development of humanist philology, he was able to bring more advanced scholarly resources to bear on the study of the Bible. In addition, his intense concern that the world should conform to God's will inclined him to look to Scripture for directions about human behavior, not only in the general prescriptions and prohibitions it laid down but also in the examples set by biblical personages. Assuming that everything in Scripture is for human edification, he included in his sermons and commentaries numerous passages of epideictic rhetoric, praising or blaming Moses and David, the prophets and apostles.

A further difference between Calvin and earlier humanists was his more explicit concern with the complexities of the human response to God's word. He was well aware that Scripture seems "often obscure," that it can be "twisted in various senses," and that even for well-intentioned readers it may sometimes appear "sterile, unfruitful, and productive of nothing but boredom," so that they feel "stuck and blocked." The result of this sensitivity was his special emphasis on the unity of word and Spirit. For Calvin, "those whom the Holy Spirit has inwardly taught truly rest upon Scripture."

"Every believer experiences in his heart," he observed, that "the certainty Scripture deserves among us is attained by the testimony of the Spirit," which is also "the Spirit of discernment." When we engage with Scripture, it leads us through ambiguity and obscurity and, at the same time, gives life and meaning to the text. Thus, the Holy Spirit is the source of that first stirring of one's own spirit, through the gospel, toward union with God.

Each of the central elements of the gospel—the incarnation and atonement, the grace available through them, the gift of faith by which believers are enabled to accept this grace for themselves, and the sanctification flowing from it—describes objectively how human beings are enabled, step by step, to recover their original unity with God. Like his predecessors among the humanists, Calvin fully subscribed to them. From the standpoint of his spirituality, they provided for the recovery of those energies with which humanity had been originally endowed by creation in God's image. The recovery of this energy Calvin described as "quickening" (*vivificatio*). "We necessary resemble the dead," he told his congregation, "until God quickens (*vivifie*) us." It comes to one through faith, which "is not an idle thing, or a cold imagination that lies suffocating in our minds, but it is effective. . . . From faith springs strength, from strength accomplishment." Faith is "full of energy." It receives additional power from the sacrament, in which "we are quickened by the true partaking of Christ" and in which "his life is transferred to us and becomes ours." The result is a heightened consciousness and newness of life. Believers become "not merely tranquil but also joyful and cheerful." Above all, however, "it is the property of faith to animate us to strenuous exertion." Faith "leads the will itself into action."

Action, then, is for Calvin the ultimate expression of the spiritual life. His position here was related to his general conviction that human beings have been created to work, one of the grounds on which he attacked monasticism. It would be contrary to our humanity "to lie down in inactivity and idleness." We should "apply to use whatever God has conferred on us." Calvin's position here parallels his conception of the life of God, in whose image humanity was created, as sustained action.

He located human activity, like other humanists, first of all in society. "No kind of life is more praiseworthy before God," he declared, "than that which is useful to society." He particularly welcomed those seasoned by social experience into the service of the church: "However much we may admire celibacy and a philosophical life remote from ordinary living, wise and thoughtful men have learned from their own experience that those who know ordinary life and are well practiced in the duties that human relations impose are far better trained and fitted to rule in the church" (Commentary on Matt 25:24; OC 46, col. 570).

But service to society was only one among Calvin's conceptions of the active life of the Christian. Living in an unusually militant age, Calvin drew, like Erasmus before him, on the tradition of spirituality that interpreted the Christian life as a ceaseless struggle with the powers of evil within both the self and the world. He summarized this conception in the prayer that concluded his exegetical lectures on Daniel:

> Grant, Almighty God, since thou proposest to us no other end than that of constant warfare during our whole life and subjectest us to many cares until we arrive at the goal of this transitory struggle: grant, I pray thee, that we may never grow fatigued. May we be ever armed and equipped for battle; and, whatever the trials by which thou dost prove us, may we never be found deficient.[4]

For Calvin, Christians must struggle against their own flesh, against the majority of the human race on behalf of the truth, and ultimately against the devil. Yet in the end there was one peculiarity of Christian warfare, since it "consists less in inflicting harm on others than in patiently bearing it." The Christian fights by bearing the cross.

Conflict, then, as a metaphor for the Christian life, merges, for Calvin, with a conception of earthly existence as, for the Christian, acquiescence in suffering. He thought human beings "more endangered by prosperity than by adversity, for they are pleased by their successes and intoxicated by their own happiness." On the other hand, such disasters as poverty, famine, diseases, and exile—the last two his own special afflictions—indeed, even death, though in themselves "curses of God" and punishment for the wicked, only benefit the children of God, who are enabled by grace to accept them as useful disciplines that "bring us to a sense of our duty." Adversity, for Calvin, tests and strengthens faith, develops patience and humility, purges the impulses of the flesh, and compels believers to raise their eyes toward heaven. He also interpreted tribulation as a means by which God "quickens" the faithful. By such means God "keeps them alert, lest they should lie asleep on the ground" or "grow sluggish with too much rest." God's judgments are "necessary to stimulate our sloth." For Calvin, rest is *only*—though only temporarily—for the wicked.

Calvin could also represent the action he identified with the spiritual life as a journey or pilgrimage, as movement toward a goal. The church, Calvin suggested, is like a tent, since God's children have "no fixed place of abode on earth" and must therefore carry their home with them. "Our life is like a journey," he asserted, "and it is not God's will that we should march along casually as we please, but he sets the goal before us, and also directs us on the right way to it." But this way was also a struggle: no one moves easily forward, and most are so weak that, "wavering and limping and even creeping along the ground, they move at a feeble pace." Yet it is also happily true that everyone can daily "make some headway, though it be slight." The singlemindedness in this conception is notable: "We must take heed that we do not turn our thoughts or mind to any other activity but, on the contrary, make it our endeavor to be free from every distraction and apply ourselves exclusively to God's calling" (Commentary on Phil 3:13; OC 52, col. 52). Calvin allows us to love this life, but only if we "travel in it like strangers, always intent on our goal."

Finally, therefore, through service, struggle, adversity, and pilgrimage, the spiritual life acquires a kind of dramatic unity as it proceeds through a series of ardent and strenuous moments from beginning to appointed end. A positive spiritual life means progress in realizing the purposes of human existence. It develops an increasingly close and confident relationship with God (faith), which finds expression in a more and more spontaneous and joyful conformity to God's will (sanctification) and in wholehearted glorification of God and appreciation of his works.

Calvin opposed the complacency sometimes associated with his followers by insisting that none has reached the goal in this life. Although he compared the career of the spirit to movement through the stages of life, from infancy to full maturity, he denied that any Christian has achieved full adulthood in this life. Here the most advanced are still, so to speak, adolescents, unevenly developed, awkward, prone to humiliating regressions yet yearning for growth and, however imperceptibly, growing into the full stature of Christ. But if believers do what they must and, as Calvin instructs, "do not cease to marvel," their faith, "weak as its beginnings may have been, will gradually advance more and more." Then "each day in some degree our purity will increase and our corruption be cleansed as long as we live in the world"; and "the more we increase in knowledge, the more should we increase in love." Meanwhile we will experience an ever clearer and more vivid sense of "God's face, peaceful and calm and gracious toward us." We will have seen him, in the beginning, "afar off, but clearly enough to know we are not at all deceived." And "the more we advance, as we ought to continue to advance with steady progress, the nearer and thus surer sight of him we obtain, which, as it continues, grows even more familiar to us" (*Institutes* 3.2.19). So the spiritual life, for Calvin as for so many before him, culminates in the *visio Dei*.

This account of Calvin's spirituality is not intended to suggest that there were not other elements in his religious thought that pointed in rather different directions. Calvin was a complex figure in a complex century, and he often expressed himself differently, according to the situation in which he found himself. But his spirituality, although the term was itself alien to him, occupied a place very close to the center of his understanding of Christianity.

Notes

1. *The Clear Explanation of Sound Doctrine concerning the True Partaking of the Flesh and Blood of Christ in the Holy Supper* (1561), in *Calvin: Theological Treatises* (Library of Christian Classics 22; London: SCM, 1954) 319.

2. Commentary on Acts 19:23–24, in *Johannis Calvini Opera quae supersunt omnia* (Brunswick: C. A. Schwetske et filius, 1863–1900) [hereafter referred to as OC] 48, col. 450.

3. *Institutes of the Christian Religion*, trans. Ford Lewis Battles (Library of Christian Classics 20–21; London: SCM, 1961) 1.7.1.

4. *Commentaries on the Book of Daniel*, trans. Thomas Myers (Edinburgh: Calvin Translation Society, 1852) 2:323.

Bibliography

Calvin's spirituality has received little explicit attention from scholars, partly because the conception of spirituality has had little place in Protestant scholarship, owing to the tendency among later Calvinists to view Calvin chiefly as a dogmatic theologian. The only work directly concerned with the subject is Richard. Highly suggestive for Calvin's spirituality is also Miles. Otherwise the subject can be best approached through Calvin's own writings. The collection published by Leith provides an especially convenient introduction to Calvin's spirituality. The most accessible edition of the *Institutes* is the translation, with an excellent introduction and notes, by Battles. Among the best general studies of Calvin is Wendel. The most recent biography is Parker.

Calvin, John. *Institutes of the Christian Religion.* Translated by Ford Lewis Battles. Philadelphia: Westminster, 1960.

Leith, John H. *The Christian Life.* San Francisco: Harper & Row, 1984.

Miles, Margaret R. "Theology, Anthropology, and the Human Body in Calvin's *Institutes of the Christian Religion.*" *Harvard Theological Review* 74 (1981) 303–23.

Parker, T. H. L. *John Calvin.* London: S. M. Dent and Sons, 1975.

Richard, Lucien Joseph. *The Spirituality of John Calvin.* Atlanta, GA: John Knox Press, 1974.

Wendel, François. *Calvin: The Origins and Development of His Religious Thought.* Translated by P. Mairet. London: Collins, 1960.

15

The Spirituality of the
Radical Reformation

TIMOTHY GEORGE

T HE RADICAL REFORMATION was a tremendous movement of spiritual and ecclesial renewal that stood on the margins of the major territorial churches, Roman Catholic and Protestant, during the great religious upheaval of the sixteenth century. This movement, however, was neither marginal nor peripheral in its basic drives and spiritual vitalities. Embracing both ecumenicity and sectarianism, violent revolution and pacifistic communalism, sublimating ascetical, mystical, and rationalist impulses from the late Middle Ages, the Radical Reformation considered as an entity posed a thoroughgoing critique of the *corpus christianum* in both its mainline Protestant and Tridentine Catholic mutations.

Yet standard treatments of Christian spirituality, by and large, have either ignored or superficially skirted the Radical Reformation. Only in recent years have the Radical reformers begun to emerge from the shadow of opprobrium cast over them by their sixteenth-century opponents. Heinrich Bullinger, for instance, called them "devilish enemies and destroyers of the church of God."[1] Luther's preferred term was Schwärmer, which recalls the uncontrollable buzzing of bees around a hive, and which the German reformer applied indiscriminately to a wide host of adversaries. Calvin's epithets were no less pejorative: "fanatics," "deluded," "scatterbrains," "asses," "scoundrels," "mad dogs."[2] Interpreting the Radicals in terms of the negatives of dissent and non-conformity has skewed efforts to understand their spirituality. A contemporary British historian of note reflects this failure in his depiction of the "true nature" of Anabaptism as "a violent phenomenon born out of irrational and psychologically unbalanced dreams, resting on a denial of reason and the elevation of that belief in direct inspiration which enables men to do as they please."[3] Social historians, Marxist and non-Marxist, have done much to situate the Radicals in the socioeconomic and class structures of the sixteenth century. However, a recent social historian of Anabaptism, who fully recognizes the spiritual force of the movement, still concludes that it was a "dangerous" abortive reform, "bent on destroying civilization."[4]

Revisionist historiography of the past twenty-five years has been preoccupied with the issues of origins and antecedents. Much good scholarship has been aimed at correcting facile generalizations of previous schools of thought and challenging what might be called a false intimacy with the historical past. Still, however fruitful this line of research has been, it has focused primarily on the external relations of the Radicals to other reform currents rather than on their own self-understanding and spiritual motivation.

The Radical groups surveyed in this chapter are sometimes lumped together as "the left wing of the Reformation." In this designation we can hear a faint echo of Luther's own accusation that both papists and Schwärmer erred on "the left and the right side," neither remaining on the path of true freedom. Luther, however, reversed the modern positioning, placing the Roman Catholics on the left and the Radicals on the right![5]

Recognizing the anachronistic use of "left-wing" when applied to sixteenth-century dissent, George H. Williams proposed "the Radical Reformation" as a collective term for all those groups of religious innovators who remained in neither the Roman Catholic or mainline Protestant churches. Following Ernst Troeltsch, Williams further divided the Radicals into three major groupings: Anabaptists, spiritualists, and evangelical rationalists. These distinct groups were in turn subdivided. For example, Williams distinguished three branches of Anabaptism: evangelical (Swiss Brethren, Mennonites, Hutterites); revolutionary (Münsterites); contemplative (Hans Denck).

For the purposes of this study, we shall follow Williams's typology because it is the most comprehensive and most durable to date. His book, *The Radical Reformation*, originally published in 1962, has been amplified and brought up to date in Spanish translation: *La Reforma Radical* (Mexico City: Fondo de Cultura Economica, 1982). Moreover, the term "Radical Reformation" has become widely accepted, even by historians who do not use it in the same way Williams does.[6]

Anabaptists, spiritualists, and evangelical rationalists all wanted to cut back through the accretions of ecclesiastical tradition, through what Balthasar Hubmaier called "the mud holes and cesspools of human dogma," to the authentic root (*radix*) of faith and order, although they disagreed among themselves as to what that root might be.[7] Precisely this, together with the fact that for the most part they were forced to develop their model of Christian life outside the confines of the established churches, gave their spirituality a distinctive cast.

By "spirituality" we mean those specific modes of existence characteristic of *homo religiosus* by which one participates in the sacred and conforms oneself to it.[8] Our purpose in this study is to give a broad profile of Radical spirituality, focusing on recurrent themes that appear in varying degrees within each of the three major groupings listed above.

Although we shall touch upon matters of doctrine and church polity, our primary aim will be to recount, as nearly as possible, the spiritual experience of the Radical reformers. Therefore, special attention will be given to primary sources, including devotional treatises, prayers, sermons, catechisms, hymns, confessions, martyr stories, letters, chronicles, and church orders. In this way the unique spiritual sensibilities of the Radicals will emerge from their own witness.

The Quest for a Sense of Divine Immediacy

Lucien Febvre has described the eve of the Reformation as an age with "an immense appetite for the divine."[9] This period was alive with all sorts of spiritual vitalities ranging from bizarre practices such as tattooing the name of Jesus over the heart and braying at Mass in honor of the donkey on which the Virgin Mary rode to the staples of mainline piety such as indulgences, pilgrimages, relics, the Rosary, adoration of the consecrated Host, and the recital of many Our Fathers. The Radicals of the Reformation shared with their age a tremendous thirst for God. At the same time, they insisted on a direct, unmediated appropriation of the divine. This led them to reject or qualify all religious *externalia* in their quest for direct access to the redeeming mystical action of God.

Luther himself transmitted to many of the Radicals the basis for their mystical orientation in the form of his editions (1516, 1518) of the famous *Theologia deutsch*. This treatise was read widely by Radicals of every camp long after Luther's early enthusiasm for it had cooled. Rather than following Luther's mature doctrine of justification with its stark insistence on the imputation of extrinsic (*extra nos*) righteousness, the Radicals harked back to a mystical union with the divine based on the immanence of God in the human soul.

Coursing through all branches of the Radical Reformation was a vehement anticlericalism, directed against both the priests and friars of the old church and the "new popes" of Wittenberg, Zurich, and Geneva. Menno Simons lambasted the Roman Catholic Church as "nothing but a human invention . . . open seduction of souls, an intolerable make-a-living and gain of the lazy priests . . . a false offensive religion and open idolatry." Hubmaier was less kind: the so-called pastors are really ass strokers, whores, adulterers, pimps, gamblers, drunkards, and buffoons whom we certainly would not have trusted to take care of sows and nanny goats![10] Behind this virulent language lay a deeper concern than mere protest against moral corruption. The clergy had interposed themselves and their ministrations or doctrines as a medium between divine revelation and the people of God.

Emphasis on the interiorized process of salvation led many of the Radicals, particularly the spiritualists, to play down the importance of the written Scriptures. "As far as I am concerned," wrote Andreas Bodenstein von Carlstadt, "I do not need the outward witness. I want to have the testimony of the Spirit within me, as it was promised by Christ."[11] Thomas Müntzer was even more emphatic: Without the Spirit within, one "does not know how to say anything deeply about God, even if he has eaten through a hundred Bibles!"[12] Though the Radicals made extensive use of the Bible, they generally refused to make a fetish out of it. They refused to tie salvation to any external aid to faith, however good and important it might be in its own right.

Some of the extreme spiritualists went so far as to suspend the observance of all outward ordinances, including baptism and the Lord's Supper, thus anticipating the Quakers of the next century. Caspar Schwenckfeld, the most representative figure of this type, conceived of the Eucharist as an inward feeding on the "heavenly flesh" of Christ. The spiritual nourishment of this mystical Eucharist had direct soteriological implications for Schwenckfeld: "Eating means . . . partaking of the nature of Christ through true faith. . . . The spiritual food changes us into itself, that is, the divine nature, so that we become partakers of it."[13] Thus, the spiritualized Eucharist became a means of progressive human deification, an immediate grasping of the divine through mystic participation in Christ's celestial flesh.

Most of the Radicals were not so drastic in their approach to what Calvin called the external means of grace. Yet for them all, true Christianity was *ipso facto* personal, experiential, individual. As we shall see, precisely this consideration lay behind the Anabaptist rejection of infant baptism. As Pilgram Marpeck put it, no one can believe for anyone else, "neither wife for husband, nor husband for wife, children for parents, parents for children."[14] One is not born into the family of God by proxy! But neither could the water of baptism in and of itself effect regeneration. The new birth consisted "not in water nor in words; but it is the heavenly, living, and quickening power of God in our hearts."[15]

An *experience* of the new birth, often involving intense emotional struggle, was a prerequisite for water baptism. Indeed, baptism was sometimes depicted as the climax of the conversion process. This seems to have been the case with the baptisms administered in the early Anabaptist congregation in the village of Zollikon near Zurich.

> Hans Bruggbach of Zumingen arose crying and shouting that he was a great sinner and that they should pray God for him. Thereupon Blaurock asked whether he desired to receive the grace of God, and he said yes. Then Mantz arose and asked, "Who will prevent me that I should not baptize him?" And Blaurock answered, "No one." So he took a dipper of water and baptized him in the name of God the Father, God the Son, and God the Holy Spirit.[16]

Menno Simons described his own conversion experience in terms that resonate with the later experience of John Wesley or the Pietists:

> My heart trembled in my body. I prayed God with sighs and tears that he would give me, a troubled sinner, the gift of his grace and create a clean heart in me, that through the merits of the crimson blood of Christ he would graciously forgive my unclean walk and ease-seeking life. . . . Behold, thus, the God of mercy . . . has first touched my heart, given me a new mind, humbled me in his fear, taught me in part to know myself, turned me from the way of death and graciously called me into the narrow path of life, into the communion of his saints. To him be praise forevermore. . . .[17]

Certainly the intensity and pattern of conversion varied greatly among the Radicals. Yet they shared a common awareness of having been illuminated or re-created or regenerated by special contact with the divine. Even Michael Servetus, an evangelical rationalist, describing the origins of his anti-Trinitarian speculations, claimed that, as a young man of twenty, he was "moved by a certain divine impulse to treat of this cause, having been taught of no one."[18] The immediacy of religious experience, a certain consciousness of salvation or divine grace in the here and now, was constitutive for Radical spirituality in all of its varied modalities.

Nachfolge Christi: Following the "Bitter Christ"

In a famous essay published in 1944, Harold S. Bender claimed that the essence of the Anabaptist movement was to be found in its concept of discipleship (*Nachfolge*).[19] Indeed, we can say that "following" rather than "faith" was the great word of the entire Radical Reformation. The Radicals flatly rejected Luther's doctrine of forensic justification *sola fide* along with Calvin's concept of absolute double predestination. Both of these formulations struck the Radicals as abstractions divorced from the reality of "living" faith. The classical Protestant position was caricatured in a hymn by Ludwig Haetzer:

Yes, says the world, there is no need
That I with Christ should suffer,
Since Christ did suffer death for me
I may just sin on his account,
He pays for me, this I believe,
And thus the point is settled.
O brethren mine, it's but a sham,
The devil has contrived it.[20]

The Radicals described the gospel of the mainline reformers as that of a "sweet Christ" in contrast to the stringent gospel of the "bitter Christ." This theme resounds through the writings of the mystically oriented spiritualists, but it is also present in the evangelical Anabaptists. In 1524, Conrad Grebel wrote to Müntzer: "We too are rejected by our learned shepherds. All men follow them, because they preach a sinful sweet Christ."[21] What did the Radicals mean when they talked of following the bitter Christ? We can discern three aspects of this idea that were central to their concept of discipleship: (1) the solidarity in suffering between Christ and believers, (2) the Christian life mirrored in the "gospel of all creatures," and (3) the necessity for utter abandonment of self (*Gelassenheit*).

Luther had posited a "theology of the cross" over against the scholastic "theology of glory," but for many of the Radicals his emphasis on the vicarious nature of Christ's suffering seemed to relegate the cross to a far distant past. For them, the passion of Christ was a contemporary process in which they had been called to participate. The suffering of Christ in Head and Members alike is a theme that permeates their writings. Hans Hut expressed it thus:

> For just as Christ, the lamb, has been slain from the beginning of the world, so also is he still crucified until the end of the world, that the body of Christ be perfected according to the length, width, depth and height in the love of Christ.[22]

This reenactment of Calvary, however, was not a ritual relegated to the altars of Christendom, but rather the daily struggle of renunciation, tribulation, suffering, and death. The unique passion of Christ the Head was thus relativized by extension in the renewed suffering of Christ in his members. There is more than a hint that the former apart from the latter cannot suffice for salvation. "Christ must still suffer more in his members," wrote Grebel. "But he will strengthen and keep them steadfast to the end."[23] By following the steps of the bitter Christ, the Radicals felt they were "filling up what was lacking in the afflictions of Christ in the flesh" (Col 1:24), for the sake of their own salvation and that of the whole world.

One of the most fascinating expressions of the place of suffering in the

Christian life was the "gospel of all creatures" propounded by many Radicals including Müntzer, Hut, Denck, Marpeck, and Servetus. The biblical basis of this motif was Mark 16:15, where the commission to preach the gospel *to* all creatures (dative in Greek and Latin) was misconstrued as the German genitive, *"aller Kreatur,"* *of* all creatures. By this expression the Radicals understood the divine revelation that was present to all in the universally suffering creation. This was not a gospel to be preached "to" all creatures such as dogs and cats, cows and calves, leaves and grass (*contra* St. Francis!), but rather a "gospel" inherent in the nature of the created order itself. Just as all creatures are subordinate to human designs, so too no one can be "saved other than by suffering and tribulation. If someone needs an animal it must first be prepared, cooked and roasted and the animal has to suffer according to the will of the one who uses it. If God would use us, we have first to be justified and cleansed within and without. . . . And this can only take place under the cross of suffering.[24]

This "gospel" is woven into the very fabric of life itself. The ordinary occupations become metaphors of salvation. When farmers plough their fields, or fishers draw in their catch, or tailors patch old clothes, or butchers prepare for their slaughtering, they are reminded by these activities of the solidarity and purposefulness of suffering in all creation. Thus they are led to embrace a life of redemptive suffering in the name and for the sake of Christ.

The art of self-abandonment implied in this theology of suffering was called by the Radicals *Gelassenheit.* Borrowed from the tradition of medieval mysticism, this term has been variously translated yieldedness, surrender, passivity, resignation, but might simply be rendered "letting-loose-of-oneself." The opposite condition (*ungelassenheit*) is one of incomposure and anxiety, "always looking for a hiding place from which you would like to escape the hand of God."

Once God's will has been accepted, the surrendered soul experiences a kind of equanimity even amid the sorest temptations and dangers. The concepts of *Nachfolge* and *Gelassenheit* come together in the example of the selfless surrender of Jesus. What was really salvific about Jesus' death was the manner of his submission. Denck observed that "Christ was so extremely resigned (*gelassen*) that, although he loves all men without measure, if it had pleased the Father, he would also have willed to suffer even in vain. Therefore this sacrifice was accordingly pleasing to the Father."[25] Jesus is the place where a Christian can observe most fully the composition and consequences of a "gelassen" life. Thus, the Christian is called to a more profound *imitatio Christi* than the mere observance of outward conformity allows. The Christian must suffer the cross *in the same way as* Christ suffered the cross. From his prison cell, Michael Sattler addressed the following lines to his church at Horb: "In this peril I completely surrendered myself unto the will of the Lord, and . . . prepared myself even for death for his testimony."[26] It is not surprising that *Gelassenheit* and martyrdom are so closely conjoined.

The Bloody Theater: A Cloud of Witnesses

The theme of suffering found concrete expression in the example of the martyrs of the Radical Reformation, whose stories, printed and sung, became a major genre of Radical spirituality. The first ceremony of rebaptism in Zurich (21 January 1525) was carried out in defiance of the mandate of the town council. From the beginning, Anabaptists were regarded as seditious and heretical. In 1527, Zwingli summed up in one phrase his great fear of the Anabaptist movement: "They overturn everything."[27] Two years later the imperial diet at Speyer (April 1529) revived the ancient Code of Justinian, which specified the death penalty for the practice of rebaptism. The Radical Reformation was ruthlessly suppressed by Protestant and Roman Catholic magistrates alike. Servetus, for example, who was both an anabaptist and an anti-Trinitarian, held the dubious distinction of being burned in effigy by the Roman Catholics in France and in actuality by the Protestants in Geneva.

Leonhard Schiemer, who was beheaded in 1528, lamented the effects of persecution. "And now that we remain as a little flock, they have driven us with reproach and disgrace into every country. . . . They make the world too small for us."[28] Jakob Hutter, leader of the Moravian Anabaptists, wrote the following letter to the governor of Moravia on behalf of the distressed brothers and sisters who had been driven off their lands:

> So now we find ourselves out in the wilderness, under the open sky on a desolate heath. This we accept patiently, praising God that he has made us worthy to suffer for his name. . . . Yet we have among us many widows and orphans, many sick people and helpless little children who are unable to walk or travel. Their fathers and mothers were murdered by that tyrant Ferdinand, an enemy of divine justice![29]

Hutter himself was executed with the sword in 1536, following prolonged torture on the rack.

A vast literature of martyrdom developed in the wake of persecution. Many treatises and sermons were in effect exhortations to martyrdom. An excellent example of this was Menno Simons's booklet to his oppressed followers, *The Cross of the Saints* (1554). Taking as his theme the beatitude "Blessed are they which are persecuted for righteousness' sake," Menno reminded his readers that they were not the first to undergo "the angry, wolfish tearing and rending, the wicked animal-like torturing and blood-shedding of this godless world against the righteous."[30] He rehearsed the biblical examples of martyrdom, beginning with Abel, and appealed to Eusebius of Caesarea's *Ecclesiastical History* in order to establish the continuity between the martyrs of the early church and those of his own fellowship. He then refuted the charge of sedition and the spurious efforts to link all Anabaptists with the violent Münsterites. In conclusion, he called upon his followers as "soldiers and conquerors in Christ" to face with steadfastness and courage the supreme sacrifice:

> Therefore, O ye people of God, gird yourselves and make ready for battle; not with external weapon and armor as the bloody, mad world is wont to do, but only with firm confidence, a quiet patience, and a fervent prayer. . . . The thorny crown must pierce your head and the nails your hands and feet. Your body must be scourged and your face spit upon. On Golgotha you must pause and bring your own sacrifice. . . . Be not dismayed, for God is your captain.[31]

As in the early church, a kind of "cult of martyrs" emerged among the Radicals of the sixteenth century. Hans Hut's ashes were gathered and preserved as relics by his disciples. There is no evidence that the Radicals deliberately provoked their own deaths or rushed with glee to the pyre as some of the early Christian martyrs seem to have done. Yet, if not possessed of a lust for martyrdom, they were nonetheless heroic in their final anguished moments. When Balthasar Hubmaier was being prepared for the flame by having sulphur and gunpowder rubbed into his hair and long beard, he cried out: "Oh, salt me well, salt me well!" When the fagots were lit he repeated in Latin the words Jesus had uttered from the cross: "In manus tuas, Domine, commendo spiritum meum."[32] Hubmaier and his wife, who was drowned in the Danube with a stone tied around her neck, were both remembered and revered as martyrs. Stories like this lent themselves to dramatic retelling. A number of martyr ballads found their way into the famous *Ausbund*, the hymnal of the Swiss Brethren that is still used today by the Amish in North America. One of these hymns, "Wer Christo jetzt will folgen nach," commemorates the martyrdom of George Wagner, who, though apparently not an Anabaptist, was accused of denying priestly mediation of forgiveness and the salvific efficacy of water baptism. We give here four of the eighteen stanzas:

> Who Christ will follow now, new born,
> Dare not be moved by this world's scorn,
> The cross must bear sincerely;

No other way to heaven leads,
From childhood we're taught clearly.

This did George Wagner, too, aspire,
He went to heav'n 'mid smoke and fire,
The cross his test and proving,
As gold is in the furnace tried,
His hearts' desire approving.

Two barefoot monks in grey array,
George Wagner's sorrows would allay,
They would him be converting;
He waved them to their cloister home,
Their speech he'd be averting.

Men fastened him to ladder firm
The wood and straw was made to burn,
Now was the laughter dire;
Jesus! Jesus! did he four times
Call loudly from the fire.[33]

Second only to the Bible, the single most important document of Anabaptist piety is *The Bloody Theater or Martyrs' Mirror of the Defenseless
Christians Who Baptized Only Upon Confession of Faith, and Who Suffered
and Died for the Testimony of Jesus their Saviour.* This remarkable book, first
published in Dutch in 1660 as a folio volume of 1,290 pages, was based on
earlier Dutch martyr books and included a wide assortment of memorials,
testimonies, court transcripts, and excerpts from Anabaptist confessions and
chronicles. In its shaping influence on Radical spirituality, the *Martyrs'
Mirror* is comparable to John Foxe's *Acts and Monuments of the Christian
Martyrs* in the Puritan tradition.

The first part of the *Martyrs' Mirror* recounts the stories of heroic Christian martyrs up to the sixteenth century. The first "Anabaptist" martyr,
according to this reckoning, was John the Baptist, beheaded by King Herod
presumably for administering the "true baptism of repentance" as well as for
condemning the loose morality of the royal court. The trail of blood leads
on through the early church fathers, the Donatists ("not strange, unknown,
erring spirits, but such people as are also in our day styled Anabaptists"),
and the various medieval sectarian groups and concludes with the death of
Savonarola in 1498.[34]

Having covered fifteen bloody centuries through the first half of the
book, the *Martyrs' Mirror* next turns to those "who gave their lives for the
truth since the great Reformation." The purpose is clearly "to unite the first
martyrs with the last," thus proving the continuance of the suffering church
through all the ages.[35]

In 1552, Cornelius Aertsz de Man, a young man of seventeen, was interrogated before his execution. The judge alleged that the Mennonite church had only been in existence about thirty years. Cornelius replied that since Christ had promised to be with his church to the end of the world, "I do not doubt that he has been the preserver of his body. . . . Although the church has been wiped out in some countries through bloodshed and persecution, it has not been annihilated throughout the world."[36]

The circumstances of the martyrs' deaths are described in gripping detail: Felix Manz drowned in the Limmat at Zurich while his mother and brother stood on the river's bank encouraging him to remain steadfast; Ottilia Goldschmidt at the site of her execution was offered a proposal of marriage three times by a young man who thought to save her life in this way; Augustine, a Dutch baker, being taken to the fire said to the burgomaster who had sentenced him, "I cite you to appear within three days before the judgment seat of God." As soon as the execution was over, the burgomaster was smitten instantly with a severe illness and died within three days. Stories like these circulated among the faithful and served to encourage those who might be faced with similar tests.

Many of the letters printed in the *Martyrs' Mirror* were written from prison to friends and family members. They show the humanity of the martyrs, who, even in their hour of distress, did not despise the ties of intimacy that bound them to their dear ones. They commend those they must leave behind to the loving care of the fellowship. Often they mention how difficult it is to leave them behind. One of the most moving examples of this genre is the letter of Janneken Munstdorp to her infant daughter, also named Janneken. The baby had been born in prison while her mother awaited execution. It is addressed as a testament "to Janneken my own dearest daughter, while I was (unworthily) confined for the Lord's sake, in prison, at Antwerp, A.D. 1573."

> My dear little child, I commend you to the almighty, great and terrible God, who only is wise, that He will keep you, and let you grow up in His fear, or that He will take you home in your youth, this is my heart's request of the Lord: you who are yet so young, and whom I must leave here in this wicked, evil, perverse world.
>
> Since, then, the Lord has so ordered and foreordained it, that I must leave you here, and you are here deprived of father and mother, I will commend you to the Lord; let Him do with you according to His holy will. He will govern you, and be a Father to you, so that you shall have no lack here, if you only fear God; for He will be the Father of the orphans and the Protector of the widows.
>
> Hence, my dear lamb, I who am imprisoned and bound here for the Lord's sake, can help you in no other way; I had to leave your father for the Lord's

sake, and could keep him only a short time. We were permitted to live together only half a year, after which we were apprehended, because we sought salvation of our souls. They took him from me, not knowing my condition, and I had to remain in imprisonment, and see him go before me; and it was a great grief to him, that I had to remain here in prison. And now that I have abided the time, and borne you under my heart with great sorrow for nine months, and given birth to you here in prison, in great pain, they have taken you from me. Here I lie, expecting death every morning, and shall now soon follow your dear father. And I, your dear mother, write you, my dearest child, something for a remembrance, that you will thereby remember your dear father and your dear mother.

And now, Janneken, my dear lamb, who are yet very little and young, I leave you this letter, together with a gold real, which I had with me in prison, and this I leave you for a perpetual adieu, and for a testament; that you may remember me by it, as also by this letter. Read it, when you have understanding, and keep it as long as you live in remembrance of me and your father. And I herewith bid you adieu, my dear Janneken Munstdorp, and kiss you heartily, my dear lamb, with a perpetual kiss of peace. Follow me and your father, and be not ashamed to confess us before the world, for we were not ashamed to confess our faith before the world, and this adulterous generation.

Let it be your glory, that we did not die for any evil doing, and strive to do likewise, though they should also seek to kill you. And on no account cease to love God above all, for no one can prevent you from fearing God. If you follow that which is good, and seek peace, and ensue it, you shall receive the crown of eternal life; this crown I wish you and the crucified, bleeding, naked, despised, rejected and slain Jesus Christ for your bridegroom.[37]

We do not know what became of little Janneken, but in her mother's beautiful will and testament we have a poignant witness to the theology of martyrdom that sustained ordinary men and women of the Radical Reformation in their efforts to follow the "bitter Christ."

Sacramental Life

The Radical reformers agreed with the mainline Protestants in rejecting the Roman Catholic doctrine of seven sacraments. They retained baptism and the Lord's Supper, but imputed to these "signs" their own distinctive meanings.

Practically all of the Radicals rejected infant baptism as a devilish invention with no basis in either the Old or the New Testament. They called it a dog's bath, a pig's bath, a filthy ablution, an idolatrous abomination and other uncomplimentary designations. This hostile attitude led to direct confrontation with the authorities, Protestant and Roman Catholic alike, for whom infant baptism was an instrument of political conformity as well as a rite of great theological importance.

The Radicals defiantly withheld their infants from baptism and on occasion even committed iconoclastic acts against baptismal fonts. In Waldshut, for example, Hubmaier's congregation dismantled the old font and threw it into the Rhine. Hubmaier then proceeded to rebaptize three hundred adults using water from a milk pail.[38]

Zwingli himself, whose softened doctrine of original sin eliminated the traditional necessity for infant baptism, had early on harbored reservations about the rite.[39] Similarly, Erasmus held that baptism might be postponed until adolescence at the discretion of the parents and further proposed a public reenactment of baptism for those who had received the rite in infancy.[40] Picking up on these themes, the Anabaptists insisted, in the words of the *Schleitheim Confession* (1527):

> Baptism shall be given to all who have learned repentance and amendment of life, and who believe truly that their sins are taken away by Christ, and to all those who walk in the resurrection of Jesus Christ, and wish to be buried with him in death, so that they might be resurrected with him.[41]

This form of adult initiation is often referred to as "believers' baptism." However, the penitential aspect is so prominent that it could just as well be called "repenters' baptism." For the Radicals, repentance always preceded faith, in contrast to the teachings of Calvin, who reversed this order and interpreted repentance as a fruit of faith.[42] Repentance marked a decisive turnabout, a conscientious saying no to one's prior lifestyle and commitments. Obviously, this kind of hearty conversion could hardly be squared with a sacramental "baby's bath."

Luther, and more extensively Zwingli, Bullinger, and Calvin, defended infant baptism as analogous to circumcision in the Old Testament. The Anabaptists regarded this as a spurious argument, for they considered the Bible to be not the record of one covenant in two dispensations, but rather two separate covenants. The New Testament took precedence over the Old in all matters of faith and church order. Thus, Jesus' own adult baptism and his commission *first* to teach all nations and *then* to baptize them (Matt 28:19–20) were taken as the normative model for Christian baptism.

Yet Anabaptist baptism retained a strong covenantal connotation in that it was the public pledge of commitment which bound the repentant believer to the congregation. Hubmaier described this aspect of baptism thus:

> In receiving water baptism, the baptizand confesses publicly that he has yielded himself to live henceforth according to the rule of Christ. In the power of this confession he has submitted himself to the sisters, the brethren, and the church, so that now they have the authority to admonish him if he

errs, to discipline, to ban, and to readmit him.... Whence comes this authority if not from the baptismal vow?[43]

In many ways, adult baptism in the Radical Reformation stood in the place of the monastic vow as a solemn pledge of commitment to an ascetic community, signifying both a radical break with one's prior life and an intention to fulfill the "counsels of perfection" not in the confines of a cloister but amid the conflicts of life in the world.

Baptism was seen also as a preparatory washing for possible martyrdom. In Hubmaier's *Catechism*, the student is made to acknowledge a threefold baptism of the Spirit, of water, and of blood. The baptism of the Spirit is the inner experience of grace that precedes the outer baptism of water, which in turn places the believer on the "narrow path" of suffering and death. Hans Hut spoke of this third meaning when he said: "The water of all tribulation is the true essence and power of baptism." This "red baptism" is also recalled by Felix Manz's comment upon hearing his sentence of death by drowning—"Ah, that is real baptism."[44]

The administration of baptism varied greatly among the different traditions within the Radical Reformation. As an illegal act, rebaptism had to be done clandestinely. There are reports of Anabaptist baptisms in houses, barns, water towers, in fields and meadows, by rivers and creeks. When the authorities heard about an Anabaptist gathering near a body of water, they suspected a baptismal service might be in progress. The most common mode of baptism was pouring. Wolfgang Ulimann, an Anabaptist from St. Gall, insisted upon immersion: "he did not wish only to be poured over with water from a dish, but to be taken altogether naked into the Rhine by Grebel and pressed under and covered over."[45] Among the evangelical rationalists, Servetus also insisted on baptism by immersion, preferably at the age of thirty in literal imitation of Jesus' own baptism. Following Servetus, and perhaps also influenced by the practice of the neighboring Russian Orthodox church, the anti-Trinitarian Minor church in Poland equated immersion with true external baptism. The Racovian *Catechesis* of 1574 states bluntly: "Where you don't dip or immerse in the water, you can have no understanding of baptism unto the death, burial, and resurrection of the Lord Jesus Christ."[46]

The Hutterite *Chronicle* described the Lord's Supper as a beautiful and gracious remembrance of the bitter suffering and death of the Lord and a fervent expression of gratitude for salvation from sin. The *Schleitheim Confession* also spoke of breaking bread in remembrance of the broken body of Christ and of drinking the cup as remembrance of his shed blood. The original Anabaptists of Zurich were radical Zwinglians on the issue of the

Lord's Supper. They and their followers repudiated all eucharistic theologies of real presence, whether Roman Catholic, Lutheran, or Calvinist. Already in 1524, months before the first rebaptisms, Grebel, Manz, and their circle in Zurich set forth details for "the Supper of fellowship" even though the city council still required the Mass to be performed in the churches. The simplicity of Grebel's liturgy would serve as a model for later Radicals. A server from out of the congregation should pronounce the words of institution. A prayer of thanksgiving but not of consecration was offered. Ordinary bread and ordinary drinking vessels were used. Private eucharistic observance and the reserved sacrament were forbidden. There should be no priestly vestments, singing, nor anything that could create "a false reverence." Positively, the Supper was at once a commemorative banquet ("it calls to mind Christ's body and blood, the covenant of the cross") and a fellowship meal ("it shows us that we are truly one bread and one body").[47]

By the late sixteenth century the Anabaptists of the Lower Rhine had not departed significantly from this pattern, except that by then the layperson had been replaced by a designated minister as the officiant:

> When the Lord's Supper was distributed the minister took the bread and broke a piece of it for each, and as soon as it was given out and each had a piece in his hand, the minister also took a piece for himself, put it into his mouth and ate it; and immediately, seeing this, the congregation did the same. The minister, however, used no words, no ceremonies, no blessing. As soon as the bread was eaten, the minister took a bottle of wine or a cup, drank, and gave each of the members of it. On this wise they observe the breaking of bread.[48]

The symbolic character of the Lord's Supper was defended by the martyrs, who were frequently questioned about their eucharistic theology. An Anabaptist from West Friesland was asked: "What do you hold concerning the sacrament?" He replied: "I know nothing of your baked God." A widow named Weynken, from The Hague, was sentenced to death by strangling because she stubbornly denied the sacramental efficacy of the Supper. On the morning of her execution, a Dominican friar offered to administer the sacrament to her. She said: "What God would you give me? One that is perishable and is sold for a farthing?" And to the priest who had celebrated Mass that day, she said that he had crucified God anew.[49]

Despite the minimalist theology implied in these testimonies, the Lord's Supper as celebrated among the Radicals was not a shallow casual observance but rather a vivid reenactment of Jesus' last meal and an anticipation of the eschatological messianic banquet. Menno Simons referred to it as the "Christian marriage feast" at which "Jesus Christ is present with his grace, Spirit, and promise."[50] Dietrich Philips, a later Mennonite, went so far as to equate the "manna" of communion with the heavenly flesh of Christ, which nourished and gradually divinized the regenerate Christians who gathered at the Lord's Table to partake of "the food of angels." The Lord's Supper, then, although interpreted primarily as a memorial, was not without soteriological implications. For this reason it became an occasion for disciplinary sanctions such as admonition and the ban in an effort to maintain a spotless community in the world of evil.[51]

Worship and Prayer

Harold Bender pointed to an important dimension of worship in the Radical Reformation when he asserted that Anabaptist congregations were not "audiences" in attendance upon a worship service furnished by a clergyman in a building belonging to the state, but a genuine fellowship of believers sharing in Bible study, prayer, and mutual admonition.[52] For many Radicals, the Christian life was a kind of uncloistered monasticism that presupposed a daily walk of holy obedience, prayer, and praise. For example, we read of a small group of Anabaptists who lived in a house behind the cathedral in Halberstadt in 1535. They would pray and sing four times a day, before and after meals, and rise twice during the night to resume their praise of God.[53] The Hutterites reportedly conformed their daily prayers to a Trinitarian schema. In the morning they prayed, "May God the Father protect me"; at noon, "May God the Son protect me"; at evening, "May God the Holy Spirit protect me." Other Radicals refused to accord any special significance to Sunday, arguing that God had made all the days of the week alike and that Christians were endowed with an "eternal Sabbath," which they should celebrate daily and without interruption, abstaining from sin and allowing God to work in them.[54]

The Radicals were reluctant to attach sacredness or holiness to any special objects, places, persons, or days. In Hubmaier's *Catechism*, the question is asked: "Where do you pray to Christ?" The respondent replies: "Neither in one place nor another. And even if someone says, 'Look, Christ is there on the altar; there he sits in the little stone or silver house,' I do not believe this."[55]

The earliest evidence for an Anabaptist meetinghouse dates from 1590. The Hutterites declined to build churches or chapels, preferring to gather for worship in a large community room such as the dining hall. By necessity many Radical conventicles were more often *ad hoc* gatherings. Menno admitted that "we preach by day and by night, in houses and in fields, in forests and wastes, hither and yon, at home or abroad. . . ."[56] Such meetings were always liable to discovery and attack by the authorities.

The form of the worship services is difficult to reconstruct, since most Radicals did not follow a formal liturgy. Scripture reading and exposition, prayer, singing, and frequent celebration of the Lord's Supper were common elements in Anabaptist worship. A church order of 1529, found in the archives at Bern, ruled that only one speaker should hold forth at a time. Peter Riedemann's *Confession* (1540) described a more formal worship structure that was used by the Hutterites. The service began with a period of silent preparation and self-examination. This was followed by a time of thanksgiving and prayer, proclamation of the word, hymn singing, and benediction.[57]

The Lord's Prayer was widely used among Radicals in all three major groupings. Hubmaier defined prayer as "an elevating of the soul to God in spirit and in truth," and he commended the Lord's Prayer as a part of catechetical instruction.[58] However, the Austrian Anabaptist Leonhard Schiemer offered a scathing parody of what the "Pater Noster" meant to nominal Christians. They pray to God "in heaven" but do not live by his commandments on earth. They ask for "our daily bread" but, having received it, they act as if it were "my" bread and live not by faith but by material gain. Some of the Radicals, such as the unitarian Camillo Renato, went so far as to eliminate all audible prayer including even the Lord's Prayer. The Spanish spiritualist Juan de Valdés, who could not quite agree with that approach, wrote a devotional commentary on the Lord's Prayer. He insisted nonetheless that prayer should be "more spiritual than verbal" and could in no wise be tied to "books or beads."[59]

Among many of those Radical groups who disparaged any form of set or "stinted" prayers, a very loose, almost charismatic, style of worship seems to have prevailed. Anabaptists in the Rems valley reportedly "fell on their faces," clasped their hands, and cried "The Lord be praised." One hostile observer likened the confusion of an Anabaptist prayer service to the "groaning and grunting of a tired old nag pulling a cart."[60] In a similar vein, Henry Barrow in England lambasted *The Book of Common Prayer*, calling it "a piece of swine's flesh" and "stage-like dialogue" and insisting that worship be characterized by the free moving of the Spirit and the spontaneous response of the people. The Barrowists, like continental Anabaptists, refused to worship in the established churches, but held their own services in various secluded spots around London. According to the report of an informant, their service consisted of Scripture exposition, extemporaneous prayer ("one speaketh and the rest do groan, or sob, or sigh, as if they would wring out tears"), the collection, and a common meal followed by a simple administration of the Lord's Supper.[61] This kind of pneumatic worship must have been common among many sects within the wide spectrum of the

Radical Reformation. Having abandoned infant baptism and the Mass, together with the formal liturgical traditions of Christendom, these reborn Christians felt free to follow the inclinations of their hearts, energized by the fresh impulses of the Spirit, wherever they might lead.

Another quieter tradition of worship among the Radicals should also be noted. In early Dutch Mennonite churches, the congregation would kneel and remain in silent devotion at both the beginning and close of the service. The practice of silent prayer was observed so that everyone could call upon the Lord "without confusion or indecent noise."

Some Swiss and Dutch Anabaptists also published collections of printed prayers. Many of these were prayers of personal devotion: morning and evening prayers, prayers before and after meals, prayers for the worried and depressed, and prayers for the sick. In 1625, Leonhard Klock published in Dutch a *Formulary of Several Prayers,* which included prayers for baptism, the Lord's Supper, and the marriage ceremony. Originally addressed to the "unanimous brethren in Prussia," this book contained a prayer that became something of a model for the later Mennonite tradition:

> Lord have mercy upon all who hate and persecute Thee and us and do harm to us. Forgive them for they know not what they do. For that reason do not hold them guilty on our behalf. We also pray for all those good-hearted people who like to listen to Thy word but lack strength to commit themselves unto thy obedience. Give them yet strength through the Holy Spirit. We pray for all those who suffer for the sacred testimony, being in prison, in bonds, pursued, exiled, despised, oppressed or else deprived of all goods and all con-solation. . . . Break, pound, and make contrite our hearts that they may shed gushing tears which Thou, O Father, mightest behold. . . . We also pray Thee to bestow upon us thy great longing and the affection of the heart, and also a sweet, devout nature, so that we in childlike love may call upon Thee, O God, as our Father.[62]

Militia Christi: The Sword and the Ban

Roland H. Bainton has observed that, when Christianity takes itself seri-ously, it must either forsake or master the world and at different points it may try to do both at once.[63] Clearly, both of these impulses were repre-sented within the Radical Reformation. The Great Peasants' War (1525) and the "Maccabean" Anabaptist uprising at Münster (1535) were the two most notable spectacles of religiously sanctioned violence within the Radical Reformation. A more moderate view of the Christian's relationship with the state was that of Hubmaier, who wrote a treatise *On the Sword* (1527), in which he countenanced the legitimate coercive powers of government, such as just war and capital punishment, and argued that a Christian could discharge the office of a magistrate without violation of conscience. (His followers were called "Schwertler" over against the pacifistic "Stäbler," who felt that as soldiers of Christ they could carry only staffs not swords.) Both revolutionary violence and real political compromise were decidedly minority positions within the Radical Reformation considered as a whole. By and large, spiritualists, Anabaptists, and evangelical rationalists alike deliberately cut themselves off from the coercive structures of society, refusing to bear arms, serve in the military, swear an oath, or hold any magisterial office.[64]

Most Radicals of the pacifist bent admitted that the "sword" was indeed ordained by God, but only "outside the perfection of Christ," as the *Schleitheim Confession* put it. That is to say, within the church the nonviolence and suffering love of Christ must be followed strictly as a witness to the world. Conversely, if magistrates desire to follow Christ, they must, quite literally, deny themselves *qua* magistrates. They must love their enemies, not kill them. Refusal of force and authority, then, becomes, along with regeneration and baptism, the *sine qua non* of admittance to the church. When asked to explain the logical inconsistency of how God could have authorized the magistracy yet prevented the salvation of any holder thereof, one Anabaptist responded in language strikingly similar to Calvin's defense of double predestination: "Since the issue of the magistracy and coercion surprises you so, namely that God ordained and instituted you and that you should yet be condemned and not saved in your office . . . my dear man, who are you to quarrel with God? Does that which is made say to the maker: Why have you made me thus?"[65]

When we look for the spiritual basis of this radical stance of nonresistance, we find the Radicals appealing again and again to the example of Jesus. Jakob Hutter assured the governor of Moravia: "We do not want to hurt or wrong anyone, not even our worst enemy, be it Ferdinand or anyone else." He further alleged that his followers would let themselves be robbed of a hundred florins rather than strike our worst enemy with the hand—to say nothing of spears, swords, and halberds. "As anyone can see, we have no physical weapons, neither spears nor muskets. No, we want to show by our word and deed that men should live as true followers of Christ." Hutter declared that it had "never entered our heads to act like the Münsterites." The Old Testament could no longer be cited as a precedent for war and bloodshed, since Christ had inaugurated a new kingdom based on forgiveness and nonviolence. The *militia Christi* is an army that sheds no blood. Its weapons are prayer, fasting, and faith. "God commands us now to beat our swords into plowshares and sickles. Wars must cease throughout the

23. *Martyrdom of Jan Smit* from Thieleman J. van Braght,
Martyrs Mirror, p. 963.

24. *Catherina Mulerin Apprehended* from Thieleman J. van Braght,
Martyrs Mirror, p. 1111.

world wherever believers are."[66] Consistent with their strategy of non-violence, the Hutterites refused to pay war taxes or revenues for executioners' wages, although they remained dutifully obedient to the authorities in all matters that did not violate their conscience.

The gospel of nonresistance was at the core of this kind of Radical spirituality. Their radical apoliticism flowed directly from their view of God as essentially noncoercive. Hans Denck asked why God did not "make us as he himself would have us?" and then supplied the answer to his own question. "The reason is, namely, that God does not wish to compel, so that his mercy might be recognized and not depised." According to Denck, Jesus is the normative model for Christians precisely because he most clearly displayed the character and intention of God. God created all persons equal to himself. Yet none so remained except Jesus, who so loved the others that he offered his own life for their sakes, *"which he must surely have learned from the Father,* since he was completely equal with the Father and heeded him in all things."[67] In this line of thought we can hear an echo of that early Christian claim that God sent his Son in gentleness and mildness, to save and persuade, not to rule as a tyrant, nor to exercise force, for "force is no attribute of God."[68]

It is significant that, in the very context of declaring the use of the sword off limits for Christians, the *Schleitheim Confession* contrasts its purpose in the world to that of church discipline within the congregation: "In the perfection of Christ, only the ban is used for a warning and for the excommunication of the one who has sinned, without putting the flesh to death."[69] In Anabaptist thinking, the authority of internal governance was in some sense parallel to the power of the magistrate. Like the pre-Constantinian church, which existed in polemical parallelism with the Roman Empire, the radical sectarians of the sixteenth century, refusing to conform to their environing culture, conceived of the church as an "alternative society" with its own instruments of order and discipline.

The "ban" was the means by which unworthy and corrupt church members were excluded from the congregation. The Anabaptists insisted upon this rite as an essential mark of the true church, which, like every living organism, had to be able to eliminate extraneous matter: "But the church without this power is as a monstrous body wanting the faculties and instruments of evacuation and expulsion of excrements, or other noisome things, and therefore is never appointed to God to live, but devoted to death and destruction."[70]

The Racovian *Catechesis* of the Polish Brethren lists five reasons for the maintenance of church discipline: (1) that the transgressor may be healed and brought back to the right way; (2) that others may be stricken with fear and kept uncorrupted by the wicked; (3) that scandal and disorder may be removed from the church; (4) that the word of the Lord be not evil spoken of outside the congregation; (5) that the glory and name of the Lord not be profaned.[71] The inability of the established churches to maintain proper discipline, along with their false doctrine and "idolatrous" sacraments, was a major reason for separation.

The remedial intent of discipline was stressed by the Radicals. The three stages of fraternal admonition enjoined by Matthew 18 were to be followed patiently before the severe act of exclusion was taken. Moreover, the formal ban was, at least in theory, only a social confirmation of a severance from Christ which had already occurred in the heart of the unrepentant member:

> No one is excommunicated or expelled by us from the communion of the brethren but those who have already separated and expelled themselves from Christ's communion either by false doctrine or improper conduct. For we do not want to expel any, but rather to receive; not to amputate, but rather to heal; not to discard, but rather to win back; not to grieve, but rather to comfort; not to condemn, but rather to save.[72]

The pastoral tone of this statement, which comes from Menno Simons's *Admonition on Church Discipline* (1541), was in fact often betrayed by the vindictive and harsh recriminations often involved in "shunning" expelled members. The practice of avoiding all social contact with the impenitent seems to have been a distinctive practice of the Dutch Mennonites. It probably originated in their efforts to distinguish themselves from the violent Münsterites. Soon, however, it came to be applied more widely to include the avoidance even of family members who were under the ban. Menno continued to counsel leniency especially in the case of an excommunicated spouse. In 1550, a dispute arose in Emden congregation of a sister, Swaen Rutgers, who refused to abstain from marital intercourse with her back-slidden husband. While some in the church argued in favor of banning her as well, Menno would not consent to such an action.[73]

Among the offenses punished by banning were heavy drinking, adultery, swearing oaths, marriage to an unbeliever, teaching false doctrines, unrelieved quarreling with spouses, and embezzling the congregation's money. Most of these were matters of personal holiness or internal congregational concern. However, the wider concern to present a pure witness to the world was not taken lightly. For example, an English tailor was excommunicated from his separatist church for charging seven shillings for making "a doublet and hose" when the going rate was five![74] The strenuous use of discipline could, and doubtless often did, degenerate into petty legalism. Yet it also contained elements of social protest that reached beyond the confines of the single congregation.

The Radical conventicles were models of what sociologists of religion call "intentional" communities. Membership was neither casual nor assumed; participation was perforce hearty and vigorous. A true visible church was at once a rebaptized company of gathered saints, *separated from* the world in its autonomous polity and eschewal of all violent connections, and a squad of spiritual shock troops *separating back to* the world through congregational discipline those members whose lives betrayed their profession.

A Gospel for Everyone: Eschatology and Ecumenicity

The adherents of the Radical Reformation were possessed of an intense eschatological fervor concerning the imminent Second Advent of Christ. Since the time of Augustine, the millennium of Revelation 20 had been interpreted widely as the present age of the church. According to this theory, the evil designs of Satan were being held in check ("chained," Rev 20:1) by Christian magistrates while the church, containing both redeemed and reprobate, awaited the final consummation of all things. By withdrawing from the official churches with their linkage to magisterial coercion, the Radicals broke decisively with this established eschatology. Interpreting their own times as the last days, the Radicals conceived of themselves as the secret bearers of the new age. Having restored (rather than merely "reformed") the church to its pristine purity, they stood, as it were, in the vortex of a historical movement destined to overthrow the powers of darkness and usher in the millennial reign. Such ideas, in bewildering combinations and often unharmonized details, sustained the Radicals as they developed their distinctive spirituality under the shadow of the end times.

The apocalyptic tone that sounds through so much of early Anabaptist literature must be set in the context of the fervent expectations that had been unleashed by the Peasants' War and the severe repression of religious radicalism that followed in its wake. Thomas Müntzer, who regarded himself as an Old Testament warrior-priest and signed his letters "Thomas Müntzer with the sword of Gideon," was beheaded following the disastrous battle of Frankenhausen (1525). A strong echo of Müntzer's teaching could be heard in the prophetic utterances of Hans Hut, a bookseller turned Anabaptist apostle. Hut interpreted the imminence of Christ's return in terms of contemporary events, "signs of the time," the most notable of which was the incursion of the Turkish armies into Christendom. By the late 1520s, they had advanced to the gates of Vienna. Drawing on the prophecies in Revelation 13 and Daniel 12, Hut predicted the return of Christ for Pentecost 1528—precisely three and one-half years after the Peasants' War. Hut set about to gather the 144,000 elect saints (Rev 7:4), whom he "sealed" by baptizing them on the forehead with the sign of the cross. At Christ's appearing, the righteous would reign on earth in a kingdom without government, without sword, and with no economic differentiation, while the wicked would be consigned to eternal punishment. By 1528 Hut was dead. His charred body (he had set fire to his prison cell in a futile effort to escape) was condemned posthumously. His movement soon splintered, although his apocalyptic message was taken up by other prophets such as Melchior Hoffman, who set a different date (1534) and place (Strasbourg) for the Second Coming—with similar results. Although both Hut and Hoffman counseled their followers to wield only the "sheathed sword"—that is, to absorb violence but not to inflict it—their drastic predictions and scathing invective against emperor, pope, and "bloodsucking anti-Christian Lutheran and Zwinglian preachers" created an atmosphere in which the overtly revolutionary kingdom of Münster could flourish.[75]

The Swiss Brethren were avowedly pacifistic from the first and were hardly, if at all, influenced by Thomas Müntzer. Yet similar kinds of apocalyptic currents can be found in their movement as well. In June 1525, a procession of rebaptized peasants from Zollikon entered the city of Zurich and paraded through its streets crying, "Woe, woe, woe, O Zurich." They wore willow twigs and ropes instead of belts, fulfilling the prophecy of Isaiah that in the last days believers would wear "a rope instead of a girdle." They pilloried Zwingli as "the old dragon" and, in the spirit of Jonah, gave the city forty days in which to repent.[76] The expectation of Christ's imminent return had become a central motivating force in the establishment of the pure church.

Michael Sattler, author of the *Schleitheim Confession*, wrote a letter from prison to his church at Horb. Drawing on the apocryphal book of Esdras as well as on the book of Revelation, he interpreted the gatherings of baptized churches as a sign that the end was near.

> Pray that reapers may be driven out into the harvest, for the time of threshing has come near. The abomination of desolation is visible among you. The elect servants and maidservants of God will be marked on the forehead with the name of the Father. The world has arisen against those who are redeemed from its error. The gospel is testified to before all the world for a testimony. According to this the day of the Lord must no longer tarry.[77]

Sattler did warn against "vain speculations" and, so far as we know, set no precise dates for Christ's return.

Anticipating the descent of the New Jerusalem, the early Anabaptists fled "out from Babylon, and from the earthly Egypt," so as not to partake of "the torment and suffering which the Lord will bring upon them" (Rev 18:4).[78]

Their hasty exodus, of course, brought considerable torment and suffering upon them in this life. As the persecutions intensified, so too did the fervency of their eschatological hope. Driven from country to country, finding no permanent home anywhere, they yearned for that "divine homeland, since we have no peace or rest in this wretched wilderness."[79]

In an apt phrase, the Belgian historian Henri Pirenne described Anabaptism as "the Protestantism of the poor."[80] The spread of an apocalyptic mood throughout large sectors of the Radical Reformation accompanied the social dislocation caused by widespread hunger, inflation, unemployment, and pestilence in the sixteenth century. We cannot claim a direct causal link here, since many Radicals in more comfortable circumstances (such as the Polish Brethren, who counted large numbers of the nobility in their fellowship) also possessed intense eschatological beliefs. Still, the larger percentage of those who flocked to the Radical conventicles were ordinary men and women of the rank and file—peasants, seamstresses, bakers, button makers, soap boilers, "tub mechanics," shepherds, and shoemakers. Paupers and people with little or no property were numerous in their gatherings. Most of these people found a respite from their bitter economic misery in a gospel that pointed beyond the hopeless circumstances of this world to an age of utter equality and plenty. Many of them, too, doubtless rejoiced at the prospect of divine justice meted out to all religious and political "big shots."

The millennial expectations of many Radicals had another profound impact on their spiritual life: it saved them from an abandonment of history and responsibility within the world. Paul Althaus has captured well the significance of this insight in his comparison of Lutheran and Radical eschatologies: "Chiliasm means *to remain faithful to this earth*; that is, it means working toward the overcoming of the demons of this world."[81] Although most of the Radicals despaired of political transformation of the world and opposed the structures of temporal power as themselves demonic in their violent *modus operandi*, they nevertheless resisted the ultimate temptation of quietism and political indifference. In their efforts to maintain a faithful witness in this present, provisional aeon, they forged a spirituality that was at once profoundly otherworldly and yet unswervingly committed to the purposes of God within history.

Before we turn to the universalistic implications of Radical eschatology, a brief word should be said about a major modification of the traditional doctrine of personal immortality of the soul. Although the Protestants eliminated purgatory as a category of the afterlife, with the equivocal exception of Luther, they all held tenaciously to the concept of immortality.[82] In his first theological treatise, *Psychopannychia*, Calvin derided the Radical concept of soul sleep and presented a lively picture of the joys of the blessed in heaven contrasted with the torments of the damned in hell.[83] The

Radicals held that, between death and the general resurrection, the soul either slept (psychosomnolence) or, more drastically, was obliterated (mortalism). In either case, they believed that they had recovered the primordial Christian eschatology, in which the dominant motif was resurrection from the dead rather than immortality of the soul.

In holding to a view of the afterlife that we might characterize as "death after death," the Radicals placed all the more stress on the *parousia* as the great final denouement of history. Although the interim between death and resurrection perforce would be a period of total extinction or dreamless sleep, the decisive last day would come "in the twinkling of an eye" as a moment of ultimate vindication and grand reunion. This expectation, together with the denial of sentient life in heaven, hell, or purgatory, may account in part for the lack of any developed funeral ritual among the Radicals. The martyrs were often buried under the gallows or in lots set aside for criminals. Others were buried in meadows, vineyards, under trees, behind sheds, in open fields. The funerals were conducted without ceremony or liturgy not only because they knew the lack of such rites would hardly affect their salvation but also because they awaited with eager expectancy the sound of the heavenly trumpet and the descent of that city which hath foundations.[84]

The Radical Reformation was a part of that great renewal of faith and learning which greatly expanded the horizons of Christian consciousness—backward toward the sources of classical and Christian antiquity, inward through new appropriations of mystical and spiritualist traditions, outward in the discovery of new continents and new races of human beings beyond the pale of Christendom, and even upward in the opening up of the heavens through the new science of astronomy and the invention of the telescope. The Radicals are not usually thought of as being in the vanguard of these developments. Their deliberate withdrawal from the main currents of political and religious life often did lead to a restrictive and exclusivistic stance. The very term by which they are best known in modern discourse, "sectarian," suggests narrow-mindedness and bigotry. Despite their separatist ecclesiology, however, they advanced a kind of "sectarian ecumenicity," which reached beyond the bounds of their provincial interests. Based on their worldwide eschatological vision, they evidenced a number of universalizing tendencies which broke through traditional restrictions and barriers and helped to enlarge the scope of redemptive and humanitarian concerns.[85]

Universal Salvation

The *Augsburg Confession* (article 17) condemned the Anabaptists for teaching that there "would be an end to the torments of the devils and condemned humans." Although this was by no means the generally accepted view among most Anabaptists, we do find an ecumenical salvific concern at several points in the soteriology of the Radical Reformation. We may point briefly to three variants of this theme.

First, the Radicals, having abandoned infant baptism as a useless trifle, taught that *all* children who had not reached an age of personal accountability were protected by the saving work of Christ. The Hutterite evangelist Nikolaus Geyersbühler did not hesitate to extend this benefit beyond the bounds of the *corpus christianum:* God does not differentiate among children born to Christians, Turks, and Jews, for all are God's creation.

Second, in an age of inquisitions and crusades, some Radicals showed a remarkable appreciation for the positive religious values in Islam and Judaism. Thomas Müntzer, who had read the Qur'an, allowed that even those born as Turks could experience a genuine moving of the Holy Spirit and the beginning of true faith. Furthermore, the Jews too have "to all outward appearances more justification than other uninformed, flighty people, for at least they are quarreling among themselves over the meaning of Scripture—a worthy controversy—and not like us over prestige and property.[86] More daring still was Jacob Palaeologus, an evangelical rationalist, who advanced the idea of an interfaith "church" composed of Jewish, Christian, and Muslim branches. Palaeologus felt that his own unitarian theology could serve as a natural point of contact with these other great monotheistic traditions.[87]

A few of the Radicals actually proclaimed the eventual salvation of all persons. Clement Ziegler, a garden preacher in Strasbourg, hoped that in the last days not only Jews but also "Turks, Tartars, Greeks, and pagans" would be saved. In the spirit of Origen (whom he cited) he announced his conviction that far-off pagans and even devils would be saved finally, even without express knowledge of Christ's historical mission. Another explicit univeralist among the Radicals, Hans Denck, was moved to "de-mythologize" hell. Hell, he explained, was the torment of the conscience which led to the acknowledgment of sin and unbelief. But this penitential process, though painful and necessary, was only temporary, for even in hell there is grace.[88]

Missionary Impulses

Although most Radicals would have looked askance at the notion of universal salvation, they all took quite seriously the command of Jesus to "go into all the world" with the message of the gospel (Matt 28:19–20). The "Great Commission" was a favorite proof text of the Radicals, not only because of its endorsement of believers' baptism but also because of its missionary imperative. The standard Protestant interpretation of this passage relegated the dominical command to the past. It had been fulfilled by the original apostolic mission and was no longer operative. The Radicals contemporized the mandate for world mission and applied it indiscriminately to all Christians. In utter disregard for the civic, territorial, and national perimeters of the established churches, the Radical reformers fanned out across Europe and even penetrated Byzantine and Muslim territory. In their conception of a world missionary apostolate, the Radicals stood closer to the revitalized orders of the Catholic Reformation than to mainline Protestantism, which did not fully "catch up" in its missionary outreach until the nineteenth century.

Most of the Radicals of the sixteenth century were displaced persons. Called out of their "rootedness in family, people, and profession into the sphere of Jesus," they saw themselves as sojourners in this world and forerunners of the New Jerusalem, which was about to descend.[89] The fusion of eschatological intensity and missionary zeal is seen in Sattler's admonition to his church to "pray that reapers may be driven out into the harvest, for the time of threshing has come near."

The Radicals recaptured the Christian missionary zeal of the early church. Like the first disciples, they too "went everywhere preaching the word" (Acts 8:4). In this sense, the Radicals, far more than the Protestant reformers, recovered the original meaning of "ecumenical." Their missionary vision included an enlarged *oikoumenē*, the whole inhabited world.

Religious Toleration

In 1612, Thomas Helwys, an English Baptist, published in London *A Short Declaration of the Mystery of Iniquity*. Dedicated to King James, one extant copy of this treatise bears the following handwritten ascription: "Hear O king, and despise not the counsel of the poor. . . . The king is a mortal man, and not God, therefore hath no power over the immortal souls of his subjects." Helwys went on to appeal for universal religious toleration: "Let them be heretics, Turks, Jews, or whatsoever, it appertains not to the earthly power to punish them."[90] Helwys and his congregation had come into close contact with the Mennonites while exiled at Amsterdam. His doctrine of toleration may well have been shaped by exposure to these heirs of the Radical Reformation.

As early as 1525, Conrad Grebel wrote to his brother-in-law Joachim Vadian, the reformer of St. Gall, appealing for toleration: "If you are not willing to stand with the Brethren, at least do not resist them; do not give to other states the example of persecution."[91] Four years before his own death at the stake, Hubmaier wrote a tract called *Concerning Heretics and Those Who Burn Them.* He asserted that "the law that condemns heretics to the fire builds up both Zion in blood and Jerusalem in wickedness. . . . Christ did not come to butcher, destroy and burn, but that those that live might live more abundantly."[92]

The achievement of religious toleration was the result of a variety of interlocking causes, both secular and religious. Certainly we cannot claim that the pleas for toleration voiced by Helwys, Hubmaier, and others brought an end to religious coercion. Yet the Radical perspective on toleration, hammered out amid persecution, was an important example of a Christian challenge to civil encroachment in matters religious.

The Radical call for toleration was related in two important ways to the spirituality we have been outlining. Theirs was not merely the cry of an oppressed sect for *its* right to religious toleration, but rather an explicit avowal of *universal* religious toleration. The forcing of persons in matters of faith is counterproductive since the character of faith is *ipso facto* noncoercive. Rulers and magistrates do not have it within their power to compel the heart. By compulsion they can only produce hypocrites, not true Christians.

The Radicals also believed that each soul stood in a unique and immediate relation to God, which religious coercion aimed to circumvent. They appealed to the inviolability of the conscience in opposing the demands for conformity. Jakob Hutter, for example, told the Moravian authorities that "God has not given the government power to demand obedience of us in matters that conflict with our conscience. Then we may say with the Apostle Peter that we must obey God rather than man."[93] As we have seen, they rejected infant baptism, which seemed to them an inevitably coercive act since it imposed a religious status on an unwilling subject. They also appealed to the sanctity of conscience in refusing to swear oaths or to bear arms. The missionary task, which they valued so highly, was another motive behind their advocacy of toleration. Hutter wrote: "We wish all the world lived like us; we would like *to convince* and turn all men to this faith, for that would mean the end of warfare and injustice."[94]

Economic Justice

Hutterite children were taught a nursery rhyme that summarized the concern for economic justice and the sharing of goods, which were central to their community life:

> Gottes Wort Wär Nit so Schwär
> Wan Nur Der Aigen Nutz Nit Wär.[95]

The Radical reformers were deeply concerned about the plight of the poor and disadvantaged, many of whom found solace and support in their close-knit conventicles. While the emphasis of mutual aid focused on the baptized community, compassion was not limited to the inner circle. Hans Leopold, a Swiss Brethren martyr of 1528, said of the Brethren: "If they know of anyone who is in need, whether or not he is a member of their church, they believe it their duty, out of love to God, to render help and aid."[96] Indeed, we may suppose that one reason why so many of the marginated members of society were attracted to the Radical congregations was the loving concern lavished upon them by the brothers and sisters.

Menno Simons felt that genuine compassion for the poor was one of the marks that distinguished his movement from that of the mainline reformers. He criticized the "easygoing gospel and barren bread-breaking" of the Protestant clergy who lived in luxury and splendor while their poor members begged for food, and the old, lame, blind, and suffering ones were shunted. In contrast:

> [The true Christians] do not suffer a beggar among them. They have pity on the wants of the saints. They receive the wretched. They take strangers into their houses. They comfort the sad. They lend to the needy. They clothe the naked. They share their bread with the hungry. They do not turn their face from the poor nor do they regard their decrepit limbs and flesh. This is the kind of brotherhood we teach. . . .[97]

At the same time, Menno denied that such benevolence implied a literal community of goods or the abolition of private property, as the revolutionary Anabaptists of Münster had practiced.

The Hutterites, however, did insist that the Christian life, rightly lived, involved the annihilation of the proprietary spirit. In Moravia they erected their pacifistic, communistic communities where, after the model of the New Testament church, all property was held in common and used as needed for the welfare of the whole group. The "servants of temporal needs" distributed the goods, while the "servants of the Word" attended to preaching and liturgical duties.

When we look for the spiritual basis of this extraordinary experiment in communal life, several motifs come together. They found biblical warrant for community of goods not only in the example of the early church at Jerusalem but also in the sending of manna to ancient Israel, Christ's feeding of the five thousand and his expulsion of the money changers from the temple, as well as the numerous Pauline warnings against covetousness and his admonition to Timothy to "do good, give gladly and have all things in common" (1 Tim 6:18). The mystical principle of *Gelassenheit* with its soteriological connotations was also interpreted in terms of a surrender or yielding up of one's temporal possessions. To hold on to the flitting treasures of this world was a prime characteristic of an unresigned will, of failure to be totally submissive to God. The "gospel of all creatures" also taught communal living since all nature—the animals, the plants, the birds, the fish—shared the common bounty of creation.[98]

Peter Riedemann, the most articulate theologian among the Hutterites, found a further justification for the community of goods within the divine nature itself.

> Community, however, is naught else than that those who have fellowship have all things in common together, none having aught for himself, but each having all things with the others, even as the Father hath nothing for himself, but all that he hath, he hath with the Son, and again, the Son hath nothing for himself, but all that he hath, he hath with the Father and all who have fellowship with him.[99]

For all of the Radicals, concern for economic justice formed an integral part of Christian discipleship, whether they followed the practice of mutual aid or the more drastic pattern of Christian communism. Inherent in their stance was an implicit critique of contemporary economic life. Since everything had been created free and in common, those who appropriated creaturely things and hoarded them for themselves were, in effect, stealing. "Of such thieves," wrote one of the Hutterites, "the whole world is full. May God guard his own from them."[100] The Radical communitarians held little hope for transforming the economic structures of their time. However, in constructing their "alternative societies" based on sharing, togetherness, and unity, they challenged the spirit of acquisition and unbridled individualism which dominated so much of both the secular and religious life of Christendom.

Human Equality

The piety and spirituality of the Radical Reformation was marked by a strong egalitarianism which matched its anticlericalism. Luther had emphasized the "priesthood of all believers," yet many Radicals found his implementation of this principle defective and half-hearted. Carlstadt, disillusioned with Luther's temporizing, divested himself of his priestly and academic attire and took up the life of a peasant-preacher ("Bruder Andreas" he styled himself) in the village of Orlamünde. Some Anabaptists refused to accord special respect to the authorities and addressed them as "ye my brethren" or as "dear men and brethren." The Hutterites made a point of addressing each other with the familiar "Du" rather than the proper "Ihr," which was reserved for God alone.[101] To be sure, their practice of equality did not always conform to their doctrine. One defector complained that the ordinary brethren were given only peas and cabbage to eat, whereas the leaders of the community enjoyed roast meat, fish, and good wine.[102]

The role of women in the Radical Reformation deserves further study. It is too much to say that Radical innovations constituted "a momentous step in the Western emancipation of women."[103] Still, believers' baptism was an equalizing sacrament qualifying both men and women for deliberations of the conventicle, missionary service, and martyrdom. "Brothers and sisters" are mentioned jointly with great frequency in the confessions, church orders, and letters of the Radicals. Women served as protectors, patrons, prophets, apostles, preachers, deacons, and hymn writers. An anonymous rhymster in England protested both the egalitarian and feminist aspects of Radical religion:

> When women preach and cobblers pray,
> The fiends in hell make holiday.[104]

The quest for human equality occasionally did rise above the patriarchal strictures of the environing culture. Jan Comenius, famous educator and bishop of the Bohemian Brethren, was inspired by the example of the Hutterites, who provided elementary education to children of both sexes. He later became an outspoken advocate of universal education, arguing that equality in learning was the prerequisite for a deepened spiritual life.[105]

* * * * *

Wilhelm Reublin, an early Anabaptist leader, leveled the following charge against established Protestantism: "Your preachers are like bad carpenters. They were able to break the pope's congregation down, but not to construct a new congregation according to Christian order."[106] Many of the Radicals went through a Protestant "phase" before embracing a more drastic program of reform. Many of the themes of Radical spirituality that we have reviewed represent an intensification or a more thoroughgoing application of genuine Protestant insights such as Luther's concept of the priesthood of all believers, or Zwingli's sacramental skepticism, or Calvin's concern for a disciplined community. In this sense the Radicals were indeed "stepchildren" of the mainline reformers. In other respects, however, they were much closer to contemporary Catholicism or Erasmian humanism than to official Protestantism. Their disdain for the doctrines of imputed justification and double predestination were echoed at the Council of Trent along with their stress on human cooperation with divine grace in the process of redemption. At the same time, mystical and ascetical impulses from the Middle Ages were blended by the Radicals into their own unique patterns of spiritual life.

Perhaps more so than with most other Christian groups, it is difficult to separate the spirituality of the Radical reformers from their ecclesiology and ethics. Unlike certain lonely mystics and some detached humanists, the Radicals were passionate about constructing "a new congregation according to Christian order." Most of the Radicals, by intention as much as out of necessity, separated themselves from empire, nation, territory, and city-state in order to restore, as one of them put it, "the old glorious face of primitive Christianity." Thus, the phenomenon of the Radical Reformation was not merely the most radicalized form of Protestant protest against the church of Rome—Protestants in a hurry, so to speak—but also a distinctive quest for a new sense of Christian community at odds on crucial points with both Protestant and Roman Catholic models. Living outside the established order, many of them accepted exile, torture, and capital punishment rather than deny their Lord, who had called them to take up their cross and follow him. This fact, as much as any other, gave a rigorist cast to Radical spirituality. One of the Anabaptists informed his inquisitor that to be a Christian was not child's play! In their prayers, hymns, and martyr stories we hear the themes of great sorrow, deep loneliness, and protest against the world of wickedness. Like the pre-Constantinian Christians, they were imbued with an intense yearning and expectancy for that "heavenly commonwealth" (*politeuma*, Phil 3:20), whose builder and maker is God.

With few exceptions, the churches established by the Radical reformers did not survive the rigors of the sixteenth century. Nonetheless, their search for the life of the Spirit kept alive a dimension of authentic Christian experience that might well have been lost or at least muffled in the more settled ecclesiastical traditions. The legacy of the Radical reformers persists, not only among Quakers, Mennonites, and their other spiritual cousins who revere their memory but also in the broader religious and humane community of seekers and saints who are still moved by their piety, courage, and hope. Among these, the philosopher Ernst Bloch has written a fitting epitaph:

> Despite their suffering,
> their fear and trembling,
> in all these souls
> there glows the spark from beyond,
> and it ignites the tarrying kingdom.[107]

Notes

1. Heinrich Bullinger, *Von dem unverschampten fräfel* (Zurich, 1531) fol. 75r.

2. John Calvin, *Treatises against the Anabaptists and against the Libertines*, trans. Benjamin W. Farley (Grand Rapids: Baker Book House, 1982) 30.

3. G. R. Elton, *Reformation Europe, 1517–1559* (New York: Harper & Row, 1963) 103.

4. Claus-Peter Clasen, *Anabaptism: A Social History, 1525–1618*, 425. For a review of recent historiography see James M. Stayer et al., "From Monogenesis to Polygenesis: The Historical Discussion of Anabaptist Origins," *Mennonite Quarterly Review* 49 (1975) 83–121, and the collection of essay in *Umstrittenes Täufertum, 1525–1975*, ed. Hans-Jürgen Goertz (Göttingen: Vandenhoeck & Ruprecht, 1975).

5. *Luther's Works*, ed. Helmut T. Lehmann (Philadelphia: Fortress, 1958) 40:129.

6. See, for example, Hans-Jürgen Goertz, ed., *Radikale Reformatoren* (Munich: Beck, 1978) 7–20; and Roland Crahay, "Le non-conformisme religieux du XVIe siècle entre l'humanisme et les Eglises," in *Les Dissidents du XVIe siècle entre l'Humanisme et le Catholicisme*, ed. Marc Lienhard (Baden-Baden: Valentin Koerner, 1983) 15–34. Williams has surveyed and responded to the scholarly discussion of his book in "The Radical Reformation Revisited," *Union Seminary Quarterly Review* 39 (1984) 1–28.

7. *Three Reformation Catechisms*, ed. Denis Janz (New York: Mellen, 1982) 135.

8. For this definition I am indebted to Otto Gründler, "John Calvin: Ingrafting into Christ," in *The Spirituality of Western Christendom* (Kalamazoo, MI: Cistercian Publications, 1976) 170–71.

9. Lucien Febvre, "The origins of the French Reformation: A badly-put question?" in *A New Kind of History*, ed. Peter Burke (New York: Harper & Row, 1973) 65.

10. *The Complete Writings of Menno Simons*, ed. J. C. Wenger (Scottdale, PA: Herald Press, 1956) 332–36; *Three Reformation Catechisms*, 136.

11. George H. Williams, *Radical Reformation*, 823. Cf. the recent discussion in Calvin A. Pater, *Karlstadt as the Father of the Baptist Movements* (Toronto: University of Toronto Press, 1984) 15–24.

12. *Spiritual and Anabaptist Writers*, ed. George H. Williams and Angel M. Mergal, 58.

13. *Corpus Schwenckfeldianorum*, ed. Chester Hartranft et al. (19 vols.; Leipzig: Breitkopf & Hartel, 1907–61) 2:574.

14. John C. Wenger, ed., "Pilgram Marpeck's Confession of Faith Composed at Strasburg, December 1531–January 1532," *Mennonite Quarterly Review* 11 (1938) 195.

15. *Complete Writings of Menno Simons*, 265.

16. Leonhard von Muralt and Walter Schmid, eds., *Quellen zur Geschichte der Täufer in der Schweiz: Zürich* (Zurich: S. Hirzel, 1952) 42–43. Fritz Blanke interprets this early phase of Anabaptism as a "revival movement"; see his *Brüder in Christo* (Zurich: Zwingli, 1955).

17. *Complete Writings of Menno Simons*, 671. I follow the translation of Cornelius J. Dyck, "The Life of the Spirit in Anabaptism," *Mennonite Quarterly Review* 47 (1973) 318–19.

18. Roland H. Bainton, *Hunted Heretic: The Life and Death of Michael Servetus* (Boston: Beacon Press, 1953) 73.

19. Harold S. Bender, "The Anabaptist Vision," *Church History* 13 (1944) 3–24. Cf. the recent study of J. Denny Weaver, "Discipleship Redefined: Four Sixteenth Century Anabaptists," *Mennonite Quarterly Review* 54 (1980) 255–79.

20. "Ei, spricht die Welt, es ist ohn Not/Dass ich mit Christo leide . . . ," *Lieder der Hutterischen Brüder* (Scottdale, PA: Herald Press, 1914) 29. The translation is that of Robert Friedmann, *The Theology of Anabaptism* (Scottdale, PA: Herald Press, 1973) 69. Cf. also the following hymn by Peter Riedemann, which stresses the necessary connection between faith

and love: "In Glauben kein Mensch Gott gefelt,/Wie und Paulus ein Zeuckhnus stelt,/Thuts den Ebreen schreiben./Noch ist goettliche Lieb das best,/Dass sich Kains andern dunckhen lest,/Es muess beynander bleiben." Quoted in Albert J. Ramaker, "Hymns and Hymn Writers Among the Anabaptists in the Sixteenth Century," (Th.M. thesis, Colgate-Rochester Divinity School, 1927) 48.

21. *Spiritual and Anabaptist Writers*, 78–79.

22. Quoted in Werner O. Packull, *Mysticism and the Early South German-Austrian Anabaptist Movement, 1525–1531* (Scottdale, PA: Herald Press, 1977) 75.

23. *Spiritual and Anabaptist Writers*, 84.

24. Quoted in E. Gordon Rupp, "Thomas Müntzer, Hans Huth and the 'Gospel of All Creatures,'" *Bulletin of the John Rylands Library* 43 (1960–61) 514–15.

25. *Spiritual and Anabaptist Writers*, 94, 102.

26. Thieleman J. van Braght, *The Bloody Theater or Martyrs' Mirror*, 419; originally published in Dutch in 1660.

27. *Huldreich Zwinglis Sämtliche Werke*, ed. Emil Egli et al., (Leipzig and Berlin, 1905) 6:46: "Omnia turbant inque pessimum statum commutant."

28. A. Orley Swartzentruber, "The Piety and Theology of the Anabaptist Martyrs," *Mennonite Quarterly Review* 28 (1954) 25.

29. Jakob Hutter, *Brotherly Faithfulness: Epistles from a Time of Persecution* (Rifton, NY: Plough Publishing House, 1979) 67–68.

30. *Complete Writings of Menno Simons*, 595.

31. Ibid., 621.

32. Williams, *Radical Reformation*, 229.

33. This appears as hymn no. 11 in the *Ausbund*. The complete hymn with German text is found in *The Christian Hymnary* (Uniontown, OH: Christian Hymnary Publishers, 1972) 418.

34. Van Braght, *Martyrs' Mirror*, 198.

35. Ibid., 411.

36. Myron S. Augsburger, *Faithful Unto Death* (Waco, TX: Word Books, 1978) 13–14.

37. Van Braght, *Martyrs' Mirror*, 984–87. The letter is reprinted in Hans Hillerbrand, *The Protestant Reformation* (New York: Harper & Row, 1968) 146–52.

38. Johannes Kessler, *Sabbata*, ed. Emil Egli (St. Gallen, 1902) 144.

39. See Timothy George, "The Presuppositions of Zwingli's Baptismal Theology," in *Prophet, Pastor, Protestant: The Work of Huldrych Zwingli After Five Hundred Years*, ed. E. J. Furcha and H. W. Pipkin (Pittsburgh, PA: Pickwick Press, 1984) 71–87.

40. *Opus epistolarum Des. Erasmi Roterodami*, ed. P. S. Allen and H. M. Allen (Oxford, 1906–57) X, no. 2853, pp. 39–42. See also Kenneth Davis, "Erasmus as a Progenitor of Anabaptist Theology and Piety," *Mennonite Quarterly Review* 47 (1973) 174.

41. Hillerbrand, *Protestant Reformation*, 131.

42. See Calvin's stated opposition to the Anabaptist ordering of faith and repentance in *Institutes of Christian Religion*, trans. F. L. Battles (Philadelphia: Westminster, 1960) III, 3.2, pp. 594–95.

43. *Balthasar Hubmaier: Schriften*, ed. Gunnar Westin and Torsten Bergsten (Gütersloh: Mohn, 1962) 145. I follow the translation in Rollin S. Armour, *Anabaptist Baptism* (Scottdale, PA: Herald Press, 1966) 43.

44. Armour, *Anabaptist Baptism*, 84; Rupp, "Thomas Müntzer," 519.

45. Harold S. Bender, "Baptism" in *Mennonite Encyclopedia* (Hillsboro, KS: Mennonite Brethren Publishing House, 1955) 1:226.

46. Williams, *Radical Reformation*, 704. The ordinance of immersion may be found in *The*

Polish Brethren: Documentation of the History and Thought of Unitarianism in the Polish-Lithuanian Commonwealth and in the Diaspora, 1601–1685, ed. George H. Williams (Chico, CA: Scholars Press, 1980) 446–60.

47. *Spiritual and Anabaptist Writers*, 76–77.

48. Cornelius Krahn, "Communion" in *Mennonite Encyclopedia*, 1:652.

49. Van Braght, *Martyrs' Mirror*, 484, 423.

50. *Complete Writings of Menno Simons*, 148.

51. Williams, *Radical Reformation*, 502–3. On the eucharistic practice of the Polish Brethren, who also emphasized the importance of discipline in connection with the Lord's Supper, see *Polish Brethren*, 461–74.

52. Harold Bender, "Public Worship" in *Mennonite Encyclopedia*, 4:984.

53. Clasen, *Anabaptism*, 146.

54. *Three Reformation Catechisms*, 161.

55. Ibid., 158.

56. *Complete Writings of Menno Simons*, 633.

57. Bender, "Public Worship," in *Mennonite Encyclopedia*, 4:985.

58. *Three Reformation Catechisms*, 144. It is interesting that Hubmaier omitted the "Protestant" doxology to the Lord's Prayer, which Luther had included in his catechisms.

59. Williams, *Radical Reformation*, 175; *Spiritual and Anabaptist Writers*, 321–22.

60. Clasen, *Anabaptism*, 92.

61. *The Writings of John Greenwood, 1587–1590*, ed. Leland H. Carlson (London: Allen & Unwin, 1962) 294. The Barrowists, one of the first Puritan sects formally to separate from the Church of England, are not usually considered a part of the Radical Reformation, although Williams (*Radical Reformation*, 787) does mention them. The English separatists can be said to be Radical in their sectarian ecclesiology (i.e., their elevation of congregational discipline to the status of an essential *nota* of the true visible church) but Protestant in their retention of infant baptism and a high Calvinist doctrine of election. See Timothy George, *John Robinson and the English Separatist Tradition* (Macon, GA: Mercer University Press, 1982).

62. Friedmann, *Mennonite Piety through the Centuries* (Goshen, IN: Mennonite Historical Society, 1949) 182–83.

63. R. H. Bainton, *The Medieval Church* (Princeton, NJ: Van Nostrand, 1962) 42.

64. George Williams identifies four types of pacifism within the Radical Reformation: (1) Erasmian prudential pacifism allowing for a rare just war; (2) evangelical conventicular pacifism based on dominical counsels; (3) suffering pacifism confirmed in persecution and martyrdom; (4) eschatological pacifism, which anticipated the ultimate divine vindication of the saints at the Second Advent (*Radical Reformation*, 226). Obviously, these are not "ideal types," since several strands of pacifist thought can often be found in the same individual.

65. Quoted in Hans Hillerbrand, "The Anabaptist View of the State," *Mennonite Quarterly Review* 32 (1958) 101.

66. Hutter, *Brotherly Faithfulness*, 70, 168–69.

67. *Spiritual and Anabaptist Writers*, 97, 102 (emphasis added).

68. *The Epistle to Diognetus* 7.3–4, in *The Apostolic Fathers*, ed. Kirsopp Lake (Loeb Classical Library; Cambridge, MA: Harvard University Press, 1913) 2:364–65.

69. Hillerbrand, *Protestant Reformation*, 134.

70. John Robinson, *A Justification of the Separation from the Church of England* (Amsterdam, 1610) 83.

71. *Polish Brethren*, 700.

72. *Complete Writings of Menno Simons*, 413.

73. John C. Wenger, "Avoidance" in *Mennonite Encyclopedia*, 1:200.

74. Richard Bernard, *Plaine evidences: The Church of England is aposticall* (London, 1610) 117.

75. Goertz, ed., *Radikale Reformatoren*, 163. Hoffman referred to the emperor, pope, and false teachers as the "höllische Dreieinigkeit."

76. *Huldreich Zwinglis sämtliche Werke*, 6:43.

77. John H. Yoder, ed., *The Legacy of Michael Sattler* (Scottdale, PA: Herald Press, 1973) 61.

78. Ibid., 38.

79. Hutter, *Brotherly Faithfulness*, 63. It is significant that, when the Hutterites revised their hymnal in 1962, they did not reprint the millenarian hymn "Vom Neuen Jerusalem," since they had long abandoned the chiliastic doctrine. See Friedmann, *Theology of Anabaptism*, 106.

80. Quoted in Irvin B. Horst, *The Radical Brethren* (Nieuwkoop: B. de Graaf, 1972) 29.

81. Paul Althaus, *Die letzten Dinge* (Gütersloh: Bertelsmann, 1928), quoted in Friedmann, *Theology of Anabaptism*, 103.

82. Luther can be quoted on both sides of this issue. In a sermon of 1553 he said: "We shall sleep until Christ comes and knocks on the grave and says, 'Dr. Martinus, wake up!'" WA 37:151. Luther's flirtation with the concept of soul sleep may well have been related to his sense of the imminence of the eschaton, which he shared with the Radicals. See the perceptive study by Heiko A. Oberman, "Martin Luther: Vorläufer der Reformation," in *Verifikation: Festschrift für Gerhard Ebeling zum 70 Geburtstag*, ed. Eberhard Jüngel (Tübingen: Mohr-Siebeck, 1982) 91–119.

83. The first edition of Calvin's work was written in 1534, although it was not published until 1542. Calvin's perspective is represented in the Scottish Confession of Faith (1560): "The Elect departed are in peace and rest for their labors: Not that they sleep, and come to a certaine oblivion: as some Phantastickes do affirme; but that they are delivered fra all feare and torment, and temptation. . . . As contrariwise, the reprobate and unfaithful departed have anguish, torment, and paine" (*Creeds of Christendom*, ed. Philip Schaff [New York: Harper & Brothers, 1877] 3:459).

84. On Anabaptist burial practices, see Clasen, *Anabaptism*, 149–50; on the implications of psychopannychism for Radical spirituality, see George H. Williams, "Socinianism and Deism: From Eschatological Elitism to Universal Immortality?" *Historical Reflections/Réflexions Historiques* 2 (1975) 265–90.

85. George H. Williams has elaborated on the theme of "sectarian ecumenicity" in *Radical Reformation*, 832–45, and in two articles: "Sectarian Ecumenicity: Reflections on a Little Noticed Aspect of the Radical Reformation," *Review and Expositor* 64 (1967) 141–60; and "Erasmus and the Reformers on Non-Christian Religions and *Salus Extra Ecclesiam*," in *Action and Conviction in Early Modern Europe*, ed. Theodore K. Rabb and Jerrold E. Seigel (Princeton, NJ: Princeton University Press, 1969) 319–70.

86. Thomas Müntzer, *Protestation oder Entbietung* (1524), quoted in Williams, "Sectarian Ecumenicity," 156.

87. Palaeologus's ideas on interfaith ecumenicity were published in *De tribus gentibus* (1572); see Williams, *Radical Reformation*, 740–43.

88. On Denck's universalism, see Packull, *Mysticism*, 42–50.

89. Walter Klaassen, "The Modern Relevance of Anabaptism," in Goertz, ed., *Umstrittenes Täufertum*, 295.

90. Thomas Helwys, *A Mistery of iniquity* (London, 1612) 69. The handwritten ascription is found on the copy now housed in the Bodleian Library at Oxford. On the relation between Helwys and continental Anabaptism, see Timothy George, "Between Pacifism and Coercion: The English Baptist Doctrine of Religious Toleration," *Mennonite Quarterly Review* 58 (1984) 30–49.

91. Williams, *Radical Reformation*, 129.

92. Henry Kamen, *The Rise of Toleration* (New York: World University Library, 1967) 60–61.

93. Hutter, *Brotherly Faithfulness*, 164.

94. Ibid., 70 (emphasis added).

95. Franklin H. Littell, *The Origins of Sectarian Protestantism* (New York: Macmillan, 1964) 96: "God's Word would not be hard, if there were not such self-regard."

96. Guy F. Hershberger, *The Recovery of the Anabaptist Tradition* (Scottdale, PA: Herald Press, 1957) 49; see also the excellent study of Peter J. Klassen, *The Economics of Anabaptism* (The Hague: Mouton, 1964).

97. Robert Friedmann, "Community of Goods" in *Mennonite Encyclopedia*, 1:659.

98. "Sie tun uns auch anzeigen / Die Gemeinschaft alles klar. / Keines nichts har für eigen." W. Wiswedel, *Bilder and Führergestalten aus dem Täufertum* (Kassel: Oncken, 1952) 3:100.

99. Williams, *Radical Reformation*, 433.

100. *Spiritual and Anabaptist Writers*, 278–79.

101. Clasen, *Anabaptism*, 176.

102. Ibid., 252.

103. Williams, *Radical Reformation*, 507.

104. *Lucifers Lacky* (London, 1641), sig. A3.

105. Joyce L. Irwin, *Womanhood in Radical Protestantism, 1525–1675* (New York: Mellen, 1979) 133–36.

106. Goertz, ed., *Radikale Reformatoren*, 100.

107. "Soviel Leid, soviel Furcht and Zittern auch gesetz sein mag, so glüht in allen Seelen doch neu der Funke von drüben, und er entzündet das zögernde Reich." *Profiles of Radical Reformers*, 9.

Bibliography

Clasen, Claus-Peter. *Anabaptism: A Social History, 1525–1618*. Ithaca, NY: Cornell University Press, 1972.

Dyck, Cornelius J. "The Life of the Spirit in Anabaptism." *Mennonite Quarterly Review* 47 (1973) 309–26.

Friedmann, Robert. *The Theology of Anabaptism*. Scottdale, PA: Herald Press, 1973.

George, Timothy. *Theology of the Reformers*. Nashville, TN: Broadman, 1987.

Goertz, Hans-Jürgen, ed. *Profiles of Radical Reformers*. Translated by Walter Klaassen. Kitchener, Ontario: Herald Press, 1982.

Klassen, John. "Women and the Family Among Dutch Anabaptist Martyrs." *Mennonite Quarterly Review* 60 (1986) 548–71.

Van Braght, Thieleman J. *The Bloody Theater or Martyrs' Mirror*. Scottdale, PA: Mennonite Publishing House, 1951.

Williams, George H. *The Radical Reformation*. Philadelphia: Westminster, 1962.

——, and Angel M. Mergal. *Spiritual and Anabaptist Writers*. Philadelphia: Westminster, 1957.

Part Two
THEMES

16

The Humanity and the Passion of Christ

EWERT COUSINS

B Y ITS VERY NATURE Christian spirituality focuses on Christ. Yet in
different geographic regions and in different historical periods,
Christians have grounded their spirituality on diverse aspects of
the mystery of Christ. In the High Middle Ages there emerged in
Western Europe a new emphasis on Christ's humanity. Although present
from the beginning, awareness of his humanity took on new dimensions:
it functioned as a catalyst of a new devotion, bringing about a transformation of sensibility, which evoked a spectrum of human emotions, such as
tender affection and compassion. It produced one of the most characteristic
and widely used forms of Christian meditation. In the field of art it effected
a shift from a stylized image of the victorious Savior to the agonizing,
bleeding human Christ on the cross. In the late Middle Ages it culminated
in an almost exclusive emphasis on Christ's passion to the point of over-
shadowing his resurrection. As it unfolded from the eleventh to the fifteenth
century, it differentiated further the Latin West from the Byzantine East and
the Middle Ages from the preceding centuries. It set a tone to Western
spirituality that has perdured, in many ways and in many quarters, even to
the present.[1]

The Humanity of Christ in Early History

Devotion to Christ's humanity has its roots in the historical existence of
Jesus of Nazareth as the center of the Christian religion. Although the
historical events of Jesus' life played a paramount role in the New Testament
writings, during its first thousand years Christian spirituality tended to
focus on the risen Lord rather than on the Jesus of history. The focus on

375

the risen Christ was set by Paul himself, who did not know the historical Jesus and who protested against restricting the apostolic privilege to those who had known Christ in his earthly life: "Even if we did once know Christ in the flesh, that is not how we know him now" (2 Cor 5:16). For Paul, the Christian spiritual life does not focus on the Jesus of history but on the risen Lord in the fullness of his paschal mystery, present to the faithful here and now. It is not easy to formulate this emphasis with precision, for the fullness of the paschal mystery includes the work of the Jesus of history and the events of his earthly life. It is characteristic for Christians to enter this paschal mystery by recalling the events of Christ's earthly life. However, in the first millennium of Christianity there did not develop anything comparable to the widespread devotion to the humanity of Christ of the High Middle Ages—with the use of the imagination in a specific method of meditation, with its extensive cultivation of human emotions, especially compassion, with its almost exclusive emphasis on the passion, and with its ramification into art and its proliferation of devotional forms in hymns, prayers, and penances.

In the Greek world, attention was directed to Christ as Logos: in his preexistence in the Trinity, as the pantocrator through whom creation was achieved, as the bridegroom of the soul and of the church, and as the risen Lord through whom the process of divinization is accomplished in the return of all things to the Father. This emphasis is seen especially in the Alexandrian school, in Clement and Origen, in Athanasius, and the Cappadocians. Although the Antiochene school turned to the humanity of Jesus, their emphasis did not produce in the East anything comparable to the Western medieval devotion to Christ's humanity.[2]

In the Latin fathers, the historical humanity of Christ did not play a central role. For example, Augustine discovered Christ through his presence as Logos in the soul. This led him to a painstaking analysis of the soul as image of the Trinity and not to a meditation on the historical event of Christ's life. In Benedictine monasticism and its derivatives, which dominated Western spirituality in the early Middle Ages, once again the focus was on the risen Lord rather than the historical Jesus. The paschal mystery was celebrated each day in the conventual Mass and throughout the year in the liturgical cycle. The second ingredient of monastic spirituality was the chanting of the Divine Office, which consisted chiefly of the Psalms. These were interpreted allegorically as referring to Christ, not primarily in concrete historical details to be imitated but in foreshadowing the paschal mystery, in which the monks were participating in their own historical existence.

Monastic Origins

Basic elements of devotion to the humanity of Christ, as it developed later in the Middle Ages, can be found in the early centuries of Christianity: in Clement of Rome, Ignatius of Antioch, Irenaeus, Origen, Augustine, Chrysostom, the Cappadocians, and others.[3] For example, Ignatius of Antioch writes to the Romans: "So far as I am concerned, to die in Jesus Christ is better than to be a monarch of earth's widest bounds. He who died for us is all that I seek; he who rose again for us is my whole desire. . . . Leave me to imitate the passion of my God."[4] However, it was in the eleventh and throughout the twelfth century that the medieval devotion to Christ's humanity began to unfold in monastic settings, among Benedictines and Cistercians. Although the main focus of early monastic spirituality was not on the historical Jesus, the roots of meditation on the life of Christ can be traced to the monastic *lectio divina*. This was a practice of private reading, chiefly of the Scriptures, which was carried out in a very slow and meditative fashion. Although it was not restricted to the events described in the Gospels nor was it elaborated into a formal method, the monks did meditate at length on those passages which present the historical events of Christ's life.[5] As it developed, it directed attention ever more sharply to the concrete details of these events. By activating the imagination, it drew the Christian into the events, even assigning him a role as an actor in the drama. Once inside the event, he responded to the scene with a variety of human emotions. This led to an identification with Christ and a desire to imitate his virtues, especially humility and poverty, along with a willingness and even a longing to suffer with Christ in his passion.

Examples of this development can be found in Peter Damien (1007–1072), John of Fécamp (990–1078), and Anselm of Canterbury (1033–1109).[6] The basic elements of this devotion are present in Anselm's *Prayers*. Although far better known for his theological treatises, such as the *Proslogion* and the *Cur Deus Homo* (*Why the God-man?*), Anselm made a major contribution to the devotion to the humanity of Christ. In fact, his *Prayers* can be seen as a companion piece on the devotional level to the theology of the redemption that he formulated in his *Cur Deus Homo*. They represent the unfolding of this devotion within Benedictine monasticism and set the tone for developments that were to follow among the mendicants and the laity in the later Middle Ages.

In his *Prayer to Christ*, Anselm speaks of remembering central events in Christ's life: "As much as I can, though not as much as I ought, I am mindful of your passion, your buffeting, your scourging, your cross, your wounds, how you were slain for me, how prepared for burial and buried." Unlike the later phase of this devotion, he does not omit the resurrection: "And I also remember your glorious resurrection, and wonderful ascension." Anselm laments that he was not present actually to see the details of Christ's suffering: "Why, O my soul, were you not there to be pierced by a sword of bitter sorrow when you could not bear the piercing of the side of your Savior with a lance? Why could you not bear to see the nails violate the hands and feet of your creator?" By asking this rhetorical question within the context of a prayer, Anselm has signaled the need for a new form of meditation that would bring the Christian back to those historical events and make the spiritual power of those events present. In formulating the question in such vivid phrases, Anselm has already provided the means to be present to the event, not in historical actuality, but in his imagination.

To enter more fully into the event, he turns to Mary, attempting to share her compassion for her suffering Son. This became a major component in the later development of the devotion, finding expression in the hymn Stabat Mater and in the paintings and sculptures of the pietà. Anselm again addresses his soul: "Why did you not share the sufferings of the most pure virgin, his worthy mother and your gentle lady?" Addressing Mary, he says: "What can I say about the fountains that flowed from your most pure eyes when you saw your only Son before you, bound, beaten, and hurt?"

Again he produces another essential element that would become the ultimate stance of the meditation on the life of Christ. He desires to become an actor in the drama: "Would that I with happy Joseph might have taken down my Lord from the cross, wrapped him in spiced grave-clothes, and laid him in the tomb." He continues: "Would that with the blessed band of women I might have trembled at the vision of angels and have heard the news of the Lord's resurrection."

Bernard of Clairvaux (1090–1153) is usually singled out as a major force in developing this devotion in the twelfth century.[7] It is true that his chief work, Sermons on the Song of Songs, is in the classical tradition of the risen Lord, drawing from the Origenist tradition of allegorical interpretation of Christ as Logos, who is bridegroom of the soul and the church. Yet even in these sermons he develops the notion of the "carnal love of Christ." "Notice," he says, "that the love of the heart is, in a certain sense carnal, because our hearts are attracted most toward the humanity of Christ and the things he did or commanded while in the flesh." Bernard advises that we should cultivate this love imaging Christ in the events of his life: "The soul at prayer should have before it a sacred image of the God-man, in his birth or infancy or as he was teaching, or dying, or rising, or ascending." Bernard gives as the principal reason why God became man that "he wanted to recapture the affections of carnal men who were unable to love in any other

25. *Crucifixion*, Monastero di S. Chiara, Assisi.

way, by first drawing them to the salutary love of his own humanity, and then gradually to raise them to a spiritual love" (*Song of Songs* 20.6). In his sermons on the feasts of the liturgical year, Bernard carries out his own advice on imaging the humanity of Christ. The feasts provide him with events upon which he meditates in detail, evoking human emotions to draw the faithful to imitation. For example, in a sermon for Christmas Day, he says: "We will reverence him in the manger, we will reverence him in the tomb. We will devoutly adore Him who became a feeble child for our sakes, who was covered with blood for us, who was buried for us" (*In nat.* [*On the Lord's Nativity*] 4). Later in the same sermon he employs his rhetorical skill to draw moral lessons from the details of the scene: "The infant Christ does not console the talkative; the tears of Christ do not console those who rejoice in worldly things; his swaddling clothes do not console those who are clad in rich garments; the stable and the manger do not console those who love the front seats in the synagogue; but perhaps they will one day see that this universal consolation descends on those who await the Lord in silence, those who weep, those who are dressed in poor clothes" (*In nat.* 4).

The method was further developed by the Cistercian Aelred of Rievaulx (1110–1167), who can be considered a master of the technique in its early phase. His skill can be seen in the following excerpt from his *De Institutione Inclusarum*, the meditation on Christ's birth, where he bids the reader: "Embrace that sweet manger, let love conquer reserve, let affection dispel fear; press your lips upon and kiss those most holy feet. Then in your mind keep the shepherds' watch, marvel at the host of angels, join in the heavenly melody singing at the same time with your voice and heart: *Glory to God in the highest and on earth peace to men of good will*" (Luke 2:14) (*De Institutione Inclusarum* 29).

Another link in the development is Eckbert (ca. 1132–1184), abbot of the Benedictine monastery of Schönau in Germany and brother and spiritual director of Elizabeth of Schönau. Like Aelred, Eckbert is a source of Bonaventure's *Lignum vitae*. A sample of his vivid use of detail in the passion is seen in the following passage: Speaking of those who maltreated Jesus during his trial, he says: "They defiled with the spittle of polluted lips, struck with sacrilegious hands, and covered in derision with a veil your honorable face, on which the angels desire to gaze, which fills all the heavens with joy, and which all the wealthy among the people implore with earnest prayer" (*PL* 158, cols. 754AB).

Francis of Assisi

It was against this twelfth-century background that Francis of Assisi (1181–1226) appeared on the scene. More than any other saint or spiritual writer, he transformed religious sensibility in the direction of devotion to the humanity of Christ.[8] Although his role in this process is widely acknowledged, it is difficut to analyze; for unlike Bernard he did not propound a theory of the "carnal love of Christ," nor are there extant sermons like Bernard's which develop a method of meditation on the historical events of Christ's life. Rather, Francis was first and foremost intent on imitating Christ in poverty and on creating a life-style based, as he believed, on the essence of the Gospel. He attempted to embody in his own person this life-style, even in concrete details. Finally, two years before his death, he received the stigmata, the marks of Christ's passion on his feet, hands, and side. His followers interpreted this as the ultimate embodiment of his imitation of Christ and the ultimate seal of divine approval.

The biography written by Bonaventure (1217–1274) describes how Francis came to the idea of his way of life:

> One day when he was devoutly hearing a Mass of the Apostles, the Gospel was read in which Christ sends forth his disciples to preach and explains to them the way of life according to the Gospel: that they "should not keep gold or silver or money in their belts, nor have a wallet for their journey, or two tunics, nor shoes, nor staff" (Matt 10:9). When he grasped its meaning, he was filled with joy and said: "This is what I want; this is what I long for with all my heart.

Bonaventure describes how Francis proceeded to carry out Christ's injunction quite literally: "He immediately took off his shoes from his feet, put aside his staff, cast away his wallet and money as if accursed, was content with one tunic and exchanged his leather belt for a piece of rope" (*Major Life* 3.1). This insight was confirmed later when Francis and his first follower, Bernard of Quintavalle, went to the church of St. Nicholas to seek God's direction. Francis opened the book of the Gospel three times: the first time to Matt 19:21, "If you will be perfect, go, sell what you have and give to the poor"; the second time to Luke 9:3, "Take nothing on your journey"; and the third time to Matt 16:24, "If anyone wishes to come after me, let him deny himself and take up his cross and follow me." "This is our life and our rule," Francis said, "and the life and rule of all who wish to join our company" (*Major Life* 3.3).

In these Gospel texts, Francis perceived the poverty of Christ's life-style and that of his disciples during the years of his public ministry. It was the life of a wandering teacher and preacher who had no permanent home, who went about his ministry unencumbered by physical possessions. This is the image of Christ that the "poor man" Francis strove to imitate with a certain radical literalness. In his approach, we see the essential elements of the emerging devotion to the humanity of Christ: a looking back to the Christ of history—here to his public ministry—a focusing on concrete details, and an imitation of Christ's virtue as embodied in these details. Although the central event here was Christ's public ministry, Francis drew attention also to the poverty of Christ's birth and death. Eventually, these two events became the central themes in the devotion to the humanity of Christ. This is not surprising, not only because of the drama of these events but also because it is precisely birth and death that establish the historicity of the human situation.

In 1223, Francis created a crib for the midnight Mass at Greccio. According to Thomas of Celano in his *First Life*, Francis contacted a friend, John of Greccio, and bade him prepare for the midnight Mass in the following way: "If you want us to celebrate the present feast of our Lord at Greccio, go with haste and diligently prepare what I tell you. For I wish to do something that will recall to memory the little Child who was born in Bethlehem and set before our bodily eyes in some way the inconveniences of his infant needs, how he lay in a manger, how, with an ox and an ass standing by, he lay upon the hay where he had been placed" (I *Celano* 84).

In 1224, two years before his death, while fasting and praying on Mount La Verna in Tuscany, Francis saw a vision of a six-winged Seraph in the form of Christ crucified. According to Bonaventure's biography:

> On a certain morning about the feast of the Exaltation of the Cross, while Francis was praying on the mountainside, he saw a Seraph with six fiery and shining wings descend from the height of heaven. And when in swift flight the Seraph had reached a spot in the air near the man of God, there appeared between the wings the figure of a man crucified, with his hands and feet extended in the form of a cross and fastened to a cross. (*Major Life* 13.3)

When the vision vanished, Francis received the stigmata, the wounds of Christ's passion, in his hands, feet, and side. Because of its miraculous, graphic, and dramatic nature, this event gave a strong impetus to the development of devotion to Christ crucified. In the course of the thirteenth century, the passion of Christ became the chief focus of emerging devotion to the humanity of Christ.

It is not surprising, then, that within the Franciscan milieu meditation on the life of Christ, particularly on his passion, should reach a classical expression in Bonaventure's *Lignum vitae* (*Tree of Life*). A more popularized version was produced by the anonymous author of the *Meditations on the Life of Christ* in the late thirteenth century. This was integrated into the *Vita Jesu Christi redemptoris nostri* of Ludolph of Saxony, which influenced *The Spiritual Exercises* of Ignatius of Loyola. This form of consciousness was by no means confined to meditations; rather it permeated hymns and devotions, painting and sculpture, and the general religious consciousness of Western Europe.

Religious Consciousness and the Historical Event

This form of meditation reached a certain crystallization in the thirteenth century. As a method of prayer, it involves, it is a true, a meditation, a contemplation, even what could be called a mysticism of the historical event.[9] But this method of prayer has more significance for the history of spirituality than simply as a practical technique. For it manifests a more basic structure of religious consciousness that emerged into prominence and permeated the religious life of Western Europe in the latter part of the Middle Ages. By viewing this phenomenon through the prism of meditation on the life of Christ, one can grasp the elements that constitute its new religious sensibility.

In the *Lignum vitae,* for example, Bonaventure meditates on events in the life of Christ in a direct and straightforward way: for example, his birth in Bethlehem and his crucifixion and resurrection in Jerusalem. Bonaventure bases himself on the Gospel accounts, activates the imagination to visualize the scenes, and invites the reader to become a participant in the action. By thus reentering into the event, the reader can come in contact with its meaning, as it reveals Christ's virtues for imitation.

Since it focuses on historical events, it differs from meditation on mythical or cosmic archetypal symbols. The one meditating perceives this event not as something in the distant past that is being viewed from the standpoint of the present. Rather he enters into the event, either as an eyewitness or as an actor in the drama of the event. He is present to the event and the event is present to him. His involvement in the event opens to him its meaning and value.

This religious consciousness has its secular analogues. For example, it underlies much of tourism. Thousands flock to sites where famous events occurred: to battlefields such as Waterloo or the Cherbourg peninsula; to the Roman forum, where great triumphs were held and where Caesar was assassinated. To visit the site of a battle often invokes a sense of being present to the event and of feeling its power at a moment when thousands clashed and died and the flow of history was altered. By being caught up in the drama of such an event, one can discern its meaning as it reveals the human struggle for power and justice. If the event is religious, then its revelatory power is greater, for to the believer it manifests God's plan of salvation history, and through salvation history God himself. For this reason, medieval Christians flocked to shrines where saints were martyred or buried.

They especially wished to make a pilgrimage to the Holy Land, to walk the streets that Jesus walked and to visit the site of his birth, his crucifixion, and his resurrection. If they could not make the physical journey, they could at least imagine they were in the Holy Land, present to the great religious events that happened there. It was this use of the imagination that produced the meditations on the life of Christ.

Christ's Nativity and Passion

The meditations in Bonaventure's *Lignum vitae* cover Christ's life from his eternal generation by the Father, through his incarnation and birth, his public life and ministry, and his passion, resurrection, ascension, and his judgment and eternal life in heaven.[10] On the historical level, we will choose two events: Christ's birth in Bethlehem and his suffering on the cross because they highlight the fundamental events of every human life: birth and death. In this way they touch the heart of the devotion to the humanity of Christ. They also highlight the two distinctly Franciscan developments of this devotion: namely, devotion to the infant Jesus in the setting of the Christmas crib and to the suffering Savior in his passion on the cross.

In his *Lignum vitae,* Bonaventure provides a technique of meditation for entering into the event of Christ's birth in a way comparable to Francis's dramatization at Greccio. He first summarizes the Gospel account from Luke 2:1–18, emphasizing Francis's perception of poverty and humility: "He chose to be born away from a home in a stable, to be wrapped in swaddling clothes, to be nourished by virginal milk and to lie in a manger between an ox and an ass." With the scene vividly set and the message revealed, he bids the reader enter into the event as an actor in the drama. In a passage that follows Aelred of Rievaulx almost verbatim (see above, p. 380), Bonaventure says, "Now, then, my soul, embrace that divine manger; press your lips upon and kiss the boy's feet." The reader is to join in with the other actors in the drama and respond as they responded: "Then in your mind keep the shepherd's watch, marvel at the assembling host of angels, join in the heavenly melody, singing with your voice and heart: 'Glory to God in the highest and on earth peace to men of good will' (Luke 2:14)" (*Lignum vitae* 4).

Bonaventure takes the same approach in dealing with Christ's suffering and death. Inspired by Francis's stigmata and his devotion to Christ crucified, Bonaventure devotes one third of the *Lignum vitae,* or a total of sixteen meditations, to Christ's passion. He draws the reader into the event by having him identify with Mary, sharing her feelings of compassion for the suffering Savior. In these meditations, there is a heightened concentration

26. Mathias Grünewald, *The Isenheim Altarpiece*, central panel: *The Crucifixion*, ca. 1515. Musée d'Unterlinden, Colmar.

on the physical details of Christ's suffering with a subsequent evoking of compassion. Addressing himself to Mary, Bonaventure says:

> This blessed and most holy flesh—which you so chastely conceived, so sweetly nourished and fed with your milk, which you so often held on your lap, and kissed with your lips—you actually gazed upon with your bodily eyes now torn by the blows of the scourges, now pierced by the points of the thorns, now struck by the reed, now beaten by hands and fists, now pierced by nails and fixed to the wood of the cross, and torn by its own weight as it hung there. (*Lignum vitae* 28)

By thus identifying with Mary, we can share Christ's suffering and penetrate the meaning of his redemptive death.

In a similar vein, the author of the *Meditations on the Life of Christ* evokes the mysticism of the historical event.[11] "With your whole mind," he says, "you must imagine yourself present and consider diligently everything done against your Lord and all that is said and done by him and regarding him." The author then directs the reader more concretely: "With your mind's eye, see some thrusting the cross into the earth, others equipped with nails and hammers, others with the ladder and other instruments, others giving orders about what should be done, and others stripping him." He focuses now on the dramatic actions: "Again he is stripped, and is now nude before all the multitude for a third time, his wounds reopened by the adhesion of his garments to his flesh." At this point he brings Mary into the drama, evoking in the reader, as Bonaventure had done, compassion for the suffering Savior through the tenderness and compassion of his mother. However, unlike Bonaventure, who remained within the limits of the Gospel accounts, the author in characteristic fashion creates a dramatic scene of his own, which is reminiscent of the scene of Francis stripped before the bishop of Assisi:

> Now for the first time the Mother beholds her Son thus taken and prepared for the anguish of death. She is saddened and shamed beyond measure when she sees him entirely nude: they did not leave him even his loincloth. Therefore she hurries and approaches the Son, embraces him, and girds him with the veil from her head. Oh, what bitterness her soul is in now! I do not believe that she could say a word to Him: if she could have done more, she would have, but she could not help Him further. The Son was torn furiously from her hands to the foot of the cross. (*Meditations* 78)

Evaluation of Devotion to Christ's Passion

By the end of the thirteenth century, devotion to the humanity of Christ was solidly established in Western spirituality, and its focus was fixed on the passion of Christ. In the later Middle Ages it exfoliated in numerous popular practices, such as the Stations of the Cross, hymns devoted to the passion, meditation on the sorrowful mysteries of the Rosary, the imitation of Christ in humility and suffering, and an increasing emphasis in the liturgical cycle of those feasts that commemorate Christ's suffering and death. This devotion spearheaded a revolution in art, becoming the focus for the shift toward a realistic depiction of Christ's humanity, leading to the great pietàs of Michelangelo and the crucifixion scenes which dominated in late medieval and renaissance art.

As the Middle Ages progressed, the passion of Christ permeated more deeply the religious psyche of Western Christendom. In the lives of the saints there are many accounts of the intensity of this devotion, even of a morbid fascination with pain and humiliation. From a psychological point of view, this late medieval devotion to the passion of Christ is one of the most problematic phenomena in the history of Christian spirituality. It is also problematic from a doctrinal and spiritual point of view. For attraction to the suffering and death of Christ became so intense in some cases that Christians lost sight of the other aspects of the Christian mysteries and of their organic interrelatedness. Emphasis on the passion led to forgetfulness of the resurrection. Focus on the suffering humanity of Christ overshadowed the Trinity and its outpouring of divine love in creation. The concentration on Christ's suffering in itself distracted the Christian from discerning the role of the passion in the scheme of cosmic redemption and in the personal and collective spiritual journey.

A striking exception to this imbalance is Julian of Norwich (ca. 1343–1416), whose visions of Christ's passion in the fourteenth century are among the most graphic in the history of Christian spirituality; yet they open the way into the joy of the Trinity and the goodness of creation. For example, she describes one of her visions as follows: "And at this time, suddenly I saw the red blood running down under the crown, hot and flowing freely and copiously, a living stream, just as at the time when the crown of thorns was pressed on his blessed head." Instead of drawing her more deeply into the experience of human pain, the vision of Christ suffering leads her into the mystery of the Trinity, which fills her with joy: "And in the same revelation, suddenly the Trinity filled my heart full of the greatest joy, and I understood that it will be so in heaven without end to all who will come there. For the Trinity is God, God is the Trinity. The Trinity is our maker, the Trinity is our protector, the Trinity is our everlasting lover, the Trinity is our endless joy and our bliss, by our Lord Jesus Christ and in our Lord Jesus Christ" (*Showings*, Long Text, 4).

How does one evaluate the devotion to Christ's passion from the standpoint of Christian spirituality? Ideally, this devotion, according to medieval accounts, was to awaken Christians to gratitude for their redemption in Christ, repentance for sin that caused his pain, and compassion for his suffering through which they were drawn into the cosmic redemptive process. Finally, this led to imitation of Christ in his suffering and in his virtues of patience, fortitude, and constancy. Even if this complex devotional consciousness were activated in a mature fashion, it still had to be linked to the larger spiritual world view and to the stages of the spiritual journey.

Since it focuses on human experience, this form of devotion can issue in a superficial sentimentalism, divorced from any deeper levels of spirit. If it penetrates beyond mere emotion to the level of moral value, it can remain superficial even here. To realize its ultimate religious possibility, it has to open itself to the deeper realities expressed in human experience and historical events: for example, the dynamism of transformation—spiritual and cosmic—embodied in the Christian understanding of Christ's death and resurrection. And even beyond this, it has to penetrate to that deeper level of mystical awareness where it experiences God himself as he is manifested in the events. In the medieval categories of Scripture interpretation, it has to move ultimately through all four senses of Scripture. Beginning with the literal or historical level, it draws out from the event its moral meaning. This was explicitly done by Bonaventure in the *Lignum vitae*, where, in his passion, Christ was presented as a model of the virtues of patience and constancy for the reader to imitate. The moral meaning is closely linked to the allegorical, which deals with Christ's work in salvation history, specifically with the transformation involved in the paschal mystery of his death and resurrection. Here the Christian moves from mere compassion for Christ's human suffering to the significance of his work of cosmic redemption from sin. At this level the Christian's ultimate response would be gratitude for God's mercy, which, according to Anselm's theory of redemption, was so great that it motivated God to take on himself the suffering that was necessarily exacted as the punishment for the sins of the human race. Thus, divine mercy subsumed into itself divine justice, bearing in the humanity of Christ the heavy burden of sin. In this way, the discerning medieval Christian could penetrate, like Julian of Norwich, through the blood and pain to the merciful love of the Trinity.

The fourth sense is the anagogic, which reveals the ultimate mystical meaning: the union of the soul with God after death or the foretaste of that union in this life through mystical experience. Through her vision of Christ's passion, Julian penetrated this level, experiencing the joy of the

Trinity. Perhaps more than any other medieval writer, Bonaventure has described the role of devotion to Christ crucified in the final stage of the spiritual journey. For him, Christ's death symbolizes what in recent spiritual writings has been called the death of the ego, that is, the finite or superficial self, and the awakening of the deeper self which is united to God. In the prologue to the *Journey of the Soul into God,* he tells how he was meditating at La Verna on the vision that Francis of Assisi had had there of the six-winged Seraph in the form of Christ crucified. In a flash he saw that the six wings of the Seraph can symbolize the six stages of the spiritual journey, and that Christ crucified is the doorway into that journey and its goal. Bonaventure observes:

> There is no other path but through the burning love of the Crucified, a love which so transformed Paul into Christ when he "was carried up to the third heaven" (2 Cor 12:2) that he could say: "With Christ I am nailed to the cross. I live, now not I, but Christ lives in me" (Gal 2:20). This love also so absorbed the soul of Francis that his spirit shone through his flesh when for two years before his death he carried in his body the sacred stigmata of the passion. The six wings of the Seraph, therefore, symbolize the six steps of illumination that begin from creatures and lead up to God, whom no one rightly enters except through the Crucified. For "he who enters not through the door, but climbs up another way is a thief and a robber." But "if anyone enter" through this door, "he will go in and out and will find pastures" (John 10:1, 9). Therefore John says in the Apocalypse: "Blessed are they who wash their robes in the blood of the Lamb that they may have a right to the tree of life and may enter the city through the gates" (Apoc 22:14). It is as if John were saying that no one can enter the heavenly Jerusalem by contemplation unless he enter through the blood of the Lamb as through a door. (*Journey,* prol. 3)

In the seventh chapter of the *Journey,* Bonaventure returns to this theme, when he deals with the passage of the soul into God in ecstasy. He bids the reader to turn his gaze on the humanity of Christ, symbolized by the Mercy Seat in the Holy of Holies in the Temple: "Whoever turns his face fully to the Mercy Seat and with faith, hope and love, devotion, admiration, exultation, appreciation, praise and joy beholds him hanging upon the cross, such a one makes the Pasch, that is, the passover with Christ." Drawing upon the allegorical meaning of the exodus, Bonaventure identifies with Christ in his death, thus passing over into the anagogic level of union with God: "By the staff of the cross he passes over the Red Sea, going from Egypt into the desert, where he will taste the 'hidden manna' (Apoc 2:17); and with Christ he rests in the tomb, as if dead to the outer world, but experiencing, as far as is possible in this wayfarer's state, what was said on the cross to the thief who adhered to Christ, 'Today you shall be with me in paradise' (Luke 23:43)" (*Journey* 7.2).

Notes

1. For a treatment of devotion to the humanity and the passion of Christ in the context of late medieval devotion, see the article by Richard Kieckhefer in this volume (chapter 3).

2. On devotion to Christ in the patristic period, see Irénée Noye et al., *Jesus in Christian Devotion and Contemplation;* also Flavio Di Bernardo, "Passion (Mystique de la)," *Dict. Sp.* 12, cols. 312–38.

3. See, e.g., Clement of Rome *Epistle to the Corinthians* 2; Ignatius of Antioch *Epistle to the Smyrnaeans 1; Irenaeus Adversus haereses* 5; Origen *In Lucam* 15.3; Augustine *Discourses on the Psalms;* Gregory Nazianzen *Oration* 37.17.

4. Ignatius of Antioch *Epistle to the Romans* 6; trans. Maxwell Staniforth, *Early English Writings* (New York: Penguin Books, 1968) 105.

5. On monastic spirituality in the Middle Ages, see Jean Leclercq, *The Love of Learning and the Desire for God: A Study in Monastic Culture* (2nd rev. ed.; New York: Fordham University Press, 1974).

6. See Peter Damien *Oratio 26;* John of Fécamp *Confessio theologica;* Anselm *Orationes.*

7. For the role of Bernard of Clairvaux in the development of this devotion, see Jean Leclercq et al., *The Spirituality of the Middle Ages,* 196–200; idem, "La Devotion Médiévale envers le Crucifié," in *La Maison-Dieu* 75 (1963) 119–21; idem, "Drogon et S. Bernard," *Revue Benedictine* 63 (1953) 116–31; idem, "Saint Bernard and the Monastic Theology of the Twelfth Century," in *Saint Bernard Theologian* (2 vols.; Berryville, VA: Our Lady of the Holy Cross, 1961) 1:1–18.

8. On the influence of Francis of Assisi, see Robert McNally, *The Unreformed Church* (New York: Sheed & Ward, 1965) 170–74.

9. I have developed elsewhere the notion of the mysticism of the historical event; see my chapter entitled "Francis of Assisi: Christian Mysticism at the Crossroads," in *Mysticism and Religious Traditions,* ed. Steven T. Katz (New York: Oxford University Press, 1983) 163–191.

10. For a detailed study of Bonaventure's *Lignum vitae* in the context of medieval devotion to the humanity of Christ, see Patrick O'Connell, "The *Lignum Vitae* of Saint Bonaventure and the Medieval Devotional Tradition" (Ph.D. diss., Fordham University, 1985).

11. For a study of the method of meditation in the *Meditations on the Life of Christ,* see Jaime Vidal, "The Infancy Narrative in Pseudo-Bonaventure's *Meditationes vitae Christi:* A Study in Medieval Franciscan Christ-Piety (ca. 1300)" (Ph.D. diss., Fordham University, 1984).

Bibliography

Sources

Anselm of Canterbury. *The Prayers and Meditations of Saint Anselm.* Translated by Sister Benedicta Ward. New York: Penguin Books, 1973.

Bernard of Clairvaux. *Song of Songs I.* Translated by Killian Walsh. Kalamazoo, MI: Cistercian Publications, 1979.

———. *The Nativity.* Translated by Leo Hickey. Dublin: Scepter, 1979.

Bonaventure: The Soul's Journey into God, The Tree of Life, The Life of St. Francis. Translated by Ewert Cousins. New York: Paulist Press, 1978.

Julian of Norwich: Showings. Translated by Edmund Colledge and James Walsh. New York: Paulist Press, 1978.

Meditations on the Life of Christ. Translation by Isa Ragusa. Princeton, NJ: Princeton University Press, 1961.

Thomas of Celano. *St. Francis of Assisi: First and Second Life of St. Francis.* Translated by Placid Hermann. Chicago: Franciscan Herald Press, 1963.

Studies

Bertaud, Emile, and Andre Ragan. "Dévotions." In *Dict. Sp.* 3, cols. 747–78.

Chatillon, Jean. "Devotio." In *Dict. Sp.* 3, cols. 702–46.

Di Bernardo, Flavio. "Passion (Mystique de la)." In *Dict. Sp.* 12, cols. 312–38.

Kieckhefer, Richard. *Unquiet Souls: Fourteenth-Century Saints and Their Religious Milieu.* Chicago: University of Chicago Press, 1984.

Leclercq, Jean. *The Love of Learning and the Desire for God.* Translated by Catharine Misrahi. New York: Fordham University Press, 1974.

Leclercq, Jean, François Vandenbroucke, and Louis Bouyer. *The Spirituality of the Middle Ages.* Vol. 2 of *A History of Christian Spirituality.* Translated by the Benedictines of Holme Eden Abbey, Carlisle. New York: Seabury, 1982.

Ledeur, Étienne. "Imitation du Christ: II. Tradition Spirituelle." In *Dict. Sp.* 7, cols. 1562–87.

MacCandless, Joseph. "Meditation in Saint Bernard." *Collectanea Ordinis Cisterciensium Reformatorum* 26 (1964) 277–93.

Merton, Thomas. "The Humanity of Christ in Monastic Prayer." In *The Monastic Journey*, 87–106. Edited by Patrick Hart. Kansas City: Sheed, Andrews & McMeel, 1977.

Noye, Irénée et al., *Jesus in Christian Devotion and Contemplation.* Translated by Paul J. Oligny. St. Meinrad, IN: Abbey Press, 1974.

Squire, Aelred. *Aelred of Rievaulx: A Study.* Kalamazoo, MI: Cistercian Publications, 1981.

Von Severus, Emmanuel, and Aime Solignac. "Méditation: I. De l'Écriture aux Auteurs Medievaux." In *Dict. Sp.* 10, cols. 906–34.

Wilmart, André. *Auteurs spirituels et textes dévots du Moyen Age latin: Etudes d'histoire littéraire.* Reprint. Paris: Etudes Augustiniennes, 1971.

17

Marian Devotion in the Western Church

ELIZABETH A. JOHNSON

THE RISE OF THE CULT OF MARY, the Virgin Mother of God, is one of the most striking features of the landscape of medieval spirituality. That landscape has a complex, composite character. One of the dangers of treating Marian devotion in a discrete essay is that it might appear as the exclusive and overriding form of the spirituality of this period rather than one often well-integrated aspect of the whole. The fact remains, however, that in a way unprecedented in previous Christian centuries the cult of the figure of Mary, beautiful Virgin, merciful Mother, and powerful Queen, became an intimate and pervasive element in the religious life of Western Christians at this time—scholars, monks, mystics, preachers, bishops, and folk alike.

There was no rectilinear development of the cult of Mary through the high medieval centuries, and differences of national temperament prevented uniformity at any given moment. Nevertheless, an overarching accelerating movement forward can be charted. In the eleventh and twelfth centuries, monastic devotion struck a new note of affective intimacy in mystical contemplation of the beauty and glory of the Virgin Mary, bringing her personal individuality to the fore. Although folk at large were drawn into this aspect of devotion through attendance at monastery festivities connected with Marian feasts, it remained primarily the monopoly of the cloister. Meanwhile, the burgeoning of towns and the ferment of intellectual life associated with the new universities began to change the social structure. A new stratum of people emerged, anxious to live the gospel outside the traditional monastic setting. The ministry of preaching to these laity undertaken by the new mendicant orders at the beginning of the thirteenth century shifted the sensibility of spirituality as a whole to a more imaginative, human level. Jesus Christ was envisioned in the poverty of his humanity in the crib and on the cross, both scenes where Mary also appears in an identifiably human role. Simultaneously, scholastic theology was systematizing an understanding of redemption that emphasized the individual's need to make satisfaction for sin. Mary then came to the fore in piety as the mother who mediated between the sinner and Christ the just judge, the mother who had a trustworthy interest in seeing to it that the saving grace of Christ would bring her children to the joys of heaven, unworthy though they might be. A plethora of devotional practices expressed and cemented the bond between the Mother of Mercy and the less-than-perfect people questing for salvation. In a last development, the fourteenth and fifteenth centuries saw the need for protection intensify as natural disasters such as the Black Death and civil and church disorders such as the Hundred Years' War and the Great Western Schism created vast insecurities in a harsh world. The all-powerful protection of Mary, who herself had borne intense suffering but was now crowned in glory, became a bulwark against dangers pressing on every side. At times her ability to rescue became the focus of devotion to the point where she functioned as an acting agent independent even of God. Even where this did not happen, ardent devotion welling up out of deep personal insecurity and encouraged by popular preaching placed Mary, Queen of Heaven and Refuge of Sinners, at the dependable center of the process of personal salvation.

The trajectory of Marian devotion through the High Middle Ages has several interrelated aspects. The active agents or prime movers of the devotion changed as the torch was passed from the monasteries to the mendicant orders to the simple clergy and to the people themselves. The figure of Mary also changed from the inspiring Virgin Mother of Christ, to the merciful mother of the people who mediated before Christ in their behalf, to the sovereign queen of heaven and earth who protected her faithful ones. The spirituality focused on her person shifted from mystical contemplation to popular imagination, the latter coupled with intense reverence, familiarity, and trust in her merciful and powerful aid.

Connecting the diversity of expressions of Marian devotion from century to century and from country to country during this epoch was one characteristic that stood out in contrast to the devotion of preceding ages. This was the full-blown personalizing both of Mary and of the individual Christian's relation to her. In the patristic era, the figure of Mary had been considered in relation to the great events of salvation history: through her obedience to God's will she had reversed the disobedience of Eve, becoming the Virgin Mother of the Savior and, in the light of his identity, the Virgin Mother of God. In the East she was praised as the great *Theotokos*, the

God-bearer. In the West her grace-filled figure was contemplated as a type of the church itself. In both, the context for thought and praise was doctrinal and liturgical.

The great *Theotokos*, imaged with her Son in hieratic art as serene, intellectual, and majestic, became the tender human mother suckling her baby. The faith-filled figure of Mary, type of the church, was personalized into Mary the individual experiencing her own joys, sorrows, and glory. This made it possible for her to assume a direct relationship to human beings as the mother of all those for whom Christ died. A strong subjective *Gestalt* characterized the piety of this age, and individuals personally experienced the fearfulness of their sinful situation and quested vigorously for the means of personal salvation. Thus, previous considerations of the role that Mary played in objective salvation history were refocused on her subjective role in the present salvation history of individual believers. From being the handmaid of the Lord whose key relationship was with Christ, Mary became Our Lady, an acting subject with an equally important relationship to the individual seeking to attain salvation. This shift from an objective, liturgical perspective to a subjective and personal one, expressed in the proliferation of newly created forms of devotion, underscores the unique character of the Marian piety that blossomed during the Middle Ages.

In exploring this development, we must be cautious about making an absolute distinction between the approach to Mary of the educated elite and that of the folk at large. Such a two-tiered model, rather acceptable in theory since Hume, would have it that the enlightened religion of the educated (monks, church leaders, scholastic theologians) was progressively contaminated and forced to change by pressure upward from the vulgar and superstitious ideas of popular religion below. Not only does this model leave unexplained the changes in popular religion itself; it also overlooks the fact that a number of educated Christian leaders through devotional preaching, the financing of shrines, etc., helped to orchestrate the rise of the cult of Mary. Although learned doctrine and popular devotion were not congruent at every point, at their best there was a dialectical relationship between them, a real historic interdependence, as both sought to express in their own unique modes the one vision of reality.

Granting that, however, there is a true sense in which Marian devotion, more than other forms of piety at the time, split off from the insights of the learned and developed a life of its own. In the universities, scholastic theology, proceeding by way of the *quaestio*, rigorously used the faculty of reason to make ever more precise distinctions and to interrelate doctrines into a vast synthesis focused on God with orderly relationships defined among all else under God. There was little room in this approach for the reasons of the heart, for affectivity and the play of love. Compounding the difficulty was the fact that the language of scholarly discourse and liturgy was Latin, although various vernaculars were developing for use in preaching and private prayer. The fissure between mind and heart ran deeply through the Marian phenomenon. The interesting result can be observed in the difference between academic works about Mary, where she is kept in careful relation to Christ, and homiletic or devotional works of the same period—even in works by the same author. Guided by the *Sentences* of Peter Lombard, scholastic theologians as a whole allotted little time and space to considerations of Mary; in the great Summas, she appeared only in relation to questions about the incarnation, and then under the rubric of things that related to Christ's coming into the world. In contrast, meditative writings known as *Mirrors* of the Blessed Virgin Mary exuberantly exulted in her own gifts and her plenitude of graces, fittingly revealed in the angelic salutation at the time of the incarnation. The Psalters of the Blessed Virgin were an even more intense expression of devotion; in them the Psalms of the Old Testament were rewritten so that their praise could be redirected from God to Mary. For example, in one Psalter uncritically attributed to Bonaventure, we read:

> Sing to Our Lady a new song: for she hath done wonderful things.
> In the sight of the nations she hath revealed her mercy; her name is heard even to the ends of the earth.
> Be mindful, O Lady, of the poor and the wretched, and support them by the help of thy holy refreshment. For thou, O Lady, art sweet and true, exceedingly patient and full of compassion. (Psalm 96/97)[1]

Thus, there were increasingly evident currents of Marian piety that were essentially a creation of popular religion.

Against this background, the highlights of three progressively interlocking aspects of medieval Marian piety roughly corresponding to its chronological development can be limned. These are praise for the beauty of the Virgin, trust in the mercy of the Mother, and pleas for the protection of the Queen.

God's Treasure

The first discernible aspect of medieval Marian devotion arose from sheer delight in the Virgin Mary. Its foundation was belief in what God had done for her and what she in turn had done to realize God's designs in the world. A humble maid, she had been especially loved by God and chosen with her faith-filled consent to be his mother. She was God's treasure, and where she was, there the heart of God was also. Contemplation of the events of her life and of her grace and virtues led people to salute her name, to sing of her beauty, and to praise both Mary and the greatness of God, who so created and gifted her. It was especially the virginal quality of Mary's maternity that attracted joyful thoughts, for this was paradoxically the means by which God drew near to earth. Belonging to no man, the Virgin shone forth at the dawn of salvation. Absolutely pivotal was the graciousness of her independent *fiat* at the Annunciation, when her conceiving Christ by the Holy Spirit was made known to her. Her purity was "so great that nothing greater under God can be imagined" (Anselm of Canterbury *De conceptu virginali* [*PL* 158, col. 451]). To glory and rejoice in her unique person was an obvious and irresistible implication. Culturally, the advent of the code of chivalry and the experience of courtly love played no little role in shaping the spirit of this devotion.

Expressions of this uplifting of the human spirit in contemplation of the Holy Virgin abound in lyrical hymns and poems, in prayers of praise, and in sermons preached on the occasion of liturgical feasts of Mary. "Nothing is equal to Mary; nothing but God is greater than Mary," praised Anselm of Canterbury (d. 1109), whose Marian prayers marked a turning point in the spiritual history of this devotion, for "God created all things, and Mary gave birth to God. God who made all things made himself of Mary, and thus refashioned everything he had made. . . . So God is the Father of all created things, and Mary is the Mother of all recreated things."[2] Everything that was new and fresh in the world was linked with her recreative presence. Through her, light entered the dark world. Through her fruitful virginity the ancient sin was overturned and the lost world found, so that rejoicing spread throughout heaven, earth, and even hell. What can one do but wonder at her, and venerate her holy virginity which is beyond all reckoning? Praise and tribute welled up from hearts filled with loving awe:

> O woman full and overflowing with grace, plenty
> flows from you to make all creatures green again.
> O virgin blessed and ever blessed, whose blessing
> is upon all nature, not only is the creature
> blessed by the Creator,
> but the Creator is blessed by the creature too. . . .
> O beautiful to gaze upon,
> lovely to contemplate, delightful to love,
> whither do you go to evade the breadth of my heart?[3]

It was especially in monasteries that such an exulting, almost mystical form of Marian piety flourished. Inside the monastery walls there were statues of the Virgin in the chapel, the refectory, the garden; there were manuscripts about her in the library. Monks said the Little Office of the Blessed Virgin Mary daily, observed Saturday as a day of fast in her honor, prayed the Ave Maria, chanted her hymns. The habit of contemplation enabled them to see through the hard shell of reality to the spiritual core within, with the result that whatever was most admired became a reflection of the Virgin's beauty: the clear pool was her purity; the mountain shutting off the horizon, her grandeur; the spring flowers, her garland of virtues. The Scriptures too were pressed into service. The Song of Songs was given a Marian interpretation by monastic writers so that the narrative allowed for contemplation of the attractive love between God the Son and Mary. Furthermore, a multitude of metaphors taken from the Old Testament were applied to her: burning bush, the Ark of the Covenant, the Star of the Sea, the enclosed garden, the blossoming shoot out of the Root of Jesse, the fleece, the bridechamber, the door, the dawn, the ladder of Jacob. All of the mystery and graciousness of God's presence were seen to rest upon her person. Virginity as the subject of meditation had a particular significance in this setting. Living, enfleshed women, fallen and dangerous to the monastic vocation, had been left outside the monastery; in the Virgin, the monk found the heavenly ideal of woman, which could solace and uplift his heart. At times this could cross the boundary of good sense and issue in sensuous meditations on the union, full of kisses and embraces, which took place at the Annunciation (Amadeus of Lausanne [d. 1159]), or in a somewhat erotic conception of the marriage that existed between God the Son and the Virgin bride (Aelred of Rievaulx [d. 1167]). More often, in the age of chivalry, the Virgin functioned for the monk as the spiritual counterpart of the worldly knight's lady, to whom he pledged his enthusiastic and honorable service and love.

Both during his life and posthumously, the monk Bernard of Clairvaux (d. 1153), ardent in piety and eloquent in style, was the major influence in developing and fostering this affective approach. Although his theological and spiritual writings give ample evidence of the Christocentricity of his own devotion, and although his own thought about Mary almost always clung to the traditional formulations of the church (to the point where he opposed the feast of the Immaculate Conception because it had not been handed on by tradition), his sermons on feasts of Mary raised the fervor of Marian discourse to new heights.[4] There was an affection in his attitude and an appeal to the hearts of his listeners, which, when coupled with his typological application of Scripture texts to her, moved a whole generation toward greater honor and praise. The classical formulation of this aspect of Marian piety appeared at the end of Bernard's second homily in praise of the Virgin Mary:

"The Virgin's name was Mary" (Luke 1:27), which means "star of the sea.". . .
Surely she is very fittingly likened to a star. The star sends forth its ray
without harm to itself. In the same way the Virgin brought forth her Son
with no injury to herself. . . . She is indeed that noble star risen out of Jacob
whose beam enlightens this earthly globe. She it is whose brightness both
twinkles in the highest heaven and pierces the pit of hell, and is shed upon
earth, warming our hearts far more than our bodies, fostering virtue and
cauterizing vice. She, I tell you, is that splendid and wondrous star suspended
as by necessity over this great wide sea, radiant with merit and brilliant in
example. O you, whoever you are, who feel that in the tidal wave of this
world you are nearer to being tossed about among the squalls and gales than
treading on dry land, if you do not want to founder in the tempest, do not
avert your eyes from the brightness of this star. When the wind of temptation
blows up within you, when you strike upon the rock of tribulation, look to
the star, call out to Mary. When you are tossed about by the waves of pride
or ambition or slander or jealousy, look to the star, call out to Mary. When
rage or greed or fleshly desires are battering the skiff of your soul, gaze up
at Mary. . . . Keeping her in your thoughts, you will never wander away. With
your hand in hers you will never stumble. With her protecting you, you will
not be afraid. With her leading you, you will never tire. When she is your
helper, you will reach your journey's end.[5]

This sermon as much as anything in the twelfth century confirmed the
value of admiring contemplation of the Virgin and bonded hearts to her in
personal affection and trust.

   This type of Marian piety was not limited to the monasteries. The people
too loved the Virgin, and through meditation on the events of her life found
a gentling and inspiring influence within the hard stresses of life. She was
Our Lady, who together with Our Lord immensely edified them and evoked
wondering praise. Since the end of the seventh century, major feast days
commemorating certain events in her life had been observed: her nativity,
her purification in the temple at the time of the presentation of the Lord,
her Annunciation, and her Assumption. In the Middle Ages liturgical
dramas enacted during the Mass on these and other feast days offered the
opportunity for graphic meditation on key events of her life. These living
pictorial representations of her encounter with the angel Gabriel or of her
showing the newborn king to the shepherds elicited awed enjoyment and
deepened awareness of her special role in the story of salvation. The magnificent cathedrals that began to rise in her honor depicted in stone sculpture
and stained glass the intrinsic quality of her presence to the faith. At
Chartres, Christ reigns alone in majesty in the center of the royal portal,
but to the immediate right he is enthroned as a small king on Mary's lap,
who is further depicted with the child in a nativity scene. In the great north
central portal, Mary's death and post-death awakening are sculpted, and

27. *Triumph of the Virgin*, Chartres Cathedral (west facade).

above both she sits crowned in majesty at the right hand of Christ. These and a multitude of other images shaped the spirituality of a people who delighted in contemplating the mysteries of her life and the beauty of her person in relation to Christ.

Although this form of praising piety was founded on the realization that Mary's goodness as Virgin and Mother redounded to the good of all, there was not much emphasis on petition to her in prayer. People loved her for herself, conceiving of her as God's greatest creation, in which they could forever discover new wonders. Common recitation of the Ave Maria, the prayer formed by joining the scriptural greetings of the angel and of Mary's cousin Elizabeth, made praising and blessing the Virgin an integral part of Christian piety: "Hail Mary, full of grace, the Lord is with thee; blessed art thou among women, and blessed is the fruit of thy womb, Jesus."[6] The dynamic was one of great feeling for her beauty of soul focused particularly on her fruitful virginity, which moved hearts to joyful praise. People's spirits rejoiced in the loveliness of Mary, with the assurance that praise of the Mother redounded to praise of the Son, who chose her and fashioned her to be his mother. Rather than being diverted from the central concerns of faith, the faithful, through this piety, reaffirmed the good judgment of God, who himself loved the beautiful Virgin Mother.

Mediatrix

A second aspect of medieval Marian piety welled up from a deep need for a trustworthy means of salvation and came to focus on the image of Mary as the Mother who could be relied upon to mediate to all the grace and mercy of God. Both the understanding that believers had of their own situation before God and a new theological understanding of Mary's role in the process of salvation interlocked, especially in preaching, and led to this attitude of trust in the Mother's merciful activity, which assumed a powerful hold in medieval spirituality.

The situation of the believer before God was a complex and none-too-comfortable one. This era was gripped by the paradox of justice and mercy in the schema of salvation. God's justice had been violated by sin, and that same justice also made it impossible for God to forgive without either punishment or satisfaction being returned to God. What the justice of God demanded, the mercy of God supplied through the incarnation and death of Jesus Christ. It was now the task of sinners to receive divine mercy in Christ, while participating in the satisfaction that he rendered to the justice of God, through their own repentant deeds and prayers. The church's penitential practices supported this understanding. It was difficult in this scheme of things to feel that one had ever done enough. A sinner stood before God and trembled, conscious of the depths of sinfulness. God was rich in mercy, but he was also the just judge. Who could withstand his scrutiny? The terrors of the judgment scene were vividly presented in church carvings and glass, with Satan mangling the damned in his jaws or leading them to the flames of hell while Christ oversaw the process as the stern, just judge. Consciousness of sin and fear of judgment were characteristics of the conscience of the era. This was indirectly abetted by the preaching of the new mendicant orders, which called the laity to a new level of personal ethical activity, encouraging them to repent and work out their own salvation through prayer and good works. How could the ordinary person pass the test and gain heaven?

The development of the theology of Mary would provide an answer. Previously, Mary had been seen as a participant in the work of salvation at the beginning of Christ's coming because her divine maternity tied her closely to the mystery of the incarnation. Now the idea developed that through her suffering during the crucifixion (her *compassio* with Christ) she had continued to participate in the salvific event; the cult of her sorrows made vivid this direction of thought.[7] As she had mothered Christ and suffered with him, so too she was glorified at his right hand in heaven. The implication of this Marian history, as Anselm eloquently realized, was that the Mother of the Justifier was also the mother of the justified: "Blessed assurance, safe refuge, the mother of God is our mother. The mother of him in whom alone we have hope, whom alone we fear, is our mother. The mother of him who alone saves and condemns is our mother."[8] Her spiritual maternity, far from being simply a juridical bond, was now considered a real relation in the order of grace.

In a broad sense, this placed Mary close to Christ in the working of salvation. Christ, like the first Adam, now had his Eve, so that Mary no longer was considered so much a type of the church as an individual woman, an *adiutorium simile sibi*. The attempt to maintain the right proportion between Christ and Mary led to the concept of mediation. This idea was strikingly captured in Bernard's image of the aqueduct: the waters of divine grace have their source in Christ, who is the wellspring of eternal life; they flow down to earth through Mary, the aqueduct. Christ came to earth through her; divine grace comes to earth through her; and human beings should return to God through the same route.[9] The general opinion grew that Mary functioned as the mediatrix between believers and Christ, as Christ in turn was mediator between believers and God.

In a more specific sense, the role of Mary as mediatrix with the mediator was focused on the human need for mercy. On the analogy of a human mother, who would not want any of her children to be lost, the mediatrix of the graces of salvation became the mother of compassion, unfailingly on the side of mercy for sinners. In Bernard's preaching on the subject, the dynamic of this development is revealed: it is fear. To be sure, he preached, "Christ alone is our gracious Savior and alone is sufficient for our salvation."[10] He is the powerful mediator between God and human beings. But in him we also encounter the divine majesty, which awakens dread. Although he is our Savior of unsurpassable mercy, we might be afraid, for he is also our judge. With Mary, however, human weakness has nothing to fear. In her there is nothing hard, nothing terrifying, no trace of indignation. She is all sweetness, charm, and tenderness. She opens her merciful arms to all in order that all, without exception, may receive of her fullness. The sinner should flee to Mary, whose pure humanity the Son also honors, for the Son hears the Mother and the Father hears the Son: this ladder is what gives the sinner hope. Indeed, God should be thanked for giving the human race such a mediatrix.

This understanding of Mary as Mother of Mercy meshed closely with the understanding of the ambiguity of the sinner's position before God. All were her children, given her through her association with Christ. Brimming over with mercy, gentleness, and loving-kindness, she lavished a forgiving mother's love on the whole brood and in particular interceded for their salvation. In scenes of the Last Judgment, Mary began to be depicted kneeling before Christ to plead for sinners—an element of grace in the midst of the ceremonial of justice. A prayer of Anselm captures this blessing:

> Lady, it seems to me as if I were already before the all-powerful justice of the stern judge, facing the intolerable vehemence of his wrath, while hanging over me is the enormity of my sins, and the huge torments they deserve. Most gentle Lady, whose intercession should I implore when I am troubled with horror and shake with fear, but hers, whose womb embraced the reconciliation of the world? . . .
> Who can more easily gain pardon for the accused by her intercession, than she who gave milk to him who justly punishes or mercifully pardons all and each one?[12]

Trust in Mary's merciful intercession thus linked Marian piety very closely to the medieval person's search for salvation. She was invoked as Refuge of Sinners, and her aid was summoned in times of temptation, in particular at the time of death. Occasionally this became thoroughly problematic, as Mary's mercy gained ascendancy over Christ's, even to the point of leaving him bereft of mercy altogether. As an anonymous writer of an influential thirteenth-century sermon wrote, the kingdom of God was divided into two zones: justice and mercy. The Blessed Virgin "chose the better part, because she was made Queen of Mercy, while her Son remained King of Justice: and mercy is better than justice."[12]

Perhaps the most potent literary influence on the growing trust in Mary's merciful intercession and the paradigm for the host of miracle stories that followed was the Theophilus legend. This legend originated in the East, was translated into Latin by the end of the eighth century, was versified by the tenth, and was put into dramatic form by the thirteenth. The recitation or performance of it helped to spread an ever-increasing belief in the never-failing efficacy of Mary's merciful intercession. In this story, a man who wished to rise in worldly power bargained his soul to the devil. Riches and success accumulated, but Theophilus became stung with remorse. When he tried to repent, however, the devil would not return the contract which had sealed the renunciation of his soul. Theophilus turned then to the Blessed Virgin with a powerfully moving prayer for her help. In negotiations with the devil, she retrieved the contract, and Theophilus died in peace. This legend had incalculable influence, appearing in poems and miracle collections, in stained glass and cathedral portal sculptures (e.g., Notre-Dame de Paris), and in the sermons of even the most serious theologians (e.g., Thomas Aquinas). It reinforced the idea that with the help of Mary's heavenly intercession even the devil could be overcome and salvation won, no matter how unlikely the circumstances.

The piety of trust in the Mother of Mercy was carried forward in widely popular recitations of other legends of her miracles. Passed on and embellished by word of mouth, these tales were eventually collected in written form to be used as recommended exempla or illustrative stories by preachers.[13] In these popular tales, Mary helped kings, bishops, and great knights, but even more the simple folk—artists, humble monks and nuns, travelers, mothers of wayward sons, clerks, acrobats. The areas of her help were many; she calmed storms, saved the drowning, aided women in childbirth, protected kidnapped children, defended the defamed and the persecuted, and received gifts from simple folk, which she rewarded with her blessing. Most important, she interceded with Christ for sinners, arranging for one to come back to life to confess her sins before dying again in grace, arguing with the devil for the soul of another, and tipping the scales in which the merits and sins of still another were being weighed. Medieval persons felt that with her they always had a chance, for she was always on their side in the exercise of mercy. Tremendous affection for her and unlimited confidence in her help were the result.

The public liturgical life of the church already venerated Mary through the cycle of Marian feasts with their hymns, prayers, dramas and processions, to which were attached indulgences and which the civil authorities helped to stabilize. As reliance on her maternal mercy grew, other expressions of private devotion proliferated. The recitation of the Little Office of the Blessed Virgin Mary was recommended for the laity, as was observance of the Saturday fast and Mass in her honor. The Ave Maria was repeated many times over accompanied by genuflections or prostrations, and this repetition was gradually organized into the pattern of the Rosary. The Ave Maria was also said three times at the ringing of the evening bells, a custom that developed into the Angelus prayer. Litanies of praise and petition were spun off from existing prayers, lengthened, and chanted. Meditations on the Mother's joys and sorrows were propagated, and in the towns brotherhoods were formed to promote her honor. The singing of the Marian antiphon Salve Regina was solemnized through its being accompanied by processions in monasteries and cathedrals. This prayer expressed to perfection the medieval person's confident attitude toward Mary:

> Hail, Holy Queen, Mother of Mercy, our life, our sweetness and our hope. To thee do we cry, poor banished children of Eve. To thee do we send up our sighs, mourning and weeping in this valley of tears. Turn then, most gracious advocate, thine eyes of mercy toward us, and after this our exile show unto us the blessed fruit of thy womb, Jesus.

Besides the plethora of developing prayers and customs, certain Marian shrines drew people's interest as the sites of special veneration. A shrine might contain a valued image of Mary or a relic such as a piece of her clothing or hair. Again, it might be the locale of an appearance of Mary or of a healing effected by her. As places where the merciful nearness of Mary might be experienced, shrines such as Walsingham in England, Chartres in France, and Our Lady of the Pillar in Spain became the goal of pilgrimages. Such journeys placed the pilgrim at risk, both physically and psychologically. Ideally, they culminated in the sacred place, where faith was strengthened, forgiveness found, favor gained, and solidarity with the hope and fear of other pilgrims established, all under the protection of the Mother of God, also the merciful mother of the pilgrims. (Wenching, thieving, and other abuses also came to be associated with these journeys.)

The burgeoning of devotions can scarcely be enumerated. In prayers and practices, people both expressed and increased their conviction that confidence in Mary was not misplaced. With intense trust they invoked the Mother of Mercy, advocate of sinners, who could be unfailingly relied upon to obtain for those who loved her the salvific grace of divine mercy. In all areas of life Mary was Mother of the people, trusted to mediate eternal and earthly blessings.

Queen of Heaven and Earth

In time, the piety of praise for the beauty of the Virgin intersected with that of trust in the mercy of the Mother in a movement of spirit that intensified both. Out of their coalescence emerged a third aspect of medieval Marian piety, one that in the end was to dominate. It glorified the Virgin Mother as Queen of heaven and earth, all the while petitioning for the Queen's all-powerful protection from dangers that threatened on every side: private and public disasters in the earthly realm, and the ever-more-likely possibility of the eternal punishment of hell. The key to the fully developed form of this aspect of devotion was the felt need for protection, for help and aid, a need almost tyrannical in the difficult life of great numbers of people.

The context for attention to Mary's protective power was the view, shared by ordinary folk and many of the learned alike, that the world was the field of activity not of the anonymous powers of sin and grace but of invisible good and evil persons. Under the one God and subject to his almighty power—although it was not always clear how far that subjection went—a host of demons and angels engaged in a perpetual warfare of opposing wills, bringing about or staving off wars, storms, pestilences, and ultimately the eternal salvation of each soul. The presence of devils in particular was very real to the consciousness of the late Middle Ages, a time gripped by a kind of satanic fever. Seducers of the soul, these evil spirits watched and waited for one bad action so that they could move in and bring a person to hell. Their tempting activity was especially strong during a person's dying hours, which offered them their last chance of victory. In life and in death, then, people envisioned themselves caught in a battle between Satan's legions and the all-powerful God, just and merciful, from whom alone one could hope for salvation. The need was strong to turn to the most effective means of help or guarantee of rescue. Devotions were built around this need: prayer to the saints, partaking of the sacraments, almsgiving, public penance, etc. In this framework, the protection of Mary, glorious Queen of heaven and earth, assumed paramount importance.

As was the case with the merciful mediation of Mary, the idea of her queenship was developed by theologians in devotional and homiletic writings more often than in formal theological works. The springboard for the idea was the belief, liturgically celebrated, in Mary's assumption into heaven when her life on earth was over. Received into heaven by Christ with a welcome commensurate to that which she gave him when he came to earth through her very being, she was crowned Queen of heaven and earth and began to participate in his power over both realms. Since this glorious Queen was also the merciful Mother of the people, her power would be used to protect the little ones of the world who honored her and called to her in their struggles. Heaven, modeled on the analogy of a feudal court, held not only the King but his Queen Mother, privy to his heart and capable of wielding influential power in behalf of her clients. The affection this could inspire was exquisitely captured by Bernard's designation of Mary's devotees as *servuli*. This diminutive of the word servant signified not so much bonded servanthood as devotedness, humility, and sense of belonging: Mary's devotees are her little pages, who follow their Lady and directly serve their beloved Queen.[14]

When devotion to the powerful protection of the Queen of heaven was kept linked with the Scriptures, the liturgy, and formal theological teaching, Mary was seen as ruling not in her own right but through her influence with Christ. Through continual intercession she obtained the flow of his graces. Moreover, she was an enduringly reliable intercessor, for how could he refuse his mother anything she asked? In time, however, especially after the fourteenth century, private piety disconnected from official teaching in great swatches. Mary was more and more assumed, at least implicitly, to operate autonomously, a counterforce to the wiles of the demons and sometimes even to the just judgment of God. She rose into a formidable power in her own right.

The growth in the perception of the Queen of heaven's power was an element in a much wider movement of the time which sought, on the basis of the divine maternity, to make the mother's status approach that of the Son in virtue and privilege. In his homily on the Twelve Stars, Bernard had already depicted Mary rising above the church of which she was the type by applying to her the image of the woman in the book of Revelation, clothed with the sun, with the moon (i.e., the church) under her feet.[15] Soon the principle that almost everything that Scripture said of Christ might be applied also to his mother was explicitly stated and began to bear fruit. Mary's suffering under the cross was the means by which she had participated in the act of redemption: therefore, the titles *salvatrix* and *redemptrix* were applied to her. Enthroned with Christ in glory she was now active in ruling the world and in making salvation effective for those who called upon her: therefore, it could be said that no one entered heaven but through her; that because she had humbled herself God had highly exalted her and given her a name above every name, after the name of the Son; indeed, that she had done more for God than God could do for himself, and at least as much for God as he had done for the whole human race (Bernardine of Siena). Full of grace and exalted above all creatures, even the angels, she and her will held sway throughout heaven and earth. There was nothing not subject to her through her Son. God himself was subject to her as a Son to his mother,

28. Jean Milhairet, *Our Lady of Mercy.* Chapelle de la Misericorde, Nice.

to whom he could refuse nothing. The Blessed Virgin powerfully balanced his justice with her mercy, placing back into its sheath his naked sword, which was raging against humankind; she gave life to mortals, purified the world, and opened the doors of heaven and hell. In some quarters, Mary in effect took over the function of Father (she so loved the world that she gave her only Son), Son (all authority in heaven and on earth was given to her), and Holy Spirit (she was advocate and illuminator of the church). Even where this did not happen, her power was understood to be enormous, and prayers for her aid became an ordinary and widespread part of Christian life. In his *Divine Comedy*, Dante (d. 1320) gave voice to this crescendo of Marian piety by depicting Mary as the guiding light who led the pilgrim to God. Enthroned in glory as beautiful and brilliant Queen, Mary mediated the beatific vision for him; the pilgrim's journey revealed that her influence penetrated the entire universe—earth, hell, purgatory, heaven. When in this period the Te Deum, a liturgical hymn of praise of God, was adapted to Mary's praise instead, it seemed only fitting:

> We praise thee, O Mother of God; we confess thee,
>   Mary ever Virgin.
> Thou art the Spouse of the Eternal Father: the
>   whole earth venerates thee.
> Thee all angels and archangels, thrones and
>   principalities serve.
> Thee all powers and all virtues of heavens and all
>   dominations obey.
> Before thee all the angelic choirs, the cherubim and
>   seraphim, exulting, stand.
> With unceasing voice every angelic creature
>   proclaims thee:
> Holy, holy, holy, Mary Virgin Mother of God.[16]

The enormity of the popular veneration that accrued to Mary in the late Middle Ages was commensurate with her power as Queen of heaven, Queen of the world, Queen and mistress of the church. Everywhere her relics and images were venerated; pilgrimages were undertaken to her shrines; prayers were offered in her honor; mystery plays starred her as the central attraction; and appeals for the exercise of her powerful protection rose up. The ever-popular miracle stories offer a glimpse into the style of her exercise of power; it was not restrained by law but moved freely with a lady's love. This was especially clear in the tales in which Mary helped the disreputable and the overt sinners, giving them a chance for salvation provided only that they were in some way devoted to her. As the compiler de Coincy pointed out, one might be a sinner, but one was "her sinner." In deathbed scenes and before the judgment seat of God, she fought for her own and never lost. In the narrations of the miracle stories, the evil ones never minded a deathbed appeal to God; but they could not bear an appeal to Mary, whom they called "that woman" (*illa mulier*), for then they would be cheated of a soul that was rightfully theirs. Say the devils in one disputed case:

> In this lawsuit, since it is a choice of evils, we had best appeal to the judgment of the high judge who lieth not. His mother will not judge aright in any plea; but God judges us so fairly that he leaves us all our due. His mother judges in such a way that we always find ourselves down when we think that we are up. She is always harming us somehow. . . . In Heaven and on earth she is the ruler rather than God. He so loves her and believes in her that he will not contradict her or disavow anything that she says or does. She makes Him believe anything she likes. If she said that black was white and muddy water clear, He would say, "It is true; My Mother says so."[18]

The Queen Mother of the judge drove the devils crazy. Her power was the power of love; although admittedly not always scrupulous in its exercise, she was eminently reliable in her protective instincts. Fervent supplication for her help was the obvious devotional expression of this conviction.

This turn to Mary's protective power gave rise to a new iconography, that of the Madonna of the protective mantle, which corresponded to the mixture of intense supplication and fervent reliance on her protection expressed in stories and prayers. Carved or painted, the Blessed Virgin stood tall and brooding, alone and without Christ. Under the umbrella formed by her draped, outstretched arms huddled a family, or a religious order, or a lay confraternity, or a king, or the populace of a whole town. Looking concerned and sometimes terrified, this whole panoply of medieval figures shrank into the shelter of her all-embracing power away from the fearsomeness of the evils that awaited beyond, be they plague, war, temptation, or judgment. Patterned on the biblical image of Christ the mother hen who would gather her brood under her wings, the image of the Lady's protective mantle implied a virtually autonomous sovereignty in her exercise of power, giving benefit to the living and the dead.

Beyond lyrical praise for the beauty of the Virgin, beyond simple trust in the mercy of the Mother, medieval Marian devotion intensified when it became a question of pleading for the protection of the Queen. There was an ever-growing popular tendency to regard Mary as one kind of infallible guarantee against all evils, even against the legitimate consequences of sin and crime. She was granted virtually absolute efficacy, and the advantage of calling on her supernatural power often took precedence over more established means of salvation such as an ethical life and the use of the sacraments. People tended to forget that, according to strict doctrine, the Queen of heaven and earth was completely relative to Christ, aiding them (if at all) only within the framework of his salvific will for the world. The multiple forms and frequent practices of late medieval Marian piety focused rather on her own glorious self, most unique of all beings, whose powerful favor could be gained by fervent and humble entreaty.

The Views of the Reformers

Even before this period drew to a close, voices were raised in critical evaluation of the state of Marian piety. The great humanist Erasmus of Rotterdam (d. 1536), for one, had shared in the devotion of the age, even pilgrimaging to Walsingham; but study of the Scriptures and the fathers of the church coupled with his own observations led him to vigorous contention against what he perceived to be popular abuses. He criticized the consistent invocation of Mary when in distress to the point of ignoring God; he opposed the idea that Christ reigning in heaven is subject to his mother; he inveighed against the substitution of candles, images, and chants to the Blessed Virgin for the living of an ethical life; he excoriated those who thought that the Virgin would be propitious to them if they sang the Salve Regina—which they did not even understand—while offending her by spending their nights in obscenities. His violent rhetoric against external practices devoid of any truly religious and moral content did not cause him to depart from the cult himself. Erasmus represents that interesting combination of honoring the Blessed Virgin while calling for correction of distortions, a combination that would appear again and again in subsequent history.

The first generation of Protestant reformers, all originally Catholic and thus nourished in a spiritual environment that stressed the cult of Mary, did not abandon Marian devotion completely. They did interpret its excesses critically as deviations from the central gospel message that human beings are saved by Jesus Christ through faith alone. Martin Luther said in later years that he had been taught the prevalent view that Christ was an angry judge and Mary the throne of grace through which redemption was mediated.[19] When confronted with his own anxiety over salvation, Luther had rediscovered Christ as the merciful and sole mediator of salvation. As a tool for continuing criticism of the massive Marian cult, he penned a praising commentary on Mary's biblical song, the Magnificat, in which he held Mary up as the model for humble faith: acknowledging her own nothingness, the humble maid put all her trust in God and was filled with gracious, unmerited gifts through the bare goodness of God. Thus, "she should be, and herself gladly would be, the foremost example of the grace of God."[19] Among Luther, Calvin, and the other reformers, Mary's role as the Virgin

Mother of Jesus Christ continued to be honored, whereas reliance on her mediation and the practice of invoking her help were banned as taking honor away from Christ, who alone mediates salvation. In later generations, Marian devotion in the Protestant churches all but disappeared, a casualty of both the new form of evangelical spirituality introduced by the reformers and the continuing polemic with the Roman Catholic Church, which continued to honor Mary with ever-increasing fervor.

In the more ecumenical spirit of recent times, Protestant scholars who have studied medieval Marian devotion continue to judge it negatively, not just for its abuses but for its basic structure, which, in their judgment, is derogatory to the centrality of Christ.[20] Particular criticism is leveled against the concept of Mary's mediation, which lessens the immediacy of believers to Christ and introduces her as a second agent in the accomplishment of redemption. Her role as Mediatrix generated a pressure that moved her from a place below Christ, to similarity with Christ, to equivalence with Christ, and finally to contrast with Christ, insofar as she was more mercifully understanding of human weakness. The result was that she gained kerygmatic priority over Christ—in effect, taking over the function of savior and becoming so glorious that she was close to being adored. Between the Mary of the Scriptures and this medieval Mary only a loose connection exists.

Although not as negative about the structure of Marian devotion as a whole as their Protestant colleagues, Roman Catholic scholars have agreed with the critique of abuses prevalent in the late medieval period. Especially deplored is the loss of focus on the mystery of the incarnation in Marian piety and its replacement with the magical idea of Mary as the "mama" who would fix everything. Instead of praise, there was demand; instead of sobriety, exuberant fancy; instead of faith, superstition. Eminent mariologist René Laurentin notes of the fourteenth century, "Repelled by a desiccated intellectualism, people sought life on the imaginative and sentimental plane. Throughout this period of decadence popular enthusiasm for the Blessed Virgin never faltered, but the adulterated fodder it was nourished on consisted of trumpery miracles, ambiguous slogans, and inconsistent maundering."[21] By the time of the Reformation, something like a purgation was long overdue.

Although theologians judge Mary's sometime usurpation of the role of Christ and the skewing of faith that results as deterioration and degeneration, other angles of interpretation are possible. Historians of religion have assessed the ascendency of the Queen of heaven as the reemergence of the suppressed mother-goddess of the prehistoric European tribes.[22] Anthropologists have analyzed it as folk appreciation of the feminine element in the world, which involves compassion, tenderness, a little capriciousness, vulnerability to suffering, and the inclination to grieve rather than punish offense. This characterization is consistent with a patrilineal system, where the patriline is the hard line of jural authority and property transmission, whereas the matriline is affectionate, soft, and providing of sanctuary.[23] Feminist writers argue that the whole phenomenon was possible only because of the projection of the patriarchal family structure into heaven, with the harsh male authority figure being tempered by the intercession of the mother, who feels loving kindness for the wayward child. More critically, they fault the medieval cult of the Virgin for fashioning an image of woman according to androcentric perceptions and needs, leaving the situation of real women unaffected by the glorification of the one.[24] Interpretations are as diverse and complex as the phenomenon of medieval Marian piety itself. For the people of the Middle Ages, devotion to the Blessed Virgin offered an experience of a female figure intrinsically related to God, along with an experience of the power of love to blot away sin and the power of mercy to ameliorate deserved justice, experiences that were not otherwise readily available in the situation of the times.

Notes

1. *The Mirror of the Blessed Virgin Mary and the Psalter of our Lady*, trans. Sr. Mary Emmanuel (St. Louis, MO: Herder, 1932) 254.

2. Anselm of Canterbury, "Prayer to St. Mary, to ask for her and Christ's love," in *Prayers and Meditations of Saint Anselm*, trans. S. Benedicta Ward (New York: Penguin Books, 1973) 120–21.

3. Ibid.

4. Both the liturgical celebration of the Immaculate Conception and the theological underpinning of the doctrine were much disputed during the Middle Ages. The breakthrough came with the insights of William of Ware and Duns Scotus (d. 1308), but even then argumentation continued and the doctrine gained a foothold only slowly. Judging from prayers, iconography, and other indicators of spirituality, the Immaculate Conception as such was not a major factor in medieval Marian piety.

5. Bernard of Clairvaux, *De laudibus beatae Mariae–Homily 2*, in *Magnificat: Homilies in Praise of the Blessed Virgin Mary*, trans. Marie-Bernard Said and Grace Perigo (Kalamazoo, MI: Cistercian Publications, 1979) 30–31.

6. A second, petitionary part of the Ave Maria originated in the fifteenth century in a variety of forms and was given a final fixed form in the sixteenth century; see Gerard Sloyan, "Marian Prayers," in *Mariology*, 3:64–87.

7. Devotion to the sorrows of Mary gradually became more pronounced and gave rise to new pictorial representations of her suffering: the pietàs, the images of her heart pierced by seven swords, and paintings of her wailing or fainting on Calvary. In the literary genre of lamentation, Mary mourned the dead Christ with a vigor unknown in the previous tradition, in an extravagant style most likely patterned on Germanic

lamentations over the dead such as occur in *Beowulf* or the *Nibelungenlied*. Sometimes her distraught grief is so realistically portrayed that her religious character is lost from view.

8. Anselm, "Prayer to St. Mary," 122. It was Anselm who had first systematized the era's understanding of God's justice vis-à-vis human sinfulness in *Cur Deus Homo*.

9. Bernard of Clairvaux, *De aquaeductu*, in *Saint Bernard et Notre Dame* (Desclée de Brouwer pour l'Abbaye de Sept-Fons, 1953) 208–13.

10. Bernard of Clairvaux, *De duodecim praerogativis beatae Mariae virginis*, in *Saint Bernard et Notre Dame*, 174–75.

11. Anselm of Canterbury, "Prayer to St. Mary, when the mind is anxious with fear," in *Prayers and Meditations*, 110.

12. This sermon was for a long time attributed to Bonaventure, but it is now seen to be contradictory to his teaching on Mary; see Hilda C. Graef, *Mary: A History of Doctrine and Devotion*, 1:281-90.

13. E.g., Johannes Herolt, called Discipulus, *Miracles of the Blessed Virgin Mary*, trans. C. Bland, with an introduction by Eileen Power (London: G. Routledge & Sons, 1928).

14. Bernard of Clairvaux, *In Assumptione. Sermo 4, Praeconium virginis*, in *Saint Bernard et Notre Dame*, 376–77.

15. Bernard of Clairvaux, *De duodecim praerogativis*, in *Saint Bernard et Notre Dame*, 178–81.

16. In *The Mirror of the Blessed Virgin Mary*, 294–95.

17. Quoted in Herolt, *Miracles*, xxxi.

18. Martin Luther, "Exhortation to All Clergy Assembled at Augsburg, 1530," *Luther's Works* (American edition; Philadelphia: Fortress, 1955–) 34:27.

19. Martin Luther, *Commentary on the Magnificat*, in *Luther's Works*, 21:323.

20. Jaroslav Pelikan, *The Growth of Medieval Theology* (Chicago: University of Chicago Press, 1978); Heiko Oberman, *The Harvest of Medieval Theology* (Cambridge, MA: Harvard University Prass, 1963).

21. René Laurentin, *Queen of Heaven*, 60; see also Jean Leclercq, "Grandeur et misère de la dévotion mariale au moyen âge," in *La liturgie et les paradoxes chrétiens* (Paris: Cerf, 1963) 170–204.

22. H. P. Ahsmann, *Le culte de la sainte Vièrge et la littérature française profane du moyen âge;* Eileen Power, "Introduction," in Herolt, *Miracles*, xi–xii.

23. Victor Turner and Edith Turner, *Image and Pilgrimage in Christian Culture*.

24. Eleanor Commo McLaughlin, "Equality of Souls, Inequality of Sexes: Woman in Medieval Theology," in *Religion and Sexism*, ed. Rosemary Radford Ruether (New York: Simon & Schuster, 1974) 213–66; Marina Warner, *Alone of All Her Sex: The Myth and the Cult of the Virgin Mary* (New York: Knopf, 1976).

Bibliography

Ahsmann, H. P. *Le culte de la sainte Vièrge et la littérature française profane du moyen âge*. Paris: Picard, 1930.

Delaruelle, Etienne. *La pieté populaire au moyen âge*. Turin: Bottege d'Erasmo, 1975.

Delius, Walter. *Geschichte der Marienverehrung*. Munich: E. Reinhardt, 1963.

Graef, Hilda C. *Mary: A History of Doctrine and Devotion*. 2 vols. New York: Sheed & Ward, 1963–65.

Katzenellenbogen, Adolf. *The Sculptural Programs of Chartres Cathedral*. Baltimore, MD: Johns Hopkins University Press, 1959.

Koehler, Theodore. "Marie (Vièrge): du moyen âge aux temps modernes." In *Dict. Sp.* 10, cols. 440–59.

Laurentin, René. *Queen of Heaven: A Short Treatise on Marian Theology.* Translated by G. Smith. London: Burns, Oates & Washbourne, 1956.

Leclercq, Jean, François Vandenbroucke, and Louis Bouyer. *The Spirituality of the Middle Ages.* Vol. 2 of *A History of Christian Spirituality.* Translated by the Benedictines of Holme Eden Abbey, Carlisle. London: Burns & Oates, 1968.

Mâle, Emile. *Religious Art: From the Twelfth to the Eighteenth Century.* New York: Noonday Press, 1958.

Manoir, Hubert du. *Maria: Études sur la Sainte Vièrge,* vol. 2. Paris: Beauchesne, 1952.

Manselli, Raoul. *La religion populaire au moyen âge: Problèmes de méthode et d'histoire.* Paris: J. Vrin, 1975.

Meier, Theo. *Die Gestalt Marias im geistlichen Schauspiel des deutschen Mittelalters.* Berlin: Erich Schmidt, 1959.

Scheffczyk, Leo. *Das Mariengeheimnis in Frömmigkeit und Lehre der Karolingerzeit.* Leipzig: St. Benno, 1959.

Sloyan, Gerard. "Marian Prayers." In *Mariology,* 3:64–87. Edited by Juniper Carol. Milwaukee, WI: Bruce, 1961.

Turner, Victor, and Edith Turner. *Image and Pilgrimage in Christian Culture.* New York: Columbia University Press, 1978.

Young, Earl. *The Drama of the Medieval Church.* 2 vols. Oxford: Clarendon Press, 1932.

18

Liturgy and Eucharist

I. *East*

ROBERT TAFT

The Setting

L ITURGY AND PIETY ARE PART of a larger historical-cultural milieu. In the medieval East this milieu was not favorable to Christian life. The divisions caused by the fifth- and sixth-century christological controversies had hardened, and Muslim conquests had reduced these divided communities to minority status in a largely Islamic world. Gone were the splendors of the urban stational and basilical rites of Late Antiquity. Liturgical life became more private, restricted to family, monastery, and church. The shrinking remnant of the Byzantine Empire saw analogous changes. The monumental architecture of the Justinianic period was succeeded by churches often miniature by comparison. The monastic victory over iconoclasm (726–843) had demoralized the secular clergy. Monasteries became richer, more autonomous, and multiplied especially in the cities; in the later centuries of Byzantium far more monastic than secular churches were built.[1] With Constantinople under Latin rule (1204–1261) after the Fourth Crusade, the secular clergy were unable to maintain the complex rite of the great church, and acquiesced in the monasticization of the offices. Still, during the Paleologan restoration (1259–1453), the church and monasteries remained a powerful force in the life of the people,[2] and the hesychast spiritual renaissance, begun on Mount Athos in this period, was to spread throughout the Eastern Orthodox world.[3] To this revival belongs Nicholas Cabasilas, lay humanist writing around 1350, whose brilliant treatises, combining the best in humanism and hesychast spirituality, make him the classic exponent of Byzantine liturgical theology during the hesychast revival.

The Shape of the Liturgy

By the late Middle Ages, the Eastern eucharistic liturgies had achieved more or less their definitive shape by filling in the basic common outline of the early Eucharist at the three "soft points" of action without words: (1) the entrance into church, (2) the kiss of peace and transfer of gifts, and (3) the communion rites and dismissal.[4] These actions acquired ceremony, chants, and prayers, as medieval liturgical development increasingly refused to let a gesture speak for itself.

The socio-political and economic situation of the period also entailed changes of scale. The compression of church life to within the walls of ever-smaller churches was accompanied by a shift toward greater symbolization. Rites lost their original practical purpose and perdured as symbolic remnants.[5] The end result was a liturgy less imperial and more intimate. No longer did its stational processions encompass the whole city within its liturgical space.[6] Its ritual, still imposing, was confined within the church building, and processions were reduced to a series of appearances of the sacred ministers from behind the sanctuary barrier.[7]

This move toward a smaller scale also entailed a certain privatization of the liturgy.[8] Not only were the once great public processions reduced to ritual turns within the interior of tiny chapels; even within the church, the ritual action withdrew into the ever-more completely enclosed sanctuary. The elevated synthronon disappeared from the apse—no longer must the celebrant at his throne be visible to all—and the great ambo in the center of the nave was displaced, reduced, even removed, as was preaching, and proclamation of the word became a ritualized formality, usually the reading of a ready text from some homiliary. The proliferation of private oratories with their clergy was a further sign of the shift away from monumental public services to the more domestic and monastic.

Liturgical Piety:
Ritual, Mystagogy, and Iconography

But liturgies have both an inner and an outer history that interact in dialectical tension, especially in the East, where the spiritual understanding of ritual contributed vitally to the development of its symbolic form.[9] Thus changes in the Byzantine Eucharist during the middle and late Byzantine periods (the introduction of particles for the living and dead at the prothesis; the development of the great entrance ritual and its symbolism; the multiplication of burial-motif troparia at the deposition of the gifts; and the elaboration of the Orate fratres text, precommunion prayers, and final rites[10]) are indicative not only of the ritual elaboration of all medieval liturgies but also of developments in piety. The offerings for the living and the dead that the people brought to the liturgy were a major expression of their part in the liturgical action. And the interpretation of the liturgy as symbolizing the earthly economy of Jesus, beginning at the prothesis with the kenosis of his incarnation (see Phil 2:5–8) and hidden life, and proceeding through the preaching of his public ministry, his appearance as Word during the procession with the Gospel or "little entrance," and in the readings of the Liturgy of the Word, reached its high point in the "great entrance," when the gifts of bread and wine were borne in while the people prostrated themselves before the appearance of the Lord being led to his sacrifice, death, burial, and resurrection in the communion of the sanctified gifts.[11] That all this had a profound effect on popular piety can be seen in the common people's attitude of profound reverence at these parts of the liturgy.[12]

Theological interpretation of this spirituality was formulated in liturgical commentaries and communicated to the masses through the ritual celebration itself, as well as in the liturgical disposition and decoration of the church building, which not only provided the physical setting of the rite but was also one of its symbolic components. Both church decoration and ritual combined to create a unitary symbolic ambience designed to provide an entrance into the mystery of salvation in Christ. Eucharist was more than a celebration of Christian table fellowship, more even than a sharing in the Lord's Word and Supper. It was theophany, a place of encounter with the very mystery of God. "Active participation" in the liturgy meant more than just taking part in the processions and chants, more than being attentive to the lessons and homily, more than just receiving communion. It also implied an ascent, through faith, from *historia* to *theoria*, from the visible symbols and ritual forms to the contemplation of the transcendent reality they contain.

Central to such a view is the conviction that the visible world is the image and manifestation of the invisible; that symbol, though distinct from its antitype, participates in and communicates its reality. This is the basis of spiritual exegesis, of mystagogy, and of iconography. What is portrayed in the literal and the visible, veils a *gnosis* perceived only by one who contemplates it with faith. By a process of anagogy one rises from letter to spirit, from the visible rites and icons to the contemplation of the mystery that is God.[13]

This "Alexandrine" method of liturgical interpretation, in which the contemplation of liturgical rites leads the soul to the mystical realities of the invisible world, represents only one strain in the later synthesis. The other, "Antiochene" strain, more attentive to *historia*, viewed the eucharistic ritual as a representation of Christ's self-oblation in his passion and death. This interpretation of the liturgical *historia* as a dramatic reenactment of the earthly economy of Jesus, crucial for almost all later Eastern liturgical interpretation, was introduced to Byzantine mystagogy by Patriarch St. Germanos I around 730 and achieved its classical liturgical expression around 1350 in Nicholas Cabasilas's *Commentary on the Divine Liturgy* (*PG* 150, cols. 367–492)[14] and *The Life in Christ* (*PG* 150, cols. 493–726).

Cabasilas makes it clear from the outset of his commentary (1.1) that everything in the divine liturgy—the lessons, prayers, chants—is meant to "turn us towards God," and "make us fit for the reception and preservation of the holy mysteries, which is the aim of the liturgy." But there is another level of liturgical signification, "another way in which these forms . . . sanctify us."

> It consists in this: that in them Christ and the deeds he accomplished and the sufferings he endured for our sakes are represented. Indeed, it is the whole scheme of the work of redemption which is signified in the psalms and readings, as in all the actions of the priest throughout the liturgy. . . .
>
> Even if one maintains that the readings and the psalms . . . were introduced in order to dispose us to virtue . . . that does not mean that the same ceremonies cannot at once urge us to virtue and illustrate the scheme of Christ's redemptive work. . . . Each symbolized some part of the works of Christ, his deeds or his sufferings. For example, we have the bringing of the Gospel to the altar, then the bringing of the offerings. Each is done for a purpose, the one that the Gospel may be read, the other that the sacrifice may be performed; besides this, however, one represents the appearance and the other the manifestation of the Saviour; the first, obscure and imperfect, at the beginning of his life; the second, the perfect and supreme manifestation.

But this representational aspect of the ritual is not an empty show. The ceremonies are meant to stimulate a personal response of faith.

> Just as the work of redemption, when it was first achieved, restored the world, so now, when it is ever before our eyes, it makes the souls of those who behold it better and more divine. I say more: it would not even have been of any use if it had not been an object of contemplation and of faith. . . . But when it was preached it created in those men of graceless soul who previously knew it not, a veneration for Christ and a faith and love which did not exist there before. To-day, contemplated with ardour by those who already have faith, . . . it makes the believers stronger in faith and more generous in devotion and love.

29. *Icon of the Three Most Venerated Liturgists and the Parasceva* (St. Basil,
St. Gregory, and St. John Chrysostom), Russian, 14th century. Private Collection.

For Cabasilas, the operation of this liturgical symbolism does not depend on some abstruse symbol system. Nothing could be more concretely realistic:

> It was necessary, not only that we should think about, but also that to some extent we should *see* the utter poverty of him who possesses all, the coming on earth of him who dwells everywhere, the shame of the most blessed God, the sufferings of the impassible; that we should see how much he was hated and how much he loved; how he, the Most High, humbled himself; what torments he endured, what deeds he accomplished in order to prepare for us this holy table. Thus, in beholding the unutterable freshness of the work of salvation, amazed by the abundance of God's mercy, we are brought to venerate him who had such compassion for us, who saved us at so great a price: to entrust our souls to him, to dedicate our lives to him, to enkindle in our hearts the flame of his love. Thus prepared, we can enter into contact with the fire of the solemn mysteries with confidence and trust.

This is no intellectualist spirituality, no lofty gnosticism of a spiritual elite, but a profoundly imaginative and popular piety.

The same theology is at the basis of Byzantine icon worship, and both of its dimensions—church and liturgy as a mirror of the mysteries of salvation, and church and liturgy as cosmic and eschatological images of the heavenly world and its worship—emerge already at the end of the early Byzantine period in the theology of the church building itself.

Byzantine churches gradually elaborate an iconographic program to express this vision to the ordinary faithful, unreached by the literary productions of a Cabasilas.[15] In the cosmic scheme, the church building and the ritual it enfolds are an image of the present age of the church, in which divine grace is mediated to those in the world (nave) from the divine abode (sanctuary) and its heavenly worship, which in turn images forth its future consummation (eschatological) when the faithful shall enter that abode in glory. In the economic scheme, the sanctuary and its altar are at once Holy of Holies, cenacle of the Last Supper, Golgotha, and tomb of the resurrection, from which the sacred gifts of the risen Lord, his word and his body and blood, issue forth to illumine the sin-darkened world.

The surfaces of the church interior become so enveloped in imagery that building and icon become one in evoking that vision of the Christian cosmos around which the Byzantine liturgy revolved. From the central dome, the image of the Pantocrator dominates the whole scheme, giving unity to the hierarchical and liturgical themes. The movement of the hierarchical theme is vertical, ascending from the present, worshiping community assembled in the nave up through the ranks of saints, prophets, patriarchs, and apostles to the Lord in the heavens attended by the heavenly choirs.

The liturgical theme, extending upward from the sanctuary, is united both artistically and theologically with the hierarchical. In fact, it is only with the liturgical theme that the symbolism of the church comes alive and appears as more than a static embodiment of the cosmos as seen through the eyes of God. A link between the divine and created worlds was forged by Christ in the covenant of his blood. This dynamic bond is expressed in both the disposition and the iconography of the church. The enclosed sanctuary wherein the mysteries of the covenant are renewed is conceived as the link between heaven and earth. Behind and above the altar, on the wall of the central sanctuary apse, is depicted the communion of the apostles—Christ the high priest, surrounded by the angels, giving the Eucharist to the Twelve. Over the altar, in the conch, is the Mother of God interceding in our behalf. With her is the Christ-child, figure of the incarnation that made this sacrificial intercession possible. Above this, at the summit of the arch, is the "throne of divine judgement," where the sacrificial mediation intercedes before God. From the sanctuary, cycles of liturgical feasts are depicted in lateral bands of frescoes that extend around the walls of the church, binding the historical past into the salvific renewal of the present.

Within this setting the liturgical community commemorated the mystery of its redemption in union with the worship of the heavenly church, offering the mystery of Christ's covenant through the outstretched hands of His Mother, all made present in the sacramental surroundings of the iconographic scheme. Even the unlettered Christian, worshiping in this setting as clouds of incense mingled with the smoking thuribles of the depicted heavenly liturgy, must have grasped something of what Symeon of Thessalonica (d. 1429), last of the classic Byzantine commentators of this era, meant in his treatise *On the Holy Temple* (chap. 131 [PG 155, cols. 337–40]):

> The church, as the house of God, is an image of the whole world, for God is everywhere and above everything.... The sanctuary is a symbol of the higher and supra-heavenly spheres, where the throne of God and His dwelling place are said to be. It is this throne that the altar represents ... the church represents this visible world.... The sanctuary receives within itself the bishop, who represents the Godman Jesus whose almighty powers he shares. The other sacred ministers represent the apostles and especially the angels and archangels, each according to his order. I mention the apostles with the angels, bishops and priests because there is only one Church, above and below, since God came down and lived among us, doing that for which He was sent on our behalf. And it is a work which is one, as is Our Lord's sacrifice, communion, and contemplation. And it is carried out both above and here below, but with this difference: above it is done without any veils or symbols, but here it is accomplished through symbols....

The Greeks have left a more developed and abundant literary and

iconographic legacy expressive of their medieval liturgical piety, but this
vision was not unique to the Byzantine tradition. True, West-Syrian and
Armenian liturgical commentators, more "Antiochene" in method, confine
themselves by and large to an exegesis of the liturgical text, with only occasional flights of allegory or expositions of ritual symbolism. Medieval
Coptic liturgical writings, almost wholly descriptive rubrical and canonical
treatises, can hardly be called mystagogy. But the East-Syrians were direct
inheritors of the spiritual legacy of Theodore of Mopsuestia (d. 428), and
their tradition of liturgical spirituality can be traced through Narsai (d. 502),
Gabriel and Abraham Qatraya bar Lipah (seventh century), and Pseudo-
George of Arbela (ninth century), to our period with Yohannan bar Zoʻbi
and Yohannan of Mosul (thirteenth century), ʻAbdišo bar Brika of Nisibis
(d. 1318), and Timothy II (Catholicos, 1318–1332).[16] These later authors
follow Gabriel Qatraya in interpreting the liturgy as "a commemoration of
the entire economy of God that was accomplished on earth through Christ,
beginning with his birth according to the flesh and proceeding gradually to
his death, resurrection, and ascension."[17] According to Bar Zoʻbi, the liturgy
is also a foretaste of our resurrection, in the likeness of the resurrection of
Christ, and the promise of eternal bliss made to all who believe. The
church, too, is part of the symbolic unity: the enclosed sanctuary is the
future and heavenly world; the nave is this world; the bema in its midst is
Jerusalem, site of the proclamation of the word. The solemn processions
between sanctuary and bema symbolize the divine commerce between
heaven and earth, which the liturgy both represents and effects.

The Liturgy of the Hours and Other Services

Though daily Eucharist never became a widespread custom in Eastern paro-
chial usage—even Hagia Sophia in Constantinople had no provision for
daily divine liturgy until Emperor Constantine IX Monomachos assigned
revenues for this purpose in 1044 (PG 122, col. 340)—this does not mean
that there was a liturgical void on weekdays.[18] Morning Praise and Evensong
were not monastic services but popular parish devotions comprising symbol, ceremony, song, and petitions for basic needs. They were the morning
and night prayers of ordinary folk, celebrated in church at dawn and at dusk
of every day.[19]

Other services such as rogations and stations for particular needs completed the devotional fare.[20] The picturesque rites of the burial of Jesus on
Good Friday also belong to this period.[21] Devotion to the passion was by
no means a medieval Western phenomenon. It was popular in fourteenth-
century Byzantium and was especially strong in Palestine and the West-Syrian

area of liturgical influence. Recently uncovered medieval Coptic *via crucis* frescoes in the church of St. Macarius at Dayr Abu Maqar in the Wadi an-Natrun witness to it in the Egyptian desert as well.

Negative Elements

All, however, was not mystagogy and anagogy, symbol and grace, in medieval Eastern liturgical life. Canonical literature testifies to widespread liturgical abuses, even among the clergy.[22] We hear of such clerical crimes as superstition, magic, sorcery, and witchcraft; simoniacal administration of the sacraments, especially the blessing of uncanonical marriages; fighting, joking, and irreverence in church; the theft of sacred objects, even obscenities, during the very celebration of the services; profanation of the sacramental gifts.[23] Little wonder that one also notes the abandonment of preaching and religious instruction. More ominous still was the neglect of the sacraments.

Decline in Frequentation of the Sacraments

Even for the devout, who were not given to such abuses, the decline in frequent communion, which began in the fourth century, had become tradition.[24] In middle Byzantine monasticism, celebration of the liturgy daily or several times a week was not uncommon, and daily communion was still the ideal. But monastic *typica* from the twelfth century to the fourteenth reveal the growth of a more restrictive policy, and by the fifteenth century instances of daily communion were noted exceptions even in monasteries. By the late Middle Ages the faithful at the divine liturgy were reduced to the status of onlookers, and communion had become an occasional act of personal devotion rather than the common sharing of the commonly offered gifts. But without communion, the divine liturgy becomes at best a symbolic reality to be contemplated; at worst, a sterile ritualism.

The Hesychast Revival

Little wonder, then, that the hesychast renewal, centered in smaller sketes rather than in the great cenobitic communities with their regimented discipline and splendidly formalized services, was not ritualist in orientation. The well-known antithesis in late-fifteenth-century Muscovy between the hesychasm of the Transvolgan followers of St. Nil Sorsky and the triumphalistic urban monasticism of his rival St. Joseph Volokolamsky is paradigmatic of this tension between interior prayer and elaborate ritual. In the late Middle Ages the need was for interior renewal rather than greater emphasis on ritual prayer, and on Mount Athos and later throughout the Slavic Orthodox world it was the hesychasts and *startsy* who responded to this need with a monastic life-style oriented more toward the prayer of the heart. The uninterrupted continuation of this type of monastic life in Scetis, Armenia, northern Mesopotamia, and in the mountains of Lebanon and Syria is further evidence that one cannot see Byzantine or Oriental Orthodox piety as exclusively "high-church" or liturgical in character. From the outset, the most authentic sources of the Christian East have always maintained that the true liturgy is within. What hesychasm did was give new life to this original vision.

During the hesychast revival it was the genius of a layman, Nicholas Cabasilas, to bring later Eastern liturgical theology back to this interior center, away from the arbitrary forays into extrinsicism and allegorism seen in the *Protheoria* (1085–1095) (*PG* 140, cols. 417–68) and in the twelfth-century *Liturgical Commentary of Pseudo-Sophronios (PG* 87³, cols. 3981–4001). Cabasilas's interpretation is in no way extrinsic to the structure and meaning of the rites, nor is his contemplation a substitute for sacramental participation, but only its prelude (1.1). For him, the liturgy is not just a rite nor a contemplation but an actual entrance into the saving mysteries through the reception of the sanctified gifts. Cabasilas was well aware of the practical demands of this spirituality. If the hidden mystery that is Christ is revealed in the incarnation, it is visible only in deed, for Jesus' humanity is like ours except for sin. This is where Christology and liturgical spirituality intersect with Christian ethics: it is only in Christ's *actions* that one can perceive his divinity, and it is only through a Christian life that one can become a true icon whereby the reality of divine life received in baptism shines through. True worship, Cabasilas makes clear in *The Life in Christ* (4.8–9), is not our liturgical service but its effects seen in our lives. "To offer Him pure homage is an effect of the holy table. . . . To live according to right reason and to tend towards virtue is to worship God."[25]

Notes

1. See Cyril Mango, *Byzantine Architecture* (New York: Abrams, 1976) 197–98 and chaps. 7–8 *passim.*

2. See Donald M. Nicol, *Church and Society in the Last Centuries of Byzantium* (Cambridge: University Press, 1979) esp. chap. 2.

3. See John Meyendorff, *St. Gregory Palamas and Orthodox Spirituality,* 56–170 *passim;* idem, *A Study of Gregory Palamas* (London: Faith Press, 1974) esp. part 1.

4. See Robert Taft, "How Liturgies Grow: the Evolution of the Byzantine Divine Liturgy," *Orientalia Christiana Periodica* 43 (1977) 357ff.

5. Ibid., 359–60.

6. In Constantinople the stational processions were still in full vigor in the tenth century; see John Baldovin, "La liturgie stationnale à Constantinople," *La Maison-Dieu* 147 (1981) 85–94.

7. See Thomas F. Mathews, *The Early Churches of Constantinople: Architecture and Liturgy* (University Park, PA and London: Pennsylvania State University Press, 1971) 111–12; Taft, "How Liturgies Grow," 359.

8. Thomas F. Mathews, "'Private' Liturgy in Byzantine Architecture: Toward a Reappraisal," *Cahiers archéologiques* 30 (1982) 125–38; Cyril Mango, "The Liturgy and the People," conference delivered at the Dumbarton Oaks Symposium, 10 May 1979 (unpublished).

9. On the history of this interplay of rite and interpretation, see Hans-Joachim Schultz, *The Byzantine Liturgy: Symbolic Structure and Faith Expression* (New York: Pueblo, 1986).

10. Most of this history is detailed by Robert Taft, *The Great Entrance: A History of the Transfer of Gifts and Other Preanaphoral Rites of the Liturgy of St. John Chrysostom* (Orientalia Christiana Analecta 200; 2nd ed.; Rome: Pontifical Oriental Institute, 1978); and idem, "How Liturgies Grow."

11. On the history of this interpretation, see Robert Taft, "The Liturgy of the Great Church: An Initial Synthesis of Structure and Interpretation on the Eve of Iconoclasm," *Dumbarton Oaks Papers* 34–35 (1980–81) 45–75.

12. See Taft, *Great Entrance*, 213–14.

13. On this question, see Taft, "The Liturgy of the Great Church," 58–75; René Bornert, *Les commentaires Byzantins de la Divine Liturgie du VIIe au XVe siècle* (Archives de l'Orient chrétien 9; Paris: Institut Français d'Études byzantines, 1966); idem, "Die Symbolgestalt der byzantinischen Liturgie," *Archiv für Liturgiewissenschaft* 12 (1970) 54–70.

14. Critical ed., Sources chrétiennes 4bis (Paris: Cerf, 1967); cited from Nicholas Cabasilas, *A Commentary on the Divine Liturgy*, trans. J. M. Hussey and P. A. McNulty. References in the text are to this work.

15. See Otto Demus, *Byzantine Mosaic Decoration* (New Rochelle, NY: Caratzas Bros., 1976); Else Giordani, "Das mittelbyzantinische Ausschmuckungssystem als Ausdruck eines hieratischen Bildprogramms," *Jahrbuch der Österreichischen Byzantinischen Gesellschaft* 1 (1951) 103–34.

16. For the Latin translation of Gabriel, see Sarhad Y. H. Jammo, *La structure de la messe chaldéenne* (Orientalia Christiana Analecta 207; Rome: Pontifical Oriental Institute, 1979) 29–48. For Abraham's work, which is little more than a resume of Gabriel's, see R. H. Connolly, ed., *Anonymi auctoris Expositio officiorum ecclesiae Georgio Arbelensi vulgo adscripta, accedit Abrahae bar Lipeh Interpretatio officiorum* (Corpus scriptorum Christianorum Orientalium 64, 71–72, 76=script. syri. 25, 28–29, 32; Rome: de Luigi; Paris: Gabalda; Leipzig: Harrasowitz, 1911–15). For Yohannan bar Zo'bi, see Albert Khoraiche, "'L'explication de tous les mystères divins' de Yohannan bar Zo'bi selon le manuscrit Borgianus syriacus 90," *Euntes docete* 19 (1966) 386–426. For the Syriac text of Yohannan of Mosul, see Elias I. Millos, *Directorium spirituale ex libris sapientialibus desumptum . . .* (Rome: Propaganda Fide, 1868). For the latin translation of 'Abdišo bar Brika of Nisibis, see J.-M. Vosté, "De expositione officiorum ecclesiasticorum," *Codificazione canonica orientale*, Fonti, ser. 2, fasc. 15: *Caldei–diritto antico* II (Vatican City: Vatican Press, 1940) 82–115. For Timothy II, see the description in Wilhelm de Vries, "Timotheus II über 'Die sieben Gründe der kirchlichen Geheimnisse,'" *Orientalia Christiana Periodica* 8 (1942) 40–94.

17. Cited by William F. Macomber, "The Liturgy of the Word according to the Commentators of the Chaldean Mass," in *The Word in the World: Essays in Honor of Frederick L. Moriarty, S.J.*, ed. R. J. Clifford, G. W. MacRae (Cambridge, MA: Weston College Press, 1973) 182, whom I am following here.

18. See Robert Taft, "The Frequency of the Eucharist throughout History," *Concilium* 152 (1982) 13–24.

19. See Robert Taft, *The Liturgy of the Hours in the Christian East: Origins, Meaning, Place in the Life of the Church* (Cochin: KCM Press, 1984).

20. See Baldovin, "La liturgie stationnale à Constantinople"; and Robert Taft, "The Pontifical Liturgy of the Great Church according to the Twelfth-Century Diataxis in Codex *British Museum Add. 34060*," *Orientalia Christiana Periodica* 46 (1980) 111–12.

21. Taft, *Great Entrance*, 216–19.

22. Nicol, *Church and Society*, 98ff.; L. Oeconomos, "L'état intellectuel et moral des byzantins vers le milieu du XIVe siècle d'après une page de Joseph Bryennios," *Mélanges Charles Diehl* (Paris: E. Leroux, 1930) 1:225–33 (text and trans. of Bryennios: 227–30).

23. Carolina Cupane, "Una 'classe sociale' dimenticata: il basso clero metropolitano," in *Studien zum Patriarchatsregister von Konstantinopel*, ed. H. Hunger (Österreichischen Akademie der Wissenschaften, Phil.-hist. klasse Sitzungsberichte, 383; Vienna: Österreichischen Akademie der Wissenschaften, 1881) 1:66–79.

24. See E. Hermann, "Die Häufige Kommunion in den byzantinischen Klöstern," in *Mémorial Louis Petit* (Archives de l'Orient chrétien 1; Bucharest: Institut Français d'Etudes byzantines, 1948) 209–15.

25. Nicholas Cabasilas, *The Life in Christ*, 126.

Bibliography

Bouyer, Louis. *Orthodox Spirituality and Protestant and Anglican Spirituality.* Vol. 3 of *A History of Christian Spirituality.* New York: Seabury, 1969.

Cabasilas, Nicholas. *A Commentary on the Divine Liturgy.* Translated by J. M. Hussey and P. A. McNulty. Crestwood, NY: St. Vladimir's Seminary Press, 1960.

———. *The Life in Christ.* Translated by C. J. de Catanzaro. Crestwood, NY: St. Vladimir's Seminary Press, 1974.

Fedotov, George P. *The Russian Religious Mind.* 2 vols. Cambridge, MA: Harvard University Press, 1946, 1965.

———, ed. *A Treasury of Russian Spirituality.* New York: Sheed & Ward, 1948.

Kovalevsky, Pierre. *Saint Sergius and Russian Spirituality.* Crestwood, NY: St. Vladimir's Seminary Press, 1976.

Meyendorff, John. *St. Gregory Palamas and Orthodox Spirituality.* Crestwood, NY: St. Vladimir's Seminary Press, 1974.

Schulz, Hans-Joachim. *The Byzantine Liturgy.* New York: Pueblo, 1986.

II. *West*

JAMES F. McCUE

THE YEARS 1150 TO 1500 DO NOT CONSTITUTE a neatly blocked off period in the history of the development of the Eucharist. Most of the features characteristic of eucharistic thought and piety during these years were already at least partially developed by 1150, and these developments would continue past 1500. Some of them were to continue in post-Reformation Roman Catholicism almost to the present. To understand these developments in eucharistic piety it will be necessary to situate them within the context of the broader changes that mark the history of Latin Christendom during these years.

Eucharistic Piety

It is clear in retrospect that from about the middle of the eleventh century the Latin church was entering a significantly new phase in its history. This transition did not leave behind it creedal or confessional divisions, and perhaps for this reason it tends to be less noted than Constantine and Nicaea or the Reformation. Yet in some ways the change is just as fundamental. Though no one could have known it at the time, Western Europe had seen the last of the large-scale invasions. The expansion into Europe of the Ottoman Turks some centuries later might lead some to anticipate the end of the Christian world, but the devastation actually wrought by the Turks in Western Europe was minor compared to the depredations of the Germans, the Normans, or the Magyars. By about 1050 these were over. By the end of the century, European armies would sally forth from Europe in a first, abortive attempt at extra-European conquest, the First Crusade. During the next four centuries Europe would go through a prolonged period of inner consolidation, until, around 1500, it would begin a period of worldwide expansion and projection of power that has so profoundly affected the destiny of the entire world.

It is from about 1050 that we see a broad movement toward centralization and rationalization in both Latin Europe and the Latin church. The most obvious dimension of this latter is the reformation and strengthening of the papacy. Theoretically, this involved an enlargement of papal claims beyond those of the patristic papacy. Practically, it involved a rapid growth of the importance of the papacy in the practical life of the churches. But the papacy is not the only institution that changed at this time. This was also the time when canonists undertook the task of making some unified sense of the many inherited traditions of church law. Similarly, theologians began the task of bringing rational coherence and system to the church's doctrinal traditions. The typical medieval theological genre, the "books of sentences," or compendia of theological opinions, took their point of departure in the multitude of apparently disparate views bequeathed by the past but aimed to bring these to some kind of systematic unity. The result of these concurrent developments was to centralize and even homogenize the Latin church to an unprecedented degree, even at a time when Western Europe remained politically and socially quite differentiated. Though doubtless the actual lived piety was more varied than the written record allows us to see, it is an important feature of the church of this time and place that it worked so hard to unify itself and that it succeeded to such a considerable degree.

This was also a period of extreme contrasts within the church. A time of growing wealth in society and in the church, it was also a time of hermits and of Franciscan poverty. Religious ideals conceded little to human weakness, and there were many who strove mightily to realize these ideals; yet it was also a time in which a *Volkskirche*—a church that included the entire society—was the generally accepted pattern of church organization. It was a common complaint among the religious leaders and elites of this time that a great deal was wrong in the church and that the lives of many bore but little resemblance to the ideals professed; yet it was also a time in which we witness great outbursts of popular religious enthusiasm. In our discussion of the eucharistic and liturgical piety of the time, we must not overlook the vast discrepancies that existed throughout this period, but neither must we allow ourselves to be so fascinated by what are commonly reckoned the excesses of the age that we overlook its impressive achievements.

This was also a period in which the sacraments became increasingly more important in the everyday life of Christians. The theological compendia devoted increasing attention to analyses of the sacraments, so that by the end of the fifteenth century it would not seem strange for a theologian like Gabriel Biel to devote perhaps a third of his theological *opus magnum* to their analysis. Above all, it was the sacraments of penance and the Eucharist that attracted increasing attention and were brought into ever-closer connection, as we shall see.

Externally, the eucharistic liturgy did not change dramatically between the twelfth century and the sixteenth. At the beginning and at the end of the period, Latin was the language of the Eucharist. More generally, it was the language of all the more solemn church services, as well as the language of the universities, of the professions, and of international communication. It was not, however, the language of the vast majority of the people, and even significant numbers of the clergy had difficulty with the language in which they performed the liturgy. But not only was the Mass celebrated in a language that most people could no longer understand; in addition, much of it was said in silence, and for a long period of time—well down into the nineteenth century—the tradition prevailed that the most sacred part would not, even in written form, be translated into the vernacular.[1]

The silence and the foreignness of the language occasioned less comment and caused fewer difficulties than one might anticipate. Presumably this was because the silence and the unintelligible but sacred language fit in with a widespread conception of sacrament in general and of Eucharist in particular. A sacrament was understood not so much as a ritual in which you took part or (using a later model) as the word addressed to you; rather, it was a power-filled act which, if the proper conditions were fulfilled, would have its effect on you. The Eucharist was an act performed by a priest in compliance with Christ's command on behalf of the people. It is striking that Peter Lombard, in a mid-twelfth-century work that was to become the standard theological textbook for the medieval universities, could call the Eucharist the *benedictio panis,* as though the words of the eucharistic liturgy were directed principally toward the bread, with the congregation presumably simply standing by. The important thing for the congregation was to meditate on the benefits to be derived from the Mass—primarily saving grace—and on the source of these benefits—the passion of Christ. The particular words that the priest was saying as part of his performance were of less immediate significance. An extreme but suggestive illustration of this understanding of the Eucharist as a power-filled act is the advice of a late medieval preacher who counsels against even saying prayers during the Mass. Even though the priest's words may be unintelligible to the lay person, he or she should not say any other prayers during the Mass lest these interfere with the power of the priest's words.[2]

In general, medieval explanations of the Eucharist fit in with this general orientation. Following in the tradition of Amalar of Metz, medieval writers tended to view the Mass as a rather complex allegory in which could be discovered all sorts of spiritual and edifying truths. In the main, the Mass was seen as a dramatic and symbolic reenactment of the life, passion, death, and resurrection of Jesus. Through this allegorization of the liturgy, a different kind of intelligibility was created, a substitute for the intelligibility that had been implicit in the eucharistic practice of an earlier age.

These patterns, as we have said, were set before the beginning of the period with which we are concerned here. There were, however, some changes in the external forms of the liturgy during the later medieval period. Two are especially important, and they are closely connected with two of the most salient features of later medieval eucharistic piety. One was the introduction of the practice of elevating the host and the eucharistic cup immediately after the consecration to enable people to see and worship them. The other was an enormous elaboration of votive Masses and of Masses for particular intentions.

Piety of Presence

Eucharistic piety of the later medieval period was primarily a piety of presence. Even though the actual reception of communion during the Mass had become quite rare during this period,[3] it was still possible for a fourteenth-century Franciscan writer to observe that "the Eucharist is the sacrament on which the piety of people nowadays is mostly based."[4] Participation in the Eucharist was, at least at the level of popular piety, more a matter of seeing and worshiping the Host than of sacramental communion.

Theological literature as far back as the second century expressed the widespread Christian belief that in some way and in some sense the body and blood of Christ were present in the eucharistic elements. But in the medieval period this traditional motif was given unprecedented emphasis and became a focus for speculation. Theological disputes of the ninth and of the eleventh centuries had focused on the issue of the presence of the body and blood of Jesus in (or, as the medieval church would eventually insist, under the appearance of) the bread and wine. These disputes ended with a strongly realistic interpretation of the sacrament clearly dominant, a view expressed strikingly in the mid-eleventh century anti-Berengarian oath:

> The bread and wine that are placed on the altar [are], after the consecration, not only the sacrament but also the true body and blood of our Lord Jesus Christ, which are not only sacramentally but truly handled and broken by the hands of the priest and ground by the teeth of the faithful.[5]

This development was not merely or primarily a matter of theological disputes and of papal or conciliar definitions. For many of the exemplary holy people of the age, the presence of Christ—the presence of God—in the Eucharist was at the center of their piety. For example, in the latter part of the thirteenth century, St. Gertrude was given to understand that each time a person looked upon the eucharistic Host with faith and devotion that person's heavenly merit would be increased. Part of the reason given for this

30. *Priest Celebrating the Mass*, Italian, 15th century.

was the fact that looking upon the Host bore a kind of analogy to the seeing—the vision—that is the characteristic state of the blessed.[6] A century later we read of St. Dorothy of Dantzig that, when contemplating the Host in the hands of the priest celebrating Mass, she would experience such rapture that at times she could no longer even see the Host. Her contemporary biographer tells us—and it is a revealing detail—that because seeing the body of Christ did not satisfy her (*non enim satiabat*) she would several times a year wish to receive the sacrament.[7]

So important did the seeing of the Eucharist become that it became a common theological topic to ask about the dispositions necessary for seeing the Host. It was generally accepted in the medieval period that anyone who had committed a mortal sin and had not adequately repented could not receive the Eucharist—indeed, would sin mortally again by so doing. The question therefore arose whether seeing the Host while in the state of mortal sin would also be sinful. The answer was regularly that it was not a sin. Quite the contrary, for those who had not adequately repented of their sins, seeing the Host could inspire in them a love for God and the proper dispositions for repentance.[8]

There were theological reasons for valuing the reception—the eating—of the Host over seeing it: eucharistic communion gave its benefits *ex opere operato*, from the power of the sacrament itself, whereas merely seeing the Host did not. However, this was a theological solution that did not altogether counteract the tendency to make seeing the focus of eucharistic piety. Indeed, in the sixteenth century, a Catholic apologist, while denying that Catholics considered adoration more valuable than reception of the Eucharist, conceded that Catholics do consider adoration less *dangerous*.[9]

The thoroughgoing literalism with which popular piety understood the reality of Christ's presence in the eucharistic elements is illustrated in the many popular legends that grew up in the Middle Ages. In Wilsnack, Germany, for example, there developed a popular local and regional devotion to a eucharistic Host that had been found covered with blood after a fire had destroyed the church in which it had been kept.[10] Another legend tells of a man who was too ill to receive the Host but who desired nonetheless to see it. So great was his desire that the priest agreed to lay the Host on his breast, whence it was seen by many actually to enter his body.[11]

The introduction of the elevation toward the end of the twelfth century was a response to an already well-developed emphasis on eucharistic presence and in turn did much to strengthen this emphasis even further.[12] The elevation, following directly upon the consecration, had as its purpose to allow the faithful to see the body and blood of the Savior present under the forms of bread and wine. Very quickly this new form of eucharistic piety took on the status of a tradition that had always been present in the church.[13] Popular piety developed an extravagant variety of claims and expectations for those who saw the Host. On the day on which you saw the Host at the elevation, you would not go blind or die a sudden death; your food would agree with you; and so on.[14]

As one might expect, these popular exuberances were criticized by many reform-minded writers during the fourteenth and fifteenth centuries, but the reformers were fighting an up-hill battle. Miracle stories were abundant and in some cases led to significant changes in practice, which were supported by the ecclesiastical hierarchy and became a fixed part of the liturgical cycle. According to fourteenth-century reports, a priest celebrating the Eucharist in the Italian town of Bolsena in 1263 was uncertain whether he had consecrated the Host. Some reports say that he had doubts about the doctrine of the real presence. The Host that he was holding began to drip blood, and the blood traced out the figure of the Savior on the altar cloth. Against this kind of thing, theological sobriety was probably not very effective. When, in the fourteenth century, ecclesiastical authorities confirmed and universalized the celebration of the feast of Corpus Christi—the body of Christ—this miracle was one of the reasons given. With the development of this feast—called, significantly, *Fête-Dieu* (the feast of God, in French)—there was introduced the practice of carrying the Host in procession outside the church building. Moreover, it was in connection with the feast of Corpus Christi that the practice was introduced of displaying the Host for adoration quite apart from the eucharistic celebration.[15] It might be said that this development of "exposition of the Blessed Sacrament" and of Benediction—the blessing of the congregation with the Host—brings to a kind of logical conclusion the development of this aspect of medieval eucharistic piety. These practices did not replace the Eucharist, but they are a kind of purified expression of what was valued most intensely in the eucharistic celebration: the presence of God.

Eucharistic Benefits

There is another important and characteristic feature of medieval eucharistic piety. Not only was the Eucharist experienced as the miraculous act by which Christ is present; it was also a very important and powerful means enabling one to achieve certain benefits. There are so many different purposes to which the Mass was put in the medieval, and especially in the late medieval, period that it is difficult to get some overall sense of the matter. Certain themes recur, however, and enable us to make some general sense of a wide variety of motifs.

First of all, the Mass was a means of attaining spiritual benefits. It was a means of grace—that is, a means by which Christians became more conformed to Christ and were prepared for a deeper sharing with God in heaven. There was a strong tendency in medieval Latin piety to think of the Christian life as an accumulation of grace, conceived of as a kind of divinely imparted energy. In general, the sacraments were seen as means of grace. The Eucharist was interpreted as the primary means through which such grace was imparted, and this was, in theory at least, its most important benefit.

The Eucharist was also the means by which the church on earth could share spiritual benefits with those who had already died but had not yet entered into their heavenly reward. This was connected with an important development in the practice of the sacrament of penance. In the eleventh century, the penitential acts that had always been part of penance came to be performed after absolution and reconciliation rather than before. This gave rise to the question of the function of these acts. They were, after all, being performed *after* the sins had already been forgiven, so they could hardly be necessary preconditions for forgiveness. But if not that, what? The answer commonly given was that, even after absolution, there remained a debt of temporal (i.e., not eternal) punishment to be paid and that the penitential acts were directed to this debt.[16] There thus arose a growing concern and fascination with the punishments that even the pious were to endure after this life, and part of this development was an increasing use of the Mass in behalf of the dead, the souls in purgatory. The doctrine of purgatory and the practice and theory of indulgences obviously owe much to this change in practice and to the efforts to make sense of this change. Masses for the dead became quite commonplace.

The Mass could provide a wide variety of other spiritual benefits as well, and many lists of such benefits have come down to us. Among the most important and most often cited were those benefits related to the growing anxiety that was so much a feature of medieval Latin Christendom. The promise was made that if you died on a day during which you had heard Mass, Christ would be present to you at the moment of death, just as you had been present to him at Mass. Even more attractive was the promise that you would not meet with sudden death or die a bad death on a day when you had heard Mass. If you attended Mass devoutly and repented of your sins, and then were to die on that day, it would be as though you had received all the church's sacraments.[17]

The benefits hoped for from the Mass were often of a more mundane sort. One would grow no older during the time that one was attending Mass. Neither would one's worldly affairs suffer through an excess of piety. Indeed, if one's faith were strong enough, one could gain more profit, in an altogether mundane sense, by hearing Mass than by working hard throughout the entire day. Seeing the Host after the consecration not only protected you from blindness; it also ensured good digestion. Such views were not, of course, accepted uncritically or universally, but the fact that they were so very much part of the folklore tells us something about the general orientation of the eucharistic piety of this time.[18]

One of the interesting stories told was of a knight who was greatly tempted to suicide. The only remedy was to hear Mass daily. One day, while on a journey, he was unable to hear Mass, through no fault of his own. As he began to experience suicidal tendencies, he asked those around him whether someone who had heard Mass that day would be willing to exchange the fruits of that Mass for the knight's horse. A young man announced himself willing, the exchange was made, and the knight was immediately freed from his suicidal depression. Later that day, as one might have anticipated, the young man hanged himself. One need not suppose that the hearers or tellers of the story would be committed to everything the story presupposed. It is not clear, for example, that it was widely believed that two people could so simply exchange the fruits of the Mass. But it does testify to the conviction that the Mass was a very powerful instrument, for good if rightly used but for ill if abused.[19]

This view of the Mass as a source of power was paralleled and reinforced by the liturgical development of the votive Mass. Since one could have all sorts of intentions satisfied by hearing Mass or even by having Mass said for one's particular intention, it was perhaps only fitting that the arrangement of the church calendar and even the liturgical texts would come to reflect something of this same orientation. The early sacramentaries (collections of eucharistic texts), the Leonine and the Gelasian, already showed trends in this direction. But it was in our period that these earlier tendencies came to their full development.

The most important of the votive Masses was the Mass for the dead. Though praying for the dead was not a medieval invention, it took on a different character in the medieval period. Prayer for the dead was seen as a means of alleviating or even canceling out the purgatorial suffering to which the dead had been consigned; and while such prayer took many forms, it was generally acknowledged that the most powerful form of prayer for the dead was the Mass. In a fourteenth century list of the fruits of the Mass we read that with each Mass a sinner is converted, a soul is freed from purgatory, and a righteous person is confirmed in good. Far more ambitious claims were made, but less important than the arithmetic is the general orientation: those who have preceded us in death are in need of our aid, and the most powerful aid we can provide them is the Mass.[20]

Exactly how the celebration of the Eucharist was thought to achieve a particular end, such as the freeing of souls from purgatory, is not altogether clear. Thomas Aquinas distinguished between the sacrifice of the Mass itself and the prayers which the faithful say at Mass and suggested that these latter and the intensity of the devotion of the participants are what differentiates the effects of one Mass from those of another (*Summa Theologiae,* Suppl., 71, 9 ad 5). But it is not clear that popular piety was particularly sensitive to such distinctions. It was common to speak of offering Mass for the dead, and it seems reasonable to suppose that this expressed the view that the Mass was something offered to God to obtain benefits that only he could provide. Though a theologian might not think that the sacrifice of the Mass was offered for a good harvest, it is not clear that nontheologians saw matters with quite the same clarity and distinctness. There may have been a fairly austere theological conception of the Mass as sacrifice, but it is an open question whether that conception was able to control or dominate popular piety.[21]

Preparing for the Eucharist

Medieval eucharistic piety was also a piety of purity and of purification. Closely connected with the emphasis on presence were attitudes of awe, of reverence, and of fear. Medieval piety surrounded the Eucharist with a whole set of purifications. It seemed altogether appropriate that one who was to touch the sacred elements would wash his hands before doing this. This seemed obvious enough that, though theologians might mention it, there seemed no necessity to develop reasons for it (Thomas Aquinas *In 4 Sent.* d. 9, q. 1, a. 4). Apparently less obvious was the view that one ought not receive communion the day after "nocturnal pollution." For this, a more elaborate argument was needed. It was not maintained that it was absolutely prohibited to receive communion under such circumstances, only that it was inappropriate.

The most important purification of all was the purification from sin. Early in the sixteenth century, Martin Luther cited Ambrose, a fourth-century writer, to the effect that since we sin daily we ought to receive the Eucharist daily. Luther reiterated this and urged that we must not think of the Eucharist as though it were a poison.[22] He was here reacting against and trying to create an alternative to a central motif in medieval eucharistic thinking. With the gradual transformation of confession of sins or penance, during the eleventh and twelfth centuries, into the rite of forgiveness of everyday sins, the spiritual landscape of Latin Christendom changed. In theology and in canon law there developed an ostensibly precise delineation between mortal sins, which radically alter one's status before God, and venial sins, which have no such radical consequences. Under ordinary circumstances, all were obliged to confess *all* of their mortal sins to a priest in confession.

The connection of all of this to the Eucharist is that it was generally held to be the case that one could not receive the Eucharist unless one's mortal sins had previously been forgiven. Indeed, if one violated this prohibition one was guilty of an additional extremely grave mortal sin. Though lists of the fruits of the Mass continued to ascribe to the Mass the power to effect forgiveness of venial sins and to remit temporal punishment due to already forgiven mortal sins, the Eucharist was no longer seen as the sacrament for the forgiveness of serious but "ordinary" sins. Moreover, the many problems that developed around the practice of confession had an impact on the manner in which the Eucharist was celebrated. One had to be purified of all one's mortal sins before receiving communion, at the risk of adding to one's sins. But this purification often proved quite difficult and burdensome,[23] so that the preparation for the reception of communion also became burdensome and often filled with anxiety. Frequency of communion had declined in the Latin church even before this development, which had usually been taken as a sign of religious indifference, but in the period under consideration even the pious were often quite hesitant about receiving communion.[24] As we indicated previously, by the end of the medieval period many considered it safer to look upon the Eucharist than to receive it.

* * * * *

Though the Eucharistic piety of the Latin Middle Ages has been severely criticized both within Protestantism and by the liturgical reformers within more recent Roman Catholicism, such criticisms should not lead us to overlook the positive role played by that piety. It would seem that this piety fostered a very strong sense of the reality and presence of God in the midst of human life, in the midst of creation. At the same time, the keen sense of sin and even of dread before God as judge would seem to have sustained an important tension. The God who was present in the Eucharist was also the mysterious one, the one who could not be taken for granted. In this piety, we see the particular form in which the Latin Middle Ages celebrated and perceived both God's immanence and God's transcendence.

Notes

1. Adolph Franz, *Die Messe im deutschen Mittelalter*, 631–37.
2. Ibid., 25.
3. On the matter of infrequent communion see Joseph Duhr, "Communion fréquente," in *Dict. Sp.* 2, cols. 1234–92.
4. Peter Browe, *Die Verehrung der Eucharistie im Mittelalter*, 22.
5. The text can be found in H. Denzinger and A. Schönmetzer, *Enchiridion symbolorum*, n. 690.

6. Edouard Dumoutet, *Le désir de voir l'hostie et les origines de la dévotion au Saint-Sacrement*, 15.
7. Ibid., 16.
8. For texts to this effect, see Dumoutet, *Le désir*, 18.
9. Ibid., 35.
10. Ibid., 81. For a fuller account of medieval eucharistic miracle legends, see J. Corblet, *Histoire du Sacrement de l'Eucharistie*, 1:464–515.
11. Dumoutet, *Le désir*, 75 n. 1.
12. Browe, *Die Verehrung der Eucharistie im Mittelalter*, 49.
13. For texts, see Dumoutet, *Le désir*, 57 n. 1.
14. Franz, *Die Messe im deutschen Mittelalter*, 56.
15. Ibid., 154.
16. On this development, see Bernard Poschmann, *Penance and the Anointing of the Sick*, 157–58.
17. Franz, *Die Messe im deutschen Mittelalter*, 64–65.
18. Ibid., 69–70.
19. For the story and its source, see Franz, *Die Messe im deutschen Mittelalter*, 71.
20. Ibid., 239.
21. On this point, see James F. McCue, "Luther and Roman Catholicism on the Mass as Sacrifice," in *Lutherans and Catholics in Dialogue*, 3:45–74, esp. 72–73.
22. Martin Luther, WA, 1.333.7ff.
23. This has often been documented. Among recent studies, see especially Thomas Tentler, *Sin and Confession on the Eve of the Reformation*, esp. 156–62.
24. See Duhr, "Communion fréquente," in *Dict. Sp.* 2, cols. 1255–56.

Bibliography

Browe, Peter. *Die häufige Kommunion im Mittelalter*. Munich: Huebner, 1938.
———. *Die Verehrung der Eucharistie im Mittelalter*. Munich: Huebner, 1933. Unaltered 2nd ed., Rome: Herder, 1967.
Corblet, J. *Histoire du Sacrement de l'Eucharistie*. 2 vols. Paris: Victor Palmé, 1883.
Denzinger, H., and A. Schönmetzer, eds. *Enchiridion symbolorum*. 32nd ed. Freiburg: Herder, 1963.
Duhr, Joseph. "Communion fréquente." In *Dict. Sp.* 2, cols. 1234–92.
Dumoutet, Edouard. *Le désir de voir l'hostie et les origines de la dévotion au Saint-Sacrement*. Paris: Beauchesne, 1926.
Franz, Adolf. *Die Messe im deutschen Mittelalter: Beiträge zur Geschichte Liturgie und des religiösen Volkslebens*. Freiburg: Herder, 1902. Reprint. Darmstadt: Wissenschaftliche Buchgesellschaft, 1963,
McCue, James. "Luther and Roman Catholicism on the Mass as Sacrifice." in *Lutherans and Catholics in Dialogue*. Vol. 3, *The Eucharist as Sacrifice*. New York: U.S. Catholic Conference, 1967.
Poschmann, Bernard. *Penance and the Anointing of the Sick*. Translated and edited by Francis Courtney. New York: Herder & Herder, 1964.
Tentler, Thomas. *Sin and Confession on the Eve of the Reformation*. Princeton, NJ: Princeton University Press, 1977.

19

Two Visions of the Church: East and West on the Eve of Modern Times

JOHN MEYENDORFF

MEDIEVAL BYZANTIUM HAS ENVISAGED its own Christian civilization as the ultimate fulfillment of history. By establishing a "new Rome" on the Bosphorus, Emperor Constantine was thought to have accomplished the divine plan that was intended in the incarnation itself: to inaugurate the kingdom of God on earth. The empire lasted an entire millennium without changing the basic content of this vision, which was nevertheless challenged internally and externally. Internally, Christian Scriptures, the liturgical tradition and the ever-present prophetic presence of monastic asceticism pointed to a different eschatology: the kingdom of God was distinct from the earthly empire and was still to come. Externally, the borders and the influence of Byzantium were shrinking and God seemed to condone the Islamic conquest of vast, traditionally Christian areas. Until the thirteenth century, the Easterners continued to envisage the Christian West as part of the God-established *oikoumenē*: the Latins were slightly erring brothers, wrongly influenced by "barbarian" ideas, but destined to rejoin a Christian Roman world, as it was conceived since the fourth century. The Byzantines were reminded of this indelible hope whenever they entered their cathedral of St. Sophia, heard liturgical affirmations of the empire's universality, and contemplated the imperial figures of Constantine and Justinian represented in the mosaic above the doors.

The tragic events of the thirteenth century seemed to have put an end to the dream. In 1204, Latin Crusaders sacked the "new Rome." A Frankish emperor sat on the throne of Constantine and a Venetian patriarch occupied the chair of Chrysostom and Photius. Furthermore, in 1240, the Mongols conquered Russia—that vast and promising missionary conquest of Orthodox Byzantium—and the daughter-churches of Bulgaria and Serbia vacillated in their faithfulness to Orthodoxy. It appeared that Byzantine imperial universalism had been replaced for good by a Latin *orbis christianorum,* headed by the pope, facing alone both the Mongol empire and the Muslim Turks. For Eastern Christians, the only alternatives seemed to be the spiritual, political, and cultural integration into Latin Christendom, or the power of Asiatic empires.

These momentous events and basic spiritual questions decisively influenced the Eastern Christian approach to eschatology and forced them to define their spiritual identity anew. Of course, in 1261 the city of Constantinople was recovered by the Greeks and, until 1453, weak Paleologan emperors attempted to maintain the waning prestige of the "new Rome," but they could do so only symbolically. The real strength and resilience of Eastern Christianity were taken up by the church itself, within which positions of leadership were occupied by representatives of a strong monastic revival, associated with hesychasm.

The Hesychast Revival

It has often been noticed that, as a contrast to the West, the Christian East never developed religious *orders* which would exercise their ministry across diocesan borders, independently of local bishops. Indeed, Byzantine canon law required episcopal jurisdiction over all local monastic communities, and Byzantine monks rarely included in their rules educational or missionary tasks, which were characteristic of the more activistic Latin orders, medieval and modern. But there were practical exceptions. For instance, the monastery of Studios, led by its great abbot St. Theodore, had become, in the late eighth century, something of a "church within the church," with a very specific program for influencing society. Similarly, and on an even wider scale, the movement most often designated as "hesychast" accomplished in the fourteenth century a widespread spiritual renewal throughout the Orthodox East. Its role can be compared, for example, with the Cluny reforms in the West. Although the ideological positions and the historical conditioning of the two movements were clearly different, a monastic leadership, progressively monopolizing hierarchical positions in the church, succeeded in both cases in establishing a set of priorities that placed spiritual values ahead of social and political contingencies.

The early history of "hesychasm" is described elsewhere in this Encyclopedia, and its doctrinal expression, as reflected in the theological writings of Gregory Palamas, is covered above.[1] However, in order to understand fully the widespread spiritual influence of hesychasm, it is important to realize that the term can be used only in a very broad sense to designate the movement that concerns us here. Hesychasts, or contemplative hermits of Mount Athos, held that divine life is immediately accessible to those who live "in Christ," and the followers of this idea included lay theologians (like Nicholas Cabasilas), political leaders, as well as ecclesiastics, who, as they reached the higher echelons of the ecclesiastical or civil hierarchies, could not be considered hermits or mystics in the usual sense of these words.[2] They were directly involved in the social, cultural, and political life of the time, pursuing concrete practical goals. But in these activities they had adopted common, and fundamentally spiritual, priorities, which explains their identity as a movement and the coherence of their activities.[3]

The decisions of the "Palamite" councils of 1341, 1347, and 1351 in Constantinople can be reduced to the basically simple affirmation that experience and knowledge of God are accessible *immediately* to all Christians; that the pursuit of such experience is an expression of the Christian faith itself; that faith is not an intellectual conjecture, but a vision of the Truth itself; that the sacramental life of the church is a necessary condition for authentic Christian experience. More technical theological problems, such as the Palamite distinction between divine essence and divine energies, were the terminological consequence, not the cause, of the experiential realism confirmed by the councils. The fact that such significant spiritual options were taken by the Byzantine Orthodox church by the middle of the fifteenth century is certainly connected with a strong revival of monasticism and a renewed recognition of monastic spiritual leadership. The revival in turn was linked with the catastrophic events mentioned earlier: the empire and the cultural pride of Byzantium had been shattered by the Latin conquests and the Turkish challenge. There was no reliable anchor of salvation left except the Orthodox church. But the church's strength was not seen in structures contingent to the empire, but rather in its eschatological, mystical, and ascetical traditions, maintained by the monks.

Around 1338, Gregory Palamas, in his *Triads* defending the hesychasts against the attacks of a south Italian "philosopher" Barlaam, provides a very symptomatic list of spiritual leaders, whom he and his disciples considered to be the models of the movement. Most prominent in the list are strong-willed and socially active bishops like Theoleptus of Philadelphia (1250–1321/26) and, particularly, Patriarch Athanasius I (1289–1293, 1303–1310). A stern and ascetic reformer, Athanasius, as patriarch, had paternalistically instructed Emperor Andronicus II on political matters, spent vast amounts on philanthropy, curbed self-serving church officials, and imposed discipline in monasteries.[4] Other patriarchs of Constantinople, especially in the period following the Palamite victory of 1347 (Isidore, Callistus, Philotheus), followed the example of Athanasius, at least in formal intent.

The priority of spiritual concerns characteristic of the hesychast movement manifested itself also in its opposition—traditional for Eastern monks—to humanistic interests in ancient Greek culture and philosophy. Not that Palamas and his disciples showed themselves to be systematic obscurantists. They did use philosophical language and concepts in their theological arguments, but they opposed the trends that began to understand Byzantium as a "Greek" state, in which Constantinople was seen as new "Athens." This emerging secular nationalism of the Byzantine intellectual elite—signaling the end of the Middle Ages—expressed itself politically in church-union attempts obtained through doctrinal surrender to Latin theology with the hope of obtaining cultural and political survival in return. Opposing such attempts, the hesychasts promoted new forms of Orthodox universalism. On Mount Athos, Greek, Slavic, Moldavian, Syrian, and Georgian monks were molded together by a common spirituality and the adoption of common values. It was inevitable, therefore, that not only the patriarch of Constantinople selected from their midst but also Bulgarian patriarchs (St. Euthymius), Serbian archbishops (St. Sava), and metropolitans "of Kiev and all Russia" (St. Cyprian) would promote in the entire Orthodox world a similar order of priorities. These included a liturgical unification on the basis of the *Ordo* ("Typikon") of St. Sabbas of Palestine, a common faithfulness to the patriarchate of Constantinople (as well as the symbolic position of the emperor, as the "emperor of all Christians"), and a common attitude of reserve toward union with the papacy, whose promoters were motivated politically more than theologically.

Not unlike Cluny in the West in the eleventh century, Mount Athos was the unquestioned center of the monastic movement, although it had no formal disciplinary power beyond its borders. The Holy Mountain, as it was called, was located in northern Greece. The entire territory of the peninsula belonged to numerous monastic communities, organized cenobitically, or in hermitages. Each community was governed by its own abbot, but all the monasteries recognized the authority of a single general abbot, known as *prōtos*. Both in the variety of monastic disciplines and in its general way of life, the Holy Mountain has survived until our own days.

From Athos, in the fourteenth and the fifteenth centuries, monasticism spread to the Balkans and Russia. This influence was carried out by traveling monks, as well as through books. Translations into Slavic were made on Athos, in Constantinople, or by Greek-speaking monks living in Serbia, Bulgaria, or Russia. The sheer volume of this new influx of Greek spiritual literature has led historians to speak of a "second" Byzantine, or south Slavic, influence on Russia (the first having followed immediately the "Baptism of the Rus" in 988). Most of the translations were works of Greek, sometimes Syrian, fathers of the classical patristic period, but also medieval Byzantine texts such as the Hymns of St. Symeon the New Theologian (d. 1022) or the writings on prayer of fourteenth-century hesychasts. The more difficult and purely theological treatises, like the works of Palamas, were beyond the grasp of most Slavic readers and were actually unnecessary since the principles of hesychasm were not intellectually challenged among the Slavs. These remained untranslated. With the exception of hard theology, the average library of a Serbian, Bulgarian, or Russian monastery of that period was identical in content to that of a Greek monastic house on Mount Athos, in Constantinople, on Patmos, or on Mount Sinai.

Perhaps the most spectacular development connected with the hesychast revival was the spread of monasticism in northern Russia. St. Sergius of Radonezh (ca. 1314–1392) was the acknowledged father of this Northern Thebaid, as it began to be called. The "lavra" of the Trinity, founded by him to the northeast of Moscow, became the motherhouse of over 150 monasteries, established by disciples of Sergius throughout the northern forests in the fourteenth and fifteenth centuries. Sergius himself could be referred to as a model by both the hermits and the partisans of community life.[5] His *Life*–the work of a disciple, Epiphanius the Wise, and an example of contemporary literary style–describes the beginning of his monastic life as one of "solitude" (*bezmolvie*, the Slavic equivalent of the Greek *hēsychia*), during which, imitating the Egyptian fathers who lived with wild beasts, Sergius befriended a bear. The biographer always stresses the virtues of simplicity, humility and brotherly love, which characterized Sergius, and recounts a few examples of mystical experiences. In addition, his love of manual work and his organizational talents helped him to become–upon direct instruction from the patriarch of Constantinople–the founder of cenobitic life in his monastery. In the spirit of the Byzantine hesychasts, his contemporaries, Sergius became involved in the social and political life of the times. Sharing the views of Metropolitan Cyprian, a Bulgarian closely linked with the ecclesiastical leadership in Byzantium, he supported the unity of the church of Russia–whose dioceses were located throughout the bitterly feuding principalities of Moscow and Lithuania–and blessed Moscovite troops before their first victorious battle against the Mongols (1380).

The history of Russian monasticism of the period is, therefore, quite consistent with the monastic ideology in the Greek-speaking lands: the mystical and eschatological emphasis leads to a sense of spiritual independence from historical contingencies, but does not imply pietistic noninvolvement or indifference to history.

Another striking illustration of the contagious spiritual zeal of the period is a revival of missionary activities. Although only glimpses of the various contemporary actions of the patriarchate of Constantinople are known, the archives testify to the establishment of new dioceses in far-away Caucasus and in Valachia, the Romanian-speaking land north of the Danube. In the newly colonized Russian north, a disciple and friend of Sergius, St. Stephen of Perm (1340–1396), having learned Greek, presided over the translation of Scripture and the liturgy into the language of a Finnish tribe, the Zyrians, for whom he also invented a special alphabet, before becoming their first bishop. Thus, the tradition of using native languages in missionary lands, exemplified by Cyril and Methodius in the ninth century, is still fully accepted in the practice of this late medieval period.

The picture of Eastern Christian spirituality in the fourteenth and fifteenth centuries would be incomplete without a mention, at least, of the developments in the field of art, which parallel the intellectual and spiritual movements of the period.

Characterizing the work of Greek artists during the so-called Paleologan "renaissance," André Grabar writes: "We see them foreshadowing the discoveries of Cavallini and Giotto, and at the same time those of the Italian painters of the fifteenth century who will revive the great style of classical painting."[6] Anyone familiar with the monuments of Christian art of the thirteenth, fourteenth, and fifteenth centuries, as they developed in Byzantium and the Slavic lands is aware of their innovative style, their new sense of movement, and their closeness to life, which stand in clear contrast to the more solemn and more severe Byzantine art of the tenth or eleventh centuries.

Some modern authors have attempted to establish a direct link between the spiritual renewal spurred by hesychasm and these artistic developments. Others, on the contrary, consider that monastic asceticism had a stifling effect on art and that the Paleologan "renaissance" reflects the new interest in classical antiquity shown by Byzantine humanists. But can either side of this simplified dilemma explain an art that was basically Christian and often monastic, without ever really becoming a "renaissance" art? Moreover, whereas the influence of antiquity is undeniable in many specific cases—such as the famous monastery of the Chora (Kariye Djami) in Constantinople—there is no reason to believe that such an interest could have motivated the Slavic patrons and artists of Macedonia, or the extraordinary achievements of the great Andrei Rublev in distant Muscovy. It is therefore more likely

31. *Icon of the Council of 1351.*

that the artistic revival, which originated in a politically moribund Byzantium and spread among the Orthodox Slavs, was an expression of the new awareness that communion with God was *possible*, that it depended on a human response to divine grace, that the Greek sense of the *humanum*, inherited from antiquity, was not suppressed but rather renewed and transfigured by the Christian experience. Thus, the message of the artistic revival reflected a Christian spirituality that, since its victory over iconoclasm, had learned to express itself in images and colors as well as in words or concepts, and which concerned not only a disincarnated human spirit but the totality of human existence, assumed by God in Jesus Christ.

East and West: The Gradual Divorce

All modern historians agree on one negative point: the schism between Rome and Byzantium, the two centers of Christendom in the High Middle Ages, cannot be associated with one particular event, or even with a precise date. It was, rather, a progressive divorce—an "estrangement," according to Yves Congar—which began with theological tensions during the period of the ecumenical councils and the development of a different understanding of the role of authority in the church. The two halves of Christendom broke communion with each other on several occasions, but were eventually reconciled, until the relatively minor incident of 1054 became *de facto* a final break between Rome and Constantinople. This does not mean that either side considered that reconciliation was impossible, but the two visions of the church were clearly moving in different directions. With the Gregorian reformation, the Crusades, the "imperial" papacy of Innocent III, rise of scholasticism and the universities, and, in the fourteenth century, the various intellectual trends that culminated in conciliarism and the Great Schism of the West, Latin Christendom considered itself to be a self-sufficient model of unity. The East, meanwhile, remained quite allergic to the institutional developments of the West, particularly to the centralized papacy, whereas the monastic theology triumphant in Byzantium in the fourteenth century emphasized the experiential, mystical, and eschatological elements of the Christian faith rather than the legal and the rational principles that dominated the ecclesial institutions and the schools of the West.

Theologians on both sides were primarily preoccupied with polemics around the issue of the Creed of Nicaea-Constantinople. Its original text, which affirmed that the Holy Spirit proceeded "from the Father" (cf. John 15:26), had been interpolated in the Latin West with the famous word *Filioque*, so that Western Christians confessed the "double" procession of the Spirit "from the Father and the Son." Whatever the original purpose of the interpolation (which began, most probably, in seventh-century Spain), its apologists were justifying it by references to the trinitarian doctrine of Augustine, who had emphasized the essential unity of the Godhead, so that the Father and the Son, being one in essence, constituted really only one source of the Spirit. In the East, meanwhile, the normative conception of the divine Trinity was that of the Cappadocian Fathers: St. Basil and his friends (fourth century). For them, the personal, or *hypostatic,* identity of the Father, the Son, and the Spirit constituted the primary Christian revelation and experience, whereas the common divine essence was in itself transcendent and unknown, being manifested only through energies.[7] Behind the issue of the *Filioque* stood, therefore, a divergence in the understanding of God. The two conceptions—the Cappadocian and the Augustinian—had direct implications for Christian spirituality.[8] They had coexisted within Christendom until the debate on the interpolation focused polemical attention upon their divergence.

Indeed, the addition of the *Filioque* to a common Creed, approved by ecumenical councils, had been effected unilaterally and raised the problem of church authority. Although it had occurred spontaneously, and, perhaps, through a misunderstanding, in remote areas of the Latin Christian world, its acceptance by the bishops of Rome in the eleventh century added a new dimension to the issue. Was the pope, in virtue of his Petrine authority, entitled to modify the ecumenical creed by himself?

The doctrinal issue of the *Filioque,* as seen by the East, became, therefore, the touchstone of a debate involving the question of papal authority—which, of course, manifested itself in many other ways, including the sanction given by Pope Innocent III of the capture of Constantinople by the Crusaders (1204) and the appointment of a Latin patriarch in the imperial city. A central issue of Christian experience was coming to the fore: Was the faith dependent upon an absolute and legally defined institutional criterion, such as the papacy? Could this criterion be trusted over and above the councils, the fathers, and, ultimately, that *knowledge* of God which, as the hesychasts were showing, belonged to every Christian within the sacramental body of the church? Did Christ give formal and absolute authority to the apostle Peter, and was this authority transmitted exclusively to the bishops of Rome? The East had always recognized a certain moral authority and a certain responsibility of the popes, and had counted on them to assure a world consensus on controversial issues, but the medieval, post-Gregorian papacy was formulating their powers in radically new ways. Beyond the political and cultural clashes of the times, two perceptions of the church emerged: in the one, the church was a God-sanctioned custodian of order and truth, demanding obedience to a visible head; in the other, order and visible unity, which earlier had been secured by the obviously fallible but practically useful power of the Christian emperors, now, with the collapse of the empire, were seen more as a mystical communion within which sacramental order and doctrinal integrity could be secured, as in the early centuries of Christianity, only through a consensus involving both the episcopate and the people.

The contrast could be observed throughout the many contacts and debates of the period. It could also be seen in the way three main Petrine texts of the New Testament (Matt 16:18–19; Luke 22:32; John 21:15–17) were understood. The Roman tradition of seeing the words of Christ addressed to Peter as applicable exclusively to the bishop of Rome was now accepted as obvious by the entire West. In the East, the Petrine passages were quite generally understood in the context of the life of each local church or even the individual faithful. For instance, Origen (third century) had seen in Peter the model of every believer: the faith makes "stones" (*petrai*) out of every Christian, who also receives the keys of the kingdom of heaven to enter therein.[9] More often, in the patristic tradition, Peter is seen as the first "bishop," entrusted with teaching and feeding the flock of his local community, as head and president of the eucharistic assembly. This tradition, expressed in the third century by Cyprian of Carthage, was based on the idea that in every "catholic" church the bishop sitting on "the chair of Peter" presides over the faithful. It was still in Byzantium the accepted ecclesiological model. The presence of the body of St. Peter in Rome, where he died, made Rome into a popular pilgrimage center and contributed to its moral prestige, but the spiritual presence of "Peter" was also an experiential reality in every church, embodied in the ministry of the local bishop. In their polemics against papal claims, the Byzantine authors of the fourteenth and fifteenth centuries do not deny the particular and, indeed, exclusive position of Peter among the apostles, but they challenge the idea of an *exclusive* succession of Peter in Rome alone. Thus, Neilos Cabasilas, a bishop of Thessalonica in the fourteenth century, wrote: "Peter indeed is both apostle and leader of the apostles, but the pope is neither an apostle (for the apostles appointed pastors and teachers, not other apostles), nor leader of the apostles. Peter is the teacher of the entire universe . . . , whereas the pope is only bishop of Rome" (*PG* 149, cols. 704D–705A).

The repeated attempts at negotiating church union were initiated by the Byzantine emperors, seeking the military and political support of the West against the Muslim threat. The attempts were welcomed by the popes, who nevertheless insisted upon the formal and definitive acceptance of both the doctrinal position and the ecclesial structure of Latin Christendom. Opposition generally came from churchmen in both Greek and Slavic lands, who demanded that union be not a simple surrender, but that it be discussed at an open and free council of the two churches. A totally new situation, which broke the deadlock, was created by the triumph of "conciliarism" in the West. Under the impact of the Great Schism, which from 1378 on opposed popes to antipopes, the superior authority of ecumenical councils over the papacy was accepted at Constance (1414–1418). Pope Martin V, the pope whose election united the warring parties of the West, endorsed the decree *Frequens*, which made the papacy responsible before a council meeting at regular intervals. This also made possible the only authentic and representative attempt at holding an ecumenical council that would include, as in the first millennium of Christian history, the delegates of both the Eastern and Western churches.

The meeting of the council successively in two Italian cities, Ferrara and Florence (1438–1440), resulted from a major papal concession to the Eastern ecclesiological perspective. Until then, the popes considered that the differences between East and West were nonnegotiable and that the East had no alternative other than to accept the faith of the see of Peter and papal authority as it existed in the West. At Ferrara-Florence, the two parties met without preconditions; indeed, the Latin church accepted that the council be considered the "Eighth," that is, that it be seen as a continuation of the common tradition that was last expressed in Nicaea in 787, at the "Seventh" council, which condemned iconoclasm. The Western theological and ecclesiological developments that had intervened between 787 and 1438 were thus implicitly put into question.

This important initial advantage for the cause of union, however, was not used properly during the long debates in Ferrara and in Florence. The spiritual gap between the two worlds and the different theological methodologies made mutual understanding difficult.

The Latin position at the council was presented and defended by heirs of Latin scholasticism, who used not only the authority of tradition but also philosophical arguments in a way that was quite unfamiliar to the Orthodox Byzantines. "Why Aristotle, Aristotle? No good, Aristotle," mumbled a bewildered delegate from distant Georgia, as Dominican John of Torquemada was debating a fine point of theology.[10] The long discussion on the issue of purgatory was another example illustrating the different approaches to basic Christian experience. Although the two sides agreed on the possibility and the necessity of praying for the dead, they understood differently the nature of "purification" required of dead souls. The legalistic view defended by the Latins insisted that divine justice needed satisfaction for sins committed for which appropriate penance had not been performed. This clashed with the Greek notion, inherited from Gregory of Nyssa, that communion with God is an endless growth in purity and that this growth, which is the purpose of spiritual life, indeed continues even after death.

But the Eastern delegation at Florence was not united. Whereas the larger number of delegates, ill-prepared for theological debate per se, was dominated by the desire to escape the Turkish menace, the intellectual spokesmen belonged to two distinct groups, which were polarized even before the debates started.

Mark Eugenikos, metropolitan of Ephesus, represented the monastic or hesychast, revival. He conceived Christian truth as fully revealed and experienced, and the Orthodox church was naturally for him the locus of that experience. In his priorities, the faith stood clearly above political expediency, and the survival of Byzantium from the forthcoming Turkish onslaught was not a sufficient price for compromise in doctrine. He was not a fanatic, however. Sincerely involved in the union negotiation and—perhaps naïvely—hoping to persuade the Latins that truth lived in Orthodoxy, he delivered the official eulogy of Pope Eugenius IV, at his delegation's arrival at Ferrara.

The other Greek party, best represented by Bessarion, metropolitan of Nicaea, stood in line with the thought of Barlaam the Calabrian, who a century earlier was the adversary of Gregory Palamas. Suspicious of monastic mysticism, Bessarion's party was passionately devoted to the thought and cultural achievements of Greek antiquity. For Bessarion, Christian revelation itself was inseparable from its incarnation in Greek Christian philosophy, and he could not conceive of the survival of Christianity under the yoke of Islam. Furthermore, the philosophical revival of Latin scholasticism, as well as the admiration for all things Greek which he discovered in Renaissance Italy, convinced him that salvation could come only from the West, the *Filioque* notwithstanding. Bessarion's views were shared by others, including particularly the metropolitan "of Kiev and all Russia," Isidore.

The eventual acceptance of a union formula by Bessarion and Isidore at the urgings of the emperor led most of the psychologically exhausted Greek delegates to sign the document as well. Mark alone refused. The decree of union endorsed the Western views of the *Filioque* issue: the Holy Spirit was defined as proceeding from the Father and the Son "as from one origin" (*sicut ab uno principio*), and the interpolation of the creed was proclaimed as "legitimate." The decree further endorsed the Western doctrine of purgatory and, last but not least, proclaimed the pope to be truly "vicar of Christ," possessing "full power" (*plena potestas*) in governing and feeding the universal church. This last term was crucial as a code word signifying the end of Western conciliarism; the council of Florence was, in fact, rejecting the regime approved at Constance, which made the pope responsible to a regularly convened council.

Thus, according to the most recent and, in general, most positive evaluation of the council of Florence, the stated goal of that assembly—the unity of East and West—was missed, and practically the entire East stood behind the rejection voiced by Mark of Ephesus.[11] Moreover, on the two issues of purgatory and papal authority, the council's decree marked not only the rejection of conciliarism but also the adoption of a theology that, a century later, would provide Martin Luther with his major reasons for opposing and rejecting the medieval Latin ecclesial system. Conceived as a major attempt at restoring Christian unity, the council ended up sowing the seed for further schisms.

The East Enters Its Dark Ages

Politically motivated and lacking that theological openness which was a necessary condition of true dialogue, the union attempts of the fourteenth and fifteenth centuries left the gap wide open between East and West. Possibly the result would have been different if the encounter had involved not only ecclesiastical politicians and scholastic theologians but more representatives of the authentic spiritual traditions—for example, in the West, the followers of Franciscan spirituality or of the school of Rhineland mysticism. It is interesting to note that recent archaeological discoveries have uncovered frescoes of St. Francis in a Greek church in Constantinople and that archaeological evidence in Ferrara has identified Italian hermits who, attending the debates of the council of Florence, were formally rebuked by representatives of the papal curia because they expressed sympathy for the positions of the Greeks.[12] This obscure information may still be a distant anticipation of the extraordinary interest, expressed by so many in the contemporary West, in the spirituality of fourteenth-century Eastern monasticism. This interest is reciprocated, for example, in the sympathetic research of the Orthodox Palamite theologian Vladimir Lossky on Meister Eckhart.[13]

In spite of such potential opportunities, the fall of Constantinople to the Turks in 1453 put an end to most direct contacts between the Christians of East and West. The West entered a period of brilliant cultural activity, but also faced incipient secularization; it undertook a remarkable missionary expansion, but suffered the tragedy of further schisms. Looking back at the history of the Renaissance and post-Renaissance periods in the West, we discover today how much Western Christendom was missing the spirituality, the ecclesiology, and the theology of the East to balance some of its more one-sided options. The Greek East, meanwhile, was forced to renounce intellectual progress and to settle within ghettoized communities in a struggle for mere survival in an Islam-dominated society. It is doubtful that the survival would have been possible without the extraordinary richness of the Byzantine liturgical experience and without the spiritual leadership, still quite alive in monasteries, provided by the followers of the hesychast revival of the fourteenth century. Russia alone soon began its development as a Eurasian Christian empire, but its church, until the nineteenth century, also remained as dependent upon the Byzantine medieval traditions for its spiritual life as the Greeks and the Balkan Slavs. Thus, Western spirituality lost much of its Eastern roots, whereas the East remained aloof and distant from events that shaped modern times.

Notes

1. See J. Gribomont, "Monasticism and Asceticism. I, Eastern Christianity," and Kallistos Ware, "Ways of Prayer and Contemplation. I, Eastern," both in *Christian Spirituality: Origins to the Twelfth Century*, ed. B. McGinn and J. Meyendorff (World Spirituality 16; New York: Crossroad, 1985) 86–112, 395–414. See also chapter 9 above, by George Mantzarides.

2. On this, see J. Meyendorff, *Byzantine Hesychasm* (London: Variorum, 1974) Introduction.

3. See the chapter "Victory of the Hesychasts in Byzantium: Ideological and political consequences" in Meyendorff, *Byzantium and the Rise of Russia*, 96–118.

4. On Athanasius, see A.-M. Talbot, ed., *The Correspondence of Athanasius I* (Dumbarton Oaks Texts 3; Washington, DC, 1975); and J. Boojamra, *Church Reform in the Late Byzantine Empire: A Study for the Patriarchate of Athanasios of Constantinople* (Thessaloniki: Analekta Vlatadon, 1982).

5. On Russian monasticism during that period, see particularly I. Smolitsch, *Russisches Mönchtum: Entstehung, Entwicklung und Wesen, 988–1917* (Wurzburg: Augustinus-Verlag, 1953) 79–100; also G. P. Fedotov, *The Russian Religious Mind*, vol. 2, *The Middle Ages: The Thirteenth to the Fifteenth Centuries*, ed. J. Meyendorff (Cambridge, MA: Harvard University Press, 1966) 195–264.

6. André Grabar, "The artistic climate in Byzantium during the Palaeologan period," in *The Kariye Djami*, ed. P. A. Underwood (Princeton, NJ: Princeton University Press, 1975) 4:7–8.

7. On this issue, see Thomas Hopko, "The Trinity. I, The Trinity in the Cappadocians," in *Christian Spirituality: Origins to the Twelfth Century*, 260–76; and chapter 9 above, by George Mantzarides.

8. The polarity between the two conceptions has been well established since the work of T. de Régnon, *Etudes de théologie positive sur la Sainte Trinité* (Paris, 1893). For recent debate on the importance of the issue, see K. Rahner, *The Trinity* (London: Burns & Oates, 1969); and D. Staniloae, *Theology and the Church* (Crestwood, NY: St. Vladimir's Seminary Press, 1981).

9. *Homilies on Matthew* 12.10, ed. Klostermann; GCS 38. (Leipzig, 1935) 85–89 (*PG* 13, cols. 997–1104).

10. The incident is reported in the memoirs of a Greek delegate, Sylvester Syropoulos; see V. Lauvent, *Les "Mémoires" de Sylvestre Syropoulos sur le concile de Florence* (Paris: CNRS, 1971) 464.

11. J. Gill, *The Council of Florence* (Oxford: University Press, 1959) vii.

12. C. L. Striker and Y. D. Kuban, "Work at Kalenderhane Camii in Istanbul, Second Preliminary Report," *Dumbarton Oaks Papers* 22 (1968) 185–93, pls. 23–26. The frescoes were probably painted during the Latin occupation (1204–1261), but they were preserved after the return of the Greeks. See also V. Lauvent, *Les "Mémoires" de Sylvestre Syropoulos*, 342.

13. V. Lossky, *Théologie negative et connaissance de Dieu chez Maître Eckhart* (Paris: J. Vrin, 1960).

Bibliography

Baker, D., ed. *The Orthodox Churches and the West.* Studies in Church History 13. Oxford: University Press, 1976.

Congar, Yves *L'ecclésiologie du Haut Moyen Âge de saint Grégoire le Grand à la désunion entre Byzance et Rome.* Paris: Cerf, 1968.

Dvornik, F. *The Legend of the Apostle Andrew and the Idea of Apostolicity in Byzantium.* Cambridge, MA: Harvard University Press, 1958.

Gill, J. *Byzantium and the Papacy, 1198–1400.* New Brunswick, NJ: Rutgers University Press, 1979.

Meyendorff, J. *Byzantine Theology: Historical Trends and Doctrinal Themes.* 2nd printing with revisions. New York: Fordham University Press, 1983.

——. *Byzantium and the Rise of Russia.* Cambridge: University Press, 1981.

——, N. Afanassieff, A. Schmemann, and N. Koulomzine. *The Primacy of Peter in the Orthodox Church.* London: Faith Press, 1963.

Nicol, Donald M. *Byzantium: Its Ecclesiastical History and Relations with the Western World.* London: Variorum Reprints, 1972.

Podskalsky, G. *Theologie und Philosophie in Byzanz.* Munich: Beck, 1977.

Runciman, S. *The Byzantine Theocracy.* Cambridge: University Press, 1977.

——. *The Last Byzantine Renaissance.* Cambridge: University Press, 1970.

20

Saints and Sinners: Roman Catholic and Protestant Spirituality in the Sixteenth Century

JILL RAITT

THIS ESSAY IS TRULY AN ESSAY, an attempt. It attempts, first, to understand what the term "spirituality" means when applied to the sixteenth century; and, second, on that basis it seeks to elaborate what spiritual principles Roman Catholics and Protestants share and what principles distinguish each from the other. I hope thereby to provide a basis for discussion of these matters and to invite the reader to pursue them further in volume 18, *Christian Spirituality from the Sixteenth Century to the Present.*

"Spirituality" is a difficult term to describe, let alone define. For the most part, Protestants have preferred "piety," a term acceptable in the sixteenth century, when Protestants suspected that beneath "spirituality" lurked monks, nuns, Jesuits, and the erroneous doctrine of works-righteousness. Roman Catholics, on the other hand, continue to take for granted the solid basis of spirituality in such giants as Bernard of Clairvaux, Teresa of Avila and John of the Cross, St. Ignatius and others who were indeed monks, nuns, and Jesuits!

To understand better what "spiritual" meant in Germany at the beginning of the sixteenth century, it is instructive to consult Altenstaig's theological dictionary, published in 1517.[1] There [Fo. CLXXXIX(r)] *pietas* is first discussed according to Bonaventure and Augustine of Hippo. "Piety is properly to be understood of the worship [*cultus*] of God," wrote Altenstaig, who then gave the classical and common uses as well, namely, care and reverence for parents and works of mercy toward the needy. In the two first cases—that is, the worship of God and the care of parents—piety participates in the virtue of justice. It is due God and parents, according to the natural law. In the instance of kindness to the needy neighbor, piety pertains to the gift of mercy and moves "from the image of God in the pious person to the service of the image of God in the neighbor." Altenstaig then notes that when *pietas* is taken in its first meaning, namely, the worship [*latria*] of God, it is synonymous with "religion." Covering all his bases, Altenstaig quotes Thomas Aquinas, who first links piety to reverence for and service to one's parents and one's country, and then cites Cicero, according to whom piety is justice toward the gods.

Spirituale [Fo. CCXLIII(v)] is given only as an adverb and is used in three ways, according to Altenstaig, who here follows Richard of St. Victor and Gabriel Biel. First, it pertains to grace and virtues. Secondarily, it pertains to spiritual actions such as preaching, correcting, visiting, praying, etc. *Spiritual* is opposed to *carnal* or more specifically, according to Jean Gerson, spiritual persons are those who go beyond the letter, ascending from earthly affections to a free and pure affection for the lucidity of truth and splendid desires for the heart of reality.

Still following the eloquent Gerson, who is himself commenting on St. Paul, Altenstaig continues. When someone commits a fault, the spiritual person gently corrects the sinner, realizing that everyone is subject to temptation. Spiritual persons are those who judge all things spiritually, who learn through suffering to be compassionate. Such persons seek not their own but look to Jesus Christ and are filled with love, humility, and piety, so that neither vanity nor cupidity can be found in them. Spiritual persons' conversations are in heaven as though they were one with the angels of God. Such persons are moved neither by blessings nor curses but in all things give good example. They would rather lose the whole world than suffer any detriment to their souls.

Two other meanings are then given by Altenstaig: namely, that when Paul speaks of the resurrected body as spiritual he does not mean that bodies will be spirits or ghosts, but rather that they will enjoy subtlety [*subtilitas*], a quality that allows bodies to pass through solid objects as did Jesus during the forty days prior to his Ascension. Lastly, again quoting Gerson, Altenstaig distinguishes between carnal and spiritual vices: the former are those which originate in the body (e.g., lust), and the latter are those conceived by the mind (e.g., anger, envy).

With the help of Altenstaig, it is possible to distinguish piety and spirituality as they were understood at the beginning of the sixteenth century.

Piety meant first giving what is due to God, parents, and country. It is one's Christian duty, one's filial obligation, one's patriotic service. Secondarily piety is shown in merciful actions toward the needy. In all cases, it has to do with actions, with Christian behavior. To be spiritual, on the other hand, is to be a certain kind of person. Truly pious persons need not be aware of the spiritual qualities that they share, but those who consciously seek to be spiritual will surely also be pious. If one looks at the extension of the terms, "pious" includes more people, among them, spiritual people. "Spiritual" comprehends fewer people, but its meaning requires that the spiritual person be also pious.

If the young monk Martin Luther were asked to apply these terms to the population around Erfurt, he might characterize most of the townspeople as "pious," with a few truly spiritual folk among them, and he might characterize the monks of the reformed Augustinian hermits as pious men trying hard to be spiritual. Among the monks were some truly spiritual men like the vicar general John Staupitz, whose compassion for the troubled Brother Martin prompted the wise direction he gave him. Staupitz advised Martin to be less demanding of perfection in himself and more trustful of the love of Christ, and to help him in these dispositions, Staupitz set Martin to studying Scripture.

The cure lay in Scripture, but it sent Martin Luther along a track that would set spirituality and the piety derived from it upon a course divergent from that of the Middle Ages, so that Luther's heirs would almost cease to use the term "spirituality" and would speak primarily of "piety." Luther insisted on two principles: (1) that sinners recognize their helplessness to fulfill the law, to justify themselves; and (2) that the despairing sinner believe God's word of promise of forgiveness sealed in Christ's death and resurrection. Justice is therefore imputed through faith and can in no way be earned or claimed as the result of one's efforts.

Luther fulminated against two kinds of works-righteousness: (1) the system of merit, congruous or condign, by which Roman Catholics believed they could earn heaven, whether their cooperation with grace took the form of doing their best before justification (congruous) or working with the infused supernatural virtue of charity (condign); and (2) the emotional meditations of the Radicals who wept at the foot of the cross instead of rejoicing in the gift of the crucified. Luther was adamant against any form of *active* righteousness. He insisted that all God wants of the sinner is surrender to the gift of faith, by which the *alien* righteousness of Christ is imputed. Then justified believers can engage in appropriate watchfulness to conform themselves to Christ, serving their neighbors gladly. Their motive should be gratitude to God for justification conferred, not an attempt to acquire merit. Luther therefore inveighed against vows, fasting, celibacy—monastic life *in toto*—which he considered to be corrupted by a desire for merit. Luther had himself experienced only frustration in his efforts to please God, to be "spiritual," by these means. Spiritual direction, which was handed down from the desert fathers through the monasteries and the work of friars like Tauler and cardinals like Jean Gerson, became for Luther the simple declaration of a minister or lay person that Jesus Christ has accomplished all that need be done: "Believe that God has truly forgiven and justified you and sin no more" are the only words of direction anyone should need. Preaching provided guidelines for living a pious life, a dutiful life of obedience to superiors and kindness to inferiors while serving God in whatever station in life one found oneself. By so doing, one put to death the "old Adam" and lived as a new person, "in Christ."

This was not, however, to assert a claim on God, for one remained a sinner, always in need of Christ's righteousness, by which alone one could be just or holy. Since part of the duty of all those justified by Christ was to obey the authorities through whom God established and maintained civil order, Luther was enraged by the uprising of the peasants, who would not be content with the government of their lords. He was equally enraged with those who claimed to be led by the Holy Spirit to the exclusion of a rightly ordered society and, even worse in some cases, to the exclusion of both Scripture and sacraments. He called these forerunners of the Radical Reformation "fanatics" or "Schwärmerei." Luther accused the Anabaptists (and others included under the general category of the Radical Reformation) of belying justification by faith, because, as Luther saw it, they sought comfort in their devotion to the crucified Christ—that is to say, in what they themselves accomplished rather than in the work of Christ for them. Devotion, thought Luther, was as much a trap as was the system of merit, for both looked to one's own work. For Luther, both attitudes were guilty of "works-righteousness."

Was Luther correct when he anathematized the spiritual exercises and rules of such sixteenth-century Roman Catholics as Ignatius of Loyola and lumped Roman Catholics and the Schwärmerei into one group labeled "works- righteous"?

Ignatius of Loyola's spirituality, in which he trained his followers, has two theological foci and one dominant practical exercise.[2] The first focal point is a deep devotion to the mystery of the Trinity. Ignatius not only meditated upon it but also, according to his diary, experienced a "vision," a profound understanding, of the three divine persons, which culminated in another penetrating "experience" of the essence of God. Before these "visions," Ignatius could only contemplate and praise God.

The second focal point, one more evident in *The Spiritual Exercises*, was devotion to the incarnation, to the revelation of God, the triune God, in the life and salvific work of Jesus Christ. The circular relations of the Trinity are, through Christ, extended into the world through creation and redemption. Through Christ, the world is drawn back to God, especially the world of human beings. This "mysticism of the mediation of Christ" is extended, in turn, to include the mediation of the angels, of Mary, of the saints, and, in a christological sense, of the created world. This larger circle of God's revelatory and redemptive work in Christ finds its center in the Eucharist, which itself expresses the role of creation (the bread and wine) raised up to a vehicle of the active presence of Christ.

The dominant practical exercise is daily examination of self, not only to probe one's conscience but also to recognize the spiritual movements of the soul. This self-examination has one purpose: to make effective an ever closer following of Christ, so that one becomes both an object of redemption and, in Christ, one of its mediators. From such careful examinations and the diaries that record them came *The Spiritual Exercises*.

The idea of *exercitia spiritualia* was not original with Ignatius and can be found at least as early as the twelfth century.[3] As Ignatius taught them, they possessed two chief components: (1) The most familiar is probably the examination of conscience. Ignatius was intent on making progress in the following of Christ. He not only made notes on his progress but also compared those notes week by week and month by month.[4] The purpose was to grow in Christlike virtues such as the practice of poverty and the exercise of humility and of fraternal charity. On one side, the method includes marking one's failings; on the other—and this is the side on which Ignatius became such a master—it is recognizing the impulses and guidance of the Holy Spirit. Both sides can be summed up as an effort to understand the movements of grace. (2) The purposes of understanding the movements of grace are, first, to praise God and, second, to distinguish grace from human impulses, rationalizations, and masked desires, as well as from promptings of the devil, which appear at first as virtuous impulses. Ignatius's careful monitoring of his own spiritual life, coupled with his growing experience as a spiritual director, is summed up in his rules for the discernment of spirits.

Are such vigorous Roman Catholic spiritual practices "works-righteousness"? Or can they be seen as a means to increased docility to and reliance upon God in Christ? For Roman Catholics, why one *intends* to do something is extremely important. (Hence Ignatius's "Rules for the Discernment

32. Michelangelo Buonarroti, *The Last Judgment*, ca. 1537-1541.
The Sistine Chapel, Vatican City.

of Spirits").[5] Spiritual direction, as practiced by Ignatius and other great saints before and after him, sought to purify those motives so that devotion to Jesus Christ and the love of God and neighbor were foremost rather than one's own benefit. But it must also be said that the care of one's own soul was regarded as a primary duty which one could not neglect. Asceticism was intended to purify one's motives by divorcing one more and more from the allure of worldly and fleshly ambitions. This was so not because the world and the body were evil—indeed, both were gifts from God—but because they so easily tended to become ends in themselves, objects of devoted worship. Ignatius therefore asks his exercitants (those making the *Spiritual Exercises*) to prefer Christ to the extent that they will accept poverty or riches, illness or health, indeed death or life with equanimity, so that *nothing* is ever preferred to the devoted service of Christ the Lord. In fact, in order to correct the tendency to put health, riches, and life ahead of God, Ignatius asks the exercitants to prefer to be poor with the poor Christ, to suffer and to die with Christ crucified rather than to commit the least sin—even to prefer the harder life and death simply because to do so is to live and die as Christ lived and died. From these preferences come the vows of poverty, chastity, and obedience as means to a Christocentric rather than an ego-centric life.

In this light—that is, a Christ-centered life—Roman Catholics have the same focus as Lutherans, however much each may disagree on the means to fulfill that life.

An additional point in assessing the role of asceticism is that it seems to be linked with spiritual progress, not only in the Roman Catholic West but also in the Orthodox East and in the great spiritual traditions of the Far East and of India. It is hard to say, therefore, that rigorous asceticism is not necessary to spirituality, when it seems that the majority of human beings in time and space have found it to be so. Could it be possible that all this striving to purify oneself, to renounce the world, and to live a life of poverty, chastity, and obedience is so much wasted effort? It goes without saying that well-informed Roman Catholics understood that none of this effort would be possible without grace. It is not a matter of "doing what one can by one's natural powers" as they exist after the fall. What Luther asked is whether any effort of that kind at all, apart from the recognition of one's sinfulness, is required. His answer is a ringing no, prior to justification. But Luther most assuredly expected Christian discipline after justification, not as a means of attracting God's grace or earning merit but as spontaneous fidelity out of gratitude to God. It is not so much that asceticism is good but that too much affection for worldly goods or for anything created distracts one from Christ and from the service of the neighbor. Goods have to be held lightly. Chastity is required in marriage as well as out. Obedience is the duty of every person who has a relationship of worker to employer, of citizen to magistrate, and so on. Luther was not antinomian.

Was Luther correct when he claimed that Radical reformers and Roman Catholics were equally guilty with regard to works-righteousness? Whether or not one agrees with Luther that any effort to acquire virtue is works-righteousness, Luther was right in seeing some likeness in Roman Catholic practice and that of some of the Radical spiritual reformers. For at the basis of much of the Radical Reformation was the conviction that human beings are responsible, that they are moral creatures, and that their morality is based upon freedom. They are expected to make right choices, and these choices should be guided by the example of Christ on the cross. This attitude of the following of Christ crucified was intensified by the actual persecution of those called Radical Reformers and their followers. They would have been unable to continue had they not before them an example to follow that gave them courage as they faced death for their beliefs. This tender love and compassion for the crucified Christ did not exclude in them gratitude for the work of Christ in their behalf. Where the Radical Reformation differed most from mainline Christianity—and especially Roman Catholicism—was in its idea of authority. It seems, then, that with regard to the second question Luther was right in seeing a similarity in the basic concern of both Roman Catholics and the Radical Reformation to seek Christ actively and to work hard to follow Christ. The question is therefore whether such "work" deserves the pejorative label "works-righteousness."

A related concern is the difference between mainline Protestants and Roman Catholics with regard to what the Christian is obliged to do to be truly spiritual. For Luther, it is to be passive under grace and active toward the neighbor; service of the neighbor requires all the asceticism necessary in one's life. For the Roman Catholic, service to the neighbor is a means of serving God, which may be either direct through the "corporal works of mercy" or indirect through prayer and other "spiritual works of mercy." Roman Catholics believe that in the beginning stages of the spiritual life one should be active, not passive, with regard to the acquisition of basic virtues like humility. One meditates and one follows the example of Christ crucified and finds strength in the sacrament of Christ's death and resurrection. These two notions, which Luther insisted should be ranked in the order of sacrament and then example, play back and forth in the life of the Roman Catholic. One receives the sacraments in order to be strengthened to follow Christ, and one attempts to follow Christ in order to grow in that Christ-likeness which makes the sacraments ever more meaningful.

Experience has also been a problem in the life of one seeking to be a spiritual person. Based on the experiential nature of Luther's conversion, a problem arose concerning the need to experience God's action. The resulting ambiguity with regard to the validity of experience in Luther's followers was resolved on the side of experience by the pietists and against experience on the part of the seventeenth-century Lutheran scholastics.[6] In the Roman Catholic tradition, direction given by trusted spiritual guides underlines the need to assess spiritual experience very carefully. It cannot be allowed to dictate the way one goes or the manner in which one prays. If one's experience is sweet, that is recognized as helpful. If the sweet experience of the presence of God is lacking, that is not to be taken as a sign of retrogression or of God's displeasure but simply as part of the spiritual life. Indeed, it can be a test of faith in which one has simply to cling to God and, in some cases, it is a far more searching test to lose even the sense that one is clinging to God. One can then only hope and believe that it is God who is doing the holding. This latter experience is that of emptiness. It is not a warm and cozy sense of being rocked in the bosom of Abraham, but is a naked faith that God is faithful and is to be trusted when there seems to be nothing else in the world or in oneself that is trustworthy. No one wrote better of this experience than the great sixteenth-century Carmelites Teresa of Avila and John of the Cross.[7]

Persevering through such "dry" periods is the acid test of one's faith, of one's love for God. Scholars have debated whether Luther's "by faith alone" is or is not radically different from the Roman Catholic "faith informed by love." That debate is too complex to be reviewed here, but it is appropriate to stress the fundamental unity of all Christians, Protestant and Roman Catholic, who believe that at the moment of justification one is sanctified by the indwelling Holy Spirit. It is this Spirit who prays for the Christian, interceding with "sighs too deep for words" (Rom 8:26). This is the same Spirit who pours God's love into the hearts of Christians and who in fact is *given* to Christians (Rom 5:5), a wonder almost beyond belief.

The *process* of sanctification may also be disputed, but not that some change occurs in the Christian who is faithful, that is, full of faith and also constant in God's service. These likenesses are profound indeed and ought to be enough to unite Christians, whether Protestant or Roman Catholic, in a Christ-centered spirituality inspired by the Holy Spirit for the glory of God.

Notes

1. Joannes Altenstaig Vendelicus. *Vocabularius Theologie complectens vocabulorum descriptiones, difinitiones* [sic] *et significatus ad theologiam utilium* ... (Hagenau: Henricus Gran, 1517).

2. See Adolf Haas, "The Mysticism of St. Ignatius according to His *Spiritual Diary*," in *Ignatius of Loyola, His Personality and Spiritual Heritage, 1556–1956,* ed. Friedrich Wulf (St. Louis, MO: Institute of Jesuit Sources, 1977).

3. See Heinrich Bacht, "Early Monastic Elements in Ignatian Spirituality: Toward Clarifying Some Fundamental Concepts of the Exercises," in *Ignatius of Loyola,* 207 with n. 27.

4. Haas, "The Mysticism of St. Ignatius," 167.

5. *The Spiritual Exercises of St. Ignatius.* There are several English translations. An easily accessible one is translated by Anthony Mottola in an Image Book edition (Garden City, NY: Doubleday, 1964) 129–34.

6. For treatment of this question, see *The Theologia Germanica of Martin Luther,* trans. Bengt Hoffman (Classics of Western Spirituality; New York: Paulist Press, 1980).

7. See chapter 12 above, by Marc Lienhard, for a similar attitude in Lutheran spirituality.

Contributors

JILL RAITT, editor of this volume, is Professor of the History of Christianity and Chair-woman of the Department of Religious Studies at the University of Missouri, Columbia. Her books include *Shapers of Traditions in Germany, Switzerland and Poland, 1500–1600* (1981) and *The Eucharistic Theology of Theodore Beza: The Development of the Reformed Tradition* (1972).

BERNARD MCGINN, collaborating editor of this volume, is Professor of Historical Theology and the History of Christianity at the Divinity School of the University of Chicago. His books include *Meister Eckhart: Teacher and Preacher* (1986), *The Calabrian Abbot: Joachim of Fiore in the History of Western Thought* (1985), *Apocalyptic Spirituality* (1979), *Visions of the End: Apocalyptic Traditions in the Middle Ages* (1979).

JOHN MEYENDORFF, collaborating editor of this volume, is Professor of History at Fordham University and Dean of St. Vladimir's Orthodox Theological Seminary in Tuckahoe, New York. He is the author of *Byzantine Theology: Historical Trends and Doctrinal Themes* (1983), *Catholicity and the Church* (1983), *The Byzantine Legacy in the Orthodox Church* (1982), *Byzantium and the Rise of Russia* (1981), and *Introduction à l'étude de Gregoire Palamas* (1959).

WILLIAM J. BOUWSMA is Sather Professor of History at the University of California, Berkeley. He is author of *The Culture of Renaissance Humanism* (1973) and "The Two Faces of Humanism: Stoicism and Augustinianism in Renaissance Thought," in *Itinerarium Italicum: The Profile of the Italian Renaissance in the Mirror of its European Transformations* (1975).

FRITZ BÜSSER is Professor of the History of Church and Doctrine, University of Zurich, and Director of the Institute for Swiss Reformation History. His publications include *Zwingli-Biographie* (1973) and *Aufsatzsammlung "An den Wurzeln der Reformation"* (1985).

CAROLINE WALKER BYNUM is Professor of History at the University of Washington. Her publications include *Jesus as Mother: Studies in the Spirituality of the High Middle Ages* (1982), "Women Mystics and Eucharistic Devotion in the Thirteenth Century" in *Women's Studies* (1984), and "Women's Stories, Women's Symbols: A Critique of Victor Turner's Theory of Liminality," in *Anthropology and the Study of Religion* (1984).

WILLIAM J. COURTENAY is Professor of History at the University of Wisconsin, Madison. His publications include "Nominalism and Late Medieval Religion," in *The Pursuit of Holiness* (1974), "Augustinianism at Oxford in the Fourteenth Century" in *Augustiniana* (1980), *Adam Wodeham: An Introduction to His Life and Writings* (1978), and *Covenant and Causality in Medieval Thought* (1984).

EWERT COUSINS, general editor of *World Spirituality: An Encyclopedic History of the Religious Quest*, is Professor of Theology at Fordham University. He is the author of *Bonaventure and the Coincidence of Opposites* (1978) and editor and translator of the volume on Bonaventure in Classics of Western Spirituality: *Bonaventure: The Soul's Journey Into God, The Tree of Life, The Life of St. Francis* (1978).

KEITH J. EGAN is Professor and Chairman of the Department of Religious Studies and Co-Director of the Center for Spirituality at Saint Mary's College in Notre Dame, Indiana, and Adjunct Professor of Theology at Notre Dame University. His recent works include "The Foundations of Mystical Prayer: The Interior Castle, Mansions 1–3," in *Medieval Religious Women* (1985) and "Teresa of Jesus: Daughter of the Church and Woman of the Reformation," in *Carmelite Studies* (1984).

TIMOTHY GEORGE is Associate Professor of Church History and Historical Theology at the Southern Baptist Theological Seminary in Louisville, Kentucky. His publications include *Theology of the Reformers* (1987), "The Presuppositions of Zwingli's Baptismal Theology," in *Prophet, Pastor, Protestant: The Work of Huldrych Zwingli after Five Hundred Years* (1984), and *John Robinson and the English Separatist Tradition* (1982).

OTTO GRÜNDLER is Director of the Medieval Institute at Western Michigan University. He is the author of "Devotio moderna atque antiqua: The Modern Devotion and Carthusian Spirituality," in *The Roots of the Modern Christian Tradition* (1984), *Social Groups and Religious Ideas in the Sixteenth Century* (1978), "Ingrafting in Christ: The Spirituality of John Calvin," in *The Spirituality of Western Christendom* (1976), and *Die Gotteslehre Girolamo Zanchis and ihre Bedeutung für seine Lehre von der Prädestination* (1965).

ALOIS MARIA HAAS is Professor of the History of German Literature at the University of Zurich. He is the author of *Meister Eckhart als normative Gestalt geistlichen* (1979), *Sermo mysticus, Studien zu Theologie und Sprache der Deutschen Mystik* (1979), and *Geistliches Mittelalter* (1984).

SERGEI HACKEL is Reader in Russian Studies at the University of Sussex. He is the author of *The Poet and the Revolution: Alekandr Blok's "The Twelve"* (1975) and *Pearl of Great Price: The Life of Mother Maria Skobtsova* (1981).

J. A. WAYNE HELLMANN, O.F.M. CONV., is Associate Professor of Theological Studies at St. Louis University and Adjunct Associate Professor of Franciscan Studies at the Franciscan Institute, St. Bonaventure University. He has published *Ordo: Untersuchung eines Grundgedankens in der Theologie Bonaventuras* (1974), and "Poverty: The Franciscan Way to God," in *Theology Digest* (1974).

ELIZABETH A. JOHNSON, C.S.J., is Professor of Systematic Theology, Religious Studies Department, The Catholic University of America in Washington, D.C. She is author of "The Symbolic Character of Theological Statements about Mary" (1985), "The Marian Tradition and the Reality of Women" in *Horizons,* and "Mary and Contemporary Christology: Rahner and Schillebeeckx," in *Église et Theologie* (1984).

RICHARD KIECKHEFER is Professor of the History and Literature of Religions at Northwestern University. He is the author of *Unquiet Souls: Fourteenth-Century Saints and Their Religious Milieu* (1984), *Repression of Heresy in Medieval Germany* (1979), and *European Witch Trials: Their Foundations in Popular and Learned Culture, 1300–1500* (1976).

MARC LIENHARD is Professor of the History of Modern and Contemporary Christianity at the University of Strasbourg (Sciences humaines) in Strasbourg, France. He is the author of *Luther: Witness to Jesus Christ. Stages and Themes of the Reformer's Christology* (1982), *Martin Luther: Un temps, une vie, un message* (1983), and *Foi et vie des protestants d'Alsace* (1981).

JAMES F. McCUE is Professor, The School of Religion, University of Iowa. He is the author of "Simul iustus et peccator in Augustine, Aquinas, and Luther: Putting the Debate in Context," in *Journal of the American Academy of Religion* (1980), "The Doctrine of Transubstantiation from Berengar Through Trent: The Point at Issue," in *Harvard Theological Review* (1968), and "Luther and Roman Catholicism on the Mass as Sacrifice," in the *Journal of Ecumenical Studies* (1965).

GEORGE MANTZARIDIS is Professor of Moral Theology and Christian Philosophy at the Aristotelian University of Thessalonica. His books include *The Deification of Man* (1984).

ROBERT TAFT, S.J., is Ordinary Professor of Eastern Liturgies at Pontifical Oriental Institute, Rome, Italy. His publications include *The Liturgy of the Hours in East and West: The Origins of the Divine Office and Its Meaning for Today* (1986), *Beyond East and West: Problems in Liturgical Understanding* (1984), and *The Great Entrance: A History of the Transfer of Gifts and Other Preanaphoral Rites of the Liturgy of St. John Chrysostom* (1978).

GEORGE H. TAVARD, A.A., is the H. G. Werner Professor of Theology at the Methodist Theological School, Delaware, Ohio. His publications include *Images of the Christ: An Enquiry into Christology* (1982), *The Vision of the Trinity* (1981), *Woman in Christian Tradition* (1973), and *Holy Writ or Holy Church: The Crisis of the Protestant Reformation* (1959).

JAMES D. TRACY is Professor of History at the University of Minnesota in Minneapolis, Minnesota. His publications include *A Financial Revolution in the Habsburg Netherlands: 'Renten' and 'Renteniers' in the County of Holland, 1515–1565* (1985), *The Politics of Erasmus: A Pacifist Intellectual and His Political Milieu* (1978), and *Erasmus: The Growth of a Mind* (1972).

SIMON TUGWELL, O.P., is Lecturer in Theology at the University of Oxford and at the Pontifical University of St. Thomas, Rome, Italy, and Regent of Studies at Blackfriars, Oxford, England. His books include *Ways of Imperfection* (1984), *Early Dominicans* (1982), and *The Way of the Preacher* (1979).

ADOLAR ZUMKELLER, O.S.A., is Director of the Augustinus-Instituts in Würzburg, West Germany. His publications include *Erbsünde, Gnade, Rechtfertigung und Verdienst nach der Lehre der Erfurter Augustinertheologen des Spätmittelalters* (1984), "Henrici de Frimaria tractatus ascetico-mystici," in *Corpus Scriptorum Augustinianorum* (1975), and "Die Lehrer des geistlichen Lebens unter den deutschen Augustiners . . . ," in *S. Augustinus vitae spiritualis magister* (1959).

Photographic Credits

The editors and publisher wish to thank the custodians of the works of art for supplying photographs and granting permission to use them.

1. Courtesy of Christine Godson.
2. Photographie Giraudon/Art Resource, New York.
3. The National Gallery of Art, Washington, D.C. The Rosenwald Collection.
4. The Cleveland Museum of Art. Gift of Mr. and Mrs. William Marlatt Fund.
5. Courtesy of The Trustees of The British Library.
6. The Metropolitan Museum of Art, New York. The Cloisters Collection.
7. The Metropolitan Museum of Art, New York. Gift of J. Pierpont Morgan, 1917.
8. Alinari/Art Resource, New York.
9. The Cleveland Museum of Art. Gift of John Huntington Art and Polytechnic Trust.
10. The National Gallery of Art, Washington, D.C. The Samuel H. Kress Collection.
11. The Metropolitan Museum of Art, New York. Gift of Felix M. Warburg and His Family.
12. Courtesy of Koninklijke Bibliotheek, The Hague.
13. Kimbell Art Museum, Fort Worth, Texas.
14. From Leonid Ouspensky and Vladimir Lossky, *The Meaning of Icons*, p. 119. Courtesy of St. Vladimir's Seminary Press, Crestwood, New York.
15. From Leonid Ouspensky and Vladimir Lossky, *The Meaning of Icons*, p. 210. Courtesy of St. Vladimir's Seminary Press, Crestwood, New York.
16. From Leonid Ouspensky and Vladimir Lossky, *The Meaning of Icons*, p. 130. Courtesy of St. Vladimir's Seminary Press, Crestwood, New York.
17. Courtesy of Stephanie Klosinski Garbacz.
18. Alinari/Art Resource, New York.
19. Photographie Giraudon/Art Resource, New York.
20. Alinari/Art Resource, New York.
21. Bildarchiv Foto Marburg/Art Resource, New York.
22. Snack/Art Resource, New York.
23. Courtesy of Herald Press.
24. Courtesy of Herald Press.
25. Alinari/Art Resource, New York.
26. Photographie Giraudon/Art Resource, New York.
27. Edition Giraudon/Art Resource, New York.
28. Photographie Giraudon/Art Resource, New York.
29. Courtesy of Stephanie Klosinski Garbacz.
30. The Metropolitan Museum of Art, New York. Gift of Louis L. Lorillard, 1896.
31. From John Meyendorff, *St. Gregory Palamas and Orthodox Spirituality*, p. 102. Courtesy of St. Vladimir's Seminary Press, Crestwood, New York.
32. Alinari/Art Resource, New York.

Indexes

Subjects

Aquinas, 27–28, 60; of Thomas à Kempis, 179, 183–84; of Thomas of Celano, 38; in the vernacular, 78–79, 145; on the Virgin Mary, 92–93, 395–98, 403; of women, 131, 134; of Zerbolt, 182; of Zwingli and Bullinger, 303, 304, 310–12

Zurich Reform, 301–4, 308, 310–12

Names

'Abdišo bar Brika of Nisibis, 422
Abu-Madyan, 2
Adam the Scot, 2
Aelred of Rievaulx, 2, 194, 380, 384, 397
Agazzari, Philipp, 68
Agnes of Prague, 37
Aiguani, Michael, 112
d'Ailly, Pierre, 76, 113, 116–19, 169–71
Aindorffer, Kaspar, 171
Albert, patriarch of Jerusalem, 51, 59
Albert of Padua, 66
Albert of Vercelli, 1
Albert Sarteano, 46
Albert the Great, 18, 128, 144–45, 160
Alberti, Leon Battista, 248
Alexander III, 8–9
Alexander IV, 37, 63
Alexander V, 113
Alexander of Alexandria, 112
Alexander of Hales, 161
Alfonso of Orozco, 71, 72
Alice of Schaerbeke, 132
Aloysius Rabatà, 58
Amadeus of Lausanne, 397
Amalar of Metz, 429
Amalric of Bene, 9
Ambrose, 260–61, 436
Amilius of Buren, 189
Amsdorf, Nikolaus von, 290
Andreas Proles, 70
Andronicus II, 441
Angela of Foligno, 31, 38, 40–41, 130, 134, 161–62
Angelo Clareno, 44, 46
Angelus Mazzinghi, 58
Anselm, 4
Anselm of Canterbury, 377–78, 396, 401–2
Antoninus of Florence, 118
Arcangela Girlani, 58
Aristotle, 246, 272, 274
Arius, 212
Arnaldo, Brother, 40
Arnold of Brescia, 9
Athanasius, 376, 442
Athanasius I, 441

Athanasius of Vysotskoe, 224
Athenagoras, 212
Audet, Nicholas, 58
Augustine, 5, 63–74, 148, 168, 183, 197, 237, 241, 244, 246, 270–71, 326, 356, 376–77, 454
Augustine of Ancona, 67
Augustinus Triumphus, 112
Aureoli, Peter, 112

Baconthorp, John, 112
Baker, Augustine, 205
Baldwin of Ford, 2
Barbara, 96
Barlaam the Calabrian, 210, 213, 217–18, 441, 450
Barrow, Henry, 350
Bartholomew Fanti, 58
Bartholomew of Pisa, 46
Basil the Great, 216, 447
Beatrice of Nazareth, xix, 132, 141, 166
Becker, Eggelinus, 118, 119
Becket, Thomas, 90
Bede, Venerable, 86, 194
Benet of Canfield, 47, 205
Bernard of Clairvaux, 1, 4, 32, 84, 141, 181, 183, 277, 378, 380–81, 397, 402, 406, 454
Bernard of Parma, 128
Bernard of Quintavalle, 381
Bernardine of Siena, 46–47, 78, 81, 83, 406
Bernardino d'Asti, 47
Berthold of Regensburg, 78
Bessarion, 450
Bibliander, Theodore, 304
Biel, Gabriel, 118–19, 270, 428, 455
Blannbekin, Agnes, 156
Bloemmaerdine, 163
Boccaccio, Giovanni, 167
Boethius, 160
Bonaventure, xxi, 31, 36, 41–45, 47–48, 84, 161, 164, 170, 205, 256, 380–84, 386, 388–89, 395, 454
Boniface VII, 101
Boniface VIII, 44, 52–53, 82
Boniface IX, 89
Bora, Katherine von, 268

Colophon

Christian Spirituality: High Middle Ages and Reformation,
Volume 17 of World Spirituality: An Encyclopedic History of the
Religious Quest, was designed by Maurya P. Horgan and Paul J. Kobelski.
The type is 11-point Garamond Antiqua and was set by
The Scriptorium, Denver, Colorado.